"A valuable portrayal of both the public and private sides of the NFL's leading coach for the past twenty years that will be in demand among sports collections." — *Library Journal,* **starred review**

"A fascinating look inside the team so many of us love to hate."
— *Washington Post*

"Ian O'Connor's biography ranks among the best in regards to the NFL . . . A comprehensive profile that manages to dig deep under Belichick's famous hoodie . . . fascinating . . . This is an important biography, as O'Connor provides a greater understanding of arguably the greatest NFL coach of all time." — *Chicago Tribune*

"Ian O'Connor's *Belichick* is a deep and substantive dive into the life of a man many recognize as one of professional football's greatest coaches. It is a football junkie's delight." — *BookReporter*

"A fascinating, unvarnished history of what made Belichick the coach he is today . . . If you want to know why Bill is the way he is, this is the book for you." — *Boston Globe*

"With deep reporting and a profound understanding of the football life, Ian O'Connor comes as close as humanly possible to solving the mystery of the great football sphinx, Bill Belichick, and his unmatched coaching career."
— **David Maraniss, best-selling author of**
When Pride Still Mattered: A Life of Vince Lombardi

"I thought I knew everything there is to know about the brilliant, secretive coach. The Hoodie would have made a model prisoner of war. He gives up nothing. And yet Ian O'Connor somehow cracked the code at Fort Foxborough, producing this compelling portrait of the coach and the man. A must-read for football buffs and anyone who appreciates leadership."
— **Dan Shaughnessy, *Boston Globe* columnist and best-selling author of**
***Francona* (with Terry Francona)**

"In *Belichick,* Ian O'Connor has delivered an excess of compelling, fresh reporting and muscled writing to construct one of our great coaching biographies. O'Connor illuminates one of sports' most secretive and mysterious figures. Fast-moving and exhaustively researched, *Belichick* will transform the way you consider the man and the Patriots' dynasty."

— **Adrian Wojnarowski, ESPN senior writer and best-selling author of**
The Miracle of St. Anthony

"A tour de force of world-class reporting and masterful, fair-minded storytelling."

— **Armen Keteyian, contributing correspondent to *60 Minutes* and**
best-selling author of *Tiger Woods*

"It is simply not possible to produce a more interesting, informative, and beautifully written biography than Ian O'Connor has in *Belichick* . . . This is the kind of gold-standard reporting that all journalists aspire to, and few actually achieve."

— **Mike Vaccaro, award-winning columnist, *New York Post***

BELICHICK

BELICHICK

THE MAKING OF THE
GREATEST FOOTBALL COACH
OF ALL TIME

Ian O'Connor

Mariner Books
Houghton Mifflin Harcourt
BOSTON   NEW YORK

First Mariner Books edition 2019
Copyright © 2018 by Ian O'Connor

hmhbooks.com

Library of Congress Cataloging-in-Publication Data
Names: O'Connor, Ian, author.
Title: Belichick : the making of the greatest football coach of all time / Ian O'Connor.
Description: Boston : Houghton Mifflin Harcourt, 2018. |
Includes bibliographical references and index.
Identifiers: LCCN 2018017251 (print) | LCCN 2018019659 (ebook) | ISBN 9780544786752 (ebook) |
ISBN 9780544785748 (hardcover) | ISBN 9780358118213 (paperback)
Subjects: LCSH: Belichick, Bill. | Football coaches — United States — Biography. |
New England Patriots (Football team) — History. | Kansas City Chiefs (Football team) —
History. | Atlanta Falcons (Football team) — History.
Classification: LCC GV939.B45 (ebook) | LCC GV939.B45 O25 2018 (print) |
DDC 796.332092 [B] — dc23
LC record available at https://lccn.loc.gov/2018017251

Book design by Brian Moore

Printed in the United States of America
DOC 10 9 8 7 6 5 4 3 2 1

To my kid sister Rita.
A Giant in life.
A lion in death.

CONTENTS

INTRODUCTION

People will long recall September 23, 2001, as a momentous date in National Football League history, and yet for a columnist who had reported from the smoldering 9/11 crime scene that was downtown Manhattan, this was no day to write about what transpired between the New England Patriots and the New York Jets. This was the first NFL Sunday after terrorists had flown hijacked planes into the World Trade Center towers, committing a mass murder of unspeakable depths. Some 60,000 fans had gathered inside Foxboro Stadium for a three-hour reprieve from the horror of it all.

I was standing on the sidelines with colleagues Adrian Wojnarowski and Gary Myers during the game's final minutes, and my story for the next morning's newspaper was already set. Joe Andruzzi, a Patriots guard from Staten Island, had three firefighting brothers among the responders at Ground Zero, including Jimmy, who had evacuated one of the doomed towers and, by an estimated 45 seconds, had narrowly escaped the fate that claimed more than 400 firefighters, cops, and EMTs. Dressed in their F.D.N.Y. helmets and coats, the Andruzzi brothers were the honorary game captains, joined on the field by their father, Bill, a former New York City cop.

No, there wasn't a damn thing between the lines or on the scoreboard that could possibly rearrange my sportswriting priorities on this day. Not even the dawning of the greatest coaching career pro football has ever seen.

Bill Belichick would lose this game to the Jets by a 10–3 count and fall to 0-2 on the season, to 5-13 in his time in New England, and to 41-57 overall as an NFL head coach. Belichick was facing a potential sixth losing season in seven years of running the Patriots and the Cleveland Browns. No matter what he tried, the coach could not temper the growing suspicion that he was just another brilliant coordinator who didn't have the leadership skills and charisma to run his own team like his former boss Bill Parcells had.

But a second-year quarterback named Tom Brady, sixth-round pick, was leading that failed final drive, after the starter, franchise player Drew Bledsoe, had taken a vicious shot from Jets linebacker Mo Lewis. I'd never heard a hit like that around any football field on any level; it sounded as if one of the dressed-up militiamen in the end zone had fired off his musket. As Bledsoe's backup trotted onto the field in the fourth quarter, looking very Ichabod Crane–ish, I thought of Brady's underwhelming career at Michigan, of his lack of mobility and athleticism, and of Michigan coach Lloyd Carr's constant (if failed) attempts to replace him with the younger and more dynamic Drew Henson.

More than anything, I thought Bill Belichick was done as a head coach.

Frankly, I wasn't terribly surprised that Belichick found himself in deep trouble a mere 18 games into his Patriots career. Cleveland owner Art Modell had fired him after the 1995 season for his apparent lack of human relations skills as much as anything else, and had advised Patriots owner Robert Kraft that he'd be making the biggest mistake of his life by giving him a second chance. In fleeing the Jets after the 1999 season, running from his contractual commitment to succeed Parcells, and reneging on his decision just 24 hours earlier to assume control, Belichick only notarized Modell's feelings. He wrote on a piece of paper that he was quitting his position as "HC of the NYJ." He handed in his chicken-scratch resignation and then gave his chickenshit reasons for it in the mother of all bizarre New York press conferences.

That public unraveling appeared to confirm the worst fears about Belichick — that he had a losing personality to go along with his losing record. I'd written a column saying that Kraft would regret this hire, for reasons beyond the first-round pick he gave the Jets as part of the compensation deal. And in the immediate wake of the 0-2 start in 2001, with the Patriots down and Bledsoe out, that prediction looked as good as gold.

It now stands as commentary more absurd than Belichick's resignation note.

On February 4, 2018, when the Patriots lost Super Bowl LII to the Philadelphia Eagles, Belichick's baffling decision to bench cornerback Malcolm Butler, hero of Super Bowl XLIX, temporarily complicated his legacy. The move angered some Patriots and exacerbated Belichick's increasingly tense relationship with his two best players, Brady and Rob Gronkowski. The Butler move was a damaging unforced error, and suddenly people were back to questioning the depth of the coach's greatness.

But one ill-conceived decision on America's biggest sports and entertainment stage could not alter Belichick's place among the game's enduring icons. Belichick has won more Super Bowls (five) than Hall of Famers Don Shula and Tom Landry combined (four). He has won 28 postseason games — eight more than the next most prolific winner (Landry). Belichick has built and maintained a 17-year dynasty (15 division titles and an average of 12.29 regular-season victories over that period) at a time when the NFL uses the salary cap, the draft, the schedule, and free agency as weapons to prevent franchises from doing just that.

Belichick hasn't just reduced the rest of the AFC East to a perpetual punch line; he has made a mockery of the league's commitment to parity. Along the way, he has surpassed Vince Lombardi as the best NFL coach of all time.

For me, as a 1982 graduate of St. Cecilia High School, in Englewood, New Jersey, and as a member of the last football team to reach the state finals at that storied school (it closed in 1986), those aren't easy words to write. Lombardi's first head coaching job — and only head coaching job before taking over the Green Bay Packers in 1959 — was at St. Cecilia, where the Carmelite priests and nuns who lorded over my youth insisted on punctuality, good penmanship, a daily regimen of Our Fathers and Hail Marys, and a lifelong devotion to this one article of football faith: Nobody will ever compare to our own Saint Vincent.

Lombardi won five NFL championships in Green Bay, including the first two Super Bowls, and in 1969, his one and only year in Washington, he led the Redskins to their first winning season since 1955. Had cancer not claimed him at 57, Lombardi likely would have established records that no coach would ever touch.

Some observers view his nine victories in ten postseason games as proof that he still belongs at the top of any historical ranking of coaches, above Belichick, Paul Brown, Papa Bear Halas, Don Shula, Bill Walsh, and Joe Gibbs. But Lombardi ruled a league that offered its players virtually no rights. It was easier back then, through the NFL's restraint of trade, to keep together a powerhouse team.

Others might move to knock Belichick down a peg or three because he "lucked" into Brady, the 199th player chosen in the 2000 draft, or because his program was sanctioned for cheating in the Spygate and Deflategate cases. Of course Belichick wouldn't be Belichick had he spent his entire career with average and aging quarterbacks. In fact, he feared he would be fired if a healthy Bledsoe saddled him with another losing season in 2001. As much as Belichick and his personnel man, Scott Pioli, would never want to see a player get hurt, never mind confront the life-threatening injuries Bledsoe suffered from the Lewis hit, they were privately thrilled they'd found a way to get Brady under center in place of a Kraft favorite whom the owner had just signed to a ten-year, $103 million deal.

Brady turned out to be an even better player than his childhood idol, Joe

Montana. But that shouldn't count against Belichick. Every legendary coach in every sport has needed a transcendent talent, an on-field, on-court vehicle for his greatness. John Wooden needed Lew Alcindor and Bill Walton. Red Auerbach needed Bill Russell. Lombardi needed Bart Starr. Walsh needed Montana.

Belichick needed Brady, and the quarterback arrived for him just in the nick of time.

On the black-ops front, hey, few dynasties are perfect. The stately Wooden won ten national titles while turning a blind eye to the UCLA booster, Sam Gilbert, who supplied the Wizard's players with extra-benefit goodies the NCAA does not allow. The Yankees of the late 1990s and early 2000s — led by the avuncular Joe Torre — fielded a full roster of significant faces across the pages of the 2007 Mitchell Report on performance-enhancing drug use, including Roger Clemens and Andy Pettitte. The Patriots? Though they acknowledged illegally filming opposing coaches' signals for years in the Spygate case, they never conceded any material wrongdoing in the Deflategate case, which revolved around the alleged improper deflation of footballs in the January 2015 AFC Championship Game rout of the Indianapolis Colts.

The league imposed substantial fines and seized first-round picks as a result of Spygate and Deflategate, and that's why Belichick's standing in the sport outside of New England isn't what it is in Massachusetts, Connecticut, Maine, New Hampshire, Rhode Island, and Vermont. Case in point: I was on the phone once with a former Maryland high school coach, Andy Borland, who had competed against Belichick's coach at Annapolis High, Al Laramore, and had been one of Laramore's best friends. Borland happened to be watching a college football game that day with a colleague who also knew Laramore. And when that colleague heard Borland was talking to an author working on a biography of Belichick, the man yelled, "Al Laramore never taught his ass to cheat, I'll tell you that. Put it in the goddamn book."

Borland immediately countered his colleague, saying, "I don't think he's a cheater, but a great coach."

Any right-minded observer of the game knows that Belichick did not become an NFL titan by bending or breaking the rules, even if it represented a part of his playbook. He won more Super Bowls than any coach dead or alive by finding, in the team-centric Brady, the perfect centerpiece of a system forever emphasizing the group's agenda over individual pursuits. Nobody's salary or seniority or résumé or draft position would determine his playing time. Belichick would put on the field the Patriots who gave him the best chance to win that week, and nothing else mattered.

Only it couldn't be that simple. Belichick is hardly the only boss in the NFL who preaches small-picture sacrifices and selflessness for big-picture gains, or the only head coach who can belt out 18-hour workdays with a nine-to-fiver's ease. So how in the world did he do this? How did he rage so successfully against the NFL machine? How did that stone-faced automaton at the podium inspire ever-changing circles of young men to compete at such a high level, practice after practice, game after game, for 17 consecutive years?

I set out to answer those questions in part because of how wrong I was about Belichick in the early winter of 2000, and because of how wrong so many longtime football men were about him. NFL officials practically begged Kraft to stay clear of him. People up and down the New York Giants organization who considered Belichick their finest assistant coach since Lombardi and Landry also believed he would fail in Foxborough, just as he had failed in Cleveland.

Belichick defied them all, and I wanted to find out how he did it. In the search for answers, in assembling this portrait of a hooded figure who has remained a mystery to most, I interviewed more than 350 people, some under cover of anonymity to protect their relationships with the Patriots' coach.

I expected nothing from Belichick as I started this project, which offered him no financial reward and no editorial control. He met those expectations. He declined to be interviewed for this book and asked a number of his friends and colleagues not to speak with me, sometimes using his longtime lieutenant, Berj Najarian, as the messenger.

Some Belichick associates were terrified to talk and apologized for being unable to share even the warmest stories of a Bill the public never saw. Some would speak only if I promised them protection. (One jokingly asked that I guarantee him immunity from future prosecution.) Some were comfortable enough in their own skin, and confident enough in their place in life, to talk freely about the man, whether he liked it or not.

I learned a lot about Belichick in the process. I learned he was a gameday reflection not only of his father, Steve, a lifer scout, but also of his high school coach, Laramore. I learned that Belichick once taught a college teammate how to cheat in lacrosse. I learned he was an immature head coach in Cleveland who did some immature things, but that he was also remarkably generous with his overworked assistants. I learned that Belichick grew from a disconnected tyrant with the Browns into a vastly underrated motivator in New England who knew how to lift players, staffers, former teammates, and longtime friends with acts of kindness and decency.

I learned that he blamed himself for the Patriots' most devastating defeat, in Super Bowl XLII, and that he always credited his players — in public and in private — for the team's most glorious victories.

This book is the yield of what I discovered through my interviews, and from the other sources I have cited in these pages. In the end, I was trying to humanize a person who had no interest in being humanized, and it proved to be the most daunting challenge of my 30-plus years in journalism.

I think it's a safe bet to say William Stephen Belichick would have had it no other way.

BELICHICK

1

THE TEACHER

By the time Steve Belichick arrived at Hiram College of Ohio in 1946 to start a full-time career in coaching, he was already something of an all-American success story. He was a college graduate out of the Pennsylvania and Ohio mill towns that had forever produced lifelong miners and factory workers, and he was an honest-to-God NFL equipment manager turned Detroit Lions fullback who had scored three touchdowns in one season before serving in World War II.

But as much as anything, Belichick was the son of Croatian immigrants who had honored his uniform and his flag by being way ahead of his time — and his country — in matters of black and white.

Belichick was an armed guard officer in the United States Navy when Samuel E. Barnes entered the officers' club one day on Okinawa and encountered a different kind of enemy within. Every white man present, except one, walked out on Barnes, who commanded a black stevedore battalion and stood among the pioneers known as the Golden Thirteen — the first 13 African American officers in the Navy. This was more than two years before Jackie Robinson made his debut at Brooklyn's Ebbets Field as baseball's first black player, and more than nine years before *Brown v. Board of Education* rendered segregated schooling unconstitutional.

Belichick knew that Barnes had been a three-sport athlete at Ohio's Oberlin College, and he told Barnes that he need not worry about the walk-out and that they should enjoy the empty club together. "He was one of the most unprejudiced persons I'd ever met," Barnes would say of the white officer who befriended him that day.

Barnes almost never spoke about his experiences in the war, or about the white seamen who crossed the street when they saw him approaching so they wouldn't have to salute a black man. He didn't tell his daughter about his place in history until the 1970s, when she found his picture in a book on African Americans in the military and called him on it. "I'm 22 years old," Olga told him. "Why did you never speak of this?" Barnes explained that "a lot of people fought in the war," and that was that. He did tell his wife about

Steve Belichick's grace and dignity, and how that had helped him advance from one day to the next.

"They were roommates," Olga said of her father and Belichick, comparing their cross-racial bond to the one between two Chicago Bears running backs in the 1971 film *Brian's Song*. "The best example I can give you, though I can't say it was the same depth of friendship because they were on the same team for years, would be Gale Sayers and Brian Piccolo in the sixties, in terms of the kind of respectful relationship they had."

Belichick saw a man as a man, and he had long embraced the virtues of equal opportunity and an honest day's work before showing up at Hiram after the war was done. He had accomplished so much for a 27-year-old raised in the Depression by a father (Ivan) and mother (Marija) who arrived in the United States around the turn of the century with next to nothing to their name — which was Bilicic before their daughter's first-grade teacher misspelled it and altered it forevermore. The 1920 U.S. Federal Census apparently listed the name as "Biliciek," though that is not how the family and the teacher came to spell it.

In 1919, Stephen Nickolas became the youngest of five children born to Mary and John Belichick of Monessen, Pennsylvania, 21 miles south of Pittsburgh. The 1920 census reported that John was the 41-year-old head of the household who had immigrated to the United States in 1901 (though his petition for naturalization said he sailed from France to New York in 1900), and that his wife, Mary, had immigrated in 1905 (though the 1930 census said she arrived in 1907). The great author David Halberstam wrote in his 2005 book *The Education of a Coach* that Mary arrived in America with no idea of her husband's whereabouts — John didn't know how to write; he'd never gone to school — and with her brother Nick Barkovic went on a hunt of Croatian communities in western Pennsylvania until she found John, working for Pittsburgh Steel.

The census reported that John and Mary had become American citizens in 1914, that neither could read or write, and that they lived on Grant Avenue, in the third ward of Monessen. The census listed the four sons in descending age — Frank, Joseph, John, and Steve — but seemed to have omitted the oldest Belichick child and only daughter, Anna. Four Croatian men aged 25 to 36 were listed as boarders and laborers in a steel mill; John was listed as a wire drawer, a thankless metalworking job that involved the use of die to make wire.

The family moved to another smokestack town, Struthers, Ohio, when Steve was a young boy. Every day, John walked more than five miles each way to his Youngstown factory job, and Steve later pitched in with his siblings to help pay the bills after their old man lost that job. Frank, the oldest boy, was a meter reader for the gas company. Among other things, Steve would become a golf caddie who made a dollar (tip included) for an 18-hole loop and a mill worker whose athletic talents gave him options not available to fellow teenage sons of undereducated Eastern European immigrants in the region.

Though he was a modest 5′10¾″ (Steve later scoffed at his listed NFL height of 5′9″) and about 165 pounds, Belichick was strong enough and swift enough out of Struthers High to play football and basketball at Western Reserve University, in Cleveland, where he was a fullback in Bill Edwards's fullback-friendly single wing. Steve was on partial scholarship; he held down various jobs, including one delivering ice over the summer, to help defray costs. Later in his college career, he worked as a janitor with a $500 income, according to census records that said his father was earning $1,300 in the steel mill, his brother Joe was earning $1,215 in the mill, and his brother Frank was earning $1,800 with the gas company.

For Steve, it was clear early on that the school was offering more than a kid who once appeared destined for a laborer's life could have dreamed of. His older brothers Frank and Joseph would spend all their working years in blue-collar jobs. Ohio records showed that before Frank died, in 1985, at age 75, he had last been employed as a supervisor of mechanics and repairers in the electric-and-light industry, and that Joseph — who died the same year, at 73 — had last been employed as a crane and tower operator in the blast-furnace-and-steelwork industry. The third brother, John, who went by John Joseph Bell, cleared a path for Steve by playing football at Pennsylvania's Geneva College, earning a master's degree at Ohio State, and becoming a successful executive with the Columbia Gas System and the York (Pennsylvania) County Industrial Development Authority, where he reportedly created more than 23,000 jobs and completed $349 million worth of projects. (John lived until 2006, dying at age 91.)

College would be the same kind of gateway for Steve. He was a three-year letterman at Western Reserve in football and basketball and a member of the Warion Society, for upperclassmen prominent in extracurricular activities. He ran for enough touchdowns to ultimately earn a place in the school's Hall of Fame. His coach, Edwards, was just starting a head coaching career that would land him in the College Football Hall of Fame; his Red Cats were that era's equivalent of a wildly successful mid-major Division I program. They went undefeated in 1938, beating the likes of Ohio Wesleyan, West Virginia, and John Carroll before crowds ranging from 10,000 to 20,000. Two years later, in Belichick's final season, Steve took a short carry over the goal line to help Western Reserve beat Arizona State in the Sun Bowl.

Edwards left the school to coach the Lions, and with Belichick fully expecting to get drafted into the military, Edwards gave him a job handling the team's equipment until his number was called. Only the coach called Steve's number before the Navy did. Edwards was trying to navigate his way around some injuries, and he wasn't happy with his fullbacks early in Detroit's season. So after watching Belichick more than hold his own while helping out in practice, the coach decided his former Western Reserve star should be added to the roster. The Associated Press reported that the move was the first of its kind in pro football "since Arnie Herber graduated from clubhouse boy into a vital role with the Green Bay Packers" in 1930.

On the afternoon of October 26, 1941, with the Packers holding a 24–0 lead in the fourth quarter at Detroit's Briggs Stadium, Belichick fielded Hal Van Every's bouncing punt on the run and made like Red Grange as he knifed through the Green Bay coverage team. The equipment manager, who was actually being paid by the players — one dollar per man every week — scored a touchdown on a 77-yard return, providing a much-needed diversion for a 1-4-1 team.

Two weeks later, after a victory over Cleveland, Belichick scored on a pair of eight-yard runs in a 20–13 loss to the New York Giants. "What I like about Steve," Edwards said at the time, "is that he tries hard every minute. We need more like him."

Detroit won two of its final three games, and Belichick completed his one and only season of pro football as a $115-a-week fullback (about an $80 increase over his previous wage) who had proven more efficient in Edwards's system than his teammates. Belichick averaged 4.2 yards on 28 rushing attempts; no other Lion was good for even 3.0 per attempt. (Byron "Whizzer" White, Detroit's biggest star and a future Supreme Court justice, averaged 2.7 on 89 carries, matching Belichick only with his two rushing touchdowns.)

The Lions ended their season on November 30. Seven days later, the Japanese bombed Pearl Harbor. Before serving in the Navy overseas, Belichick played on an all-star team at the Great Lakes Naval Station, in Illinois, where he blocked for Bruce "Boo" Smith, the Heisman winner out of Minnesota, and still took his fair share of handoffs. "Smith, Belichick Lead Massacre" read one United Press headline over a story recounting Great Lakes' 42–0 victory over Purdue in 1942. One of Belichick's two touchdowns in that game came on a 35-yard interception return.

The following year, Steve ended up on the coaching staff at Southwestern Louisiana Institute, and then left for the war in Europe. He was reportedly commander of a merchant marine gun crew before being transferred to the Pacific. Belichick was discharged on March 5, 1946, according to records, some six months after the formal surrender of Japan. Okinawa, where Belichick was based with Sam Barnes, was scheduled for use as a staging area for an invasion of Japan that likely would have caused more than a million American casualties.

Upon his return to the States, Belichick had thoughts of picking up his NFL career where he left off in Detroit. He figured he might have a shot to play for Paul Brown, who had won a national championship at Ohio State after building a powerhouse team at Washington High School, in Massillon, Ohio. Brown was now running the startup Cleveland Browns of the startup All-America Football Conference, designed to rival the NFL, and his friend Edwards thought Belichick was the best fullback he'd ever had.

"However, I got messed up when one of Coach Brown's assistants misunderstood me," Steve would say. "Coach Brown was still in the Navy at the time when this assistant asked me at Great Lakes whether I wanted to play [pro] ball. I told him that I did, but he told Coach Brown that I was undecided, and Coach Brown doesn't operate that way — you either do or you don't. Anyway, this coaching job opened up for me at Hiram College and I took it."

Hiram was a small liberal arts school in northeast Ohio, better known as the former home of the 20th president of the United States, James Garfield, than as a place to chase athletic glory. Steve's teams were an odd mix of battle-scarred men, in college thanks to the GI Bill, and undeveloped boys, none on football scholarships. Hiram wasn't Notre Dame or Michigan. The players were generally too small and too slow to play major-college football, but the servicemen — some in their late twenties — had a distinct physical and mental advantage over the 160-pound teenagers, who were in awe of them.

The ex-servicemen made up more than half the team. Some were married, some were close to 30 years old. They were often housed in the de facto barracks near the field, and one player said it wasn't uncommon for a rowdy poker game among the older crowd to end with someone's fist or head coming through one of the rooms' paper-thin walls. "The war veterans were generally wonderful to be around," said a younger teammate. "But in those barracks, if things got out of hand, you might hear one of them say, 'You high school guys had better shut your fucking mouths or I'm going to put my fist down your throats.' And those servicemen had all the girls. They ran the campus. We had no chance against them."

Kir Karouna, a bench player from New York City, pointed out that age sometimes worked against the soldiers and sailors on Belichick's team. "We were running around the track to warm up once," Karouna said, "and the fellow next to me was in the invasion of Normandy and Utah Beach. I said to him, 'How come you're huffing and puffing?' And he said, 'Look, wait until you get to be 26.'"

Belichick was around the same age as a number of his athletes, and yet he commanded nearly universal respect. The players remembered him as big-chested and broad-shouldered, with a boxer's nose that had been broken too many times to count while he played football in leather helmets with no facemasks. Steve usually wore baseball pants that looked like knickers, a T-shirt or sweatshirt, and a ball cap. He didn't like socks worn from the knee down, and he told his players they would never wear them. "And we never did," one said.

The coach wasn't what anyone would call a screamer, but he knew how to get his team's attention. "Steve was very thorough in watching film and pointing out what should've been done," Karouna said. "It wasn't a shouting session even when we lost a game, which wasn't a rarity. He'd say, 'If you did this or did that, the outcome would've been different.' I think most players liked him."

At least until his emotions bubbled over at the sight of sloppy execution. Upset one afternoon over his players' inability to properly run a play in practice, Belichick took the ball himself and asked a linebacker to try to tackle him. Belichick ran at full speed, without pads, and sure enough, the linebacker, in full pads, did as he was told. "I don't remember much about the collision," said Jack Kerr, an end from Pittsburgh. "I only remember that there was one."

The way another of Belichick's players, Richard Dean, remembered it, the coach was mostly angry at the defensive line. "Steve was one tough cookie," Dean said. "No one dared tackle him. He got the ball from the quarterback and ran it himself and . . . went through the line like greased lightning."

Nobody was allowed to drop a forward pass in one of Steve Belichick's practices; that would really draw his ire. But, by and large, the relationship between the tough-love coach and his undermanned student athletes was an exceedingly healthy one. In fact, Belichick was well liked across the entire campus. He was a physical education instructor who was made an honorary member of Phi Gamma Epsilon, Hiram's oldest Greek social club. He was a coach who inspired his teams with the depth of his knowledge. Kerr, who doubled as a punter, said Belichick "taught me more about kicking a football than I ever knew."

Hiram played home games before crowds of a few hundred people and almost always lined up against bigger, superior opponents. To toughen up the Terriers, Belichick sometimes had them run or push a blocking sled up the hill that led to the locker room. Don Nunnelly, a lineman from Alabama, said the coach had a drill known as "Murderers' Row," a term borrowed from the 1927 Yankees of Ruth and Gehrig. The drill was lacking in subtleties. A ballcarrier and a defender stood about five yards apart, with tackling dummies on the ground marking their tight boundaries. "A lineman had to tackle the guy going full speed," Nunnelly said, "and if you didn't tackle him, you had to stay there until you made the tackle."

Belichick understood when he took the Hiram job that he would be unlikely to duplicate the success his mentor, Edwards, had at Western Reserve. Playing mostly against small Ohio and Pennsylvania schools, the Terriers had produced only six winning seasons between 1904 and the temporary wartime suspension of football in 1943, and yet in his first year Belichick managed a record of 5-3 and consecutive victories over Kenyon, Grove City, and Ashland.

He wasn't afforded much off-season time to focus on improving the football program: Belichick also coached basketball and track and field and just about everything else at Hiram — often without the help of any assistants — if only because that's what coaches at small schools back then were expected to do. Belichick traveled with his basketball team in three packed station wagons and was no less dedicated to that sport than he was to football. He even watched Hiram's intramural competitions in his perpetual search for talent, and he pulled out of that rec league a 5'11" guard from Cleveland with some leaping ability, Robert Ingram, who called Belichick "the best coach I ever played for."

Steve ran a balance of half-court and fast-break basketball, and he was not opposed to working the officials in an attempt to get a call. "He had a presence," Ingram said. "When he spoke, you listened. He wasn't a massive man, but he was a big man with plenty of muscle. You wouldn't want to tangle with him, and I never saw anyone challenge him."

At least one athlete did challenge his judgment, if not directly. Wally Kosinski arrived on campus in 1948, Belichick's final football season, with a rocket arm that would later catch the eye of none other than Paul Brown. Kosinski was about 6'2" and 205 pounds, which was big for a quarterback in those days, and Belichick favored the smaller, quicker Jerry Hess.

Jack Kerr, the punter and end, said Kosinski could cover 70 yards in the air with a pass. The would-be quarterback came in with a slightly lower estimate. "I could throw the ball sixty yards through the air and through a rubber tire," Kosinski said. "I had an arm and accuracy second to none."

Belichick didn't agree with that scouting report; he wanted Kosinski to play halfback. "And I couldn't run my way out of a paper bag," Kosinski said. "I thought he was so wrong on his assessment of me . . . I think Steve Belichick was a tremendous football guy, and I have nothing untoward to say about him that way. I don't want to get into politics, but Croatia cultur- ally is very close to Poland and I was a Polish kid, and we Eastern Europe- ans usually look out for each other. But that didn't work with Steve Beli- chick. He was a tough hombre. He was tougher than nails."

Kosinski would be installed as the starting quarterback by Belichick's replacement, Al Pesek, and later signed a $5,000 option contract with the Cleveland Browns while doing intelligence work for the Air Force that in- cluded a trip to Germany and an assignment to spy on the Russians. When Kosinski returned to Hiram (the Browns were training there) to tell Brown the Air Force needed him longer than expected and that he was no lon- ger interested in pro football, he said the legendary coach "had his glasses down on his nose while he was looking at something on his desk. He hardly ever looked up at me. The whole meeting took a total of four minutes, and then he looked up at me and said, 'Well, that's your decision. Goodbye.' That was my encounter with Paul Brown."

In the late 1940s, Belichick had more pleasant and meaningful interac- tions with the Cleveland coach. Steve was proud of his association with Brown, through Edwards. Life at Hiram was good for Belichick, even if his winning percentage in football wasn't to his liking. He followed that 5-3 opening year with a most promising start to the 1947 season, an 8-7 road victory over Thiel College of Pennsylvania. The Terriers tackled punter Sam Scava in the end zone in the fourth quarter, snapping Thiel's 15-game winning streak before a stunned and dismayed crowd of 2,000. But Hiram won only one more game that year, then went 1-5-1 in '48, when the Terriers were outscored by a 126–39 margin. Belichick had better luck on the bas- ketball court, starting with a 5-11 record in '46 before improving to 7-10 the next year and then going 12-8 in the '48–49 season, with Hess as his best player.

But Steve's greatest day at Hiram was, without question, the day he met Jeannette Ruth Munn, a 1942 Hiram graduate who taught Spanish and French at the school. Munn was vibrant, Belichick was gruff. By all ac- counts Jeannette was a looker, and at least a couple of Belichick's players thought she was a bit out of Steve's league. "She was a very beautiful, petite lady," said one. Many of Belichick's players actually didn't know their coach was seeing Munn, and one who did know thought the couple might've been keeping it quiet because of a written or unwritten policy discouraging in- tra-faculty relationships.

Richard Dean, who played football and basketball at Hiram, said he didn't think anyone on either team knew that Steve was dating Jeannette. Dean had Munn as his Spanish teacher and described her as "very good, very pretty, and very nice . . . She got along with everyone."

And then one day, Jeannette Munn was gone. She took off with Steve for Nashville, Tennessee, after Edwards left Brown's side as an assistant in Cleveland and accepted the head job at Vanderbilt University, where he'd give Belichick his first shot at the big time. The Commodores competed with heavyweights in the Southeastern Conference — they'd won their last eight games the previous season and outscored those eight opponents by a margin of 307–26 before their coach, Red Sanders, left for UCLA.

Edwards assigned the backfield to the man he described as a hell of a back, and yet he didn't sound terribly excited about it; he initially planned for Belichick to coach the freshmen. "I could have gotten several men for the job, but not the man I wanted," Edwards was quoted as saying. "I want a southerner." As a northerner replacing a popular North Carolina boy and Vanderbilt graduate, Edwards might've been playing to some of the locals who thought they were still fighting the Civil War. "I feel it would be better that Steve handle the backs this fall since he knows them," he continued. "Then I think I can get the man I want after this season and have him here when we begin practice next spring."

The Commodores went 4-4 in the SEC in 1949 and 5-5 overall, not the worst-case first-year scenario for a coaching staff that had a tough act to follow in Sanders. On August 18, 1950, before his second season at Vanderbilt opened, Belichick married Jeannette at the Memorial Presbyterian Church in West Palm Beach, Florida, where Munn's parents, Leslie and Irene, lived on 33rd Street.

Some of Jeannette's friends were less than thrilled with her choice of a life partner. "When we got married," Steve said, "her friends went berserk. They couldn't figure she'd marry a football coach. They figured maybe a concert pianist or a music teacher."

Steve and Jeannette were married by Dr. H. Hansel Stembridge, according to the Belichicks' certificate of marriage, dated August 22, 1950. Jeannette wore to her wedding a blue satin frock, a headdress of pink roses, and a shoulder-length veil. A black-and-white photo in the *Palm Beach Post* showed her carrying a bouquet of white roses and chrysanthemums as she left the church arm in arm with Steve, who looked every bit as rugged in his light-colored suit and dark tie as she looked stunning in her dress.

At the time, as a highly regarded scout and teacher of the game, Steve had every right to believe he was on track to become a big coaching star in the upper reaches of major-college football. So on the day he got married, Steve had no idea he had already worked his final game as a head coach — at Hiram, where he finished a combined 32-41-2 in football and basketball.

He would be a college assistant, an excellent one, for the next 40 years.

But that didn't mean Steve would spend the rest of his career making his bosses look smart and wondering what might've been, wondering what it would've felt like to run his own high-powered program. Steve would get to feel that feeling, and to live that life. A Belichick would become a head coach again, and he'd be responsible for moments on the football field, more than a few of them, that were a little bigger than snapping Thiel College's 15-game winning streak.

William Stephen Belichick, named after Bill Edwards and his own father, was not yet four years old when Steve Belichick was hired by the United States Naval Academy, in February of 1956. Edwards and Belichick had been fired at Vanderbilt after four disappointing seasons, at least by their employer's unrealistic standards. (Vanderbilt maintained the toughest admissions standards in the SEC, making it difficult to recruit top talent.) They were fired, essentially, Steve felt, because they couldn't beat Tennessee.

Belichick landed at the University of North Carolina under George Barclay, and after three consecutive losing seasons he was thrown a life preserver by Navy coach Eddie Erdelatz, who had an opening and asked Belichick to fill it, for a salary of $7,000. Steve, Jeannette, and young Bill moved to Annapolis and started a love affair with the academy and the town that would carry on for decades.

Bill had already shown a great eagerness to do whatever his father was doing. He idolized Steve, loved following him into practice, into scouting meetings, or into the film room. By age six, Bill was a Baltimore Colts fan who watched their epic 1958 NFL title game victory over the Giants on his maternal grandparents' black-and-white TV in Florida. But football was more than a source of joy and amusement to the boy. Steve said that his six-year-old son was already tracking down and distance and memorizing the Midshipmen's plays. By the fourth grade, he said, Bill was already becoming proficient in working the projector and breaking down Navy's game films.

"He wasn't a pest," Jeannette said of her son. "He was there to learn."

The Belichicks had white walls and blue curtains in their home — "very conducive to watching film on the wall," Bill would say years later. Only Jeannette, the language teacher who spoke seven languages, wasn't about to let her only child completely lose himself in a mind-numbing blur of 16-millimeter clips of opposing formations. She read books to Bill at the kitchen table. Sometimes Bill would read a chapter out loud and then his mother would read the next one. If the boy didn't understand a word or a scene, Jeannette stopped and explained it to him.

"A lot of what I learned from her was how to be a teacher," Bill said years later. "And how to, you know, explain things, or try to boil it down so that I could understand it . . . So when I started breaking down film, that a lot of the little things became important to me. And it was always instilled in me that it was important to write neatly, to do things the right way, the way they were supposed to be done."

Bill's favorite childhood read was *Winnie-the-Pooh.* He liked it so much, he said, "I almost read the cover right off the book." Bill liked the Hardy Boys mysteries and one of the first sports books he read, *Pennant Race,* Jim Brosnan's diary of the long-shot 1961 Cincinnati Reds. He later read and adored Jerry Kramer's diary of the 1967 Green Bay Packers, *Instant Replay,* and any other chronology of a sports season he could get his hands on.

Football was his narrative of choice, and for obvious reasons. "He wanted to be with me," Steve said, "and I wanted to be with him." Joe Bellino, the Navy running back from Winchester, Massachusetts, who won the 1960 Heisman Trophy, remembered a six-year-old Bill hanging around the practice field and the field house, where his father ran weekly night sessions dissecting the upcoming opponent he'd just finished scouting.

Bill sat in the back and watched his old man diagram formations for the players — many of whom played offense and defense and some special teams, too — and lay out the best available plan. *Here's what they're going to do . . . This is a key . . . Here's this backfield set . . . Here's this guy's stance.* Steve Belichick might not have been a part of many winning coaching staffs early in his career, but he was already developing a reputation as an advanced scout without peer.

Sometimes, when Navy was facing an overmatched opponent, Steve would say, "The turning point in this game is going to be the coin flip." It was his way of keeping his players and colleagues as loose as possible.

"Steve introduced the offensive and defensive game plans, and he was very meticulous," Bellino said. "I can remember him saying quite clearly on a number of occasions, 'Guys, we can beat this team. All you have to do is play the game as I plan it.' Steve picked out the opponent's weakness and attacked it, and we won many games on the minute details that he introduced on Mondays . . . He'd notice the opposing team's offensive linemen, how they lined up, whether a guy's right foot was back or parallel with his left foot and how that could determine whether it was a run or pass play or a run play to the right or left. That's how he game-planned for every team."

Early in the 1960 season, Navy played a game it appeared destined to lose at Washington, the nation's third-ranked team and a 44–8 winner over Wisconsin in the previous season's Rose Bowl. Belichick scouted the Huskies and thought they were vulnerable to swing passes to the left side. After Washington botched an attempted punt late in the fourth quarter while holding a 14–12 lead, and after the Huskies sacked Navy quarterback Hal Spooner for an 11-yard loss, Spooner threw one of those Belichick swing passes to Bellino, who took it 19 yards to the Washington 16 and ultimately set up the winning field goal in the closing seconds. The Huskies wouldn't lose another game the rest of the season.

"Steve was like a general," said Bellino, who would serve in Vietnam. "He was a guy you wanted to lead you into battle . . . For us, what Steve Belichick said was gospel."

As it turned out, young Bill Belichick felt the same way about Joe Bellino. A nine-year-old Billy attended Bellino's graduation ceremony, Steve said, "and when the cadets all threw their caps into the air, he just walked over and picked up one without looking. There must've been 700 caps on the ground, and he picked up his idol's, Joe Bellino's."

Bill cherished life around the academy as a boy, even as his father and the other coaches put in endless workdays. Roger Staubach, the 1963 Heisman Trophy winner at Navy, played catch with Bill after practices ended and the receivers had left for the night. Every week, Ernie Jorge, a Navy assistant, sent young Belichick the team's plays in a package labeled "Bill's Ready List," which the boy took into his room and studied and studied and studied some more.

Steve Belichick was sure never to force football or coaching onto his son, but Bill, even at age five, had wanted to ride along with his father to scout William & Mary in Virginia. He later wanted to draw up schemes in his bedroom at night. He wanted to analyze plays on film by down and distance and to absorb everything from Steve's coaching friends when they gathered at the house. He wanted to take snaps from Tom Lynch, team center and captain and the future academy superintendent.

Bill wanted advice from Wayne Hardin, who had played college ball at Pacific for Amos Alonzo Stagg and had become Navy's 32-year-old head coach in 1958. When Bill was about 12 and starting to play organized football, he asked Hardin what position he thought suited him. "Tell you what," the coach told the boy. "Turn around, bend over, and snap the ball to me."

Bill's first snap was a bit soft. His second attempt was firm, delivered with purpose. "Don't change it," Hardin told him. He advised Bill to keep watching Lynch and to copy everything he did.

Hardin had a son, Gary, who tagged along to practice with his friend Bill. To pass the time while their fathers worked, sometimes Gary and Bill wrestled on the field-house mats or played on the basketball court or ran around the track. Wayne Hardin laughed when he observed Gary and Bill watching his players run through drills. Steve's boy was so focused on what the coaches were saying and how the units were responding to them. "Billy was eating it up," Hardin said, "while my son was looking in the sky and waiting for the golf course to clear out."

Gary Hardin would grow up to become a professional golfer, good enough to play on tour, and he could see as a grade-schooler that Bill had other designs. They did golf together as kids on the Navy course (Bill ended up caddying for Spiro Agnew, the Maryland governor and future vice president of the United States), with limited success. "We used to hit into the water a lot," Gary said. They both played some YMCA-level football, Gary said, and there was no doubting who was more serious about the game.

"Bill was already looking at football as a career, even at that age," Gary said. "We spent a lot of time together and stayed at each other's houses. We'd play chess and other strategy-type games. Bill was very into the strategy aspect, and we'd draw up football plays and defenses that we watched our dads come up with . . . Bill knew where he was going much quicker than most. He didn't waste any time. Every practice and film, he was putting stuff away in his memory."

Bill's father was too nervous to watch the Midshipmen play in person, so he was more than happy to spend his Saturday afternoons on another campus, searching for any game-day minutiae that might give Navy a competitive advantage the following week. He effectively scouted Army every week, as Army–Navy was everything to his bosses, peers, and subordinates in Annapolis. But when he wasn't gathering intel on West Point, Steve Belichick was identifying vulnerabilities in every opponent on the schedule.

"He always came up with something," said Wayne Hardin, who said Belichick made a difference — *the* difference — in a 1958 game against Michigan when they were both assistants under Erdelatz. The Wolverines had a talented two-way halfback who, when playing defense, raced aggressively toward the line of scrimmage if he saw a running back coming his way. Belichick told the other Navy coaches that if they ran a play-action pass toward this defender, he could be beaten over the top.

The targeted Michigan player had been hurt, but up in the press box Hardin saw him suddenly enter the game on defense and told his Navy staffmate, Jorge, to relay Belichick's play to another assistant, Dick Duden, down on the sideline. "We need that play right now," Hardin barked to Jorge. "He may not be in there after this play." But in the fog of competition, Duden didn't get the message. Hardin angrily reached for the phone. "I went nuts," he said. "I told Duden, 'Don't say anything. Just tell the quarterback that's the play.' And he did. Touchdown — we won the game."

Joe Tranchini had completed the 85-yard scoring drive by throwing a 36-yard pass to Dick Zembrzuski with 5:05 left. "No Michigan defender was within 15 yards of him," read the United Press International dispatch.

Instead of walking into the winning locker room with a bounce in his step, Hardin was terrified. He tried to hide as the celebration broke out around him. He thought he might've overstepped his bounds by forcing the call that had just toppled Michigan. Word had gotten around that Hardin had delivered the order from the press box, and had done some yelling and screaming in the process, but the players and coaches only thanked him for coming up with the decisive play. "I didn't call it," Hardin told them. "Steve called this play last Monday."

Steve Belichick lived for these moments, and so did his son. Bill traveled with his old man on scouting trips, and he never forgot the way Steve outworked the four or five other scouts in the press box with him. Steve was up there with his pencils, his charts and binoculars, and he wrote down the substitutions in his book, wrote down the play, and then immediately moved on to the next play. Bill was mesmerized. "To go to a game and watch him scout a game was an unforgettable experience," he would say years later.

"You would have other scouts asking, 'What happened on that play?' He was just so good at it. When the game would be over and we would be driving home, we would talk about the game, but he saw every play. The scheme and the defense, the pattern that they ran, the coverage they were in, who blitzed. He had a great vision. He taught me what he watched for."

Steve decided to write a book on his strategy and philosophy in analyzing teams and players, and his wife played the role of editor. Jeannette repeatedly instructed her husband to better explain his points, to avoid jumping from A to D while skipping the B and C that the average fan and reader needed. "If I can understand it, I'll type it," Jeannette told Steve. "And somebody else could get it. And if I don't understand it, then we gotta rewrite it."

The result was the 1962 book *Football Scouting Methods,* which became a manual for those who wanted a doctorate in game-day reconnaissance. Steve spoke to the importance of in-person observation, even though he wrote, "In this day of modern science and transportation, it is possible for a scout to come back to his school with the movies of the game he saw some twenty-four hours before."

Steve ran a summer camp with Jack Cloud, a Navy coach and former NFL player, that revolved around discipline and conditioning, and his off-season workouts were known to bring even the sturdiest young Middies to their knees. Bill was there with his father for as many drills as possible. He did everything with Steve, at home and on the road, including shop for bargain books at used-book stores or at the Salvation Army. "If they were over a buck," Bill said, "then we'd pretty much write 'em off." Steve was known around the academy for his frugality. He was an immigrant steelworker's boy and a son of the Depression, after all.

Steve Belichick taught his only child much about life, about family, and about football — he was a leading scholar in all three fields. But the truth was, on the subject of how to be a head coach, Steve realized over time that it wasn't his thing. His boy would need another strong role model on that front, and as he prepared for the rite of red-white-and-blue passage that was high school football, Bill Belichick was about to meet him.

2

BIG AL

Al Laramore, head football coach at Annapolis High School, went unde-feated in 1966, the year desegregation sent some black students from Wiley H. Bates High School to Annapolis and sent some white students to Bates. The schools were separated by only a couple of blocks. They shared the same football field and nothing else.

In this separate and unequal environment, Bates didn't have the funding to fully equip its players. Alan Pastrana, star quarterback of the 1962 An-napolis team and a future member of the Denver Broncos, attended a Bates game in 1962 and watched three of its players leave the field and hand their helmets to incoming teammates. "It was so strange," Pastrana said. "They were there, and we were here. There was no interaction at that point, and that's just the way it was."

Desegregation finally started to tear down the walls between the two worlds, and in 1968, after Bates had transitioned into a junior high school, one of its white students showed up at Annapolis High to play center for Laramore's football team. His name was Bill Belichick.

Bill had done some growing up since his days as a child in the back seat of his parents' car, proudly identifying the Fords, Chevys, and Buicks on the highway before his dad could. His boyhood in a beautiful waterfront town was all but borrowed from a Rockwell painting. He was a Baltimore Colts fan who met Johnny Unitas at his dad's football camp and snapped a ball to him, and who also met the coach, Don Shula, a friend of his father's. Bill went to a Colts game or two every December, after his old man's season ended at the academy, especially if the Browns or the Bears were the oppo-nents. He hung out with Navy's Heisman winners, Joe Bellino and Roger Staubach. He sat on the family's porch with his dad and fellow assistant Er-nie Jorge while the men drank beer and talked football. He listened atten-tively to the Navy coaches who visited his home and absorbed their lessons on handling adversity, and he marveled at the players' discipline, selfless-ness, and respect for authority.

Bill had good, sports-mad friends like Mark Fredland, son of a Navy professor, and Gary Hardin, and he had a father with manageable ambitions and a secure job (Steve became a tenured associate professor in physical education) and a mother who was happy to feed his insatiable appetite for football knowledge. When Jeannette wasn't reading her cherished copies of *The New Yorker*, she was doing her own breakdowns of opponents. "She had as much football knowledge as little Bill did at one point," Bellino said. "I think she might've coordinated all of Steve's notes. She probably viewed the game films as much as Steve did."

Steve had already confirmed Bellino's suspicions. "I don't think there's a woman in the country who knows more about football," he said of his wife. "She can tell you the second-string quarterback with the Rams or who coaches at Texas–El Paso."

This was Bill's charmed life on Aberdeen Road, at least until his experience at Bates High turned turbulent. As the only child of a man who had helped integrate a wartime officers' club by welcoming Sam Barnes, Bill came out of a household built around respect for all colors and creeds. But as a student at Bates, Bill often witnessed conflict along racial lines. He would later say that because the white and black neighborhoods were so different, "there was a lot of beating up of kids and that kind of thing. I was young. It was all over my head."

Gary Hardin had moved with his family to Philadelphia, and he'd call Bill to get updates on what was happening at school. "I'd get reports from him that one of our friends had gotten beaten up," Hardin said. "It was a violent, awful time . . . I was a new guy in a new atmosphere, and Bill was in a town he knew that was changing all around him."

The integration of the Annapolis and Bates student bodies initially didn't solve much of anything. The 1968 assassination of Dr. Martin Luther King Jr. led to rioting in Baltimore, a little more than 30 miles away, and eventually to the presence of a Black Panther Party office in Annapolis. Alan Pastrana's younger brother, Ron, a running back, said there was often trouble brewing between whites and blacks on school grounds. "Oh, my God," he said, "there was rioting, arrests, bottles flying across the parking lot, and the police didn't want to do anything. On the football field, there was no color line, but in the parking lot there was."

Against this distressing backdrop, Laramore, a former star tackle in college, believed his team was a symbol for what black and white could achieve when working together. The coach was proudest when his best player, Archie Pearmon, a black defensive end, was named winner of the Jim Rhodes Memorial Trophy, awarded annually to the most outstanding player in Anne Arundel County, beating out a number of accomplished white candidates. At a January 1969 banquet, Laramore said that it was a privilege to coach Pearmon, and that his classmates at Annapolis High looked up to him.

One white teammate who became a lifelong friend of Pearmon's, Bob Bounelis, confirmed Laramore's contention that there was no racial discord between white and black football players in the locker room or on the field. But there would be severe racial disturbances at the school in 1970, when some black students — a number of them moved by *The Autobiography of Malcolm X* — decided they should make a statement on Abraham Lincoln's birthday, February 12. The students had boycotted classes the previous month and gathered in the school cafeteria to voice their complaints about a white power structure that didn't make enough room for African American educators in the administration, or for African American studies in the curriculum.

The high school protesters wanted to model their actions after the college protesters raging against the war in Vietnam, and when they were confronted by administrators, trouble ensued. A UPI report quoted police describing Annapolis High as being left in "shambles" and said that "students went on a rampage, tearing down bulletin boards and smashing windows, desks and other furniture." At least 20 students were reportedly expelled as a result, including Carl Snowden, later a civil rights and community leader who successfully sued the FBI for illegally monitoring him from the time he was a teenager at Annapolis.

If the school's athletes needed a sanctuary from the escalating tensions, they found one in Al Laramore's locker room. Back at Annapolis High for his junior and senior years, Bill Belichick saw in Laramore a unifying, nononsense force who didn't tolerate divisions of any sort among his players. Big Al, as Laramore came to be known, was an important role model for young Belichick, who watched as his high school coach discriminated against only one kind of player: those who couldn't help him win a ball game.

A grizzly bear of a man, the 6'3", 300-pound Laramore stood as an imposing figure in the school hallways and operated as a de facto police force of one, respected equally by students white and black. On the team bus, he commanded the same kind of respect. The Annapolis Fighting Panthers sometimes stopped at a fast-food joint after a victory on the road, and the players would be engaged in loud, triumphant chatter while tearing through their burgers and fries until the moment their coach stepped on the bus.

"And then there was total silence," Ron Pastrana said. "He would look at his assistant and say, 'Are we all here?' If the answer was yes, he sat down and then everyone could start talking again. And half the team was minority and half wasn't, but you couldn't tell on that bus. When you looked on the bus, it was integrated. The school cafeteria wasn't — it was black on that side, Jewish in this corner, WASP in another section. But on Laramore's bus, everyone was one."

Pastrana said the black players often led the team in song on Laramore's bus. One of them, a defensive back named Wayne Blunt, said the coach treated the black athletes on his team with the same consideration granted the white athletes. Blunt was one of seven children, and he was thinking of quitting football to focus on helping his family pay the bills. Laramore visited the Blunt home to talk to Wayne's mother. He paid for her son's football shoes and helped him get a part-time job as a short-order cook that he could fit in after practice. Blunt got paid every Saturday, and after he'd collected two or three paychecks, his parents made sure he reimbursed his coach.

"Al wanted me to play for him. He kept after me," Blunt said. "That made me feel really good." As for the racial problems at school, Blunt maintained that they were tempered by athletes of different colors working together in highly functioning units. "And look," Blunt said, "there was no more problem when Al got involved." One story, later passed down to Laramore's twin sons, Dan and Dave, and perhaps embellished over time, had Big Al wielding a baseball bat as he guarded the gym that day the protesters were ransacking classrooms, ready to defend what he'd worked so hard to build.

Laramore's larger-than-life presence — and the image of him as a white sheriff standing tall in what had been a largely white domain — didn't stop him from establishing credibility in the black community as an equal-opportunity distributor of playing time. In later years, when his sons were in elementary school, Laramore took them along for rides while dropping off some of his black players after practice. These were places, Dan Laramore said, "where no white person would go, even a fireman wouldn't go. My brother and I and Dad would go in there, and we were accepted because of who my dad was." And for good reason: Big Al would become the first Annapolis basketball coach to field an all-black team, despite heavy resistance from the locals. "If there was pressure to put a white kid or two on the team," his son Dan said, "he resisted it."

In fact, a close friend of Laramore's believed that Big Al's health suffered under that pressure. Laramore endured bouts of depression in the 1970s and '80s that required hospitalization, a fact his son Dave wanted on the record to show the kind of tenacious fighter his father had been. ("This is the same person," Dave said, "who once had a mild heart attack in the middle of a game and didn't tell anybody.") Big Al ultimately became the first Maryland high school coach to win state titles in three sports — football, basketball, and lacrosse. "And I think each year after he suffered from depression, he won a state championship," Dave said.

One of Laramore's black basketball players, Kenny Kirby, who became an alderman in Annapolis, said Laramore made it known in 1971 that he was going with the best 15 players available to him, regardless of color. "He made that crystal clear to everyone," said Kirby, a 6'6" forward and later a team captain. According to Kirby, the players knew that Laramore had suffered "some stress problems and psychological problems" as a result of the objections voiced by white administrators and fans over the makeup of his roster. Laramore was temporarily replaced as Annapolis's football coach in 1972 (for the stated reason of an illness), and as basketball coach early in 1973 — by former Detroit Pistons star Eddie Miles — before returning for the close of the season and a run into the state playoffs. The fact that Laramore wouldn't blink and effectively compromised his own health in defending his all-black basketball team, Kirby said, "made you believe in him that much more."

On the football field a few years earlier, Laramore had already earned his players' trust. His culture of inclusion, a young Bill Belichick thought, represented the ideal of what a team was supposed to be. "It's the great thing about sports," Bill would say. "Race didn't have anything to do with it."

The Panthers' program was a pure meritocracy, which meant that Belichick had to work his way onto the Panther Stadium field. Bill wasn't big, and he wasn't fast, and he wasn't athletic. "He was a great help to the coach, telling others what to do," Jeannette Belichick said. "But he was slow, like his mother . . . He knew where he was supposed to be, but it was hard for him to get there."

Laramore found plenty that he liked in Belichick anyway, even if the kid couldn't move as quickly as his father did. The coach realized that his center could see the entire field like few teenagers could, and knew every teammate's assignment on every play. They formed something of a partnership, Laramore and Belichick, two Baltimore Colts fans who appreciated sound fundamental football. If Bill saw in his father a perfectionist's attention to detail, and in Navy coach Wayne Hardin a willingness to be bold and creative on special teams ("That wasn't lost on us as little guys," Gary Hardin said), he saw in Al Laramore an emphasis on toughness and simple execution.

Laramore's approach would have a lasting impact on Belichick, who later acknowledged what millions of young football players across the country understood — that, outside of your parents, few people can influence and shape you like a good high school coach. Bill was impressed that Laramore could run four plays, two base defenses, and the same punt and kickoff returns over and over and still dominate an opponent. Belichick saw that the game could be mastered through a relentless commitment to the basics.

He also saw that a head coach didn't need to be a big talker or showman to get his point across. Laramore wasn't one to waste words, and when speaking to local reporters from the *Evening Capital* and the *Baltimore Sun* who covered the Panthers, he generally kept it short and semisweet, volunteering nothing outside the narrow boundaries of the message he wanted to see in print. The coach was quick to blame himself for losses and to credit his players for victories, a habit greatly appreciated by Belichick and his teammates. In return, when his players were quoted in the press, Laramore expected them to remain humble and to talk about the team, not themselves. He was a devoted admirer of Vince Lombardi who wanted — no, demanded — a Lombardi-like program built around Old World values of sacrifice and grit.

In fact, Laramore's son Dave later said that when he read about the Packers legend, "it was like *Wow, I feel like I'm living with him.*" Back at St. Cecilia's, in New Jersey, Lombardi had been a self-made high school basketball coach, and he coached those kids in sneakers and shorts just as he coached his kids in helmets and pads. Laramore operated the same way, expecting his basketball players to fully commit to his football values.

A Belichick classmate and basketball team member, Leslie Stanton, likened Laramore's style to that of a different old-schooler: Woody Hayes at Ohio State. "Three yards and a cloud of dust," said Stanton, who remembered his basketball coach forever running drills emphasizing the bounce pass, the chest pass, and proper layup form. As far as nontraditional dribbling was concerned, Kenny Kirby said, Laramore had an unbreakable rule. "If you needed to go behind the back or between the legs to get somewhere on the court, he allowed it," Kirby said. "But you had to prove to him that you knew when to do it, and that it wasn't just showboating. He was a fundamentals-first person. He couldn't stand showboating at all."

On the football field, beyond the expected prohibition on end-zone celebrations, Laramore believed in a lot of running, a lot of sweating, a lot of three-a-days in the summer, and plenty of full-contact drills in the fall — which shaped young Belichick's vision of how to properly prepare a football team. Big Al's philosophy was as simple as the Panthers' white helmets, with their single solid stripe down the middle and jersey numbers above each earhole. "Our slogan was 'Hit or be hit,'" Ron Pastrana said. Other people around Laramore, including his wife, Dorothy, the school librarian, said another of his favorite sayings was "My way or the highway."

Laramore believed in playing seniors over juniors, and juniors over sophomores, and in making practices harder than the games. He expected his linemen to block downfield, play after play and series after series, because he expected his ballcarriers to regularly plow their way into the secondary. Al Laramore, Pastrana said, "wanted one thing out of his team: reckless abandon."

Line up with a purpose, block with fury, pound the ball through the defensive front, and then do it all over again. Laramore did not often deal in the currency of deception. He thought execution and determination would trump the opponents' pre-snap knowledge of what was coming their way. One Annapolis player said Laramore sometimes shouted in the play call from the sideline and didn't care if the opposing sideline heard it.

"We lined up in the same formation 99 percent of the time," said Tom Terry, the starting quarterback. "We had two tight ends, one wingback or wide receiver, Bill Belichick at center, myself, a fullback, and a halfback. On 24 Quick Trap, that play goes directly up Bill's backside, and the fullback took the ball. We ran 22 Power 90 to 95 percent of the time to the right or up the middle, because nobody would stop it. We had a very good offensive line, and we'd throw it occasionally here or there because we had a track star at receiver, Bill Mason."

The Panthers hit the blocking sled and ran through the Smitty's Blaster and used the rope pulley to harden their developing bodies. If a kid said something even slightly out of turn, Laramore immediately ordered the smart-ass to run a lap. Laramore could get loud and angry in a hurry, but he wasn't one to constantly berate his players, an approach that made a mark on Belichick.

Big Al liked smart players and good listeners, and he found both in young Bill. Belichick was an earnest student and a lunch-pail athlete who spent his summers waiting tables and working for the Mayflower moving company when he wasn't helping at his dad's football camp. Though his teammates and classmates didn't identify anything truly exceptional about him, Bill did stand out at Annapolis in a curious way.

"Oh, man," Ron Pastrana said, "Billy was always with a beautiful girl." One in particular was Deborah Lynn Clarke, Bill's high school friend and future girlfriend and wife. Debby was a cheerleading captain and the daughter of Doris and Stuart Clarke. Stuart was an Army veteran of World War II, the first personnel director at the NASA Johnson Space Center, in Houston, and one of the men involved in picking the original Gemini astronauts. Bill was sports editor of the yearbook when Debby worked on the staff. Next to her yearbook photo, she quoted the William Blake line "Exuberance is beauty."

"Debby Clarke, all those good-looking girls in school — Billy was always on it," Pastrana said. "I don't know what it was about him. He wasn't chiseled. He was a quiet, ordinary lineman. Maybe Billy had a good car or something, I don't know."

If nothing else, Bill had a good thing going with the football team. He was proud to wear his A.H.S. Football sweatshirt, proud to be part of the program. He wasn't among the most prominent Panthers as a junior, but he developed into a senior starter on a winning team and did enough with his limited skills to earn his teammates' unconditional respect.

"Bill stuck his nose in everything," Blunt said. "He wouldn't back off you."

Sometimes Belichick drove his blue Volkswagen Bug to summer practices with his backup, Bob Bounelis, who recalled the starting center as a young man of very few words. They had first met as seven-year-olds in a Naval Academy boxing clinic. Bounelis arrived that day in a T-shirt and long pants and was summoned into the ring with Bill. "I got one lucky shot in and knocked him down," Bounelis said. "He humiliated me the rest of the day, and then we became fast friends."

When they were high school seniors, Bounelis had no problem sitting behind Belichick. He thought his friend had earned the first-string job going away. "Bill was the catalyst to keeping everything moving on offense," Bounelis said. "Bill knew what he was doing better than anybody else."

Terry, the quarterback, remembered Belichick as very small in stature in high school, about 5′9″, but thought of him as a perfect deliverer of the football. There was good reason for that: Bill had spent hours upon hours snapping balls into a target he'd draw on his basement wall. "Bill shook the entire house with that ball banging against the wall," his father said.

Sometimes at practice, Laramore dunked a ball in a bucket of water, to simulate game conditions in a rainstorm, and handed it to his center. Bill made a clean snap to Terry every time. Whether the ball was wet or dry, the quarterback said, "we never had any problems with any fumbles or anything like that. I don't remember dropping a single snap." Soaking a practice ball to prepare players for miserable game conditions was a coaching method Belichick himself would later adopt.

Chris Carter, a gifted tailback and safety, had played a lot of ball with Belichick growing up and was by far the superior athlete. He shattered the Annapolis single-season rushing record with more than 1,200 yards as a senior and twice ran for four touchdowns in a game; at one point he was the only white starter on the school's basketball team. But Belichick impressed Carter as an advanced tactician who thought his way around the football field. "We had a pretty good offensive line," Carter said, "and Bill was the leader of that offensive line. He was the signal caller, and his size was not a hindrance . . . He was always one of those guys who always had something good to say before the crew would go out for the game. He was not a rah-

rah guy, but he had good, solid information. He got a lot of that from his dad."

Perhaps Belichick's most conspicuous on-field moment during his senior season unfolded against Bel Air High School. Annapolis had a 5-0 record entering that game and had outscored its opponents by a 158–66 margin. Bel Air took an 8-0 lead before the Panthers fumbled on their way into the end zone, and before Belichick, No. 50, alertly pounced on the loose ball to apparently give his team a touchdown. "Everyone was jumping around," Terry said. Only there was a problem: The official on the scene ruled that in the mad scramble to retrieve the fumble, Belichick had not gained control of the ball before he touched the back line of the end zone. In other words, it was a touchback, not a touchdown, giving the ball back to Bel Air.

"No, no, no," the ref barked at Belichick. "You're out of bounds."

To the surprise and dismay of some of his teammates, Belichick responded, "Good call, ref. That's the right call." Laramore's reaction? "Al wanted the touchdown," Terry said. "He didn't like it as much."

Annapolis lost that game, then got crushed by Good Counsel in the next one, 52–6. The Panthers rebounded with decisive victories over Andover and Glen Burnie, which had shared the county title with the Panthers the previous year. Laramore would never let a season get away from him without putting up a hell of a fight. He knew how to reach his boys in his pregame talks, often citing everyday life challenges and connecting them to the team prayer. "It didn't make any difference what faith you were," said one colleague. "It was like he would be talking to each person in that room individually, looking them square in the eye. I could see it in their body language. They were ready to play, brother. I mean, those kids had damp eyes. They could not wait to get out of that room. You better not be standing in the doorway or your ass was going to get run over."

Annapolis was all set up for another season-ending duel with a Severna Park team that had ruined its hopes for an outright championship in '68. Before that road game in Belichick's junior year, Laramore was quoted in the *Evening Capital* as saying, "We'll be there at 11 a.m. and ready to play." That was the extent of his public expressions of confidence.

Laramore never wanted his team shooting off its collective mouth — he once gave one of his captains a look that could kill for predicting victory at a pep rally. But Big Al did want people to know that he would play any team, anywhere. And he wanted to play and beat the Severna Park Falcons more than he wanted to beat anyone. "For whatever reason," Bounelis said, "Severna Park had our number."

On November 22, 1969, Annapolis and Severna Park met for a Saturday afternoon contest in Panther Stadium; school officials had decided against continuing the series on Thanksgiving Day. Annapolis took the field before a packed and energized crowd, hoping to avoid a defeat that, for the second consecutive year, would leave the Panthers with only a share of the county title.

Severna Park scored first on a Mike Thompson six-yard run in the first quarter, setting a tense tone. But a big Carter gain in the third quarter preceded Scott Crandall's eight-yard touchdown, making it 6–6. (Both teams' two-point-conversion attempts failed.) The Panthers wanted to avenge the '68 defeat, but they knew that a tie would give them sole possession of the championship. They preserved that tie with two goal-line stands, finishing with a 6-0-1 league record (8-2-1 overall) and another testament to Laramore's standing as one of the very best coaches in the state.

His departing center, Belichick, still had a season left to play in lacrosse, a sport that had occupied a firm place in his heart since he began playing it around the seventh grade. He would be a starting defenseman on an 8-2 team that lost the county title to unbeaten Severna Park. The Falcons' coach, Ron Wolfe, raved about the impact Belichick had on the group.

"Bill had a great stick," Wolfe said. "He was physical for his size, and he knew how to compensate for his lack of speed with positioning on the field. He got to where he had to be . . . It was like having a coach on the field."

Al Laramore always said the same thing about Belichick. He told his wife that Bill's extreme intelligence was a valuable asset at a time when Big Al didn't have even one assistant coach helping him. Laramore ran the Panthers all by himself, so in practices and in games he needed a few reliable teenage advocates to cover his back while he was tied up with this or that unit. Chris Carter was one. Belichick was another.

"He treated us almost as equals," Carter said of his coach.

This had a tremendous effect on Belichick, who would talk about Laramore's influence on him for years to come. Big Al would go on to break records at Annapolis High over the better part of the next two decades, before his life was tragically cut short by a heart attack. Little Bill? He would carry Laramore's lessons with him on his journey into manhood. For his farewell to Annapolis, Belichick quoted the 17th-century English poet Abraham Cowley next to his senior yearbook photo.

"I would not fear nor wish my fate," read the passage, "but boldly say each night, / tomorrow let my son [*sic*] his beams display / or in the clouds hide them; i have lived today."

Bill had decided to attend one of the nation's most prestigious prep schools, Phillips Academy, in Andover, Massachusetts, for a year of postgraduate study. As for college, Belichick told his father he wanted to find another school in New England.

"You've never even been to New England," Steve Belichick shot back, ignoring the summer trips to Nantucket his son had made with Mark Fredland.

"Yeah," Bill said, "but I've done some studying and found there are more good schools in New England than anywhere else, and I want to see them."

So, 350 years after the Pilgrims arrived on the *Mayflower,* Bill Belichick would go ahead and discover New England. It was a place that would dramatically change his life.

3
ANDOVER

Bill Belichick was staying late after practice to work on his snaps, which was not in itself a profound development. He was the new starting center on the football team at Phillips Academy, and he had already proven himself to be diligent in his approach to the game.

But this was a rainy day before the season opener, and the grass was wet, and a fellow offensive lineman and two-way starter named Dana Seero was struck by a sudden thought. Phillips had lost a game the previous season because its center had snapped a rain-soaked football over the punter's head, sending it rolling a good 30 yards in the wrong direction, and here was Belichick making sure the same thing did not happen two years in a row.

Was Belichick, a fresh postgraduate arrival, somehow familiar with the story of this crushing 1969 defeat? Or was he just doing what a coach's son ordinarily does by using a set of circumstances — in this case, a passing storm and an ample supply of footballs — to give himself and his team a competitive edge?

Seero didn't believe Belichick had any knowledge of the 1969 season at Andover, and it didn't matter. Either way, the four-year Andover player had never before seen anyone on his team make such productive use of bad weather. *This is good,* Seero told himself as he watched Belichick put in the extra work. *This way, if it rains, he'll be dialed in and we won't lose the damn game.*

In later years, Seero thought Belichick was embracing a militaristic view of football that rainy day, honed by watching his father coach Naval Academy students who were taught in the classroom and on the field that every detail needed to be addressed with life-or-death urgency. Young Belichick also learned from the Midshipmen that authority figures were to be respected, not questioned, and that a player should celebrate a team's achievements rather than waste time celebrating himself.

The time he spent around disciplined and mature young men had helped make Belichick college-ready straight out of Annapolis. But according to

David Halberstam's *Education of a Coach,* Belichick decided he'd spend a year in prep school if he couldn't get into Yale, Dartmouth, Amherst, or Williams. After Belichick went 0 for 4, he ended up at Phillips, where Steve Belichick's staffmate at the academy, Dick Duden, had been a legendary player.

The all-boys boarding school, widely known as Andover, was founded in 1778 (George Washington sent his nephews there) and was notarized by Paul Revere, who engraved Andover's official seal, which includes images of an active beehive and a flowering plant and the Latin mottos FINIS ORIGINE PENDET ("The end depends on the beginning") and NON SIBI ("Not for self"). The school was tucked in the northeastern part of Massachusetts and was known for its green grass and blue blood.

Andover had a gorgeous campus with a colonial vibe, a majestic bell tower encased in brick and dedicated to the 85 Andover men who died in World War I, and a physical plant superior to those of many liberal arts colleges on the East Coast. America's ruling class and society elites sent their sons to Andover, the second home to what would be the Bush dynasty from Texas — George H. W., George W., and Jeb would all attend — and to future scholars, philanthropists, and Wall Street financiers. It was a hell of a place for a ham-and-egger like Bill Belichick — former caddie, furniture mover, and busboy — to go to school.

Some tension naturally existed between the preppies and the townies, and occasionally word filtered out about a Friday night fight between the groups. Only two and a half miles separated Phillips from Andover High School, and there was some interaction between the two (the Andover track team would practice at the Phillips indoor facility), but the schools were effectively worlds apart. One working theory, said Seero, was that Phillips "always accepted one big, tough townie a year to keep the rest of the townies away from campus."

Seero was a working-class student and a local who figured he'd end up like his brothers: as a football captain at the very public Andover High. "But poor, dumb Dana Seero from Andover High had good grades, played the trombone, and was pretty good at football, and I went to Andover," he said. "It's a terrific school that prepares you for a lot of things. There are incredibly talented people there, and they don't give a fuck if your name is Bush or Seero or Belichick. They only care if you can deliver the goods. And if you can't handle never being the best at anything while you're there, don't go there."

Belichick found out quickly that he wouldn't be even close to the best at anything at Andover. He'd had solid grades at Annapolis, but he wasn't at the top of his class, and, by his own admission, he devoted more time and energy to sports than he did to his schoolwork.

At Phillips, Belichick had no choice but to work harder than he'd ever worked in his young life. The school offered little support — and certainly no babying — for even the most pampered incoming students; Phillips all but advertised itself as a sink-or-swim place. "And if you sank, that was too bad," Seero said. "That means you didn't belong at Andover, and off you go."

Belichick was ill prepared for the rigors of the Phillips curriculum, and he was, at times, in awe of the academic prowess of his fellow students. As the football team manager, Timothy Gay, put it, "Even the jocks were smart at Andover." Belichick was very much out of his element and out of his league. He described the typical Andover student as "light-years ahead of me" and told himself he needed to pick it up if he didn't want to be left behind.

Coming from his conservative upbringing, Belichick also experienced at Phillips a culture shock of a different kind. College campus protests over the war in Vietnam, the bombings in Cambodia, and the shootings at Kent State (where National Guardsmen killed four students and wounded nine) inspired at Andover a sense of rebellion that challenged the headmaster, John Kemper, a West Point graduate and career Army man. Students had been pushing back on decades-old restrictions on hair length and smoking, on required attendance at chapel, and on the mandatory dress code of jackets and ties. (They all received, on arrival, a 30-page book of rules on behavior and penalties for violations.)

Over time, the Andover administration backed off on its restrictions and allowed for the new environment of encouraged expression that Belichick encountered in the fall of 1970, when he became part of a student body of 879 boys. Recreational drug use was rampant on campus — the tall and entitled Andover tennis star Jeb Bush was among the regular marijuana users — and the school newspaper, the *Phillipian*, proudly announced that it was "uncensored" and that its faculty adviser "never sees the paper until after it has been printed and distributed." The paper featured editorials that Belichick said he found "outspoken." Overmatched by the academic demands, taken aback by some by the student freedom and liberalism he never saw at the Naval Academy, Belichick was a postgraduate, or PG, in need of a kindred spirit. He found one in a bespectacled boy born in Waltham, Massachusetts, named Ernie Adams, the son of a Navy officer. Ernie was a mad football scientist in training.

Adams had attended Brookline's Dexter School, the former home of John F. Kennedy, whose son John Jr. would end up at Andover 13 years after his father's assassination. At the time Belichick met Adams, who had arrived at Andover in the fall of 1967, Ernie was most likely among the only two or three teenagers in America outside of Annapolis who had read Steve Belichick's book, *Football Scouting Methods,* cover to cover. (Miraculously enough, Andover teammate Evan Bonds had also read it.) "I do remember Ernie telling me at one point he was very excited . . . to know Bill was coming as a PG," said Gay, the team manager. "He ran up to Bill all excited and said, 'Let's talk about your dad's book.'"

Adams was thrilled to find that Bill was Steve's son, and Bill was thankful to have something in common with a classmate who was a budding Latin scholar and whose intellect was clearly superior to his own. Adams played beside his new friend on the line, at left guard. If Belichick felt a bit intimidated by the collective IQ of even Andover's football players, Seero, the right tackle, said he shouldn't have been. "Bill shows up for two-a-days and walks down the hallway of the dorm and meets a guy who happens to be Ernie Adams," Seero said, "and Ernie is practicing conjugating Latin verbs . . . I've got news for you: Ernie was the only guy doing schoolwork that week on the whole football team. Ernie was the one academic freak."

Bonds, the right guard, might've qualified as well; he was already advancing an academic career that would culminate in a Ph.D. in musicology from Harvard. But Bonds, Belichick, and Adams were as serious about studying football as any boy on that campus was about studying anything. While other Andover students were reading the classics, Bill and Ernie were going to the library to rummage through back issues of *Sports Illustrated* and read about football.

It was a daily obsession, not a hobby. They watched film, talked strategy, drew up plays in their rooms, and lost themselves in the minutiae of the game. Lou Hoitsma, a math teacher and assistant football coach, marveled over how rare it was for boys of that age to devote so much time to the philosophies and formations that might or might not work in a particular week.

Adams and Bonds and the other students who had been at Phillips for years could feed their football addictions and still manage their classwork with little difficulty. Belichick did not have that luxury. The son of a woman who had taught French in college, Belichick thought he could handle French 3 at Andover as easily as he'd handled four years of the language at Annapolis. His first assignment was to read *Les Misérables,* and he needed to look up every word of it. "Math was the same way," Belichick said. "I needed extra help every day. I'd turn in a paper I would have gotten an A on in high school, and it would come back with red marks all over it."

Young Bill had better luck in anthropology, a class he initially had no interest in taking and ended up adoring. "I remember really wanting to go to that class," he said. "I realized that going off the beaten path sometimes isn't a bad thing. Andover gave me an appreciation of a lot of different things."

He was grinding in the classroom just as surely as he was grinding on the football field, where Steve Sorota, the longtime head coach, had a way of seamlessly integrating the one-year postgraduates into his program. Belichick was particularly impressed with Sorota's ability to keep the incumbents happy while sometimes replacing them with PGs, who were often regarded as ringers.

A smallish man, Sorota was a former teammate of Vince Lombardi's at Fordham, but he was not a practitioner of Lombardi's game-day decorum. He was forever a taciturn figure on the sideline, a thinker in rimless glasses, and a mental error by one of his players was more likely to be met with a piercing glare than a shout of "What the hell is going on out here?"

Gay said Sorota "never waved his arms. He just stood there and managed things." In fact, said Stratis Falangas, the left tackle, "I don't think I ever heard Sorota raise his voice."

Despite the clear academic priorities, they took their football pretty seriously at Andover, where Sorota presided over a varsity team and as many as six junior varsity teams. Sorota was a tough guy from a tough town — Lowell, Massachusetts — but he wasn't Al Laramore at Annapolis. "It was not 'my way or the highway,'" said Tim Callard, one of his assistants. And Sorota wasn't married to a singular style of play, either.

He analyzed his roster year after year and analyzed his opponents week after week and installed new schemes that best fit his personnel. "Back in Annapolis," Belichick said, "we had four running plays and two pass plays. It was a completely different story at Andover. We had a lot of plays and options."

They also had a lights-out quarterback in Milt Holt, a one-year postgraduate student from Hawaii who called his own plays. He had a cannon for a left arm and nimble feet that seemed quicker, more dazzling, because he wore white shoes while the rest of the team wore black. Holt had insisted on wearing white, and Sorota, realizing that the quarterback had talent rarely seen in Andover, thought it would be a good idea to relent.

Sorota ran practices that were light on contact and heavy on film work, organization, innovation, and just plain thinking. Sometimes he'd go up in the stands and watch as his boys ran through their drills. "He would be looking at things," Seero said, "more like a manager than a coach you'd find at most high schools."

It was clear early that Belichick, wearing No. 50, would be a de facto assistant coach for Sorota on the field, just as he was for Laramore. Gay, the team manager, who later became a physics professor at the University of Nebraska, recalled that during a break in the middle of a game, he saw the head coach initiate a meeting with his center.

"I do vividly remember that Coach Sorota sidled up to him," Gay said, "and sidling away after getting information. I never saw Coach Sorota do that to another player."

Belichick had earned that trust by nailing every one of his blocking assignments, and by correcting on the fly teammates who had better memories when taking an advanced calculus exam than when trying to pick up blitzers. "I would ask Bill who to block," said Falangas, the left tackle, "and he'd get tired of me asking. He didn't have an awful lot of patience for people who didn't know their assignments, and that would be me . . . He let me have it once. He told me, 'Block that guy.' He told the guy, 'You're going to get hit,' and I ended up being the one who got hit instead.

"Not many people knew what the backs or receivers would do, but Bill was attuned to everything . . . That gave the team an awful lot of stability, too. He anchored that front line out of his will and intelligence more than his size."

Dwarfed by the 6'3", 225-pound Seero, the 6'3", 190-pound Bonds, and even the 6'2", 200-pound Adams, the 5'10" Belichick weighed in around 180, making him the smallest man on the line. He was quick out of his stance, and some teammates thought he was more athletic than he gave himself credit for. Not that Belichick would ever say so. "He was a quiet person," Falangas said, "never one to brag. In fact, I never knew his father was a coach [at Navy] until after Bill graduated."

Falangas recalled Belichick once growing angry over something an assistant coach said. Though Seero and others maintained that they never heard the remark, Falangas said the assistant referred to Belichick as the "weak link" on the line. "That pissed him off immensely," Falangas said. "By no means was he a weak link. I'm sure it was in jest. Bill never made a mistake."

Belichick's job was to cleanly deliver the ball to Holt, a wondrous dual-threat athlete booked for Harvard, and deliver it he did. Bill was already an advanced student of the game. When he wasn't practicing football, he was talking it with Adams. They feverishly shared notes as if they were co-authors working on the first draft of a football encyclopedia.

Belichick was the better athlete, but Adams was the more powerfully built player, a guard who relied on his brute strength and technique. "Ernie executed our trap plays," Seero said, "and he was much stronger than the guys he played against. But he wasn't the guy to make a downfield block on a broken play or get downfield with someone on an end run."

Together, Bill and Ernie were quite a pair. They played a lot of bridge together, at least when they weren't debating the merits of one defensive scheme over another. "Ernie," Seero said, "had a madras jacket he wore for many years, but many of us did as well. He migrated to tweed somewhere along the line." Ernie wore the clothes a suburban father of four wore in the 1950s. He had a distinct Boston accent and was friendly and outgoing at the time, easy to interact with, while Bill often looked at the negative side of things. "Dour Bill," some teammates called him.

"I remember most of us were writing long essays or doing experiments in a physics lab," Gay said, "and Bill and Ernie were breaking down plays, and so it was clear they were football gurus . . . People didn't just say 'Bill's the genius.' It was like 'Look at Bill and Ernie — they are total football guys.' They were a team from the get-go."

Bruce Poliquin, a backup halfback who later became a congressman from Maine, recalled that he often saw Ernie and Bill together in the dining hall, the library, and the common campus areas, with Ernie usually carrying a football and Bill a clipboard. Dan Lasman, a backup lineman and one of only two lower middlers, or sophomores, on the varsity, saw the two of them poring over game films as he walked through the gym and toward the locker room. Belichick and Adams never ripped into the younger backup when he made mistakes on the practice field; Lasman felt only guided and instructed by them.

"Ernie was a notch below Bill as a player," Lasman said. "Ernie seemed so accepting of what he was, and never tried to be somebody he wasn't. He was completely nonplussed by his ability compared to the other, clearly more gifted athletes on the team. That wasn't the point for him. He loved to play football."

And this would turn out to be a great season to play football at Andover, even though the school paper forecast a rebuilding year. Phillips opened with a 26–12 victory over the Tufts freshmen and a 28–22 victory over the Williams College freshmen, and yet it was the third game that strongly suggested that Andover might have the makings of a special team. Sorota took his players on the road to New Jersey for a meeting with Lawrenceville, which had toppled Andover the previous fall, and a coach, Ken Keuffel, who taught a master class in the single-wing offense.

To some members of the Andover team, the Lawrenceville kids seemed four or five years older. Phillips beat them anyway, and suddenly there was chatter about running the table and finishing 7-0. Writing up the Lawrenceville game story for the *Phillipian* was a student named H. G. Bissinger, who went by the byline Buzzy. Bissinger, who would later be known as Buzz, would become a Pulitzer Prize–winning reporter and the bestselling author of *Friday Night Lights*. It was another reminder that everyone at Andover was heading somewhere.

Phillips blew out Mount Hermon and Deerfield by a combined score of 60–6, improving its record to 5-0 and creating a feeling of exhilaration among the players. Belichick and his fellow offensive linemen were getting their due for keeping their quarterback upright and clean, and for blowing open holes for the running game. Through it all, Sorota kept his even disposition perfectly intact. Belichick and the rest of the Andover players watched him carefully, watched how he handled in-game success and adversity as if they were one and the same. Sorota's tone helped them remain balanced and in the moment.

Andover was two games away from its first perfect season since 1959, and Sorota kept to his weekly routine of contained hitting in practice and plenty of film work. Every Sunday, Callard, who doubled as a tough-as-nails religion teacher, picked up the film of the previous day's game at the nearby drop-off place, the police station in Stoneham. Callard watched the tape first before handing it over on Sunday evening to the head coach, who spent Monday doing his own review.

Callard had played on the offensive line at Princeton and, though he worked more with Adams and the other guards and tackles than he did with Belichick (Sorota liked having the centers work with the quarterbacks), he noticed something unmistakable on those films. "Other kids would forget something on a play," Callard said, "but I can never remember Bill Belichick missing an assignment. Bill wouldn't always make an outstanding block, but he always had the right man . . . Obviously he was thinking all the time."

Andover improved its record to 6-0 with a 21–0 thrashing of Dartmouth's "B" freshman team, and the victory elevated the stakes for the final game of the season, prep football's answer to Harvard vs. Yale: Andover vs. Exeter, the team in blue against the team in red, the longest-running rivalry in American high school football. They started competing in 1878, 100 years after Andover was founded and 97 years after Exeter opened 35 miles to the north in New Hampshire. Visiting teams once traveled by stagecoach to the opposing campus. To students and alums at each school, it was the only game on the schedule that truly mattered.

A lot of great young Andover men from great American families had battled in this game, and almost all of them would take the memories of victory and defeat to their graves. This was an unbeaten season on the line. Andover could not possibly throw it all away by falling to a 3-2 Exeter team.

As always, the campus came alive the Friday night before the game at the traditional pep rally, which ended with the burning of a wooden A. The following day, fans packed the Brothers Field stands at Andover for the 90th edition of the rivalry. Bissinger was covering for the *Phillipian,* and this was the one time a game between old-money boarding schools in the Northeast could even remotely approach the madness that defined the culture of West Texas high school football he'd write about 20 years later in *Friday Night Lights.* (It was Adams who suggested Odessa's Permian High as the foundation for his book.)

Led by the cheerleaders and band members, Andover students marched to the field Saturday and were rewarded with the first home victory over Exeter since 1958 to secure the perfect season. The 34–8 rout was the lead story on the front page of the *Phillipian,* under Bissinger's byline, the first time the football team led the weekly newspaper all year. Holt was spectacular throwing and running the ball, Tom Mulroy caught nine passes for 149 yards and two touchdowns, and the defense delivered two goal-line stands. What a game, what a day, what a lifetime memory. Thirty years later, when his daughter, Amanda, enrolled at Phillips, Bill Belichick would give her a framed 1970 pennant that carried the score of the game, with Andover's 34 in a bright shade of white and Exeter's 8 in a dim shade of gray.

In the end, Holt was the chief reason why a team expected to go 3-4 finished 7-0. The triumph belonged to Sorota, too, and his calm and cerebral approach, not to mention his willingness to alter his system when necessary to best serve his kids. Decades later, Andover players could see the impact their head coach had on their PG from Annapolis, Belichick. Sorota was flexible on offense and defense. He was never emotional on the sidelines, and yet he was very demanding of his players. He believed that nothing in football, or in life, was deserved.

In the fall of 1972, his senior season, Dan Lasman would be demoted by Sorota before the Exeter game for poor play and replaced by a friend. It was a humiliating experience for him, but Sorota knew he needed to send a message to his player and his team. On cue, a freshly motivated Lasman came off the bench and played one of his better games in helping Andover again beat Exeter.

Lasman learned a hard boyhood lesson that week—that you need to work for everything you get—and Sorota was the man who hammered it home. In that sense, Lasman said, "Bill Belichick would become a modern-day Sorota. They're different people, but in some ways Bill would become kind of the son of Sorota."

By the time lacrosse practice started, Bill Belichick had finally figured out how to survive and sometimes thrive at Andover. He was a B student at a school where a middle-class public school student from Maryland needed an A-plus effort to get that B.

"It really took me about half a year before I got straightened out up here," he would tell an assembly of students three decades later, "both academically, athletically, socially. I was just pushed to a much higher standard than I'd ever been before, and I wasn't really sure how to react to that at times. But gradually I understood the program and understood what was expected and how to achieve it . . . It started to really hit me as to really how special this was and how much I was getting out of it."

As Vietnam raged on and American boys kept coming home in body bags, Andover remained a campus on edge. If Belichick wasn't engaged in the turbulent political atmosphere on campus, the same could be said of his classmate Jeb Bush, whose father, George H. W. Bush, had lost his bid for the Senate in Texas before being appointed by President Nixon as ambassador to the United Nations. Jeb reportedly spent most of his four years at Andover disconnected from any and all discourse on Vietnam and other third-rail political issues, and he admittedly smoked pot, drank alcohol, and underachieved in the classroom before meeting his future wife while studying in Mexico and finally cleaning up his act.

Many years later, as a Republican candidate for president of the United States, a job his father and older brother, George W., had won, Jeb Bush said he had never smoked marijuana with his classmate Belichick. "I remember him being a football geek even back then," Bush said.

Belichick was not a rebel with or without a cause, but he did let his hair down a bit — literally and figuratively. "Bill's hair," said Seero, "was about the length of the early Beatles'."

Back home in Annapolis, his old man was not a fan of the look. Steve Belichick was a proponent of Naval Academy guidelines, and as Bill made his way through Andover and then through four years of college, Steve had only two problems with his only child.

"I thought his hair was too long and his music was too loud," Steve said.

Steve didn't need to worry about what was becoming of his boy. Bill was never going to trade in his preferred Andover subculture — the jocks — for a place with the party boys known as the freaks. He was too busy with Ernie Adams and Evan Bonds breaking down film from their undefeated football season as part of a second-term project, and his primary spring-term objective was to try to help Phillips lacrosse go undefeated, too.

Bob Hulburd was head coach of the lacrosse team, and he was an Exeter grad, of all things, and a former All-American at Princeton. Though he wasn't known as an innovator, Hulburd was efficient, well organized, and hell-bent on having the best-conditioned team in New England. He learned the importance of physical and mental toughness in the United States Navy, in which he served during World War II. Hulburd was a communications officer on one of the first LSTs — tank landing ships — to land at Normandy, in part because German was one of the seven languages he spoke. (He would later chair the German department at Andover.) Hulburd lost his close friend and Princeton lacrosse teammate Tyler Campbell in France, and never fully recovered from it.

"I would say D-Day and lacrosse were the two most important things in his life," said his daughter Holly.

Hulburd ran his practices at game speed, one reason why he'd pieced together 16 consecutive winning seasons and three straight New England prep school titles entering the spring of 1971. Tim Callard, who was also one of Hulburd's assistants, said the head coach worked mostly with the offense and encouraged his boys to move the ball rapidly and do a lot of cutting. Callard conceded that Hulburd "was not a great strategist," but said he connected with his boys by trusting them and empowering them during games.

Andover had a dozen lettermen returning in the early spring of 1971, making it difficult for Belichick to crack the starting lineup. Belichick had been a defenseman at Annapolis, but Paul Kalkstein, another Hulburd assistant, said the PG went out for the team as an attackman in an attempt to secure more playing time. Kalkstein became one of Belichick's most ardent supporters. Though the assistant felt that Bill was slowed by a knee injury, he firmly believed his advanced stick skill was an asset the team could use.

Hulburd thought his returning attackmen were better options, and Kalkstein kept nudging him to get Belichick into the game. "I never saw Bill without the knee injury, and he was not fast," Kalkstein said. "But he was always in the right place . . . He had skills beyond a lot of kids, because he grew up playing in Annapolis, and we had kids who had never played or had only played a couple years and were great athletes who didn't have his skills."

Belichick just happened to arrive at Phillips the year the school fielded what might have been its most talented lacrosse team ever — the roster was loaded with athletes and midfielders who could run all day long. Bill was the fourth attackman who, according to Dana Seero, his teammate in both sports, "easily could've started. If he'd been there two years, I suspect he could've beaten out one of the guys."

Belichick earned an ample supply of playing time anyway, in the sport that many believed was his true passion. Kalkstein said that the fourth attackman never complained while on the sideline. As a raw, bone-chilling

Massachusetts winter gave way to the regenerative promise of spring — Andover players sometimes had to shovel snow off their field after returning from break — lacrosse season represented too much fun to complain about anything. Lacrosse didn't share football's place of prominence at Andover — the crowds were much smaller, sometimes numbering a few dozen family members and friends — but that hardly mattered.

Hulburd was a reassuring voice of reason during games, and a man who adored lacrosse every bit as much as Belichick did. And Kalkstein was always there to remind young Bill just how talented he was with his stick.

Andover would finish the season 10-1 overall and 6-0 against prep school competition; its only loss came at the hands of the powerful Brown University freshmen. "Bill was on the same level as the Brown freshmen," Kalkstein said. Belichick would account for seven goals and nine assists on the year, punctuated by an 11–2 victory over Exeter, the rival that had dominated Andover in the years before Hulburd took over the lacrosse program, in 1956. Hulburd consistently beat his alma mater, and finished his head coaching career after the 1971 victory over Exeter with four straight New England prep titles and a three-year unbeaten streak at home.

As it turned out, this was the first time Bill Belichick played a role in a New England sports dynasty. It wouldn't be the last.

Bill Belichick planted his hands around the football, lowered his head below his knees, and peered through his helmet and the gap between his arched legs. He was a college sophomore at Wesleyan, in Middletown, Connecticut, and he was about to snap the ball on a practice play that would extinguish his love affair with the game.

On the field with Belichick that day was a senior, Tom Tokarz, who remembered Bill walking through the front door of the Chi Psi fraternity the year before wearing an Andover shirt, cutoff sweatpants, and soccer shoes with no socks. Belichick was holding a lacrosse stick, and he was accompanied by his good friend from Annapolis Mark Fredland, who was already a member of the frat Bill was about to join.

Belichick didn't quite fit at rowdy Chi Psi, and yet he had something of a pied piper effect on fraternity enrollment. The year before, Fredland's freshman year, only four young men had pledged at Chi Psi, including a lacrosse player named Chris Diamond, who said "Greek life and the frats were out" while many students were consumed by the serious campus business of Vietnam protests. But in the fall of 1971, Diamond said Belichick was an endearing and popular enough figure to help recruit a Chi Psi class of some 20 members. "In a subtle way," Diamond said, "Bill was like an alpha male, and he attracted friends."

Among many other frat brothers and teammates, Bill later made the acquaintance of Scott Langner, the son of a Birmingham, Alabama, judge. Langner realized a childhood dream by playing freshman ball for the Crimson Tide and their legendary coach, Paul "Bear" Bryant. Langner's father played for the Tide, and his cousin David would become a legendary figure in the Alabama–Auburn rivalry by returning two blocked Bama punts for fourth-quarter touchdowns to give Auburn a 17–16 victory in the 1972 Iron Bowl.

Bear Bryant preferred his football players to be bigger than the 5′8″ Scott Langner, so the linebacker decided to transfer to a small-time school where he could crack the lineup. Someone recommended Wesleyan, of all places, and into Belichick's life he stepped.

"What I remember most," Langner said, "is Bill loved to eat . . . We always listened to music: the Grateful Dead, the Allman Brothers, Moody Blues, and people like that. It was all hippie music."

Langner decided that Belichick, who also played squash at Wesleyan, wasn't much like the football players he knew at Alabama. "Bill was a serious person," he said. "He wasn't a jock, if you know what I mean. There weren't a lot of jocks [at Wesleyan]."

Langner was one of them, a thick, blond-haired hellion on and off the field. Though he got along just fine with Belichick, he had a bit of a problem with his teammate between the lines. "Bill was a center," Langner said, "and I played linebacker. I hated centers."

It showed in practice. "Scotty would charge into Bill, and Scott was 215 pounds, while Bill was maybe 185," said Belichick's freshman coach, John Vino. "Langner would charge into him on long snaps or on any snaps . . . Scott Langner was a terror, and when the ball was snapped you had to get out of his way. He didn't care if you were on his team or the other team. He just wanted to hit you."

He just wanted to make his fellow Cardinals see stars. Langner's quickness and strength more than made up for his lack of height, and he played with a kind of athletic ferocity rarely seen at a small liberal arts school considered an academic equal to some members of the Ivy League. Tokarz recalled that Langner "let out this bloodcurdling yell every time he hit somebody. He kind of terrorized some of the younger guys."

Wesleyan players called Langner "the Wave," an apparent reference to his Crimson Tide roots. Langner thought of himself as a Division I athlete at a Division III school, and sometimes he acted that way. Like the night, later in his time at Wesleyan, when he'd grow sick and tired of the fraternity's soda machine swallowing money without spitting out a cold drink. Langner said this thievery went unchecked for about two months before he decided to go upstairs and grab his shotgun.

He did a lot of hunting as a kid, and he told people that his white German shepherd, Caesar, had served as his hunting dog. Around 1 a.m. that night — "When nobody was up but me and my dog Caesar," Langner said — the Wave approached the soda machine, armed and dangerous. Chi Psi was a jocks' lodge known for its *Animal House* culture, for being the wildest frat on campus. (Belichick was viewed as one of its few mild-mannered residents.) "We drank a lot," Langner said, "played poker, a lot of pool. We played pinball. Sometimes we disturbed the fraternity next door."

One football teammate called Chi Psi "a hell-raising community." With his loaded shotgun, Langner was taking the hell-raising to a new extreme.

"I shot the machine about twice," Langner said. "It woke everybody."

Including Belichick, who was said to have been sleeping on a nearby couch. The man who was Belichick's assistant lacrosse coach and soon-to-be head coach, Terry Jackson, said he'd been told Bill was indeed sleeping on a downstairs sofa — near the soda machine — at the request of a roommate who had a friend staying over. Then the shots rang out. "Bill went upstairs as fast as Bill could go," Jackson said, "and chased the roommate's friend out and recaptured his bed."

Tokarz was working security that night and happened to be the first authority figure on the scene. He recalled that there was a joke "suicide note" attached to the soda machine that said something to the effect of "I was stealing money. I don't deserve to live. I'm committing suicide." On arrival, Tokarz found Langner and his poor Caesar "curled up on his shoulder, scared as hell from the noise concussion. The gun was still there, and the soda machine was bleeding Coke and other liquids."

Langner appeared before a Wesleyan student judiciary board and was contrite enough to escape expulsion and end up with a penalty that included probation and mandatory attendance at a summer gun safety course. Belichick, Diamond said, was the one who "helped Scott get a light sentence."

Unlike the Wave, Belichick had plenty of roster climbing to do as a sophomore. Vino had him as a freshman in football and lacrosse, and he thought of Bill as a likable, brainy kid with a dry wit, average line skills, and above-average consistency as a long snapper. Bill also carried himself with a style that mirrored his times. "His hair was very long," Vino said, "and so was mine. We were all like the Beatles at that time." A couple of teammates described Belichick's bowl cut in the front and shoulder-length hair in the back as a Prince Valiant haircut.

That description came with a disclaimer. "He had a Prince Val," said teammate Frank Levering, "but he was not quite as good-looking as Prince Val." Levering thought of Belichick as quiet and reserved, as someone who never volunteered anything. "You could be right there, three feet away from him," Levering said, "and get the feeling he was not even aware of you." Levering had played on a state championship high school team out of a small North Carolina town, and he thought many of his teammates there were far more gifted than Belichick.

In a football program that revolved around a singular mission — trying (and often failing) to beat Williams and Amherst, the other members of the so-called Little Three academic powers — Belichick did excel in conflict resolution. "He was the mild one in that [frat] house," Vino said. "He was the voice of reason even when there was no reason. And if there was an argument on the field, he would be the arbitrator."

But on this one play in this one practice early in Belichick's sophomore year, his voice of reason was not heard. He was the center on a point-after attempt, and the Wesleyan coaches thought they'd spotted a weakness up the middle in the upcoming opponent's kicking unit. They wanted the first-string defense to get some work on this purported weakness against their own teammates, and Belichick, a backup, was identified as the specific point of attack.

Bill Macdermott, the head coach, had been a good player at Trinity College and was well liked by his team. Macdermott was relentlessly enthusiastic and emotional and was almost always moved to tears by victories and defeats big and small. It became a running joke among the players: *How long is it going to take this time for Mac to start bawling?*

Macdermott's preferred side of the ball was offense, and he loved to grade his players after every play, every scrimmage. His staff included Herb Kenny, the Wesleyan basketball coach and former St. Bonaventure football player, and Pete Kostacopoulos, who was about to start a long and distinguished career as the Cardinals' head baseball coach. Kostacopoulos, or Kosty, ran the defense for Macdermott. Kosty was known to be a crusty type who chewed a lot of tobacco. Fellow assistants knew not to stand downwind from him when he was up in the press box.

Players had differing opinions of Macdermott and his assistants, their styles and expertise. "But there were no villains on the coaching staff," Levering said. The players respected Kostacopoulos's knowledge of the game and his ability to get the most out of them. Linebacker Art Conklin, for one, thought Kosty was a strategic genius, and one who let you know about it when you played like shit. Belichick struggled in one scrimmage while playing linebacker, according to Conklin, compelling Kosty to come up with this mocking evaluation on his postgame rating sheet: "Bill, the scrimmage started at 10 in the morning. It's now five o'clock, and you have yet to make a tackle."

So Kostacopoulos, a hard-ass, was acting as an overseer for this particular hard-ass play. "I happened to be standing behind the defense," he said — standing there as his two toughest linebackers, Langner and Conklin, were getting ready to unload on Bill Belichick.

As he had at Andover, Belichick had established himself as a long snapper who stayed after practice to work on his craft, and as a coach in training who saw things less insightful teammates didn't see. Tokarz played in the defensive secondary as a senior, and he recalled Belichick shouting out the opponent's pass play from the sideline before the snap. Belichick would notice that a receiver had lined up close to the sideline, signaling that he was going to run an in pattern. Sure enough, Belichick nailed the call and Tokarz was all over the intended receiver to force an incompletion. In many ways, Tokarz thought, his younger teammate was a more advanced football mind than some of the Wesleyan coaches.

Kenny said Belichick "did everything nobody else wanted to do," and never made a mental mistake no matter what position he was asked to hold down. If Kenny had any problem at all with Bill, it related to his Andover training. "We treated the prep school kids a little differently than the public school kids," Kenny said. "We thought public school kids were a lot tougher than the preppies."

Kenny recalled that Belichick spent extra time with him after practice. Sometimes in the morning, Bill would stop in the assistant coach's office to go over a scouting report. "That's unusual for a kid not playing much, especially at Wesleyan," Kenny said. "They don't have the free time to do what Billy did."

But even in the world of small-time college football, a backup is often deemed expendable and put in harm's way. On this day, multiple witnesses said Wesleyan was working on a dangerous technique that required multiple defensive players to engage the center. It was unclear how many reps were run at Belichick's expense, but it was clear to nearly every witness that this dress rehearsal was a really bad idea.

"It's a tough play to run live against your own team," Tokarz said. "I thought we might've done that dummy drill to practice that. Coach decided to do it live, and, yeah, it was unfortunate. We all thought that [it was a mistake]. I don't know anybody who thinks any different."

Lenny Femino, a 5′5″, 165-pound freshman from Salem, Massachusetts, who could bench-press 325 pounds, was off to the side watching from only ten feet away when he thought to himself, "Holy shit, this is practice. In a game, you've got to find your opponent's weak spot and hit the gap and go, but this is just practice . . . I wouldn't want to be Bill right now."

Conklin, the 5′10″, 210-pound linebacker out of Newtown, Connecticut, said that Kenny had devised a new scheme to block kicks, and that it involved putting two tackles in front of the center, with a third defensive player positioned behind those tackles. "It was 100 percent Herb," Conklin said, "and [Macdermott] just blew the whistle." The linebacker said that Langner dropped down as one of the tackles next to a teammate named Bill Wilson, and that, by design, the two set their sights on Belichick.

Helmet lowered and eyes facing his holder and kicker, Belichick was made vulnerable by the nature of the task. He snapped the ball and then braced himself to be hit.

"As soon as the snap occurred," Conklin said, "they were supposed to wrap their arms around [Belichick's] legs and [rise up and] get into his shoulder pads and knock him over, and I was supposed to run over him and get directly onto the kicker and block the PAT. It wasn't just one time — we must've done that ten times, twelve times . . . It was stupid, and I think it was illegal. We did it over and over and over again. I ran over Bill, like I said, a dozen times . . . The next day Bill was in a cast."

Kostacopoulos remembered the sequence this way: "We were working against PATs, and one of our players submarined him, and he got [Belichick's] knee and he got hurt. I remember the play . . . I know people talked about two guys converging on him. It wasn't a drill. It was a technique that this person on defense — I don't remember who it was, but he was going to submarine his way in there and give the center a hard time."

Kenny worked on special teams, and decades later he said he didn't remember running this play over and over the way Conklin described it. Though he said the technique in question wasn't new in college football circles, he conceded, "It was probably new to us." Kenny recalled that another Wesleyan player was initially snapping the ball during the PAT practice before he replaced that player with Belichick. "I said, 'Come on, Billy, you've got to come snap,'" Kenny said. "He was a little reluctant. He got hurt, and he always blamed me."

Conklin said the coaches repeated the PAT block attempt so often that day that he couldn't recall the specific play that injured Belichick. Whichever play it was, one player said the sound of contact and pain instantly rose above the collisions taking place up and down the line of scrimmage and brought everything to a halt.

"You heard it," Lenny Femino said, "and you heard Bill. I remember him screaming. The screaming was awful. He was flopping on the ground. It was not good . . . You didn't see the broken leg. I just heard it and you knew he was injured and you knew it was bad and everything stopped."

Others who were there described Belichick's injury as a serious knee injury. Tokarz confirmed Conklin's account that three defensive players, not two, had crashed into Belichick and that one went high and two went low, leaving Bill done for the year. "Bill was an excellent snapper; he was the right guy to do that," Tokarz said. "And you've got three guys blowing him up in practice trying to block the kick . . . The guys who hit him felt terrible. They felt horrible, all three guys."

By all accounts, Belichick was raging mad over this unnecessary injury caused by a hazardous technique. Jackson, his lacrosse coach, said Bill had a temper that most people never saw, and that Jackson himself saw only once or twice. Once was Belichick's reaction to this play and this season-ending injury. Bill was so angry, he didn't bother returning to the team for his junior year.

"It tore up Bill's knee while they used him as a guinea pig," Jackson said. "Tore up his knee and forced him to give up football. He was hot under the collar. He was burning inside. He never forgave those coaches . . . He just never spoke to those football coaches again. He explained to me what had happened, and I can't say I blamed him."

Kenny disputed that account. He said Belichick was mad at him for "maybe about a week," and that he did not feel moved to apologize to his player. "That's just football," he said. "That's what happens. I never apologized, and we got along well after that."

Either way, Conklin said Belichick never complained to school officials about the events that led to his injury, nor did he involve his father in the matter. Don Russell, the former Wesleyan football coach who was now the athletic director, confirmed that Belichick never brought the incident to him and never mentioned it in any conversations decades later.

"They could've made a stink to the university," Conklin said of Belichick and his father, "but Bill sucked it up and accepted a lost season.

"He just took it and never said another word."

Bill Belichick's relatively silent boycott of the football team, or its coaches, didn't survive his senior season. He decided he missed the sport enough to give it one last go, and returned in the fall of 1974 as a repackaged tight end and linebacker/defensive end hoping the position change would increase his playing time. Bill had to know that was a long shot. He'd effectively missed two seasons of football, an extended absence that would be tough to overcome even at the Division III level.

This much was clear: His younger, superior teammates did hold him in high personal regard. Bill Weiss, a freshman center, recalled that Belichick "commanded a lot of respect from the guys on the team. People would listen to him when he would talk. He had a certain presence about him."

Paul Nelson, a freshman who started over Belichick at tight end, spoke of how fiercely Bill competed in blocking drills. Jeff Gray, a sophomore who was moved to center and who could bench-press nearly 400 pounds, felt that Belichick seemed older than his years and that, from his sideline view, he had an advanced understanding of what was happening on the field. Gray didn't like to long-snap, but the strongest man on the Wesleyan team did like to watch Belichick perform the task because of his precision and eagerness to do it flawlessly time after time.

Pat McQuillan, a captain on the 1974 team, remembered Belichick taking a Wesleyan course taught by Macdermott in football theory, or football coaching, and writing a 50-page dissertation on a defensive scheme. It was a shame that Belichick's body couldn't keep pace with his mind. As a rising sophomore, before he got hurt, Bill had little chance to beat out a converted center named Bob Heller, who would become a two-time Kodak Little All-American. As a returning senior, he had little chance to beat out a defensive end named John McVicar, who would also become a two-time small-college All-American.

McVicar was a 6'4", 200-pounder from Broomfield, Colorado, who was a long, lean, and explosive athlete, a pass rusher out of central casting. The first-string tight end, Nelson, went head to head against McVicar in practice. "He was like Ted 'the Mad Stork' Hendricks, the spitting image," Nelson said. "He had long arms, and you couldn't get into his body. He'd stonewall you off the line of scrimmage. I never had much problem blocking anybody except him."

McVicar appreciated the fact that a senior, Belichick, would pull a freshman aside — especially one like McVicar who was playing ahead of him — to offer tips on an opponent's formations and tendencies. "Bill," McVicar said, "was starting to coach right there."

McVicar was also well aware of his backup's considerable talent deficiencies. Belichick saw some playing time here and there over the Cardinals' first seven games, five of them losses, before replacing the injured McVicar for the final game of the season, against longtime rival Trinity. McVicar was suffering from a severely sprained ankle, and his absence allowed Belichick to assume a significant role against 6-1 Trinity in the last football game he'd ever play.

Nelson said Belichick was a plugger who could usually hold his own whenever he replaced a starter. Bill couldn't hold his own against Trinity before the home crowd of 4,000. At halftime, McVicar said, Macdermott and his assistants discussed what to do about one area of defensive weakness that was hurting the cause.

"The discussion," McVicar said, "was if me on one leg was faster than Bill on two. It was an even footrace. I was able to play that game with a heavily taped ankle and couldn't put much weight on it. But we were getting killed on this corner that Bill was playing, because he just couldn't pursue that fast. They were attacking the edge and it was like 'This is killing us.' He just didn't have the footspeed. They could outrun him, then the cornerback ended up as the first line of defense. I played some in the second half, but I wasn't able to do much better [than Bill]. I couldn't run at all."

Trinity won the 74th meeting between the two schools, 21–15, to leave

Wesleyan with a 2-6 record. The Cardinals' final points of the season effectively told the story of Belichick's college football career. Quarterback Brad Vanacore, a sophomore who was Bill's designated little brother in the Chi Psi fraternity, threw a touchdown pass to Nelson, the freshman who started over Bill at tight end. Vanacore then threw the two-point conversion pass to Ralph Rotman, the freshman who beat out Bill as the second-string tight end. Belichick had also lost the long-snapping competition to Weiss at the start of the season.

"Bill kept running into stone walls," Nelson said.

Yet Belichick was still going to leave his mark as an athlete at Wesleyan. Some of the same teammates who played ahead of him in the fall would watch from the stands and the bench as he outperformed and outsmarted a frustrated series of opponents in the spring.

Bill Belichick, economics major, chose in Wesleyan a school known for its liberal worldview (especially relative to Williams and Amherst). The school was years ahead of most colleges in aggressively recruiting African American students, and it was the kind of place where a football player might be more interested in writing poetry than launching himself into a blocking sled.

Frank Levering, an offensive lineman who later became a poet, an author, and a Hollywood screenwriter, described the Wesleyan of the early to mid-seventies as "a place where there was a lot of drugging going on, and a lot of casual sex, which came as a shock to me. I didn't grow up in a culture like that. The smell of marijuana was very much in the air every day. But not so much the football players. They were very conservative guys, by and large."

Belichick fit that definition. He did party while listening to the Dead and Bob Dylan, and he did make trips to Mardi Gras in New Orleans in a canary-yellow Subaru ("An awesome car," Chris Diamond said), and he did persuade Debby Clarke, his high school friend, to set aside her elementary education studies at Alabama's Birmingham–Southern College for a few days to join him at Mardi Gras and become his steady girlfriend.

"The rebellious years," Belichick called them.

Bill did also get himself drunk on at least one occasion. The night before a big football game, Conklin recalled Belichick, still wearing his leg cast, drinking to excess and losing his balance, then falling into a trash can. When Belichick woke up in his bed the next morning, his friends told him jokingly that he'd slept right through the game.

But all in all, Bill tried to keep the debauchery at Chi Psi under some degree of control. According to the college newspaper, the *Wesleyan Argus,*

Belichick was serving as president of the frat in 1973 when some 30 to 45 of its members urinated on the Beta House frat, where five windows were broken. The *Argus* reported that Belichick "expressed concern and said such an incident would not occur again."

Diamond said the mass urination on Beta was a Chi Psi tradition, and that Belichick did what little he could to keep it under control. "Nobody wanted to be president of the frat house; we were having too much fun," Diamond said. "Bill volunteered. He held the place together through a couple of rough moments."

One time, as Thanksgiving neared, Diamond, Langner, and a couple of hungry Chi Psi brothers stole Belichick's freshly cooked turkey out of the fridge in the middle of the night. They stuffed a smallish frat brother into the dumbwaiter and lowered him downstairs behind locked doors to pull off the heist. They stripped the turkey bare to make sandwiches, then returned the carcass to the fridge for Belichick to find the next day.

Other nights, the boys used the dumbwaiter to break into the kitchen to make themselves hamburgers. Bill handled the pranks with ease, as he himself could enjoy a laugh at a friend's expense. "He was a needler," Conklin said. "He'd needle guys and was constantly on them . . . In one incident, Bill needled to a point where he almost came to blows with someone, so that was a part of his character, too."

So were common sense and common decency. Chi Psi hosted a stag party one night for a frat brother who was getting married, and someone had convinced a female Wesleyan student to jump out of a cake. As the party turned a bit rowdy, Belichick was smart enough to help Conklin escort the female student onto the fire escape, out of the frat, and back to her room.

By and large, Bill carried himself as a focused, serious-minded student who understood his purpose on campus. He was clearly at Wesleyan to get an education (Lenny Femino did hear him speak eloquently about Napoleon for 20 minutes in a seminar), though the Andover experience had reduced this esteemed university to a relative layup. People who knew Belichick figured he'd end up as a successful executive at a big firm, living the Wall Street dream, even as he was already inquiring about entering his father's business, the business of coaching.

In the end, Belichick made his greatest impact at Wesleyan on the lacrosse field. He was a known lacrosse commodity coming out of Annapolis and Andover, and for a while it looked as if he might play for the coach who would become an institution at Williams, Renzie Lamb, who said he had Belichick's name on a list of ten or twelve recruits he submitted to the admissions department. "And if I got one or two of them in," Lamb said, "I'd be as happy as a pig in shit."

Though Bill was academically fit and appealing as a two-sport athlete, said Lamb, who later worked with Steve Belichick at the Naval Academy, he didn't make the cut. (He'd added only two points to his SAT score after enrolling at Andover, a source of comic relief to his father.) At Wesleyan, Terry Jackson, head soccer coach, moved up from his lacrosse assistant's post to head coach for Bill's junior and senior seasons. Jackson admitted that he initially knew little about the sport, and Lamb said there were times he tried to help his Little Three opponent with suggestions during games.

Many of the students who went out for lacrosse at Wesleyan had never played the game in high school, making Belichick the exception. Jackson surrounded the lead-footed midfielder with football players who had speed, and hoped Bill's stick skills and field vision would complement their raw athleticism. The plan worked.

Don Russell, athletic director, watched Belichick play lacrosse and immediately realized he was "running the show. Always a leader on the field every time. Bill was our leader, and that was it, right from the beginning." This came as no surprise to Russell, who had received a phone call from Navy assistant football coach Rick Forzano, a colleague of Steve Belichick's, recommending Steve's son for Wesleyan. Forzano had told Russell that young Belichick was a good kid, a slow but smart football player who knew how to handle a lacrosse stick.

An AD at a small school like Wesleyan can bounce from game to practice to game to practice, and Russell watched Belichick play squash for Coach Don Long before "crowds" of a dozen friends, frat brothers, and stray faculty members. But he particularly enjoyed watching Bill work his way around a lacrosse field.

Belichick adored the game — he was often seen outside Chi Psi with his stick, throwing the ball around — and he taught the novices around him how to play. "Bill was my first lacrosse coach," said Pat McQuillan. "Bill's campus dorm room looked like an equipment cage. Bill had everything in his room — equipment, jerseys, lacrosse sticks, balls . . . I got pretty good coaching at a very reduced rate."

An accomplished soccer coach with some basketball experience, Jackson was smart enough to defer to Belichick and to Bill's buddy from Annapolis, Mark Fredland, a gifted attackman. In turn, Bill never abused the privilege in attempting to tell his coach how to run the team. He would visit Jackson in his office and leave him with some ideas to ponder. Bill would babysit Jackson's children, and help him move from one house to another. They were good friends beyond their sound coach-player relationship.

Jackson had a strong rapport with most of his players, and he'd taken some lacrosse instruction in Florida to better understand how to put them in a position to succeed. "Bill would do some things in practice," he said, "like skip-passing to people and passing from midfield to behind the goal, that I'd never taught, basically. But we let him do it. They got added to the program."

Belichick often resorted to the skip pass — one that bypasses a nearby teammate in favor of one on the opposite side of the field — when an opponent applied defensive pressure or doubled the ball, leaving a distant man open. Bill wasn't merely a facilitating point guard who saw the entire court on the fast break; he was also Wesleyan's toughest player. He broke his thumb playing lacrosse, and after a Wesleyan doctor refused to clear him to return, Belichick made an appointment with Russell. He asked the AD if it would be OK for him to seek a second opinion, and Russell was impressed with the young man's maturity in even making the request. Second opinions weren't in vogue at the time. "I don't know how many kids would've thought of that," Russell said. Bill found a doctor in Annapolis who greenlighted him before the postseason tournament to play with a soft, removable cast, and Wesleyan's physician approved.

Jackson only once saw Belichick lose his cool in lacrosse the way he did when he suffered the season-ending football injury; it was during a brawl against Bowdoin in which Bill was "livid" over some alleged offense committed against a teammate. Otherwise, Belichick operated with cool efficiency while probing an opponent's weaknesses. "Bill is the smartest player I've ever coached in lacrosse, without question," Jackson said.

Bill was also a selfless recruiter. In an attempt to improve the roster, he persuaded athletic kids with no experience to give the sport a chance, even kids like John McVicar, the freshman who had beaten out Belichick in football his senior year. Jackson thought lacrosse was Bill's "first love right from the beginning" and that Bill didn't miss playing football after his injury as much as he missed being a part of football. "But he transferred everything into lacrosse while he was at Wesleyan," Jackson said.

Everyone on the team ribbed Belichick about his lack of foot speed. They all got another laugh at Bill's expense when he accidentally scored on his own goal. Mike Sanfilippo, the starting goalie, had taken a penalty in one game, and the versatile Belichick was forced to replace him. Bill didn't like playing in net, Sanfilippo said. But Belichick grabbed a goalie stick and, while attempting to clear a ball, lost control of it when an opponent delivered a wraparound check from behind, sending the ball bouncing into Wesleyan's net. "Bill scored against us," McQuillan said, "though I don't know if he'd ever admit it."

Belichick more than compensated for that sequence with the intel he often gathered on opponents. In a critical 7–6 overtime victory over Williams in 1974 — a season that saw Wesleyan sweep its Little Three rivals — Sanfilippo recalled Belichick warning him that a certain Williams player preferred to shoot high. Sure enough, that player had a clear shot at the goal on a breakaway in the game's decisive possession, and on Belichick's instructions Sanfilippo guessed high and made the save.

Belichick also made plays with his stick that some of his teammates found hard to believe. On a snowy early April day in '74, Belichick cut across the field against a loaded Bowdoin team and caught a clearing pass with the back of the head of his stick, ran toward the Bowdoin goal with the ball in this unusual position, finally flipped it in the air and caught it with his net, and then dumped it to an attackman.

In that same game, Belichick also used his knowledge of the rulebook as a lethal weapon. He realized early that Bowdoin star Josiah Spaulding Jr. was playing without a chinstrap, and he informed the officials of the violation. At an imposing 6'3" and 225 pounds, with long hair and an unwieldy beard, Spaulding said he was known as "a seventies hippie playing lacrosse." He was also known as the product of a prominent local family. His father, Josiah, had lost a bid for the U.S. Senate to Ted Kennedy in 1970, and his mother, Helen, was a direct descendant of James Bowdoin, the second governor of Massachusetts and the man for whom the college was named.

Spaulding thought he looked funny wearing a chinstrap, but now he had no choice. Somehow Bowdoin hadn't packed an extra one for the game, forcing the oversize attackman to run athletic tape through his helmet earholes and around his beard. "It was extremely uncomfortable," Spaulding said. Bowdoin lost the game, 10–7.

The two teams met again in the ECAC New England Regional Championship game, and this time around Spaulding secured sweet revenge. He had four goals and an assist in Bowdoin's 15–7 victory, but it was one particular goal that Spaulding would remember forever.

The ball was down near the Bowdoin net, and Spaulding was watching from afar and standing beside the much smaller opponent guarding him, the two of them waiting for the action to come to them. Suddenly that Wesleyan defenseman, Belichick, took his stick and swung it hard into Spaulding's left leg, just below the knee, knocking him to the ground. An enraged Spaulding pulled himself to his feet and threw a hard right hand that landed underneath Belichick's helmet and knocked him down. The officials didn't see either infraction.

Meanwhile, Bowdoin's goalie secured possession of the ball and saw his biggest and best attackman wide open down the field. He fired the long pass as Belichick tried to gather himself, and Spaulding caught it on the run and scored. "I was scoring goals left and right on him," Spaulding would say of Belichick.

Wesleyan finished 8-4 that year, and then 8-3 in 1975, when Belichick returned from his thumb injury before the Cardinals lost to Middlebury in the ECAC playoffs. "Obviously," wrote his hometown paper, the *Capital,* "Belichick was a leader in how to live right in his four years at Wesleyan, since he was elected co-captain of the school's 1975 varsity lacrosse team."

But as much as Jackson thought Belichick cherished his time playing lacrosse, the coach conceded that football "never really left his inner soul." Bill decided he didn't want to parlay his Wesleyan and Andover degrees into a corporate job, though his father said he twice met on campus with Procter & Gamble for a possible spot in its management trainee program. Bill decided he wanted to follow his dad's lead, like he had as a young boy.

Bill had gone to a national coaches' convention with his old man in the hopes of networking, and Steve Belichick worked his considerable connections hard. He called Lou Holtz at North Carolina State. "And he said he'd love to have him," Steve recalled.

Holtz later reported that the opening he'd reserved for Bill was closed by new budget realities under Title IX legislation that mandated increased funding for women's sports. Steve Belichick knew some of the Baltimore Colts' assistants, including George Boutselis, who put in a word for Bill with their head coach, Ted Marchibroda. Baltimore's head coach also heard from his own son Ted, who had played high school ball for one of Steve's teammates at the Great Lakes Naval Station.

Herb Kenny, the Wesleyan football assistant and head basketball coach, also said he recommended Bill to Marchibroda, Kenny's former teammate at St. Bonaventure. Despite his role in Belichick's football injury, Kenny said Bill walked into his office one day and asked if he'd call the coach of his hometown Colts.

"I called him and I said, 'Ted, I've got a kid who's really thorough and I think he'd be good for you,'" Kenny recalled. "Ted said, 'Coach, I don't have anything, but I could use a person to break down film . . . I don't have any money. I'll try to do the best I can for him.'"

Bill Belichick interviewed with Marchibroda and told him he wanted to work 14, 16 hours a day, and that he'd do anything his boss asked of him. "Obviously," Belichick told him, "I have a long way to go, so put me to work." Marchibroda thought the kid sounded sincere enough and took him up on it.

"I got three meals, a bed, and a lot of football," Belichick said, "and that was all I really wanted at that time."

And just like that, Bill Belichick had landed his first coaching job. He didn't have to start his career in high school or college—the Division III backup was heading right for the pros.

What kind of coach would he be once he got there? An exchange Belichick had with John McVicar offered a hint. McVicar had never even seen a lacrosse game while growing up in Colorado, and when he brought his stick home during vacation breaks, his friends thought it was some kind of newfangled fishing pole.

Belichick knew McVicar's size and speed could help Wesleyan, so he schooled him in the finer points of the game. One day, Belichick asked McVicar to let him take his stick home for the night.

"And he restrung my stick so the ball would stay in there better," McVicar recalled. "He taught me how to make my lacrosse stick illegal and then fix it before the ref could catch you. He strung it loose, the depth of the pocket. In those days, the depth could be no deeper than the ball. He made it extra deep. If someone on the other team said I had an illegal stick, Bill showed me how to pull a string to tighten it up and then hand it to the ref."

Speaking many years later, McVicar, a liver transplant surgeon, laughed at the memory. "He told me how to use an illegal lacrosse stick," Bill Belichick's old teammate said. "If you ain't cheating, you ain't trying.

"It doesn't surprise me, or wouldn't at all," McVicar continued, "if he tried to use every advantage he could to win an athletic contest."

5

BILLY BALL

At 23, Billy Belichick thought he had the best unpaid job in the world. The Baltimore Colts were his childhood team, and he could still name their starting lineups on both sides of the ball. He had met the likes of Johnny Unitas and Alex Sandusky while working at his father's football camp, and that famous horseshoe logo on his shirt meant everything to him.

They all called him Billy then, and that was the only downside to the gig. Belichick told the players that he didn't like to be called Billy, that he'd appreciate it if they called him Bill. "Worst mistake he made," said Bruce Laird, the strong safety. "Billy" it was going to be.

Belichick was getting to work for a rookie head coach named Ted Marchibroda, an overwhelmingly decent human being in an often indecent profession, and he was not being asked to collect dirty jocks and towels from the locker room floor. Marchibroda had worked as offensive coordinator under Washington's George Allen, who enjoyed the luxury of having more assistant coaches than he could count. The Baltimore general manager, Joe Thomas, was known for his frugality and his insistence on employing a smaller staff, which created an opening for Billy to expand his role.

"When [Marchibroda] had his seven assistants," Belichick said, "he could have used another ten guys . . . But I think we scrimmaged the Redskins four times, and there were guys on that staff that I really had more responsibility than . . . the ninth, tenth guys on the staff and all that. Not that I knew anything, but we just didn't have that many people. So I was doing the stuff that they were doing."

Billy lived for free at the Howard Johnson's near the airport, with Marchibroda and assistants George Boutselis and Whitey Dovell. "I had a fella I knew was running the HoJo," Marchibroda said, "and he said he could get some rooms for the coaches if I could get him a couple of passes for his boss. And I did."

They met for breakfast around seven every morning, and Marchibroda always picked up Billy's tab. The Colts' coach covered enough of Billy's meals and expenses, Steve Belichick would say, that he should've been able to write off Billy as a dependent on his taxes.

The younger Belichick drove the older coaches from the hotel to the office in the morning and back again around midnight, and he saw this task as a blessing instead of a burden. Billy did a lot more listening than talking on those drives, and he realized just how little he knew about what it takes to coach in the pros.

"So not only did I, in my first year, get the whole experience of, from the minute you walk in the office, the coaching, the players, and the meetings and all that," Belichick would say. "There was also the being involved with the head coach and the offensive line coaches, special teams coach, on an off-the-field basis of 45 minutes each way in the car."

Marchibroda immediately realized that as soon as he put Billy in a room to do a job, he wouldn't see him again until that job was done. He had Billy doing film breakdowns for Maxie Baughan, the defensive coordinator, helping out with special teams, running the scout team, working the Xerox machine like mad, and sending films to opponents. Sometimes Billy's girlfriend, Debby, made the drive up from Annapolis in her mother's Dodge Swinger, but his leisure time was measured in minutes, not hours. Belichick would write up and draw every play on a card and then, on the outside edge of the card, check off every category that play fell under. Then he'd apply what he called the ice-pick method.

"If it was first-and-10, plus territory, gain of over four yards, screen pass, halfback was the receiver, the defense ran a blitz, whatever categories it fell into," Belichick said, "then I would check those off. I would take the hole punchers, so there were like 200 holes around the edge of the card and I would punch out the holes that I had checked off. Then you have a whole stack of cards here, slide the ice pick in there for third down, and boom, all the third-down cards drop out. Then you take all those cards and look at them and put them all back together, put the whole deck of cards back together, stick the ice pick back in there, and all the screens fall out . . . I would do like 200 of those. Screens and third down and red area and goal line and short yardage, and what they ran against blitzes and what they ran from slot, and what they ran from motion. All of that."

The work wasn't always so monotonous and free of emotion. Sometimes Belichick was asked to inform players that they'd been cut from the team, an assignment that inspired some to call him "Bad News Bill." This couldn't be comfortable work for a college boy who had grown up idolizing the very men he was charged with firing.

But Joe Ehrmann, third-year defensive tackle, was among the Colts who were struck by the way Billy handled that job and carried himself around the facilities. He wasn't only mono-focused and committed to everything Marchibroda wanted him to do; he was unafraid of the dark side of coaching. If an established player had to be sacrificed for the betterment of the team, Billy was willing to honor the process.

"I had a great deal of respect for the young guy," Ehrmann said. "He wasn't intimidated . . . His goal wasn't to be the most popular guy in that camp, and he wasn't. There was a job to do and he did it, whether it was driving coaches around or cutting players . . . I don't remember him spending a lot of time or energy going out of his way to attach himself with the players. He didn't feel any pressure to be liked."

Marchibroda was likable enough for the entire staff anyway. Only 44, he came across as a mentor, as someone older than his years. Players didn't fear being disciplined by him as much as they feared disappointing him.

Marchibroda thought it was critical to empower everyone in the building. During his first day on the job, he introduced himself to a secretary in the coaches' office, Maureen Kilcullen, and asked her, "What have you done today to help the Colts win?" She thought he was crazy. Over time, Kilcullen realized that Marchibroda wanted her to believe she was just as important to the cause as his star quarterback, Bert Jones, and his star running back, Lydell Mitchell.

This collaborative culture emboldened Billy Belichick, too. He was allowed to make his share of mistakes, including the one he made after Marchibroda handed him his old Redskins playbook.

"One of my jobs was to white-out 'Washington Redskins' and type in 'Baltimore Colts' on it and then Xerox it off," Belichick said. "It was literally the same: the same offense, and Maxie Baughan was the same defensive coordinator, and it was the same defense. I remember there were a couple pages somehow that snuck into the playbook that 'Redskins' didn't get whited out, and I heard about it on that."

Marchibroda's staff had a hell of a task in front of it, as the Colts were no longer what they had been in Unitas's prime. Baltimore was coming off three consecutive losing years, including a 2-12 season in 1974 that started with Howard Schnellenberger as head coach and ended with the GM, Thomas, replacing Schnellenberger for the final 11 games. The Colts didn't win even once in their home ballpark, Memorial Stadium.

They opened training camp at Goucher College after practicing the year before at a high school, McDonogh, where Ehrmann said players showered and dressed in a makeshift locker room under metal bleachers while trying to survive the fumes from a propane heater. It didn't take long for Billy to make his mark at Goucher. Three or four weeks into camp, Thomas approached him and said, "You are doing a pretty good job. We're going to start paying you."

Thomas told Billy he'd start making 25 bucks a week. After taxes, he'd be bringing home a whopping $21.22. "Don't spend it all in one place," Thomas told him.

The Colts had to wait for the Orioles to end their season in the American League East to take up full-time residence in Memorial Stadium in late September (Earl Weaver's team missed the playoffs in 1975), leaving them to conduct some of their business at McDonogh. When the Colts were housed at Memorial, sometimes the grounds crew needed to prepare the field for the Orioles or cover it because of wet weather, forcing the football team to be shifted to an alternate site. Belichick recalled the Colts, in uniform, hitting the walk button and crossing 33rd Street like a junior varsity team to practice at the Eastern High School field, which, he later said, "had two blades of grass, dirt, glass, rocks."

Of course, Memorial was no picnic even on the sunniest of days. On warmer days early in the season, the bowels of Memorial could feel about as comfortable as the boiler room of a submarine. Belichick worked right outside Weaver's office, in what he described as a cinder-block closet. Jones, the quarterback, thought the locker room was nothing more than concrete walls and cold, dreary, wet concrete floors.

"We all had pets," Jones said. "Whatever critter came by that day."

Bruce Laird's favorite locker room pet was a cockroach the size of a small rodent. Players would come off the field, shower, and then shake their clothes to get the roaches out before getting dressed. Staffers would unlock a door to a storage room, turn on the light, and then wait a minute before entering so whatever was inside had time to scatter.

Belichick couldn't believe that the stadium didn't even have a suitable weight room, or that the team didn't have a strength coach. "There was a little universal gym that had four or five stations," he said, "and that was it."

As the season wore on, the field was so worn down that the grounds crew painted the dirt green to project the illusion of grass. But to the Colts, if Memorial Stadium was a dump, it was *their* dump. The team had moved there in 1953 and had played in Memorial through *Brown v. Board of Education,* the Cold War, the assassinations of Jack and Bobby Kennedy and Dr. Martin Luther King Jr., the riots in Baltimore, and the civil rights movement.

"Back then at Memorial, everyone would come together," Ehrmann said. "The CEO would sit next to the cabbie . . . That was the beauty of that 1975 team that galvanized the community. We learned how to meld those two cultures, black and white. One day the music in the locker room is country and western with Bert, the next day it's soul music with Lydell and the other black players. It was a magical time in terms of relationships."

The '75 Colts had to repair the broken trust between the franchise and a fan base that was already sick and tired of losing. Baltimore opened the season by routing the Chicago Bears, 35–7, holding a rookie named Walter Payton to no yards on eight carries. But the Colts returned to form by losing their next four games, leaving Marchibroda to publicly complain that his team had played without passion in extending its losing streak. In the locker room, the head coach embraced a more hopeful tone when he told the Colts they would advance to the playoffs if they ran the table over their final nine games.

Ken Mendenhall, center, emerged to tell Marchibroda's secretary, Kilcullen, what the head coach had said. She laughed. Everyone in and around the building figured the Colts were staring down the barrel of another painfully long season. Marchibroda and his staff didn't surrender to any such inevitability.

They worked absurdly long hours in their effort to save the season. The team didn't provide catered meals to the staff, so the coaches would work until dinnertime, leave the building and walk to a restaurant, and then return to work some more. Baughan said that he sometimes slept overnight on his office floor, and that he taught Belichick "how to sleep on his desk when he got tired." Jones, the quarterback, recalled seeing Billy asleep on the training room table. This was the George Allen way, passed down to Marchibroda and Baughan: Allen defined leisure time as five or six hours of sleep.

The time invested didn't go to waste. The Colts blew out Joe Namath and the Jets at Shea Stadium, beat the Cleveland Browns by two touchdowns, and then signaled for the first time that they might be capable of something special. They were playing the 5-2 Bills in Buffalo, and O. J. Simpson scored the game's first three touchdowns.

Buffalo was up 28–7 in the second quarter when Jones caught fire, hitting Roger Carr for 89 yards and leading the Colts on a staggering run of 35 consecutive points to ultimately prevail 42–35. For the first time that season, Marchibroda had ripped into his team at halftime. He had good reason to be pissed off. "There was a point in that game," Belichick would say years later, "where I honestly think the only person on the field that thought we could win was Bert Jones, and he kind of played and willed the team to win, and it kind of caught fire after that."

Jones was the Louisiana-born, rifle-armed son of Dub Jones, the former Cleveland Browns star. He could do things with a football that stunned

Belichick, who was taken with the quarterback's athleticism, shoulder flexibility, and arm strength. "As a pure passer," Belichick would say, "I don't think I could put anybody ahead of Bert Jones."

Jones thought highly of Billy, whose $25-a-week wage had been raised to an obscene $50 a pop. The quarterback and the young assistant were what Jones called "tendency people," or football guys who wanted every bit of information they could get before every snap to improve their odds of success on that play. Though Jones saw Billy as the equivalent of a graduate assistant in college, he knew him to be an integral part of the team.

"He was like a walking computer," Jones said, "before there were computers."

Belichick was as detail-oriented as any of the veteran coaches on staff. He would break down the 16-millimeter films and feed data to Laird, the signal caller at strong safety. Billy passed on information about the splits of opposing tight ends, or certain movements, or "tells," in a player's positioning or body language that could tip a play. Belichick's information on what the opponent would or wouldn't do was, in Laird's words, "incredibly accurate."

In one game, Billy told Laird that when a certain team lined up in slot formation, and when a certain receiver lined up inside the numbers on the slot side, that receiver would run an out route almost every time. "That's pretty powerful information to have," Laird said. "And sure enough, it was true.

"He was such an introverted guy and so quiet," Laird continued, "I rarely had a lot of conversations with him, other than to look at his information and tell him after the game when we came in, 'Hey, man, that was great. That was unbelievable' . . . I think he would've made me a much better player if he stayed. I know he made me better in 1975. Billy realized the game is a game of chess, not just brute strength."

The Colts blew out the Jets at home, beat the Dolphins, Chiefs, and Giants by a combined 51 points, and then outlasted Miami in overtime and New England in regulation to claim the AFC East with a nine-game winning streak. "It was the greatest turnaround in NFL history," Belichick said, "from 2-12 to 10-4." It was a victory of cohesion and competitiveness over sheer talent, and it would come to be known as the Miracle on 33rd Street.

The romance between this great football town and its fabled football franchise had been rekindled. The Colts were back, and everyone was deliriously happy. Everyone but the GM who had pieced the team together. Joe Thomas was upset that Marchibroda was getting most of the credit for the renaissance, and his PR man, Ernie Accorsi, had to remind him that former New York Yankees executive George Weiss got elected to the Baseball Hall of Fame despite the fact that his manager, Casey Stengel, got most of the public credit for the Yanks of the fifties.

"You're going to have to live with it," Accorsi told him. The PR man would also tell Thomas, "You have Harry Truman's balls and Lyndon Johnson's thin skin, and that's a bad combination."

The rest of Baltimore wasn't too worried about the GM's hurt feelings. Early in the season, Belichick estimated that there "weren't 17,000 people in the stands." The winning changed everything. Three-quarters of the way through the year, Belichick said, the Memorial ticket lobby was so packed that the team couldn't move through that area. "So we had to go out through the [Orioles'] dugout," Belichick said, "out onto the field, and come back in that way or it would take us a half hour to get through the lobby, with everybody asking for autographs. I mean, it was a madhouse."

Baltimore's spirited charge into the postseason would run smack into a brick wall, or, rather, a Steel Curtain. Pittsburgh was the defending Super Bowl champ, and in the middle of a run that would leave the Steelers with four championships in six seasons. The Colts' chances of pulling off an upset were severely compromised when Jones suffered an arm injury early in the game. His backup, Marty Domres, completed only 2 of 11 passes and was intercepted twice. Somehow the visitors were up 10–7 in the third quarter before Terry Bradshaw overcame a first-half knee injury and two interceptions of his own to run for the touchdown in the fourth quarter that gave Pittsburgh a two-score lead in what would be a 28–10 victory.

Marchibroda assured his Colts afterward that they'd lost to a better team. The Steelers had a dominating defense and Hall of Famers on both sides of the ball, and a coach in Chuck Noll who would become the first to win four Super Bowls. Belichick had great appreciation for Noll's intelligence, his diverse interests away from the game, and his talent for consistently fielding physical and fundamentally sound teams. By watching the 1975 Steelers at work, even at Baltimore's expense, Belichick finished a one-year educational experience that was worth far more than 50 bucks a week.

Billy said he learned more football in the dungeons of Memorial Stadium that year "than any place I've ever been. It was like a graduate course in football." Belichick so impressed Marchibroda and his assistants that the Colts hired one of his old teammates from Wesleyan, Tom Tokarz, to take up his apprenticeship the following season.

Not that the Colts ever wanted to lose Billy. Marchibroda saw how often players such as Jones, Laird, and linebacker Stan White used the young aide as a resource. "Nobody complained about Billy," Marchibroda said. "Nobody had anything negative to say. I saw the players wanted information as soon as they saw Billy. I knew he was doing the job, and the players were glad to have him there. Before practice, they were going up to talk to him. They wanted to get his firsthand knowledge."

According to Marchibroda, Belichick wanted a $4,000 salary and a car to return to the Colts for a second year, and Thomas wouldn't give it to him. Detroit Lions coach Rick Forzano, a Paul Brown disciple and former staffmate of Steve Belichick's who once stayed at the family's Annapolis home, stole him away with an offer of $10,000 and a new Thunderbird.

Billy left for Detroit, and the relationship between Marchibroda and Thomas turned sour, in part because the head coach fought for Billy and the general manager let him walk. Thomas would be out after the 1976 season and off to run the San Francisco 49ers, who went 7-23 in his two seasons as GM.

If Billy made an exceedingly positive impression on Marchibroda and most of Baltimore's coaches and players, he did little to impress one highly regarded figure in the organization: Maureen Kilcullen. On Wednesday mornings, she recalled, Billy started his advance work on the opponent to be played a week after that upcoming Sunday's game.

"I thought he was kind of surly," Kilcullen said. "My encounters with him were mostly him coming into the office to give me some kind of scouting report or game plan. He just wasn't very talkative. I was the only woman there, so that could've been a different dynamic . . . If Billy was going to piss anyone off, it would be a peon, me, someone who wasn't going to hire him. Maybe that's the way he was. I didn't particularly care for it."

Billy had the responsibility of sending game film to that week's opposing team. And if the films were supposed to be delivered by Tuesday, sometimes they didn't arrive until Wednesday.

Kilcullen was the one fielding phone calls from angry, shouting coaches who demanded to know where their films were. "It drove me freakin' nuts," she said. Kilcullen would try to get Billy on the phone, but he dodged her calls. Kilcullen thought the young assistant was merely being a pain in the ass.

But with the passage of time, Kilcullen came to wonder if Billy's unwillingness to perform a simple task in a timely fashion had been something else. She couldn't speak to his true motivation then, but maybe there was a reason the opposing coaches waited an extra day before they got their hands and eyes on those films.

"Maybe," Kilcullen said, "it was inches with Bill . . . Then he'd push the envelope somewhere else another inch, and then another."

Maybe in his rookie year in the NFL, Billy Belichick was reaching for a competitive advantage for the very first time.

Rick Forzano had a 10-year-old Billy breaking down film for him at the Naval Academy. Forzano specifically remembered a young Belichick looking at tight ends and receivers when he turned on the projector in Annapolis, so he decided that in addition to assigning him some special teams work, he would put him in charge of tight ends.

Billy's arrival in Detroit had a bit of a full-circle feel to it, as his father had played for the Lions. Steve Belichick had put in 20 years at the Naval Academy, and he no longer harbored the dream of becoming a head coach, or of working anywhere but Annapolis. Steve had passed on a couple of offers to be an NFL assistant, and he'd fully embraced the tenured academy life of a teacher and coach who helped make men out of the young Midshipmen and did everything in his power to make Army the second-best team on the field once every fall.

Steve was happy scouting opponents, working with the punters and the younger players, running the field-house steps to stay in shape, and watching his only child do what Steve never did: coach in the NFL. "Billy had a lot of his dad's traits," Forzano said. "Detail, discipline, a very dry humor. He can cut your legs out from underneath you and you don't know it. Steve was good at that. The apple doesn't fall far from the tree."

Forzano thought Billy could see things most assistants and scouts couldn't see. He had Billy doing extensive work on the kicking game, on ways to attack the opposing kickers and to protect Detroit's. "I think he was always finding that little edge," Forzano said. "He was in the film room more than a Hollywood producer."

Forzano had become the Detroit head coach after his predecessor and boss, Don McCafferty, died of a heart attack in July 1974. The Lions' owner, William Clay Ford, hired Forzano over two assistants with NFL head coaching experience in Bob Hollway and Eddie Khayat, who had coached the St. Louis Cardinals and the Philadelphia Eagles, respectively, and over future NFL head coaches Raymond Berry (a Hall of Fame end with the Colts) and Jerry Glanville.

The players saw Forzano as tough, energetic, and hardworking. "But a lot of us thought Hollway or Khayat would or should get the job," said linebacker Jim Laslavic. "We were all surprised when Rick took over. So he was up against it a bit."

Another Detroit assistant, Wally English, said Ford's hiring of Forzano, who had a 17-43-1 overall record at the college level, created a fracture on the staff. Khayat and Hollway lasted only one season with Forzano, and English recalled that Khayat, a former ten-year NFL player and amateur boxing champ in Mississippi, had backed his former boss into a corner at the Senior Bowl and engaged him in a heated discussion.

Forzano went 7-7 in 1974 and '75, then added to his staff the likes of Ken Shipp—who had worked as offensive coordinator with Joe Namath and Archie Manning—and Fritz Shurmur (defensive line) and Joe Bugel (offensive line), who later stood among the league's finest assistants. And Billy Belichick.

"His father said, 'Don't call him Billy; call him Bill,'" English said. "I guess [Billy] indicated he was a younger guy . . . Everyone respected Bill, even though he was a Forzano guy. Forzano gave him a lot of leeway when he got to that kicking game stuff. He would let Bill talk to the whole team. Even though Bill didn't have the title, he was like the special teams coach."

Much as he had in Baltimore, Belichick quickly earned the respect of players with his knowledge of X's and O's. He was 24 years old, younger than most of the Lions, and it didn't matter. "Billy was a whiz kid," Laslavic said. "I don't remember anyone ever messing with Billy, even though the players were older than him. He was too serious about his work."

Shipp, a respected offensive coordinator and passing game innovator, had given his phone-book-thick playbook to Belichick to study and told him there would be a quiz on its contents in a couple of weeks. Shipp was skeptical of Billy's chances of passing the test; the kid had devoted most of his time and energy to defense in Baltimore, after all. But when Belichick ultimately took the five-hour test, Shipp was stunned by the results. "He damn answered everything," the offensive coordinator recalled.

In his two years in Detroit, Belichick was educated by veteran coaches who handed down lessons learned while working with great players in great programs. Shipp taught him how pass patterns needed to be adjusted based on particular coverages. Shipp's replacement the following season, Ed Hughes, showed him the Dallas Cowboys system he'd helped run while working with Tom Landry and Roger Staubach—the protections, the passing and running game, the shifts and motions the Cowboys liked to run.

Glanville had worked with Steelers defensive coordinator Bud Carson at Georgia Tech, and he gave Billy a glimpse of the defensive philosophy and Cover 2 scheme that shaped Pittsburgh's dynasty. Jimmy Carr had been a cornerback on the only team (the 1960 Philadelphia Eagles) ever to defeat Vince Lombardi's Green Bay Packers in the postseason and had served as a defensive coach with Minnesota, Chicago, and Philadelphia. He was among the first to utilize nickel packages, zone blitzes, and other newfangled schemes. Shurmur and Bugel would later win a combined three Super Bowl rings.

Belichick took from all these men. "And that sucker would work 24 hours a day," Bugel said. "It was unbelievable to watch. I told him when I left Detroit, 'Billy, you're going to be a great, great coach.'"

Belichick was not afraid to challenge his older colleagues. Once a backup to Johnny Unitas at the University of Louisville, English was coaching Detroit's running backs when Billy attempted to correct him on a run play to the weak side, with the fullback lined up behind the quarterback and the halfback lined up behind the left tackle. English wanted the fleet fullback, Horace King, to carry the ball, and he wanted the halfback to either block outside or inside depending on what the tackle did with his man. But Billy didn't think the halfback should play off the tackle's block; he wanted the halfback to go inside each and every time.

He explained that if the linemen took big splits, his way was all but guaranteed to work. "Bill was coaching me, 12 years his elder," English said, "on how I should coach running backs . . . I respected that he had the balls to bring me in the office to draw that up."

English didn't take his advice, and kept the play as he designed it. Belichick did get his revenge in another forum, though: He regularly beat English in racquetball games by hitting the ball low, off the sidewall, in places his opponent couldn't reach.

If Belichick had a best friend on the staff, it was Floyd Reese, the 28-year-old strength-and-conditioning coach and a former UCLA star, who presided over the kind of weight room and weight program that didn't exist in Baltimore. They were ambitious grinders who hung out together, who traded ideas on how to finally improve the Lions' fortunes on Sundays. (Detroit had appeared in one playoff game since last winning the NFL championship, in 1957.) Reese would find himself asking a question in a staff meeting that made the older coaches stop and think, only to hear Belichick follow up a few minutes later with a question that was three levels more advanced than Reese's.

"I was always trying to catch up to Bill," he said.

Meanwhile, the Lions were always trying (and failing) to catch up to the Minnesota Vikings in the NFC Central. Detroit lost three of its first four games in '76, all to divisional opponents, and Forzano handed in his resignation three weeks after his owner, Ford, blitzed him and GM Russ Thomas with a win-or-else ultimatum. The Lions introduced as Forzano's successor their own personnel guy, Tommy Hudspeth, whom the *Detroit Free Press* described as a "45-year-old non-drinking, non-smoking Mormon (one wife, three children)." Hudspeth had been the head coach at Brigham Young and the University of Texas–El Paso, and he promised that the Lions would throw the football.

New England was the next opponent on the schedule. The 3-1 Patriots had just completed a 48–17 blowout of an Oakland Raiders team that would go 13-1 and win the Super Bowl. The week before that victory, the Patriots defeated the two-time defending champion Steelers in Pittsburgh. Detroit–New England appeared to be a mismatch, and the worst possible opening-act scenario for Hudspeth.

But Billy Belichick was always thinking up different schemes at his home in nearby Birmingham, and he had an idea for Shipp and his new boss. While working for the Colts, Belichick had watched film of the Los Angeles Rams' 1974 playoff victory over the Washington Redskins. Rams coach Chuck Knox used what he called an "ace" formation, which included two tight ends, two wide receivers, and one running back. Rams receiver Lance Rentzel said that the Redskins were confused by an alignment that was directly responsible for his team's first touchdown — a ten-yard pass to tight end Bob Klein that punctuated an eight-play, 72-yard drive.

Belichick approached Shipp. "Look," he said, "I know we haven't ever used this formation, but, you know, I studied this formation when I was at Baltimore last year. I think this is really going to give the Patriots a problem. Can we take a look at this?"

This is why Belichick thought two tight ends would dramatically improve Detroit's odds of winning a game it had no business winning: "New England," he would later recall, "had just beaten the Raiders by 31 points playing a lot of Cover 3 in their 3-4 defense . . . Back then in the conventional pro set, it was very hard to get three receivers out to the weak side, because to do that, you'd have to release both backs. Against a 3-4, you just couldn't get them out quick enough. But if you switched to a balanced two-tight-end, two-receiver set, then you already have a guy at the line of scrimmage that can get to the weak side of coverage very quickly."

The Lions looked at it, debated it, then used it. Detroit had two talented tight ends in Charlie Sanders and rookie David Hill, and they were versatile enough to be split or used off the line as wingbacks. As it turned out, the Patriots had little idea what to do with the two of them. Greg Landry, Detroit's veteran quarterback, completed 15 of 18 passes and threw for three touchdowns in this 30–10 rout, all three to Hill and Sanders. Landry also found Horace King underneath for six completions and 45 yards. Hudspeth credited his assistants for discovering on film that New England's linebackers liked to drop deep in pass coverage.

Belichick noticed that the Lions were loose, confident, and energetic against the Patriots. "You could have probably gotten the Lions and 40 points if you wanted to put money on that game," he would say. "But that day was different. There was a boost of energy. There was a power surge. There was a confidence that just wasn't there even a few days before. You never know how change is going to affect a team."

Belichick was referring to the change of leadership. And even though Hudspeth didn't call the plays, didn't wear a headset, and didn't do much beyond staying out of the way—UPI described him as "seemingly little more than an interested spectator as he wandered along the sidelines"—his presence in Forzano's place clearly had a positive emotional impact on the team.

Chuck Fairbanks, New England's coach, would forever refer to the double-tight-end formation as "Detroit" after this loss, changing the Patriots' in-house language for many coaching staffs to come. Hudspeth? He went 5-5 that season and then got fired after going 6-8 in 1977.

Belichick was back in search of a job. He took two truths from that upset victory over the Patriots that would stay with him for the rest of his career. The first was his belief that nobody should be afraid to deploy a tactic simply because it cuts against the grain of conventional thought.

The second was about self-confidence, and Belichick's sudden awareness that he was on to something big. He looked at how his formation, his idea, had destroyed the 3-1 Patriots, and he came to a reasonable conclusion.

"OK," the young Detroit assistant said. "I can coach in this league."

Bill Belichick arrived in Denver in 1978 a married man. He'd exchanged vows at the Naval Academy the year before with Debby Clarke, and they found a place in the Denver suburb of Morrison.

Professionally, everything felt different, too. Unlike the Colts and Lions, the Broncos had just made a trip to the Super Bowl, albeit a losing one, on the strength of their vaunted Orange Crush defense. They represented Belichick's first legitimate chance to win a ring.

Bill ended up working with two defensive coaches, in Richie McCabe and Joe Collier, who would make a lasting impression on him. McCabe was a former NFL defensive back and a secondary coach who took to Bill and almost immediately starting telling people he was going to be a head coach someday. Collier introduced Belichick to the 3-4 defense, and had his 26-year-old aide breaking down film, though his forecast for Bill's career was a little cloudier than McCabe's.

"You wouldn't visualize him [being a head coach] because his personality wasn't outgoing," Collier would say decades later. "You didn't look at him as a potential head coach. I looked at him as a potential coordinator, which I thought he'd be great at."

In fact, Denver's rookie head coach, Red Miller, recalled that Belichick was "the most dour young man I've ever been around" and that he "wasn't the best-dressed kid."

Bill didn't have much interaction with Miller, who worked primarily with the offense and the offensive line, yet he did log enough hours to spend some nights sleeping at the office. He helped out Marv Braden, the special teams coach, and filmed Denver's workouts. Sometimes he caught Bucky Dilts's punts in practice, and talked to Jim Turner, the kicker, about his methods of warming up. He spent as much time as he could in Collier's room, soaking up every last detail about the 3-4. Babe Parilli, quarterbacks coach, said Belichick visited him to go over pass-play reads and progressions. Parilli enjoyed the give-and-take, but, like Collier, he thought Bill's personality (or lack thereof) didn't match up with the profile of a future head coach.

Braden gave Belichick a piece of advice to help him relate better to players. They were watching film one day when Bill saw something he didn't like out of one of the Broncos, and ripped into the guy. It wasn't a big deal, Braden recalled, but he wanted the young assistant to know that coaches with short fuses often say things they quickly regret.

"Don't downgrade the players too much," Braden told Bill. "It's the same guys you're downgrading on Wednesday that you practice with on Thursday and play with on Sunday. You've got to keep them up. You can discipline them. You can correct them and drive them and give them more oomph than they think they've got. But don't be too caustic."

Belichick shared an eight-by-ten office with John Beake, personnel man, in a tiny brick building that served as the Broncos' headquarters at 5700 Logan Street. Beake thought the young assistant learned a lot from Collier about how to be a smart and tireless worker.

Collier even schooled Belichick in racquetball, regularly beating him in staff matches. Carroll Hardy, player personnel director and a former big-league ballplayer who was the only man ever to pinch-hit for Ted Williams, also taught Bill a few lessons on the racquetball court. Hardy often stood in front of Bill to reduce the size of his target, and Bill would hit him with the ball because he couldn't get it around him. "I got the best of Bill Belichick," Hardy said, "and he didn't like it. He got mad. He smashed his racquet pretty good against the wall. He did a little cussin' along with it."

Though Belichick stayed in Denver for only one year, he was given an advanced education in coverage concepts by Collier, who presided over a defense defined by its closing speed, not its size. Ultimately, the Orange

Crush defense of Lyle Alzado, Tom Jackson, and Randy Gradishar couldn't replicate its 1977 success. The Broncos finished 10-6 and got blown out by Pittsburgh in a divisional playoff game, 33–10.

Though he enjoyed skiing with Debby, Belichick wasn't happy in Denver. He missed living near the water, and he wanted bigger responsibilities than he had with the Broncos. He thought only briefly about leaving coaching for law school. He spoke with the first-year head coach at Air Force, Bill Parcells, about a role at the academy, but Parcells was already burdened by what would be the first of many stay-or-go crises in his career. Braden had known Parcells since his high school days; he'd tried and failed to recruit Parcells's brother, Don. So Braden visited with the Air Force coach and talked him through his choice between staying at the academy and leaving for a position with Ray Perkins's New York Giants.

Parcells chose the Giants. Meanwhile, Belichick had his brilliant friend from Andover, Ernie Adams, whispering in Perkins's ear, too. Adams and Perkins had worked together with the New England Patriots, and Ray was so impressed with the way Ernie broke down film that he promised to hire him once he became a head coach. Sure enough, Perkins said, Adams was the first man he called after he was appointed by the Giants. And one of Adams's first contributions was telling Perkins he knew of someone who could help him win.

"His name is Bill Belichick," Ernie told him.

"OK," Perkins said. "What's this guy's deal?"

Ernie spelled out Bill's background, and Perkins was interested. He told Adams that he was about to take a trip to San Diego, where he'd worked as the Chargers' offensive coordinator, to take care of some personal matters, and that Ernie should set up a meeting with Belichick out there.

"Everything gave you the feeling that this guy was going to get it done, or he was going to ask somebody for help to get it done," Perkins said of their meeting in a hotel. "He was going to do the job either way."

Before Perkins made a decision on whether Bill Belichick should be his special teams coach, he wanted to hear Bill's answer to a simple question that he asked every job candidate he interviewed. Perkins listed three words: *consistent, right,* and *fair.* He then asked Bill which word did not apply to the playing of a football game, or any game.

Belichick didn't hesitate. Not even for a second.

"Fair," he said.

"You're right," Perkins told him. "And you're hired."

6

LITTLE BILL

Shit rolls downhill.

Bill Belichick made that claim in a meeting in 1979, his first year as a New York Giants assistant under rookie head coach Ray Perkins. Belichick was a special teams coach and defensive assistant, and Perkins, once a teammate of Joe Namath's at Alabama and a blind believer in the Bear Bryant way, had just reamed out his staff over some real or imagined breakdown.

"Perkins was shitting on them," recalled linebacker Harry Carson, "so the coaches were shitting on us. I'll always remember that expression, 'Shit rolls downhill.' That came from Belichick."

Hired by Perkins, who made his mentor Bryant appear timid and soft in comparison, Belichick arrived in the New York area on the same flight as Parcells. The Giants hadn't appeared in a playoff game since 1963, and they were fresh off eight consecutive losing years. The 1978 season had been particularly painful; the Giants lost seven of their final eight. They fumbled away a game to the Philadelphia Eagles in the closing seconds when they could've taken a knee to run out the clock (Philly's Herm Edwards scooped up the loose ball and ran it into the end zone), and the fans couldn't forgive the folly of what would be called the "Miracle at the Meadowlands." Soon enough they were hanging owner Wellington Mara in effigy, burning tickets in the parking lot, and flying a banner over the stadium that read 15 YEARS OF LOUSY FOOTBALL — WE'VE HAD ENOUGH.

The conservative Mara had been feuding with his uninhibited nephew and business partner, Tim, over how the organization should be run, and NFL commissioner Pete Rozelle mediated by suggesting that George Young, formerly of the Dolphins and Colts, take control of football operations. Young's first two significant moves in 1979 were the hiring of Perkins and the drafting of a quarterback from Kentucky's Morehead State, Phil Simms, whose selection with the seventh overall pick in the first round was met with a robust round of boos.

The Giants' attempt to regain credibility and stabilize the franchise took a hit when Parcells, the first-year defensive coordinator, resigned after four months on the job. His wife, Judy, didn't want to move their three daughters from the Colorado Springs area, where he had been the head coach at Air Force for one year. Parcells took a sales job with a land development company, and Belichick stayed behind with a group of football players who had very little use for him.

"I have to say that secretly we sort of looked at him like 'What does he know? He's never played the game. He's a lacrosse player.' He wasn't really one of us," Carson said. "When you look at another guy who has played linebacker, you look at him with a certain amount of respect, because he's been there and he knows what ramming it up there and taking on a blocker means. He knows what it's all about . . . But with Belichick, the subject of playing Division III football never came up. The subject that came up was: He played lacrosse. He didn't play football."

Belichick's non-career as a football player wasn't the only thing that bothered some Giants. George Martin, a former 11th-round draft pick who became an impactful starter at defensive end, said the 27-year-old assistant was "very nerdy to most of us" and years later compared him to a character in the sitcom *Family Matters*, Steve Urkel, the bespectacled geek. John Skorupan, outside linebacker, said the Giants took every opportunity to remind Belichick that he had done nothing, at that point, to earn their undivided attention and respect. "We did abuse him," Skorupan said. "There's no doubt about that. He was a smaller guy, younger than us, and we certainly knew that he didn't play in the NFL. He was kind of roly-poly, and he was watching films all the time and he was very intense about it. He'd say, 'OK, it's time for special teams,' and we'd moan and groan and give him a hard time."

In those days, starters were often used on special teams, usually against their will, and the young assistant paid the price for it. With sunscreen on his nose and flip-flops on his feet, sporting a seven-dollar haircut, Belichick was a frequent source of locker room and lunchtime conversation among the players. "He was a guy we mocked, we made fun of," Martin said, "because we saw him as a peer age-wise." The veteran defensive end and team leader also echoed what some of Belichick's past colleagues had privately grumbled about — that Bill was landing jobs because of his father's standing in the profession.

"We knew his dad was an accomplished coach," Martin said, "and we thought he was a young whippersnapper who was riding his dad's coattails and hadn't earned the right to be in the NFL . . . His dad showed up at practice, and we almost gave more attention to his dad. In our estimation, [Steve Belichick] earned the right to be respected. He came there to validate his son, and that was the wrong thing to do for us veterans."

Asked if Giants players had said this to Bill Belichick's face, Martin said, "Actions speak louder than words. We didn't have to tell him. When a coach tells us to turn the lights on and nobody moves, that's disrespectful. When he tells you to go to the weight room or do this and you do it at a snail's pace or ignored him or laughed at him, that's disrespectful . . . He'd come over to the sideline and we were lounging around and he'd say, 'Get the hell up and get out of here.' And we didn't move. We neutered him and totally disrespected him.

"I'm ashamed to say we did a lot of that when Bill came on the scene. That's the price of admission and initiation."

It was a price Belichick was willing to pay.

Martin, for one, had no use for Perkins, who was as lean and mean as a 1-iron and had cold, penetrating blue eyes that could make a man twice his size buckle at the knees. Perkins coached the game the way he played it — hard — and the Giants didn't appreciate his draconian approach to discipline and conditioning, or his lack of bedside manner. "He was actually vehemently hated by the vast majority of the team at that time," Martin said, "and he seemed to revel in it."

Belichick wasn't hated like Perkins. In fact, as much as the Giants initially saw him as something of a pathetic figure, they soon realized that their new special teams coach wasn't one who would easily back down.

"To Bill's credit," Martin said, "he was undeterred and undaunted by the ridicule or by the lack of respect we showed him. He came in with a focus, and the fact that he was smart really caught our attention. He went from ridicule and laughter to getting our attention . . . Even at that young age, he had an insight that was absolutely uncanny. It seemed like every game he saw our opponents' Achilles' heel and would implement something that was pure genius and find something to give us an advantage."

Belichick had impressed Perkins before he started to win over the players. The head coach sat in on Belichick's first meeting at his first Giants training camp; that special teams meeting was the equivalent of a full team meeting, because just about everyone on the roster had some role in the kicking game. Perkins wanted to see how the players reacted to Belichick, especially the ones who were known to challenge authority.

Sure enough, one such player acted in a way that Perkins described as out of line. The head coach wouldn't specify the exact nature of the remarks or behavior, but he suggested that the player, Gary Jeter, was trying to humiliate the new coach running the meeting. Belichick completely shut down the offending Giant, told him he'd been part of the problem the previous season, and ordered him to either act professionally or leave the room.

"I was tickled to death," Perkins said, "so I got up and left. By me leaving the room, I think I told everybody in there I was pleased with the way he handled it. And I didn't worry about Bill ever again."

As he started to find his footing and his voice, Belichick still projected a vibe to some of being in over his head. John Mara, the oldest of Wellington's 11 children, was an attorney at the time of Belichick's arrival and an occasional visitor to practice, years before he assumed control of the club. Mara thought the new special teams coach seemed very young, almost like a little kid. He most certainly did not fit Mara's idea of what an NFL assistant coach should look like.

"He dressed in flip-flops and jeans and sweatshirts," Mara said. "My only impression of him was that he looked out of place." Mara's brother Chris, who worked in player personnel, recalled the subject of Belichick's disheveled appearance coming up in conversation during golf outings with linebackers Brian Kelley and Brad Van Pelt. "They always joked about him and laughed about him," the scout said. "And a lot of that had to do with the fact Bill just didn't look the part of a serious coach."

But then the owner's sons watched Belichick go to work. "He was very engaged in what was happening on the field," John Mara said, "and was always talking to players in a group and individually . . . never really yelling or screaming. You would have to look for him to find him on the field. He kind of blended in . . . He looked like the student as opposed to the teacher, and all of a sudden he's out on the field with guys who looked older than he was, and he's leading them around."

Harry Carson watched Belichick put the stopwatch on punter Dave Jennings to record his hang time and noticed that the special teams coach was thorough and passionate about everything he did. Over time, Perkins saw the Giants respond to Belichick, approach him with questions, a sign that they respected his aptitude for the game. The head coach also saw Belichick become quicker to jump on a player who wasn't giving maximum effort in a drill.

Unfortunately, the Giants had too many players who too often inspired the wrath of the coaching staff. They just weren't very good, and Perkins knew it. The Giants started the season 0-5 and never fully recovered. Simms, the rookie quarterback, did replace Joe Pisarcik and did win his first four starts, offering a beaten-down fan base the next best thing to a winning team: hope. The Giants went 6-10, then fell to 4-12 in 1980. Amid the mind-numbing blur of losses, Perkins remembered Belichick pushing him to try some onside kicks in an attempt to jump-start the team. (They tried two against the Eagles, recovering both, in a Monday night game in 1980, but still lost, 35-3.) One more sub-.500 season away from getting fired, Perkins was involved in two moves early in 1981 that forever altered the fortunes of the franchise.

He rehired Bill Parcells, who had been miserable without football and had returned to the NFL the previous year as a New England Patriots linebacker coach. And he supported George Young's decision to use the second pick in the draft to take a linebacker named Lawrence Taylor out of the University of North Carolina.

The Giants already had Pro Bowlers Carson and Van Pelt at linebacker, along with Kelley, and there were players who thought the team shouldn't be adding to a position of strength when it had so many holes to fill. In fact, some defensive players were angry over what the Giants planned to pay Taylor and grumbled about a possible walkout.

There would be no boycott in East Rutherford; the 6′3″, 237-pound Taylor was the Giants' best player the first time he stepped onto the practice field. Dave Klein of the *Star-Ledger* of Newark asked Parcells what he planned to do with him. "What we're going to do with Lawrence Taylor," the defensive coordinator answered, "has never been done before."

As it turned out, Parcells was the one who ultimately put Taylor in Belichick's hands. Though Belichick had been hired to run special teams, Parcells asked Perkins if he could use him on defense. Eleven years older than Belichick, Parcells had played Division I football at the school now known as Wichita State and had worked at seven different colleges, including West Point, where he befriended a smoldering young basketball coach named Bob Knight. Parcells knew the difference between a good coach and a fraud, and he could tell early on that Belichick was very good at explaining what had happened on a particular play.

"I thought he had very good potential," Parcells said. "He was a coach's son, and I liked that. I knew his father when I was at Army and his father was at Navy. We had similar roles, we exchanged film with each other, and his father was the one who introduced me to Bill when I coached at Vanderbilt and we were playing at Army. I liked Steve very much, and . . . I thought Bill certainly had a lot of potential there, and so we phased him into the defense."

The way Perkins remembered it, the transition from a 4-3 defense to a 3-4 defense was part of Parcells's motivation to ask for Belichick's help. The day he was hired as the Giants' coach, Perkins had said, "Show me a Super Bowl champion and I'll show you a team that doesn't play 3-4 defense." But Perkins did play some 3-4 as early as 1979 — he used it when the 0-5 Giants beat the 5-0 Buccaneers — and he knew he needed to take full advantage of the Giants' biggest strength on defense. "Bill Belichick started helping out with the linebackers," Perkins said, "and everything he did turned to gold."

That first year Belichick worked with Parcells, a year after the Giants were ranked 27th out of 28 teams in points allowed, they finished third in the same category. Only Belichick wasn't infallible. He'd already earned his standing as an innovative special teams mind, and yet he made one move that angered and befuddled his co-workers. After the Giants took a late three-point lead in a critical 1981 game against NFC East rival Washington, Belichick ordered kicker Joe Danelo to attempt a squib kick to keep the ball away from dangerous return man Mike Nelms. Danelo wanted to try to kick it out of the end zone, but Belichick wouldn't budge. The Redskins recovered the squib, tied the game on a field goal in the final seconds, and then won it in overtime. Perkins blamed himself for the decision but said he was "influenced by too many people." Of Belichick's call, an emotional Danelo said, "I don't understand it at all."

The Giants survived the gaffe and made the playoffs for the first time in 18 years — the first season Belichick, Parcells, and Taylor spent together — and even won a wild-card-round game over Philadelphia. After the NFL players' strike of 1982 reduced the season to a nine-game mess, Perkins left the Giants to succeed Bear Bryant at Alabama, and the two Bills got promoted: Parcells to head coach, and Belichick to linebackers coach and de facto defensive coordinator. Big Bill and Little Bill. Belichick was 31 years old, only eight years out of Wesleyan, and already he was running a defense for a flagship NFL franchise.

Parcells didn't officially name Belichick coordinator in 1983, even though he was very much in control of the unit. "He was coaching the defense," Parcells explained, "but my [third year] was when I named him coordinator. I thought it would be better. I was a defensive coach, and I just thought it was going to be less pressure on him if I did it that way, and waited some time to name him after giving him the responsibility."

Parcells almost never got the chance to make that appointment official. The Giants were his dream job as much as Alabama was Perkins's. Parcells grew up in Hasbrouck Heights, New Jersey, a few miles from the team's current home. He was 13 when he saw his first Giants game at the Polo Grounds, in 1954, and he cried his eyes out four years later after listening to the radio call of the Baltimore Colts' Alan Ameche scoring in overtime to defeat the Giants in their epic Championship Game in Yankee Stadium. For Parcells, landing the Giants job at age 41 — only four years after he thought he was quitting football for good — was an overwhelming experience.

But he made a bad choice to start the 1983 season, and it nearly proved fatal to his career ambitions. Parcells decided his first-string quarterback

should be Scott Brunner, who had replaced an injured Simms in 1981 and
'82, instead of the former first-round draft pick who had returned from a
knee injury. As a result, the Giants would win three games out of 16 and
compel Young to try to hire University of Miami coach Howard Schnellenberger.

Schnellenberger stayed at Miami, and Young begrudgingly stayed with
Parcells. Belichick had an offer from the defensive coordinator of the Minnesota Vikings, Floyd Reese, his old Detroit colleague and friend, to coach
the Vikings' secondary, but he ultimately decided he didn't want to leave
the New York area and the badly wounded Parcells, to whom he felt indebted. Of even greater consequence, Lawrence Taylor backed out of a deal
to play for Donald Trump and the New Jersey Generals of the new United
States Football League and accepted a revised and greatly enriched contract
with the Giants.

Parcells was angry at Young entering the 1984 season, and he was angry
at himself for going soft on his underachieving players and for acting like a
coordinator instead of a head coach. Parcells started hunting for confrontation with his players and assistants, and nobody was safe. If he was going to get fired, he was going to hit some people hard on the way out. The
approach worked, too. Parcells made Giants players and coaches uncomfortable, pressing them every day to chase perfection. He wasn't a genius
tactician. Instead, Parcells discovered that his most valuable asset was the
force of his personality. Great coaching, especially in a violent sport gov-
erned through the power of non-guaranteed contracts, generally involves
persuading athletes to do things their hearts and minds advise them not
to do. Bill Parcells could impose his will on his athletes and his assistants.
That was his gift.

He showed it even as a defensive coordinator, when he chewed out a
linebacker for dropping into the wrong area in pass coverage, only to have
the secondary coach, Fred Glick, tell Parcells that the linebacker had actually done as he was taught. "Even though he was wrong," Glick said, "Parcells said, 'Don't ever correct me again.' He didn't want to be corrected in
front of players. I don't think Parcells ever thought he was wrong."

So he ripped into his quarterback, Simms, and his best player, Taylor,
along with everyone else, while slowly building a championship-level team
out of the ashes of the '83 season. The Giants finally assembled a line that
could protect the quarterback, and an offense that was designed to do something more than stay out of the defense's way. "Our direction on offense,"
said receivers coach Pat Hodgson, "was not to lose the game. For Bill Parcells, it had always been defense first, special teams second, offense third."

Extreme tension sometimes existed between the defensive players and coaches and their colleagues on offense. Ron Erhardt, offensive coordinator, once walked into a unit meeting and told his players that if they didn't turn the ball over against certain opponents, "maybe we can tie them 0–0." When the Giants fielded an offense that could make the defense proud, they went 9-7 and 10-6 in 1984 and '85, winning one playoff game each year before running into the 15-1 49ers (in '84) and the 15-1 Bears (in '85), both eventual champions. Along the way, Parcells also engaged in full-contact drills with his finest assistant coach.

On the chalkboard and grease board, Bill Belichick had an answer for just about everything. "On special teams," Hodgson said, "he had all sorts of gadget plays. He was very creative with the things they'd do. We'd put ten guys out there and run a guy onto the field, hesitate, wave him off, snap the ball, and then he'd go down the sideline. We had hideout plays, every kind of gadget you could think of when needed. Then he went to the defense and they fought battles, Big Bill and Little Bill."

Opposites don't always attract. Parcells was a physically imposing man, a loud and proud Jersey Guy with the temper of an overheated motorist stuck in Shore traffic. Belichick was a physically underwhelming, charisma-free automaton. Parcells didn't hesitate to seize his advantage in size, volume, and position on the food chain to verbally assault Belichick in front of insiders and outsiders alike.

Kevin Gilbride, a future NFL head coach, was working for the Ottawa Rough Riders of the Canadian Football League when he witnessed one such assault. Belichick was meeting with Gilbride inside Giants Stadium — Little Bill was often generous with his time with outside coaches looking to pick his brain — when Big Bill stumbled upon the scene and exploded.

"He just ripped Belichick for meeting with me, just fiercely ripped his rear end," Gilbride recalled. "I felt horrible. I didn't know what the deal was. We'd been to summer camps and had been on the sideline and watched practice. I don't know if Parcells looked at me as a potential threat, but I wasn't even in the NFL. But when Parcells ripped Bill, it didn't even faze [Belichick]. He said, 'Don't worry about it.' He asked me, 'You want something for lunch?' At the time, I felt embarrassed for Belichick . . . Obviously this wasn't the first time it happened. He became inured to this type of treatment to develop thick skin. And the more I got to know Parcells, the more I understood this wasn't a one-time thing."

Parcells was not a one-dimensional bully when it came to motivating his subordinates; he was too smart for that. He knew he had to build up players and coaches after he tore them down. One assistant coach described public embarrassment followed by a private apology as "something that happened all the time with Big Bill." Parcells had a knack for saying a reassuring word at the most opportune time.

Parcells's playing past also helped his relationship with his team. Unlike Belichick, he'd been a good enough college linebacker to get drafted into the NFL (seventh round, Detroit Lions, 1964). He loved the jock life, the camaraderie, the feeling young men share when they accomplish something as a unit in a sport as dangerous as football. Parcells tried to re-create that bond he'd known in his college days with the Giants he was putting in harm's way.

"We could give it to him and he'd take it," Carson said. "We'd horse around . . . Bill loved being in the locker room, and that's one thing a lot of people don't know. He enjoyed being around the guys. He got a lot of energy from being around the guys, and being one of the guys. And that's how the whole Gatorade thing got started with us — because he was razzing on Burt."

Jim Burt, the nose tackle who started the tradition of dumping a bucket of Gatorade on a winning head coach.

"Bill got under Burt's skin," Carson said, "and Burt got so pissed off with Parcells as he was riding him that at the conclusion of a game against Washington, Burt came to me and said, 'Parcells is such a cocksucker. Let's get him.' I said, 'What do you mean *Let's get him?*' He said, 'Parcells is your boy. If I did something to him, he'll have my ass. But if *you* do something with him, he's not going to do anything. So let's get him.' I said, 'Get him with what?' He said, 'Let's get him with Gatorade.' So we did it together, and there were no ramifications." Of course, the fun could last only so long. Parcells had made his decision after the 1983 disaster to be true to himself, to be an unapologetic hard-ass, and there was no turning back from that. Phil McConkey, backup receiver and return man, absorbed his share of verbal abuse for dropping a punt or for some other not-so-venial sin. McConkey maintained that Parcells feared no Giant player or coach, except one: his young tight end. "He was deathly afraid of Mark Bavaro," McConkey said. "But he picked on everyone, including the staff. He would absolutely yell at Bill Belichick in front of players. I think Parcells went too far with Bill, but he did that with a lot of people."

Big Bill was once heard screaming into his headset, "Don't you start giving me any shit, Belichick. Your ass will be out in the fucking parking lot." Parcells often told his assistant that something was "screwed up," but when Belichick pressed for a specific correction, Parcells would bat away the request and order Little Bill to figure out the fix on his own.

If there was one place Belichick could strike back at his boss, it was on the racquetball courts in the bowels of Giants Stadium. During his time with the Giants, Bill was an avid jogger and stationary bike rider who also competed in what he called a late-night "huff and puff" hockey league for men in their thirties and forties. Despite the endless hours at the office, he found time to add racquetball to his fitness regimen. He couldn't beat Randy Dean, a backup quarterback in 1979 who recalled occasionally seeing "a mangled racquet in the garbage" after an angry Belichick had lost, and he struggled to beat his friend Dave Jennings, the Pro Bowl punter. But Little Bill didn't have much trouble in lunchtime matches with the immobile Big Bill. Parcells would lose to his assistant, light up a cigarette or two, and then step back onto the court and lose again.

Carson, the team captain, had a front-row seat for many one-sided Big Bill–Little Bill clashes of a different kind. He'd jog to the sideline during a stoppage in play, or between downs, and stand between the two coaches as they figured out what to do on the next snap. "And Belichick is flashing a signal to the signal caller," Carson said, "and Parcells would say, 'I don't want that.' And Belichick would say, 'But Bill —' and Parcells would raise his voice. 'I don't want that, Belichick. Just play the fucking thing the way I said to.' They're both on the sidelines on headsets, both looking at the field, and they're communicating to one another and whoever was up in the booth . . . [Belichick] would always take it, because he was the defensive coordinator and Parcells was the head coach."

These battles of the Bills, Martin said, were almost always fought in the heat of game-day competition and not on the practice field. But by the 1986 season, when the Giants established themselves as a deadly serious championship contender by going 14-2, Martin detected a not-so-subtle shift in the Parcells-Belichick dynamic.

To understand that shift, one needed to understand just how badly the Giants' defensive players wanted Parcells to remain as their coordinator in 1983. "We were absolutely pissed off that we'd lost Parcells from a defensive perspective to be the head coach," Martin said. "We felt abandoned almost to the point of having an uprising . . . We were cocky and dominant, and we attributed that to Parcells, who had a personality. You could engage him, he was fun, he would kid with you, and he knew about your personality and family. There was that relationship with Parcells. Not so with Bill Belichick. There was absolutely no fluff, no bedside manner. He was strictly business. He was never going to ask you how your kids were doing, how was your wife's birthday party, what your summer was like. He was incapable of that."

Parcells assured the unit's leaders that Belichick was perfectly capable of doing the job, and that Little Bill had Big Bill's full support. Martin said it took the Giants' defense about a year to accept Little Bill as a worthy de facto coordinator. Despite Belichick's youth and lack of a distinguished playing career, the Giants eventually embraced the fact that Little Bill's relentless attention to detail was an asset that put them in a position to succeed.

Not that players didn't continue to defy him in their own way. Lawrence Taylor was busy on Sundays redefining the standards of NFL greatness, so he didn't have much time or use for Belichick in film sessions during the week. Little Bill's monotone delivery had earned him the nickname Captain Sominex, and he had a great talent for putting LT to sleep.

Carson described how Belichick would be scheming away at the front of the room while Taylor lay flat under a nearby table. Sometimes LT claimed he had a bad back and needed to lie on the floor while watching film. Sometimes he wore sunglasses, too, just to make it easier to wall off all of Belichick's breakdowns. "He's got his eyes closed," Carson said of Taylor, "and when the lights go off to watch film, everybody's sort of in their own little world. So Lawrence would fall asleep while Bill was diagramming plays. The table would be in the front of the room, and the projector was on the table. Lawrence would have his eyes closed, but somehow he'd be alert and able to answer all the questions Belichick would pose to him."

Carson sat in the back of the room in a La-Z-Boy recliner. As soon as the lights went off, he said, and Belichick started droning on, it was difficult for everyone to stay awake. Legs up, Carson would flip his hoodie over his head and start listening to the jazz or rock or religious music in his headphones. If he happened to hear Belichick over the music, he'd answer his questions.

The coach found ways to get his necessary points across. Joe Morris, the running back from Syracuse, was once ripped by Belichick in a film session for missing a tackle on kickoff coverage.

"I really thought it was never going to work out for him," Morris said. "I was embarrassed. He clearly pointed out my failures as a player, and no player wants to be taken down a peg . . . And I said, 'Bill, from that day on, I never want to be embarrassed in a film session again, so I'm going to make sure any effort you see on film is my best effort.'"

Years later, Morris told Belichick, "I thought you were a dick at first, but let me tell you something: You made me a better player."

Belichick made a lot of players better, even the future Hall of Famers. Morris recalled Carson missing a tackle in a game and Belichick making him hit a tackling dummy over and over in the next practice. The coach couldn't believe the linebacker hadn't made the tackle in question, and asked him how a Pro Bowler could be so sloppy in his technique. Carson was pissed about the commentary and the requirement to do this drill.

"But he did it," Morris said. "And Harry never closed his eyes on a tackle the rest of his life . . . There has to be an affinity for someone who makes you get better."

And this is where some light is shed on that shift in the Parcells-Belichick relationship. Little Bill had earned the respect of his defensive players through accomplishment — theirs — and therefore grew less inclined to be the kind of tackling dummy for Big Bill that Little Bill had put in front of Carson.

"It was almost like a father and son," Martin said, "where the son comes on and he's completely obedient to the father. He makes certain he follows instructions to a T, he's not one step out of line, and eventually that son realizes he has his own platform, his own voice and responsibility, and he comes into his own. It was nice to see Bill Belichick stand up to Parcells and say, 'Goddammit, I'm the coordinator and I'm going to make this call.'

"They had a lot of fiery exchanges," Martin went on. "Parcells was reluctant to give up his command of the defense. It was around 1985 or '86 where Belichick started not being afraid to stand up to Parcells. All Belichick needed was the support of the players . . . That's when the pendulum swung and we went from Parcells guys to Belichick guys."

And yet Big Bill would always be the emotional leader of the Giants, their undisputed heartbeat, the master of pushing the right human buttons at the right time. He wanted to keep the game as simple as possible for his players, wanted them to focus not on newfangled X's and O's but on the effort they were expending against the men lined up across from them.

Parcells did give Belichick freedom in how he coached his defense, and remained open-minded to the nuanced changes the coordinator would make. "Occasionally there were some times I had to restrain him," Parcells said, "because he was very cerebral and he had a lot of ideas, and a lot of them are very good. You have to be able to transmit them to the players, and sometimes I erred on the side of *A little less is better, and let's rely on execution. We have good players — let's let them play.*"

More and more, the defensive players came to view Belichick as the brains of their operation. Carson said that when defensive players took the field, they were so thoroughly tested and prepared by Belichick, they just had to react to what they saw. "We didn't have to think about anything," the linebacker said. "When you think about stuff, that's when you're dead." Belichick did the thinking for them, and made them faster to the ball.

Belichick used punters and kickers in practice to run the upcoming opponent's plays against the defense. He'd show them a card that detailed where they should line up and what routes to run, and if one of the punters or kickers made a misstep, he pounced on the offending Giant and demanded that his defense get a better look. On the flip side, if an offensive or defensive starter was taking a lazy-minded approach to punt, field goal, or extra-point reps in practice, Belichick went after that starter with the same fire and urgency.

In the end, no matter how anyone looked at it, the two Bills made a formidable pair. Their '86 team opened the playoffs with a 49–3 destruction of the 49ers, defined by Burt's vicious hit on Joe Montana, who threw a pick-six to Taylor on the play before heading to the hospital with a concussion. Belichick had advised Parcells to play more man-to-man coverage against Montana the night before the game. During the game, Belichick had rattled Montana with a scheme that called for Taylor and either Carson or emerging star Carl Banks to shoot through the center-guard gap to produce immediate and intense pressure on the star quarterback.

The following week, the Giants hosted the Redskins in an NFC Championship Game that was played in cold, howling winds. The irrepressible mayor of New York City, Ed Koch, was already on record saying he had no interest in hosting a ticker-tape parade for what he called a "foreign team." (The Giants had left the city for the New Jersey swamplands more than a decade earlier.) The Giants were more concerned about the blustery forecast than about the blustery mayor. They needn't have worried. In winds gusting up to 30 miles per hour, the Redskins would go 0 for 14 against the home team's defense on third down, and 0 for 4 on fourth, while managing a grand total of 40 rushing yards on 16 attempts in a 17–0 defeat.

A stunning scene unfolded after the Giants clinched their first trip to a Super Bowl, and their first appearance in a championship game since 1963. Wearing a red Giants jacket, a gray hoodie underneath, and a look of boyish glee stretched across his face, Belichick left the field on the shoulders of Greg Lasker, a safety, and Pepper Johnson, a linebacker. Little Bill had his left hand planted on Lasker's head and his right hand planted on Johnson's right shoulder pad. The assistant who had been ignored, mocked, and disrespected by his players was now being carried off the field under waves of swirling paper and garbage — the ticker tape Koch promised they'd never see.

The picture ended up on the front page of the *New York Times*. Yes, Little Bill Belichick had hit the big time. His family and friends all saw the picture, and he figured he must've collected 100 copies of that *Times* front page. He was 34 years old, and he was two weeks away from stepping onto the Rose Bowl field in Pasadena, California, to face the Denver Broncos for a chance to make the Giants champions for the first time in 30 years. And as fate would have it, that game would be decided, in large part, by a Navy man shaped by a college coaching lifer named Steve Belichick.

· · ·

Before facing the Broncos in Super Bowl XXI in Pasadena, Bill Belichick had to come up with two plans: (1) a plan to keep quarterback John Elway in the pocket and (2) a plan to keep Lawrence Taylor awake.

The Giants had barely beaten the Broncos at home in the regular season, and only because 6′4″, 245-pound George Martin shed a blocker, rose up to deflect an Elway pass with his right hand, caught his own rebound, broke an attempted Elway tackle in the open field, and rumbled his way home for a 78-yard touchdown. Parcells called it the best play he'd ever seen.

In the days preceding the big game, LT felt the same way the Vegas odds-makers did — that the Giants stood little chance of losing. They were riding an 11-game winning streak and were fiercely determined to make up for their shutout loss to the Bears in the '85 playoffs. Sean Landeta, who had all but whiffed on a punt against those Bears and gifted them a touchdown the day before his 24th birthday, symbolized the Giants' resurgence by rebounding with a Pro Bowl season. Mark Bavaro had also made the Pro Bowl, playing through a fractured jaw and carrying half the 49ers' defense on his back on a catch-and-run during a comeback victory at Candlestick Park. Simms had thrown five touchdown passes against no interceptions in the two playoff victories, and the Giants' linebacker corps had become even more dominant with the emergence of Carl Banks, their first-round pick in 1984.

So Taylor wasn't about to sit at attention when Belichick started going over some adjustments in the way the Giants would defend Elway. "Lawrence had his cap down over his eyes, sunglasses on," Martin said, "and Bill calls him and Lawrence doesn't respond. He calls him a second time and Lawrence doesn't respond. So Bill walks across the room right in front of LT, lifts his glasses up, and Lawrence is sound asleep. This is the week of the Super Bowl. That's Lawrence . . . Bill did coach him differently, but with that kind of talent, every coach did. You don't want to poke that bear unnecessarily. Bill was standing on a long line of individuals who gave that broad latitude to Lawrence."

Though the Giants had in Taylor the kind of defensive force the sport hadn't seen, their spirit in this game, and in this entire postseason, would be best embodied by a tiny, undrafted castoff, Phil McConkey, a receiver and return man who had learned a ton about football from Bill Belichick's father. The son of a Buffalo cop who worked two jobs on the side to pay the bills, McConkey was all of 5′10″ and 145 pounds when he showed up in Annapolis in the spring of 1975 and met Steve and Bill, who was on his way from Wesleyan to the Baltimore Colts. McConkey thought his own father was tough, but Steve Belichick positively terrified him.

"He was one gruff human being," McConkey said. "Steve was not a man to sugarcoat anything. He ran the off-season program on the basketball court, and all I remember is lining up garbage cans for guys to throw up in. We just ran and ran. Shuttle runs, basketball drills, gassers, calisthenics. Steve was the toughest coach I ever had, by far. He wasn't only preparing us for football, but to be combat officers in the U.S. Navy, to be responsible for your life and many more lives."

McConkey did five years in the Navy before leaving the service and taking a shot at the NFL that started with a 1984 workout with Steve Belichick at the academy in Annapolis. McConkey had learned from Steve how to properly stretch before running, how to properly catch a punt, how to watch film, how to do everything. He never wanted to let the old man down.

McConkey twice ran the 40-yard dash in 4.4 seconds on Navy's practice field while Steve Belichick timed him, and Steve called his son and recommended the Giants give this nontraditional 27-year-old prospect a serious look. McConkey made the team by diving for the ball in practice, bloodying himself in the process. On one such dive, in his first camp, McConkey wrestled the ball away from the Giant who was covering him, and did so right at Belichick's feet. "McConkey," Little Bill sighed, "you're a pain in my fucking ass." The long shot thought it was the best compliment he ever received.

The Giants released McConkey after the 1985 season, then reacquired him in a trade with Green Bay four games deep into '86. The return man had remarkable hands and balance; he could hold three balls under each arm and still catch a seventh. Big Bill and Little Bill insisted that he always catch punts in the air, not on the bounce, something that was forever preached by Steve Belichick, too. On days Steve showed up at Giants practices, Parcells often asked him to keep an eye on a certain player or a certain technique or drill. Landeta said that Steve was the first coach ever to tell him that the return team rarely benefited when the ball touched the ground. As it turned out, McConkey, one of Steve's guys, saved the Giants an untold amount of yardage by absorbing brutal hits on the dead run while following that line of thought.

McConkey caught a 28-yard touchdown pass from Simms in the divisional playoff rout of San Francisco, and he caught enough punts against Washington in the windblown NFC title game for Parcells to tell him he'd saved the Giants at least 100 yards in field position. Yet his Super Bowl performance was the one everyone would remember. It came on a sun-splashed day in Pasadena, where the Giants were thrilled to be 2,400 miles away from a bitter North Jersey winter. Simms knew he was going to have a big day in warm-ups when the ball came flying out of his hand. He ended up nearly pitching a Don Larsen game in this Super Bowl, completing 22 of 25 passes for three touchdowns and winning the MVP award in a 39–20 victory.

McConkey was the unlikely Giant who dramatically changed the game when it was still in doubt. The Broncos were trailing 16–10 in the middle of the third quarter when their left-footed punter, Mike Horan, let one rip. McConkey always thought the ball's flight path from a left-footed kicker was devilishly unpredictable, so he had Simms, a right-handed thrower who kicked with his left foot, punt to him in practice. On cue, McConkey caught Horan's punt and returned it 25 yards to set up a field goal that gave the Giants a two-score lead.

On their next possession, the Giants ran a flea-flicker and Simms found McConkey wide open behind a confused and flat-footed Denver secondary. The play covered 44 yards before McConkey got upended just before the goal line; Joe Morris carried the ball across on the next snap. The Giants held a 26–10 lead entering the fourth quarter, then turned it into a rout when a Simms pass into the end zone bounced off the hands and facemask of Bavaro and into the waiting grasp of McConkey, who scored the Super Bowl touchdown he so desperately wanted on that earlier 44-yard catch.

The Giants were Super Bowl champions at last. Fresh from his Gatorade bath, Parcells gathered his players in the locker room and shouted, "The rest of your life. The rest of your life, men. Nobody can ever tell ya that ya couldn't do it, because ya did it."

At some point in the celebration, Bill Belichick was hit by a sudden thought. He wondered if this would be the final time he'd have a moment like this in his NFL career. So he made his way back onto the Rose Bowl field for one last look at the scoreboard, one last look around the building. He took it all in — the sights and sounds of victory — and then got stopped near the locker room by security guards who didn't recognize him and who likely figured he was too young to be the defensive coordinator of the world champs.

Little Bill finally made it onto the winning bus. At 34, he'd reached the summit of professional football because of a loving father who had taught him the trade, and who had delivered him an undersize, overlooked player from Navy schooled in the Steve Belichick way.

Bill Belichick's grim disposition inspired some players to call him "the Voice of Doom," though Bill Parcells shortened it to "Doom." Big Bill said he liked to call Little Bill "Doom" because he was "always predicting negative things."

Funny. Not so funny was the fact that George Young, the Giants' GM, thought Doom's personality and human relations skills didn't match up with those required of a head coach. In a Giants Stadium conference room in the late 1980s, Young made it clear to everyone present that Little Bill would not assume control whenever Big Bill stepped down.

"I was there when he said it," Chris Mara recalled. "He said, 'He'll never become the Giants' head coach' . . . George, like others, said, 'This is an ex–lacrosse player. He's a disheveled-looking mess most of the time.' George was big on that other stuff as far as appearance, which is why he was so high on Ray Perkins, who took command of everyone around him and was a born leader. I just don't think he saw that in Bill Belichick."

Young had grown up in a tough Irish Catholic part of Baltimore, the Tenth Ward, and he had no use for the suburban Baltimore kids who flocked to lacrosse. A star high school and college (Bucknell) tackle in his day, Young thought lacrosse players weren't real athletes. "The only people who play lacrosse," he used to say, "are the people who could afford those sticks. The athletes couldn't afford those sticks."

Young told associates that what he wanted in a head coaching candidate was intelligence, a high energy level, and something to prove. Belichick checked off all three boxes. "But George believed he'd struggle with the media because he didn't have that engaging personality," one of those associates said. "That was part of the reason George wasn't that high on him as a head coach."

Belichick didn't have much experience in major press conference settings, as Parcells was such a large and all-consuming media presence. Yet nearly all the beat writers, columnists, and TV and radio reporters who covered the Giants actually thought Belichick was a valuable and available source of information and insight. Peter King, Bob Papa, Dave Klein, Vinny DiTrani, Bob Glauber, Hank Gola, Mike Eisen, Mark Cannizzaro, and Greg Garber — media members who would spend decades covering the Giants and the NFL for outlets in the New York area and nationwide — all thought Little Bill helped their understanding of the sport and the Giants' place in it.

In the 1980s, Giants coaches and players would chat informally with media members on a routine basis during their training camps at Pace University in Pleasantville, New York (through 1987), and Fairleigh Dickinson in Madison, New Jersey, and during the season at Giants Stadium. Parcells knew better than most how to work a media room; he'd tell writers to "put your pens down" when he wanted to fill them in on background. Belichick knew how to play the game, too. He'd often stop as he walked through the locker room to educate writers and broadcasters in need. Klein, of the *Star-Ledger*, said Belichick was the best football coach he'd ever dealt with, on or off the record.

"You could go up to Bill at any time to get any answer on anything," said Glauber, then of Gannett newspapers in Westchester County, New York. "I'd often go up to him and say, 'Bill, on this certain play in the game, what happened on this play? Why did it work?' He had a pencil behind his ear and he'd grab my notebook and start scribbling with a pencil and give me the formation. So he would be very, very helpful . . . We almost shared a bond in that we were kind of in the trenches and Parcells was the dictator. There was a little bit of camaraderie there because of that."

Gola, then of the *New York Post,* described Belichick as a great source who pointed a reporter in the right direction. Another New York–area writer agreed but said that Belichick "wasn't going to be a Deep Throat to sabotage Parcells." King, then of *Newsday,* recalled many pleasant locker-room conversations about the game with a Belichick who was "very loquacious and very open. He was not a curmudgeonly guy." DiTrani, of the *Record* of Bergen County, New Jersey, recalled Belichick being cold to him for a couple of weeks after he wrote a critical column about the 1981 squib kick against Washington, but, like Gola, he generally found Little Bill to be a helpful not-for-attribution compass on the stories of the day.

George Young either didn't know or didn't care about Belichick's strong relationship with the local media; the GM just didn't think he had the requisite makeup to serve as the public face of the franchise. Young didn't think that Little Bill had the leadership skills of the receivers coach, Tom Coughlin, or the same intellect as the running backs coach, Ray Handley.

Some executives in other corners of the league had different ideas. By the end of the 1990 regular season, two years after Belichick had interviewed for the Cleveland Browns job and a year after he'd interviewed for the Phoenix Cardinals job, Little Bill was drawing renewed interest from the Browns and the Tampa Bay Buccaneers. Even though his proud, self-made leaders, Harry Carson and George Martin, had retired two seasons earlier, and even though Lawrence Taylor had been suspended for repeated drug use that same year and was living just as recklessly off the field as he was known for playing on it, Belichick presided over the league's No. 1 defense.

The way he managed the high-maintenance Taylor had a fair amount to do with that, which was ironic. Back when Parcells promoted Belichick to defensive coordinator, Taylor had gone into Big Bill's office and told him, "I'm not listening to this motherfucker. Are you kidding?" LT would describe Little Bill as "a total pain in the ass" and as the "driest-humor son-of-a-bitch you've ever seen." Taylor would add that as much as you want to be sitting next to Belichick on Sunday afternoons, "you don't want to be near him" any other day of the week.

LT once jumped out of his seat in a meeting in response to a stinging

Belichick critique and bolted out of the room. According to linebacker Steve DeOssie, Taylor told Belichick, "Look, you little motherfucker. You never hit anybody when you were at Wesleyan or wherever the fuck you went to school. I'd be surprised if you ever saw the goddamn field. I'm sick of this." Belichick continued on with his meeting, and Taylor found a soft couch so he could take a nap.

But what struck DeOssie the most was the difference between how Belichick interacted with LT and other players and what he'd experienced in Dallas. As a five-year member of Tom Landry's Cowboys, DeOssie knew the coach-player dialogue as a one-way street. The coach told the players what to do, and the players did it. Landry, DeOssie said, "was like Moses coming down from the mount with the Ten Commandments."

Parcells, by contrast, had encouraged a free-flowing exchange of criticisms and profanities. "Some of the things Simms said to him on the sideline were fucking amazing," said tackle Karl Nelson. "Parcells said that anything said on the sideline during a game, good or bad, is over as soon as the game was over. He said things to assistants on the sideline that would make a sailor blush."

When Belichick followed Parcells's lead in defensive meetings, DeOssie initially was afraid to contribute to the discourse. He'd been taught in the Landry system to always submit to the coach's authority. "It wasn't just Lawrence going off on Belichick," he said, "but Belichick going off on Lawrence, too. It was never a one-sided verbal beatdown when it came to Giants coaches and players. It could get personal, but it was never really personal. Wives and children were off-limits, and everything else was up for grabs. It was like an airing of grievances in medieval times.

"But it wasn't only guys going off on each other and trading insults. Belichick was one of the first coaches I ever saw who actually sought input from his players instead of just saying *Do this, do that*. Bill saw the value in what his players were seeing on the field, and that was usable information for him."

In his own way, Taylor was always an astute provider of that information and a reliable asset, despite his chaotic personal life. He wrote in his autobiography that he started using cocaine and crack at least three times a week during the 1985 season, that his wife once had to kick open the door of a drug den to get him out, that he smuggled a teammate's clean urine into the bathroom — via an aspirin bottle tucked into his jock — to beat drug tests, and that he used golf courses as his personal detox centers. Though Parcells started clearing out what he considered some bad influences in the locker room two years before he won the Super Bowl (he said in his own autobiography that he knew of 20 to 30 Giants who used drugs between 1983 and 1986), Taylor was spared, for seemingly the most obvious reasons. "Parcells knew where his bread was buttered on that one," Karl Nelson said.

Parcells angrily denied that he had turned a blind eye toward Taylor's behavior. Either way, even in his diminished state, Taylor performed at a once-in-a-generation level and proved to be among the smartest, most instinctive players Belichick had ever seen. LT had a knack for identifying the critical plays in a game that demanded he find his superhuman gear. "Some guys," Belichick would say, "you look at those plays and you kind of say, 'C'mon, this is the biggest play of the game,' and that's not his best play. I don't think I ever said that about Taylor."

Belichick motivated Taylor by pumping up pass rushers on other teams, or by praising the one player — running back George Rogers — who was taken ahead of him in the draft. Fully established as one of the finest coordinators in the league, and a potential head coach, Little Bill wasn't afraid of conflict with anyone, Parcells included. He even teamed with Parcells once to dress down Giants linebackers coach Al Groh. According to Parcells's good friend and former high school basketball coach Mickey Corcoran, Belichick noticed in one practice, which Corcoran attended, that Groh was letting a player coast through a drill.

"Belichick said, 'Look at this goddamn asshole farting around,'" Corcoran recalled. "He got all over the guy. It was Al Groh, a good coach. He pissed off both Belichick and Parcells, and Belichick noticed he wasn't coaching a guy the right way and he told Parcells. They were both pissed. Parcells started screaming at Groh, too."

Little Bill started flexing some Big Bill muscle. In 1989, after Landeta met Jon Bon Jovi at the China Club, in New York, the punter invited the diehard Giants fan to practice, and drive to Giants practice in his Ferrari the rocker did. Bon Jovi became close friends with Belichick, who one day saw four men he didn't recognize — including two invited interns from the New Jersey Nets — standing near Bon Jovi at practice.

"Suddenly Belichick comes over and looks at the other guys and says, 'Who the fuck are you?'" recalled one of the Nets interns, Brian Walker. "They didn't have much of an answer, and Belichick told them, 'Get the fuck out of here.' Then he turns to us and asks the same question. We showed him our credentials and he allowed us to stay."

Whether or not George Young saw it, Belichick was starting to take on the personality of a head coach. But before he became one, Little Bill would vie for a title against the first NFL head coach to give him a job.

• • •

The Giants had just beaten the two-time defending champion 49ers for the 1990 NFC championship without scoring a single touchdown. They had eliminated the dynastic duo, Joe Montana and Jerry Rice, with Matt Bahr kicking his fifth field goal on the final play, a week after he'd suffered a severe concussion on a tackle against the Chicago Bears.

They had just booked a trip to the Super Bowl with a backup quarterback, Jeff Hostetler, who had taken over after Phil Simms broke his foot in the 14th game of the season, against the team the Giants were now about to face, the Buffalo Bills. And they didn't want to leave their Candlestick Park locker room.

"We didn't want it to end," Steve DeOssie said. "There was more hugging and intensity in that locker room than anything I've ever seen."

DeOssie had snapped the ball on the winning kick, and had shouted at his delirious teammates to avoid hitting Bahr in the head in the celebration. After the ball passed by the left upright, and after Belichick and Parcells jumped into each other's arms, former Giants kicker Pat Summerall told his CBS audience, "There will be no three-peat." The Giants boarded their buses and headed to the airport for a trip to Tampa, site of the Super Bowl.

Nearly everyone described it as the most joyful flight of their lives. Players danced to blaring music in the aisle of the plane, players and coaches were drinking, and Parcells — his shirt unbuttoned at the top and his tie knot hanging loose — looked into a camera and said, "Happy New Year's, guys. We're going to the show."

Belichick had played a 3-4 defense with split-safety coverage against the 49ers a week after switching to a four-man front against the Bears, and suddenly he needed to come up with something entirely different for a Buffalo Bills offense that looked unstoppable. After the Giants' plane landed in the predawn hours in Tampa, Belichick immediately went to work on his most unconventional plan yet. Just as they had been against San Francisco, the Giants were big underdogs against Buffalo. The Bills had led the league in scoring during the regular season, with 428 points, and they'd scored 95 in their first two postseason games, destroying the Los Angeles Raiders in the AFC title game, 51–3. They had future Hall of Famers at quarterback (Jim Kelly), running back (Thurman Thomas), and receiver (Andre Reed and James Lofton). They also had at the controls of their no-huddling K-Gun offense the man who'd decided in 1975 that a 23-year-old Wesleyan grad was worthy of a job with the Baltimore Colts: Ted Marchibroda.

"I am really happy for Billy," said Buffalo's offensive coordinator. "I just wish I didn't have to coach against him from the other side."

Belichick said that he thought often of Marchibroda in the days before the Super Bowl, and that he knew Marchibroda thought often about him. Little Bill had learned so much about the league from the coach, and he'd also learned a ton about the coach himself. He remembered that his first boss had Bert Jones call his own plays in Baltimore, and figured he'd have Kelly do the same in Tampa. According to author David Halberstam, Belichick didn't believe Kelly was among the league's best quarterbacks at reading defenses and seeing through disguises used to make one look like another. And since Belichick was already one of the sport's preeminent tweakers and adjusters, a coordinator who changed his alignments almost on a weekly basis, this appeared to be a critical mismatch in the Giants' favor.

The Giants led the league in fewest points allowed. (Belichick always judged a defense on points allowed, turnovers forced, and yards allowed, in that order.) Little Bill's unit had held the Bills to 65 rushing yards on 24 carries and a reasonable 212 yards in the air in Buffalo's 17–13 victory at Giants Stadium in December (though Kelly had left that game in the second quarter with a knee injury).

Belichick knew the Giants could contain the Bills and make this fast-breaking team play the Giants' half-court game, if he could persuade his proud men to embrace what would seem on the surface to be an emasculating scheme. Belichick told his unit that if it allowed Thomas to gain 100 yards or more rushing, the Giants would end up as Super Bowl champs. Pepper Johnson heard his coordinator say it this way: "I will quit this business if Thurman Thomas runs for over 100 yards and we lose."

Belichick was delivering this edict to the same defense that had surrendered 100-yard games to only two running backs in the past two years. "Guys like LT, Carl Banks, Leonard Marshall — that pissed them off," defensive back Everson Walls said. "They were like 'What? Hold up, Bill. We're not going to let these guys punk us.'"

Players all over the room were shaking their heads and shooting incredulous looks at one another. Belichick had to sell it, and sell it hard. "I think the running game was the least of our concerns in that game," he would say. "Thurman Thomas is a great back; we knew he was going to get some yards. But I didn't feel like we wanted to get into a game where they threw the ball 45 times."

So Belichick came up with a plan to primarily use two defensive linemen, Leonard Marshall and Erik Howard, and sometimes a third, and drop as many as eight Giants into coverage. He was inviting the Bills to run the ball, and to bleed the clock in doing so. Belichick knew that Marchibroda and Buffalo's head coach, Marv Levy, preferred to throw underneath the

Giants' coverage. "Pepper and Carl and Lawrence and those guys—that's what they live for," Belichick said. "Go ahead, you can catch it for four or five yards, but you're going to pay the price. And that's the way we wanted to play."

Punish the receivers. Force the run. Keep Kelly and the offense off the field. Make the Bills more uncomfortable than they'd been all year. Over time, the defense came to accept Belichick's vision as the proper method of attack.

Some veteran Giants knew this was a much-easier-said-than-done proposition. Mark Bavaro said he'd watched Buffalo beat L.A. by 48 points in the AFC title game with an offense that made the Giants' look Jurassic in comparison. "I remember in the Candlestick locker room saying to myself, *Do we really want to win this game and go get embarrassed in the Super Bowl?*" Bavaro said. "As good as San Francisco was, Buffalo was something we hadn't seen before, scoring that many points . . . But that was always tempered by the fact that Belichick was on our side. That gave us a lot of confidence that he'd find a way."

The Giants barely worked on offense all week, even though they were facing Bruce Smith, who had 19 sacks on the year and had replaced LT as the most feared defender in the game. Parcells had asked Taylor to start a practice fight with Giants tackle Jumbo Elliott to get him fired up for Smith, but other than that, the entire focus was on getting the defense ready for the pace of Buffalo's no-huddle attack.

"We told our offensive players all week long they needed to hold the ball and get first downs," said Fred Hoaglin, the offensive line coach. "Didn't tell them to score. Just hold the ball and keep it from them. We had two huddles on offense in practice, and the coaches would go in one huddle and that team would run a play, and then we'd walk over to the other huddle and call another play. And we'd do it in rapid fashion for ten minutes, fifteen plays, stop and take a break and do it again and again. That's all we did in practice. We had no offensive practice overall, and that concerned me. But we knew we needed the defense to practice at that kind of pace."

Belichick had his group in Olympic shape, and he was so laser-focused on the monumental challenge at hand that in a Wednesday meeting with the media, when he was asked for a third or fourth time about his reported candidacy for the Cleveland Browns job, he snapped. He used profanity to hammer home the point that he was thinking only about the Buffalo Bills. "No more questions about head coaching jobs in this league," he said. "Period."

When the Giants made their Super Bowl Sunday arrival, they found a Tampa Stadium that had been converted into something resembling a military state because of the ongoing war in the Persian Gulf. The security presence was massive. Armed soldiers were everywhere, and Tom Coughlin remembered staring at a helicopter gunship hovering above the press box. Tens of thousands of fans waved small American flags in the stands. Whitney Houston sang a rendition of the national anthem that left many of the hulking men around her shaking or in tears, feeling goose bumps on top of their goose bumps, before four F-16 fighter jets roared across the sky.

The Bills won the coin toss, and, despite Belichick's wishes and plans, they threw the ball on the first three snaps. The good news? They didn't get the ten yards required for a first down and were forced to punt. On the Giants' sideline, Elliott turned to Hoaglin and joked about Buffalo's hurry-up offense. "Fred," he said, "what was that? The hurry-up-and-get-off-the-field offense?"

The Giants took the ball, worked the clock with their run game, and kicked a field goal on their 12th play. The tone had been set. The Giants possessed the ball for a remarkable 40 minutes and 33 seconds of the 60-minute game, 34-year-old Ottis Anderson ran like he was ten years younger, and Jeff Hostetler, second-string quarterback, managed the game like a first-string conductor. Hostetler had waited nearly seven seasons to get a chance to play, and he'd told his wife, days before Simms went down, that he was frustrated enough to retire. He'd come a long way since 1984, when, in a 7-on-7 drill in his first year, he accidentally bounced a pass off the back of Belichick's head. "His stuff went flying," Hostetler said, "and as a rookie I'm thinking, 'I'm done now.' But afterward, all the defensive guys were giving me high fives because a lot of guys said they'd wanted to do the same thing. He was so mad at me. I can't repeat what he said."

By the night of January 27, 1991, Belichick had long since forgiven Hostetler, who gave the defense a chance in Super Bowl XXV to make Little Bill's scheme a winning one. Thurman Thomas indeed cleared 100 yards (135 on 15 carries, including a 31-yard touchdown on the first play of the fourth quarter), and the Giants' 2-3-6 and 2-4 and 3-3 nickel packages indeed held the Bills' passing game to reasonable gains. The linebackers and secondary had also pounded Buffalo's receivers; Banks, who had recovered from wrist surgery, was among the difference makers. Andre Reed conceded that he'd never been hit so hard in his life. "They bruised up my whole body," he said.

Belichick used Walls, a career cornerback with Dallas, at safety and asked him to do something he'd never done: act as the play caller in the secondary. It was a fascinating move. Belichick always thought Walls was a wildly unorthodox man-to-man cover guy, the most unique defensive back he'd coached, but Belichick told Walls he wouldn't change his footwork or technique because they had worked so well for him in Dallas. And yet here was Belichick suddenly asking the ten-year veteran to embrace a brand-new responsibility. If the pace got too hectic for him, Walls would look to the defensive coordinator, his outlet, for help.

"I'd never played safety until Bill Belichick, the mad professor, saw me as a guy who could do it," Walls said. Inside the final two minutes, with the Giants holding a 20–19 lead, Walls made the open-field tackle on Thomas that likely prevented an 81-yard touchdown run and ultimately forced Buffalo to send out Scott Norwood to try a 47-yard field goal with eight seconds left.

The kicker who landed the Giants in this game, Matt Bahr, approached Parcells on the sideline. "Bill," he said, "[Norwood] hasn't made one from 47 yards on grass all year. He's going to overkick it."

As Norwood lined up near the right hash mark, some players on both sides of the field held hands. Some knelt, and some stood. Some looked, and some turned away. In the crowd, Norwood's wife, Kim, had tears in her eyes as she held the hand of Janine Talley, wife of Buffalo linebacker Darryl. Ann Mara, wife of Giants owner Wellington, held her rosary beads and prayed for Norwood to miss while Bills officials stared at her from an adjacent box.

Her prayers were answered. Norwood launched his kick wide right into infamy, and the Giants players and coaches erupted as Norwood staggered off the field. With four seconds still on the clock, DeOssie grabbed a video camera to shoot the sights and sounds of victory. Soon enough, he was thanking Belichick for the opportunity to be part of the special night he'd just scripted with a game plan that would end up in the Pro Football Hall of Fame.

"In the two years I played for Bill Belichick," said DeOssie, the former Tom Landry player, "I learned more football than in my previous 15 years playing football combined."

Belichick found Bon Jovi taking photos of the madness in the locker room. Bill and the other assistants would join Parcells and the team at the hotel that night for a party highlighted by the hilarious scene of Coughlin muttering the words "world fucking champs" over and over. (Parcells had those words stitched onto Coughlin's souvenir Super Bowl blanket.) Big Bill won his second championship with an all-time staff that included five future NFL head coaches (Belichick, Coughlin, Romeo Crennel, Groh, and Ray Handley), a former NFL head coach (offensive coordinator Ron Erhardt), and a future head coach at Notre Dame (assistant special teams coach Charlie Weis).

Coughlin was on his way to Boston College, and the 49-year-old Parcells was on his way to a temporary retirement that would be announced in a stunning news conference in May. In between, Belichick had no choice but to walk away from a franchise he never wanted to leave.

Upon his arrival in New Jersey in 1979, Wellington Mara had co-signed a loan for Belichick so he could buy a house. Bill had spent years taking a knee near the Giants' bench, imploring his players to do more while taking his marker and drawing up his plan on a grease board. Little Bill wanted nothing more than to keep showing up at Giants Stadium on Saturday mornings to ride the bike and study three or four tapes of the next team on the schedule.

Yet even after Belichick toppled his first NFL mentor, Marchibroda, in the Super Bowl, George Young still wanted no part of him as a head coach. The GM wanted one of the other assistants to replace Parcells whenever Big Bill decided to leave, and with Coughlin booked for Boston College, it was Handley, a position coach not exactly in leaguewide demand, who was first in line.

Belichick's road to a head coaching job would have to run through Cleveland. Harry Carson wrote a letter of recommendation on Little Bill's behalf to Browns owner Art Modell. Parcells told Modell that Belichick was "going places in this business." Big Bill had spent some time preparing his best assistant for this moment, grooming Little Bill to run his own team. He solicited Belichick's opinion on many global Giants decisions and educated him on contracts and player discipline. "Bill, here's the situation I'm in right now," Parcells told Belichick. "Someday you'll be in this position."

But the subject of what Little Bill did in Super Bowl XXV was a bit of a sore spot with his boss. Of that game plan, Parcells would say years later, "I don't know whose idea that was to put it in the Hall of Fame. If anything should be in the Hall of Fame, it should be Ron Erhardt's game plan. We had the ball for 40 minutes and some seconds. That takes work, consistent play. We were only on defense for 19 minutes. To me, we had a good plan against them. It was well thought out, a couple of things we did, the two-man lines in that game. But I'm not diminishing anything. I'm just telling you. I don't know how that happened. I'm not knocking anyone here."

The truth is, Belichick agreed that his strategy had been successful because the Giants' offense stayed on the field forever. "We didn't have to play that much defense," he said. "That really helped."

The Cleveland Browns cared about none of that. The Browns cared about none of George Young's concerns, either. They needed a head coach to wake up the echoes, and they decided to hire the man a former Notre Damer, Mark Bavaro, described as "the biggest football geek or nerd that's ever stepped foot in the NFL."

Some 45 miles from where his father had landed his only head coaching job, at Hiram College, Bill Belichick would run his own team for the first time. Steve Belichick used to bring his young son to Cleveland Browns camp at Hiram so he could watch Jim Brown, Lou Groza, and Gary Collins. They were true Cleveland greats, young Bill thought, and all these years later he suddenly had a chance to join them.

7

CLEVELAND

In January 1989, Ernie Accorsi met Bill Belichick for lunch at the Marriott in Mobile, Alabama, site of the Senior Bowl. The general manager of the Cleveland Browns needed a head coach, yet at the start of the interview he did not consider the 36-year-old defensive coordinator of the New York Giants a serious candidate for the job.

Some five and a half hours later, Accorsi left that meeting shaking his head. He recalled, as a college kid, watching a young Jack Kennedy in his first presidential debate and thinking Kennedy had been preparing himself for the White House since he was ten years old. Accorsi had a similar feeling about Belichick. He'd never met someone who had so clearly started preparing to be an NFL head coach when he was such a young boy.

Marty Schottenheimer had just lost another heartbreaking playoff game, this one to the Houston Oilers, before rejecting owner Art Modell's mandate that he hire an offensive coordinator and getting himself run out of town. Accorsi had now lived through two epic AFC Championship Game losses to the Denver Broncos, forever known as the Drive and the Fumble, both of which propelled to the Super Bowl the very quarterback Accorsi had drafted for the Baltimore Colts in 1983: John Elway. The Stanford star had bluffed that he would quit football and play for the New York Yankees if the dreadful Colts kept him, and Colts owner Bob Irsay blinked by dealing him to Denver against Accorsi's wishes.

The GM hadn't recovered from the fact that the quarterback he'd drafted No. 1 overall was the one who denied him two trips to the Super Bowl. Accorsi ignored the warning signs that the aging Browns needed to be rebuilt, and he decided he needed a veteran coach to take one last shot at stealing a title.

But the young Belichick floored him. They met at noon and blew right through the Senior Bowl practice they were both expecting to attend that afternoon. Belichick locked his eyes on Accorsi's the whole time and spelled out his vision for giving Cleveland its first NFL championship since 1964.

Decades later, Accorsi would call it the most impressive job interview he'd ever conducted.

"You were ten strokes behind," the GM told Belichick near the end of the meeting. "But you just shot a 64 and made it close."

Accorsi would've hired him if he'd been able to persuade Modell to approve it. He would've hired Belichick if he'd been ready to start over with the Browns. Only the GM thought he could squeeze one more run through that rapidly closing window of opportunity. Bud Carson, 58-year-old defensive coordinator of the New York Jets and former architect of the Steel Curtain defense in Pittsburgh, seemed like a strong win-now choice, and Chuck Noll swore by him.

Carson got the nod, in part because Accorsi worked with him in Baltimore and thought he was a football version of Earl Weaver — crusty, cantankerous, and brilliant. In his first season, 1989, Carson actually led the Browns into contention but lost the AFC title game to — who else? — Elway's Broncos. In year two, Carson disintegrated and was fired after a 42–0 home loss to Buffalo that Modell called "an embarrassment to all of us." The second time around, Accorsi wasn't going to swing and miss on Belichick. Modell liked Mike White, the quarterbacks coach of the Los Angeles Raiders, and Accorsi brought in former Browns assistant Bill Cowher, who had gone with Schottenheimer to Kansas City. Cowher aced his interview, but Accorsi still favored Belichick, and Modell wasn't about to hire a Schottenheimer guy anyway.

As the Giants were making their push toward their Super Bowl matchup with Buffalo, Accorsi got word to Belichick that he was his first choice. Mike Lombardi, his pro personnel director, also had numerous conversations with Belichick, Accorsi said, though the GM hadn't asked him to engage the candidate. John Madden's on-air praise of the Giants' defensive coordinator also got Modell's attention.

Modell and his wife, Pat, ultimately met with Belichick and his wife, Debby, for dinner at the owner's home. Modell's son David, a team executive, and his wife, Olwen, were also present. The next day, David Modell raved to co-workers about Belichick's binderful of ideas for the Browns, and told people his mother loved the candidate. "He's got a plan," David quoted his mother as saying, "not like the other guys in the past."

Art Modell was sold. He listened to the recommendations he got from Accorsi, Harry Carson, and Bob Knight, the three-time national championship basketball coach at Indiana, who had met Belichick through his former colleague at West Point, Bill Parcells. Modell and Belichick came to terms on a five-year contract between midnight and 1 a.m. on February

5, 1991, that made the 38-year-old the league's youngest head coach by six years. When Belichick and his new boss met with the news media later that day, Modell made it clear that Knight's phone call had influenced his decision.

"He spoke very highly of Bill's integrity," Modell said, "his sense of honor and discipline . . . I thought it was extraordinary coming from Bobby Knight, a man I've respected from afar."

Belichick arrived at his Browns presser in a dark suit, white shirt, and red tie. Behind him walked Debby, cutting a handsome figure in a conservative pink dress. They sat at a conference table cluttered with an unwieldy knot of microphones and tape recorders. Belichick sat in the middle, to the right of his wife and to the left of his boss. Accorsi, a former sportswriter and team publicist, had given the new coach a scouting report on the area media. The GM told Belichick that two major newspapers covered the team, the *Plain Dealer* and the *Akron Beacon Journal,* and that he thought the *Beacon Journal*'s coverage was especially negative.

"I knew what Bill's personality was like," Accorsi would say, "but I didn't care. Even though I had a PR background, I didn't care. I wanted to win, and that's all that mattered to me. My impression of him was absolutely nononsense and all business. [The media] wasn't even a factor. Coming off of Bud, who was insecure and thinking people were against him, this guy came off as cocksure and he didn't give a shit."

For his first press conference as a head coach, Belichick had written key words to talking points on his left palm. Modell introduced the tenth coach in Browns history, and the youngest since the legendary Paul Brown was hired at 37.

"I know there will be some questions about my age and experience relative to this job and this type of responsibility," Belichick said. "You know, when I came into professional football, I was 23 years old with the Baltimore Colts, and I heard those same questions then, and the next year with the Lions and then the Broncos, and so forth . . . I feel like all those questions have been met. I'll stand by my record.

"I feel like I've been in coaching for 30 years, through my father and the people I've met with him."

Modell explained that he had given Belichick a five-year deal — two years more than he preferred to give coaches — because he wanted stability at a time when the Browns were in some disarray. He also maintained that Belichick would have 24/7 access to him, that he would be more involved in running football operations than past coaches, and that he would have "total consultation and input" into Accorsi's supervision of the draft — all things that had to be a bit unsettling to Accorsi, who was losing influence with Modell after sticking him with Carson.

"It's a gamble," Modell conceded of his Belichick hire. "For every success story, I'll point out ten failures. Maybe I've struck gold on this one."

Bill and Debby Belichick were starting this adventure with their two children, six-year-old Amanda and three-year-old Stephen. "We're ready for a change," Debby said. "This has been Bill's ambition for some time." Debby said Bill no longer brought home game films to review, and she described her husband as having tunnel vision when it came to his professional and personal lives. "When it's football season and when he's coaching," she said, "that's what he does. It's like a file cabinet. Pulls out the drawer, pulls out 'football,' he sticks it back in. And he comes home and he pulls out 'family.' Very organized person."

And this seemed like a very organized process. The Browns needed a head coach who could lead them to their first Super Bowl appearance, and they'd just hired a coordinator who helped the Giants win two Super Bowls and who had contained a Buffalo offense that was advertised as unstoppable.

The fan base certainly bought in. Ticket sales picked up heavy steam in the immediate wake of Belichick's hiring, and Modell said a dinner crowd of 500 stood and cheered at the mention of his name three nights after the coach's press conference. Modell had given his man exactly what he wanted — power and security — and on the surface it looked like a perfectly sustainable NFL marriage.

In reality, the owner and the coach were wildly different human beings. At heart, Art Modell was a self-made showman. He was a Brooklyn-born son of an electronics retailer who went bankrupt in the Great Depression and died when Art was a teenager. He dropped out of high school, worked as an electrician's helper in a New York shipyard for 57 cents an hour, and served in the Army Air Corps during World War II. Modell became a successful TV and advertising executive who bought the Browns in 1961. Two seasons later, in a reported clash of personalities, Modell fired the franchise namesake, Brown, and his seven championships (four in the old All-America Football Conference) in the middle of a bitter Cleveland newspaper strike that tempered fan backlash. Modell was a driving force behind the TV network deals that ultimately turned the league into a multi-billion-dollar juggernaut, including the birth of *Monday Night Football,* and he booked preseason doubleheaders in his stadium that helped turn the exhibition season into a moneymaker.

Some people thought he was funny enough to be a stand-up comic.

Modell was a media charmer who liked a little panache, a little style to go with his substance. If there was anyone on the planet who embodied the opposite approach, it was the man Modell had just hired.

On Bill Belichick's first day of work, there were small signs of potential trouble to come. In a nod to Belichick's youth and defensive expertise, Modell compared Bill to Don Shula, who went from defensive coordinator of the Detroit Lions to head coach of the Baltimore Colts at age 33. "I hope the analogy holds up in years to come," Modell said, "because Shula, next to Lombardi — maybe including Lombardi — is probably the greatest of all time."

Belichick's response: "To be compared to Don Shula is really a joke. The guy is a Hall of Fame coach, and I've never coached one game in this league. I hope he's not insulted."

Modell also stated that the Browns, holders of the second overall pick in the NFL draft, were interested in possibly selecting Notre Dame's Raghib "Rocket" Ismail. Though nearly every team coveted the explosive playmaker, Belichick would never publicly reveal the identity of a prospect he might be considering.

The day after his announcement, Belichick showed up for work at 6 a.m., earlier than the Cleveland staff was accustomed to arriving. He interviewed some of the holdover assistant coaches and met one-on-one with beat writers covering the club, in an attempt to start building some mutual trust. At the time, there were no strong signals that the existing policies of full access to players, coaches, and staff would be coming to an end.

"It was like his opening pitch," said Tony Grossi, of the *Plain Dealer*. "He extended his hand and he was very nice. We were like, 'Oh, all right, this is great.'"

In the eighties, Sam Rutigliano was a quotable and gregarious media favorite. His successor, Schottenheimer, always made time for reporters, and his successor, Carson, was a grandfatherly presence and a big believer in the freedom of the press; he was honest to a fault. Belichick would turn out to be something completely different, and the Cleveland media would either learn to live with it or not.

Belichick had more important matters to tend to. He boarded a flight for Indianapolis and the NFL Scouting Combine to look for some players who could win the Browns a championship, and to see if an old friend from the college ranks would be willing to run his defense. His name was Nick Saban.

Bill Belichick stood before the 1991 Cleveland Browns in an auditorium at Lakeland Community College, 25 miles outside of Cleveland. Belichick was holding his first training-camp meeting as a head coach, and he spoke for about three minutes, no longer. Brian Brennan, an eight-year veteran with the Browns, remembered the speech vividly a quarter century later, if only because the new coach was so clearly in control.

This is what Brennan remembered Belichick telling his team, in part:

> I've been a ball boy in the league. I've been a special teams coach in the league. I've coached defensive halfbacks. I'm currently coming to the Browns as the defensive coordinator of the world champion football Giants, and I'm now the head coach. And I'm going to tell everybody in this room right now that there's no question we're going to win, and you're either going to be a part of this team or you're not. And if you've played more than five years in this league, I respect you. If you haven't played five years yet, in my eyes you still have a lot to prove. All right, break. Offense, stay here; defense, go there.

It was going to be a long, hot summer at Lakeland Community College, and Belichick had set up his camp specifically to see who would melt and who would not. The Browns were going to practice twice a day, and they were going to constantly engage in full-contact drills. This was not going to be Bud Carson's camp.

Carson smoked in meetings, and his players sometimes smoked in the locker room. At halftime of the 1990 season opener against Pittsburgh, rookie defensive end Rob Burnett looked on in amazement as four prominent Browns each held smoldering cigarettes in one taped-up hand and markers in the other to draw on a board. "I'm like *Where am I? A law firm or office building, or am I at halftime of a Steelers game?*" Burnett said. "These guys are smoking cigarettes and drinking coffee. That was my introduction to the NFL."

Burnett said Carson was late for more practices "than I've ever seen in my entire time playing football." Belichick wanted dramatic change in Cleveland, and he hired a tough-guy coordinator to help him with the transition. A former defensive back at Kent State, Nick Saban had been an assistant at Ohio State when he first got to know Belichick. Saban later worked at Navy with Steve Belichick, whom he and fellow Navy assistants called "the Emperor." In his first go-around as a head coach, at Toledo, Saban went 9-2 in 1990, before resigning to go to work for Steve Belichick's son. He was a 5'6" ball of fire. The day he resigned at Toledo to take the Cleveland job, Saban said, he cried for the first time since his father died, 18 years earlier.

On the other side of the ball, Belichick inherited an excellent receivers coach, Richard Mann, who had a deeper understanding of offense — especially on protections and the adjustments needed on blitzes — than any receivers coach Bill had encountered. Belichick also brought back into the league his old friend Ernie Adams, who had spent the previous five football seasons making a Wall Street killing as a municipal bond trader. Adams had been the Giants' director of pro personnel before leaving the NFL, and it was often said that he'd left because he was bored and needed a fresh challenge. But neither Giants GM George Young nor coach Bill Parcells was as enamored with Adams's ability to memorize a playbook in a day or two as others seemed to be, and Young wanted Adams gone so he could hire Tim Rooney, former personnel man for the Steelers and the Lions, a move Young later called one of the smartest he ever made.

Accorsi knew Adams from their college scouting days: They had frozen their asses off together on the roof of the University of Maryland press box while scouting Clemson quarterback Steve Fuller. Adams had already established himself as a man of mystery, a coach and personnel guy who preferred to blend into the background. Three or four days after the Browns hired Belichick, Young called Accorsi and the two executives had this exchange:

YOUNG: Tell me, has there been an Ernie Adams sighting yet?
ACCORSI: As a matter of fact, he just appeared.
YOUNG: How did he?
ACCORSI: I think he just came through a floorboard. He just appeared.

Over time, Accorsi came to see Adams as a legitimate genius in a sport where that term was thrown around as casually as a wet towel in a locker room. "I can tell you this," Accorsi said. "Every time I talked to Bill, I turned around and Ernie was right there."

Belichick was going to need all of Adams's brainpower and all of Saban's rage to rebuild a declining cast of entitled veterans from teams that had lost three conference title games to Denver in four years. He was also going to need Bernie Kosar, the beloved quarterback and local boy from Boardman, Ohio, to recover from the ten-touchdown, fifteen-interception season he'd had in 1990.

Things would've been easier for Belichick back in New Jersey, where he could've been the head coach of the defending world champs. Parcells had abruptly walked out on the Giants in May, partly because of health concerns and partly because he simply felt it was time to move on. Young, as expected, replaced him with Ray Handley, a math wizard who said he'd been banned from a casino in his hometown of Reno, Nevada, for counting cards at the blackjack table, and who twice nearly left the Giants for law school.

Nobody saw Young's choice as being any more charismatic than Belichick. Asked to react to the Handley appointment, Belichick congratulated his former staffmate and said it had been "a pleasure" to work for Parcells. He called his former boss "instrumental in my development and philosophy as a coach. I can only hope to be as successful as Bill in my new role with the Cleveland Browns."

Toward that end, Belichick had started trying to get his soft and ill-conditioned Browns into Giants shape, Belichick shape, in the weeks after he took office. "Dear goodness gracious," said the kicker Matt Stover. "All you have to do is ask people about that off-season conditioning program . . . Everyone was going, 'Wow.'"

The rookie head coach carried the punishing workouts into the summertime heat of training camp. "Just a straight bloodbath camp," Rob Burnett said. The defensive end recalled week after week of two-a-days, long practices in full pads, starting in the morning with what he called "the coffee-and-doughnut drill."

The coffee-and-doughnut drill, Burnett explained, involved a linebacker and a defensive lineman on one side and an offensive lineman, a fullback, and a ballcarrier on the other. "You have a ten-foot space with cones, and you can't go outside the cones," he said. "Basically, it was nothing but collisions, head-on collisions. We did it right after stretching, that first drill. We called it the coffee-and-doughnut drill because if you weren't awake, you were awake after that.

"That was college and high school stuff," Burnett continued. "We're professionals. We didn't need that drill."

Belichick thought otherwise. He thought the Browns needed to get tougher, sturdier. Joe Morris, the former Giant who was playing his final NFL season in '91, said the coach had very real concerns with the amount of practice time some Browns missed with injuries, and with the power wielded by the team doctor, John Bergfeld. "Bill said, 'Joe, I've got to take this team from the doctor,'" Morris recalled. "I said, 'You're right.'"

The players weren't the only ones having a rough go early in camp. The reporters who regularly covered the team — men and women who had grown accustomed to dealing with relatively friendly, agreeable faces behind the head coach's desk — were suddenly facing all kinds of restrictions. Belichick announced that the locker room would be closed to the news media throughout camp, that interviews would take place only in an auxiliary gym, and that interview requests needed to be made in writing. Reporters were barred from team flights to and from games and were told they weren't allowed to call players in hospital rooms. Belichick also announced that the team's medical staff would not be permitted to comment on injuries or a player's physical condition. Upon review of these new terms of engagement, *Plain Dealer* columnist Bill Livingston called the camp "Fort Belichick." *Akron Beacon Journal* beat writer Ed Meyer described it as "Stalag Belichick."

The Browns and Giants took part in joint practices at the Browns' camp, and some of the New York–area writers who enjoyed a regular on- and off-the-record dialogue with Belichick in his days under Parcells were stunned at how secretive and uncooperative he'd become in a matter of months. "Coming away," said one writer, "all of us were saying, 'Holy shit, this guy has changed.'"

Modell wasn't happy with Belichick's approach to media relations, yet the owner wasn't about to pick an unnecessary fight with the man he predicted would "return us to the old days of glory." Beat writers and columnists were on their own. The *Plain Dealer*'s Tony Grossi landed a heavy blow on Belichick over his policies and his threat to bar reporters from practice if they dared to report anything they saw on the field.

Grossi pointed out in his column that Belichick was far more pleasant and expansive when answering questions on his four radio and TV shows, which paid him more than $200,000 a year. Belichick had a weekly half-hour radio show on WKNR-AM, a daily five-minute show on the Browns' flagship radio station, WHK-AM, a weekly spot on WJW Channel 8, and a weekly half-hour show on WOIO Channel 19. After the coach refused to answer a benign question and a benign follow-up about sitting significant players in a preseason game against Minnesota, and then answered a similar question three nights later on one of his shows, Grossi wrote, "Are we to surmise from Belichick's act so far that he will only be civil for a price? Do reporters have to wave $20 bills at him for post-game comments?"

The columnist reported that in their earlier days together with the Giants, Young had sent Belichick to a class to improve his people skills. It was becoming clear to the Cleveland media that the new Browns coach didn't exactly ace the class.

Belichick spent the summer wearing a godforsaken rubber sweat jacket that resembled a trash bag. He cut the sleeves off his jackets and windbreakers, and he wore cutoff sweatpants, too. He was lifting weights, jogging, working the stair machine (at the highest possible resistance), riding the stationary bike, and sweating every bit as much as his players, yet somehow poring over notes and tapes during his workouts.

His staff was expected to maintain a brutal schedule, too, a pace that would've left many of the players doubled over trash cans and losing their lunch. Those demands were the same at the bottom of the organizational flow chart as at the top. At the bottom, a 26-year-old coach with college and World League experience named Phil Savage was hired as a quality control assistant to help on one side of the ball. He'd accepted a $20,000 salary until the day Belichick walked up to his desk, introduced himself (Savage wasn't interviewed by the head coach when he landed the job), and told him he would instead be handling offense *and* defense and doing the work of two quality control coaches instead of one. Belichick didn't offer to double Savage's wage. He gave him a $5,000 raise for the additional workload, then walked him down the hall to meet Saban.

"Seven months later," Savage said, "I was ready to give him a refund."

A couple of weeks into the preseason, Belichick called Savage into his office and told him his film breakdowns weren't meeting the team's needs. Belichick threw on a tape and started analyzing the splits of the offensive linemen and receivers, the linemen's stances, the quarterback's head movements, the depth of the running backs — every conceivable detail about the 22 men on the field. Belichick spent 20 minutes on one play, and a stunned Savage did the math in his head. Three plays an hour, 60 plays on offense, 60 plays on defense — that's 40 hours for one game! The young staffer thought he'd never again sleep or go to the bathroom.

"He said, 'We'll train you, and then we can train the next slapdick who comes in here,'" Savage recalled. "We hired Kevin Spencer in December. I was never more thankful to have someone else come on the scene to help. It was a long, long year.

"That was the hardest I ever worked," Savage continued. "Bill gets on the treadmill of football and he doesn't see seasons. It's just one day stacked on top of the other, whether it's training camp or the regular season or free agency or draft prep. He gets on the treadmill and he starts walking, and you say, *OK, can I keep up?* And he keeps going and going and going and going."

Young staffers were required to work up what Belichick called "the pads" — detailed diagrams of every movement from every player on every play. Browns staffers and assistants had the damnedest time keeping up with him. Even Saban, who could never sit still. Steve Belichick recalled working with him at Navy and thinking Saban was a brilliant football mind but also a nervous, nail-biting wreck. Steve joked that he watched Saban wear out ten miles of carpeting while pacing during a three-minute phone call.

Saban had worked for a man in Houston, Jerry Glanville, who didn't allow his assistants to fraternize with peers on other teams. To maintain his relationship with Bill Belichick, then with the Giants, Saban would quietly meet with him in different places to exchange ideas. "West Point seemed like a place that we could hide out," Saban said. "So we went there and stayed for weekends, stayed in a hotel up there, and talked ball."

They were kindred Croatian spirits born six months apart, Belichick with roots in the western Pennsylvania steel mills and factories, Saban in a West Virginia coal-mining town, Monongah, that in 1907 had been the scene of an explosion that killed 362, the worst mining disaster in American history. Football had changed the arc of their families' narratives and given them a chance to become rich and famous men.

They both believed in the 18-hour workday, which made them a perfect match in Cleveland. Years later, Saban described his four seasons under Belichick as the toughest of his career for a reason: The head coach, quite literally, drove him into the ground. One late night, after yet another full day of Browns practices and meetings and film sessions, a gaunt-looking Saban staggered into a room and told Savage and a few others, "Guys, I can't go another minute. I promise you I'll be here at 5:30 in the morning. I've got to get out of here." And then Saban dropped all the way to the floor and slumped against the wall, a totally beaten man.

As good a secondary coach as his players and co-workers had ever seen, Saban could be just as demanding on the slapdicks beneath him — on Savage and others. Unlike Belichick, the defensive coordinator had a volcanic temper that could erupt at any minute. Saban was an equal-opportunity ripper, shredding young assistants for making errors in film breakdowns and jumping on young players for blowing assignments in coverage.

"Bill was very sarcastic but much more low-key," Savage said. "He's going to come in and needle you with a really sarcastic comment and make you feel an inch tall and feel like the biggest dummy. Nick would just rip you apart with a barrage of verbal [insults]. Bill would just come in and shrug his shoulders and say, 'This is the worst film breakdown I've ever seen in my entire NFL career.'"

No, Little Bill was not a Big Bill–styled screamer, though he once treated a Browns assistant the way Parcells had treated him in the heat of a game. On his headset, Belichick told the assistant to "shut the fuck up," and the assistant wanted to climb down from the press box and strangle him on the spot, before cooler headsets prevailed.

Belichick did demand that his subordinates show up early for meetings and practices. Dom Anile, a holdover scout from the Rutigliano-Schotten-heimer-Carson days in Cleveland, found out the hard way after the 1991 draft. Belichick had just promoted Anile to director of college scouting. Anile thought this was his big career break, and one day — the first day of practice after that draft — he was on the phone with an agent trying to get some bodies into camp.

Anile finished his call and headed out to practice. Players were merely stretching; they hadn't started any drills. But when Belichick spotted Anile walking toward him from the field house, he made an urgent beeline for the scouting director and cornered him near the sideline.

"You're late," Belichick barked.

"Practice hasn't started yet, Coach," Anile responded.

"You're late," Belichick said again.

"I have no excuses," the scouting director said. "I will never be late again."

And Anile never was.

"According to the Vince Lombardi and Bill Belichick clock," Anile said, "I was late, because you're supposed to be ten minutes early."

Modell said that he'd never seen anything like Belichick's work ethic, and that at times he advised him to slow down and catch his breath. In mid-August, the Browns moved into their state-of-the art, $13 million complex in Berea, which included four beautiful grass fields. After a couple of weeks, Belichick asked the grounds crew to tear out some grass on one field and install some dirt to simulate the infield at Cleveland Municipal Stadium, which the Browns shared with the Cleveland Indians. Some of the crew members felt like crying; they were in the business of growing grass, not ripping it out. They did as Belichick told them, and afterward realized that it made perfect sense.

"If you look at old films of what that [Municipal Stadium] field looked like before Bill got here," said Tony Dick, a member of the grounds crew, "nobody cared if there was grass there or not, and that goes back even to the eighties. That field was awful — the game field especially, and the practice field, too. But when Bill got here, everything had to be perfect. Before games, he would go out there and say, 'Hey, we have to take an eighth of an inch off the grass.' We would have lawn mowers on the field right before the game, as people were coming into the stadium. He wasn't maniacal; he just wanted everyone to do their job correctly."

If some influential figures in the building looked down on the groundskeepers, Belichick wasn't one of them. "He thought more of us," Dick said, "than anyone else in the organization."

Dick was a full-time college student at nearby Baldwin Wallace, and yet he worked 80 to 100 hours a week, at eight bucks an hour, trying to make Belichick's fields look exactly as he wanted them to look. The coach even found a constructive use for the dirt that was dug out for the Berea facility and piled high next to the building to be hauled away.

"Bill told them not to haul it away," Dick said. "They turned it into a ramp. They eventually called it Mount Belichick. It was probably a 20-foot-tall mountain of dirt, and they rolled it into a ramp, seeded it, and he used it as a conditioning hill . . . Bill was looking for an edge and had a mountain on the side of the facility and put the fat guys on it."

Michael Dean Perry, younger brother of Chicago Bears cult hero William "the Refrigerator" Perry, was among the "fat guys" who would ultimately spend some time scaling Mount Belichick. Perry also happened to be the Browns' best player, a Pro Bowl defensive tackle who had managed a career-high 11.5 sacks in 1990. Perry ended his contract holdout on August 27, his 26th birthday, five days before the season opener against Dallas. He immediately found out he wasn't in the shape he thought he was in.

Belichick had him run in a way the 6′1″, 290-pound tackle wouldn't soon forget. The Browns' coach mandated that his players run gassers — sprints the width of the field, 53 yards from sideline to sideline and back. Two back-and-forth trips equaled one rep. "After I ran those gassers that everybody's talking about," Perry said, "I felt like going to bed and never getting up again."

Cleveland desperately needed Perry and an improved pass rush after its first-round draft pick, UCLA safety Eric Turner, went down with a stress fracture in his leg, leaving an already battered secondary decimated. Belichick had to use a trash can to climb over an eight-foot stone wall at a locked-up UCLA field to work out Turner before the draft; the safety vaulted the wall in a single bound and then blasted Belichick in a contact drill after the Cleveland coach insisted he deliver his best shot. "He pounded the crap out of me," Belichick said. "But he didn't knock me down. No matter how much it hurts, you never show it."

Belichick had done everything humanly possible to prepare the Browns to be what they hadn't been the previous year under Carson: competent. He impressed his most important player, Kosar, with his command of concepts that didn't revolve around his specialty, defense, and with his presence in offensive meetings that Carson hadn't attended. But the 1991 Browns weren't the 1990 Giants. They weren't even the Browns of the eighties. It was going to take time to make Cleveland a contender, to build a team worthy of its association with Paul and Jim Brown. And there would be a considerable amount of pain suffered along the way.

Bill Belichick had coached 32 games as head coach of the Cleveland Browns, winning 13 of them, and yet his biggest victory unfolded three days after the 1992 season ended. That was the day the New York Giants fired Ray Handley, George Young's choice to replace Bill Parcells. The same George Young who had told those closest to him that he would never hire Belichick to coach the Giants.

The bookish Handley was emotionally ill-equipped to handle the top job, and he began losing his grip on it the day he stormed out of a news conference when pressed by a reporter about his preference at quarterback—Jeff Hostetler or Phil Simms. Even Belichick, as brutal as he could be to the Cleveland media, with his mumbling and dismissive nonanswers, had never done that.

Belichick had to be enjoying this Young/Handley shit show from afar. He also had to be taking a measure of satisfaction in the performance of his Browns defense. In 1990, Belichick's Giants unit had held opponents to a league-best 211 points, while the Browns surrendered what would be a decade-worst 462 points. In 1992, Belichick's Browns (with an assist from Saban) gave up 275 points, while Handley's Giants allowed 367.

Slowly, surely, Cleveland was making progress that was ripped right from the loose-leaf pages of Belichick's three-ring binders. He kept all his pro personnel information in blue ink, said scout Chris Landry, and all of his scouting information in red ink. Belichick never stopped studying those binders. At 4:30 one morning, Landry dropped a completed report on a table in what he thought was the vacant head coach's office, only to hear Belichick's voice from the desk behind him. "Scared the crap out of me," Landry said. And then Belichick immediately asked the scout to look at film of some preseason games. Of course, the head coach never asked his subordinates to look at more film than he himself had watched, often with a lollipop in his mouth.

In going 6-10 in '91, the Browns lost six games by four points or less. They won seven games the following year, despite the fact that Kosar twice broke his ankle. After a miserable 1990 under Carson and interim replacement Jim Shofner, Kosar, when healthy, had played fairly well in two seasons under Belichick, throwing 26 touchdown passes against 16 interceptions and completing 63 percent of his attempts. But there were rumblings that tension existed between the quarterback and the coach over the conservative nature of the offense.

This much was clear: Belichick was now in total control of the Browns' football operations. Realizing he was steadily losing his voice in the organization, Accorsi had resigned in the spring of 1992. The GM admitted that he'd made a mistake almost immediately after hiring Belichick when he told the rookie coach that he was pursuing the job of president of the Green Bay Packers, which Accorsi saw as the best front-office job in football. Belichick didn't say much of anything in response. In retrospect, Accorsi wasn't sorry that he'd been honest with his coach. He was sorry that he was looking into another job.

"That wasn't fair to Belichick," Accorsi said. "*I just got my first head coaching job, I'm really into this, and the GM's looking to leave.* So he couldn't possibly trust me after that. I wasn't all in . . . This guy's thinking, *My GM's leaving,* and then he really wanted complete control. Totally justified."

Accorsi would be remembered in Cleveland mostly for the deal with Buffalo that landed the first pick in the 1985 supplemental draft used to take the University of Miami's Kosar, who wanted to play for the Browns, the team stationed 80 miles from his Boardman home. The GM left Cleveland impressed with Belichick's skill as a talent evaluator, with his ability to relay his personnel preferences to the scouts, and with his philosophy on offense.

"He knew how he wanted to play," Accorsi said. "He said, 'We've got to play the game in the middle of the field. People always try to take away the edges . . . You've got to have the courage to throw the ball in the middle of the field.' I'd never heard that before. He was a creative thinker."

Belichick had already formed a partnership with Mike Lombardi, a scout for Bill Walsh in San Francisco before Accorsi hired him in 1987, and he would lean more on Lombardi with Accorsi out; the personnel man was a significant voice in developing the Browns' grading system. Belichick would expand the role of Ozzie Newsome, the former tight end who had moved into the front office, and, as always, he'd seek the counsel of his friend from Andover, Ernie Adams, the offensive assistant who was working with running backs and tight ends. Adams, among other duties, had been heavily involved in the 1991 draft.

Belichick had also brought in a young coach from Murray State, in Kentucky, named Scott Pioli, whom he'd befriended during his Giants days, to work as an assistant in pro personnel. Out of Washingtonville, New York, a college player at Central Connecticut, Pioli made the 90-minute daily drive to the Giants' camp at Fairleigh Dickinson–Madison, where his best friend's girlfriend was working security. She introduced him to Belichick, who was impressed with the kid's hustle and his stated desire to learn everything he could about the profession. The coach offered him a home on the sofa in the suite he shared with his colleague Al Groh. Five years later, Pioli was making $16,000 to scout talent, drive Belichick to the airport, and do whatever the Browns' head coach asked of him. Belichick would sometimes stuff hundred-dollar bills in Pioli's ashtray and tell him to fill up his gas tank and buy himself a good meal.

But Belichick was leaning mostly on Belichick. He was putting this overwhelming challenge on his own shoulders. He'd replaced a brand-new indoor field with another indoor field he preferred, costing Modell a pretty penny, so his players would have better footing in practice. He'd interviewed more than 100 potential assistants for his staff and worked out hundreds of college prospects and available NFL players known as Plan B free agents — those players not among the 37 protected by each team.

Belichick pulled the Browns out of National Football Scouting, which pooled general draft information for different teams, to take sole ownership of his personnel evaluations. He was reportedly granted the resources to hire as many as ten scouts after Accorsi's resignation, and he put in his own numerical and letter grading system to measure prospects, with an assist from Dallas Cowboys chief scout Gil Brandt, who visited with him a few times to discuss the Cowboys' system. Dallas was the first NFL franchise to use computer analytics in grading talent, emphasizing data loaded into an IBM machine over some grizzled scout's gut instinct, and Brandt was willing to meet with Belichick, Saban, and Lombardi in Berea to share some of the Cowboys' secrets.

"We went through what we did and how we did it," Brandt said, "and I think they pretty much adopted the system we used, because it was a pretty good system. It was a way to evaluate players by having something tangible so that there were characteristics we used, position specifics we used, a numbering system we used, and a grading system we used to help you identify players. When you saw the numbers for the successful ones and the non-successful ones, it jumped out at you."

Though one Browns official downplayed how much the Dallas system influenced Belichick and his method of evaluating prospects, Brandt was kind enough to open a window on his franchise that his host in Berea never would've opened for an NFL competitor. He explained how the Cowboys identified and then developed young talent in their system. Years later, Belichick would thank him by saying that Brandt belonged in the Hall of Fame. "He'd probably be the first guy I would put in there," Bill said.

When it came to information, Belichick was always a taker, never a giver.

The Browns ended up using a grading scale on which 8.0 represented the projection for an immediate day-one starter and potential Hall of Famer. A 5.5 would be an undrafted free agent from a smaller school, a 5.6 an undrafted free agent from a bigger school, and a 5.7 a "make it" player, or someone who could make a roster. A 6.0 would be a potential starter who needed development, and a player between 6.6 and 6.9 would be a first-year starter with elite physical skill. Any prospect graded at 7.0 or higher would be a Pro Bowl–level talent.

The system was designed to highlight the players who had the necessary physical tools to play professional football, and to put numerical limits on those who were deficient in any of those areas. "Bill likes cornerbacks that are big," said scout Chris Landry. "If you're under 5'11", that guy can't get over a 5.5 grade, even if he has great production and all the other areas match up."

The letter grades were equally important, as they identified perceived flaws. In a scout's report, the letters printed before the numerical value signified a physical deficiency. The letter *B* told the reader that the player didn't have bulk. An *S* announced a lack of speed, and a *T* branded the player as tight, or not fluid. The letters printed after the number signified a nonphysical deficiency, such as *c*, which represented a character issue. "Or an *m* was a mental guy," Landry said, "not mentally strong . . . Bill would want further definition on that."

Bill would want his scouts to tell him what a player was likely to do for Cleveland, not what round he should be drafted in. Height, weight, and speed were always the most critical measurables, but a prospect with no letters after his number grades earned a more serious look. Belichick's goal was to build a roster around Pro Bowl players in their mid- to late twenties, and to build a new version of the Giants—a big, physical team that welcomed the opportunity to play in the wind and the cold. In pursuit of this goal, he was amazing colleagues with his professional stamina and single-minded approach to the craft. He would often be seen in a dark meeting room watching film while on one exercise machine, or highlighting notes—with the cap of the highlighter wedged in a corner of his mouth—while on another.

"People who showed up at nine or ten o'clock in the morning in suits and ties might complain about Bill," Tony Dick said. "But when we were there at two or three in the morning shoveling snow to get coaches into the parking lot, we'd see him show up at three in the morning after leaving at midnight. He knew when everyone was arriving at, and leaving, that building. Nobody knew more about that than Bill Belichick."

Early on, Belichick was winning over people in the building and around town. Kosar praised him in the newspapers. The fans loved it when he punctuated his very first home victory, over the Bengals, by making his way to the Dawg Pound—the end zone bleachers that housed the most rambunctious fans—and rotating his fist before mocking Bengals coach Sam Wyche for calling the AFC Central a three-team race between Cincinnati, Pittsburgh, and Houston. "Maybe he's right," Belichick said in a rare public jab at another coach. "Maybe it will still be a three-team race."

As much as he was working Saban and his fellow assistants to the bone, Belichick also earned their undying appreciation for giving them all, or much, of the money he was making from his TV and radio shows above his reported $400,000 wage. The head coach also was known for his hundred-dollar handshakes — where he'd slip a staffer or a secretary a Benjamin as if he or she were the maître d'. Chris Landry said it wasn't uncommon to find an envelope in the top drawer of his desk filled with more cash than he'd earned in his paycheck. One of Cleveland's later scouting assistants, John Lombardi, grandson of Green Bay Packers legend Vince Lombardi, said Belichick would pull him out of a hallway and into an office and hand him money or a steakhouse certificate. Belichick even brought into the office a hairstylist and paid for all staffer haircuts. His generosity was widely considered his best character trait, especially among the youngest members of the organization.

But his first two years were marked by conflict, too, and not just with the media. Reggie Langhorne, wide receiver, was the first significant player to test Belichick's authority. Langhorne was a camp holdout who had been demoted on the depth chart, and when he refused to run routes for the scout team, Belichick fined him and made him inactive for the road game against the Giants. Belichick had also fined the receiver for being one or two pounds overweight. "I think he was smacking me around," Langhorne said, "and I'd been in this city seven years and I felt there was no way he was going to bully me."

The receiver spoke of the tug-of-war between a rookie coach trying to establish his system and entrenched veterans who'd had success under Schottenheimer doing it a different way. Langhorne conceded that Schottenheimer could also act like a dictator at times. "But I could talk to Marty," he said. "Most guys on the team could talk to Marty. This guy, no."

Langhorne didn't play a second season for Belichick, and neither did fellow receivers Brian Brennan and Webster Slaughter, who also complained about their roles in the offense. For the most part, Belichick had semifunctional relationships with Slaughter and Brennan. In fact, he rewarded Slaughter's efforts in camp one day by sending him into the locker room to put on flip-flops, return to the field, and sit back and watch practice. On another camp day, Belichick broke up a fight between Slaughter and cornerback Raymond Clayborn. "And then we're standing there, still angry and saying things," Slaughter would recall, "and Bill broke the ice by saying, 'OK, which one of you guys hit me?' Everyone bust up laughing. He had a dry sense of humor. I really got him. I really understood him . . . He's probably my favorite head coach to play under."

Yet Slaughter signed as a free agent in Houston. In the seven seasons after Kosar was drafted, in 1985, Slaughter, Brennan, and Langhorne combined for 918 catches and 73 touchdowns for Cleveland in the regular season and postseason. Belichick's quarterback would have to get by without a lot of familiar firepower.

On defense, Belichick was having serious trouble reaching the kind of understanding with his best player, Michael Dean Perry, that he'd reached with Lawrence Taylor. Perry wanted to play the attacking, shoot-the-gap style Carson had him play, and Belichick wanted him to adhere to more restrictive two-gap principles. Perry and Belichick had also quarreled over his weight and the origin of the tackle's knee injury. "When Belichick first came in," Perry said, "we didn't see eye to eye. We don't see eye to eye right now, and we probably won't in the future." By late in the 1992 season, the Pro Bowler was asking for a trade.

One day, Belichick called the training room and Perry answered. As he handed the phone to the team trainer, Bill Tessendorf, Perry held the receiver away from his mouth and said, "It's Hitler. Little Hitler." Belichick heard it and laughed. "The reason he called him Little Hitler," recalled Perry's fellow defensive lineman Anthony Pleasant, "was because Bill was trying to kill us in Cleveland all the time in practices."

Perry was riding the stationary bike during practice once when a teammate asked him if he was injured. The tackle answered that he was feeling just fine. When the teammate naturally followed up by asking why he wasn't on the field, Perry responded, "I'm not playing for that fucking guy."

It was never easy suiting up for Bill Belichick. Tommy Vardell, the first-round pick in 1992, ended a brief training-camp holdout and walked straight into a buzz saw. He called his first couple of days in camp "insanity" and recalled full-contact practices as long as three hours in the heat that were followed by conditioning runs up the hill. Vardell was a California kid out of Stanford who was used to the dry heat and cool breezes off the Pacific, not the humidity off Lake Erie. It wouldn't be until later in Vardell's career, when he played for other teams, that he realized the Belichick pace in camp was, in his words, "pretty crazy."

Fullback Ron Wolfley, a four-time Pro Bowler as a Cardinals special teamer, arrived in 1992 to some startling sounds. Belichick demanded that the Browns run sprints or gassers, and some players responded by disguising their voices and shouting, "Fuck you," or "This is fucking bullshit"—figuring Belichick wouldn't be able to identify the culprits amid the noise of the stampede.

Wolfley thought this open disdain for the primary authority figure was poison for the football team. The fullback adored Belichick's style. "And I say this as affectionately as I possibly can: He was a bit of a sociopath, and I loved it," Wolfley said. "He didn't care about your family. He didn't pretend to care about your family. He didn't ask about your family . . . He'd leave you alone. You go out there and do your job and, I kid you not, he wouldn't talk to you. I loved that about him."

Wolfley said Belichick ordered the players to run five gassers in a certain time, with a one-minute rest between each gasser. The fullback trained and trained for this test, and still got sick on his fifth and final turn. "When I crossed the finish line, I barfed," Wolfley said. "And as I went down and was holding my knee, I see these lizard-skin boots backing away from me. The guy in the lizard-skin boots was Bon Jovi. I almost barfed on his boots, and I'm thinking, *How in the world does Bon Jovi hang out with a guy like Bill?*"

Perry and other disgruntled Browns would say that Belichick was trying too hard to be Parcells, and that he lacked the people skills to pull it off. But one of the old Giants who ended up in Cleveland, Everson Walls, maintained that Little Bill had little choice but to take on some Browns. "I've never been around players who griped so much," Walls said. "In New York, the climate there was all about toughness. Michael Dean Perry was a great player, but he was always bumping heads with Bill about practice, running, injuries. He was a problem."

He wasn't the only one on the defensive line. Belichick asked Burnett and Pleasant to put on weight and become more user-friendly in a two-gap scheme, and Burnett thought that directive was a mistake. He thought Accorsi had drafted the defensive ends to use their athleticism to contain John Elway on the edges and finally reach a Super Bowl. Though Belichick had a history of switching up his schemes on nearly a weekly basis, as he had in the Giants' most recent postseason drive to a title, Burnett also thought his coach was too careful and predictable in using his Cover 2 scheme, a zone defense developed by Steelers coach Chuck Noll that requires two deep safeties to split the field.

Burnett maintained that Saban agreed with him, too. "Nick was so pissed with Bill," he said. "He wanted to do so many things and he was hamstrung by Bill. I used to meet with Nick all the time, and Bill would not bend as far as changing defenses. He stayed as vanilla as ice cream . . . I said, 'Nick, why don't we run this? Why don't we run that?' Because we had all this stuff. I was in love with the game. To Nick I was like 'Oh, man, remember in training camp when they couldn't block us on this blitz?' He goes, 'I know, I know. But sometimes I put it in the game plan and Bill won't run it on Sundays' . . . We maybe used a tenth of Nick's playbook."

Burnett was more frustrated than Saban with the head coach. "Bill would condition us during the season; it was high schoolish," Burnett said. "*Come on, man, we're pros. You're going to make us run six gassers because you didn't like the last team session for today?* Bill, that's how he was. A micromanager. My biggest learning experience during that time came through Nick Saban. I owe a lot of my knowledge defensively to Nick . . . We would do things in practice. We'd do a lot of Nick's stuff in practice, and they couldn't touch us. But game time came, we'd only play a certain number of defenses and we'd blitz once. We'd play not to lose, Cover 2, and never put the other offense on their heels."

Another old Giant whom Belichick brought to Cleveland, Mark Bavaro, surveyed the widening circle of complainers and decided his coach was "outnumbered." That became more apparent when Scott Galbraith, a tight end who played his college ball at USC, weighed in with his assessment of the coaching staff.

"Bill Belichick was a certifiable crazy freakin' madman," Galbraith said. "We hit every day, all day. Marathon practices . . . In the locker room, we thought Belichick was short-lived, another Modell cheap quick fix. We were convinced that he was going to be a flash in the pan. Belichick could not relate. We knew this son of a gun would not last long. I mean, who would play for this asinine jackass? Who would do that? In the locker room, we had no respect for Bill Belichick at all."

Galbraith called the Browns' offense "prehistoric, elementary, almost impossible for Bernie to succeed in." Years after he retired and became a pastor and team chaplain for the NBA's Sacramento Kings, Galbraith said he probably needed to seek forgiveness for the hatred he felt for Belichick over his two seasons in Cleveland.

He was clear on the original source of that hatred — Belichick putting an assistant Galbraith found unqualified in charge of his career. The tight end called his position coach, Ernie Adams, "a joke" who offered no clear roadmap to improvement. "He'd say, 'Hey, Scottie, you gotta catch that ball,'" Galbraith said. "Or 'Hey, Scottie, you gotta get that block.' I'd say, 'OK, Captain Obvious, I was trying. But do you have the principle on how to complete that block next time, or are you just saying I have to get that block?' But after a while it was hopeless."

Galbraith was close to Kosar, and after the Browns cut the tight end days before the start of the 1993 season, he asked the quarterback for a favor. Galbraith's agent had told him Belichick was hardly giving a favorable report to teams that might be interested in his services, so Galbraith asked Kosar to ask the coach to knock it off. The quarterback agreed, approached Belichick, and then called his friend back. Galbraith said Belichick's response, as relayed by Kosar, went like this: "Tell Galbraith to shut the fuck up. I don't have time to talk about his sorry ass."

Galbraith signed with the Dallas Cowboys and was so grateful his former quarterback took his cause to Belichick, he decided he'd spend the rest of his life willing to run into a burning building for Bernard Joseph Kosar Jr., the most popular and powerful of all Browns. Kosar was the local boy who made good, a Hungarian American star in an Eastern European stronghold, Cleveland, that lived and died with its football team.

Kosar won division titles in his first three seasons and in four of his first five, and he set a league record in the 1990 and '91 seasons for most consecutive passing attempts without an interception (308), supplanting the legendary Bart Starr. The quarterback had earned a certain status in the organization, and sometimes he used that status to his advantage.

Bavaro remembered a unit meeting in 1992 when Gary Tranquill, quarterbacks coach, was drawing up a play in the facility's auditorium. Tranquill was in midthought, telling his Browns about a particular play — "This is how we're going to do it" — when Kosar interrupted by saying, "No, we're not."

Bavaro couldn't believe his ears. He turned to face Kosar, who was sitting behind him.

"I think we really should," Tranquill responded.

"No, Coach, we don't do that here," Kosar said. "We're not going to do that."

Bavaro felt like he'd stepped into a scene from *North Dallas Forty*. He personally liked Kosar, and thought him to be a good quarterback. "But that was the attitude from Bernie," Bavaro said, "and the other old-timers there. 'This is our team.'"

As it turned out, the 1993 season would determine who did and did not control the Cleveland Browns. Belichick had taken on other prominent Browns, but he'd never taken on Bernie. This fight would be different. This one would be a heavyweight championship matchup, and the two combatants would end up covered in each other's blood.

8

MISTAKES BY THE LAKE

In 1993, the Cleveland Browns were 3-0 for the first time since 1979, and life was good for their head coach. Bill Belichick had missed out on his most coveted off-season free agent, Reggie White, but he had added to his roster a three-time Pro Bowl nose tackle, Jerry Ball; a former No. 1 overall pick at quarterback, Vinny Testaverde; and one of his old New York Giant favorites at linebacker, Pepper Johnson. Belichick had also convinced Art Modell that he didn't need to bow to public opinion and hire an offensive coordinator to energize what had been a methodical attack.

Modell even declared that Belichick would be "the last head coach I've hired" and said he felt so good about his man that if the Browns weren't contenders by the end of his contract, in 1995, "I will get out of football and leave Cleveland . . . If I did make a mistake, I have nobody to blame but myself, and it's time for me to move on and get out of town."

The owner conceded that Belichick wasn't the easiest guy to like ("He's no Don Rickles, let's face it"), but the 3-0 start, highlighted by a *Monday Night Football* upset of San Francisco and punctuated by a road victory over the Los Angeles Raiders, had Clevelanders suddenly thinking Belichick was more likable than they'd previously thought. His most recent first-round draft pick, "Touchdown" Tommy Vardell, out of Stanford, rushed for 104 yards on 14 carries against the Raiders and temporarily made fans forget the popular veteran Kevin Mack, who had retired and unretired over the summer before being exiled by his head coach. In the end, Belichick ran down the sideline and bear-hugged Eric Metcalf, who scored the winning touchdown with two seconds left.

Belichick had claimed after the 1992 season, a 7-9 season, that it would be "a real serious, almost criminal act to deviate from the direction and progress that we've made." After three games, it seemed he might actually have a point.

BELICHICK HAS TOUCH OF MIDAS, read one *Plain Dealer* headline.

But one crisis he couldn't avoid involved the most important position in the sport. A struggling Bernie Kosar had to be benched in the fourth quarter of the Raiders game for Testaverde, who erased a 16–3 deficit and led the Browns to the dramatic victory. Under most circumstances, this would've been viewed as a triumph for Belichick, whose off-season faith in Testaverde had been validated.

Only these weren't normal circumstances. Kosar was king in Cleveland. Like Modell, Bernie had a cozy relationship with the local media and often called writers to tell his side of a particular story, on or off the record. Kosar forever belonged to the city and its people — often the target of jokes from elitists on both coasts — ever since the day he walked into a University of Miami press conference in a loose tank top and tight shorts, sunglasses buried in his curly dark hair, and said of his decision to leave the Hurricanes for the NFL, "It's a question I think of me basically just wanting to go home."

Kosar avoided the regular 1985 draft and maneuvered his way into the supplemental draft, and the Browns maneuvered their way into the first supplemental pick to grab him. Even without a Super Bowl appearance, the marriage had been a blissful one. Wearing No. 19, Johnny Unitas's iconic number, Kosar had become nearly as revered in Cleveland as Johnny U was in Baltimore. At 6'5", he was gangly and awkward and lacking in athleticism and speed. He had a sidearm delivery and almost never stepped into his passes; he preferred opening up his shoulders and planting his lead foot to his left, like a baseball hitter stepping in the bucket. He won in spite of it all with smarts, competitive intensity, and a talent for staying clear of the interceptions that derailed his former Hurricanes teammate Testaverde over his six seasons with Tampa Bay.

"There's not going to be a quarterback controversy," Art Modell said after Testaverde replaced Kosar against the Raiders. "I'm not going to let it happen. I told Bernie Kosar in no uncertain terms that he's our No. 1 quarterback, and that's exactly what Bill Belichick told him."

Modell had just given the quarterback a contract extension through 1999 that would pay him an average of $3.85 million a season. He often likened Kosar to a son, and their relationship was an issue Belichick had to deal with. The coach temporarily tabled that concern by immediately naming Kosar the starter for Cleveland's next game, against Indianapolis, keeping the fan base in a healthy frame of mind. The town was alive with the possibility that its cherished Browns were finally back in business as a serious threat to win the AFC Central, and Belichick seemed to be settling in for a long run in the chair once occupied by one of his coaching heroes, Paul Brown, the innovator he'd describe as "the father of this game."

Though Belichick remained wildly uncomfortable and borderline noncompliant in press conference settings, there were small signs that he was making an effort with at least a couple of local media members. He had established a friendship with Channel 8 sports anchor Casey Coleman, son of Cleveland and Boston broadcasting legend Ken Coleman and soon-to-be voice of the Browns. The coach even allowed Coleman to spend a week with him in the 1992 season, starting with the broadcaster and his camera crew showing up every day at Belichick's Brecksville home at 5 a.m.

Mary Kay Cabot of the *Plain Dealer* was another influential media member who was granted access beyond the bare Belichick minimum. The Browns' PR man, Kevin Byrne, thought the coach respected reporters he believed to be hard workers, and Cabot, a twentysomething on her first NFL beat, was already known as a tireless reporter. Cabot was struck by just how much Belichick cared about the fans' perception of him. He would sit down with her and review every negative reference to him in her stories, highlighted in yellow by Byrne, and explain why he thought "Voice of Doom" and similar grim references didn't paint an accurate picture of him.

"It really did sting," Cabot said of Belichick's reaction to criticism. "I do believe that kind of thing did matter to him early on."

Belichick would occasionally invite Cabot to sit in on Monday film sessions also attended by Coleman. If the coach figured he couldn't make inroads with other media members who regularly skewered him, he thought Cabot was worth the investment of time. Belichick showed her things on tape she never would've seen from the press box, and she found his knowledge of the game to be staggering. Though they had their share of shouting matches — Belichick later called Cabot at 7 a.m. to scream at her for reporting that receiver Michael Jackson wouldn't play that week, thereby tipping off the New York Jets — the coach invited the writer to join him, Coleman, and Mike Lombardi on a private jet for a pre-draft trip to meet a prospect in New Jersey.

Belichick also opened a window for Cabot into his family life, allowing her to interview his wife, Debby, who was clearly interested in softening her husband's public image. Bill and Debby had three children by then — Brian, the baby, was born in 1991, on November 25, Kosar's birthday — and Cabot found Belichick to be a loving father who was pained by the fact that he couldn't see his kids from Monday through Friday during the season, and who had them at the facility on Saturdays. In other published stories, friends said that Belichick drove Amanda, the oldest, to ballet class and Stephen, the middle child, to karate class, and that sometimes Amanda joined in when her father was going over plays at home. "She just thought he hung the moon," Cabot said.

The writer also found in Debby and Bill a couple who cared about the community. The Belichicks effectively saved the Zelma George homeless shelter for women and children by starting a foundation to fund it and by arranging for holiday events for the residents. "They did a lot of charity work around here," Cabot said. "They were very involved, and he really tried. At a certain point he just basically gave up," by which Cabot meant not the charity work, just any meaningful attempt to improve his public image. "At a certain point he was like 'Screw it.' Especially after the Kosar thing."

The Kosar thing. Despite the conflicts with Michael Dean Perry and other prominent veterans, and the fact that some offensive and defensive players (and Nick Saban) thought he was too conservative with his game plans, Belichick's program appeared to be arriving. He was winning some games and winning over some supporters. He was hosting Bon Jovi at practice. He was coexisting (if barely) with Perry, who had walked out of training camp. He was even getting strong reviews from a beloved figure in Cleveland, 37-year-old linebacker Clay Matthews, a four-time Pro Bowler who, along with linebacking partner and two-time Pro Bowler Mike Johnson, preferred Belichick's defensive system to Bud Carson's all-out attack. "We were shooting a lot more threes [under Carson], in a basketball analogy," Matthews said. "I don't think that best suited us."

But the Kosar thing remained an angry-looking cloud system that hovered above everything Belichick had worked for in Cleveland, until it exploded and unleashed an apocalyptic storm. The first benching of Kosar led to the second benching of Kosar the next week, at halftime of a 23–10 loss at Indianapolis, where Testaverde, of all people, criticized Belichick's decision to pull the starter. Kosar was pulled again during the following week's 24–14 loss to the Dolphins, a game in which Miami lost Dan Marino for the year to a torn Achilles tendon, and afterward Belichick named Testaverde the first-string quarterback going forward, before Modell weighed in with his "unqualified and unequivocal support" of the move.

Testaverde was built like a Greek god and blessed with rare athleticism and a cannon for a right arm. "The guy could've probably played linebacker, defensive end, running back, quarterback, tight end, safety," Belichick would say. Kosar? He looked like a weekend softball player and he was physically beaten to hell. Years later, Bernie would estimate that he'd suffered dozens of broken bones and torn ligaments in his NFL career, and Lord knows how many concussions. He had to stand among the league leaders in anti-inflammatory meds, and he guessed that he'd been knocked unconscious 20 times. He also lost a bunch of teeth from hits absorbed when he wasn't wearing a mouthpiece, which leads to another reason Belichick picked Vinny over Bernie.

Kosar didn't wear a mouthpiece because he had one of the sharpest and quickest minds in football, and he had to communicate clearly with his teammates at the line of scrimmage when he recognized a certain defensive formation and the need to call an audible. Belichick had said before the season that there would be "more emphasis on the quarterback calling the plays than we've had in the past," which was music to Kosar's ears. Only Belichick was never a big fan of Bernie's audibles. Nor was Bernie a big fan of Belichick's pedestrian, pound-the-ball offense. In fact, the two of them had long been engaged in a battle for play-calling control.

Two of Kosar's most recent audibles had resulted in touchdown passes — a 30-yarder to Jackson near the end of the first half against San Francisco and a 14-yarder to Jackson against Miami. Nevertheless, Jerry Ball said that at halftime of the San Francisco game, in Cleveland Municipal Stadium, players in the locker room could hear Belichick next door shouting at Kosar, "I don't give a damn. When I tell you to do something, you do it."

So Kosar was out and Testaverde was in. Three nights later, at the monthly meeting of the Greater Ashland County Browns Backers, the *Ashland Times-Gazette* reported that Jackson had lit into his head coach for being unable to relate to players, for failing to run a functional offense, and for failing to hire an offensive coordinator. "If Belichick would let Bernie call his own plays," he said, "you'd see a different offense." The receiver said that if a player questioned Belichick, he would "write you right out of the game plan." Jackson also complained about the ex-Giants on the roster ("We are becoming the Cleveland Giants") and about the presence of new team consultant Jim Brown, whom he called "kind of like a little spy" for his friend Belichick, who had met the Browns legend at an NFL alumni golf tournament and had become a supporter of, and participant in, Brown's Amer-I-Can program for gang members in need of reform.

Testaverde brought order to the chaos by throwing three touchdown passes in a 28–17 victory over Cincinnati that lifted the Browns to 4-2 and inspired Modell to reveal that he'd extended Belichick's contract two years, through the 1997 season. The owner insisted that the quarterback situation had nothing to do with the announcement, and that his coach had earned the extension as he neared the midpoint of his five-year deal.

"I think he's been treated unfairly by the media and fans," Modell said, "and I wanted to show my unwavering support for him. The players and the media will have to get used to having him around." The owner predicted that his Browns would be a playoff team for a long time to come, and he maintained that he had no problem with Belichick's call to continue on without an offensive coordinator.

It seemed Belichick was running the offense by committee, with quarterbacks coach Gary Tranquill, running backs coach Steve Crosby, and Ozzie

Newsome chipping in. (Newsome had been promoted to assistant to the head coach/offense/pro personnel and was said by Modell to have a strong voice in the offense.) Tranquill had Steve Belichick and Saban on his staff at Navy, and had played college ball at Wittenberg for Bill Edwards, Steve's college and pro coach and Bill's godfather. Tranquill had also worked under Woody Hayes at Ohio State, and he was there when Hayes got himself fired for punching a Clemson player at the Gator Bowl. He'd seen all kinds of coaches come and go, and when he arrived in Cleveland, in 1991, as part of Bill Belichick's staff, he viewed Bill as "a typical defensive coach who didn't know anything about offense and tried to be involved. That's what I thought. I just had had enough of that after three years."

One game in particular captured the dysfunction of the offensive protocol. Belichick was frustrated with Tranquill and the play calling and decided to put Ernie Adams in the hot seat in the booth upstairs. According to a witness who thought of Adams as an exceptional strategist, it was a complete disaster. With Mike Lombardi in the back of the press box calling out colors to identify different sets, this person said, Adams crumbled under the pressure.

"Lombardi would yell out, 'Silver, blue,' whatever the formation was," the witness said, "and Ernie was slow getting the plays off. He panicked. He'd say, 'Jesus Christ, Bill, I don't know what the fuck to call' . . . I don't care if they say it's not true, but Ernie Adams called plays that night. He was the fucking offensive coordinator . . . The thing was too big and too fast for him."

Through it all, as quarterbacks coach, Tranquill remained the buffer between Belichick and Kosar/Testaverde. The assistant found Kosar to be perhaps the smartest player he'd ever been around when it came to understanding defenses and his teammates' strengths and weaknesses.

Kosar was also a legacy player, the most significant Cleveland Brown since Jim Brown, and he required a lot of heavy maintenance. "He'd been there for so long, and he was kind of set in his ways," Tranquill said. "He was probably a guy who wanted to do things the way he'd been doing them all the time, and I don't blame him for that . . . He was very outspoken. I was caught in between.

"It was a tough situation," Tranquill continued. "I just kind of remained aloof. We weren't very good, number one. We didn't have a lot of really good players on offense at that time. We were still trying to do some things we shouldn't have tried to do offensively, and it just kind of festered. It was a no-win situation."

And so, as a result, nobody won. Testaverde went down with a shoulder injury in the fourth quarter of a 28–23 victory over Pittsburgh, made possible by Metcalf's punt-return touchdowns of 91 and 75 yards, giving the Browns sole possession of first place. They played Bruce Springsteen's "Glory Days" on the Municipal Stadium speakers, and the 37-year-old Matthews, a Brown since 1978, said the team had taken a big step toward the glory days of the eighties.

Only Kosar was suddenly back under center, something Belichick never again wanted to see. One windy day in Berea, after Bernie threw some fluttering passes to nowhere, the coach and his staff watched film of the practice afterward and spotted something hard to believe. Michael Jackson, receiver, had run an end-around and thrown the ball 60 yards in the air.

"Bill rewinds the tape all the way back to Bernie barely getting it beyond 30 to 35 yards," recalled Phil Savage, coach and scout. "And in his colorful communication skills he says, 'What the fuck? Guys, look at this. This asshole barely cracks 35 against the wind, and we've got a receiver who just launched it 60.' You could get a sense he was building a case in his mind that Bernie was at the end.

"Tranquill was in a tough position. He was the middleman, and he got caught in a vortex. He was close to Bernie, and Bernie thinks he can play and Bill thinks he's washed up. Tranquill said to [Belichick], 'If you want to fire him, that's your prerogative. But let's not sit here and ridicule this guy.'"

During the Browns' bye week, Belichick suddenly cut two respected veterans, cornerback Everson Walls and linebacker David Brandon, shaking up his team despite its 5-2 record. Belichick would shake up the entire city, state, and league on November 8, Black Monday, the day after the Browns lost yet another game to John Elway's Broncos. Elway was tremendous, as always, and Kosar was something less than that. Down 29–7 at home, with thousands of fans already out in the parking lots, Kosar ran the final play of his Cleveland Browns career.

Leroy Hoard, running back out of Michigan, was a big admirer of Kosar's ability to overcome all of his physical shortcomings. With Bernie, Hoard said, "you kind of had to close your eyes and wait for it to happen." Kosar threw the ugliest passes with the ugliest form. He'd plant his front foot to the left, as if he were throwing to that side, and then fool the shifting defense by spinning the ball down the middle of the field. Somehow, some way, the damn thing found its target. Bernie was the great improviser, and in what would be his final huddle as a Brown he was going to do some improvising with Belichick's call. He was going to come up with a play that he would later say he just "drew up in the dirt."

"We were in the huddle, and Bernie gets down on a knee and looks up at Jack [Michael Jackson]," Hoard said. "'You're supposed to run a corner on this play, but I want you to take three steps to the corner and, if it's Cover 2, hit the seam and go to the post. That ball will be in the air.' I'll be damned, that ball was in the air and Jack came out of that break and it was a touchdown. Imagine the face on your coach, who's so organized, with everyone on the same page, to see that play as a touchdown. Bill had to think, *If I let this fly, how far is this going to go?*"

Belichick wasn't about to let it fly, not anymore. Metcalf said Kosar was famous for looking over at the sideline from the huddle and ignoring the plays the coaches wanted him to run. In this case, people on the sideline said Belichick screamed obscenities at Kosar, who then returned fire. One starter who disagreed with Kosar's stubborn approach to play calling, who saw it as insubordination, heard Belichick shout at the quarterback, "Run the play, motherfucker." So Belichick met with Modell that Sunday night. The coach walked upstairs to the owner's office after every home game to share thoughts on the wins and losses, to decompress, but there would be no winding down this time.

Belichick and Modell met for three hours that night and, with the backing of Jim Brown and Mike Lombardi, who had been promoted to director of player personnel, the coach convinced Modell that Kosar not only was shot physically, but was playing for himself. It wasn't an easy sell. Modell had watched Kosar play a full half against Miami on a broken ankle the year before and nearly pull out a victory in what the owner, as well as Dolphins coach Don Shula, said was the gutsiest thing they had seen. Bernie was his quarterback, his guy, his football son.

Modell went home that night saddened by what he was about to do. He called for a meeting of the entire staff the next morning, and when the owner entered that meeting room, he told the assistants he wanted to go around the table and hear their opinions on whether Kosar should stay or go. Savage was in the room, and he recalled that John Mitchell, defensive line coach, was called on first.

"No way he was going against Bill," Savage said of Mitchell. "Each coach fell in line. [Receivers coach] Richard Mann advocated for Bernie but said he's not the same guy. Everyone said Bernie's not the same guy."

Modell had his answer. "Once we make this move," he told the group, "the fires will be roaring tonight."

Kosar was summoned to Modell's office around 11:30 a.m.; the quarterback figured his boss wanted to talk about the offense. When he entered and saw Belichick, he realized that this wasn't going to be a shoot-the-shit session about expanding the passing game. Kosar was told he was fired. "It was a painful experience for Bernie and myself," Modell said. "We talked to him. I talked to him." Kosar then asked if he could talk to Modell alone. Belichick left the room, and quarterback and owner spent their last 20 minutes together as employee and employer.

When word got out, fans reacted as if Modell had fired Paul Brown all over again. The Browns' switchboard lit up with ticketholders demanding their money back, and angry fans called and faxed the local papers and radio stations to vent about Belichick, who described the move as "the most difficult decision I've ever made or been a part of." Belichick spoke of his respect for Kosar as a person and competitor but pointed out he was 5-11 in his last 16 games.

"Basically," the coach said, "it came down to his overall production and the diminishing of his physical skills."

Kosar was deeply hurt by the claim that he couldn't be a winning quarterback anymore, and he ripped Belichick for running off Reggie Langhorne and Webster Slaughter, who had caught a combined 21 passes for 338 yards and two touchdowns for Indianapolis and Houston the previous day. Kosar said the Browns had attempted to portray him as uncoachable, a notion he called bullshit.

"How ironic is it that my last pass was a 38-yard post pattern for a touchdown, huh?" he asked.

Modell had no choice but to go along with this in support of a coach he'd already predicted would be the last one he hired. As he walked into the press conference with Belichick, he turned to the PR man, Byrne, and said, "You know, a lot of owners would be in the South of France today."

The front-page headline in the *Plain Dealer* the next morning read SACKED, in big, bold wartime type next to a picture of Kosar, in uniform, bowing his helmetless head. The four lines of subheads on the front page read this way:

BROWNS BOUNCE BERNIE
HE'S LOST IT, BELICHICK SAYS
I HAVE NOT, KOSAR INSISTS
FANS IN A FRENZY

The Kosar firing took up almost the entire front page, save a story on the upcoming Al Gore–Ross Perot debate over NAFTA on CNN's *Larry King Live*. Inside the pages of the *Akron Beacon Journal*, a 20-year-old student at Baldwin Wallace was pictured holding a sign that read CUT BELICHICK, NOT KOSAR! and she was reported to be among a dozen students protesting outside the team's Berea facility.

"I took my window facing the street, where I watched film," Savage said. "I took a handkerchief and waved it outside the window like a white flag."

One of the players hit the hardest was Kosar's center, Steve Everitt, a first-round pick out of Michigan who had grown up a Hurricanes fan in Miami. He idolized Bernie and considered the opportunity to be his teammate a dream come true.

"When that happened to Bernie," Everitt said, "it was like a relative had died. The mood was awful on the team."

It was just as bad around the city. Times were so tense, Belichick's children, who attended the private Old Trail School, in Bath, were no longer riding the bus to school, in order to stay clear of teasing classmates.

"It was hard on us," Debby Belichick would say. "There were threatening calls made to the office, and the kids had people watching them on the playground at school. We had people watching the house, and it became so absurd that I'd look out the window and wonder, *Hmm, should I make them some lunch?* I wanted to laugh about it because it was so ridiculous, but we actually had to be very careful."

The Belichick children wouldn't be attending any more games in 1993. Though the shocked players didn't have a choice, many of them couldn't understand why, with Testaverde injured and the Browns still holding a share of first place, they would have to play the next four games without an established quarterback. Todd Philcox, the healthy alternative, had one career start to his name.

"Why would you do that," Michael Dean Perry asked, "when we had no other quarterback?"

"I believe cutting Bernie at that point was a mistake," said kicker Matt Stover. "I felt they should've benched him."

"We're 5-3," Eric Metcalf said, "so for us, that's what felt kind of silly at the time . . . Bernie didn't change the play into an unsuccessful play. He made it happen. You can call it insubordination all you want, but he gave us opportunities to win. I thought that's what it was all about."

"We had enough issues," Rob Burnett said, "so don't cut him. Cut him after the season. We thought nobody was safe after that, but we already knew that. The Bernie thing was unnecessary, but Belichick was running around with the sickle."

Over two weeks, the sickle had claimed Walls, Brandon, and then the biggest available victim, Kosar.

"We had a winning record," said Anthony Pleasant, "and all of a sudden he made all those cuts and we went downhill from there."

It wasn't fair to Philcox, who simply wasn't qualified to handle the immense responsibility just dropped in his lap. In the quarterbacks' room, he'd watched Kosar decipher defenses and predict alignments as if he were a veteran coordinator. On the field, he'd watched Kosar "chewing out a guy's ass" whenever a teammate wasn't meeting Bernie's standards of effort and execution.

But Philcox saw what everyone else saw in the Kosar-Belichick relationship. "They certainly butted heads," he said. "It was obvious, and you could see it escalating to a degree." The fallout had Philcox starting on the road against Seattle. Tranquill and Savage rode next to each other on the team bus that day. Tranquill turned to his friend and said, "What in the world is going on? The end of time is upon us."

On the very first play from scrimmage, Philcox dropped back to pass and had the ball knocked from his hand by Seattle's Terry Wooden. Robert Blackmon scooped it up and ran it into the end zone. Fourteen seconds into the game and the Browns were already down a touchdown in what would be a dispiriting 22–5 defeat. Philcox completed 9 of 25 passes for 85 yards. He fumbled twice, threw two interceptions, and was sacked for a safety.

"He was in a tough situation," said Belichick, the man who put him there.

Meanwhile, new Dallas Cowboys quarterback Bernie Kosar — acquired as insurance behind the injured Troy Aikman — completed 13 of 21 passes for 199 yards and a touchdown and avoided any interceptions or sacks in leading his team to victory over the Phoenix Cardinals. Kosar suddenly had a chance to win the Super Bowl ring that had eluded him in Cleveland, and the Browns suddenly had a better chance of missing the playoffs.

Modell and Belichick were sitting ducks, all alone on an island surrounded by hostile seas. Everyone felt free to take a shot at them. Gary Danielson, an ESPN broadcaster and an ex-teammate of Kosar's with the Browns, was introduced to a Cleveland scout named Terry McDonough when they crossed paths at the University of Kentucky before a Wildcats football game. Danielson opened their conversation by saying, "I'm one of Kosar's best friends. You cut him. Your head coach is a jerk and I hope you lose every one of your games." Caught by surprise, McDonough didn't get a chance to gather his thoughts and respond until seeing Danielson again ten minutes later.

"Hey, Gary," he called out. "Did you mean what you said about Coach Belichick?"

"Yeah," Danielson said.

McDonough, who cut a thick, intimidating figure, jumped out of his chair and chased a cowering Danielson out the door while screaming obscenities at him and threatening to kick his ass.

Not many Clevelanders remained quite as loyal to Belichick. At the Browns' next home game, their first since Bernie was bounced, tens of thousands of pissed-off fans showed up to protest this unfathomable mistake by the lake. Fans outside the stadium sold BILL SUCKS T-shirts, Kosar masks, and BOOT BELICHICK bumper stickers. Signs hung inside read CAN THE LITTLE MAN and WILL ROGERS NEVER MET BILL BELICHICK, and a banner tethered to a plane flying above the stadium read JUMP ART AND TAKE BELICHICK WITH YOU. GO BK.

Modell knew that cutting Kosar would temporarily change the way the fans looked at the coach and the team, but he'd underestimated the impact of the move. "Bernie did a masterful job of making us look villainous on that," said Jim Bailey, Browns executive vice president. "I don't blame him at all. We didn't realize he was that good at it."

The Browns next lost to the Houston Oilers; of course they did. Philcox threw four interceptions, and when it was over, three police officers escorted Belichick off the field. A mob of some 200 to 300 fans gathered outside the Browns' locker room and repeated a chant first heard in the fourth quarter, "Bill must go," along with "We want Belichick." The fans might as well have been carrying torches and pitchforks. They were shouting and banging on metal trash cans along the concourse, and when the losing coach appeared, a circle of cops with billy clubs led him to the postgame interview room, housed in a nearby trailer.

Belichick could still hear the calls for his head as he took the podium and faced the news media. His wife cried while watching the televised scene from her loge. "To quote Buddy Ryan," Bill said, "if you listen to the fans, you will be up there with them. I have to do what I think is right, and I've been doing that. I know this team is headed in the right direction."

The security detail led him safely back to the locker room. Belichick lost three of his next four games, leaving him 1-5 since making the most difficult decision of his football life. Before one of those post-Bernie games, Debby Belichick was helping collect canned goods for a charitable cause while a man was selling a BILL SUCKS T-shirt ten feet away and an FBI agent was watching her in response to the phoned-in threats.

The head coach of the Cleveland Browns was taking hits all over the league. In a *Houston Chronicle* column, under the headline "Browns' Belichick Unpopular with Everyone," respected NFL writer John McClain wrote the following:

"In 14 years of covering the Oilers, I never have seen a coach work harder at being a cold fish than the Browns' Bill Belichick. He possesses the worst communicative skills of any coach I have interviewed . . . In the wake of the Bernie Kosar debacle, Browns fans are finding out what most of the players and reporters who cover the team knew — that Belichick is an insecure control freak with a little man's mentality. The chip on his shoulder is the size of a football, and anyone who even thinks about questioning his authority is given a bus ticket out of town."

Gary Tranquill didn't question Belichick's authority. He only questioned Belichick's qualifications to be heavily involved in the offense. He thought his boss treated him very well personally, but professionally he felt suffocated. "I managed it for three years," Tranquill said, "and it got to a point where I just said, 'This is not worth it. A lot of things are going on here that's not the way it should be.' And I decided it was time for me to leave."

So he left Cleveland after another 7-9 season, becoming the latest casualty of the Belichick regime. Modell was growing impatient. He was already on record saying he would "get out of town" if he had to fire this head coach. Only a winning season in 1994 might prevent all that from happening. But then again, maybe not.

Art Modell told associates that he felt like Professor Henry Higgins, the Rex Harrison character in *My Fair Lady* who tried to teach the Aubrey Hepburn character, a Cockney flower girl named Eliza Doolittle, how to lose her working-class accent and talk like a duchess. Bill Belichick was that kind of project.

Modell's wife, Pat, told her husband to buy the coach some suits and get him out of those dreadful cutoff sweats. Pat told Art to tell Bill to sit up and stand straight in press conferences, to speak clearly, and to comb his hair now and then. But turning the Browns' head coach into a refined gentleman would be harder than turning the Browns into serious contenders.

In the film room and on the practice field, Belichick was in the habit of referring to opponents and even his own players as "fucking assholes." Belichick didn't berate people in a Parcellsian way, but some of his players thought he was the most profane coach they'd ever had.

"I don't think he's going to run a seminar on public relations," Art Modell said.

This would become readily apparent to those who worked with Belichick on his weekly *Browns Insider* TV show, which was often filmed on Tuesday or Wednesday morning at 4:30 or 5:30, the coach's preferred hour. Belichick's cohost was Jim Mueller, who had a good working relationship with the coach.

"We tried to soften Bill's personality," Mueller said, "so the fans could see he's not just this gruff guy with one-sentence answers."

Belichick had a photographic memory, or something close to it, and he could read a page of a script once and spit it back out. Sometimes during the show's walk-through he'd read a question in the script that he didn't want to answer on camera, like this one: "When you're driving in your car, what music do you listen to?" A perfectly harmless question for a Jon Bon Jovi friend who loved rock music, of course, yet Belichick wanted no part of it.

"What do you want me to say when I'm asked this?" he asked a crew member.

"Why don't you say what you listen to in the car?" the crew member responded.

"I'll tell you why," Belichick said. "It's nobody's fucking business what I listen to in the car. It's nobody's fucking business where my wife gets her hair done. It's nobody's fucking business where my kid goes to school, and it's nobody's fucking business that I even drive my car. So what do you want me to answer?"

"Bill, you're friends with Bon Jovi. You're friends from back in New Jersey, and you went on tour with him. OK?"

Belichick was asked the $100,000 question during the taping, and everyone on the set held their collective breath. Asked what music he listened to in his car, Belichick answered with two words: "Bon Jovi." Those two words, nothing more. Mueller wanted to know if they should reshoot the exchange and was immediately told by the crew that there would be no do-over.

The Browns kept trying with Belichick. They understood that in the cold grayness of winter in places like Cleveland, Green Bay, and Buffalo the locals desperately needed something to warm up to, something to lift their spirits. They knew that their owner, Modell, would invite fans into the huddle if he could, and that Belichick would rather keep them as far away from his team as possible.

So they brought in a comedian, Mike Veneman, to lighten up their show. Veneman did a cooking segment with Belichick that opened with the coach wearing a Browns sweatshirt and introducing what he called his "BBPBJ" recipe. "Bill Belichick's Peanut Butter and Jelly Sandwich," he said. "How divine," replied Veneman, wearing a white apron. Belichick proceeded to spread peanut butter on both slices of raisin bread (he said his mother liked to use raisin bread), explaining how that approach prevented the jelly from leaking through the bread. "That's why you're the head coach," Veneman said. "It's forward thinking like that. I've never seen that."

Belichick actually thought that segment was funny. "Other than that," a crew member said, "it was awful."

Belichick was the ultimate long-term project. One off-camera stunt that many didn't find humorous could've gotten the coach in trouble with the league. In an apparent attempt to lighten the mood among his players, Belichick allowed two exotic dancers to appear before them, according to six people in the room. The witnesses provided different accounts of what the women did. One defensive player said the dancers "got totally naked." Another defensive player said they were wearing outfits that resembled Playboy Bunny outfits. "They didn't strip down or anything," that player said, "but some guys thought it went too far."

A third player said he left the room when he saw the women arrive and someone else roll out Visqueen on the floor, suggesting a potential act he did not care to witness. One offensive player said the women didn't strip down naked. "It was hilarious, and it was to make a point," he said. "No titties were exposed, I will tell you this."

All witnesses agreed that some players remained in their seats and enjoyed the entertainment, others remained in their seats and ignored the women, finding their presence silly and uninteresting, and others walked out of the room in protest of something they found in poor taste. One player estimated that half a dozen Browns walked out.

One of the Browns who left the room thought Belichick was trying to bond with the team and had just picked the wrong approach.

"Desperate people do desperate things," said one defensive player. "Bill was trying to do anything to loosen up the team . . . It turned some guys off . . . I didn't feel right about it. I didn't think it was appropriate at that time."

"He saw how frustrated and tired we were," another defensive player said of Belichick, "and he thought this was going to make us happy. It didn't make me happy. I didn't need to see that. I'd rather go home. I don't think a lot of the guys needed it."

One offensive player said the female dancers had been brought in as part of a rookie show. NFL teams had long staged training-camp talent shows that were tied to relatively benign rookie hazing. Sometimes these NFL talent shows could get a little raunchy and things could get a little carried away, in the middle of a long, brutal camp.

"It wasn't crazy like a strip show," the offensive player said. "We laughed. I was happy about it. We were tired of looking at each other all day. So this was something better to look at."

Another offensive player said that veteran Browns were booing rookie performers one night, and that Belichick responded by telling the rookies they'd have to rise early and run the hill if they didn't pick up the entertainment a notch. "I think more than anything, bringing in the dancers," the offensive player said, "that was one of the nights that the rookies were supposed to do something. I don't know if Bill did it. I think it was the rookies that did it. We laughed."

Some Browns executives were later made aware of the appearance of the female dancers in the facility but took no apparent action against their coach. As it was, Belichick couldn't afford to take another direct public relations hit. Bud Shaw, *Plain Dealer* columnist, recalled a training-camp day when Belichick was asked on live TV about the number of defensive backs he planned to keep. The coach just buried his head in his hands for what felt like two minutes before finally looking up and saying, "Six. I don't know."

This from a man whose wife once cut out newspaper articles that mentioned him as a Giants assistant to put in a scrapbook. This from a man who handed out playbooks to his team that included a page titled "Cooperating With News Media," which opened with these two paragraphs:

Reasonable cooperation with the news media is essential to the continuing popularity of our game and its players.

It is important that each coach and player be courteous and prompt in associations and appointments with radio and television broadcasters and newspaper reporters. Please recognize that each member of the media, like you, has a job to perform.

The Belichick playbook included pages on the running-hole numbering system (even numbers to the defense's left, odd to the right), the defensive signal system (including calls "Steeler 1 Lock" and "K.C. Red Dog"), and master's degree research from ex–Browns assistant John Teerlinck on how athletes react to stimuli. It included calls for the "Under" alignment (including "Under Viking" and "Under Wide"), the "Over" alignment ("Over Stack Viking"), and the 4-3 ("4-3 Solid" and "4-3 Plus"). It included a "Cover 2" summation that said the defense was designed to "allow very few touchdown passes" and to "force the ball to be thrown short and outside," and that listed audibles including "White" (Cover 2), "Larry" (zone left), and "Roger" (zone right).

For Belichick, the most pertinent page in the Cleveland playbook concluded with this paragraph: "The media is a direct link between you and the fans who support our game. Therefore, it is important to you and this organization that you present yourself to the media in a manner and style in which you yourself would like to be received and treated."

And yet team executives were forever worrying about the damage Belichick might've been doing to the brand with his daily disdain for the sporting press. "Bill just had no respect for the media, or didn't demonstrate any," Jim Bailey said. "Those guys were very tough — a tough media at that time — and he just couldn't bring himself to cooperate very much . . . I never confronted him; I know our PR guys did. We always felt he could've made life easier without hurting the franchise . . . He would come in and slouch down in his chair and stare down at his shoes and mutter one-word answers. It was a really difficult situation."

On the other hand, Ernie Adams told the *Beacon Journal*, local reporters and columnists needed to accept part of the blame for the way Belichick treated them. "To read some of this stuff," he said, "you would have thought that Bill was down there in the bunker at the end of World War II with Eva Braun."

The players were among the constituents who yearned to experience a kinder, gentler, more human side of their boss. Perry was among the team leaders who occasionally led a boycott of Belichick's mandate to practice in full pads.

Before the Monday night game against the 49ers, Perry and Ball decided they couldn't allow their boss to go ahead with a third consecutive day of hitting. They ordered their teammates to leave their pads in their stalls and head out for stretching. Belichick made his way to the field with his practice plan in hand and found his players in helmets and shorts. He looked down at his paper that said they were supposed to be dressed in full pads. He threw up his hands, rolled up the paper, and walked up to Clay Matthews and Mike Johnson, who pointed toward Perry and Ball, who were stretching in the back row.

"Bill got back there to us, fuming," Ball said. "He came over to me and Michael Dean and said, 'If we don't win, it's going to be your ass.' And we beat the 49ers . . . We had some motivation for that game."

The scene captured the disconnect between Belichick and his players. "Technically," Metcalf said, "we were his guinea pigs. It was his first deal. It was a tough group to have as your guinea pigs." The old guard, he meant, had been entrenched and perhaps more than a bit entitled. Belichick could've done more to bridge the gap. Burnett recalled that whenever the coach passed players on his walk from facility to field, or field to facility, he avoided a typical exchange of pleasantries. "As soon as guys would go, 'Hey, Coach,'" Burnett said, "he would look the other way."

Sometimes Belichick ignored front-office types, too. One midlevel executive was sure he was about to be fired after he approached Belichick in the hallway, only to have the head coach look through him and walk away as if he weren't even there. (The executive wasn't fired.)

Belichick was wearing out the people he worked with, including Saban. The defensive coordinator was looking a bit run-down by the 1994 season; he seemed to have aged in his four-year term at the rate of a United States president. He told one associate he had no use for his boss's restrictions on assistants talking to the news media. Saban dearly wanted to land a big-time head coaching job, and he wanted more freedom to talk to get his name out there. "I'm not going to be Bill Belichick's defensive coordinator forever," Saban told the associate, who said there was less communication between Saban and Belichick in '94 than there had been in their three previous seasons together.

"At the end of the day," Rob Burnett said, "[Belichick] didn't allow Nick to be the best . . . Nick expressed some frustration. At the end, it wasn't the best relationship."

But their Tuesday game-plan meetings, coaches and scouts said, were a thing to behold; their genius for football was on full display. Belichick always encouraged his assistants to offer their opinions, even if — or especially if — they conflicted with his, and he went back and forth with his coordinator over this or that scheme. Belichick and Saban did share a philosophy of building a defense around big, bruising players in the middle of the lineup. And with their defense leading the league in points allowed, eventually surrendering only 204 (30 points fewer than the second-ranked defense in Pittsburgh), Belichick and Saban also shared a frustration with an offense that was improving and finally had an official coordinator — Steve Crosby, who had been a de facto coordinator late in '93 — but was still not ranked among the league's top ten in points scored.

That frustration contributed to Saban's own dour moods. He was a small man with "the voice of a 6′5″, 280-pound guy," said safety Louis Riddick, and he ran as hot as Belichick ran cold. Riddick said the head coach "had a way of undressing you in a meeting room when watching tape," usually with a laser beam pointing out a player's mistakes. Steve Everitt, center, said Belichick often made the Browns laugh with his stinging critiques about everyone from his own players to opposing assistants. "He'd be like 'There's no fucking way Al Groh is going to come in here and beat us. Fucking Al Groh, you've got to be kidding me,'" Everitt said. "He'd be like 'Vinny, we're not playing fucking Georgia Tech next week.' That's how he knew how to push guys' buttons. It was fun to watch."

By contrast, Saban was almost never fun to watch or to be around. He was always rocking back and forth in his chair, as if preparing to launch himself into someone's sorry ass. "Not good enough — *do it again!*" Saban screamed over and over in practice. He often used poor Phil Savage as his personal tackling dummy, verbally blasting him at every turn. The coordinator also used Savage and a couple of other slapdicks, or slappies, George Kokinos and Jim Schwartz, to landscape the property around the pond in his yard. Scouts sometimes were sent on "Saban rehab" assignments to look at small-college talent. "Saban rehab," said one Browns staffer, "was just getting away from him."

Schwartz ran the team's tape room, where Belichick and Newsome and the rest of the coaches and personnel men regularly returned the tapes they'd taken out to watch. "Not Saban," the staffer said. "Belichick could be a dick when it was time to be a dick. Saban was a dick all the time."

Nick used to chew Red Man tobacco, and during one set of warm-up drills he accidentally spat a huge wad of chew all over safety Bennie Thompson's leg and didn't bother to apologize. During one film session, Saban went on a tirade after watching a pass rusher on another team break through the line, fall down, and then make little effort to get up while the opposing quarterback was preparing to throw the ball. "He just laid up there like a freakin' fish," one veteran in the room said of the fallen pass rusher, "and [Saban] goes, 'I want you sons of bitches to roll and give [the quarterback's] ass a surgical knee.' That's what he said. He goes, 'Hit the ground and start fucking rolling and give his ass a surgical knee.' And I was like 'What did he just say?'"

The NFL was never for the faint of heart, and in the end Belichick needed Saban on that defense as much as Parcells had needed Belichick with the Giants. The coordinator was so thorough, so detailed, so good, he was as valuable as any playing member of his unit. Riddick said Saban taught at a Ph.D. level, telling the defensive backs how their feet should be set, where their eyes should go once the ball was snapped, and then the second place they should go while the play unfolded. And as volatile as he could be during the week, Saban was just as composed on Sundays.

"He yelled and screamed and spit and motherfucked you; he just was very rude and condescending," Burnett said. "But on game day he was about as calm as an Olympic pool . . . whether we were winning by 20 or losing by 50."

His defense didn't even give up 13 points a game in '94, which was a very good thing for his boss. The only way Belichick was going to win over the team and the town, especially after the Kosar firing, was to win, and win big. And in year four of his program, his vision started to come into focus at last.

Belichick never stopped grinding in search of even the slightest competitive advantage. He slept overnight on a couch in his office, using an afghan his wife had knitted for him back in his assistant days in Denver, just to get an earlier start on the game plan in the morning. He pored over newspaper clippings from the market of his upcoming opponent to find a revealing quote or injury update — something, anything, that might give the Browns an edge that Sunday. He held long Saturday afternoon meetings with his staff during the season — home or away — that his secondary coach and future coordinator, Rick Venturi, called "unheard of." He made sure the cafeteria was stocked with healthy food for the players, even as he enjoyed eating buckets of Johnson's Popcorn from the boardwalk in Ocean City, New Jersey, Mike Lombardi's hometown.

Belichick didn't ask his assistants to work longer hours than he did. "I don't know if he ever went home," said Woody Widenhofer, linebackers coach. Belichick had dinner served at the facility so the coaches could refuel and work deep into the night. The offensive and defensive staffs watched film together, and they watched both sides of the ball so an offensive coach could offer his opinion on what the defense was doing, and vice versa. That made the nights longer than they were in most corners of the NFL. "I'd never seen that before," Widenhofer said.

Sometimes Belichick wanted to make changes to game plans at midnight, and wanted them made right away. He didn't slow down in the off-season, either. Venturi recalled one Friday, a couple of weeks before the draft, that was supposed to precede a rare weekend off. Suddenly Belichick summoned the defensive staffers for a 5 p.m. meeting to assign them film review of about a dozen college prospects who were likely to go undrafted. Thinking of his weekend plans, and hoping Belichick could wait until the following Tuesday or Wednesday for the reports, Venturi asked him when he wanted the work completed. Belichick shot his assistant a look. "As soon as possible," he said. The weekend off became a weekend on.

The grind took a toll on everyone who tried to keep up with Belichick's pace. "I got into coaching for fun," Widenhofer told a co-worker. "And this isn't fun."

Fun simply wasn't a part of Belichick's assistant-coach playbook. Kirk Ferentz was working at the University of Maine when he interviewed for a job coaching the Browns' offensive line. Belichick subjected him to a stone-faced interrogation like he'd never before faced, and Ferentz was sure he'd failed miserably, before getting a second call and, ultimately, the offer. The upside? Everyone agreed that Belichick let his assistants coach on the field, didn't suffocate them, and gave them room to succeed or fail.

He had put together what turned out to be an all-star squad of future NFL and major-college head coaches and NFL executives. Saban, Ferentz, Scott O'Brien (special teams), and Pat Hill (tight ends, offensive line) were among the very best at what they did. Hill was tough enough to have challenged 250-pound linebacker Pepper Johnson to a fight. Eric Mangini, a graduate of Belichick's Wesleyan, where Mangini set sacks records as an undersize noseguard, was a ball boy, and Thomas Dimitroff was a grounds-crew member who watched film with Scott Pioli, pro personnel assistant, while covered in grass clippings and paint. Schwartz was a personnel scout who worked on research projects. The young slappies made their football contributions when they weren't running out for cigarettes for the secretaries and staffers, or taking the coaches' cars for oil changes, or grabbing a few hours of sleep nearby at the no-frills Acadian apartment complex.

And of course there was Ernie Adams. Modell famously said he'd pay anyone $10,000 if he or she could explain what, exactly, Adams did for a living, but Belichick thought his friend was worth a whole lot more than that.

Adams wasn't the only former Giant who was part of Belichick's team. Though the likes of Joe Morris, running back Lee Rouson, Mark Bavaro, and Everson Walls had come and gone, Johnson and Carl Banks were together again in 1994, giving Belichick a combined 20 years of NFL experience at linebacker. The coach had a lot of talent on his front line, too, and a philosophy against substandard offensive lines — rush five defenders to force weak pass protectors to go one-on-one — that worked more often than not.

The '94 Browns won eight of their first ten games, with the defense allowing ten or fewer points five times, and with serviceable quarterbacking from Vinny Testaverde and his new backup, Mark Rypien, who had been a Super Bowl MVP for Washington. They suffered two painful losses in one weekend — the loss of Saban to Michigan State, as head coach, on Saturday, and then a loss in Municipal Stadium to Belichick's former employer, the Giants, the following day. Saban had overcome his boss's media relations policy after all, but he did stay on for the rest of the season. Belichick appointed a secretary to help him with his Michigan State business while Saban remained committed to the Browns.

A week later, in the best showing of Belichick's head coaching career, the Browns beat the two-time-defending-champion, Troy Aikman/Emmitt Smith/Michael Irvin–led Dallas Cowboys on the road in December when Dallas tight end Jay Novacek was stopped inches short of a game-winning touchdown on the final play. "Hopefully," Belichick said afterward, "we'll play these guys again." He was talking about Super Bowl possibilities for his 10-4 Browns, who gave a game ball to Modell and clinched a wild-card playoff berth when Buffalo lost the next day. And yet this football town couldn't fully embrace this football team. By all accounts, the 1994 Browns were the least loved playoff team in the history of Cleveland sports.

The animus centered around one man. Michael Dean Perry shot down the notion that players were growing more comfortable with Belichick's style. "Deep down," he said, "guys are no happier with him. It's just a smoke-screen because we're winning . . . You just don't feel comfortable with him."

Belichick maintained that his fan mail was more supportive than the media coverage of him might suggest. Then again, he swore he didn't much care. "I saw this city run Lenny Wilkens out of town," he said of the former Cavaliers coach, "and, basically, Marty Schottenheimer. There was a lot of negativity about the Cavs when they lost to Michael Jordan — whose fault is that? I don't mind not being the flavor of the month."

Yet the fans did. Winning used to be enough in Cleveland, but no more. Tony Jones, left tackle, explained it this way:

"People just can't forget the Bernie thing, and they hate the coach."

The coach did what he could to overcome the hate. He established a simple method of defeating his opponents: identify their strengths and then scheme the best way to neutralize them.

"Bill is the most practical football coach I've ever worked with," Venturi said. "He's never going to ask his players to do something they can't do. We'd spend hours before we ever put up an X and an O on Monday or Tuesday, studying matchups versus teams, and at the end of the day he'd say to us as a staff, 'OK, these two guys don't beat me . . . and I don't want to have this discussion again on Sunday.' And then he'd let you go at it."

Even though he was a believer in the height, weight, and speed measurables, Belichick pressed his assistants to think creatively, and independently, when evaluating talent to potentially add to the Cleveland roster. He once had VHS tapes distributed to every coach and scout that purported to highlight a pass-rushing prospect named Rodney Spinks, at Northern State. The staffers did their evaluations and met in the draft room with Belichick to go over their reports. Almost everyone in the room had serious concerns about Rodney Spinks. Terry McDonough was about the only evaluator at the table who liked Spinks, despite the substandard competition he was facing at Northern State. McDonough said the kid reminded him of Leon Lett, of the Dallas Cowboys, a seventh-round pick out of Emporia State, in Kansas, who would develop into a two-time Pro Bowler.

As it turned out, Rodney Spinks *was* Leon Lett: Belichick had come up with a phantom player from a phantom school to see if his evaluators could rise above their preconceived notions about no-name prospects from nowhere conferences.

The head coach also challenged himself to fortify his roster under the NFL's brand-new salary-cap system. Out was Plan B free agency (the players fought against its restrictions in federal court), and in was a less confining form of free agency and a hard $34.6 million cap. Belichick figured it out, despite some uninspiring results (at best) with his grading system in the draft. True, the Browns had picked a few winners in 1991 — Eric Turner in the first round, defensive tackle James Jones in the third, and receiver Michael Jackson in the sixth. They found a dependable center in Steve Everitt in the first round in '93. Belichick and Lombardi also found a productive receiver, Derrick Alexander, with a compensatory pick at the end of the first round in '94.

But they had missed badly throughout much of the '92 draft and needed to compensate later with undrafted free agents such as Orlando Brown and Wally Williams (a pair of Rodney Spinkses), who grew into starters on the offensive line. (Brown had so wanted to impress the Browns during a workout at South Carolina State that he blasted Scott Pioli in a blocking drill and nearly knocked him over.) Belichick honored his commitment to finding players in the middle of the field by making his first three first-rounders a safety, a fullback, and a center, taken with the second, ninth, and 14th overall picks, which seemed high for those positions.

The Browns didn't have a 1,000-yard rusher on the roster, nor did they have a 1,000-yard receiver. They overcame their deficiencies with a defense that beat the mighty Cowboys on the road and allowed 258 fewer points than the Cleveland defense Belichick and Saban had inherited in 1991.

At 11-5, they had earned an honest-to-God home playoff game. The New England Patriots were the opponent, and they were coached by someone who didn't need a scouting report to understand the strengths and weaknesses of Bill Belichick.

When Bill Parcells was between NFL jobs and working a Browns game for NBC Sports, he had one question for Cleveland staffers. "Where's Doom?" he would say.

Parcells found Doom on New Year's Day 1995, in a rematch of a regular-season game between the Browns and the Patriots that was won by Belichick. (Parcells won their first meeting, in 1993.) Big Bill and Little Bill had talked once a week during the season, sharing information on common opponents and supporting each other on various issues, including the Kosar crisis. "Our relationship is certainly much different than when we were working together," Parcells said. In other words, it was much better.

"He did a tremendous amount for me," Big Bill said. "Many of the things he created defensively we're still using, and we've expanded on them."

For his part, Little Bill called Parcells a good personal friend and raved about the experience of working under him. "I'm glad he feels I gave something back, because he certainly gave me a lot," Belichick said. "Bill's meant an awful lot to me and my career, not just on the football field but dealing with a lot of things off the field . . . I think we have a pretty full relationship all the way across the board, and I respect and cherish all the parts of it."

Now Belichick had a better understanding of the pressures confronting an NFL head coach, and of how they could drive a man like Parcells to berate Little Bill and his fellow Giants assistants. But the improved relationship with Big Bill did nothing to temper Belichick's desire to beat him. In fact, some ex-Giants always wondered if the connection between Parcells and Belichick was really all it was made out to be.

Mark Bavaro pointed out that Steve Belichick was really the one who had taught Bill how to coach. "So I don't think Bill was really a Parcells guy," Bavaro said. "Bill was always his own man, and knowing that while looking back on some clips of them arguing and butting heads, it's much more understandable. Probably Bill at the time, when Parcells was yelling at him, he was thinking to himself, 'I could probably do a better job than you if you give me those headsets.'"

Parcells was the two-time Super Bowl champ and newly named Associated Press coach of the year when he entered Cleveland's Municipal Stadium on New Year's Day, so Belichick had more to lose. Little Bill was still trying to survive. He was still trying to prove that he could have a long and prosperous future as an NFL head coach, and that the post-Kosar culture he'd established in '94 was sustainable. A playoff victory over a Parcells team riding a seven-game winning streak would do a ton for his cause.

"He didn't make it personal with Parcells," said Rick Venturi, secondary coach. "But I know it was. We all felt it was."

Belichick made that clear on the third-quarter drive that decided the game. With the score 10–10, Leroy Hoard ran ten yards for a touchdown. "I got to the sideline," Hoard said, "and [Belichick] was going crazy. And, like, whoa. That was the most excited I ever saw him."

Patriots quarterback Drew Bledsoe threw his third interception of the day in the fourth quarter — the tenth pick of the year for Eric Turner — which set up the Matt Stover field goal that effectively sealed it. Afterward, Parcells hugged Pepper Johnson, Carl Banks, and, of course, Belichick, who told the losing coach, "That's a hell of a job this year, Bill." Belichick would say Parcells was the reason he had gotten the chance to be a head coach.

"In some respects," Big Bill said, "I thought I was playing myself defensively."

"I didn't want to play him," Little Bill said, "and he didn't want to play me. Because one of us had to lose."

Belichick was basking in the victory for obvious reasons. Testaverde, the quarterback he had picked over Kosar, had delivered a terrific, interception-free performance in his postseason debut. Turner, his first draft choice in Cleveland and the No. 2 overall pick in '91, had just made the biggest play of his Pro Bowl year.

"When Bill beat Parcells," Rob Burnett said, "I just saw a glow I'd never seen in that guy. He looked like his first child was born."

That glow would last for only a week. The Steelers had beaten Cleveland twice during the regular season, and they were just too strong for the Browns in their divisional playoff game at Three Rivers Stadium, winning by a 29–9 count. The Browns had lost six games all year, three of them to Pittsburgh and one to Denver. They still hadn't figured out a way to overcome the opponents who forever haunted them.

Burnett, who credited Belichick for easing up on the players before the New England game, criticized him for going too hard before the Pittsburgh game. The defensive end said that the players were sent out for practice "in full pads like animals that week," and that Belichick needed to realize that his players were going to break down if they were constantly asked to go live in drills.

Yet in the immediate wake of the Pittsburgh loss, Belichick wasn't concerning himself with what might hold Cleveland back. In his wrap-up press conference, the coach cited examples of Super Bowl champions who had rebounded from crushing playoff defeats the prior year.

"I've been involved in two of those," Belichick said.

He planned on being involved in a third. Of course, there were plenty of examples of contenders who never recovered from postseason defeat, and the Browns would try to avoid that fate without the help of two of their biggest defensive stars — Saban and Perry, who would be cut for salary-cap savings and later signed by Denver.

By the middle of the 1995 season, those losses would be completely irrelevant. Bill Belichick's Browns were about to discover the meaning of true adversity, the kind that would make even the firings of Bernie Kosar and Paul Brown seem like relatively good days at the office.

On October 27, 1995, when Art Modell secretly boarded a private jet at Baltimore/Washington International and signed a 30-year lease to play in Johnny U's abandoned football town, he rendered himself dead to hundreds of thousands of Browns fans who believed his pledge to never move their team. Modell also destroyed any chance the Browns had of salvaging their season and honoring the Super Bowl predictions made by *Sports Illustrated* and others.

Modell had his reasons for leaving Cleveland. He was in debt, and he had no interest in following his father's path into bankruptcy. He'd watched as taxpayer money helped build new downtown venues for the Indians and the Cavaliers, franchises that didn't have the same hold on the city that the Browns did. He'd been engaged in fruitless negotiations with the city for years in an attempt to refurbish the team's leaky, creaky stadium, which had been built in 1931 and still looked the way the Browns' owner described it — like an "old barn." Modell suffered what he called enormous losses on the ballpark, the Indians had cost him money by moving out (Modell had taken control of Municipal from the city in the mid-1970s), and the advent of NFL free agency had left him in dire need of luxury boxes and club suites to compete. The owner said he needed $175 million in tax dollars to renovate the stadium and give him a Lake Erie home worthy of the area's revitalization. The city wouldn't or couldn't meet his demands. At the time, the Browns were a disappointing 4-4 but still in the mix for a possible playoff berth. On Friday night, November 3, after WBAL-TV, in Baltimore, broke the story that Modell was scheduled to announce the franchise's move that Monday, the owner effectively confessed in a conference call with the *Plain Dealer* and the *Akron Beacon Journal*. He declared his promise that he'd never abandon Cleveland "null and void" and said he'd "blow my stack" if he heard one more complaint that he hadn't given the city a chance to keep the team. "I've been waiting six years for something to happen," Modell said, "and if there's something in the 11th hour where a rabbit can be pulled out of a hat, then I'll know and I'll change my tune."

The people of Cleveland didn't see a rabbit, just a rat. The joy of watching the Indians play in a World Series for the first time in more than four decades was replaced by overwhelming sadness and rage. Mike Snyder, of WTAM, called Modell at home in the early morning — Art always answered before the second ring — and got him out of bed and on the air. Modell wouldn't deny that the move was happening, and Snyder got angrier as the interview unfolded, just like his listeners.

The Browns were routed by the Houston Oilers (who, ironically, were leaving Texas for Tennessee) that Sunday before only 57,881 fans, many of whom spent the day filling Municipal with obscene chants about Modell, who missed his first home game since buying the club for $3.925 million in 1961. The owner had received death threats and was advised not to attend, so he traveled outside the 75-mile radius of the TV blackout to watch with his son David. Modell wasn't there in person to see the fans hold up signs mocking him, to see the Dawg Pound loyalists pointing up at his empty loge and screaming for justice, or to see his football players play as if they'd already packed their bags.

Bill Belichick called the non-effort "embarrassing." Jim Brown said the only time he'd experienced a worse feeling inside Municipal Stadium was when his 1963 Browns played the Cowboys two days after President Kennedy's assassination in Dallas.

The following day, Modell attended a news conference with Maryland governor Parris Glendening and Baltimore mayor Kurt Schmoke and made official a deal that included a rent-free $200 million stadium to be completed next door to the Orioles' park at Camden Yards after his yet-to-be-named franchise played two seasons in Memorial Stadium, old home of the Colts. The team name, the Browns, was about the only thing that Modell wouldn't be allowed to take with him. Baltimore had lost its beloved Colts to Indianapolis in 1984, when owner Bob Irsay had 15 Mayflower trucks load up the operation and flee town in the dead of a snowy March night, and 11 years later Baltimore was striking back, at Cleveland's expense.

"I leave my heart and part of my soul in Cleveland," Modell said. "But frankly, it came down to a simple proposition: I had no choice."

Modell and his family would never again be seen in public in Cleveland. The owner left Belichick, his assistants, and his players to cover the tab. With Modell already in Baltimore for the announcement, Jim Bailey, who had grown up watching the Browns on his grandfather's little black-and-white TV, had called a meeting of the entire organization in the team auditorium to officially deliver the news. Bailey turned toward Belichick as he spoke. "Bill looked like Bill always looked," he would remember. "You've seen that face: the same look he always has. He doesn't show his emotion much. He was in the front. I saw shock on everyone else's face."

Modell did sneak into the Browns' Berea facility for one quick pep talk, though he didn't meet with the Cleveland media afterward. This would be the last time Modell set foot in the Cleveland area. His PR man, Kevin Byrne, relayed the speech his boss gave to the players, which included a vote of confidence in Belichick. "Bill will be your coach in Baltimore," Modell said, via Byrne, "and hopefully, for many years after that."

The players immediately quit on Modell and Belichick, and the season descended into chaos. It was a season that had started with the ill-fated decision to give $17 million to Andre Rison as the alleged missing-piece playmaker to a championship team. (Modell said he had to take out a loan in his wife's name to pay Rison.) It was a season set ablaze by the announcement of the franchise's move before Rison poured gasoline on the fire by saying he couldn't wait to get to Baltimore.

Browns fans were cheering for the visiting teams, and there were reports of bomb threats at the stadium and the Browns' facility. Modell and Belichick were hung in effigy, but only the coach was around to answer for a crisis of someone else's design. "The owner was nowhere to be found," Belichick would recall. "He was in Baltimore. Kind of felt like you were on a deserted island, fending for yourself."

The environment was so hazardous to the team's mental health after four consecutive defeats that Belichick decided to fly his 4-8 team to San Diego two days earlier than planned. Some 2,400 miles away from home, the coach showed both his punitive and softer sides. Rob Burnett said Belichick practiced the Browns in full pads for two hours on Friday, normally a light walk-through day, after being dissatisfied with Thursday's practice. The defensive end would later tell his coach on the flight back to Cleveland, after San Diego's 31–13 victory, that he'd erred in pushing the team so hard. "I said, 'Bill, listen, we're human,'" Burnett recalled. "I always had to say that to him. 'We are human beings, flesh and blood and bones and water, and having to see everything live is not the answer.' He didn't really answer. He was kind of lawyerish. At one point he said, 'Maybe we shouldn't have gone that long Friday.'"

But earlier that week in San Diego, Leroy Hoard said Belichick gave credit cards to coaches and ordered up vans to transport players and told them to have some fun on the coaches' cards. Steve Everitt recalled that Belichick actually met up with the players. "Bill would come out and hang out with us," the center said. "He knew where we were going to be. He'd show up and talk to the older guys."

Down three touchdowns in the Chargers blowout, Belichick absorbed some ridicule for calling timeout with one second left to allow Matt Stover to kick a 40-yard field goal. The kicker was touched. Belichick had to know he would be mocked, and yet he was willing to take the hit to reward a player who was having a good year for him.

"I go out there and make the field goal," Stover said, "and I looked at him and said, 'Wow, Coach, wow. Thank you. That says a lot.' That means he had my back."

On December 17, the 4-10 Browns hosted the 6-8 Bengals in the final football game ever played in Cleveland Municipal Stadium. Fans who had shown up over the years in rain, sleet, and snow had come armed with things to throw onto the field, and with crowbars, wrenches, and saws to cut out pieces of the stadium just as cleanly as Modell had cut out their hearts. Browns sponsors didn't want to be associated with anyone as radioactive as Modell, so all of their signage in the stadium was covered in black. Phil Savage recalled that the black spray paint had fuzzy edges to it, making the covered advertisements look as if they'd been burned. "The stadium looked like it had been put on fire," Savage said.

Though security guards and cops were everywhere, and police choppers circled above, the game took on the feel of a lawless event. Belichick actually felt fear on a football field for the first time. Anytime a team crossed midfield during the game and headed toward the end zone in front of the Dawg Pound, the officiating crew turned that team around and pointed it toward the opposite goal, to avoid the debris being thrown from the Pound. Cleveland and Cincinnati were essentially playing the equivalent of a half-court basketball game.

For once, the Browns played like the Super Bowl contenders they were supposed to be. Testaverde threw two touchdown passes. Earnest Byner, the tragic figure responsible for "the Fumble" in the bygone loss to Denver, had returned to Cleveland after five seasons of exile in Washington and delivered, in this game, his first rushing performance of at least 100 yards in three years.

In the fourth quarter of what would be a 26–10 victory, all anyone could see and hear was the raw sights and sounds of a construction site. Fans used their saws to cut out wooden benches and their tools to unfasten seats and either throw them onto the field or take them home.

As the game ended, players and coaches were being instructed to retreat to their locker rooms as soon as possible. But some Browns stopped and headed for the Dawg Pound, where grown men were weeping like newborns. The players were crying, too. Byner paid his respects, and those who saw him embrace the fans and slap their hands on a victory lap said it appeared as if they were absolving him of his mortal AFC title game sin. Everitt, a 6′5″, 310-pound hulk with rock-star-length hair and a pro wrestler's countenance, was as emotional as anyone as he buried himself in an unwieldy tangle of fans grabbing at him, slapping his shoulder pads, and pulling on his jersey. They didn't want to let him go. They didn't want to let the team go.

The field was littered with the nuts and bolts and batteries and garbage hurled from the stands. One family in a Dodge caravan pulled out of the stadium parking lot with three rows of seats — 30 seats in all — strapped to the roof with bungee cords. About an hour after the game had ended, Jim Mueller, the co-host from Belichick's *Browns Insider* show, decided to take his son onto the field for one last look around. The stadium was practically empty, but Mueller noticed a middle-aged man walking around the upper concourse with his arm inside his trench coat. The man walked down near the baseball dugout, entered the field, and walked by Mueller and his son with his arm still tucked inside his trench coat. The broadcaster wondered if the stranger was carrying a weapon, a gun, maybe.

"Then he walked out into the end zone," Mueller said, "opened his coat up, and laid a single red rose down on the turf. And then he turned around and walked past us into the stands with tears in his eyes.

"That's a Cleveland Browns fan, and that's what happened to this city."

Art Modell fired Bill Belichick by phone on Valentine's Day 1996, with two years and $1.6 million left on his contract.

"Valentine's Day," the coach's son Stephen would comment years later. "How many coaches get fired on Valentine's Day?"

Stephen was eight years old when Modell made that phone call, and he would later say the firing had an "enormous" impact on him. Stephen's father was his hero. He had a life-size photo of his dad on the wall of a bedroom he shared with his younger brother, Brian.

Bill Belichick likely made this day inevitable the moment he decided to fire the hometown hero, Bernie Kosar, who by then was finishing his career as Dan Marino's backup in Miami. When Belichick heard that Kosar was holding some silly, endless grudge against the *Washington Post's* Christine Brennan over something she'd written while covering his Miami Hurricanes teams in the 1980s for the *Miami Herald,* Belichick sent Brennan a letter. (He'd sent the sportswriter another handwritten note a decade earlier, to thank her for a feature she wrote on his father.) "Don't worry," the coach wrote to Brennan. "Bernie doesn't like me, either." If Belichick had shown a little more of that humor and humanity in Cleveland, he might've survived the move to Baltimore.

As it turned out, the karma was all wrong for Bill Belichick and the entire organization throughout 1995. The Browns were all set to take Penn State tight end Kyle Brady with the tenth pick in the draft (Brady said Cleveland had called Penn State's equipment manager for his helmet and shoe size) before the Jets stunned everyone and took him at No. 9, sending Belichick and his personnel director, Lombardi, into a tailspin. They panicked and traded their pick to San Francisco and dropped down to No. 30, where they selected Ohio State linebacker Craig Powell, a complete bust who played all of nine games in his career. Fortuitously for the franchise, if not its outgoing coach, that trade did secure the draft choice that Modell's new team, the Baltimore Ravens, would use to select future Hall of Famer Ray Lewis, two months after Belichick was fired.

In all, Belichick drafted 41 college players for the Browns, and 40 of them failed to make even one Pro Bowl throughout their careers. The Browns often held early, desirable picks in each round, thanks to their losing records, and yet Belichick and Lombardi failed to convert them into championship-level depth. Their second-round pick in '91, Auburn guard Ed King, never made any discernible impact. Their second-round pick in '92, San Diego State receiver Patrick Rowe, finished his career with three catches for 37 yards after he tore up his knee in a preseason game. Their second-round pick in '93, Florida State defensive lineman Dan Footman, spent only two years of his NFL career as a primary starter (though he did have 10.5 sacks for the Colts in 1997). Their third-round pick in '94, Romeo Bandison, never appeared in a game for the Browns before he was cut in his second season. Their six drafted players in '95 started a combined 24 NFL games in their careers; Georgia quarterback Eric Zeier accounted for half of that total, and he went 4-8 in his starts.

The draft wasn't the only story to tell about this failed regime. One team official said that the Browns had brought in "a lot of questionable guys" beyond Andre Rison, and that the departures of veteran linebackers Clay Matthews and Mike Johnson following the 1993 season left a character void that showed up in 1995. "When things did go south," the official said, "we had no internal fortitude."

During the '95 season, said defensive coordinator Rick Venturi, "we had a million breakdowns." Venturi was one of them. As Saban's replacement, Venturi was drinking coffee by the gallon and working around the clock when he suffered what he called "a brownout" while Cleveland was scrimmaging Chicago in the blistering training-camp heat in Platteville, Wisconsin. "Worked myself into oblivion," Venturi said. He blamed himself, not Belichick. He said he was out three to four weeks.

That summer, Belichick annoyed some in the organization — particularly Jim Bailey — by hiring a young staffer, Mike Tannenbaum, as an extra set of eyes on the salary cap. Only Browns executives on the business side didn't want another set of eyes on the salary cap. Bailey confronted Belichick on Tannenbaum's presence, told the coach he couldn't "hire guys on my side of the building," and warned that Tannenbaum wouldn't be given any access to his cap information.

Bailey described Belichick's relationships in the building as "edgy," dating all the way back to the Ernie Accorsi days. Yet according to Bailey, Modell initially planned to bring along Belichick to Baltimore, as he'd promised the players. Early in the off-season, Belichick himself thought he'd be making the trip to Baltimore, where it had all started for him with the Colts in 1975.

Ultimately, those edgy relationships ended up changing Modell's plans. "The transitional time was very difficult," Bailey said, "and we had a lot of things going on with our finances, with the league, and Bill was demanding that attention be paid to football operations, just like normal and without regard to all the other things. He wanted commitments to coaches and players, and we weren't in position to do that. We were dealing with banks, financing, the league — it was a big state of flux. It got real testy and tough, and Bill was mad at us, and we were mad at him.

"Art said, 'I think we're going to have to make a change. I hate to do it, but this can't work.' And I couldn't disagree with him. I felt the team could do pretty well under Bill, but all the extraneous stuff got in the way."

So Modell made the call from his West Palm Beach, Florida, residence, and told Belichick he wouldn't be coaching a short drive from his Annapolis childhood after all. Nobody was surprised to learn that they quarreled over what Modell would say publicly about the firing, and over how much blame he'd be assigning Belichick for the 5-11 record.

"We've had some success with Bill, including an 11-5 playoff team in 1994," Modell said in the statement he eventually released. "However, I believe to get to the next level, a change at head coach is necessary." The owner spoke of the respect he had for Belichick's work ethic, yet he also spoke hopefully of the fresh start that Baltimore allowed.

Belichick put out his own statement — not on Browns letterhead — thanking Jim Brown for his friendship and loyalty and the fans for their support. "I will always cherish the many memories of being part of the rich tradition and history of the Cleveland Browns," Belichick said.

And that was that. The old Browns center, Mike Baab, remembered Belichick standing in front of the team in his first meeting after getting hired in February 1990 and shouting, "I've worked too long and too hard for this chance to let you guys fuck it up for me."

The players didn't end up fucking it up for Belichick as much as the owner did, or as much as Belichick fucked it up for himself. In a cruel twist of fate, Modell hired Ted Marchibroda to return to Baltimore and replace the kid from Wesleyan he had agreed to take on in 1975. Belichick talked to his good friend Jimmy Johnson, the Miami Dolphins' head coach, about running his defense, but instead he agreed to accept an offer from his former boss Bill Parcells to join the New England Patriots as assistant head coach and secondary coach; Al Groh was already in place as defensive coordinator.

Belichick cleaned out his office in Berea and left the facility for the final time. Terry McDonough, a scout on his way to Baltimore, looked out from a second-floor window as Belichick headed to his car with a backpack strapped to his shoulders.

McDonough felt a sense of sadness and waste. He shook his head and said to himself, "There goes a very good football coach."

9

BORDER WAR

Bill Parcells reacquired Bill Belichick after his firing in Cleveland, and voilà, the New England Patriots surrendered a total of nine points in two playoff games to give Big Bill a chance to become the first head coach to win Super Bowls with different franchises. With Belichick in Cleveland, Parcells had gone 21-27 in his first three seasons in New England. Big Bill liked to say you are what your record says you are, and his record said he needed Little Bill by his side.

The Patriots were set to play Brett Favre's Green Bay Packers in Super Bowl XXXI in New Orleans, and yet the game had been reduced to a mere afterthought. Win or lose against Green Bay, Parcells wanted out from under Patriots owner Robert Kraft, who was just as fed up with the head coach as the head coach was with him. So, in the days before his AFC Championship Game victory over Jacksonville, Parcells put himself very much in play with his former employer the Giants, and he planned to take Belichick with him on a potential return trip to New Jersey. In fact, Giants GM George Young told his preferred candidate, Arizona Cardinals offensive coordinator Jim Fassel, that he should root for the Patriots to beat the Jaguars because he didn't think ownership wanted to wait until after the Super Bowl to make the hire.

Wellington Mara had watched Parcells's New England team overcome a 22-0 deficit to beat his team in Giants Stadium, 23-22, to close out the regular season. He badly wanted Parcells to return, but his 50-50 partner, Bob Tisch, was sensitive to Young's position. Young didn't personally like Parcells any more than he liked Belichick, he didn't think Big Bill had the energy for the job anymore, and he told Mara in early January 1997 that he'd resign if Parcells returned.

Young strongly favored Fassel or Belichick's former defensive coordinator in Cleveland, Michigan State's Nick Saban, whom the GM described as one of the most impressive candidates he'd ever interviewed. Mara and his son John, a Giants executive, reluctantly agreed that it wasn't fair to force Parcells on Tisch, and that they should go along with Fassel for the good of the partnership. Young was summoned to John Mara's office and told that he could hire the Arizona coordinator, who had flown into town on a private jet under the assumed name Jeff Smith and checked into a New Jersey hotel.

"I think that's the first time I ever saw George sprint down the hallway," John Mara said of the rotund GM.

Minutes later, the phone rang in Mara's office. Tisch was calling to say that he'd had a change of heart and that if his partners really wanted to hire Parcells, he wouldn't stand in their way. John told his father, and Wellington shouted, "Get George now." Only by the time John tracked down Young, it was too late. He'd already offered the job to Fassel, and the Maras weren't about to tell their new coach that there had been some terrible misunderstanding.

That left Parcells with one appealing option: the New York Jets, who had fired the bumbling Rich Kotite and were coming off a 1-15 season. The Jets were appealing because 82-year-old Jets owner Leon Hess was desperate for a winner and more than happy to give Parcells the personnel power Kraft had stripped from him and handed to front-office man Bobby Grier, who selected Ohio State receiver Terry Glenn in the 1996 draft, over Parcells's objection that the team should pick a defensive player.

Will McDonough, of the *Boston Globe*, a friend of Kraft's and Parcells's, had blown the lid off Super Bowl week before the alcohol started flowing on Bourbon Street when he opened his breaking news story on Monday, January 20, 1997, with this paragraph:

> Bill Parcells will coach his last game for the Patriots Super Bowl Sunday, but what happens next may turn into an ugly situation between him and team owner Bob Kraft concerning Parcells' contract.

McDonough reported that Kraft would be seeking compensation from any team that hired the coach, and that Parcells's agent, Robert Fraley, was contending that his client's expiring contract allowed for no such thing. Kraft and Parcells were making the Art Modell–Bill Belichick marriage in Cleveland look blissful by comparison. Parcells had been hired in 1993 by James Orthwein, who had purchased the team from Victor Kiam in 1992 with the intent of moving it to St. Louis. Kraft was the man who, two years later, prevented the New England Patriots from becoming the St. Louis Stallions, and inherited Parcells in the process.

The son of a Boston dressmaker who hoped he'd become a rabbi, Kraft ascended out of a family of modest financial means; the Krafts didn't even own a car. Robert was a class president on an academic scholarship at Columbia, a Harvard Business School graduate and longtime season-ticket holder who made his fortune in the paper-and-packaging industry after taking control of his father-in-law's company. Kraft got the break of a football fan's lifetime when the owning family of the Patriots and their stadium, the Sullivans, lost a bundle promoting Michael Jackson's Victory Tour in 1984, forcing Sullivan Stadium into bankruptcy and starting a team-ownership domino effect — from Billy Sullivan to Kiam to Orthwein to Kraft — that forever changed the NFL.

Kraft bought an option on 300 acres of land surrounding the stadium in 1985. Against the wishes of his banker, Kraft bought the building out of bankruptcy for $25 million in a 1988 deal that included the lease requiring the Patriots to play there through 2001.

Built for a lousy $7.1 million, the stadium was a godforsaken dump with a long history of plumbing issues. It made baseball's ghastly Shea Stadium, in Queens, look like the Taj Mahal, and Kraft's banker thought the place would end up as a white elephant if the team moved out of Foxborough. But Kraft was a natural-born risk-taker, a guy who'd make a ten-dollar bet on the street with only five dollars in his pocket. As a young entrepreneur, he took over a struggling paper mill in Newfoundland by guaranteeing a sale of 200,000 tons, even though he didn't have the financial wherewithal to make any such guarantee. Kraft later turned that company, International Forest Products, into a global juggernaut with business interests in more than 90 countries.

Kraft had grown up a fan of the Boston Braves, his first love, and he was saddened when they moved to Milwaukee in 1953. He didn't want to see the Patriots end up in St. Louis, and he relied on his experience as owner of the Boston Lobsters, of the World TeamTennis league, in blocking that move. The Lobsters played in Boston University's Walter Brown Arena in the mid-1970s, and though Kraft's product and advertising were putting fans in the seats, the university pocketed the concessions and parking revenue. From that bum deal, Kraft learned the value of controlling a team's venue.

With control of what had been renamed Foxboro Stadium, Kraft declined Orthwein's $75 million bid to buy out the lease and move the franchise in 1994 and instead offered Orthwein $172 million for the team, a record price in American sports. Kraft's wife, Myra, thought her husband had lost his mind.

Kraft knew he was crazy for paying that kind of money for a team with a lousy Q rating, stuck in a lousier ballpark, but he couldn't help himself. He'd become an instant fan when the Boston Patriots were born as an American Football League franchise in 1960, back when NFL-starved New Englanders regularly watched the New York Giants on TV and adopted them as their own. He'd watched the Patriots play at Boston University, Fenway

Park, Boston College's Alumni Stadium, and Harvard Stadium. He bought season tickets for his family in 1971, the year the team moved into what was then Schaefer Stadium, where he sat with his sons on those dreadful metal benches above the end zone in Section 217, Row 23, Seats 1 through 6, and dreamed of someday running the club.

In 1994, he bought the franchise that had won one playoff game in ten years in the old AFL and three playoff games — all in the 1985 season — in 24 years in the NFL. Their games were often subjected to TV blackouts in the market for failing to sell out. They were 19-61 over the five seasons preceding Kraft's purchase, and running a distant fourth in a sports-mad market hopelessly devoted to the Red Sox, Celtics, and Bruins. The day after Kraft was made their official owner, the Patriots sold nearly 6,000 season tickets in the middle of a winter storm, or nearly 5,000 more than their previous one-day record — set when Parcells was hired. They would sell more than 40,000 season tickets and sell out every home game for the first time. Kraft's man-of-the-people vibe was appealing to the masses, even if it wasn't appealing to Parcells, his most important football asset.

Parcells didn't like the fact that his boss was a much more visible presence than the Giants' Wellington Mara, and that Kraft clearly enjoyed the newfound spotlight. ("I had stardust in my eyes," the owner admitted years later.) Kraft didn't like the fact that Parcells barely acknowledged his wife and, after boarding the team plane, refused to talk to the banker who had loaned Kraft the money to buy the franchise. From there, Kraft's decision to strip Parcells of his personnel power and to back Grier in the draft room in favor of Terry Glenn inflicted, in the coach's eyes, irreparable harm on the partnership. Parcells asked the owner to remove the final year from his contract. Kraft obliged and absolved Parcells of any financial penalty for the amended deal, but he maintained the right to seek compensation if Parcells tried to coach another team during that year.

Parcells and Kraft were becoming Jimmy Johnson and Jerry Jones all over again. Their personality clash wasn't helped by the fact that the owner's wife compelled her husband to cut a 1996 fifth-round draft pick, Christian Peter, after reading reports of his violence against women at Nebraska, or by the fact that Robert and Myra Kraft were angered by the coach's mocking reference to Glenn as "she."

Even though the Patriots were days away from playing the Super Bowl, and even though Parcells and Kraft held a joint news conference in New Orleans in a farcical attempt to project a unified front, the coach was already out the door. The Giants had opened that door for the Jets, and Kraft later came to believe that an informal deal between Parcells and Hess had been in place in December. Years later, Parcells would rail against a report in the book *Patriot Reign* that said his hotel bill for Super Bowl week showed dozens of itemized calls from his room in the team hotel, the New Orleans Marriott, to Hempstead, New York, home base of the Jets. "That was total horseshit," Parcells said. "Some Patriots officials want to make it look good by saying, 'We had phone records.' If I talked to the Jets, do you think I'm stupid enough to talk on Patriots phones?"

In a rare public rebuke of the man who promoted him with the Giants, and who threw him a lifeline after his firing in Cleveland, Belichick would tell author Michael Holley that he believed Parcells was distracted enough that week to affect New England's preparation. "I can tell you firsthand, there was a lot of stuff going on prior to the game," Belichick said. "I mean, him talking to other teams. He was trying to make up his mind about what he wanted to do. Which, honestly, I felt [was] totally inappropriate. How many chances do you get to play for the Super Bowl? Tell them to get back to you in a couple of days. I'm not saying it was disrespectful to me, but it was in terms of the overall commitment to the team."

The entire week revolved around the Parcells-vs.-Kraft narrative, not the Patriots-vs.-Packers narrative, and in the end the better team with the better quarterback and better organizational chemistry won, 35–21. Favre threw two touchdown passes, including the 81-yarder to Antonio Freeman in the second quarter that gave Green Bay the lead for good. Drew Bledsoe, the No. 1 overall pick in the 1993 draft, threw four interceptions — four more than Favre threw — while Parcells kept repeating the mistake of kicking the ball to Desmond Howard, who ran free the entire game and scored the game's final touchdown on a 99-yard kickoff return.

Parcells didn't even fly home with his losing team. He resigned that Friday, and conceded in yet another strange press conference — with Kraft sitting up there with him — that the owner's choice to diminish his role in personnel had played a part in his exit. Parcells quoted a friend who told him, "If they want you to cook the dinner, at least they ought to let you shop for some of the groceries." He accepted NFL commissioner Paul Tagliabue's ruling that the Patriots owned his coaching rights for the 1997 season, and that they would be owed compensation for trading those rights.

Kraft called his daily dealings with Parcells's ego "a handful," and he was very clear about his terms for trading that handful to the New York Jets. "I'm not playing chicken," the owner said. "I'm not bluffing. I'm not even threatening. I'm just saying, 'Guys, if you want Bill Parcells as your coach in '97, make sure your No. 1 draft choice is there in its current position' . . . How would you like to be the guy that Bill Parcells left and you've got to face him twice?"

Truth was, Bill Belichick would've done almost anything at that point to face Parcells twice a year in the AFC East. Little Bill wanted Big Bill's job with the Patriots as much as he had wanted Big Bill's job with the Giants. Belichick spoke at length with Kraft on the flight home from New Orleans, the flight Parcells had skipped. Little Bill wanted to build a championship program that he envisioned but couldn't build in Cleveland, and he wanted to do that in Foxborough, a formless town wedged between Boston and Providence. He wanted to work for Kraft, too. After Belichick's playoff victory in Cleveland over Parcells and the Patriots, Kraft showed up in his locker room to congratulate him. "In my whole career," Belichick would say, "I cannot recall any other owner, executive, or coach doing this to my team."

Kraft liked Little Bill, liked him a lot. New England's defensive players, especially the defensive backs, had raved about Belichick's ability to coach them up, and Kraft thought he had a better understanding of the salary cap than Parcells did.

Only the owner couldn't bring himself to hire someone so closely aligned with the man who'd just made a tumultuous break from the franchise. One night when the Krafts were having dinner with the Belichicks, the owner told Little Bill why he couldn't have Big Bill's job. Debby was said to be less understanding of Kraft's reasons than her husband was, but the sides parted amicably, and with a sense that they might someday meet again to do business. Kraft hired the agreeable and energetic Pete Carroll, the former Jets coach, who represented everything Parcells was not, and Belichick participated in a shell game designed to help Kraft's AFC East rival land Parcells.

The plan executed by the Jets' president, Steve Gutman, was simple: The team would hire Belichick as an interim one-year coach, then reduce him to Little Bill again when Parcells was liberated from his Patriots deal to coach the 1998 season. The Jets didn't even bother seeking permission from the Patriots to talk to Parcells. Big Bill and Little Bill signed up for the scam, Parcells was made a Jets consultant, and then Belichick would be made Parcells's eventual successor after Big Bill coached another two years.

"You sure you want to do this—be a temporary coach?" Hess, the oil baron, asked Belichick.

"I want to do this as much as I want to do anything in my life," Little Bill replied.

The Jets introduced Belichick as their new head coach in a packed press conference at the team's Long Island headquarters at Hofstra, and they added to the absurdity of the event by having the lurking and looming Parcells speak by phone, Wizard of Oz–like, to the gathered reporters. "Bill and I will work in concert as we always have," Belichick said, "and I think we'll be successful." Parcells swore that he wouldn't have the final word on personnel in his strange new role. "I will just act in an advisory capacity," he said.

The Patriots released an angry statement calling the arrangement "a transparent farce." Leon Hess tried to negotiate with Kraft from a counterfeit position of strength, and Kraft kept insisting he wanted the Jets' first-rounder, the No. 1 overall pick, and argued that Parcells was more valuable than any of the college players expected to go at the top of the draft.

Meanwhile, Belichick started hiring some of his former Cleveland staffers, such as Scott Pioli and Eric Mangini, with Mike Tannenbaum on deck. He stole a truckload of assistants from the Patriots, including former Giants coaches Al Groh, Romeo Crennel, Mike Sweatman, and Charlie Weis. Belichick, the substitute teacher, was clearly trying to leave his mark on the curriculum before the headmaster returned.

"I am not waiting around for Bill," he said. "When I took it, I had the understanding it was full speed ahead and I am making the decisions to put the organization in the best situation to win in 1997. I am in charge of the Jets' operations to try to strengthen the football team."

Belichick allowed that he'd run the same offense and defense as the Patriots ran under Parcells, and that he'd install the same media policy for assistant coaches, who wouldn't be allowed to talk to reporters. "If you guys don't behave," he told media members through a smile, "I won't let you talk to Bill Parcells."

Belichick represented the Jets at the pre-draft combine in Indianapolis, where he said he was hoping to re-create the winning environment he'd had with the Giants. He met with Pioli to determine what the Jets could and couldn't do under the salary cap. He met with draft prospects, too, including an Ohio State linebacker named Mike Vrabel. According to Jets executive Pat Kirwan, a former coach and scout who had become the team's director of player administration and was in place before Belichick arrived, Belichick reacted to the linebacker in a way he almost never reacted to a prospect.

"Vrabel comes in," Kirwan recalled, "and right away I never saw Bill Belichick light up like this. He's always all business and intimidating to the player, but he was all lit up and having a great time talking to Vrabel. They were really engaged. Bill says, 'Look, I don't have a pick where you're going to go. We're going to miss you, unless I figure out how to get one. But I promise you this: The first time you're a free agent, you're going to play for me.'"

Kirwan thought of Belichick as the most effective interviewer of prospects he'd ever come across. He saw the coach as an evaluator who could run a penetrating one-on-one and quickly get to the essence of a player without turning the sit-down into a police interrogation. Kirwan recalled Belichick meeting with a talented defensive lineman at the '97 combine who had a reputation for being an underachiever. Belichick wanted to test the kid to see if he was accountable for his disappointing play and, perhaps, worth a gamble in the draft. As the player entered the room, he presented his hand for a handshake that wasn't going to happen. Belichick ignored his gesture, told the kid to sit down, and turned out the lights.

"The tape comes on, and it's programmed so the kid is playing shitty on the tape," Kirwan said. "Bill is saying, 'Tell me what happened here, and here, and what went wrong on this play, and why did you do that here.' After ten minutes, the kid cracked and started blaming his coaches, saying, 'They didn't use me right.' You can only imagine where this is going. The lights go on, and Bill goes, 'Hey, we'll be in touch.' The guy leaves, and Bill says something to the effect of 'That guy will never play for me.'"

Kirwan remembered the first time Belichick sat with him, while Parcells remained in limbo. Little Bill told him that he'd learned a lot in Cleveland, that he never got out and spent enough time with the fans, and that he would do things differently the next time around. Belichick also went over every Jet on the roster with Kirwan, asking him how much each player engaged the media. He wanted to know the identities of the talkers and the locker room leakers.

"He also prepped for me by reading anything he could get his hands on in newspapers from two months before," Kirwan said. "He looked at guys ripping Kotite. If they ripped Kotite, he felt, 'ultimately they'll rip me.' So he got rid of some guys. They didn't last long."

Belichick didn't last long as the Jets' head coach, either. The Little Bill–Big Bill circus was a terrible look for the league, and Tagliabue knew he couldn't let the circus carry on for long. The commissioner also knew it was good for business to have Bill Parcells as a head coach on the sidelines every Sunday, up front and center, rather than as an unseen mystery consultant. Tagliabue listened to the arguments from both sides in a midtown Manhattan meeting and then ruled that the Jets should send four draft choices to New England, including their 1999 first-rounder, but not their No. 1 overall pick that spring.

Parcells had agreed to a six-year deal, including at least four as head coach, and said he couldn't wait to honor the faith that Hess had put in him by surrendering four picks over three years. Belichick? His second go as an NFL head coach had lasted six days. He had a six-year contract of his own as assistant head coach and defensive coordinator, and the promise of being the next man up whenever the impetuous Parcells decided once again that he'd had enough.

"That was the plan we came in with," Belichick said. "I was racing around for six days, trying to get as much in place as I could."

And in the early days and weeks of the new administration, Parcells was asking questions about some of the hires made while he was still serving only as a consultant. "All these young kids running around," Kirwan said of the Piolis, Manginis, and Tannenbaums, "they were really Belichick guys . . . Parcells asked me all the time about the young guys Belichick brought in. I told him they were doing great, don't worry about it."

Parcells needed to control everything, and for those six surreal days, anyway, he couldn't control Belichick. When order had finally been restored and Parcells had finally taken his place as head coach and general manager, the Jets were in the hands of the best 1-2 coaching punch in the NFL.

Parcells and Belichick would do their share of winning with the Jets; that much was certain. But things had changed for Big Bill and Little Bill since their Giants days, and it soon became clear that the functional side of their partnership was on borrowed time.

On the afternoon of September 12, 1999, the New York Jets appeared to have won the Bill Parcells trade with the New England Patriots, their opponent that day in Giants Stadium. With Parcells as their coach the previous season, the Jets had won their first division title since the AFL–NFL merger, in 1970, advanced to the AFC Championship Game for the first time in 16 years, and established themselves as a popular choice to reach the Super Bowl for the first time since man had walked on the moon.

In only two seasons, Parcells had turned a 1-15 hoax of a team into a serious contender to win it all. The Patriots of Pete Carroll were holding their own, reaching the playoffs in his first two years, after 10-6 and 9-7 regular seasons, but the four draft choices they had acquired in the Parcells trade (linebacker Andy Katzenmoyer, receiver Tony Simmons, running back Sedrick Shaw, and offensive lineman Damon Denson) would start a combined 28 regular-season games in their NFL careers. To make matters worse, the Jets had pilfered New England's star running back, Curtis Martin, by way of a poison-pill clause in the $36 million contract Parcells offered the restricted free agent.

Kraft had desperately wanted his former coach to fail in his new job. In fact, after Giants coach Jim Fassel won the 1997 NFL Coach of the Year award, he ran into the New England owner at the league meetings. "Kraft gave me a big hug," Fassel recalled, "and said, 'Man, you made my life. You got Coach of the Year, and Parcells was across the river.' Kraft hated Parcells. *Hated* him."

The border war had boiled over by the time New England arrived in the Meadowlands for its fifth meeting with the Bill Parcells Jets, who had won three of the first four against the Pete Carroll Patriots. Kraft had feared that Parcells would prove to be worth more than a draft pick at the top of the first round and, much to his dismay, his fears were being confirmed. The Jets had held a 10–0 lead in the third quarter of the AFC Championship Game at Denver eight months earlier before John Elway and Terrell Davis took over, and the visiting team starting playing loose with the ball in the Mile High winds.

This was going to be the Jets' year, finally, more than three decades after Joe Willie Namath won their one and only Super Bowl title by honoring his guarantee of an upset victory over the mighty Baltimore Colts. Elway had retired. Parcells had fortified his win-now time by signing a parade of older free-agent veterans. Big Bill was going for it, and if there was going to be a rebuilding price to pay with the roster down the road, Little Bill, his contracted successor, would be the one to pay it.

Belichick's former quarterback in Cleveland, Vinny Testaverde, was returning from the best season of his career, and he was inspired to try to win a ring for the memory of his father, Al, who had died of a heart attack on Valentine's Day. The Jets were loaded on offense, with Testaverde and Martin in the backfield and former No. 1 overall pick Keyshawn Johnson on the outside. They had a defense that had allowed a mere 266 points the year before, second best in the league, and they had an unmatched power couple on the sideline in Parcells and Belichick.

But the Jets couldn't even get through the 1999 opener with their season intact. They were driving on the Patriots in the second quarter when Martin fumbled the ball and Testaverde made what appeared to be a benign move to try to recover it. He collapsed in pain and immediately grabbed at his left ankle. His Achilles tendon had snapped, and he knew it the second it happened. Testaverde pounded his fist into the turf. He was done for the year, and so were the Jets. "It was like a piece of every one of us was being carted off the field with him," Martin said.

The Jets lost six of their first seven games before a meaningless 7-2 close to the season left them out of the playoffs and, at 8-8, in a last-place tie with the Patriots in the AFC East. The Testaverde injury had made the evolving Parcells-Belichick relationship more relevant than the games.

That relationship had appeared strained as early as 1997, their first season together with the Jets. One prominent starter said that Parcells berated

Belichick in front of the players, leaving the defensive coordinator muttering under his breath. Nobody was surprised. In their post-Giants time together, Big Bill had something new on Little Bill. Parcells wasn't just the boss anymore. He was the boss who had watched his most valuable subordinate fail in his attempt to be the boss in Cleveland, a truth that gave Big Bill a bigger hammer to wield.

"Oh, yeah, Parcells berated Belichick right in front of me one time," recalled Ray Mickens, reserve defensive back. The Jets were running through their Friday dress rehearsal for a Sunday game, and Big Bill expected things to go smoothly after some long hours on the practice field.

"He got the red ass on Friday," Mickens said, "if anyone made a mistake . . . We made four mistakes in a row [on defense], and on all four Parcells didn't say anything. He just sat over there. He starts turning red on the first and second mistake, and the next play comes and . . . he gets redder. After the fourth one, he just goes off on Belichick, just literally. I cannot even say what he said — I don't want to repeat it. He just went off in front of all of us on Belichick. I've seen that happen a lot from Parcells. He's tough on all his coaches, players, the trainers . . . It wasn't a personal thing. It's just the way it was."

Belichick weathered the storms, as always, and made his unit better, as always. Mickens said he had no idea how much he didn't know about football until he met Little Bill. Belichick was the first coach who told him to sit in on receivers meetings to learn how they're taught to beat defensive backs. The first coach who told him to survey the offensive backfield at the line of scrimmage, and to understand how he could find clues to the receivers' pass patterns in the positioning of the running backs.

Neil O'Donnell, starting quarterback in '97, had competed against Belichick's Browns for five years in Pittsburgh and found him to be an extremely difficult defensive coach to beat, especially on third down. O'Donnell recalled that when they were co-workers on the Jets, Little Bill was a quiet, even-keeled assistant who liked to jot down notes to himself on a piece of paper. The quarterback also thought that on the practice field, Belichick tried to keep his distance from Parcells, whose verbal assaults were relentless, especially those directed at his offensive coordinator, Charlie Weis.

"Belichick would just go on his way," O'Donnell said. "He wouldn't change. He wouldn't let Parcells rattle him. You hear so much about how close they were, and I really question that. It was a weird relationship between Belichick and Parcells. They didn't really interact much. Parcells was in meetings with the defensive side of the ball, but you never saw them even on the practice field talking much . . . They didn't seem close at all."

One Jets executive who had extensive dealings with Big Bill and Little Bill confirmed that the two were not what anyone would describe as friends. "I think they tolerated each other because they thought each other was pretty good," the executive said, "and because Parcells saved Bill's career after he was fired in Cleveland."

But there was tension between Belichick and his crew from Cleveland and Parcells and his loyalists, like Dan Henning and Dick and Todd Haley. None of this was helped by Big Bill's talent for ripping into Little Bill at the drop of a headset. David Halberstam reported in *The Education of a Coach* that a successful Belichick blitz in one game — a call at first opposed by Parcells — inspired Big Bill to scream into an open microphone, "Yeah, you're a genius, everyone knows it, a goddamn genius, but that's why you failed as a head coach — that's why you'll never be a head coach . . . some genius." Halberstam described the barrage as "deeply shocking" to all the coaches who heard it and as "the cruelest words imaginable."

One scout heard something similar during a Jets practice, when a defensive breakdown compelled Parcells to shout at Belichick, "Dammit, this is why your ass got fired in Cleveland." Big Bill and Little Bill were wildly different people, and the gulf between them was growing wider by the week.

Belichick didn't want to be Parcells's assistant for much longer. He didn't want to be anyone's assistant for much longer. He was doing some things behind the scenes to improve his odds of succeeding as a head coach the next time around — if there was going to be a next time — and media relations was part of his private rehab program. Just as he had with the Giants in an earlier life, Belichick established good working relationships with some of the beat writers covering the Jets. Parcells had made his assistants off-limits to the media, if only to reinforce his authoritarian rule and to stem the tide of information on the exploding phenomenon that was most concerning to Big Bill: the Internet.

But understanding that he needed to repair the bridge to the news media that he'd firebombed in Cleveland, Belichick was helpful to reporters looking for background, context, and maybe an off-the-record confirmation or two. He took a liking to a young PR staffer named Berj Najarian, a confidant of Keyshawn Johnson's. Belichick generally had no use for PR people, but Scott Pioli told him he should try to get to know Najarian. The coach and the intern often worked out on the treadmill side by side, and they talked about ways Little Bill could better deal with the media while working around Big Bill's restrictions.

Belichick knew he had to give something to get a return on the back end that could help clear a pathway to the top job. An example: Rich Cimini, of the *Daily News,* was tasked every week with drawing up one of the opponent's favorite plays so it could be printed in the Sunday morning edition.

So after the press room cleared out every Thursday night, he'd call Belichick and ask the coach if he could stop by and diagram the Xs and Os for him. Sure enough, without Big Bill or anyone else knowing, Little Bill would appear with that familiar pencil behind his ear and draw up a play on a card, which Cimini transferred to Xerox paper and faxed to his office.

Belichick also agreed to sit with Cimini for a story on how he'd broken down tape before the 1998 season opener against San Francisco. Little Bill dissected Steve Young's game for the writer, and shockingly mocked the 49ers' offensive line ("They can't block anybody") and identified the pass rush as the key to victory ("To me, this is the way to beat San Francisco") on the record, before the game was played. Belichick had a stack of VHS tapes with him; he'd spend more than 100 hours studying the 49ers before the Jets lost to them in overtime, on Garrison Hearst's 96-yard touchdown run. During the film session, Little Bill joked with Cimini about Big Bill's likely reaction if he ever stumbled upon this scene.

"He wanted to get out from under Parcells's thumb," the writer said, "and get his name out there and get some credit."

Belichick filled in for Parcells as head coach of the AFC team in the Pro Bowl, and while in Hawaii — where league rules requiring head coaches to be available to the media trumped Big Bill's gag order — Little Bill gave his first interview in five months and told Cimini that he had no plans to pursue other jobs around the league. (Belichick had engaged in serious talks with Al Davis about coaching the Raiders after the 1997 season.) "I'm happy where I am," Belichick said. "I'm excited about the future of the Jets. I think we've made good strides in two years, and I think we can get better."

A year later, so much had changed. Little Bill was worn out working for Big Bill, and the one owner he really wanted to work for — an owner who would give him personnel control — was suddenly in the market for a head coach. Robert Kraft thought sunshiny Pete Carroll had effectively turned the Patriots' facility into Club Med, where accountability was a part-time thing and where players felt free to be late for meetings and to take complaints directly to the personnel chief, Bobby Grier. Kraft fired Carroll after an 8-8 season, and he was ready to do what he couldn't bring himself to do after the stormy Parcells exit three years earlier — hire Belichick. Only there was a problem. When it came to the Patriots and the Jets and Big Bill and Little Bill, there was always a problem.

Parcells had resigned after the Jets finished their season with their fourth straight victory, over Seattle, and after their fans chanted at the coach, "One more year." By contract, Parcells's exit automatically made Belichick his successor (though Big Bill planned to keep a front-office role). Little Bill had pocketed a $1 million bonus from owner Leon Hess, who had died in May, to remain on board and wait for Parcells to resign and/or retire, and he was fully expected to fulfill his obligation. Yes, there were questions about Big Bill's resignation, and why he told team president Steve Gutman he was leaving Sunday, about an hour after the final game.

Did Parcells merely realize that the Jets' championship window had slammed shut on his fingers, and that he didn't need a few days or a week to see that it was the perfect time to walk away? Or did Parcells know that the Patriots were about to seek permission to interview and hire Belichick, and that he needed to quit immediately to trigger the clause that made Little Bill coach of the Jets?

One Jets official said he believed Parcells "had no intention of stepping down" until he realized he could lose Belichick to the Patriots. Either way, after New England sent a fax to the Jets on Monday morning requesting the opportunity to talk to Belichick, Parcells crumpled it into a ball and threw it away. Big Bill figured there was nothing to talk about. He told Little Bill on Saturday that he was 99 percent sure he would retire, and Parcells said Belichick responded, "I've been waiting for this." Kraft would have to find his replacement for Carroll somewhere else.

But when Parcells met with Belichick on Monday, he was surprised to learn that his defensive coordinator had some concerns about his promotion. Eight months after Hess's death, the sale of the Jets still hadn't gone through to either of the two billionaire finalists, Cablevision founder Charles Dolan and pharmaceutical heir Robert Wood (Woody) Johnson IV, and Belichick was frustrated by the delay. Of course, Belichick was also uneasy about Parcells's continued role in the organization, especially after getting word through back channels that he would be offered complete control in New England. Big Bill swore that Little Bill would have the final word on personnel decisions, but, given their shared history, it was a hard claim to buy.

"Maybe if you feel that uncertain about it," Parcells told Belichick, "you should think about not taking this job."

So Belichick thought about it. An emotional Parcells met with the players in the team's auditorium to tell them he was stepping down.

One of the Jets' defensive ends, Anthony Pleasant, who had played for Belichick in Cleveland, sat next to Little Bill when Big Bill told the team he was leaving. "Belichick was sort of surprised that it was announced he was taking over for Parcells, and he didn't agree with it," Pleasant said. "I can recall Parcells asking Belichick in the team meeting, did he have anything to say, and Belichick said, 'No.' You could tell he wasn't happy about it at all."

Parcells had a scheduled news conference in which he would make his resignation public, and the Jets' longtime PR man, Frank Ramos, came up with the idea that Big Bill should introduce Little Bill as his successor immediately after his announcement. Ramos ran his proposal by Gutman, and then by Parcells. "Why don't you ask Bill Belichick about that and see what he thinks?" Parcells responded.

"I think if you told him that's how we're going to do it," Ramos said, "that's how it will be."

"You go talk to him," Parcells insisted.

Ramos found Belichick and shared his idea about Parcells introducing him in his retirement news conference. Little Bill told the PR man that he didn't want to intrude on Big Bill's day, and that he'd do his own announcement on Tuesday. In a statement to the media, Belichick apologized for being unavailable for comment.

Ramos had been with the Jets for 37 years; he was working for them before Joe Namath was drafted. So he'd been around long enough to know something wasn't right. Ramos expressed his concerns to Gutman, who grew nervous about the handoff from Big Bill to Little Bill even as Belichick was meeting with staffers about current Jets and players to chase in free agency.

The team president had every right to be nervous. Years later, Parcells would write in his autobiography that Belichick had found him in the coaches' locker room around 6 p.m. and informed him that he wanted to consider New England's interest in him, given the uncertainty of Jets ownership. Angry, Parcells reminded Belichick that the late Hess had given him a $1 million bonus to stay and honor the terms of his contract. "He made a deal, and then tried to get out of it," Parcells wrote. "A deal's a deal. You want out? You're going to pay. Simple."

Of course, Parcells had already established himself as a coach who knew how to maneuver his way out of a contract like nobody else in the NFL. He'd used Belichick as a stooge in his own successful shell game to jump from the Patriots to the Jets, but he wasn't about to let Belichick run a misdirection play of his own from the Jets to the Patriots.

Little Bill remained determined to liberate himself from Big Bill once and for all. He went home that night and talked things over with Debby and their three kids, and arrived at the team's Long Island facility to a newspaper headline calling his absence at Parcells's press conference "a PR blunder." It was plenty more than that. Belichick showed up for work Tuesday morning preparing to stun the football world.

He actually held a half-hour staff meeting at 10 a.m., talked about the Senior Bowl for college prospects, and scheduled another meeting for the following week. Most of the players were excited to have Belichick continue the Parcells program, minus the booming Parcells volume. Victor Green, safety, had purchased him a crystal paperweight at Tiffany's the day before that set him back a few hundred bucks. Testaverde told reporters that Belichick had grown since their days together in Cleveland.

"I see a different coach," the quarterback said. "I know for a fact he's ready to take on this role and be successful. Some of his ways have changed . . . his demeanor, the way he talks to the players."

Belichick decided to blow off some steam with a workout, and he ended up on the treadmill next to the one occupied by Kevin Williams, a second-year cornerback and return man out of Oklahoma State. Williams had just been released from a New York hospital after suffering from a rare bacterial infection that traveled from his throat to his lungs and nearly killed him. He'd been in a coma for 15 days, had lost nearly 40 pounds, and had been on a respirator. His agent and the Jets waged an unseemly battle over whether the team needed to pay the full balance of his contract.

Williams was beginning what would be a long and somewhat bitter comeback, but he harbored no ill will for the man who was succeeding Parcells. "We loved him," Williams said of Belichick. "We all wanted him to be the head coach."

That fateful day, with Belichick at his side working the treadmill, Williams thought the coach seemed a bit somber. "I could tell something was wrong with him," the cornerback said, "but I had no clue what was wrong."

For once, Belichick wasn't in the mood to talk about the pros and cons of various defensive schemes. He looked at Williams and said, "All you can do, Kevin, is get up and try to do the best you can every day. Be the best person and the best player every day. And sometimes that's still not enough, but that's all we can do as people."

Williams assumed Belichick was talking about him and his recovery from a near-death experience. He had no idea the coach was waxing philosophical about his own career. Williams remained on his treadmill for a while after Belichick left the room, and soon enough he'd look up at a TV monitor and discover exactly what his coach was trying to tell him.

"I couldn't believe it," Williams said.

Nobody could.

On his way to a 2:30 p.m. news conference scheduled as his official introduction as head coach, Belichick had a few stops to make inside Weeb Ewbank Hall, named for the franchise's only Super Bowl–winning coach. He told Parcells and some co-workers that he was stepping down. He found Gutman and handed him a piece of loose-leaf paper that contained the handwritten scribblings of a man desperate to get out. The note informed the incredulous team president that Belichick was resigning "as the HC of the NYJ."

Dressed in a dark gray suit that reflected the mood of the day, Belichick made his way to the facility's auditorium, where Ramos told the gathered media members that the man of the hour had an announcement to make. His hair, shirt collar, and tie knot askew, his face glistening with sweat as he stood before a backdrop of Jets and Cadillac logos, Belichick read from a resignation statement that looked and sounded more like a ransom note, and then put on a show before a flabbergasted audience that wouldn't soon be forgotten.

"Due to the various uncertainties surrounding my position as it relates to the team's new ownership," Belichick said, "I have decided to resign as the head coach of the New York Jets."

His time as the counterfeit coach of the Jets — after the 1996 season — had lasted six days. His time as the genuine coach of the Jets lasted only one. This wasn't Pat Riley breaking his contract with the New York Knicks four years earlier with a faxed resignation and a getaway trip to Greece; Riley had won four championships as head coach of the Lakers before executing his outrageous escape from New York. Belichick? He'd proven nothing as a head coach before running away from a team in the biggest market that was only one season removed from reaching its sport's final four.

Belichick then went on a 25-minute filibuster to nowhere. Little Bill agreed that he had a deal in place to succeed Parcells, but he contended that Hess's death and the continued two-man duel to determine the new owner had changed the circumstances "so significantly it wouldn't be fair to make a half-hearted commitment with all these questions in the back of my mind."

Belichick was concerned that a new owner could mean a new general manager and a new power structure. As to why he wouldn't merely wait for either Johnson or Dolan to emerge as his employer, Belichick said, "We were supposed to have a new owner by December 15, and now it's January 4. It's not fair to the organization to drag it out until the middle of February."

Parcells didn't bother to attend the presser, and Belichick took advantage of his absence by mocking his former boss. Big Bill had been threatening to retire and hand over the controls to him for a dozen years, Little Bill said, and he'd learned not to take him seriously . . . until the previous day. "Until Monday morning," Belichick said, "when he made me aware that this was the final decision and not 80 percent, 90 percent, 83 percent, 77 percent . . . It had gone as high as 99, but I've seen it back off and come back again. Until it was 'This is what I'm going to do,' that's really when I started to think, 'OK, well, now that means this is what I've got to do.'"

Belichick said he yearned to spend more time with his family, even as his lawyer was already looking over his contract in the hopes of making him free to pursue another 18-hours-a-day job. Belichick also maintained that his treadmill time with Kevin Williams had suddenly given him a fresh, broader perspective on life.

"That kid has gone through so much," he said. "Thinking of the commitment that Kevin has made just to live and what it takes to win and compete at a high level in this league, I looked out at the fields and thought of all the players and practices and all the game plans and all the decisions . . . all those things, and I went up to my office and wrote the letter."

Belichick was using a player's near-death experience as a shield. It was not his finest hour.

The 50-minute presser defined perhaps the most bizarre day in the history of a franchise that often led the league in bizarre days. Gutman took the podium after Belichick walked out and assured reporters that the coach's contract had been modified "on at least five occasions in the last three years" to address every management and control issue he'd raised. The team president called the existing contract "unambiguous" and surprised many in the auditorium by suggesting more than once that Belichick was in a state of personal chaos.

"We should have some feelings of sorrow and regret for him and his family," Gutman said. "He obviously has some inner turmoil."

The NFL then announced that the Jets' contract was binding, and that no NFL club was permitted to talk to their one-day wonder without the team's permission. Belichick had already planned to file a grievance with the league so he could pursue the New England job, leaving Parcells enraged over the way this was playing out.

Big Bill thought Little Bill owed him his loyalty. Parcells's high school basketball coach and lifelong father confessor, Mickey Corcoran, summed up his former player's feelings about Little Bill this way: "Parcells made [Belichick's] career. After he fell on his ass in Cleveland, he grabbed him right up. Without Bill Parcells there is no Belichick."

Tagliabue, the commissioner, would have to officiate this dispute, just as he'd officiated the dispute between the Jets and the Patriots over Parcells three years earlier. Meanwhile, one week after Belichick's resignation, Woody Johnson won the right to purchase the Jets with a bid of $635 million. He immediately tried to persuade Parcells to return to the sidelines.

That wasn't going to happen. Parcells wasn't going to return to his vacated job, and Belichick wasn't going to return to his, either. They ended up face-to-face on the 38th floor of a Times Square building in an eight-hour hearing to determine Belichick's status. Big Bill testified for more than an hour, and Little Bill for more than three. Charlie Weis testified for only three minutes but reportedly revealed that he had heard Parcells tell Gutman that Belichick wouldn't gain the full personnel control that was outlined in his contract. Feeling betrayed by an assistant he'd hired for the Giants in 1990, when Weis's last two jobs had been selling long-distance phone service in South Carolina and coaching New Jersey high school football, Parcells threw Weis out of the Jets' facility for good the very next day.

Tagliabue eventually ruled in favor of the Jets, swatting away Belichick's claim that he never actually took over as head coach by citing more than ten discussions between Big Bill and Little Bill about putting the succession plan in place after the 1999 season. Belichick was then about to withdraw an antitrust claim against the team and the league after a federal judge denied his request for a temporary restraining order that would've granted his freedom. In fact, U.S. District Court Judge John Bissell chided Belichick for locking himself in a prison of his own design.

"He had a head coaching position with the New York Jets, highly compensated, with the prestige, the title, the exposure, the market, and the team that certainly should have provided to him adequate rewards," Bissell said. "It was he who turned his back on that."

Parcells knew that he was holding a big hammer — that he could force Belichick into exile by compelling Kraft to hire Jacksonville Jaguars defensive coordinator Dom Capers. So on January 25, three weeks after Little Bill quit, Big Bill called Kraft's office and identified himself as Darth Vader. The Patriots' owner knew it was an ominous villain of a different kind.

They talked for the first time since their acrimonious divorce. They even reminisced and laughed, and agreed that each could've handled things differently before and after their Super Bowl loss to Green Bay. And when they got down to business, Parcells told Kraft he needed his first-round draft pick in exchange for Belichick. He wanted a first-rounder for a coach with a losing record just a year after Green Bay got a second-rounder from Seattle for the right to hire a Super Bowl winner, Mike Holmgren.

Baltimore Ravens owner Art Modell, who'd lived the Belichick experience in Cleveland, was among the many league observers who couldn't believe the asking price. Modell had warned Kraft that he shouldn't make Belichick his football coach. "If you do it," Modell said, "you'll be making the biggest mistake of your life."

Executives inside NFL headquarters, including Belichick's old friend George Young, the former Giants GM who became the league's senior VP of football operations, strongly encouraged Kraft to hire someone else. Columnists in New York wrote that Little Bill's method of escape exposed him as an unworthy candidate. (BELICHICKEN — JETS BETTER OFF WITHOUT QUITTER, read a New York Post headline.) Friends in the Boston media sent Kraft tapes of Belichick at his mummified worst in press conference settings in Cleveland. Though the owner was alarmed by what he saw on those tapes, Kraft kept hearing from Patriots defensive backs such as Ty Law and Lawyer Milloy that Little Bill was a keeper. The owner kept going back to Belichick's early command of the salary cap and his willingness to consistently communicate with Kraft during the 1996 season when Parcells would not.

The risk-taker couldn't resist his hunch; Kraft called back Parcells to say he was ready to do the deal. The owner had thought about the fickle nature of draft picks. He thought about using his 1998 first-rounder from the Jets — received as compensation after they stole away Curtis Martin — on running back Robert Edwards, who would follow up a great rookie season by wrecking his knee and his career playing flag football in the sand at the Pro Bowl in Hawaii.

In Kraft's opinion, Belichick was a safer bet. So Kraft agreed to build their transaction around New England's first pick in the 2000 draft, No. 16 overall. Early the following morning, Parcells called a flabbergasted Belichick to give him the OK to contact Kraft, and to make sure he secured at least four years in his contract.

A cease-fire had been established in all Jets–Patriots hostilities. Parcells faxed a letter to Kraft at his International Forest Products office in Boston. The letter read as follows:

Dear Bob:

This letter is intended to memorialize our conversation from last night, which occurred around 11:00 pm.

The New York Jets hereby grant permission to the New England Patriots to talk to Bill Belichick about any position they desire.

If Bill Belichick accepts and assumes a position with the New England Patriots, and reports to work on or before Monday, January 31, 2000, then the New York Jets trade to the New England Patriots their 5th round pick in the 2001 annual NFL selection draft, and their 7th round pick in the 2002 annual NFL selection draft, and the New England Patriots trade their 1st round pick in the 2000 annual NFL selection draft (16th overall), their 4th pick in the 2001 annual NFL selection draft, and their 7th round pick in the 2001 annual NFL selection draft.

Formal trade papers will follow, and all copies will be filed with the league office.

Sincerely,

Bill Parcells

Kraft and Belichick started finalizing their deal by phone around 10 a.m., and the coach who was facing a season on the bench jumped into his car and made the four-hour drive from his Long Island home to a hotel in Mansfield, Massachusetts. Kraft picked up his new coach at the hotel and drove him in his Lexus to the team's facility in Foxborough, where some cameramen were waiting near the plowed-off snow at the gate. The Patriots introduced their new head coach at 6 p.m.

"Hopefully this press conference will go a little better than the last one I had," Belichick said in his opening remarks, drawing a rare hearty laugh from his audience. He thanked reporters for gathering at a late hour, on short notice. "I know the last three weeks have probably been trying for all of you," the new coach continued, "but that's all behind me. I'm tremendously excited to be here and to be a part of the New England Patriots organization. This is a first-class operation."

Belichick described the previous three weeks as "quite an ordeal," though he denied that he was fleeing Parcells more than he was fleeing the ownership uncertainty now embodied by Woody Johnson. "If I wanted to get out of Bill's shadow," Belichick said, "I wouldn't have come to New England. There's a shadow up here, too." Out of his failed five-year term in Cleveland, Belichick said he'd learned to delegate more and put a greater focus on big-picture tasks.

Kraft was overjoyed about having landed the man Parcells had first persuaded him to take on as an assistant, over budget, four years earlier. The owner and Belichick started mapping out their plans over dinner at the Capital Grille, in Chestnut Hill. Meanwhile, a number of columnists and respected football voices weren't quite as thrilled with the move. Paul Needell, of the *Star-Ledger* in New Jersey, wrote that the Patriots' owner was the clear loser in the trade. Across the river, one New York columnist wrote that Kraft would regret the day he hired Belichick. Up in Boston, *Herald* columnist Karen Guregian named nine coaching legends, including Parcells, whom she found worthy of a first-round pick, and Belichick didn't make the cut.

Parcells? He rejected the notion that he'd outfoxed Kraft, and stated that he would've paid the same price if put in Kraft's situation. Big Bill said he was glad Little Bill was back in the game.

"The Patriots got a good man," Parcells said. "He'll be a formidable adversary."

Big Bill had no idea.

10

BRADY

The NFL was back to playing football 12 days after the 9/11 terrorist attacks, and Bill Belichick was already telling confidants that he feared for his job. Part of his stated concern was an extension of his natural pessimism — Bill Parcells had nicknamed him Doom for a reason. Belichick liked to tell people his team sucked whether or not he believed it to be true.

This time around, he had real cause to worry. He'd coached 17 games with the New England Patriots and lost 12 of them, and his most recent game had been a dispiriting road loss to a lousy Cincinnati team to open the 2001 season. Belichick was ripped afterward for failing to challenge a questionable spot on Drew Bledsoe's fourth-and-two quarterback sneak, which had come up an inch short in the final minutes. Meanwhile, he was locked in an energy-draining stare-down with his most productive playmaker in 2000, Terry Glenn, who had been suspended for four games over substance abuse, and for the remaining 12 games by Belichick for leaving camp, before winning a grievance and his reinstatement to the active roster in Week 5.

Robert Kraft was already confessing to associates that maybe he should've listened to Art Modell, that maybe he should've kept that first-round pick he surrendered to land Belichick, and that maybe he would have to fire his coach at season's end. He'd gotten rid of Pete Carroll after Bill Parcells's replacement won an average of nine games over three seasons, and here was Belichick starting his second season on a miserable note after winning only five. Carroll didn't have complete personnel control in New England, and he had advised Kraft, upon exit, to give that power to his successor. Now Kraft was wondering if he'd made a big mistake in following Carroll's advice.

So Belichick carried this heavy baggage onto the Foxboro Stadium field before the second game of 2001, a home game against his old friends the New York Jets, who felt a much more profound burden as high-profile representatives of their devastated city. Belichick had shown a proper human touch in the wake of the attacks by suspending operations and allowing his players time away to be with their families. Now that the Patriots and the Jets had reassembled for football, the man who had quit the latter to join the former appeared to have put his money on the wrong horse.

Years later, multiple sources would say that in a pregame conversation, Belichick told the Jets' rookie head coach, Herm Edwards, that he was likely on his way to getting fired for a second time. One Jets coach, Mike Westhoff, said Belichick told Edwards, "I don't know if I'll make it through the year. We stink." Edwards insisted that this hadn't happened. The Jets coach did say that Belichick's offensive coordinator, Charlie Weis, had expressed concerns to him about the state of New England's program while the two spoke on the field before kickoff. Edwards declined to offer specifics, but Weis had already shared with others that the staff thought Bledsoe was running the locker room and resisting some of the culture changes Belichick was trying to install. "We don't have veteran guys believing in our system," Weis told one coach.

This had hardly been Belichick's vision when he took over in 2000 and attempted to toughen up what he found to be a soft, flabby, and mentally weak team. For starters, he tried to work the New England holdovers and newcomers into his idea of peak physical shape. The Belichick-Parcells idea of what peak physical shape meant didn't always jibe with the definition of the term around the league. Kevin Williams, the recovering Jet who was on the treadmill next to Belichick the morning of his resignation, ended up with Dave Wannstedt's Miami Dolphins late that 2000 season and discovered that not every NFL head coach was as maniacal in his approach.

"Those guys in Miami, they would have died playing for Parcells and Belichick," Williams said. "Wannstedt had those boys on cruise control. I was like 'What, you can actually be like this?' You can actually jog through practice?' It was crazy."

A number of Patriots had felt the same way about Carroll, a born-and-raised, sunglasses-and-sandals Californian who was laid-back enough to allow staffers to enter his office without invitation and initiate conversation about football, philosophy, pickup basketball, or life. The players initially took to this style, of course, because they felt liberated from Parcells's despotic methods.

But after winning ten games and a playoff game in year one, Carroll's Patriots won nine games and lost their first-round playoff game in year two, and then went 8-8 and missed the postseason in year three. The lack of discipline was slowly eroding what the Parcells-Belichick Patriots had established in their run to the Super Bowl, and Belichick had returned to restore some law and order. Naturally, he met with some resistance.

"A lot of guys maybe don't want to say it, but they didn't want to play for

Belichick when he came in," said Michael Bishop, a backup quarterback in 2000 who had been drafted by Carroll. "It was his way or the highway, and I think some guys preferred the highway."

Belichick had fired strength-and-conditioning coach Johnny Parker, a former colleague with the Giants and the Patriots, right after he accepted Kraft's offer, and four months later he fired Bobby Grier. He tossed former first-round pick Andy Katzenmoyer from the first team meeting for showing up late. In another meeting, he called out another former first-round pick, Tebucky Jones, a safety who had an impressive 40-yard-dash time out of Syracuse. "Tebucky," Belichick said, "you ran a 4.43 at the combine, but you really run a 5.0, because you don't know where the fuck you're going."

Nobody was safe. In one film session, an assistant coach criticized an opposing quarterback for looking at the exact spot where he wanted to throw the ball, prompting his boss to stop the tape. "You're joking, right?" Belichick asked the assistant. "How the fuck do you think he gets the ball there? He has to look where he's throwing."

Marc Megna, a noseguard from the University of Richmond who was drafted by the Jets in 1999 and was trying to make the Patriots as a linebacker in 2000, recalled being shocked over the quality of players Belichick was willing to cut. Though he didn't need the reminder, Megna said Belichick constantly told him, "This isn't fucking William & Mary we're playing" whenever he committed an unforced error in camp.

A long shot from Fall River, Massachusetts, Megna thought he had made his hometown team in the final preseason game against Carolina, when he ran free and blasted Panthers quarterback Dameyune Craig for the sack. He was thrilled with himself as he headed to the sideline. He was basking in the biggest moment of his football life, and fully expecting a hearty attaboy from his coach, before Belichick stopped him cold.

"Come on, Marc," he sniped, "you've got to get the fucking ball out." Megna didn't even get a "good job" out of him. He was waived three days later, though brought back late in the season.

It would be a long season for all involved, which wouldn't have been hard to predict at the start of training camp. Belichick installed a grueling conditioning test that, according to the team, required quarterbacks, linebackers, fullbacks, and tight ends to run twenty 50-yard sprints in seven seconds a rep, and for tailbacks, wide receivers, and defensive backs to run twenty 60-yard sprints in eight seconds a rep. Offensive linemen had to run sprints of 40 yards in six seconds, with a half-minute break between reps. The results were less than encouraging.

"We have too many guys who are overweight," Belichick said, "too many guys who are out of shape, too many guys who just haven't paid the price they need to pay at this point of the season. I think it's basically a situation where you can't win in this league with 40 good players when the other team has 53. You need to match them, and I guess I haven't done a very good job of getting through to the players on what they need to do to prepare for an NFL season."

Belichick immediately ripped off a series of fines for ill-conditioned players that ran into the tens of thousands. Tony George, a defensive back and diabetic, was among those who failed the test after completing 19 of the 20 sprints; he later explained that he was in danger of suffering a diabetic coma and yet hadn't stopped running earlier because he didn't want to use his diabetes as an excuse.

Belichick had warned the Patriots that there would be no excuses for failure. Damien Woody, second-year starter on the offensive line, said the new coach delivered a grim speech to open the 2000 camp that was short and bitter and left "jaws dropping all over the room." Belichick told his players that they shouldn't ask for breaks, because they wouldn't be given any. "There is no light at the end of the tunnel," he told them. When Belichick walked out of the room, Woody thought to himself, *Oh, my God, what are we in store for?* The message was clear: The Patriots were no longer being coached by Pete Carroll.

And then Belichick started running his players hard and ordering them to crash into one another at full speed, over and over again.

"It was honestly a living hell," Woody said. "It felt like we practiced in pads for three and a half weeks straight. It was crazy . . . Not many human beings could withstand that first Bill Belichick training camp.

"He wouldn't let anything go all year. Any little detail . . . Imagine being in pads and practicing two and a half hours and the coach blows his whistle and tells you to start it over right from stretching. When you've got something like that going on, and you're getting tested at night in meetings, it's physical and mental warfare. Who is going to be left standing?"

Belichick tested everyone, from the few big names on the roster to the undrafted players fighting for the last couple of spots. Shockmain Davis, a receiver from Angelo State, recalled dropping a corner-route pass from the sixth-round pick, Tom Brady, in a preseason game and having Belichick rewind the tape over and over in front of the team. Davis said that he had to dive for the ball and that the defender interfered with him, but the coach didn't care. "We've seen you make this play eight million times," Belichick barked, "and you mean to tell me you couldn't catch this ball?" Belichick wouldn't stop rewinding the damn tape. "You just want him to move on to the next guy," Davis said. "You don't want to be that guy in the team meeting after the game. He's going to expose you."

The Patriots were all exposed early in that regular season. They lost their first four games, and they didn't score more than 19 points in any of them. New England finally broke through in Week 5, when Bledsoe passed for four touchdowns in a road victory over Denver and earned AFC Offensive Player of the Week honors. Only the good vibe didn't last long: The quarterback made a couple of bad throws in his next practice. "And Bill looked at him," recalled one veteran starter, "and said, 'Stop thinking about your fucking awards.' And Drew just said [sarcastically], 'Yeah, that's what I was thinking about.' I've never seen a head coach talk to a franchise player like that."

Even in the worst of times, Carroll was hell-bent on keeping his players upbeat. His successor had no use for that glass-half-full dogma. One player said that some Patriots thought Belichick had too quick a hook, and that they played hesitantly and in fear of making a mistake. "There were a lot of people unhappy," the player said. Another Patriot said Belichick once gathered the players and told them they needed to conform to his ways or they would "cease to exist here."

One veteran who had spent time elsewhere with what he described as a user-friendly franchise raged against New England's small-time operation — players had to drive to an off-site practice field, and incoming players were often housed in the nearby Endzone Motor Inn — and called the team's leaky, creaky stadium and relatively primitive facilities "pretty freaking brutal." He said the culture inside the organization was no more agreeable. "I just felt there wasn't a lot of warmth in the building. If you asked for anything, it was a problem. If you asked the equipment manager, 'Hey, can I get another pair of socks?' he'd be like 'What happened to your other socks?'"

This veteran said that typical tough-guy coaches of losing NFL teams usually try a kinder, gentler approach in midstream to salvage something of the season. "But not with Belichick," he said. "It just got worse and worse and worse." The player said that the full-contact hitting during the team's bye week was extreme, and that two weeks later the coach took out his frustrations on his 2-8 team after a trip to Cleveland, in its second year with the expansion Browns filling the void left by Art Modell's move to Baltimore. Cleveland fans mocked their former coach with "Belichick sucks" chants and a large BELICHICK 2-7, YOU STILL STINK sign, in a 19–11 Browns victory lowlighted by Bledsoe's three lost fumbles.

"Worst performance we had all year," the veteran said, "and that Monday I expected some pullback from this tyranny. And he comes in and he's like 'All right, you heard those fans on Sunday. OK, I do suck. But here's what you motherfuckers did.' And then he has the lights turned off, and then the film goes on and it's ten straight minutes of nothing but screwups and bad plays. I thought, *This is crazy. How much lower can you get?* . . . The overall mentality was that he was creating unity among the players, except that they were all unified in their hatred toward him. It was almost a strategy — that the disdain for him would bring them together."

Truth is, Belichick had in place a wide circle of executives, coaches, and aides who would go on to do big, important things in the NFL. He had an assistant head coach, Dante Scarnecchia, who would become as great an offensive line coach as the game had seen. Belichick had at the very bottom of his staff a local kid who used to fetch morning newspapers for Parcells, Mark Jackson, who would ultimately run the Villanova athletic department during a time when the Wildcats were winning two NCAA basketball titles.

But at the time, the quality of teaching wasn't yielding classroom results. Belichick had twice lost to the hated Jets, and before this season mercifully ended he'd be thoroughly embarrassed by three of his best players — cornerback Ty Law, receiver Troy Brown, and the reinstated Terry Glenn. The Patriots had beaten the Bills in Buffalo in near blizzard conditions, and Glenn had cited his fear of flying in wintry weather in refusing to take the team charter home that night. Belichick allowed Brown and Law to stay with Glenn as long as they made it to Foxborough in time for an early-afternoon meeting. Only the three ended up in a strip club that night on the other side of the Canadian border, and on Law's drive back, with a female companion, around 5:30 a.m., U.S. customs officials stopped his car and found the drug Ecstasy in his baggage. The cornerback maintained his innocence and ignorance — he said that the baggage belonged to a relative and that he had no idea illegal drugs were stashed inside. Law was fined $700 by authorities and suspended for the final game of the season by Belichick, who repeatedly told inquiring reporters that he saw the case and the penalty as an "internal matter."

The episode did nothing to support the notion the Patriots were more disciplined under their new coach than they had been under Carroll. Of course, the Patriots lost that final game — at home, to Wannstedt's cruise-control Dolphins, who clinched the AFC East title. Belichick watched the playoffs at home for the fifth time in six seasons as a head coach, and after the New York Giants routed Minnesota in the NFC Championship Game, he called his former general manager in Cleveland, Ernie Accorsi, who in 1998 had succeeded George Young as the Giants' GM. Accorsi said it was the very first call he got that Monday morning.

"Congratulations," Belichick told him. "And I want to apologize for fucking that thing up in Cleveland."

"You didn't fuck it up," Accorsi assured him.

But it was an open question as to whether Belichick would fuck it up in Foxborough. His off-season was actually shaped by a personnel move that seemed to betray the idea that he had autonomy over his roster. Bledsoe had been sacked 100 times and thrown nearly the same number of interceptions (34) as touchdowns (36) over the 1999 and 2000 seasons, and yet the Patriots signed him to a ten-year, $103 million deal. Though it was likely Bledsoe wouldn't earn anywhere close to that figure — contracts aren't fully guaranteed in the NFL — the agreement represented a major investment in an immobile quarterback who had just been subjected to some fan and media calls for his benching in favor of the more elusive Bishop. Robert Kraft was heavily involved in the negotiations; he personally called Bledsoe to close out the deal. The owner loved the quarterback, and the quarterback loved him back. Bledsoe described Kraft as a mentor, and the owner hoped to make him a Patriots lifer and keep him as the face of the team as it prepared to move into the new stadium being built next door. Their relationship reminded veteran Belichick watchers of the one shared by Modell and Bernie Kosar in Cleveland.

By the time the delayed second game of the 2001 season arrived, Belichick was about as ready to move on from Bledsoe as he was to move on from Kosar in 1993. In Cleveland and New York, Belichick never thought Bledsoe was a particularly difficult quarterback to game-plan against. But even he couldn't possibly make the switch one game deep into a $103 million contract. So after a moving pregame tribute to 9/11 victims and emergency responders at the World Trade Center, including the three firefighting brothers of New England guard Joe Andruzzi, all survivors, Bledsoe took the field with an 0-1 Patriots team that looked quite different from its 5-11 predecessor.

Just as Belichick had made more than two dozen roster changes from Carroll's last team to his own first team, he made more than two dozen from 2000 to 2001, all with the help of his trusted aide, Scott Pioli, who had taken Grier's seat in the cabinet. Pioli had met Belichick in his Little Bill days with the Giants, when Pioli was a football player at Central Connecticut State, and had followed him to Cleveland and later to the Jets. Though Pioli would marry Bill Parcells's daughter, he chose to follow Belichick again, to New England, after Little Bill's nasty divorce from Big Bill.

Kraft never thought he'd hire a member of Big Bill's family, not after the way he had left the Patriots for the Jets following the 1996 season. "Parcells fucked us," Kraft told a fellow owner. "And I let Belichick talk me into hiring Parcells's son-in-law. That's how much I trusted Belichick's opinion of people."

While he was coaching linemen at Murray State, Pioli had been offered a personnel job by Belichick in Cleveland. His boss at Murray State, Mike Mahoney, thought of Pioli as a terrific recruiter and evaluator and advised him to turn down the Browns and stay in coaching. Pioli didn't listen; he'd harbored a dream of someday running an NFL team. Now he was Belichick's personnel chief in New England, trying to build a big, physical, weatherproof contender.

With help from Andy Wasynczuk, a Kraft executive from the Parcells and Carroll days, Pioli made bargain-basement deals with a truckload of veteran free agents. The GM and Belichick felt good about the players they'd landed in the off-season, including a defensive end they had with the Browns and the Jets, Anthony Pleasant; an 11th-year linebacker they had with the Jets, Bryan Cox; a running back from Buffalo, Antowain Smith; a special teams madman from Miami, Larry Izzo; and a linebacker who had disappointed in Pittsburgh, Mike Vrabel, whom Belichick had promised he'd sign ASAP when he saw him at the 1997 combine.

Belichick and Pioli also felt good about their most recent top two draft choices, defensive end Richard Seymour and offensive tackle Matt Light, though the Patriots were criticized in some corners for ignoring their glaring offensive needs with the sixth overall pick by taking Seymour instead of Michigan receiver David Terrell. The team was still using a revamped version of the scouting system put in place decades earlier by former coach Chuck Fairbanks and Bucko Kilroy, a former All-Pro lineman turned scout and executive who was regarded as a founding father of player evaluation and who worked with Gil Brandt on the Dallas Cowboys' computerized method of grading prospects. That system had not produced much help in the 2000 draft; nine of the team's ten picks in that draft would ultimately combine for zero Pro Bowl appearances and all of three seasons as primary NFL starters. The lone exception was Tom Brady, a 6′4″ quarterback out of Michigan and San Mateo, California. He was the 199th overall pick of the draft, and when the announcement was made, Brady said he "had to look on a map to see where the New England Patriots played, because I had never been this far east."

He'd spent his rookie year as a fourth-string player in dire need of adding weight to his flagpole frame. In the preseason of that year, one teammate said, "I remember thinking to myself, *It's really a shame Tom's not going to make this team. He's a good player.* I was shocked he made the team." Inactive for 14 games in 2000, Brady had returned for his second year bigger and stronger, if not faster. (He was clocked at 5.28 in the 40 at the draft combine, where his running style evoked a panting insurance broker chasing after a cab.) Brady was so sharp in the preseason, he jumped ahead of Bishop, who was waived, and veteran Damon Huard, who had won five of six starts in Miami and been signed to a three-year, $3 million deal to back up Bledsoe. The receivers thought Brady threw a light, catchable ball. Belichick was struck by how he took control of his rookie class, including the defensive players, with a firm on-field presence and a commitment to film study and post-practice workouts that went unmatched.

"Tom has a lot of natural leadership," Belichick said the day he promoted Brady to second-string.

Bledsoe was still the starter, and Belichick was still a coach unsure whether his team had the fortitude to avoid a repeat of 2000. He lost himself in his job, as always, and if he came up for air once in that summer of 2001, it was for a concert featuring Jon Bon Jovi at the Tweeter Center, in Mansfield, where Bill and Debby gathered with some staffers. Belichick was a card-carrying rock-and-roll fan — he'd taken his Cleveland staff to see Pink Floyd — but nobody touched Bon Jovi, whom Bill and Debby had followed around Europe when he was opening for the Rolling Stones. For this show at the Tweeter Center, Belichick invited ball boy Zak DeOssie, an Andover student and the son of former Giants linebacker Steve DeOssie. They sat about 16 rows back, dead center, and when Bon Jovi performed "Livin' on a Prayer," the ball boy saw Belichick singing along and getting into it with the crowd. "He wasn't swinging from chandeliers," DeOssie said, "but he was certainly enjoying it."

The good times were fleeting. Belichick had a large anchor placed in the locker room to remind the players of the dead weight his ill-conditioned team had carried around the year before. To show his players the ultimate exercise in teamwork overcoming long odds, Belichick took them to a Providence theater to see a film about the early-20th-century explorer Ernest Shackleton, whose men somehow survived a nearly two-year ordeal after their ship was crushed by ice and sank in the Antarctic.

The 2001 Patriots confronted real-world adversity of their own before the season started, when their quarterbacks coach, Dick Rehbein, died of heart failure during camp after passing out on a treadmill and again during a hospital stress test. Rehbein had a good working relationship with Bledsoe and had done more campaigning on Brady's behalf, before the 2000 draft, than anyone in the organization. Rehbein had Brady reading biographies on everyone from General George Patton to former Giants quarterback Phil Simms to learn more about leadership.

"He made you look forward to coming to work," Bledsoe said of his late position coach, "even in the hard times."

Belichick and Weis took on Rehbein's responsibilities with the quarterbacks; Romeo Crennel, Belichick's former staffmate with the Giants, Patriots, and Jets, had taken over the defense in the off-season. After the Cincinnati loss in Week 1, the Patriots were desperate to beat the Jets in their home opener to establish a degree of stability in Belichick's program. Michael Felger, beat writer for the *Boston Herald*, had written in July of a "genuine feeling in Foxboro that the Pats will surprise a lot of people in 2001" because, among other reasons, Belichick and Pioli made sure there were "fewer bad players" on the depth chart than there were in 2000. An 0-2 start would pour a keg of cold beer on that optimism.

As it turned out, the Patriots and Jets played a game lacking in aesthetic value, especially from an offensive perspective. The Jets' Vinny Testaverde threw the ball 28 times for a lousy 137 yards and no touchdowns. Bledsoe did connect with Troy Brown on a 58-yarder, but he accounted for a grand sum of 101 yards on his other 27 attempts, along with two interceptions — including one in the end zone to kill a fourth-quarter drive — and no touchdowns. He also took a damaging delay-of-game penalty on a fourth-and-goal at the 1. Curtis Martin, the star back Parcells had pilfered from the Patriots, was the only man all day who carried the ball across the goal line, giving the Jets a 10–3 lead late in the third quarter.

Facing a third-and-10 at his own 19 with time melting away in the fourth, the 6'5" Bledsoe tried to salvage something out of nothing in a most unconventional way: with his feet. He felt the rush, scrambled out of the pocket to his right, and then headed down his own sideline for the first-down marker. As he was pursued by Shaun Ellis, the player the Jets had landed with the first-round pick New England sent them in the Belichick trade, Bledsoe ran, or trotted, in an upright and reluctant way. Just as a lunging Ellis got a piece of the Patriots' quarterback from behind, Jets linebacker Mo Lewis launched his right shoulder hard into Bledsoe's upper torso, two yards short of a first down, separating the quarterback from the ball and sending him flying out of bounds. It was a perfectly legal, if vicious, tackle that made a frightening noise.

"It sounded like someone had been hit by a truck," said Jets defensive coordinator Ted Cottrell.

Brady would call it "one of the hardest hits I'd ever seen. I could hear it. His entire facemask was turned around on his head and it was bent." Brady also said that if he got hit the same way, "I'd be in the hospital for a month." Bledsoe actually returned to the game for one more series, which ended in a second Marc Edwards fumble — all while a torn blood vessel was spilling blood into the quarterback's chest and abdomen. Of course, the Patriots' medical staff wasn't aware of the seriousness of the injury at the time, and it wasn't until Bledsoe was sent to Massachusetts General that the hemothorax was discovered and doctors realized their patient could've died from internal bleeding.

Before he'd even learned of the severity of Bledsoe's condition, Belichick reprimanded himself in his postgame news conference. "I shouldn't have put him out there," he said of Bledsoe's final series. "Watching him play, he wasn't himself. He got his bell rung. When I went over to him, he seemed coherent and said he was OK. But after watching him, I didn't think he was. I told him what decision I had made. He understood."

Yes, he understood why Belichick approached Tom Brady on the sideline and said, "Drew's out and you're in." Starting at his own 26 with 2:16 left and the Jets ahead by a touchdown, Brady completed five of his first six passes for short but productive gains, driving New England into Jets territory before an Andruzzi holding penalty sent him back across midfield. Brady erased that mistake by running for nine yards and then hitting receiver David Patten for 21, bringing a Foxborough crowd to life for the first time in his career. But as the clock worked against him, 29 yards away from pay dirt, Brady threw four consecutive incomplete passes to end the game and leave the Patriots devastated at 0-2.

As the teams walked off the field, the Jets' backup quarterback, Chad Pennington, was struck by the look on Brady's face. "He was completely dissatisfied with the result," said Pennington, a first-round pick in the 2000 draft and a prospect taken 181 spots ahead of Brady. "You could see in his eyes he expected to lead his team back . . . I saw in his demeanor in the game, his focus, drive, his eyes, body language — nothing about him said he was a sixth-round pick who was just happy to get a couple of reps."

Belichick was more concerned with the final score than with Brady's performance. "I felt like the team really deserved better," he said, which was a most un-Belichickian thing to claim about a loss defined by four New England turnovers. His team appeared to be a Cleveland-size mess. Belichick was 5-13 overall as Patriots coach, he couldn't generate any offense, and his stated intention of focusing more on the macro than the micro in his second head coaching stop wasn't translating into on-field success. Beyond that, one locker-room divide was suddenly deepening over the sight of Bryan Cox playfully interacting with his former Jets teammate John Abraham after Bledsoe was leveled. Pepper Johnson, a Belichick assistant at the time, would later write in his book *Won for All* that the scene "haunted us for some time" and inspired some to wonder about Cox's loyalties.

"A lot of guys were hurting after the loss to the Jets," Johnson wrote, "and some began thinking that we had these ex-Jets on the team who didn't give a damn about born-and-bred Patriots players. Even a lot of our coaches had come over from the Jets with Belichick . . . In addition, the ex-Jets were angry because they knew how some of their teammates felt, and they thought it was unfounded."

On the drive home from the stadium that night, agent Mark Lepselter, who had just placed his client Patten in New England, recalled listening to sports talk radio proclamations that Belichick was done in Foxborough, or should be done. Lepselter was among many who thought Belichick might be a couple of bad losses away from the end of his head coaching career, but his focus was on Patten, an undrafted receiver who had once lugged bags of coffee beans for a living and was trying to establish himself as a legitimate NFL starter in his fifth year. "And now you're wondering if your client is going to catch any footballs," Lepselter said. "We didn't have a clue about Tom Brady, or even know who he was."

Nobody did, not really. Tall and dimpled, Brady looked the part of a leading man and, despite being a sixth-round pick, projected first-round faith in himself. One day, after he was drafted, Brady was leaving the stadium and carrying a pizza box when he came upon Kraft and attempted to introduce himself before the owner cut him off.

"I know who you are," Kraft told him. "You're Tom Brady, our sixth-round pick out of Michigan."

The quarterback looked the owner in the eye.

"And I'm the best decision this organization has ever made," Brady said.

At 0-2 in 2001, Kraft was not a believer in that prophecy. Bledsoe was his boy, and now the franchise player was being replaced by an untested quarterback who'd had an uneven career at Michigan. Kraft couldn't afford this twisted turn of fate, not with a new stadium going up. Three years earlier, when he couldn't make a deal with Massachusetts lawmakers, Kraft had agreed to move the team to Hartford after Connecticut officials promised to build a $350 million stadium as part of a deal that could ultimately be worth $1 billion to him. He walked away from that deal of a lifetime five months later in order to keep the team in Foxborough, in an agreement that required him to contribute as much as $325 million of his own money.

As the Patriots were preparing to host the Indianapolis Colts in Week 3, the first start of Brady's career, a dour-looking Kraft approached linebacker Ted Johnson, lowered his head, and pointed toward the construction site of his new stadium. The owner didn't say much, and he didn't need to. "He was worried that nobody would sign up for season tickets," Johnson said.

Belichick was worried more about his career, and so were the people he brought with him to Foxborough. He'd hired Ernie Adams out of NFL exile, a second time, to be his shadow adviser and another set of Andover eyes. He'd taken Pioli from Parcells, and he'd turned over the offense to Weis, whom Parcells had dispatched over his perceived betrayal. He'd given the defense to Crennel and the defensive secondary to Eric Mangini, his fellow Wesleyan grad and a low-level Browns and Jets aide who had the look of an up-and-comer. He'd also hired Berj Najarian, the young PR man with the Jets who had played baseball at Manhasset, Jim Brown's high school on Long Island, and then at Boston University, before interning with the New York Knicks.

The Knicks' PR chief, John Cirillo, said Najarian "had the look of success" and "a great confidence and composure" when handling tasks that would normally be assigned to higher-ranking staffers. Najarian had grown close with Belichick by keeping the same round-the-clock schedule while they worked for the Jets. Frank Ramos, the Jets' PR chief, said he'd see the two side by side on treadmills before he left for his early-morning run. "I thought Berj did a very good job," Ramos said. "Very conscientious. The hours never meant anything to him." Belichick thought he needed his own de facto publicist, which he hadn't had in Cleveland, where he felt isolated in his endgame struggle with Modell and those who worked for him. Kraft wasn't about to move out his own media guys, Don Lowery and Stacey James, but he did allow the coach to hire someone to serve as his consigliere.

Najarian became Belichick's chief of staff, and one of his early moves was to arrange meetings between his boss and influential Boston media members, including some who had been critical of the Kraft hire, to help bridge the chasm between the coach and the press. One *Boston Globe* columnist, Michael Holley, had written weeks earlier that Belichick had lorded over awful drafts in Cleveland, and that his hiring would leave the Patriots "looking like the ruins of Rome." Najarian had some work to do.

Upon his arrival in 2000, Belichick sat down with the *Globe*'s Ron Borges for a humanizing, 4,400-word magazine piece that detailed his life on Nantucket—his Wesleyan lacrosse teammate, Mark Fredland, helped Belichick build three homes there, including two used by his parents and in-laws—and quoted old classmates and friends talking about a softer side the coach kept hidden from public view. Belichick also did a sit-down in Nantucket with *Globe* columnist Dan Shaughnessy for *ESPN the Magazine*, though he insisted on doing the interview at an airport inn—no home visits allowed.

"They were trying to make nice and repair his damaged Cleveland reputation," Shaughnessy said of Belichick and Najarian. The writer recalled Belichick arranging salt shakers on the table to diagram plays and using his wife, Debby, as a prop to illustrate a blocking technique; Shaughnessy thought the coach came off as more likable than his reputation suggested. Belichick met with another columnist, Steve Buckley of the *Herald,* in the coach's grim Foxboro Stadium office — the writer likened it to a high school guidance counselor's office — and told him he was among the few who wrote about his stormy New York escape and actually got it right.

Whatever goodwill came out of Belichick's marginally lighter approach to media relations wasn't going to last unless the Patriots started winning football games. One league official said that Belichick had been "toxic" when he started in New England and that the FOBs (Friends of Bill) who left the Jets to join him "were almost committing career suicide going with him. He was hated. Well, maybe not hated, but he wasn't liked around the league, and his friends weren't liked, either."

So all of Belichick's men felt a profound sense of urgency at 0-2, with the $103 million quarterback just starting to recover from his life-threatening bleed. In fact, one team official said that some members of the coaching staff and front office were "secretly happy" that they could get Brady on the field without upsetting Kraft, who all but considered Bledsoe his fifth son. Of course, they weren't happy that Bledsoe was seriously hurt; they'd never wish that on anyone. But Belichick, Pioli, and others wanted to play Brady, and they couldn't figure out how to get that accomplished. Now they had their opening. Now they had an opportunity to dramatically alter the dynamics of the program. Now Belichick could move on from Bledsoe and avoid a sequel to the Kosar fiasco that had caused him such irreparable harm in Cleveland.

"I don't think we're talking about John Elway here," Belichick said of Brady, "but I don't know how many of those there are. He's got a good NFL arm. I really don't think I'm going to be standing here week after week talking about the problems that Tom Brady had. I have confidence in him."

Brady had earned that trust by surviving a most improbable journey to a starting position in the NFL. In 1991, as a teenager in San Mateo, California, the brother of three older sisters who were terrific athletes, Brady was a backup on an 0-8 freshman team at Junipero Serra High School that scored two touchdowns all year. He was a pear-shaped 6'1" sophomore who got a break on the junior varsity when the kid ahead of him, Kevin Krystofiak, quit football to focus on basketball. The JV coach, Joe Hession, thought Brady looked more like an offensive tackle but gave him a shot at quarterback anyway. In the first quarterback start of his life, a scrimmage against Pinole Valley, the 15-year-old Brady took such a fierce pounding that Hession felt like quitting and drowning his sorrows at the nearest bar.

Neither the coach nor the player quit. Through constant film study and footwork and jump-rope drills to improve his small-college speed and agility, Brady made himself a big-college prospect. He won only 11 of 20 games as a two-year varsity starter but threw the ball convincingly enough to earn a scholarship offer from Michigan. Some of his coaches wondered if he should take the safer, closer option at Cal–Berkeley, or even if he should pursue baseball — the Montreal Expos would pick the left-handed-hitting catcher with power in the 18th round in the 1995 draft. But Brady fell in love with Ann Arbor, much to the dismay of his father, Tom Sr., who needed eight weeks of psychological counseling to deal with the fact that his only boy would be playing some 2,100 miles from home.

Actually, Brady would be sitting — not playing — some 2,100 miles from home. "I got to Michigan, I was seventh [string]," he said, "and I had a hard time getting to be number two. And when I finally got to be number one, there was someone else they wanted to be number one."

Drew Henson, everybody's all-American. A fourth-year junior, Brady had thrown all of 20 passes over his first three years as a student. He'd earlier told his head coach, Lloyd Carr, that he was seriously weighing a transfer to Cal. "Tom pretty much had his plane ticket purchased and was ready to go," said his friend and fellow quarterback Jason Kapsner. Brady reconsidered and returned to Carr's office to tell him he'd decided to stick it out. And now the 6′4″, 220-pound Henson, a three-sport phenom from nearby Brighton High, had come along just when Brady had ascended to first string. At a Michigan team autograph session, about 500 people lined up from midfield to the end zone to spend a fleeting moment with Henson — who had set national career high school records with 70 home runs and 290 RBI and who had already banked $2 million to play minor league ball in the summer for the New York Yankees — while the ignored Brady stood in the stadium tunnel with a student assistant named Jay Flannelly. Brady signed three autographs that day, tops, and never took his eyes off that endless line to Henson.

Brady was such a non-star at Michigan that one prominent booster waiting near the team bus one day with a Sharpie and a souvenir program didn't want him to sign the program, because he coveted only the autographs of legitimate NFL prospects. As an athlete, Henson was everything Brady wasn't. Carr felt so much pressure to play the freshman that he had him share first-team snaps with Brady in the late summer of 1998, after the fourth-year junior had beaten out Kapsner and Scott Dreisbach in the spring for the job vacated by Brian Griese, who had led the Wolverines to the national championship.

Carr named Brady the starter, yet he immediately said the golden-boy freshman would also get to play. For most of his two seasons as Michigan's starter, Brady dealt with the ever-looming specter of Henson, who held a hammer over Carr. The kid had the New York Yankees as leverage, and a father who was representing him while working for the global juggernaut that was IMG. Students, alums, boosters — they all wanted to see Henson, even with Brady as a senior co-captain in 1999. Carr started that season playing Henson in the second quarter as part of a rotation that had him going with the hot hand in the second half. Despite knowing that one mistake at the wrong time could cost him, Brady eventually played Henson back to the bench for good. He'd win 20 of 25 games and effectively go the distance in his final start at Michigan, an epic 35–34 overtime victory over Alabama in the Orange Bowl that saw Brady overcome two 14-point deficits and throw for 369 yards and four touchdowns — he threw 46 passes against the Crimson Tide, while Henson threw one.

And yet only one NFL executive called Carr about Brady before the draft in the spring: Bobby Grier of the New England Patriots, who had worked with Carr at Eastern Michigan. "Bobby," Carr told him, "there's no doubt in my mind that Tom Brady will be a starting quarterback in the NFL."

Carr raved about his quarterback's toughness. He recalled watching an overmatched Brady take hit after hit during his first scrimmage as a freshman — "He got the hell beat out of him," said the Michigan coach — and pulling himself up and quickly rejoining the huddle time after time. Brady had overcome a lot in his five years in Ann Arbor, including Carr's reluctance to give him the ball full-time, and the coach thought the weathered adversity would make his quarterback a better pro than his showing at the draft combine suggested.

Carr figured the Patriots would be a good fit, too, because he thought highly of Belichick. As Michigan's defensive coordinator in the late eighties, Carr spent a day watching film with Belichick in the Giants Stadium dungeon; he called it one of the best days of his coaching career. He was struck by Belichick's versatility, his knowledge of every defensive and offensive position on the field, and his willingness to take follow-up questions over the phone. Carr said that Michigan made a number of changes to its defense based on Belichick's recommendations, and that the Giants' assistant helped his career.

A dozen years later, Belichick liked Carr's quarterback, and so did Scott Pioli. But nobody in the Patriots organization liked Tom Brady as much as Dick Rehbein did. Belichick had asked the assistant to take a look at two quarterbacks — Brady and Tim Rattay, at Louisiana Tech — for a possible selection later in the draft. Rehbein thought one was clearly better than the other. "Twenty years from now," Rehbein told his wife, Pam, after returning from his scouting trip to Michigan, "people will know the name Tom Brady . . . Someday this is going to be a Joe Montana or Brett Favre."

Rehbein told his boss to find a round, any round, to draft the kid. Belichick was a bit concerned that Carr kept trying to find ways to replace

Brady with Henson, and he already had a nine-figure player at quarterback in Bledsoe and two backups in Bishop and ten-year veteran John Friesz. Brady would be a nice piece to add to the roster, but in Belichick's mind he was certainly not a must-have prospect.

As the draft unfolded, after Pennington went to the Jets in the first round, Brady missed out on a couple of opportunities to go where he thought he belonged in the early to middle rounds. His hometown team, the 49ers, took Hofstra quarterback Giovanni Carmazzi with the 65th overall pick. Ten picks later, the Baltimore Ravens took Louisville's Chris Redman, despite the fact that their offensive coordinator, former NFL quarterback Matt Cavanaugh, had lobbied hard for Brady. In the fifth and sixth rounds, three more quarterbacks came off the board: Tee Martin, Marc Bulger, and Spergon Wynn.

A New York Giants scout named Whitey Walsh was another big fan of Brady's, though he thought the quarterback "looked kind of emaciated, with no muscle definition." Walsh was imploring Giants GM Ernie Accorsi to take the Michigan quarterback before it was too late. "He was very forceful," Accorsi recalled, but nobody in the draft room was moved. Rehbein grew nervous as round after round passed without New England selecting his guy. Belichick took an offensive tackle (Hawaii's Adrian Klemm), a running back (Arizona State's J. R. Redmond), another offensive tackle (Michigan State's Greg Randall), a tight end (Boise State's Dave Stachelski), a guard (Missouri's Jeff Marriott), and a strong safety (Virginia's Antwan Harris) before he arrived at his seventh pick of the draft, No. 199 overall — one of four compensatory picks granted the Patriots after they lost four players in free agency. Six quarterbacks had been chosen by other teams over the first 198 selections, and none were named Tom Brady or Tim Rattay.

On April 16, 2000, his 48th birthday, Belichick decided the former seventh-stringer in Ann Arbor should be his fourth-stringer in Foxborough. One of New England's scouts, Jason Licht, was in the draft room when Belichick made the call. "When that pick came up, Bill was just 'OK, it's Brady.' He doesn't do cartwheels or get very excited, but I do remember on that Brady pick him being a little more intense."

Rehbein felt something more overpowering. "We got him, we got him," he breathlessly told his wife over the phone. Nobody was quite sure what, exactly, the Patriots were getting. Except Rehbein. And Brady. His Michigan friend Jay Flannelly, who called him about an hour after he was drafted, remembered the quarterback sounding relieved, overjoyed, and confident that his time with the scout team would be short.

"I'm going there to take Bledsoe's job," Brady told him.

Upon first inspection in Foxborough, veteran Patriots weren't sure what to make of the rookie quarterback. Willie McGinest, a defensive end and linebacker and a starter since 1994, said he thought Brady "needed to get his ass in the weight room and get in shape. We were all joking with him and messing with him about his combine tape."

Redmond, a third-round member of Brady's draft class, said he remembered the quarterback "being about the worst athlete you could ever put in an NFL uniform." Yet everyone raved about the quarterback's relentless film study, his almost instant mastery of the playbook, and his commitment to working with scout-team receivers late at night. Rehbein couldn't get over how quickly and thoroughly Brady could draw up a play and articulate its options in his first days and weeks as a pro. The quarterbacks coach was so fired up about the kid they'd just drafted that he'd tell his family about him over dinner. "My dad would talk about Tom Brady almost as if Tom was his own kid," Betsy Rehbein recalled. "He would talk about Tom driving this yellow Jeep Wrangler, making fun of this little boy he was watching grow up."

Brady grew up faster than any talent evaluator could've expected. Brady and Bishop, the former Kansas State star, often hung out on the players' nights off, and one night in 2000 they looked each other in the eye and made a pact between friends that went like this: *If either one of us takes the starting job from Bledsoe, he has to promise to never give it back.* Now in his second year, after adding about 25 badly needed pounds in the weight room, Brady had Bledsoe's job by default. Belichick had spent more time with him in the weeks after the Rehbein tragedy, and his belief in Brady had grown by the classroom session. Out of a fear of another team poaching him off the practice squad, Belichick had kept Brady on his 53-man roster in 2000, at a time when nobody was compromising roster depth at another position for a fourth quarterback. Now his faith was beginning to pay off.

To observers on both sides of the field, Brady looked pretty good in relief of Bledsoe in the loss to the Jets. But the mood among fatalistic New Englanders accustomed to bad fortune when it came to their football team, never mind their haunted baseball team, didn't allow for any silver lining with this storm cloud. Once again, their Patriots had 5-11 written all over them.

Tom Brady had just taken his team down the field on a dramatic 60-yard scoring drive — capped by his touchdown pass to Jermaine Wiggins — near the end of regulation to tie the San Diego Chargers, and the vast majority of the 60,292 fans in the house feared what might happen next. They expected Doug Flutie, former Boston College magic man, to take the ball in overtime and secure a victory at Foxboro Stadium for the 13th time in 14 tries as a collegian and pro.

The locals had so much belief in Flutie, the Heisman Trophy winner from Natick, Massachusetts, who threw the most memorable pass in college football history, his Hail Mary to beat the Miami Hurricanes. So if Patriots fans were pessimistic about their team's chances, it had everything to do with Flutie and little to do with lingering doubts about their own quarterback.

In fact, Brady had managed to split his first two games in relief of Bledsoe. He beat Peyton Manning and the Colts in his first start by a 44–13 count, though he wasn't asked to do much with the offense. He played interception-free football, while Manning, the No. 1 overall pick in 1998, was intercepted three times. (Two were returned for touchdowns.)

Brady didn't look so prepared the following week, when he contributed to a 30–10 loss to Miami by taking four sacks and dropping a snap, which was kicked by a teammate and picked up by the Dolphins' Jason Taylor, who carried the ball into the end zone. "So much for that quarterback controversy," read the lead in a *Herald* column by George Kimball, who wondered if Huard should start against San Diego. Brady turned emotional in his postgame news conference when describing how much he hated to lose and how disappointed he was in the team's effort that week in practice.

Belichick held a little ceremony after that blowout loss that involved the burying of a football and the supposed dawning of a new day. "It may sound corny," said Jerod Cherry, special teamer, "to have a bunch of grown men getting motivated with the symbolism of burying a football and kicking dirt over the first part of the season. But it worked. Bill showed transparency at that meeting by telling guys, 'We're all in this together . . . We've got to come together as one.' And from that point on, we did just that."

Angered and embarrassed by the perception that he'd been exposed against Miami, Brady came out firing away against San Diego, completing 33 of 54 passes for 364 yards, 2 touchdowns, and no interceptions. (He hadn't been picked off in 114 career attempts.) The way he responded late in regulation and again in overtime, after Flutie shockingly went three and out, left an indelible impression on Belichick. On first down from his own 23 in overtime, Brady detected a San Diego blitz that he'd studied with Weis in the lead-up to the game and called an audible. He took the snap and fired the ball down the right sideline for Patten before the Chargers' rush could level him, drawing a pass interference call that awarded New England 37 yards and placed the ball on the San Diego 40. Brady completed a couple of short passes to give his kicker a better look, and Adam Vinatieri ended the game with a 44-yarder.

Brady didn't just win for the second time in three starts. This time he proved he could carry the team on a day when the running game was dreadful (29 yards on 24 carries) and the special teams were worse. "He put himself on the map," said Huard. "I like his attitude," said Terry Glenn, who had returned from his drug suspension to catch seven passes from Brady for 110 yards and a touchdown. "He has a really good, take-charge attitude, something you need at that position."

But it was Belichick who was most generous in his assessment of Brady's performance. The head coach who had never believed in public displays of affection raved about his quarterback.

"I can't say enough about Brady," Belichick gushed. "Tom had a great day throwing the ball, spreading it around, getting all the receivers involved. Tom has a game presence that's good."

Belichick's preseason feelings about the kid were being confirmed. For the first time as a head coach, he thought he might have someone with the makings of a special player at the most crucial position in all of American team sports. He'd have five more games with Brady, three of them victories, before confronting the most important decision of his career. The Bernie Kosar Decision, Part II.

When the Patriots lost to the St. Louis Rams on the night of November 18, falling to 5-5 after consecutive victories over Atlanta and Buffalo, there was a significant difference in the play of the two quarterbacks. Kurt Warner, the grocery store clerk turned Super Bowl champ and two-time league MVP, passed for 401 yards and three touchdowns, while Tom Brady passed for 185 yards and one score. Drew Bledsoe, cleared by doctors to return, watched from the sideline in a blue windbreaker. The former No. 1 overall draft pick could've died after that hit by Mo Lewis, and the Patriots would've been foolish to accelerate his transition back into the lineup.

But after the 24–17 loss to St. Louis, Bledsoe figured it was time for him to take his share of snaps with the first team offense in practice. Belichick had promised him he would get a fair crack at winning back his job from Brady, and during his rehab Bledsoe was consistent in saying he was confident he could do just that. And Brady's performance had slipped of late, as if defensive coordinators were starting to adjust to him.

Brady had beaten Peyton Manning a second time by throwing three touchdown passes and no interceptions, yet he was intercepted four times in a loss at Denver and was sacked seven times (while passing for only 107 yards on 27 attempts) in an ugly victory over Buffalo. The Patriots might've defeated 7-1 St. Louis, the league's best and most explosive team, had An-towain Smith not fumbled at the Rams' three-yard line late in the first half and denied his team a two-score lead. Brady did little to help their odds of pulling off the upset.

St. Louis coach Mike Martz, offensive coordinator of the 1999 title team and the brains behind what was known as the Greatest Show on Turf, called New England a legitimate Super Bowl contender and the most physical op-ponent his Rams had faced all year. Maybe that's why Belichick said he didn't plan on making any changes in preparing for his next game, against New Orleans. Nobody would've been surprised had Belichick decided to go with Brady, who was 5-3 as the starter, against the Saints while monitor-ing Bledsoe's work in practice and then making a call in two or three weeks.

Only that's not what he did. The next day, Belichick told his quarter-backs that he'd made his final decision on his first-string quarterback for the balance of the season, barring "something unforeseen." At the time, he realized the magnitude of the stakes. "There was friction in the locker room," said one New England starter, "and it was amplified times a thou-sand when Drew got healthy . . . You wouldn't believe how much tension was in that locker room." The majority of players, including many of the younger Patriots, favored sticking with Brady. Some of the old-guard Patri-ots wanted to turn back to Bledsoe.

Though the decision to cut Kosar in 1993 had contributed to Belichick's firing two years later, the coach figured he'd get a second chance in the league, and Kraft had given him that chance in Foxborough. Belichick wasn't going to get a third shot at it. If he made the wrong choice on Brady/ Bledsoe, it would cost him his career as a head coach.

In his office, Belichick told the two quarterbacks that he was going with Brady for the final six games. A source close to Belichick said that before Bledsoe's injury, the coach was preparing himself to take on the battle with Bledsoe and his chief benefactor, Kraft, to get Brady under center, and that there was no way he was turning back now. Belichick thought Brady was a quicker thinker on the fly, and more willing to take the safe play over an un-necessary gamble down the field. Bledsoe wasn't accustomed to Belichick's demand for accountability on every decision he made in a game, and it wore on him. Though Bledsoe had the stronger arm, Brady was buying the passing progression Weis was selling — first read, second read, throw the checkdown, over and over. Brady had also shown a greater commitment to working with teammates in the off-season; in fact, he'd never missed a workout.

Bledsoe was livid when he heard the news. He thought his coach had lied to him. Belichick wasn't worried about that as much as he was worried that the practice snaps Bledsoe had taken the previous week hurt Brady's preparation against St. Louis, and that any future sharing could've hurt the team in the coming weeks.

Bledsoe took his case to Kraft. Much as he loved his franchise player and wanted to avoid the embarrassment of having his $103 million investment on the bench less than one full year into a ten-year deal, Kraft was too smart to get in the middle of this one. If he had been perceived as a meddler in the Parcells days, those days were over. Kraft had hired Belichick to run football operations, and picking the starting quarterback was perhaps the most essential part of football operations.

The following day, Bledsoe addressed the news media at his locker. Nobody wanted to see him go through this, not even Brady's most ardent backers. Bledsoe was one of the good guys in the NFL. He'd always carried himself with dignity, even when some pockets of the fan base started to turn on him.

Only on this day, before a hungry horde of reporters, Bledsoe would have the hardest time staying positive. He'd lost nearly half his body's blood after that Lewis hit, and then come all the way back, only to receive this permanent demotion. Asked if he was hurt or frustrated upon hearing Belichick's decision, Bledsoe let out a half laugh and said, "Next question." He had the same response when asked how he could compete with Brady without getting snaps. Bledsoe never acted like this with the news media, or with anyone else for that matter. His feelings of betrayal were getting the best of him. Asked if he was assured he'd have an opportunity to return from his injury to the starting lineup, he said, "That's what I was told."

Bledsoe said he'd remain a team player and do everything he could to help Brady, whom he liked and respected. The two quarterbacks had golfed together and had spent plenty of time at Bledsoe's house. Brady called his elder "one of the toughest guys I've ever been around" and "a great friend and mentor." As competitive as the two quarterbacks were, they shared something of a big brother–little brother relationship.

Only things were different now. "I look forward to the chance to compete for my job, and I'll leave it at that," Bledsoe said after Brady was named the starter. *My job.* Belichick had taken it away and handed it to a kid who was making a lousy $298,000.

Belichick did what he could to soften the blow. He spoke of how Bledsoe was a consummate professional, of how the 29-year-old quarterback did more for the New England Patriots franchise than anyone before him. The coach later conceded that after Bledsoe suffered his injury, he might've erred in how he painted the future to him. Belichick said there might've been "a little gap in the understanding of what an opportunity would be."

He also acknowledged, "Maybe I shouldn't have made the commitment to Drew."

The Belichick-Bledsoe relationship was fractured for good. Not that the coach ever had a firm appreciation for a quarterback who didn't make decisions quickly enough for his liking. During one film session, Belichick grew tired of the image of Bledsoe patting the ball in the pocket before finally delivering it. "Drew," the coach said, "stop jacking the ball off and throw it."

Belichick said Brady would remain the first-stringer even though the quarterback's game had recently shown some cracks. "He's done a reasonably good job," Belichick said. The endorsement was lukewarm at best, when measured against his assessment of Brady following the San Diego game. But Belichick knew he wasn't giving the ball to Todd Philcox this time. After the death of Dick Rehbein, Belichick took control of his regular quarterback meetings, and his permanent appointment of Brady made those meetings awkward. Bledsoe and the coach barely spoke to each other.

Belichick could live with the tension in the meeting room. He knew in his heart he'd made the right call. He'd always been struck by Brady's retention of minute playbook details, by his recognition of defensive schemes on film, and by his ability to slow down the game and see the entire field in real time.

"From day one," Belichick said, "you asked what happened after a play and he'd tell you eight things that happened. You go back and watch the film, and there are the eight things that he said happened, and that's what happened on the play. You can see every one of them."

In the end, Belichick was betting his career aspirations on this beautiful football mind. Tom Brady would not let him down.

The season was over with 1:43 left in the divisional playoff game, played in a nighttime snowstorm at Foxboro Stadium, the final contest ever staged in the charmless place. The Oakland Raiders had a 13–10 lead and possession of the ball after Charles Woodson separated it from his former Michigan teammate Tom Brady and Oakland linebacker Greg Biekert recovered the fumble. Belichick was heading into the off-season with a strong belief that he had finally found his long-term quarterback and that he had established a program built to last.

The Patriots had won their last six regular-season games to claim the AFC East title, beating two of their head coach's former employers — the Jets and the Browns — in the process. Belichick was so happy to finally beat the Jets, he all but acted like a Times Square tourist on New Year's Eve. "That's the first time I've ever seen him hug anyone," said linebacker Roman Phifer.

Belichick was struck by how hard his players had competed all year. "We didn't really think of ourselves as anything special," he said. Neither did the league: The NFL had originally scheduled the Patriots for a bye week after their 16th and final game, which their coach took as a sign of disrespect. Belichick thought the schedule makers were telling his players, *You guys will be out of it, so you can go ahead and start your vacation early. Go ahead on home.*

New England had effectively clinched a playoff berth with its 20–13 victory over Miami in the last regular-season game played in Foxboro Stadium, highlighted by a 23-yard pass from running back Kevin Faulk to Brady, of all people, and punctuated by the sight of Belichick and his players doing a victory lap around the field and high-fiving their fans in a show of appreciation. "I'm a real veteran of closing down these stadiums," Belichick said in a cute reference to the near-apocalyptic endgame at Municipal, in Cleveland.

"What a coaching job Bill has done," said Phifer. "You appreciate it from the outside, but in here it's amazing to watch week after week."

An 11-year NFL veteran and another former Jet, Phifer embodied the hodgepodge nature of a defense that included an undersize college defensive end (Tedy Bruschi) at inside linebacker, a Steelers castoff (Vrabel) on the outside, and a pass-rushing defensive end (Seymour) who was an unpopular first-round pick with a fan base pleading for offensive help. "We're not the Steel Curtain or the '85 Bears or anything like that," Vrabel said. The Patriots were opportunistic defenders who could switch from a 4-3 set to a 3-4 and back to a 4-3 again on consecutive possessions. Crennel, the defensive coordinator, believed his unit found strength in its flexibility and versatility and actually performed better when challenged to adjust from one scheme to the next. As for the divide Pepper Johnson believed existed between the ex-Jets and others in the locker room, Bryan Cox, the former Jet whose loyalties were questioned after the Bledsoe injury, helped to bridge the gap the following week with a big hit on Colts receiver Jerome Pathon that announced the arrival of a new day in Foxborough.

The Patriots closed out the regular season with a 38–6 rout of the Panthers, made possible by the pick-sixes contributed by Ty Law and Otis Smith, both of whom also had pick-sixes in the September blowout of Peyton Manning's Colts. Smith and Lawyer Milloy poured a bucketful of ice water on Belichick, who had won a division title for the first time, and the delirious players put on their AFC EAST CHAMPIONS caps and T-shirts. "Now the season starts again," Belichick said of the playoffs. And that new season, Dan Shaughnessy wrote in the *Globe*, was destined to be a prosperous one. He opened his column this way: "Might as well face it: The Patriots are going to the Super Bowl."

It seemed that prediction was about to die a painful death in the heavy snow a couple of weeks later, when Oakland's Woodson raced in untouched from the left side of the defense, blasted Brady, and knocked the ball from his hand. Replays clearly showed New England's quarterback attempting to tuck the ball into his body — not attempting to pass it — when he lost control. The Raiders started celebrating as a furious Brady was pulled up from the frozen field by his teammates, his jersey all askew.

Referee Walt Coleman was getting prepared for Oakland to run out the clock when his replay buzzer went off; the play was subject to review. Buried deep inside a blue hooded jacket, Belichick betrayed no hint of the stunning reversal to come. Coleman made his way to a sideline camera, slapped on a headset, and reviewed the video evidence, which confirmed that Rule 3, Section 22, Article 2, Note 2 applied to the Brady hit. The rule stated that "any intentional forward movement of his arm starts a forward pass, even if the player loses possession of the ball as he is attempting to tuck it back toward his body." The purpose of the rule was to make life easier for game officials by not making them determine a quarterback's intent when his arm is moving forward. Coleman returned to the field, faced the Oakland sideline and a crowd that had already surrendered, and made the ruling public.

A stone-faced Belichick, snow resting on the top of his hood, listened with his mouth agape as Coleman told his captive audience that the called fumble had been changed to an incomplete pass, and then lifted his right hand and snapped it downward. Raiders coach Jon Gruden, snow resting on his visor, started running and screaming over the absurdity of it all.

The Raiders were as angry as they were stunned. "Ball came out — game over," Woodson said. "It kind of took the air out of a lot of guys." The crowd was suddenly alive with possibility even before Brady completed a 13-yard pass to Patten to the Oakland 29. The Patriots gained but one yard on the next three plays before sending out Vinatieri to attempt a desperation 45-yarder. "You can't get any tougher than that kick," Belichick said, "in four inches of snow."

Chilled breath billowed from the players' helmets and the coaches' headsets. This surreal snow-globe scene reminded weathered New Englanders of a 1982 game against Miami played in virtual whiteout conditions. The Patriots won that game, 3–0, after their coach, Ron Meyer, sent out a snowplow manned by an inmate named Mark Henderson — on work release for the day — to clear a spot for kicker John Smith to make the deciding field goal. Two decades later, there would be no furloughed inmate available to help Adam Vinatieri. He was an undrafted kicker out of South Dakota State who had played overseas with the Amsterdam Admirals before Bill Parcells gave him a shot in New England, where Vinatieri declared himself a special player the day he ran down Herschel Walker on a kick return.

As he lined up the attempt, Vinatieri decided to take small steps on his approach to the ball to avoid slipping and falling. He had beaten Buffalo the year before in overtime on a brutal wintry day, but that kick into the elements was a 24-yarder. This attempt was an entirely different proposition. Vinatieri knew he couldn't deliver a high and majestic kick in the driving storm, so he told himself to just make sure he lifted the ball above the hands of the defenders. Vinatieri was thinking he needed to hit a 3-iron instead of a 9-iron, and on contact he wasn't sure if he'd hit the ball hard enough. "But when the officials stepped forward and raised their hands," Vinatieri recalled, "I said, 'Oh, my God, I made that kick.'" Twenty-seven seconds remained on the clock. Under the circumstances, it might've been the most improbable kick in NFL history.

Of course, the Raiders stood no chance in overtime. The Patriots won the coin toss, and Brady, who had completed nine consecutive passes on the fourth-quarter scoring drive that cut Oakland's lead to 13–10, immediately moved his team deep into Oakland territory by completing eight consecutive pass attempts (the first six to J. R. Redmond and Jermaine Wiggins) before Vinatieri was asked to close it out. The kicker and his holder, Ken Walter, starting using their feet to clear the spot of the attempted field goal.

"No snowplow in sight tonight," the CBS play-by-play man, Greg Gumbel, said on the air. And when Vinatieri nailed the 23-yarder on the 15th play of the overtime drive, to send the Patriots to the AFC Championship Game, the hooded Belichick turned toward Brady, raised his arms high, and pulled him in for a hug as if to kiss him. Belichick hugged another player, and then joyously bounced onto the field, pumping his right fist toward the sky. Foxboro Stadium had been scheduled for demolition on December 23, the day after the final regular-season home game, against Miami, and here were the euphoric — if frostbitten — fans threatening to tear down the place on January 19.

"They just will not — will not — quit," an emotional Belichick said of his players afterward. "These guys just keep fighting until their last breath."

The whole night, start to finish, was a referendum on the winning coach. Belichick had built a team that held up under near-Arctic conditions. He had drafted Seymour, who penetrated the line and blew up Oakland's third-and-one handoff that could've given the Raiders a first down and a chance to run out the clock. Belichick had studied tape of that 2000 game played in a Buffalo blizzard, a game that saw Wiggins manage back-to-back 17-yard catches on the winning drive in overtime, and decided to make the robust tight end a significant part of the game plan against Oakland. (Wiggins finished with 10 catches for 68 yards.) Belichick had honored his special teams roots by fielding a unit capable of pulling off one of the all-time special teams plays in Vinatieri's 45-yarder.

Belichick had made the defining choice of the season when deciding that Brady should replace Bledsoe permanently, their salaries be damned. Brady completed 26 of 39 passes for 312 yards against Oakland and scored on a six-yard rushing touchdown in the middle of the fourth quarter. After his quarterback erased a ten-point deficit in the final eight minutes of regulation, masterfully running the no-huddle offense, Belichick had enough faith in him in overtime to call his number — and not Vinatieri's — on a fourth-and-four from the Oakland 28. Brady delivered with a six-yard fastball to Patten, who made the catch from his knees.

The quarterback had already earned a Pro Bowl appearance in his first season as a starter, and now he stood one game away from the Super Bowl. Of his overturned fumble, soon to be known as the Tuck Rule Play, Brady said, with a Cheshire cat's grin, "I was throwing the ball, definitely. And even if I wasn't, that's my story and I'm sticking to it."

Belichick's story? The man who had turned a 5-11 record in 2000 and an 0-2 start in 2001 into a spot in the AFC Championship Game learned a couple of hours before kickoff that he had lost NFL Coach of the Year honors to the Chicago Bears' Dick Jauron, who finished 13-3 before losing in the divisional round of the playoffs to Philadelphia.

And that was OK. Jauron could have his well-deserved honor — and his place in front of the TV watching the rest of the tournament. Belichick coveted only one trophy, and suddenly that one was almost close enough to touch.

11

CHAMPION

Pittsburgh Steelers safety Lee Flowers plowed hard into the back of Tom Brady's lower legs, and the New England Patriots' quarterback buckled at the knees, twisted his body backwards, and collapsed in a heap. This was late in the first half of the AFC Championship Game, and Bill Belichick's program was about to be put to the ultimate test.

The Patriots held a 7–3 lead when Brady completed his 28-yard pass to Troy Brown, his final throw of the day. On this sunny, unseasonably warm day in western Pennsylvania, with the home team cast as heavy favorites to win, Brady's injured ankle forced Belichick to do something he never wanted to do: bet his Super Bowl hopes on Drew Bledsoe, who hadn't seen action in 125 days.

Funny how things work out: Bledsoe had a premonition that he'd play in this AFC title game, and now that premonition had come to be. He hadn't appeared in relief since his rookie year, 1993. He ran out to his old huddle and told his teammates, "Look who's back!" His first pass was a bullet to David Patten, good for 15 yards. Bledsoe always had a hell of a right arm, much stronger than Brady's. But on the second play, Bledsoe's poor judgment reminded fans of how he'd lost his job in the first place. He broke the pocket and ran upright for the right sideline, where Pittsburgh's Chad Scott blasted the lumbering quarterback just as the Jets' Mo Lewis had in the second game of the year, sending him flying. Only this time Bledsoe popped up and cut an animated path back to the huddle.

The hit woke up Bledsoe, made him feel like a football player again, after four months off. He immediately found Patten for another ten yards and a first down at the Pittsburgh 11. On the next snap, with three receivers flooding the zone to the right, Bledsoe side-armed a pass into the deep corner, one of his favorite places to throw the ball. Sure enough, he found Patten for a touchdown, then turned to his bench and extended his arms in what-did-you-think-of-that form. The Steelers made it a game in the end, but they weren't winning after a magical four-play sequence like that.

Bledsoe later wept as he took a knee to run out the clock on a 24–17 victory. His father, Mac, had surprised him by flying into town to watch a game his son wasn't supposed to appear in, and when they made eye contact, Drew cried again. It had been an emotionally taxing season and day. Bledsoe had lost his quarterbacks coach, Rehbein, during camp, nearly lost his own life on the football field, and then lost the only job he ever wanted. On the afternoon Bledsoe would temporarily regain his job, the Patriots made honorary captains of Rehbein's wife, Pam, and daughters, Betsy and Sarabeth, and no player was more touched by the gesture than the veteran quarterback, who had started establishing a scholarship fund for the Rehbein girls the morning after their father died.

Belichick, Kraft, and Charlie Weis, Rehbein's close friend, had visited the family's home in the immediate wake of Dick's death. Pam Rehbein was moved when, after New England's 38–17 victory over Indianapolis in October, Belichick credited her husband with the acquisitions of Brady and Patten, who had caught two touchdown passes against the Colts totaling 97 yards, thrown one for 60 yards, and rushed for a 29-yard score. "Dick loved working for Bill," Pam Rehbein said. "There were no Mickey Mouse games with Bill. He knew what he wanted done and he let it be known. Dick absolutely loved that about Bill . . . Sometimes coaches will tell you one thing, it doesn't work out, and then it comes back to bite you. Dick said that never happened with Bill."

In the final moments of an AFC Championship Game victory over Pittsburgh that his team dedicated to Rehbein's memory, a beaming Belichick lifted his youngest child, Brian, into his arms. The coach then engaged in a group hug with his older son, Stephen, and his running back, J. R. Redmond. A year after the Patriots finished in last place in the AFC East and put their head coach in harm's way, they were going to the Super Bowl.

On the Heinz Field podium, relieved that Pittsburgh's Joey Porter had dropped what should've been a fourth-quarter interception and pick-six, Bledsoe held the conference trophy high and pumped it three times. As much as the moment belonged to him, it belonged to the man who had benched him, too.

Belichick's baby, the special teams unit, made the difference by scoring two touchdowns in a one-touchdown game. Moments after CBS analyst and former Giants quarterback Phil Simms said on the air that the Patriots "think they have a decided advantage in special teams, especially with their punt return team," Brown sliced down the heart of the field to score on a 55-yard return. In the third quarter, Brown scooped up a blocked field goal on the dead run at his own 40 and, just before he was brought down near midfield, lateraled it to Antwan Harris, who took it the rest of the way.

Brown was drafted by Bill Parcells in the eighth round of the 1993 draft, and had developed into the perfect Belichick player. He had started only seven games over seven seasons with Parcells and Pete Carroll; he'd started 28 games, caught 184 passes, and become a Pro Bowl player in two seasons with Belichick, who thought the quiet receiver was among the best lead-by-example players he'd been around. "Oh, man," Belichick said, "that guy is some football player." Only on Belichick's Patriots could an AFC title game be saved by the 198th pick in a draft (Brown) after the 199th pick in a different draft (Brady) went down.

Of course, Belichick was blitzed about who would make the Super Bowl start in New Orleans: Brady or Bledsoe, both of whom told reporters they should ask the coach. On cue, Belichick said that Brady could've conceivably played in the second half against Pittsburgh, and that a healthy Bledsoe was the better bet. He saw no need to offer up information that didn't need to be disclosed. He'd have only one week to prepare for the Super Bowl — the 9/11 postponements and makeups had forced the NFL to wipe out the second week between the conference championship games and the biggest spectacle in American sports — and New England would spend that week working as discreetly as possible.

The Patriots pulled away from Heinz Field and headed for the airport. When they arrived in town to play the Steelers, Damien Woody had said, "It seemed the whole city of Pittsburgh was in our hotel. People with Terrible Towels, Steelers jerseys, like the whole city was trying to intimidate us. And when we won that game, it was like a ghost town. We didn't see cars on the road, nothing. It was like Pittsburgh was wiped off the map. Like the whole city was gone."

Long after they left Heinz Field behind, the Patriots discovered that they'd be facing the St. Louis Rams, who'd defeated the Philadelphia Eagles in the NFC Championship Game. Rams coach Mike Martz had predicted after his November victory over Belichick that his team might see the Patriots again, and those turned out to be the words of a prophet.

In only two seasons, Belichick had proven he was worth the first-round pick and all the headaches attached to his stormy departure from the Jets. Now came the hard part. Now he had to figure out Kurt Warner's St. Louis offense over seven days, just as he'd figured out Jim Kelly's Buffalo offense over seven days in a different life. Only Little Bill wasn't working for Big Bill anymore.

This time Little Bill was Big Bill.

Bill Belichick picked Tom Brady over Drew Bledsoe all over again. In New Orleans, after watching Brady work out on his healing left ankle, the coach made it official. "Tom Brady demonstrated in practice that he is fit to play," Belichick said. "He will be our starting quarterback on Sunday."

What a remarkable journey for Brady, who entered the league so unentitled he eagerly took a job making $500 at a teammate's football camp. Asked years later what he knew about a young Brady, the Rams' superstar back Marshall Faulk said: "I knew about him what everybody else knew about him: He sucked and he couldn't beat out Drew Henson."

Belichick knew different. Though his was the popular move among Patriots fans (by Monday afternoon, 81 percent of 60,000 voters in a Boston .com poll had stated their preference for Brady, if healthy, over Bledsoe), Belichick never much cared for public sentiment. One of his assistants said that Bledsoe was never seriously considered as the Super Bowl starter, that Belichick merely wanted to show him some respect and, of course, to take a quick look at Brady on that ankle.

That assistant also said Bledsoe's performance in Pittsburgh hadn't necessarily helped his cause. He completed only 10 of 21 passes for 102 yards and almost lost the game on Porter's near pick-six. The New England staff thought Bledsoe showed heart and poise in overcoming his inactivity and managing the magnitude of a conference championship game, but the assistant said he'd actually made a bit of a mistake on his touchdown pass to Patten. Bledsoe made the more difficult first-down throw, the assistant argued, while Brady would've settled for hitting an open Charles Johnson in the flat. Though the assistant's assessment that Johnson would've easily scored was questionable — a Pittsburgh defender was in the vicinity — it underscored Belichick's feelings about Bledsoe.

"That was Bill's problem with Drew in a nutshell," the assistant said. "That's one reason Tom had so much success with Bill, and vice versa. The right reads are made, and there's no complaints."

Only this week, New England's biggest quarterback dilemma involved the quarterback suiting up for the other team. Kurt Warner was the best in the league (4,830 passing yards and 36 touchdowns), and he ran an offense that had scored more than 500 points in three consecutive seasons. St. Louis also had the best all-around running back in football, Faulk; a great left tackle in Orlando Pace; devastating weapons at receiver in Torry Holt and Isaac Bruce; and speed up and down both sides of the ball. The Rams were coached by Martz, who drove a Porsche and wanted his team to play faster than his car. Martz had been Dick Vermeil's offensive coordinator on the 1999 team that was led by the former Arena Football League quarterback who used to stock shelves at a Hy-Vee in Cedar Falls, Iowa, for $5.50 an hour. "Kurt Warner came off the street," Vermeil said, "and [Martz] made him NFL player of the year."

The 2001 Rams led the league in 18 offensive categories. "How do we stop a team that has two MVPs in the same backfield?" Belichick said of Warner and Faulk, who had combined to win the past three league MVP awards. New England's defense had surrendered the sixth-fewest points in the NFL but ranked 24th in yards allowed. The Patriots as a whole, said guard Joe Andruzzi, were "a bunch of nobodies put together," and proud of it.

So the Patriots were heavily favored to lose another Super Bowl in New Orleans, where their 1985 team was crushed by the Chicago Bears of Mike Ditka and Buddy Ryan and where their 1996 team was done in by Brett Favre and the in-house soap opera starring Bill Parcells and Robert Kraft. Following a quick stop home, Belichick and the players arrived the day after their upset victory in Pittsburgh, while the coordinators remained in Foxborough an extra day to work on the game plan. Belichick spent the flight to New Orleans talking to Ernie Adams about their plan to contain Faulk. After they landed, the head coach didn't specifically warn his team about Bourbon Street and the French Quarter; rather, he established a midnight curfew for most of the week and merely reminded his players to exercise good judgment and always remember they were representing something bigger than themselves.

"There was a lot of chatter during the week that the Rams were staying out late," Damien Woody said, "no curfew, late partying . . . We were zeroed in, zoned in, and from the things I heard, the Rams were really enjoying themselves."

Though his Patriots were generally a monument to low-maintenance living, Belichick had one high-maintenance issue to deal with. Lawyer Milloy was complaining about the size of his hotel room, and his coach solved the problem by giving the safety his suite — complete with a Jacuzzi and a treadmill that had been installed specifically for Belichick. Once that crisis was averted, the Patriots were in a favorable place spiritually and emotionally.

Five years after his absurd joint Super Bowl presser with Parcells, Kraft appeared content to bask in his coach's shadow. Belichick appeared content, period, after spending his previous two Super Bowls in attack-dog mode when writers asked about his interest in the Cleveland job (January 1991) and about Parcells's reported interest in leaving the Patriots (January 1997). Belichick came across as relaxed; he occasionally even cracked a smile while tending to the nonstop media obligations during the week. And why not? His 2000 Patriots had finished dead last in the AFC East, and here he was a year later, the toast of the entire sport.

"Have I lightened up a bit? I probably have," Belichick told reporters. "In Cleveland, I might've been a little too rough on [the players] at times. In the end, my intent isn't to try to have conflict, or try to be iron-fisted, or tyrannical, or anything like that — but to just try to get it done, get through a message. However that's interpreted, I'll leave that up to you guys."

Before he even reached the postseason tournament, Belichick had made a bit of a stunning admission about his grim approach to media relations during his time with the Browns. "I watched what Bill [Parcells] did with the New York media when I was there, and maybe I tried to do some of those things," he said. "And he was in a position where, honestly, he could get away with some things that other people can't get away with. And I don't think I really realized that . . . I tried to do some of the things he did. And they came out a lot differently when I did them than when he did them. It was a miscalculation."

Nobody much cared anymore. Parcells was out of the league, and Little Bill was one of two coaches left with a shot at winning it all. Belichick and Martz spent the week complimenting each other for making brilliant in-game adjustments. The two men weren't close and had never worked together, but Belichick was the only head coach to call Martz with congratulations after the Rams clinched their division title. As the big underdog with the more impressive pedigree, Belichick represented the more interesting story. Of the 53 players on his roster, only 15 were there the day Belichick was hired in 2000, when the Patriots were some $10 million over the salary cap.

He had 21 veteran free agents, six rookies and first-year free agents, and three waiver pickups on his Super Bowl team. His front-office guy, Scott Pioli, knew the Patriots needed an overhaul of attitude, character, intelligence, and toughness. He told Belichick he could find Belichick players, pro's pros, and he brought in the experienced likes of Cox, Phifer, Pleasant, Patten, Mike Compton, Bobby Hamilton, Otis Smith, and Larry Izzo.

"Not a turd in the bunch," said one Patriots official.

Pleasant was an intriguing acquisition. He had seen the worst of Belichick firsthand in Cleveland, and he initially had reservations about joining the Jets, in part because Little Bill was a part of Big Bill's staff. Before signing with the Patriots, Pleasant spoke with some of his old Cleveland colleagues — Pioli, Pepper Johnson, and Eric Mangini — and they all assured him that Belichick had changed for the better. Pleasant took a trip to Foxborough to see for himself.

"He wasn't the same guy he was in Cleveland," Pleasant said. "He wasn't practicing like it was boot camp, the way he was in Cleveland. He tried to take care of players. He listened to the players. I think he got a better understanding as far as the body can't continue to take a pounding, pounding, pounding, that the body needs to recover. His mannerisms were different.

He seemed more seasoned as a head coach, more mature. He just had a different mind-set than he had in Cleveland."

Pleasant thought the Cleveland Belichick "didn't listen to anybody" and acted as "a know-it-all with a chip on his shoulder." He told Belichick's old friend with the Browns, Michael Dean Perry, that the coach was especially careful with the older players during the week to preserve them for Sundays. "Mike," Pleasant told Perry, "you wouldn't believe what Bill is doing."

Cox was another veteran who saw personal growth in Belichick, his defensive coordinator with the Jets. "Bill had an issue not just with communication," the linebacker said, "but with presentation. He was all football and nothing else, from what I saw . . . The man evolved. He was more personable. He'd find you, ask you how your family was doing. I really believe he got better as his children grew older and he had to communicate more with them . . . You knew the man could coach; he also became a total person."

Turns out he had a soft touch after all. Belichick didn't just dial back the kind of relentless full-pads hitting that can wear a team down to the nub by Thanksgiving. He also became a much better delegator, more like his former boss. Parcells would focus on big-picture tasks such as motivating players and controlling the daily media message, and allow Little Bill to run the defense. Much as he was criticized for trying to act like Parcells in Cleveland, Belichick had to act more like him in New England.

"When he first came here," Charlie Weis said, "I ran the offense, he ran the defense, and the one thing he wasn't allowed to do was really manage the team. Then, when he brought in Romeo this year and turned over the defense to Romeo and other guys, that allowed him to become a head coach, and I think he's really flourished. His personality has come out as he's gotten more familiar with guys on both sides of the ball. When you're a coordinator, you're not supposed to have a personality. You're only supposed to teach them what to do."

Weis later told reporters, "You don't know Bill. He's not going to ever let you see him . . . You're missing the guy who went on tour with Bon Jovi over to Europe. This guy's got more personality than anyone knows."

If the press didn't often see it in his news conferences throughout the season, the players saw it in meeting rooms and on the practice field. Pleasant, the 12-year veteran, knew better than any Patriot that a transformation was taking place. In the middle of the season, he stopped in Belichick's office to deliver a message the coach had never heard in Cleveland.

"I just saw something in him, saw it in his eyes," Pleasant said. "I just felt compassion for him, and I just saw in his heart he really wanted to win very, very badly. And I felt after all the negative things said about him as a head coach, after what happened in Cleveland, that I really wanted it for him . . . I told him, 'Coach, my goal is seeing you win a championship.'"

Belichick had climbed a mountain every great coach has to climb. For the first time, his players wanted to win for him as much as they wanted to win for themselves. Now all he needed was a winning strategy against a more talented opponent. For starters, to acclimate the defense to the blazing speed of the St. Louis wideouts, Belichick had the scout-team receivers line up three yards in front of the line of scrimmage. He also ordered his outside linebackers and everyone else within reach of Marshall Faulk to prepare to hit him, jam him, and maul him whenever he tried to release outside into a pass pattern. (Faulk had caught more than 80 passes for four consecutive seasons, for a total of 26 touchdowns.)

A coaching assistant, Ned Burke, ran the New England scout team charged with giving the starters another preview of Faulk's talent. "Our poor backup running backs," he said. "Mainly Kevin Faulk. He was the guy who could most duplicate what Marshall could do." For good reason: Kevin was Marshall Faulk's cousin.

As a game-plan team forever making adjustments to its schemes, New England felt it had an advantage over the Rams with one week instead of two to prepare for the Super Bowl. "We put in a whole new playbook for whoever we were playing every week," Burke said, "and we're used to doing it quickly. We knew the Rams were a system team."

Belichick hammered home to his players that they were entirely capable of beating the Rams; they only had to execute the plan. Just as he had been certain the Giants would upset Buffalo 11 years earlier by punishing its receivers and letting Thurman Thomas have his way on the ground, Belichick was sure his Patriots would prevail if they met the Rams' finesse with physicality.

The November loss to St. Louis actually had been the turning point in the season — many players later said they believed they could beat anyone after nearly beating the league's elite team. The Patriots had won eight straight since that night. So in a team meeting on the eve of the Super Bowl, Pleasant said, Belichick told the players, "I've got a plan on how we're going to beat them. Don't let them throw the ball deep on us. Just play the deep ball, and let them catch everything underneath us. But no big plays on us." Belichick spoke of beating up the Rams' receivers, making it hard for them to get into their routes, and disrupting the timing that was so critical to Warner's success.

But Belichick talked more about the great running back than the great quarterback. In their regular-season matchup in November, Faulk had rushed for 83 yards and caught seven passes for 70 yards and a touchdown. Up seven, the Rams ran out the final 7:37 on the clock because New England couldn't stop Faulk. It was another reminder of why Belichick had called the trade in 1999 (when he was with the Jets) of Faulk from Indianapolis to St. Louis "one of the happiest days of my life." He just wanted that matchup nightmare out of the AFC East. (The Colts moved to the AFC South through the league's expansion and realignment in 2002.)

In the days before the rematch in New Orleans, Belichick did a sit-down interview with ESPN's Chris Berman, one of the national media members he liked and respected. When the interview was done, Berman asked his producer and camera operator to leave the room. The broadcaster and coach chatted about strategy for a few minutes before Belichick looked Berman in the eye and said, "Marshall Faulk will not beat us in this game."

The Patriots embraced his confidence. Intense preparation breeds extreme faith, and Belichick's players were telling people they had never had a coach so detailed in his approach.

"In my whole time in New England," Redmond said, "there's never been a time when I stepped on the field and every single player on our side of the ball did not know exactly what the defense was going to do." Redmond, a third-down back, spoke of writing 12-page reports on what the defense did in all passing situations, on the strengths and weaknesses of certain defenders (*Is he athletic? Is he a bull-rush guy? Does he like to jump around?*), and on the college backgrounds of opposing linebackers and safeties, from first string to third string. "Real-ass reports," Redmond said. "I did less in college than I did with Bill Belichick, every single week, and that's why the only mistakes I ever made were physical, not mental."

On February 3, 2002, Super Bowl Sunday, the Patriots were reveling in their standing as long shots. The Rams were favored by 14 points, and New England's one skill player who could run with them, Terry Glenn, had been suspended again by Belichick for missing meetings and practices and had long been reduced to what George Orwell would call an unperson. Belichick wasn't sweating it. The afternoon before the game, he sat in his office with a couple of old Wesleyan friends, Jim Farrell and Mark Fredland, and spent what he called "probably the most relaxing hour of that entire week for me . . . We just sat and talked about what for us were the good old days."

The next day, Belichick was so calm when meeting with Kraft before the game that the owner walked out of the locker room believing his team would win. Two hours before kickoff, Belichick was so confident that he had prepared his team to pull off one of the biggest upsets in NFL history, he sat down on the Patriots' bench next to ball boy Zak DeOssie and talked about everything except the Rams.

DeOssie wasn't only a fellow Andover boy and the son of a linebacker who had helped Belichick win a title; he was also a good friend of the coach's daughter, Amanda, his former schoolmate at Phillips. During training camp, Belichick allowed DeOssie, a quarterback at Phillips, to use the weight room and run the conditioning test with the team. Belichick had him learn how to be a long snapper. He even used the kid as an extra arm in seven-on-seven drills, worked on his form, and told him he wanted to send him back to Andover a much better player.

Now they were together again at the Super Bowl, with kickoff approaching, and Belichick was talking to the kid about the Andover team, about his classes, about campus life. They chatted for 25 minutes, and not once did Belichick mention the Rams or the Super Bowl he was about to play.

"It was just a father talking to his daughter's friend," DeOssie said. "That's all it was. He was totally prepared for the game, and he wanted a little normalcy.

"I think he knew he had done everything he possibly could."

The New England Patriots had the ball on their own 17-yard line with no timeouts and 81 seconds to play in Super Bowl XXXVI. The St. Louis Rams had just scored two fourth-quarter touchdowns to erase a stunning 14-point deficit and make it a 17–17 game, and Bill Belichick was now facing a question that would shape the rest of his career.

Should he go for the win and trust that his young quarterback wouldn't commit a fatal turnover, or should he run out the clock and take his chances in overtime? Up in the Fox television booth, the sport's most prominent analyst, John Madden — a Super Bowl–winning coach with the Oakland Raiders who was influential enough to create his own video-game dynasty, *Madden NFL* — had the answer for Belichick. He said the Patriots had to play for overtime. "I don't think you want to force anything here," Madden said. "You don't want to do anything stupid, because you have no timeouts and you're backed up."

Just about everything had gone right for Belichick and his 14-point underdogs, who started meeting the Rams' star power with a unified front in the pregame, when the Patriots insisted (against league resistance) that they be introduced as a team rather than as individuals. Damien Woody said the energy in the tunnel before that team introduction was unlike anything he'd ever felt. "We were like a bunch of crazed dogs," he said.

Another good omen: One of Belichick's childhood heroes at the Naval Academy, Roger Staubach, was joining former President Bush for the opening coin toss.

Belichick had been most concerned about St. Louis establishing its superiority in the first five minutes, but New England's defense immediately rattled the Rams on the first possession with some meaningful hits. On the second play, following a Warner incompletion, Tebucky Jones drilled Holt on his leaping 18-yard catch. For the Patriots, the pain was worth the gain.

The hits kept piling up across the first half. Chased from the pocket, Warner overthrew Holt on the sideline, and the receiver took another big shot from Jones. The quarterback completed a three-yard pass to Bruce, who was popped by Ty Law. Warner's lip was bloodied, and his team's belief in itself was bruised. The first play of the second quarter said everything about the Patriots' strategy and the way this game was unfolding.

Willie McGinest, an athletic marvel at 6′5″ and 270 pounds, lined up to Warner's left and, after the snap, delivered a shot to receiver Az-Zahir Hakim, nearly knocking him over and disrupting his route. McGinest then continued to rush the quarterback, who ultimately threw high to Hakim over the middle, where it seemed half the Patriots' roster was waiting for him. Though Roman Phifer hit teammate Terrance Shaw hard in the head as they converged on Hakim, the ferocity of New England's approach was becoming more evident with every play. A minute later, Lawyer Milloy put a convincing hit on Rams tight end Ernie Conwell, who didn't hold on to the ball.

Belichick said he'd learned from his father and Bill Parcells that "the most important thing on defense is to get 11 guys out there that can tackle." The Rams were starting to believe there were 15 Patriots out there ready to put them on the ground. In the middle of the second quarter, Mike Vrabel blitzed from Warner's right, raced untouched to the quarterback's spot, and clubbed Warner in the head (no flag was thrown) as he followed through on his pass toward the right sideline. The ball was picked off by Law, who ran 47 yards for the first touchdown of the game.

When the Rams tried to regain control before the end of the first half, New England met their finesse with more force. Receiver Ricky Proehl, a 12-year veteran, made a 15-yard catch and started to drop to the turf just as safety Antwan Harris flew in helmet first to pop the ball out and into the hands of teammate Terrell Buckley. Five plays later, from the St. Louis eight-yard line, Brady attacked a vulnerability that Belichick had noticed in practice two days earlier at Tulane University. The coach realized that the Rams played tight and tough defense near the goal line, and he figured they could be beaten on a quick out-and-up pattern. So Brady pump-faked to his right toward Patten, who then snuck behind the suckered cornerback, Dexter McCleon, and made a tumbling catch in the back of the end zone that mirrored the catch he made against Pittsburgh in the AFC Championship Game.

Much to the surprise of almost everyone watching, the Patriots were holding a 14–3 lead over the Greatest Show on Turf. New England players later said they saw shock on their opponents' faces. "You know how they say every boxer has a plan until they get punched?" Redmond said. "That's what the Rams looked like. It looked like they got punched and said, 'Uh-oh.'"

The Rams were so desperate for a big play with 31 seconds left in the half, they sent out Faulk — with one career kickoff return to his name — to field the kick from Vinatieri. On the broadcast, Madden said he'd seen Faulk practice kick returns the day before, during the Rams' walk-through at the Superdome. The analyst wasn't alone. Also present for that dress rehearsal were some Patriots staffers who were setting up video equipment. One of the videographers, Matt Walsh, told the defensive coaching assistant, Brian Daboll, that he'd seen Faulk being used in this unconventional way. So Belichick was sitting on this Mike Martz curveball, too. Vinatieri sent his high kickoff away from Faulk, to the running back's left, and Faulk raced over to catch it on the fly just before his momentum carried him out of bounds at the six-yard line. Faulk's first and last kickoff return of the game netted the Rams one lousy yard.

Belichick was calm during the extended halftime as he assured his team that St. Louis would play the rest of the game with a renewed purpose. On the Rams' first series of the second half, the Patriots again hit Warner in the head — Phifer caught him after knocking down the pass attempt off a delayed blitz. A Super Bowl MVP two years earlier, when he threw for 414 yards and two scores against Tennessee, Warner wore a mask of confusion and despair. With more than six minutes to play in the third quarter, the Patriots had used five defensive backs on 10 plays, six defensive backs on 15 plays, and seven defensive backs on three plays. Half the time, Warner didn't know what he was looking at. He unnecessarily burned two of his three timeouts in the third quarter before throwing his second interception, this one right to Otis Smith, who had used his hands to help Holt trip and nearly fall flat, with the ball in the air. Vinatieri nailed a 37-yard field goal to give New England a 17–3 lead.

The crowd was alive with the anticipation of an historic upset, the biggest since Joe Namath and the Jets from the old AFL beat the NFL's Baltimore Colts, who were 18-point favorites, in Super Bowl III. Despite the fact that Belichick kept putting extra defensive backs into play, Martz insisted on throwing the ball and keeping it out of his best player's hands. Faulk would end up with only 17 carries and four receptions, or 21 touches. Over the Rams' eight-game winning streak leading up to the Super Bowl, he had averaged 28 touches and had four games with at least 25 carries and three with at least 30.

St. Louis also helped New England's cause by declining to use the no-huddle offense to speed up the tempo of a game clearly being played at the Patriots' preferred pace. Not that the Rams believed their wounds were all self-inflicted. Many of them thought referee Bernie Kukar and his crew allowed New England far too much latitude in how it defended a faster team. Faulk described the Patriots' strategy against him this way: "So pretty much it was like, wherever the fuck he was, hold him, grab him, tackle him. That was the plan. Other teams did it, but there was something about the Super Bowl. In the Super Bowl, they stopped throwing flags."

The Patriots were penalized five times for 31 yards, the Rams six times for 39. As he had with the fast-breaking Buffalo Bills in the Gulf War Super Bowl, Belichick wanted to drag the fast-breaking Rams into a half-court game. One way of accomplishing that, of course, was to constantly foul them. As Warner would recall:

> I really believe going into that game, that Bill told his guys, "Hey, we're going to do whatever we can early in this game. We're going to hold them. We're going to grab them. We're going to be physical with them. And we're going to force the officials to throw a bunch of flags on us in the first half." Because what we know is, the NFL does not want the Super Bowl dictated by a bunch of flags thrown in the first half and the game stopping. They want the flow of the game to go. And so I believe they went with that approach. And then finally, in the second half, there were some flags starting to be thrown and they had to loosen up a little bit and we were able to have a little bit of success.

One such flag saved the Rams from utter disaster. On fourth-and-goal at the 3 with more than ten minutes to play, Warner fumbled as he tried running for the end zone, and the loose ball was scooped up by Jones, who ran 97 yards down an exploding Patriots sideline for a touchdown that would've made it 24–3. Only McGinest had put a bear hug on Faulk as he tried to release into a pattern on the left side, and the officials nailed him on it. The linebacker was clearly emotional after a score that would've sealed a championship was taken off the board. "I was upset," McGinest said, "but I made a play that was in the game plan. I was out there to harass him. That was my job."

Warner called the Belichick strategy "a genius approach," because the officials had responded exactly as the coach suspected. They didn't want to be the central figures in the Super Bowl, so they called only the penalties on the Patriots that they had to call. Two plays after they called the foul they had to call on McGinest, Warner scored on a two-yard run to make it a ball game.

New England went three and out and gave the ball right back to St. Louis, and suddenly it appeared as if Belichick and Crennel were running low on ideas. The Rams drove into Patriots territory, helped by Warner's 30-yard pass to Proehl, and Belichick felt the need to intercede. Even after McGinest sacked Warner and left the Rams facing the long odds of third-and-25, Belichick called his final timeout. His defensive players were exhausted, and they needed his help. Those players thanked him by forcing St. Louis to punt.

Only another three-and-out from Brady broke the New England defense, and probably for good. The Rams needed just 21 seconds to cover 55 yards in three plays. Warner hit Proehl on a soft throw to his left, and the receiver stopped on a dime, cut to the inside, and blew past a lunging Jones on his way into the end zone. The score was 17–17 with 90 seconds to play. The Greatest Show on Turf had finally arrived, and it had the Superdome rocking like it had for U2 at halftime.

And now Belichick confronted a momentous decision after Troy Brown returned the kick only to New England's 17. He knew his defense was done stopping the Rams for the night. He turned to Weis and asked him what he thought. "I think they've got all the momentum," the coordinator said. "I think we should go down and try to score."

"OK," Belichick responded. "Call something safe. If we get a first down here, we'll go ahead and be more aggressive. Let's make sure we don't start off with a sack."

Sitting with Ernie Adams in the press box, Ned Burke, the offensive coaching assistant, heard the exchange between Belichick and Weis. They all believed that Brady wouldn't make the big mistake. The quarterback was so calm, cool, and collected, he had fallen asleep on the locker room floor after arriving at the Superdome early.

"As far as what I could hear on the headset," Burke said, "it was total confidence between Bill and Charlie that Tom would get it done, and that doesn't always happen in NFL games. You could hear their confidence. Bill is a skeptic, and he generally at that time was a more conservative play caller than Charlie was. Charlie would always tell him, 'Hey, we're going to start out the series with this,' and Bill would hem and haw and say, 'Nah, let's just get some positive yards.' That's just Bill's personality. That trait didn't come out. It wasn't typical of Bill's doom and gloom. It was like he sensed, *This is our chance to do it.*"

On the first play, out of the shotgun, Brady barely avoided the Rams' Leonard Little and the sack by stepping up and finding Redmond for five yards. "I don't agree with what the Patriots are doing right here," Madden said on the broadcast. "I would play for overtime." Actually, Belichick was playing to avoid overtime. Brady found Redmond again, this time for eight yards. After spiking the ball with 41 seconds left, he threw yet another pass to his running back, who did a brilliant job navigating would-be Rams tacklers and getting out of bounds at the New England 41 to stop the clock with 33 seconds left. "And now I kind of like what the Patriots are doing," Madden said.

He liked it almost as much as Redmond's Uncle Ben, who predicted the day after Bledsoe's injury that the substitute quarterback who had impressed him, Tom Brady, would lead the 0-2 Patriots to a championship.

Vinatieri untangled his foot from some television cords and practiced kicking into a net near the New England bench. Wearing his headset and a blue long-sleeve team jacket with a red stripe, Belichick paced slowly back and forth, betraying no emotion. After an incompletion, Brady made the biggest play of the drive when he ran 64-Max, All-In, which called for three receivers to line up to the right and run patterns to the left at varying depths. Brady completed a 23-yard pass over the middle to the receiver running the shallowest route, Brown, who made it to the sideline to stop the clock. Twenty-one seconds to go, ball on the St. Louis 36. Brady wanted to get a tad closer for Vinatieri, so he threw a safe ball to Wiggins for six yards before rushing to the line and spiking the ball with seven seconds left.

"I'll tell you," Madden said on the air, "what Tom Brady just did gives me goose bumps."

The Rams couldn't stop New England from running down the clock on this drive; they'd wasted their timeouts earlier trying to decipher Belichick's ever-changing defenses. And now the head coach of the Patriots was one 48-yard field goal away from pulling off the monumental upset. St. Louis had won 16 of 18 regular-season and postseason games, and seemed certain to win a second championship in three years. Before the game, Proehl looked into an NFL Films camera and said, "Tonight, the dynasty is born."

Belichick got 92 desperately needed rushing yards on 18 carries out of Antowain Smith, a near-flawless execution of the game plan from his defense, and the requisite cautious and dependable performance from Brady. The Patriots didn't surrender a single turnover, and the Rams surrendered three, including Law's pick-six. On this night, it was clear that Belichick and his staff had outcoached Martz and his.

The Patriots had bottled up the best of the best in Warner, who was fighting through a thumb injury, and the indomitable Faulk. The Rams' offensive coordinator, Bobby Jackson, called the quarterback and the running back the two smartest players he'd ever had in four decades of coaching. Faulk, he said, could come off the field after a failed play and explain exactly what went wrong with the blocking up front. "He saw everything," Jackson said. "It was unbelievable what that guy saw."

And yet Faulk and the rest of the Rams couldn't see the best way to attack a defense that was dropping everybody and their brothers into coverage. Belichick and Crennel were initially planning to play more man-to-man coverage, but they decided in the middle of the week to play more zone and use the two safeties in Cover 2 to provide deep help and allow the corners to be ultra-physical with Rams receivers off the line. St. Louis had averaged 31.4 points in the regular season and four times had scored more than 40 (including in its playoff victory over Green Bay), and yet the team didn't score a touchdown in the first 50 minutes of the game. Warner didn't throw a touchdown pass until 58 minutes and 30 seconds had expired.

The ball was on the right hash mark. For this field goal attempt, Belichick sent out an undrafted long snapper from Sacramento State (Lonie Paxton), an undrafted holder from Kent State (Ken Walter), and an undrafted kicker from South Dakota State (Vinatieri). He was standing in the middle of an event witnessed by tens of millions of people, and yet Belichick was all alone with his thoughts. He had started his NFL career as a barely paid gofer. He had been disrespected by players in his early days with the Giants. He had been detested by players, reporters, and fans in Cleveland who called for him to be fired. He had been cast as a loser by league executives and columnists who thought he'd be a sure failure in Foxborough after fleeing the Jets. He had been booked as the next NFL coach to be fired after he lost 13 of his first 18 games with the Patriots, including the first two of this season.

Now he needed perhaps his best player, Vinatieri, to come through one last time. When the kicker walked onto the field, he felt a surge of extreme confidence. "It felt like the movies," he said, "when you see a pitcher on the mound and everything calms down and gets quiet. I know there's a million things going on, but for me it was more about just focusing on your job." He'd been 24 for 24 in domed stadiums, and nothing would ever be the same in New England if he could extend his streak of perfection. From the spot of the expected hold, Vinatieri took three steps backwards, then two side steps to his left before swinging his right foot behind him. He was ready to decide what the great *Miami Herald* columnist Edwin Pope — who had covered every Super Bowl — would call "the best Super Bowl ever played."

The snap was true, the hold was pure, and Vinatieri launched the ball high over the outstretched arms of the Rams' interior linemen. It felt so good, Vinatieri later told his old kicking coach, Doug Blevins, that he had to pick up his head early and watch. Belichick ran out onto the field, near his own 24-yard line, to get a better view of this beautiful kick sailing right down the middle and through the uprights. Belichick threw up his hands toward the Superdome roof, and almost immediately his daughter, Amanda, was right there with him, along with Lawyer Milloy, who would lift him off the ground. Belichick pulled Milloy in with his right arm and Amanda in with his left, pulled them in tight.

"The happiness on Bill's face," said Burke, the offensive assistant, "was more palpable than I'd ever seen."

Little Bill had won a Super Bowl all his own. He was nobody's coordinator or protégé as the red, white, and blue confetti fell around him. He would call the moment "surreal." He would call this takedown of St. Louis "a miracle."

The devastated Rams would call it something else after they staggered off the field. "A sick feeling" was the way Proehl described it. "They cart you off like cattle to get the stage on for the winners, and then you hear the celebration through your locker room." Asked to identify the difference in the game, Proehl said, "Bill Belichick. It's that simple. He is a great football coach, and his team knew everything we were going to do."

During the postgame ceremony, Belichick held the Vince Lombardi Trophy high with his left hand. His 83-year-old father, Steve, joined him on the makeshift stage; Steve found himself standing next to Brady, who had both hands planted on his backwards-turned championship cap as he shook his head in disbelief. Steve's son said that when he handed the team to Brady in the wake of Bledsoe's injury, "the Super Bowl was the farthest thing from our minds."

Now the Super Bowl trophy was right there in Belichick's hands. He said his players' selflessness was the reason they had won, and he thanked Kraft for giving up that first-round pick and hiring him when so many thought he was positively mad to do so.

The Patriots partied deep into the night. At some point during the postgame celebration, Belichick was approached by Jason Licht, the team's national scout. "Wow," Licht said, "that was awesome. Now what?"

"*Now what?*" Belichick responded incredulously. "We win more."

Belichick retreated to the hotel bar to celebrate with his wife and friends, stayed up until 4:30 in the morning, then conducted a Monday morning press conference before flying back home with his team. The next day, 1.25 million fans lined the streets of Boston for a parade celebrating the franchise's first title since its birth as the Boston Patriots, in 1960, and the city's first championship team since the 1986 Boston Celtics.

Before the Patriots made their way to the parade route, Belichick was already conducting business for the 2002 season. He approached linebacker Ted Johnson, a starter for most of his seven seasons, and said, "Before we get on the bus, I just want you to know — don't read anything into it — I put you on the expansion draft list."

Each team had to make five players available for the incoming Houston Texans to choose from, and Belichick didn't see the need to wait to inform his. *Damn,* Johnson thought. He couldn't even make it to the parade unscathed.

It was just a small reminder that Bill Belichick wasn't only going to win championships. He was going to win them his way.

12

BIGGER BILL

Tom Jackson had a little bit of history with Bill Belichick. Jackson was a Pro Bowl linebacker for the 1978 Denver Broncos, and Belichick was a low-level assistant learning about the 3-4 from Joe Collier, defensive coordinator of the Orange Crush, and spending a lot of time wishing the Broncos would give him bigger responsibilities than he had.

So when Jackson used his ESPN platform on the popular pregame show *Sunday NFL Countdown* to attack Belichick on the morning of September 14, 2003, he drew a significant amount of blood. This criticism wasn't coming from a TV guy who had spent more hours in the makeup room than any locker room, or from some newspaper columnist who had never even put on the pads and experienced the living high school hell of a nutcracker drill. This was coming from a man who had competed in 201 regular-season and postseason NFL games and had established himself as a thoughtful voice in his second career.

Jackson was talking about the New England Patriots the Sunday after they'd lost their season opener in Buffalo by a 31–0 score. Belichick had released his captain and popular strong safety Lawyer Milloy five days before that game over a salary dispute, and Milloy had immediately signed with the Bills and contributed a sack of Tom Brady, five tackles, and a forced interception to the rout. Milloy had long been an emotional leader for the Patriots, and his teammates were furious over Belichick's decision to release the four-time Pro Bowler so close to the start of the season.

To get under the $74.6 million salary cap, Belichick wanted Milloy to take a bigger pay cut than he was willing to take. The coach said it was the toughest decision of his career. He called Milloy, who had made 106 consecutive regular-season starts, a "casualty of the system" and also conceded that he wasn't replaceable. The year before, Belichick had sent another popular Patriot, Drew Bledsoe, to Buffalo, but the circumstances were entirely different. Bledsoe wanted out after losing his job to Brady, and Belichick was so certain that New England's former franchise player no longer presented a credible threat to the Patriots that he allowed him to stay in the division, trading him to the Bills in April 2002 for a first-round pick.

Milloy, on the other hand, was still a valuable starter. "Has it ever been this quiet in here?" Tedy Bruschi, another heart-and-soul type, asked reporters in the locker room after Milloy's release. "I don't think it has. I think 'shocked' is the word . . . You sort of just shake your head and ask yourself *Why?*" The Patriots then staggered, zombie-like, through the game in Buffalo and lost for the first time in three meetings with Bledsoe.

Milloy couldn't help but deliver this shot to his former coach's rib cage after the shutout: "I miss my teammates, I miss the fans. It's unfortunate that they're stuck with an organization that deals away players, good players. There's no loyalty there."

The Patriots had missed the playoffs in 2002, had lost eight of their seventeen games since upsetting the Rams in the Super Bowl, and had just watched their coach coldly cut the first player to run to him to celebrate his greatest victory. The safety didn't record an interception in 2002, his tackles were down, and his 30th birthday was approaching, but it appeared that Belichick had underestimated Milloy's impact on his teammates. He thought he needed to make a business decision, a brutal one, and now it seemed he'd forgotten how important the human heartbeat is in sports.

"Bill Belichick is pond scum again," wrote Kevin Mannix in the *Herald*. "Arrogant, megalomaniacal, duplicitous pond scum."

Belichick was bloodied and on the ropes when Tom Jackson threw his roundhouse punch. Sitting in his ESPN studio across from Chris Berman, a friend of the Patriots' coach, Jackson started to speak as the question HAS BELICHICK LOST HIS TEAM? appeared on the screen beneath his image. Jackson looked straight into a camera that was transporting his message to football fans from coast to coast and said, "I want to say this very clearly: They hate their coach, and their season could be over, depending on how quickly they can get over this emotional devastation they suffered because of Lawyer Milloy."

Jackson would later explain to colleagues that he was speaking in a general context, that he was trying to say any NFL coach would face locker room backlash after cutting a popular starter so unceremoniously. Regardless, Patriots players assailed his take as completely erroneous. Rodney Harrison, the former San Diego safety who had replaced Milloy, called Jackson's claim "one of the stupidest things I ever heard." The broadcaster would later admit that he never spoke to any Patriots players before delivering an opinion that was presented as fact.

Belichick was furious with Jackson and said he wouldn't dignify his comments with a response. The analyst wasn't the only ESPN employee Belichick had an issue with. Greg Garber, who had covered the Giants as a newspaperman in the 1980s, had wanted to talk to the coach about the Milloy fallout in the days after the Buffalo loss. He didn't want to have to ambush him with some jagged-edged questions in his daily press conference.

As a Giants assistant, Belichick had taken Garber into the film room to show him what different coaches were doing. Garber made his request through Belichick's gatekeeper, Berj Najarian, in the hope that their history might make a difference, and he was disappointed to find out that it didn't. So the reporter asked his tough questions in the presser, and Belichick never talked to him again.

The world champion coach was a world-class grudge holder. Yet those close to Belichick understood why he was so angry, and so protective of what he'd built. Back in his Denver days, Belichick had been told by the special teams coach, Marv Braden, to make sure he didn't "downgrade the players too much" during the week, because they needed to play inspired football on Sundays. For all of the player-relations errors he committed in Cleveland, Belichick thought he'd made great strides in that area. He had the proof, not just in the form of the Lombardi Trophy but in what his ex-Brown and current Patriot Anthony Pleasant had told him during the 2001 championship run. Pleasant saw a more caring and compassionate coach in Foxborough than he saw in Cleveland, and for that reason he told Belichick he wanted to win a ring for him.

And then suddenly the coach was cast again in the role of a hater and forced to defend the way he ran his program. It had been a long, trying year for Belichick, who nearly had to attend a second funeral for an offensive coordinator in two seasons. Charlie Weis almost died in the 2002 preseason after undergoing gastric bypass surgery designed to shed weight (Weis weighed more than 300 pounds) and to improve his life expectancy after burying his father at age 56. Weis suffered severe internal bleeding after the stomach-stapling procedure and was given his last rites by a Catholic priest before making a dramatic recovery. Belichick took over the quarterbacks until Weis could return to work, but that position — held down by Tom Brady — wouldn't be the problem as the Patriots came crashing back to earth.

The defense was the problem, especially the defense against the run. The 2002 Patriots allowed more rushing yards than 30 out of 31 fellow NFL teams, and they couldn't run the ball themselves. (They finished 28th in rushing yardage and scored only nine touchdowns on the ground; the league leader, Minnesota, scored 26.) They did open the season with three consecutive victories, but those were followed by a streak of four consecutive losses that set a dispiriting tone for the second half of the season.

Most of the low-budget free agents signed in the spring hadn't breathed any new life into the cause. The Patriots looked like a tired team, and by season's end Brady's right arm — forced to throw 601 passes, or 188 more than he threw in 2001 — was dangling like a wet towel from the shoulder he separated in the Week 17 game against Miami. New England's roomier, upgraded workplace inside Gillette Stadium (the new place was supposed to carry the name of CMGI before the Internet company ran into financial trouble) did nothing to reinvigorate a team clearly suffering from a Super Bowl hangover; in fact, if anything, the Patriots' relative penthouse might've made them too comfortable at the office.

Belichick had been creative in his attempts to keep his much-feted players motivated. In August, a year after he took his team on a preseason trip to Providence to see an IMAX film on the polar explorer Ernest Shackleton, Belichick took his players to see a documentary on Bill Russell, who had won 11 championships with the Celtics, including eight in a row. Russell himself walked onto the stage after the film ended, and the floored Patriots gave him a standing ovation. The Celtics great spoke to his captive audience about the need to stay focused and hungry in pursuit of a second straight title.

Belichick knew he had to stay on top of his players now more than ever. Victor Green, defensive back, said the Patriots frustrated their coach early in the season by constantly using the word *swagger* in the news media. "One day in a team meeting," Green recalled, "Belichick says, 'Guys, stop with the fucking *swagger*. I'm tired of that word anyway. What the fuck is that? Swagger?' He never wants players to get comfortable with success."

This was always a 24/7 proposition for Belichick, even in the off-season, when the Patriots' coach was an omnipresent watchman at the team facility. Grey Ruegamer, center, recalled going out late one Friday night for beers with friends and then working out at the facility the next morning. He didn't see any cars in the parking lot, so after he headed in for a post-workout steam, he was surprised to see a figure sitting at the far end of the sauna. Belichick.

"My mind is racing at this point," Ruegamer said, "and I'm like *Holy shit*. I say, 'Coach, good morning.' He just looks at me and says, 'Grey,' and that was it. That was it for 15 to 20 minutes, and I'm thinking, *I must smell like a brewery, and he's got to be noticing this. Do I say something? Anything?* I was freaking out the whole time. He was absolutely an intimidating presence . . . A lot of times he just looked at you and you felt that intimidation.

You could be the only two dudes in the hallway, and you'd say, 'How are you doing?' And he'd just look right through you like you'd just shit on his shoes."

Belichick had the same presence in the auditorium for team meetings. Whenever he started quizzing his team on the opposition, fear was in the air. "Every kid who was ever in math or English class," said tight end Christian Fauria, "and the teacher starts walking around randomly asking questions even though nobody has their hand up knows that feeling. *Should I keep my head down and write notes, or make eye contact and dare him to ask me a question?* That was the mentality . . . It was 'Who's the backup safety? What school did he go to? How did he get there?' Who's looking at the backup safety? But you needed to know if the first guy got hurt, if he took his place, what were his strengths and weaknesses if he came into that situation . . . Nobody wanted to be embarrassed in front of their peers."

On the practice field, regardless of whether the Patriots were making a championship run or just trying to stay above .500, Belichick was forever twirling a whistle in his hand and chasing a perfect day of preparation. J. R. Redmond recalled being about two hours deep into a sloppy practice, with about 12 minutes to go in the session, when Belichick decided he'd seen enough of his team going through the motions. "He blew the horn," Redmond said, "and we started practice all over from the stretch . . . We went over the plays we messed up again and again."

Redmond said the 2002 Patriots were on the field five hours that day. The running back ended up with Bill Callahan's Oakland Raiders in 2003 and found an entirely different culture in place. "If we had a 15-play period of practice," Redmond said, "and maybe nine of the plays had a busted assignment or a snap-count screwup or some issue, we wouldn't repeat that play. We just went to the next period. After having one or two practices like that, or a week of practice like that and then playing in the game, that's a huge difference. We never had one practice like that in New England."

But as much as Belichick pressed his players on the details and tried to will them into the postseason tournament, they won only nine games and failed to qualify. The same Patriots who had beaten the Jets by 37 points on the road in Week 2 lost to them by a 30–17 count at home in Week 16. "At the end of the game," said Jets quarterback Chad Pennington, "you could tell they were tired, weary, from two straight years of winning the Super Bowl or trying to defend it . . . You could tell there was a little wind out of their sails."

On January 26, 2003, the day Super Bowl XXXVII was played between the Oakland Raiders and the Tampa Bay Buccaneers, Belichick surprised friends and strangers alike by publishing an op-ed piece in the *New York*

Times that was headlined "O.K., Champ, Now Comes the Hard Part." Paid the *Times*'s standard $450 for his thoughts, Belichick applied his dry wit to the column in cobbling together 37 thoughts on just how uneasy lies the head that wears the crown. Among Belichick's warnings to the eventual winning coach, Tampa Bay's Jon Gruden:

> Several of your players (and their agents) will come looking for a little extra at contract time. After all, didn't they make Fantasyland possible? Of course they did. Be ready . . .
>
> You'll stand in front of your team and talk about how different it is being champs, even though you can't truly know the difference yet . . .
>
> You'll notice that all your opponents know your team a little better than they did this season: they'll hit you a little harder and play a little better when you show up. Deal with it . . .
>
> Remember, the Smart Coach/Moron Coach Meter, which is currently way off the charts in the right direction, can be very moody.

Nobody was about to call Belichick a moron for failing to make the playoffs on the championship rebound. Though he disagreed with the popular notion (and the numbers) that said the Patriots were a wildly inconsistent group, Belichick understood that changes had to be made in the off-season. He performed a makeover on his defensive secondary while keeping three-time Pro Bowl corner Ty Law in place, and he traded for four-time Pro Bowl nose tackle Ted Washington. Belichick wasn't shy about his intentions when he spoke to those he was recruiting to his team.

He invited John Thornton, a defensive tackle for the Tennessee Titans, to make a free-agent visit after he was done spending time with another suitor, Marvin Lewis, of the Cincinnati Bengals. The Patriots were already famous for their no-frills approach to recruiting before Belichick showed up a little late for his meeting with Thornton. The coach was sweating through his cutoff shirt — he'd clearly just come from a workout — and he held a half-eaten apple in his hand. Thornton was impressed by the fact that a Super Bowl–winning coach knew every last detail of his college and pro careers. "He was like an encyclopedia," Thornton said.

Belichick didn't overdo it with the sales pitch. While Bengals coaches were repeatedly calling Thornton to persuade him to sign, Belichick simply told him, "We want you. Come start for us at left end. We're going to win a Super Bowl, and you'll be part of it."

Cincinnati offered a lot more money than New England did, and that made the decision easy. Before Thornton left Foxborough, Belichick told him that if he didn't sign with the Patriots, they would draft a defensive lineman and win the Super Bowl with that player instead. And with the

13th overall pick in April, Belichick selected 6'5", 300-pound Ty Warren of Texas A&M.

One major free agent Belichick did land was Rosevelt Colvin, who'd had 21 sacks in his previous two seasons in Chicago. Colvin had grown tired of Windy City weather and wanted to go play in a market with a warm climate or a domed stadium. Foxborough offered neither, so when Colvin's agent called with news of Belichick's interest, his client said thanks, but no thanks. He also didn't want to be coached by a branch of the Bill Parcells tree.

"I don't want to be yelled at every single day," Colvin told his agent, Kennard McGuire, who persuaded his client to make the trip anyway.

Arguably the league's most coveted free agent, Colvin recalled a Patriots staffer picking him up at the airport in a white Ford Taurus. "It's overcast," he said, "trash everywhere on the highway . . . No limo, not like a Lincoln Town Car, but a car they probably use to shuttle guys on the practice squad back and forth to the airport."

When they arrived at the Patriots' facility, Colvin said, there was no welcoming committee at the door. "Nobody was there other than Berj Najarian," he said. "All the lights are off. There's nothing going on at the facility at all. Berj asked me if I needed anything to drink. 'Are you sure? Water? Let me take you on a tour.' Berj took me to the locker room. It was dark; he didn't turn anything on. I went to talk to Belichick for an hour. We sat down and talked and then I said, 'I appreciate you bringing me in.'"

Colvin then folded himself inside the same white Ford Taurus for the ride back to the airport to take the next flight out of town. He told his agent, "I'll pass." Belichick and his personnel chief, Scott Pioli, were growing a bit tired of the narrative that they'd made only bargain-basement buys in free agency during their time in Foxborough, so they responded with the best offer Colvin received: $30 million for seven years. The linebacker quickly forgot all about his desire to play in a tropical climate. The Patriots also signed cornerback Tyrone Poole, for $8 million over four years, and Harrison, a two-time Pro Bowler, for $14.5 million over six years, after taking him to the local Ground Round.

"Yeah, they really wined and dined me," Harrison joked.

Pioli thought that if the coach wanted serious-minded grinders in New England, he should treat them that way from the start. Though the players accepted and even embraced Belichick's approach, they still couldn't accept the Milloy firing, and proved it in Buffalo. In this second game of 2003, a road game against the Eagles, either they could rally around the coach who had just enraged them or they could make a very wise man out of Tom Jackson. The Patriots didn't have to forgive and forget; they only had to prove that they remained willing to play hard for Belichick.

And they did that in a 31–10 victory that saw Brady throw two touchdown passes to Fauria and one to Deion Branch. The Patriots forced six turnovers and sacked Eagles quarterback Donovan McNabb seven times. Bruschi, who had been openly critical of the Milloy move, returned an interception for a touchdown. Were these the actions of a team that truly hated its coach?

Larry Izzo, New England's best special teams player, profanely dismissed Jackson's claim before adding, "I don't know another coach in the league who has the support of his players more than Bill, and we went out and showed that today."

The Patriots lost Colvin for the year to a shattered hip, which could've been a devastating, season-defining development for many teams. New England won six of its next seven games anyway, suffering another big injury (Ted Washington broke his leg against the Jets) before hosting another 7-2 team in a nationally televised night game that was billed not as a battle of contenders but as a battle of Bills.

Parcells vs. Belichick. Big Bill vs. Little Bill. The two men were barely on speaking terms, and that was OK. Their teams were prepared to do the talking for them.

They had split four games when Little Bill was in Cleveland and Big Bill in New England, though Belichick won their only postseason meeting. They didn't know it at the time, but this Cowboys–Patriots clash would be the last time Belichick and Parcells would stand across from each other on NFL sidelines. Predictably enough, the buildup to this heavyweight fight focused on their nasty divorce in New York.

"I have no hard feelings about anything," Parcells maintained before his fifth and final showdown with Belichick.

Parcells later wrote in his book that he had called Belichick after his Super Bowl victory over the Rams and the call lasted less than a minute. Maybe Belichick was better at holding a grudge, or maybe he was worse. Either way, Belichick wasn't quite as effusive in his praise of his former boss as he was before they met in that playoff game on New Year's Day 1995, when Little Bill said that Big Bill "did a tremendous amount for me."

Privately, according to author Michael Holley, Belichick told his players before the 2003 Patriots–Cowboys game, "Don't get distracted by irrelevant aspects of this game. Belichick versus Parcells? We're both assholes. We started coaching together when some of you were in diapers . . . Don't get into Belichick versus Parcells. If you want the easy way out, tell them that I won't let you comment."

Publicly, Belichick told reporters, "We worked together for a long time and we shared a mutual respect. Not all decisions are easy, but as coaches, we often have to make difficult decisions. There was a lot that went into it, and given all the circumstances, I felt I made the right decision. We have a professional relationship and we had some success together. Bill always gave me the latitude to run the defense within certain general parameters, but we've all moved on with our careers."

Belichick and Parcells never really had more than a professional relationship, which was permanently damaged by the Jets mess. On a cold night in Foxborough, the deep pregame freeze between head coaches was evident for all to see.

"It was almost comical," wrote Dan Shaughnessy in the *Globe*. "While the teams went through their extensive warm ups, Belichick and Parcells paced, hands in pockets, pretending not to notice one another. There were times they were within five yards of each other, but there was no handshake, no greeting. Together for so many years with the Giants, Patriots, and Jets, Belichick and Parcells are foxhole buddies no more and the good people at ESPN relayed the big chill to its national audience."

The game unfolded as expected, with two great defensive coaches lording over the two defenses that would finish the season 1-2 in points allowed. The Patriots scored the only touchdown in a 12–0 victory, though it really wasn't a fair fight. Belichick had Tom Brady and Parcells had Quincy Carter, who threw three interceptions — three more than Brady did. Little Bill was also playing with the core of his 2001 title team. Big Bill? He was rebuilding a Cowboys team that had gone 5-11 three straight seasons under Dave Campo.

The final score was a mere sidebar to the postgame handshake — assuming there would be a handshake. Cameramen closed in on Belichick and Parcells as they came together on the field, and Big Bill surprised some witnesses by wrapping Little Bill in a hug. Parcells congratulated his former assistant on the victory. "I told him I thought he had a good football team," Belichick said, "and I wished him well. And I do."

When questioned about the hug, an irritated Parcells said, "People in the media can try to drive a stake between us, but that's not going to happen. He did a helluva job for me." Parcells added that he thought the Patriots had "a good shot" to win it all a second time.

Belichick didn't know it that night, but after he left Gillette Stadium, his 3-2 record against Parcells would remain in place for eternity. Parcells still held a 2–1 lead on the big-picture scoreboard, the one that really mattered: Super Bowl titles won as a head coach.

Little Bill still had time to do something about that.

· · ·

On his way to another AFC Championship Game, Belichick had humbled the Buffalo Bills of Lawyer Milloy and Drew Bledsoe, beating them by the same 31–0 margin that had favored Buffalo in its season-opening rout of New England. Belichick had also shredded Tom Jackson's they-hate-their-coach claim by winning 13 consecutive games, including a tight playoff victory over the Tennessee Titans — settled by another Adam Vinatieri game winner — played in brutal Foxborough conditions.

Belichick had even weathered another controversial move he made that had a negative impact on a popular player. Richard Seymour, team captain and Belichick favorite, had missed two December practices to attend his grandfather's funeral in South Carolina. His coach seemed to believe that Seymour missed one practice too many. On his return, the right defensive end was told that the starter at his position in the 3-4 that Sunday, against Jacksonville, would be Jarvis Green. Seymour sat the first quarter, came on like a man possessed in the second quarter, and contributed seven tackles, a sack, and a forced fumbled to New England's tenth consecutive victory.

Seymour was angry and hurt. "Very disappointing," he called the demotion. Larry Izzo had twice missed two consecutive practices after his father's death, and yet he wasn't docked any playing time. "It was a coach's decision," Belichick said of the Seymour benching. "Sorry to hear everybody can't understand that, but I do what I think is best for the team. That's all." Belichick reiterated the following day that he had the "utmost respect for Richard Seymour," one of his very best players, and all wounded parties agreed to move on to the postseason push.

On his way to an AFC Championship Game matchup with Tony Dungy and Peyton Manning, Belichick saw nothing but green grass in front of him. Parcells and the Cowboys had been eliminated from the playoffs, and the Milloy-Bledsoe Bills hadn't even qualified for the field. Belichick was running low on scores to settle before he received a request for a one-on-one interview — through Berj Najarian — from Mark Cannizzaro, of the *New York Post*, who told Najarian he wanted to talk to Belichick about a critical column he was writing on former Jets president Steve Gutman. The same Steve Gutman who'd watched Belichick's bizarre resignation presser and effectively said the coach had lost his mind.

The Jets still hadn't appeared in a Super Bowl since the 1968 season, and Gutman — widely regarded as an overmatched accountant with no discernible football expertise — was an inviting target if Belichick wanted to take a shot at him. As it turned out, he did. Belichick apparently spent the night marinating over what he wanted to say, then had Najarian invite Cannizzaro into a side room the following day after his usual briefing with the news media. The writer asked the coach what he thought of Gutman's characterization of him upon his exit.

"I'm going to make one comment and we can close the book on it," Belichick said. "I can't think of anybody in professional sports — and certainly in my 30 years of professional football — who has said more and won less than Steve Gutman."

Belichick had rarely taken his eye off the ball like this, never mind in the middle of a playoff week. He'd been waiting years for his opening on Gutman, and he seized it. Belichick also said that he knew he was making the right decision when he left the Jets for New England, and that his fears about the uncertain future of the organization all came to fruition.

His payback complete, Belichick turned his attention to a worthy adversary, Manning, the son of former New Orleans Saints quarterback Archie Manning. The Patriots had beaten the Colts, 38–34, in a wild game at the RCA Dome in November that was decided by a goal-line stand in the final seconds. The Colts had established a long history of failure in the presence of the Patriots; they'd lost 11 of the past 13 meetings, dating back to their pre-Peyton days.

Only this was a different Indy team showing up at Gillette Stadium to play for the right to go to the Super Bowl. The Colts had scored a combined 79 points in their playoff victories over Denver and Kansas City, and Manning, who had been 0-3 in the postseason before 2003, had completed 44 of 56 passes for 681 yards, eight touchdowns, and no interceptions in those games. The Colts had been so explosive on offense, they didn't punt the ball once against the Broncos or the Chiefs.

"I don't think I've ever seen a team run through the playoffs like they have," Belichick said. The same man who had schemed the high-flying 1990 Bills and 2001 Rams back to earth had a plan, and a defense, that could neutralize a dome team that preferred a fast track. In their previous seven home games, the Patriots had shut out three opponents and given up a total of 36 points.

This game was a clash of opposites. Manning was All-Everything at Tennessee, and the first pick in his draft. Brady wasn't even his own coach's preferred choice to start at Michigan as an upperclassman. On the coaching front, Belichick was the disagreeable grinder who never met an 18-hour workday he couldn't turn into a 20-hour workday. Colts coach Tony Dungy was the neighborly voice of reason who brought a sunshiny dose of humanity to the workplace. "You know me," Dungy said. "I'm not one of those guys who sleeps in the office. I'm not one of those guys who feels you have to do that to get the job done."

The Patriots had little fear of Indy's scoreboard-tilting speed, dazzling as it was to the rest of the league. Damien Woody, the valuable guard lost to a knee injury in the Tennessee victory, captured his team's feelings about the Colts this way: "They put up all these flashy stats, but when someone punches them in the mouth, can they take a punch? We felt no, they couldn't. So we punched them and they couldn't counterpunch, and we felt we could beat them up."

As contrasting styles often make for great rivalries, Patriots–Colts was starting to show real promise. This was their first playoff showdown, and Indianapolis tight end Marcus Pollard added to the intrigue when he declared that if the Colts kept playing like they had been, "they might as well just hand us the rings." Belichick pounced on that line, just as he always pounced on far more benign observations made by upcoming opponents in an attempt to sharpen his team's edge. "Nobody hands you a ring," he reportedly told his players. "I don't care how much money you have; you can't fucking buy one. You have to play and you have to earn it." Belichick was said to have pulled out his Super Bowl XXXVI ring and held it above his head for emphasis. As much as he micromanaged his own players' public comments and reminded them that they gained nothing by flexing their muscles in the media, he loved it when bulletin-board material emerged from some other coach's locker room.

"Not only don't we say anything stupid; we don't think anything stupid," Brady said of Pollard's remark. "We don't need to go out there and talk. We let 13 games in a row say it for us."

They did their talking with a 14th in a row, too, using the same tactics that Belichick's bygone Giants had used in the Gulf War Super Bowl against Buffalo and that his Patriots had used in the indelible Super Bowl upset of St. Louis. New England manhandled Manning's outstanding receivers, Marvin Harrison and Reggie Wayne, leaving people up and down the Colts' organization apoplectic over the lack of penalties called, and put enough pressure on the quarterback to intercept him four times and sack him four times.

Down seven with less than two minutes to play, Manning threw a fourth-and-10 pass to Pollard, who was held by linebacker Roman Phifer. No penalty flag was thrown. When New England's 24–14 victory was complete, Colts GM Bill Polian ran after the officials as they headed for the tunnel. A member of the competition committee, Polian said he would spend much of the next league meeting in the spring making sure officials started calling defensive holding "much closer to the way [the rules] are written."

Vinatieri kicked five field goals, Antowain Smith rushed for 100 yards, and Jarvis Green—who'd had 4.5 sacks in his first two regular seasons combined—delivered three of New England's four sacks after Belichick correctly figured he'd make an impact against a Colts offensive line focused on more prominent pass rushers. Ty Law accounted for three of New England's interceptions, and the safety Belichick had put in Milloy's place, Rodney Harrison, gathered in the fourth and forced a fumble, further validating his coach's decision to go with the slightly older and slower player.

As it was, Belichick was the Patriot most responsible for setting the early tone against Indy. On his first possession, facing a fourth-and-one from his own 44, Belichick decided to go for it. Brady walked up to the line with a handful of different play options to choose from, and he picked the right one: The quarterback gained two yards for the first down, and ultimately completed the 65-yard drive with a touchdown pass to David Givens.

The Patriots were heading back to the Super Bowl because they had defeated one league co-MVP, Tennessee's Steve McNair, and then another, Manning, who fell to 2-8 in Foxborough and 0 for his last 4 against Brady and Belichick. Belichick's plan against Peyton was simple: Make his defensive linemen active in his passing lanes and, if possible, make Manning throw on the move, as he wasn't the same quarterback when his feet weren't set. Oh, and don't be fooled by the amount of shouting and mad gesturing Manning was doing at the line of scrimmage; he wasn't audibling nearly as much as it seemed.

New England was near flawless in its execution. To a man, the Patriots said afterward that they were sick and tired of hearing about Manning and an offense that played faster than the Indianapolis Motor Speedway. "Peyton this, Peyton that," Harrison said. Manning had a quarterback rating of 156.9 in his previous two playoff games; he posted a 33.5 against New England.

With an assist from Romeo Crennel, his earnest defensive coordinator, Belichick had dismantled yet another offensive machine. So the Patriots headed for Houston and a date with the NFC-champion Carolina Panthers, in an attempt to make history with a 15th straight victory, while Peyton Manning headed home. It wouldn't be the last time Belichick sent him there.

Dressed in a blue team windbreaker and not the gray Reebok hoodie he'd started wearing in November, Bill Belichick was doubled over with his hands on his knees as Adam Vinatieri was about to attempt a 41-yard field goal with eight seconds left in Super Bowl XXXVIII. The Patriots and the Panthers were locked in a 29–29 tie inside Reliant Stadium, and Belichick had everything on the line with this kick. He had already won a championship, yes, but he would become an historic figure in professional football with a second one.

He would be remembered as an all-time great with a second one.

This time around, Belichick had two weeks to prepare for the big game, one of the many reasons New England was the prohibitive favorite and the Panthers were assigned the underdog role given the 2001 Patriots. Belichick was already hailed as a chess master who knew best how to attack and contain his opponent's most prized pieces, and his postseason experience gave him a decided edge over Carolina's John Fox, who was in the playoffs for the first time as a head coach and who had needed only two seasons to turn George Seifert's 1-15 Panthers into a title contender.

Life was good for Belichick on and off the field. His rocker friend, Jon Bon Jovi, had dedicated a song to him, "Bounce," the title track of an album dedicated to the resilience of New York and the country in a post-9/11 world. (Years later, Bon Jovi would offer $50,000 at a fund-raiser for Hannah and Friends, a nonprofit for special-needs families inspired by Charlie Weis's daughter, if Belichick and Weis would join him onstage to sing a few lines of "Wanted Dead or Alive." They agreed, and performed as badly as advertised.) In the winter of 2004, the singer wasn't just a sports fan anymore; he was the new owner of the Philadelphia Soul of the Arena Football League, a real football man just like his friend.

"Look," Belichick said, "I like his music, he likes football. So that's a good thing." When they were together, the chemistry between them was obvious to everyone at the Patriots' facility, from players busy practicing to others rehabbing injuries. "The only time Bill Belichick was distracted at practice was when Bon Jovi was there," said Rosevelt Colvin. "Then he didn't care what anyone was doing."

Belichick hadn't lost a game since September 28, when Washington beat New England by three points, and for that he was named NFL Coach of the Year. Belichick credited the pro's pros on his roster for his success, and never hesitated in praising the veterans drafted in Parcells's time, including Willie McGinest, Tedy Bruschi, and Ty Law. But he needed to use 42 starters this season — Patriots players lost 103 regular-season games to injuries, including Ted Washington's six games to his broken leg — and to stitch together a patchwork offensive line that included a rookie and fifth-round draft choice (Dan Koppen), a guard who opened the season on the practice squad (Russ Hochstein), and a tackle who was active for one game in 2002 (Tom Ashworth). That line hadn't allowed a sack all postseason.

Belichick was concerned about the Carolina defense and what it might do to his line and skill people. "He beat us down mentally throughout the entire two weeks about this defensive group," Deion Branch said. "It gave me this little chip. I know for a fact I was going to show Coach, 'We can defeat these guys.' He wasn't saying we couldn't do it, but it was a mental challenge for us . . . Trust me, practice was the worst. We'd be in a stance, and a coach would be behind us holding our jersey when Tom snapped the ball, and we couldn't run five yards. 'This is what they're going to do. They're going to hold you.' Coach made the game so much easier for us."

On the other side of the ball, Belichick's defensive secondary wasn't affected at all by the loss of Milloy. In the regular season and postseason combined, Law had nine interceptions; Tyrone Poole had six; Harrison, who led the team in tackles, had five; and rookie Eugene Wilson had four.

Dan Reeves, an NFL head coach for 23 consecutive years before he was fired by Atlanta, said he watched a number of Patriots tapes and decided they "scheme as well as anybody I've ever seen." New England would need all of Belichick's creativity against the Panthers, who allowed only 36 points in their three playoff victories and who featured a running back, Stephen Davis, who had rushed for a career-high 1,444 yards.

The Patriots' coach respected Fox and his Carolina staff, including Parcells's old friend, offensive coordinator Dan Henning; strength coach Jerry Simmons, who worked under Belichick in Cleveland; and another member of that old Browns staff, Scott O'Brien, who might've been the league's finest special teams coach. Belichick actually owned four season tickets to Panthers games, dating back to their first year in existence, 1995, when he bought them to show support to then–Panthers GM Bill Polian and personnel man Dom Anile, another ex-Clevelander. Now it was time for Belichick to do everything he could to devalue those tickets.

In a pregame speech to his players in a hotel ballroom, Belichick planted the Super Bowl XXXVI Lombardi Trophy on a table and declared that it represented a team. "That's what it symbolizes," he said. "Not the guy who leads the league in punting, not the guy who's got 15 sacks, not the guy who's got 1,200 yards rushing. It represents the team that's the toughest, smartest, most confident team. If you think back on our season, no matter what tough spot you've been in, in the end, the reason why you won is because you identified the situation, you heard the call, and you did your job. That's what execution is about. This game is about execution. There's one champion — it will be us if we play well."

But Belichick was also pissed off over the amount of talking Carolina had done. Richard Seymour and Panthers defensive tackle Brentson Buckner got into a heated on-field exchange in the pregame that was joined by other players, and tensions were sky-high. When Belichick addressed his players before they took the field, he had angrily rejected the notion that the 2003 Panthers were the equivalent of the 2001 Patriots and that they were about to secure the same result. One player told the *Globe*'s Michael Smith that the message went like this: "They're not us. They'll never be fucking us. They'll never be champions. We're the fucking champions, and the trophy is coming back where it belongs."

This was a seething Belichick the players almost never saw or heard. "To me," said tight end Christian Fauria, "it was the most passionate I've heard him. You could tell it was personal . . . Bill wasn't busting a cooler and didn't have his veins popping, but he was very calculated and direct with his words and message."

The Patriots were again introduced as a team, not as individuals, and engaged the upstart Panthers in what some would consider another Super Bowl classic. Brady was tremendous, completing 32 of 48 passes for 354 yards and three touchdowns while that patchwork offensive line didn't allow him to get sacked. Carolina quarterback Jake Delhomme was nearly Brady's equal — he threw for 323 yards and three touchdowns — but he was sacked four times. The Panthers stayed right with the Patriots by scoring on big plays, including an 85-yard pass from Delhomme to Muhsin Muhammad — who had 141 yards on only four catches — that gave Carolina its first lead, 22–21, in the middle of the fourth quarter. (The Panthers failed on their two-point conversion attempt.)

It was a strange game. New England and Carolina did no scoring in the first and third quarters, and lit it up in the final three minutes of the second and all of the fourth. Belichick also made a rare disastrous mistake on a stage so big, choosing to squib-kick to the Panthers after a Brady touchdown pass to David Givens with 18 seconds left in the first half. "Can I say one more time how much I hate the squib kick?" Belichick's former co-worker with the Giants, Phil Simms, said on the CBS broadcast. Carolina recovered, and after the Patriots gave up a 21-yard Davis run, John Kasay kicked a 50-yard field goal on the last play of the half to cut New England's lead to 14–10.

The halftime show would feature another unforced error when Justin Timberlake exposed Janet Jackson's breast before 143.6 million witnesses in what he later called a "wardrobe malfunction." The Patriots and Panthers had a tough act to follow, and they didn't disappoint. New England took a 21–10 lead early in the fourth quarter, and Carolina receiver Ricky Proehl — who had scored the tying touchdown for the Rams in the Super Bowl two years earlier — said the Patriots started "talking junk. They were like 'OK, we're getting ready to put the final nail in your coffin.'"

The Panthers suddenly emerged from their casket by scoring on a 33-yard DeShaun Foster run and again — after Reggie Howard intercepted Brady in the end zone — on the Delhomme heave to Muhammad, who beat the rookie Wilson down the field and finished him off with a stiff-arm. Fox made the mistake of chasing points and going for two after both touchdowns, failing both times, and New England responded with a 68-yard drive.

Trailing by a point in the closing minutes, Brady called 136 X-Cross Z-Flag on second-and-goal from the one-yard line. In other words, he called Mike Vrabel's number. The linebacker had caught a touchdown pass against San Diego in 2002, but this was different. This was late in the fourth quarter of a Super Bowl that was nerve-racking enough to inspire Belichick to admit, "I was having a heart attack out there." Vrabel already had two sacks, and his second-quarter strip of Delhomme had led to a Seymour recovery and ultimately New England's first touchdown.

The coach had turned a kicking-game afterthought with the Pittsburgh Steelers into a burgeoning star. Belichick loved Vrabel's versatility, intelligence, instincts, leadership skills, and effectiveness on special teams. "One of the toughest players I've ever coached," Belichick said, "mentally and physically." Vrabel was also a jokester who could get away with saying things to Belichick few others could. Sometimes he'd give the coach advice on what defensive calls he should make. "Mike," Belichick would tell him, "when you're a coach and you're calling the defenses, you should go ahead and do that."

More than anything, Vrabel was a football player's football player. "We had a roomful of guys like that," McGinest said of the linebackers. "We had guys in there who didn't need playbooks . . . Vrabel's one of the smartest guys and players I've ever been around."

Vrabel would catch ten touchdown passes over the years for Belichick, so the coach bristled when someone described the linebacker's pass routes as gadget plays. "He was part of our goal-line offense that was a standard formation," Belichick said. "It was a standard play."

Lined up to Brady's left, Vrabel ran a crossing pattern that compelled two defenders to run into each other, leaving the 6′4″, 261-pound tight end open. Brady didn't hesitate in throwing his way. Big, hulking men who aren't in the habit of catching footballs often use their bodies as a backstop when trying to gather in a pass. Vrabel didn't have that luxury, or that need. He was an athlete, after all. He extended his arms and caught the touchdown pass with his hands. Kevin Faulk's two-point conversion run made it 29–22 New England, with 2:51 to go.

The Panthers responded as if they were anything but first-timers in the Super Bowl. A schoolyard quarterback who projected a fun, draw-'em-up-in-the-dirt vibe, Delhomme led Carolina down the field. Harrison broke his arm on that possession, weakening the Patriots' secondary, and right away Delhomme hit Proehl for 31 yards, to the New England 14. Three plays later, he found Proehl again for a 12-yard touchdown. Fox didn't go for two this time; his Panthers made it 29–29 with 68 seconds left.

"The Patriots were the superior team," Proehl said years later. "They were just a great football team, and they looked at us in the pregame like 'This is going to be a joke.' You felt that as a player on the other side . . . But after I scored, I felt like *We've got this game. They're on the ropes* . . . They were looking at each other and yelling at each other, and you could sense the tide turning. *They've got guys pulling up with cramps, and we're going to win this game.*"

The Panthers' mood immediately darkened when their kicker, Kasay, booted the ball out of bounds, advancing New England to the 40-yard line. Brady opened the drive with an incompletion but then worked around an offensive pass interference call with throws to Troy Brown (who was playing through a broken nose), Daniel Graham, and Deion Branch (who had ten catches for 143 yards and a touchdown) to reach the Carolina 23 before Belichick used his last timeout with nine seconds left. Vinatieri trotted out to attempt to kick the Patriots to another parade.

"To see them get into field goal position, you want to throw up," said Proehl, who had seen this movie before with the Rams. "I was just sick to my stomach. What are the chances of this happening?"

But Proehl had no idea that across the field, two Patriots also felt sick to their stomachs: Belichick and his accidental 38-year-old long snapper, Brian Kinchen, his former tight end with the Browns. The team's regular long snapper, Lonie Paxton, had gone down with an injury, and so had his replacement. Belichick had arranged for a late-season tryout and, though Kinchen hadn't played in the NFL in three years (he was teaching Bible classes) and had airmailed a snap over the holder's head during his audition, he beat out three other candidates to land the job.

In the freezing cold during the Tennessee playoff victory, Kinchen had snapped a ball into the ground and started a downward spiral that left him a broken athlete. He lost all confidence in his ability to perform the task, and his snapping problems became much like the throwing problems Chuck Knoblauch and Rick Ankiel experienced in baseball. His special teams coach, Brad Seely, got all over him, and so did offensive coordinator Charlie Weis, who, like his former boss Parcells, had a piercing sense of humor. Kinchen resorted to lobbing the ball for the sake of accuracy, and Weis told him one day, "Man, you really showed your age. You could've timed your snaps with a sundial."

The long snapper locked himself in his hotel room at night, dressed in his full uniform, and practiced dozens of snaps into the pillows he stuffed beneath his window. Even that didn't work; he bounced nearly every snap he tried to deliver the next day. He called Scott Pioli four nights before the Super Bowl and asked to be cut, and Pioli relayed the request to Belichick, who knew he had no better options available so close to showtime. During practice the following day, Kinchen caught Belichick's eye from a distance, and the coach gave him a thumbs-up. "Never in his lifetime had Bill given me the OK sign," Kinchen said. "It was so not him. But that was his way to let me know he was watching and that everything is going to be just fine."

Only on Super Bowl Sunday, everything was a million miles removed from fine. During the pregame meal, Kinchen was working a hard bread roll with a steak knife when he badly cut up his index finger. Belichick was beyond angry with the rented long snapper who had proven to be more trouble than he was worth. "Stitch it up, put a tourniquet on it, whatever you want to do," the coach told Kinchen. "But you know what? You're playing. It's a Super Bowl."

And play in the Super Bowl Brian Kinchen did. He bounced two balls to holder Ken Walter, on a punt and an extra-point attempt, and Walter handled the bounces like a big-league shortstop. As Kinchen exited the field after the extra-point bounce, near the end of the first half, an incredulous Belichick chased after him. "Brian," he barked, "do you realize this is the Super Bowl? You do know you're not doing the job we hired you to do correctly, right?" Long snapping was the one football skill Belichick had mastered as a player, and he'd be damned if he was going to lose a championship because one of his Patriots couldn't perform the task. Kinchen felt humiliated. "I felt like saying, 'You called me,'" he remembered. "'Shut up and let me do my job or just don't pick up the phone next time.'"

Kinchen prayed and prayed that the Panthers wouldn't tie it on their final possession, and that it wouldn't come down to a Vinatieri field goal attempt in the closing seconds. "So imagine the anxiety I felt," Kinchen said, "when it did." As he prepared to snap the ball, Carolina called time out. The Panthers weren't trying to ice the kicker as much as they were trying to ice the snapper.

Kinchen paced about and thought of Bill Buckner, the Red Sox first baseman who helped blow the 1986 World Series by missing a simple ground ball from the Mets' Mookie Wilson. He thought of Trey Junkin, the long snapper who had come out of retirement the previous year, at 41, and lost a playoff game for the New York Giants on a botched delivery in San Francisco. Finally, Kinchen told himself that, unlike Junkin, he would fire the snap as hard as he could and hope for the best.

This was why Belichick was doubled over, hands on knees. This was why Belichick said he felt like he was having a heart attack. Vinatieri had already missed one field goal in this brutally physical game and had another one blocked, and it was clear that Kinchen's weeks-long meltdown had affected him. Vinatieri had made 31 of 35 indoor kicks in his career; strangely enough, all four misses had come at Reliant Stadium. But he had proven himself to be one of the NFL's signature clutch players two years earlier with his remarkable field goal against Oakland and then his title clincher against St. Louis. He believed he would make this kick against Carolina, if only Kinchen gave him a chance.

Terrified of the moment and the potential consequences of failure, Kinchen lowered himself over the ball, near the right hash mark, grabbed it with both hands, and cut it loose. He heard the thud of foot meeting ball and watched the 41-yard kick sail straight through the uprights with four seconds to play. He quickly scanned the field left to right for any sign of a flag, and when all was clear, he dropped his elbows to his side and screamed from his toes like he'd never screamed in his life, exposing every vein in his arms and neck.

Meanwhile, Belichick rose from his stance, dispassionately slid his headset down to his neck, and signaled with his right hand for his kickoff team to bring it in. The Panthers did nothing of consequence with that kickoff, and Belichick and his Patriots were Super Bowl champions one more time. The players and coaches wrapped one another in liberating hugs, and soon enough the Patriots were on the podium, lifting the Vince Lombardi Trophy.

Kinchen screamed at Belichick four or five times until the coach finally turned to him. "I told you I'd get it done," the long snapper shouted. Belichick nodded his head. In the locker room afterward, Kinchen embraced Belichick's wife, Debby. "I shouldn't even be talking to you after what you put Bill through," she joked.

Belichick agreed to an ESPN interview with his friend Chris Berman, but he declined to shake Tom Jackson's hand when he arrived on the set. Even after winning it all, Belichick was always on to the next opponent.

Brady was the MVP, again, even though he'd spent much of the season using painkillers and limiting his practice reps for a right shoulder that would require surgery in the off-season. But this second title and 15th consecutive victory were about Belichick and his program. He used his Pro Bowl pass rusher, Seymour, as the lead blocker on New England's first fourth-quarter touchdown. He used his linebacker Vrabel as the receiver on New England's second fourth-quarter touchdown. He had to finish the game with two backup safeties, Shawn Mayer and Chris Akins, in place of the injured Harrison and Wilson, and with a long snapper who had forgotten how to snap the ball.

More than anything in 2003, Belichick had to win back his players after cutting one of their most respected teammates, Lawyer Milloy.

"This will be an unforgettable season for me," Belichick said.

He had another one coming right behind it.

◄ At Annapolis High, "Bill knew what he was doing better than anybody else."

Annapolis Senior High School. The Wake, 1970. Annapolis: Graduating Class of 1970. Print. Archives, Annapolis High School Library.

▲ One Phillips coach said he couldn't remember Belichick, No. 50, ever missing an assignment.
Trustees of Phillips Academy, Andover, Massachusetts

▲ At Wesleyan, Belichick wore a Prince Valiant haircut and made his greatest impact on the lacrosse field.
Wesleyan University Library

➤ A dangerous drill and a serious leg injury ruined Belichick's college football experience.
Wesleyan University Library

◄ Big Bill Parcells was always looking over Little Bill Belichick's shoulder while winning two Super Bowls with the Giants.
Arthur Anderson / Getty Images

➤ The odd couple in Cleveland, Art Modell and Bill Belichick. It was doomed to fail.
Bettmann / Getty Images

▲ Belichick paid the price for isolating himself in Cleveland and having no allies in the end.
Mitchell Layton / Getty Images

▲ Little Bill no longer wanted to work for Big Bill, so he put on quite a show when he quit on the Jets.
Al Pereira / Getty Images

▲ Robert Kraft was a natural-born risk taker. His big gamble on Belichick paid off.
Darren McCollester / Getty Images

➤ Bill and Steve Belichick get Gatoraded after the third Super Bowl victory, nine months before Steve's death.
AP Photo / David J. Phillip

➤ Walking the red carpet, the lord of the rings.
KMazur / WireImage / Getty Images

⌃ Belichick and Brady always had a purely transactional relationship . . . the best one in the league.
Elsa / Getty Images

◀ Roger Goodell was angry that Belichick didn't express enough public contrition for Spygate.
Jim Davis / the Boston Globe via Getty Images

▲ Walking out on Super Bowl XLII, his most devastating defeat, while there was still time on the clock.   *Harry How / Getty Images*

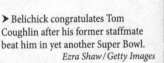

▲ After Spygate, Eric Mangini remained dead to his former boss forevermore.
Matt Sullivan / Getty Images

➤ Belichick congratulates Tom Coughlin after his former staffmate beat him in yet another Super Bowl.
Ezra Shaw / Getty Images

▲ "How in the world does Bon Jovi hang out with a
guy like Bill?"
Patrick Smith / Getty Images

▲ The chief of staff, Berj Najarian,
never leaves Belichick's side.
Maddie Meyer / Getty Images

▲ No. 44, Barack Obama, honors No. 4 for Belichick and the Patriots.
Mark Wilson / Getty Images

▲ The Andover assassins, Belichick and Adams, always hunting for an edge.
Barry Chin / the Boston Globe
via Getty Images

▲ "So it sure has been a pleasure," Peyton Manning told Belichick after their last competitive rodeo.
Doug Pensinger / Getty Images

◄ Those in the know thought Linda Holliday lightened up her longtime boyfriend . . . as much as one could.
Ethan Miller / Getty Images

➤ Belichick and Brady. The greatest of the great.
Christian Petersen / Getty Images

◄ In triumphant and turbulent times, Belichick and Kraft had to defend their long friendship with President Trump.

Chip Somodevilla / Getty Images

▲ No coach had ever won five Super Bowls, and yet Belichick burned for No. 6.

Wendy Maeda / the Boston Globe *via Getty Images*

► Belichick wearing his father's fedora. A cold arrival in Minnesota for Super Bowl LII, and a chilly offseason to come. *Elsa / Getty Images*

13

DYNASTY

Scott Pioli had been named Executive of the Year by the Pro Football Writers of America in 2003, meaning he'd come a long way from his days as a college kid shadowing Bill Belichick at Giants camp and crashing overnight in his room. Robert Kraft had been apprehensive about hiring Bill Parcells's son-in-law, or any relative or friend of Parcells's, for that matter, but Pioli had turned out to be a major acquisition.

He had started studying the game as an undersize but barrel-chested defensive lineman at Central Connecticut State, where he watched 16-millimeter film of opponents on the white bedsheet he taped to his apartment wall. Pioli had been a high school class clown in Washingtonville, New York, a small village 60 miles north of Manhattan that was home to big-city firefighters and cops, and then a party boy at Central. His position coach, Frank Leonard, loved his football intelligence and toughness and was the one most responsible for straightening him out in college. "They were about ready to run his ass out of there," Leonard said. "He could have fun, you know what I mean, like a lot of young people. Sometimes maybe he didn't know where to draw the line. I helped him a little on where to draw the line."

If nothing else, Pioli was always deadly serious about football. He became a graduate assistant at Syracuse, working with offensive coordinator and line coach George DeLeone, and later an ace recruiter at Murray State. Over time, Pioli prodded the San Francisco 49ers into granting him an interview for a personnel opening, before Belichick called to say he had a job for him in Cleveland. The 49ers offered Pioli a $25,000 wage, and Belichick offered $16,000 and undefined job responsibilities. To the average applicant, this would've been a no-brainer. To Pioli—hey, nobody in the 49er organization had ever offered him a pullout sofa to sleep on.

Pioli started out as a gofer in Cleveland and gradually developed into a negotiator and personnel expert. They formed a hell of a team over the years, Belichick the Bon Jovi fan and Pioli the Springsteen fan. Pioli had no regrets about choosing a job with his mentor in New England rather than with his father-in-law, Parcells, in New York. "Scotty is a very loyal guy," Leonard said. "I think it was a tough decision for him. I know it was tough for him."

It was the right call, and the Patriots already had two Super Bowl trophies to prove it. Belichick and Pioli had assembled a cast of athletes who eagerly embraced a program defined by self-sacrifice. When Pioli became Belichick's chief personnel officer, they built their system of evaluation around the pursuit of intelligent, high-character players who prioritized football above everything other than their families and their God.

Belichick and Pioli knew that everyone in the NFL had talent, so they needed to use other measuring sticks to separate the Patriots from the non-Patriots. "The big thing I'd say we look for, which would try to differentiate the players for us, are players with passion — guys that really love football," Belichick would say years later. "As we all know from our jobs, if you love what you're doing, you don't feel like you're working. If you don't like what you're doing, then every step of the way is just painful torture. We don't want people who are in football because of the lifestyle it brings or the opportunities [or rewards] from it. We want people who are in our business because they love doing it."

Belichick and Pioli wanted people who loved practice, too, not just the games. Unlike professional baseball, basketball, and hockey, professional football is played only once a week. NFL players practice five days (usually with Tuesdays off) for every game on the schedule. The players who want to improve over those five days will naturally approach things differently than those who merely endure practice. "As it relates to people," Belichick would say, "it's trying to bring people into the organization that share a similar philosophical outlook to the game, and have a passion for the game, that we in the organization have. That's really where it starts."

The Patriots wanted players who didn't point the finger of blame at teammates and coaches. In this context, among many others, New England struck gold with Tom Brady, a franchise quarterback who loved practice, loved his job, and hated lazy-minded excuse making. Brady burned to be great, and he understood how important it was for him to act as the most accountable Patriot. He also understood the value of empowering every man on the roster.

Scott Farley, an undrafted free agent from Division III Williams, assumed that the superstar quarterback had no idea who he was, and had no good reason to care. One day, Farley was walking near the cafeteria when Brady passed him, said hello, and addressed him by name. Farley was startled and suddenly inspired. "A moment like that can go a long way for a guy like me," Farley said. "I'm like a nobody, and I felt wanted, respected, and that I meant as much as anyone else there."

When a team's most important player is invested in the entire roster and is also its most dedicated player in the film room, good things happen. Brady had thrown a critical block for a receiver, Bethel Johnson, on a third-and-13 catch in the playoff victory over Tennessee as Johnson cut across the field for a 14-yard gain on what would be a touchdown drive — a risk-your-body choice that meant more to Johnson than the 41-yard touchdown pass Brady had thrown him on the first possession.

Jerod Cherry, a special teamer, used to carpool with Brady, and he often bore witness to the young quarterback's prodigious work ethic. In the wee hours of the morning, after a one-point Monday night loss at Miami near the end of the 2004 season, Cherry was getting treatment at the team facility when he saw only one other player still in the building. It was Brady, carrying a stack of films and trying to get better despite a résumé that included two Super Bowl rings and a combined 38-12 record as a starter in the regular season and postseason.

Brady used to ask one of his backups, Jim Miller, to watch his feet on his dropbacks during practice and to challenge him if his technique was flawed in any way. Rohan Davey, another backup quarterback, studied Brady closely and thought his primary source of motivation was written all over him. "You hear about guys that have that chip," Davey said. "Tom had won two Super Bowls and he still had a chip . . . He really felt disrespected, like 'I can't believe you guys passed me over in the draft for all these other guys.'" All real and imagined slights were fuel for Brady's fire. One late night in 2002, around 2:30 a.m., Brady called the rookie backup he sometimes referred to as "Shaq" because of his size (245 pounds) and college affiliation (LSU).

"Shaq, what are you doing?" Brady asked.

"Shit, I'm sleeping," Davey answered.

"Nah, nah, get on the film and turn on play 26 and tell me what that defense is. I've been looking at it for 30 minutes and I can't figure it out."

Brady was always a force of encouragement for the lesser lights around him, a valuable tool for a coach such as Belichick who treated special teamers as if they were starters. Davey felt he was held accountable for the game plan, as a rookie, "the same as if I were Tom, probably even more." Belichick was big on percentages when it came to opponents' tendencies, Davey said, asking players questions like "On third down and two, what percentage of the time do they blitz?" Or "If we come out in a three-receiver set, what percentage of the time do we expect them to line up in this defense?"

Davey had played for Nick Saban at LSU, and he thought Saban and Belichick were similar in that they both "had a disdain for stupidity." As he had in Cleveland, Saban showed his displeasure immediately on the practice field, while Belichick was more likely to wait and make his harsh corrections in the film room. "He never made you feel comfortable," Davey said. At the same time, Belichick never let any team member feel like he was an irrelevant part of the big-picture goal.

"Bill made everyone, whether you played five plays or a hundred plays, feel like their contribution mattered," Cherry said. "He gets everyone to understand that if you're a practice squad guy or the starting quarterback, your input contributes to the winning. And when you feel empowered like that, you want to give your all."

Belichick, from Wesleyan, would make Farley, from Williams, feel even more at home with some good-natured NESCAC sparring during practice. The Patriots were working on a Cover 2 scheme one day when Farley jumped a dig route while another receiver ran free behind him on a post pattern. Standing behind the defense to get a deep safety's view of the play, Belichick barked, "Farley, you're not playing the Tufts Jumbos anymore." Accountability, for New England, was a one-size-fits-all proposition.

Over the years, Belichick had proven he would go anywhere and talk to anyone who could lead him to the team-centric players he craved. While he was still in Cleveland, Belichick visited with Jerry West, the great Los Angeles Lakers executive and former player. West said Belichick asked him about managing a salary cap, and about the Lakers' draft philosophy and how that might apply to what a football coach was searching for in the college game. "He is really, really sharp," West said. "The questions he would ask, some I had no answer for."

Belichick visited Saban at LSU. He developed a friendship with Jimmy Johnson, who coached the Miami Hurricanes, the Cowboys, and the Dolphins, after the two met at the Kentucky Derby while Bill was in Cleveland and Jimmy in Dallas. Over the years, Belichick would visit Johnson at his home in the Florida Keys to fish, drink beer, and, of course, talk shop. Johnson had won two Super Bowls with the Cowboys and a national title with the Hurricanes, and he had valuable insight to offer on draft picks and personnel moves. Belichick wasn't only the best coach in the NFL; he was the best listener and brain-picker, too.

"He knew more about my draft than I did," Johnson said.

Belichick would later visit with New York Yankees GM Brian Cashman and manager Joe Torre to find out everything he could about how they prepared their players during the dynasty years. Cashman wanted to pick Belichick's brain, too, but the football coach asked so many questions about their baseball approach that it remained a one-way conversation — just the way Belichick always preferred it.

The Patriots' coach funneled all of his acquired information into a singular vision for how to shape his team. Jason Licht, the New England scout and personnel man who left for the Philadelphia Eagles in 2003, said Belichick made it clear to his evaluators that they weren't to define themselves as mere talent collectors. He wanted his scouts to determine how coachable prospects were, and whether their intelligence matched their passion. "Our goal was not to get the most talented 53," Licht said. "It was to get the right 53. I learned from him that 90 percent of the reason a high draft pick or prized free agent doesn't work out is because of what's above the neck."

Hired by the previous regime, Licht recalled his first staff meeting with Belichick as something of an intimidating experience. He decided that if he was going to go down in front of the new boss, he would go down swinging. Licht decided to be fearless in expressing strong opinions on prospects, even if those opinions ran counter to the reports of older scouts in the room. When that happened, Licht said, "you could see that Bill's ears perked up, and he was looking you up and down like he was taking note that this guy put time into it and is giving me a pure evaluation."

Belichick treated his scouts the same way he treated his players and assistants. Every man mattered. Every member contributed to the team's winning and losing.

"When you scouted for Bill Belichick," Licht said, "you had to be at your best when you were giving your opinions on players. We're talking draft meetings now, and here's the head coach knee-deep in the season, and usually it's 'I'm not going to have to really give a lot of evidence on why I like a certain player. He's going to have to take my word.' But it's not the case with him. There were times in October when I'd come off the road and he'd run into you in the hall and ask about a defensive tackle at Alabama or North Carolina. He'd say, 'Man, I really like this guy. He's a high pick and can start right away.' And then he'd say something like 'Did you happen to see him against Appalachian State? What the hell happened to him there?' And you're like 'What? When did he have time to watch that?'

"But he did," Licht continued, "so you had to know everything about that player . . . On a Tuesday night when you're typing out a report at midnight after going to Auburn, you can't throw just anything down. He will read every single word that you write."

Licht said Belichick wanted size at the obvious line positions, but that he also wanted skill-position players who were willing blockers and who had a physical stature about them. "He wanted guys that played big," Licht said, "and size comes across in different ways. It doesn't necessarily mean height . . . but a guy who could take a lot of shots and had a thickness to him."

Kevin Faulk, running back and return man, was a perfect example of this kind of player. Even though he was drafted out of Louisiana State by Bobby Grier and Pete Carroll, the 5′8″, 202-pound Faulk became a Belichick favorite, in part by shedding arm tackles attempted by bigger defenders. Faulk was the kind of resourceful situational player who helped separate the Patriots' program from all others. When Belichick arrived, Faulk asked him what he needed to do to work on his ball-security and blitz-pickup issues. He worked his ass off on his weaknesses, turned them into strengths, and became a reliable third-down option.

"When the game was on the line," Belichick said, "he was always in the game and he was always in the eye of the storm, and that really speaks more to me to the value of the player than whose name is in there on the starting lineup on the first play of the game."

Faulk was a productive receiver out of the backfield, but he scored only two points for the 2003 Patriots. Those two were scored in the final minutes of the Super Bowl.

Belichick coveted more and more players like Faulk, who accepted a far different role in the NFL than he had in college. "Instead of embracing the role that your team wants you to have and needs you to have," Belichick said, "some players want a role that they want to have and then sometimes that's a little bit of a conflict." The Patriots didn't want conflict makers, but conflict avoiders. They wanted leaders, too, intangible players such as Faulk who set examples in preparation and dependability even for teammates who received more playing time at his position.

"Toughness, intelligence, work ethic . . . you don't get that out of a vertical jump," Belichick said.

Fundamentals were everything to Belichick, and he was a big believer in practicing situational football. He'd charge his players and assistants to respond to a certain score and time left on the game clock. He'd teach his players to tap the ball into the field of play when the other team fumbled, and to tap it out of bounds when a Patriot coughed it up — simple things that some players said they weren't taught elsewhere.

Patriots needed to be versatile, too. Belichick watched what Bill Parcells did with Jeff Hostetler in the 1980s, when the quarterback was stuck behind Giants starter Phil Simms. Hostetler caught a pass, ran the ball, and blocked a punt before he ever threw a pass in a game, a story Belichick would later share with his team. So he never hesitated to ask offensive players to play defense, and vice versa. Troy Brown was moved to the secondary. Mike Vrabel was moved to tight end. Richard Seymour was moved to fullback.

One day in camp, Belichick approached 5′11″, 275-pound defensive lineman Dan Klecko, son of former New York Jets great Joe Klecko, and told him to get ready to be a fullback, an outside linebacker, and a change-of-pace noseguard. Klecko got some work at middle linebacker, too, and his college coach at Temple, Bobby Wallace, told him he was catching good-natured heat from people wondering why Belichick was getting so much more out of his guy.

Belichick could even make an offensive lineman out of an NCAA heavyweight wrestling champ with no college football experience. Out of Cal State–Bakersfield, Stephen Neal said he'd been "sitting on my couch with my dog" before he persuaded the Patriots to give him a tryout. He asked New England's equipment guys for the kind of hip pads he was required to wear in high school — the equipment guys had to tell him that the Patriots didn't wear hip pads — and he needed to ask other linemen where to line up in the huddle and what to do on every play. Belichick waived him, re-signed him, and ultimately started him at right guard. People were only surprised that Belichick didn't turn Neal into a slot receiver.

More proof that, as much as anything, the Patriots were viewed by design as interchangeable parts. "A guy who comes in and wants his name on a scoreboard that says 'Joe Blow, No. 28' is probably not going to be a New England Patriot," Belichick said. "A guy who wants to play for a team and not worry about being a star is likely to be one."

Even though Belichick would become more of a delegator than he was in his Cleveland days, he could still walk into any position room and take it over on the spot. It was rare for head coaches with defensive backgrounds to run quarterback meetings, but Belichick could easily do it while still managing the frequent interruptions from secretaries and staffers ("What type of meal do you want for the team flight to Oakland?" . . . "This player just became available; you have any interest in him?"). Belichick would also meet with his quarterbacks every Saturday in his office, where they'd sit on his couch. "Sometimes we'd talk in depth about game plans," said Jim Miller, "other times about politics, a movie, or what's going on in life. He really cares about his players."

He really cared about putting them in an optimum position to win.

"Most head coaches who are defensive guys couldn't call one offensive play in the playbook," Miller said. "Bill could call an entire game."

So, yes, he expected his Patriots to have more than a working knowledge of positions they didn't play, and of opponents who appeared buried on the depth chart. "I remember we were playing a preseason game and he'd come in and ask you a question about their roster, like 'Who is the backup nickel?' — in a preseason game," said Kliff Kingsbury, a quarterback drafted in 2003 before landing on injured reserve. "Some cat who is not going to make the team, and he's asking you where he's from, what university he played at, what technique is his favorite technique, and he expected you to know it. He wanted you to be on edge and know that type of stuff. And if you give the wrong answer, he gives you that look and shakes his head."

Belichick didn't wait to set this tone until after Thanksgiving, when teams started making an urgent postseason push. "Every day he says it's a big day," Brady would recall. "He says it in May. He says it in July. He says it in December. We joke about it a lot. He never comes in and says, 'Eh, you know, this day doesn't really mean that much.'"

The head coach thought it was vital that New England's message to the players was consistent. He'd talked to players from other organizations who complained about the coordinator wanting one thing and the head coach wanting another. Or about a conflict between the front office and the coaching staff over how the player should approach the game. Belichick wanted incoming Patriots to know that they didn't have to worry about any such conflict. "Whatever message I'm giving you," he told them, "that's the way it's going to be."

He sent the ultimate message by way of his own commitment to the job: Belichick logged more hours in the building than anyone. He usually started before 6 a.m. on Mondays, with the responsibilities that day of reviewing game film, meeting with staff, talking about the players' game-day grades, meeting with the players, sending them onto the field for a light workout, and meeting with staff about the next opponent, before leaving around midnight. He would return before dawn on Tuesday to start all over again on the game plan, with no letup in sight until Friday. The Patriots were week-to-week chameleons with their schemes, which only made more work for Belichick. "His preparation is second to none," Brady would say. "Sometimes we come in on Wednesday morning to get the game plan and it doesn't even look like our playbook." So the coach had credibility when demanding maximum effort. His 2001 team was 3-4 when he handed the players a sheet that, among other things, explained how a 99.9 percent effort by the United States Post Office and the airline industry would result in 400,000 lost letters and 18 plane crashes every day.

When Belichick saw 99.9 percent effort in practice, he'd shout, "Take off," and nobody needed a translation. "You never wanted to hear those two words from him," Colvin said. "That means you'd better start running laps."

As a coach who never subscribed to the notion that on-field berating was a mandatory part of his job, Belichick made the vast majority of his player corrections with a penetrating look in team meetings, or with his biting critiques in the film room. No Patriot ever wanted to be the leading man in one of his Monday morning movies. New England could win by three touchdowns and Belichick would still hunt down the two or three plays that, under different circumstances, could've cost the Patriots the game, or their season.

If he saw a breakdown on third-and-short or fourth-and-short, Belichick would often say things like "You mean to tell me you can't get us an inch here? This doesn't mean enough to you to get an inch for us in this situation?" Or his classic response to mistakes exposed by the film: "That's not what we're looking for."

Though Belichick did embrace feedback from Brady on game-plan adjustments, on plays the coach incorporated during the week that Brady didn't think would work on Sunday, the quarterback never received favored-nation status in these film sessions. Dan Klecko, undersize noseguard and oversize fullback, said that Belichick wasn't afraid to treat his franchise player "like he's Dan Klecko." Brady once assumed the starring role in a weekly showing of film lowlights after committing the not-so-venial sin of throwing a pass into triple coverage that was picked off.

"And the next day Belichick says, 'There you go, Brady, throwing it into a fucking team meeting,'" Klecko said. "You're sitting there, you just got your ass kicked, and you're trying not to laugh . . . but you're like *Did he really just say that to Tom Brady?*"

He'd say it to anyone, any week, any season. Belichick would try all sorts of things to inspire his players and to break up the grind and drudgery of camp and a long, painful season. He'd show them classic boxing matches or introduce them to Bill Russell or tell them stories about watching Jim Brown and coaching LT. He had rookies get up and sing in front of the whole team and do a three-man barrel roll over one another on the practice field while giddy veterans poured water on them to create a mud pit. Contrary to popular perception, Belichick even kept his schemes as simple as possible. "He let the players play," said safety Shawn Mayer. "Everything was a very easy game plan to execute. If we had any issue with anything, we just checked to Cover 2 or Tampa 2 and just played football."

But the details mattered to Belichick more than anything. Bethel Johnson had been a running back until his senior year of high school, and he said Belichick was the first coach to teach him how to run proper routes. He was having trouble mastering the comeback route — the Patriots thought it took him too long to get out of the route — before Belichick told his speedy receiver that he was running too fast into his break. "You don't run a 4.2 on the route," he told Johnson. "You come out of it running a 4.2." Belichick persuaded him to slow down and control himself on the first half of the pattern, then explode once he planted his foot and broke to the sideline.

The good news? This kind of precise coaching showed up in the box score. The bad news? It also showed up in the film room.

Cherry recalled walking into a Monday morning showing of lowlights, after a New England loss, without any reason to believe he'd be singled out for the result. "The last person on earth I imagined it would be was me," Cherry said. He was a special teams player, after all, and his minor error wouldn't have made any other coach's top ten reasons why this particular Sunday went south.

Then again, there was a reason Cherry called playing for Belichick "the hardest thing you'll ever do, but the best thing you'll ever do." No coach had ever cared more about special teams than the former prep school center who stayed after practice to work on long snaps in the rain. "He shows a lowlight of me not properly downing the football at the one-yard line," Cherry said, "and he says the following: 'This play right here sums it all up. This play.' Me screwing up. I say to myself, *How in the world is my one play the culmination of the entire game being lost?* It was improper technique. My feet were on the goal line."

Meetings revolving around that weekend's opponent were only slightly more fun. Belichick would fire questions at the rows of Patriots before him to find out who had done their homework and who had not. Occasionally he'd slip in a question that was tantamount to a prank, like the time he asked a rookie what state Kansas City was in. (The kid responded, "Kansas," of course, and Belichick shot him a you've-got-to-be-kidding-me look.) Sometimes a smart-ass player who knew an answer might do some show-boating by adding extra and unnecessary information to his answer, drawing a half smile out of the coach.

Belichick wanted players who were energized by the challenge of finding the puzzle pieces and putting them together. He'd give them written tests, and the players who aced them were valued Patriots. Belichick didn't care if they'd fail with every other organization in the sport.

When studying college talent, the Patriots were forever hunting for players who looked and acted like Patriots. A dynasty in a different sport, the New York Yankees, had a similar philosophy. The scout who signed a teenage Derek Jeter, Dick Groch, used these words to open the summation in his official report: "A Yankee!" As much as Jeter looked like a Yankee before he signed with Michigan (he abandoned a full scholarship for George Steinbrenner's money), Tom Brady looked like a Patriot while playing at Michigan. New England saw in the quarterback an accurate passer, a leader, a winner (with a 20-5 record as a starter), and someone who managed the Drew Henson circus with the poise and maturity of a pro.

New England was among a small handful of franchises that didn't subscribe to the two major scouting services, Blesto and National, which pool information on thousands of college players. Belichick was not in the business of sharing information; he was in the business of gathering it. Over all other standards, he wanted college prospects measured against Patriots on the current roster. If a certain college safety was better than, or equal to, the safeties in New England's secondary, Belichick was interested.

He had learned some hard lessons from his Cleveland days when it came to the draft. Belichick had taken too many gambles on athletic players who looked the part but who weren't overly productive for their college teams, and he wasn't prepared when the Jets took the player he wanted in 1995, Penn State's Kyle Brady, one pick ahead of him, at No. 9. Thomas Dimitroff, the ambitious former grounds-crew worker in Cleveland, had been brought in as New England's director of college scouting and was considered a rising star. But Pioli was the front-office voice Belichick listened to above all, and just about every NFL owner envious of the Patriots' stunning success had an eye on him. Belichick didn't want to lose him in the worst way. In New England, they almost never disagreed on a player they drafted or a free agent they signed.

"It's not a matter of him caving in to me or me caving to him," Pioli said. "It's what we know. It's not about me proving myself right and Bill wrong. It's about coming to the right decision."

And the results began to show; Belichick's drafts in Foxborough were far better than they'd been in Cleveland. Richard Seymour and Matt Light, their top two picks in 2001, became invaluable members of the defensive and offensive lines. The three receivers taken in 2002—Daniel Graham (first-round tight end), Deion Branch (second-round wideout), and David Givens (seventh-round wideout)—all became starting postseason targets for Brady. The 2003 class included finds such as fourth-round corner Asante Samuel and fifth-round center Dan Koppen. The 2004 class was headlined by nose tackle Vince Wilfork, the 21st overall pick, who would develop into a five-time Pro Bowler.

Pioli and his scouts studied thousands of college players, eliminating the vast majority of them before things turned serious at the pre-draft combine in Indianapolis, an unseemly meat market where the job applicants are poked and prodded and tested and almost literally stripped to their core. New England put the prospects it deemed worthy on a front board in its draft room, with the rest relegated to a back board.

The Patriots found enough true Patriots at the combine, in the draft, and in free agency to win 21 consecutive games over the 2003 and 2004 seasons, steamrolling the record of 18, set by five teams. Seymour and Rodney Harrison dumped a bucket of water on their coach after they won their historic 19th straight, a 24–10 victory over Miami, and, having downplayed the milestone's significance before the game, the Patriots finally conceded that they did care about the record.

"I did tell the team that I was proud of what they did," Belichick said, "and that they could be proud of what they accomplished, and that no other team in pro football has done that."

The Patriots extended their streak to 21 before finally losing at Pittsburgh in their seventh game. They won seven of their final eight, including a blowout in Cleveland just days after the firing of yet another Browns coach, Butch Davis. Belichick hadn't coached a game in Cleveland since his first Patriots team lost there in 2000, when Browns fans taunted their former coach with "Belichick sucks" chants. He returned the favor with a vicious 27-point beatdown that included late blitzing of a rookie quarterback, Luke McCown; the sight of Tom Brady throwing a deep touchdown pass while holding a 35–7 lead; and the sight of Belichick reinserting running back Corey Dillon into the blowout so he could pick up the two yards he needed for a 100-yard game. Belichick swore that payback wasn't at hand, but people close to the coach knew better.

The Patriots finished 14-2 on the strength of a brilliant defense, an opportunistic Brady, and a running game greatly enhanced by the newcomer Dillon, a three-time Pro Bowler in Cincinnati who rushed for 1,635 yards and a dozen touchdowns and elevated the Patriots from 27th in rushing yardage, in 2003, to seventh. Dillon actually represented the kind of character-issue players New England preferred to avoid — he'd been in trouble with the law throughout his youth, had been arrested on domestic assault and DUI charges, and had once thrown his helmet, shoulder pads, and cleats into the stands in Cincinnati in the hope of securing a trade. When Belichick would pepper his team with questions about where this player or that coordinator attended college, or what looks a certain rival might give near the goal line, Dillon was out of his league.

"When he was asked questions," Roosevelt Colvin said, "he was just guessing at the answers. Everyone knew Corey didn't know the answer."

Game day was a different story. Belichick gambled that the Patriots' culture could make a responsible person and player out of Dillon, at least in the short run, and the running back responded with the best season of his career.

The Patriots had everything they needed to win a third Super Bowl in four years. They had the coach, the quarterback, the front office, the defense, and the running game to make them a dynasty in a salary-cap era designed to dismantle dynasties before they were fully formed. They also had a secret weapon, a franchise player who was a mystery even to the vast majority of people inside the franchise.

Out of Andover, Ernie Adams wrote a letter to the football coach at Northwestern, Alex Agase, an All-American college and pro player who had seen action as a Marine on Iwo Jima and Okinawa and had earned a Purple Heart. Adams asked if there might be an opening on the Wildcats' staff, and Agase did what most major-college coaches never would: He answered the letter.

Agase told Adams he could serve as team manager, with a shot at more prominent assignments if he proved worthy of the challenge. And once he was on campus, in the fall of 1971, the curly-haired kid with thick glasses and a thicker New England accent proved more than worthy. Adams had spent most of his practice time with the team chasing footballs and setting up tackling dummies and cones. A Northwestern assistant, Jay Robertson, who had served as an infantry officer in Vietnam and as Wildcats captain under Ara Parseghian, often noticed Adams moving unusually close to the live drills to carefully observe the coaching that was being done.

One day, Agase summoned Robertson to his office and handed him a thesis in a cardboard binder that was titled "Treatise on the Dropback Pass." Robertson read it without knowing the identity of the author and decided, "Goddammit, this is deep stuff." Big Ten schools weren't proficient in the dropback pass at the time, and Agase had little interest in turning his program into an aerial show. Yet he wanted Robertson to know that the new team manager was responsible for the advanced breakdown on the passing game he'd just absorbed.

"I was amazed," Robertson said.

Agase asked Robertson to evaluate Adams over the winter and find out if he could help the Northwestern staff. Robertson took the kid into the downstairs meeting room known as "the Dungeon," a onetime ticket office in the old stadium that had tables, chairs, film projectors, a fridge, a toilet, and not much else. Coaches went down there to study their team and the opposition in peace. "I gave Ernie the keys to the Dungeon," Robertson said, "which was probably the happiest day of his life at Northwestern."

Adams showed up at the football offices carrying a black briefcase nearly every day after classes and lunch, and then he'd disappear into the Dungeon. He immediately learned the coaches' terminology and broke down films of Big Ten opponents. Robertson and a Northwestern colleague, Bill Dudley, took Adams to the Notre Dame spring game to see if he could scout Parseghian's Fighting Irish live. They sat in two dusty photographers' boxes above the press box, Ernie in one booth and the coaches in the other. When they compared notes at halftime, Robertson and Dudley had added to their diagrams a phantom play—one the Irish hadn't run in their intrasquad spring game—just to see if Adams was paying attention. The coaches showed Ernie the bogus card and pressed him on why his diagram of that sequence didn't match up with theirs.

"And he said, 'No, I remember this play. The referee fell down,'" Robertson recalled. "We'd just drawn a fake play, and Ernie had such vivid recall and documented the extra tidbit that the referee fell down, which he did, we knew we didn't have a chance. Dudley and I looked at each other and folded our cards and said, 'Ernie, the rest of the game is yours. And we're going to get hot dogs.'"

Parseghian was known for throwing all kinds of formations and plays at scouts working his spring game, in an attempt to overwhelm them, but Adams didn't blink. The kid was so good, in fact, that Agase reassigned Robertson and made Dudley and Adams his scouts. Ernie wasn't old enough to rent a car, and Robertson had to teach him how to make hotel reservations and fill out expense reports. Some Northwestern coaches resisted the presence of this bookish wonderboy, who did most of his work on defense. Pat Naughton, a defensive coordinator who could give out an ass-chewing with the best of them, blitzed Adams when he suggested he had some intel on Illinois coach Bob Blackman from his days at Dartmouth. Over time, Naughton came to realize that young Ernie could answer questions that older staffers couldn't. "And Ernie's play that he talked about Blackman running at Dartmouth?" Robertson said. "Illinois ran it, and that exonerated Ernie."

Adams was in charge of the scout team, and when Naughton asked him to run an upcoming opponent's third-and-five play, Ernie consulted the cards he'd written up and ran the precise play. Ernie was also responsible for the scout team's motivation and huddle discipline, never an easy task for a college underclassman in charge of older schoolmates who were bitter over their lack of playing time. "Ernie somehow mastered that job and never had a rebellion," Robertson said. "I think those kids knew they had something special."

Those kids took to the student dressed in his gray T-shirt and purple shorts, the student who busied himself sniffling and wrinkling his nose and pushing up his glasses while excitedly reading from his play cards. Adams could coach talent and scout talent, but the Northwestern coaches wanted to see if he could recruit talent. Robertson took him on a trip to a Chicago-area high school, where the coach ushered his college visitors into a back room, lit a cigarette, and summoned into the room a young player who seemed too small for the rigors of Big Ten football. The coach had his player take off his shirt and flex his muscles, and Robertson, a bit embarrassed, wrapped up the visit with an empty pledge that they'd keep an eye on the player.

On the drive back to the Northwestern campus, after a couple more recruiting stops, Robertson looked over at his passenger. Adams was lost in thought behind a bleak expression. Robertson could tell that the episode of the high school player removing his shirt had disgusted Adams, whose initial goal was to either coach under Steve Sorota at his alma mater, Andover, or to become a college assistant. Adams had just realized he didn't have the personality or the desire to recruit.

"Ernie," Robertson said to him in the car, "it looks like the NFL or nothing, doesn't it?

"You're so right," Adams responded.

Agase was replaced at Northwestern by former Indiana coach John Pont, and Ernie then won over Pont and his Indiana staff faster than he'd won over Agase and his. Upon graduation, in 1975, Adams persuaded New England Patriots coach Chuck Fairbanks to give him an unpaid job after he learned two Patriots playbooks in four days. Ernie had a photographic memory and an ability to write up scouting reports more thoroughly than any Fairbanks had seen in his 20 years of coaching. He was ahead of the curve in splicing together film clips for more efficient study of, say, an opponent's goal-line defense. "We were the only ones doing it," Ernie said. A former Fairbanks assistant, Ray Perkins, hired him as an offensive assistant and quarterbacks coach immediately after getting the Giants job in 1979, and Ernie, in turn, recommended that Perkins bring on his old Andover friend Bill Belichick.

Adams didn't exactly impress NFL quarterbacks with his own throwing arm in practice. "But there wasn't anything that got by Ernie," said Randy Dean, one of his quarterbacks with the Giants and at Northwestern. "He was a great resource coverage-wise or on technique or on certain things he'd seen on film."

Though Belichick successfully navigated the transition from Perkins to Bill Parcells and remained with the Giants until he was hired by Cleveland after the 1990 season, Adams somehow lost his way. He was named the Giants' director of pro personnel, at age 29, in May 1982 — when the *New York Times* made it a point to report that he'd "never played college or professional football" — and then let go in favor of Tim Rooney three years later. "He was forced to find another career," Robertson said. Adams was working as a municipal bond trader on Wall Street when Belichick hired him in Cleveland, and as an investment analyst when his Andover classmate hired him in Foxborough. Belichick kept bringing Ernie back from the NFL dead.

Adams's media guide bio said his responsibilities included "researching special assignments for both the coaching staff and the personnel department," but Ernie was involved in far more than that. Adams attended every Patriots practice and game, and from the coaches' box he communicated directly to Belichick, headset to headset. He could tell Belichick what he was seeing on the field, or whether to challenge a questionable call on replay. He was active in draft preparation and had a draft-day seat in a decision-makers' room that had fewer bodies in it (in order to maintain a streamlined focus) than most around the league.

Adams had nearly instant recall on teams, players, and game situations from the past. He studied film and statistics and assumed a prominent role in personnel decisions, game planning, and halftime adjustments. He was a big contributor to the successful plan of attack against Marshall Faulk in the Super Bowl XXXVI victory over St. Louis. In the Super Bowl XXXVIII victory over Carolina, Adams advised Belichick to accept a defensive penalty on second-and-goal at the Panthers' 4 rather than risk a challenge on a potential Brady touchdown pass to Christian Fauria that was ruled out of bounds. The Patriots scored on an Antowain Smith carry on the next play.

"I stick my finger in as many pies as possible," Adams told the *New York Times* in a rare interview. "It's important that I don't have everyone in the organization thinking I'm in their way. If I come to a conclusion on something, I go to Bill and give it to him . . . My responsibility is to do whatever I can think of to help us win. Part of it I make up as I go along. Bill and I work together. If I think I can help us win, my job is to do it.

"The reason we're successful here is everyone is on the same page. We sing from the same hymn, the same notes. No one deviates."

Above everything else, Adams was a devoted son. He lived with his mother, Helen, until her death, in September 2004. "And when his mom was dying of cancer," Robertson said, "he stopped by her hospital room every morning at some ungodly hour to pay his respects, and then did so on the way home. He was unbelievable. He's really a remarkable guy."

Adams sometimes worked more than 100 hours a week. He was everywhere, and yet his goal was to be seen and heard by as few people as possible. Tom Brady said that very few Patriots knew anything about him. Scott Farley, training-camp safety, said that Adams was the only person at the team facility he was never introduced to.

"He was a man of mystery, certainly," Farley said. "He was always within earshot of Coach Belichick, but you wouldn't know the difference between him and one of the first-year trainers. If you haven't been a part of the organization, you would think he's a guy just kind of walking around and taking everything in. I'm sure there's a lot that goes on behind those glasses of his that is a part of the success . . . It was like *Where's Waldo?* He's there, but he's not there."

It was becoming more and more clear that Belichick and Adams were pro football's answer to Noam Chomsky and Stephen Hawking. In what might be the best two-word description of a living human on record, author David Halberstam called Adams "Belichick's Belichick." Though he projected the vibe of a nutty professor dressed in khakis and a windbreaker, Adams was known to friends as being every bit as competitive as his former Andover classmate. "Ernie's a guy that I have the confidence to bounce pretty much anything off of," Belichick said. "I think he's got a great football mind and he's been a very valuable resource for our organization and for me personally."

Back in the bad old days in Cleveland, Adams wasn't met with such universal praise. One of the Browns tight ends he worked with, Scott Galbraith, called him, among other things, "a joke." But, like Belichick, Adams was fielding the kinds of endorsements in New England that were making any Cleveland criticisms moot.

"He knows more about professional football than anyone I have ever met," Brady said.

Yet Adams was never made available to the general news media, even during pre–Super Bowl sessions that included mandatory access to all participating assistant coaches. Adams wasn't an official coach, and his vague title allowed Belichick to keep him off-limits. Occasionally a New England coach or player would offer up a useful nugget about Adams — on the subject of opponents, Brady said that Ernie once advised him to "make them defend every blade of grass"— but that was about it. In a league that shared among its members everything from revenues to pre-draft scouting reports, Belichick thought the less shared about his Andover classmate, the better.

Adams was never much of a talker anyway. His first boss at Northwestern, Agase, asked Jay Robertson to probe the depths of Ernie's football knowledge, and decades later Robertson felt he hadn't come close to hitting rock bottom. In hindsight, Robertson realized it was odd how things had unfolded at Northwestern. During all his time spent at the Wildcats' football offices, Adams never brought up the fact that he was close to Bill Belichick, son of the longtime Navy assistant Steve. Robertson was among the coaches who had read Steve Belichick's scouting book.

"But Ernie said he had one friend involved in football as much as himself, and that was Evan Bonds," Robertson recalled. Bonds was a fellow Phillips lineman and football nerd who attended Duke and later earned a

Ph.D. in musicology from Harvard and a faculty position at the University of North Carolina. "Ernie talked a lot about Bonds," Robertson said. "But he never discussed Bill Belichick with me."

The Patriots were preparing to play the Philadelphia Eagles in Super Bowl XXXIX, and Bill Belichick was reaching again for a motivational tool that was, in many ways, beneath him. Twisting printed headlines and quotes into something sharper than a butcher's knife was a tactic used by every meathead high school coach in America trying to whip his athletes into a frenzy, and yet Belichick did it as much as anyone in the NFL. He understood that football was the ultimate game of emotion, and that an enraged, disrespected team was more likely to sacrifice body parts in the pursuit of victory.

"Let me just read you a little something here; I thought this was kind of interesting," Belichick said to a hotel ballroom's worth of players sitting in rows of armless conference chairs, most of them dressed in casual shirts and jeans. He'd gotten his hands on information printed in a *Philadelphia Inquirer* story headlined "In Case of a Win, a Major . . . Event; Just Don't Call It a Parade," and reportedly referenced in an email from an Eagles official to the Boston Red Sox delegation that had just celebrated an historic, ghost-busting title. The *Inquirer* article explained that superstitious city officials weren't calling the event planned for Tuesday at 11 a.m. a victory parade. "We're being deferential to the Eagles," managing director Philip R. Goldsmith said. "They've asked us to be cooperative and not talk about it." City officials wouldn't go on the record with details of the planned celebration, but *Inquirer* sources anonymously filled in some blanks. The Eagles were expected to ride the parade route in double-decker buses, and military jets were scheduled to perform a flyover.

Of course, when Belichick shared these details at the team's hotel, he left out some important context. "At first," the coach told his players about the city's plans, "I couldn't believe it. But it's actually true. Talking about the Philadelphia parade after the game. All right, it's 11 o'clock in case any of you want to attend that. It's going to go from Broad Street up to Washington Avenue, past City Hall, then down the Benjamin Franklin Parkway, and it will end up at the art museum."

Never mind that every city — Boston included — plans a potential championship celebration days in advance of a championship game. Belichick knew the sport he was playing, and he knew the room he was working.

"That level of disrespect," receiver Bethel Johnson said of the scheduled parade, "added fuel to our fire."

"It was absolutely a great motivating factor," said offensive lineman Russ

Hochstein. "Bill had a great way of painting us as the underdog whether we were or not, and in that Super Bowl I sure felt like it after that, and I think my teammates did as well. It was 'Hey, we've won two Super Bowls in three years, and here they are planning their parade route.' Bill threw that out there, a lot of guys grabbed on to that, and it was like 'Whoa, maybe people do think we're going to lose.' Bill had an uncanny way of doing that. He'd find a quote or a small snippet in the newspaper and use that to motivate us."

Belichick had dealt from the same motivational deck earlier in the postseason, starting with New England's 20–3 divisional round victory over the quarterback (Peyton Manning) and the AFC rival (Indianapolis Colts) they positively owned. In the leadup to that game, Belichick told his players that the Colts — in anticipation of a victory over New England — had called the Steelers looking for an extra 1,500 tickets to the AFC Championship Game in Pittsburgh. That real or imagined claim likely wasn't necessary after mouthy Colts kicker Mike Vanderjagt, who had criticized Manning and Tony Dungy two years earlier for not showing enough emotion, said he thought the Patriots were "ripe for the picking." The kicker who missed the 48-yard field goal that would've tied the Patriots in the final seconds of the season opener also told WISH-TV, in Indianapolis, that New England was "not as good as the beginning of the year and not as good as last year."

The Patriots were angered by the remarks, and didn't need Belichick to pile on as kickoff approached. But pile on he did, just in case his players weren't angry enough. According to one of the backup quarterbacks, Jim Miller, Belichick played video of Vanderjagt's remarks in a team meeting on the eve of the game. "He held up the Super Bowl ring from the year before," Miller said, "the last world championship . . . He said, 'Guys, you know how hard it is to win.' This is Saturday night in the hotel, and normally you show film reminders and go over things. And Bill got everyone together and showed that video, the Vanderjagt thing, and that was it. We broke and got our snack. That's really all he said."

New England didn't allow a single touchdown to the No. 1 offense in the league, whose two-time MVP quarterback had just set an NFL record with 49 scoring passes. Belichick called Manning "the best quarterback I've coached against." Yet Manning was now 0-7 in Foxborough, while Brady was 7-0 in the postseason. The Patriots rushed for 210 yards (Corey Dillon delivered 144 of them) to Indy's 46, and even though they were missing three defensive starters, in Seymour and cornerbacks Ty Law and Tyrone Poole, and using receiver Troy Brown in the secondary, the Patriots baffled Manning with looks he hadn't previously seen.

The Patriots–Colts narratives were firmly in place. Indianapolis was a finesse team built around small, quick players, while New England countered with power and physicality the Colts couldn't handle. Manning was a stat machine and a dome player missing some intangible needed to win the big one, especially the big one in Foxborough, while Brady was the more industrious leader and winner. Dungy was a nice guy you'd want as a next-door neighbor, while Belichick would sell his firstborn for a first down in a close game.

The Colts had complained about all of New England's grabbing in the secondary in the AFC title game the previous winter, compelling the league, in the off-season, to reestablish its commitment to keeping receivers clean and scores up. So the Patriots mocked them after this latest playoff defeat and dared them to push for some other rule reinforcement. "What are they going to do next?" Brown asked.

The Colts watched New England go into Heinz Field and tear apart the team that had ended its record 21-game winning streak on Halloween night. Brady was run-down with the flu, and the wind chill off the river on this night was minus 1, but his two touchdown passes (including a 60-yarder to Deion Branch) and Rodney Harrison's interception of rookie Ben Roethlisberger and 87-yard interception return for a score shaped a 41–27 victory that snapped Pittsburgh's own 15-game winning streak. Belichick had actually been surprised to see the Steelers advance past the New York Jets in the previous round. On a call to his friend Herm Edwards, the Jets' coach, to solicit inside information on Pittsburgh, Belichick revealed that he'd predicted to his players all week that the Jets would upset the Steelers, who prevailed in overtime. Imagine what Belichick would've done with that information during the week if he were Pittsburgh's coach and a future opponent had said that about his team.

Either way, the New England coach pushed the right buttons before that game. He felt that his players weren't sure they could win in Heinz Field, where the Steelers had them down three touchdowns late on Halloween. So he was more emotional than usual when he gathered them before the game to tell them how confident he was that they would beat Pittsburgh.

"I'm speechless," linebacker Ted Johnson said. "He just has it, whatever it is. He just finds a way. The way he motivates us, the way he can get a team ready mentally and physically. He's so tuned into his players . . . He just says and does the right thing at the right time."

Dressed in a ghastly hooded sweatshirt that was becoming his signature article of clothing, much like Vince Lombardi's camel-hair coat, Belichick was reminded that he was also 9-1 as a head coach in the postseason (including his 1-1 record in Cleveland), matching the postseason record of the Green Bay Packers' legend, widely regarded as the profession's greatest ever.

"It's very flattering to be mentioned in the same breath with Vince Lombardi," Belichick said. "That's why the trophy has his name on it. I don't think I deserve it."

Football fans everywhere would feel differently if he won his third Super Bowl title in four years.

As they began their slow-death march up the field, the Philadelphia Eagles were a slumping, fading advertisement for the greatness of the New England Patriots. They were down ten points with 5:40 left in Super Bowl XXXIX, in Jacksonville, and they did not have the willpower to even act interested in getting the two scores needed to send the game into overtime. They did not bother to deploy the standard no-huddle offense used in these situations. Upon completing their short, uninspired passes, they walked back to the huddle they shouldn't have been forming in the first place with all the urgency of middle-aged brokers playing in a Sunday beer league.

The Eagles would give all sorts of strange non-excuses for why they had descended into a prevent offense at the worst possible time. The most popular one? A gassed Donovan McNabb puked in the huddle and couldn't get his bearings; McNabb said that never happened. On the opposite sideline, backup Patriots quarterback Rohan Davey said he was busy checking the ticking clock. "We were all perplexed," Davey said. "They all looked like they were going slow. All of them looked sluggish and lethargic. It just wasn't Donovan."

Either way, no matter how beneficial this was to the Patriots, Bill Belichick and his staff and players couldn't believe what they were seeing. The Fox broadcast team of Joe Buck, Troy Aikman, and Cris Collinsworth took turns expressing amazement over Philly's slow fade to black. "How many Philadelphia fans are screaming at the TV, saying, 'Hurry up'?" Buck commented with 3:46 left, after the Eagles had advanced the ball 15 yards in two minutes of game time. The one Eagle who seemed to care as much as the Patriots — Terrell Owens, of all divas — was playing at a high level on one leg after a late-December surgery on his fractured fibula and injured ankle. Other than that, Philadelphia coach Andy Reid had on the field a team of men who seemed to be hopelessly lost.

And this is where the Eagles advertised New England's greatness. The Patriots were so much better equipped for the interminable journey that is a Super Bowl Sunday than the novices in their path. They wore out the Eagles by having a far better understanding of just how much longer a Super Bowl is, from start to finish, than a regular-season or playoff game. The pomp and circumstance. The never-ending halftime show. The Patriots had a full grasp of the spectacle, and of the need for players to pace themselves and to eat more during the day and during halftime to maintain their energy. The Eagles had reached the NFC Championship Game the previous three years and lost all three times, and in the Super Bowl they didn't know what they were getting into. "We came out smoking," said one team official, "and then we ran out of gas. I really think it was a nutrition deal. I think our team ran out of steam and it hurt us."

Belichick had experienced five Super Bowls as a head coach and assistant before this one in Jacksonville, and he'd told friends in the business that a team would be foolish to burn a lot of energy early in the game. "It's a total marathon," he said. "You're going to win the game in the fourth quarter. Just get your guys to the fourth quarter."

The Eagles did finally score on that absurdly long drive to pull within a field goal, but with only 1:48 left they were forced to try an onside kick that was recovered by New England's Christian Fauria. The Patriots went three and out, but their third consecutive left-footed punter under Belichick, Josh Miller, pinned Philadelphia at its own four-yard line with 46 seconds to play. Slow again after a one-yard completion to Brian Westbrook wasted precious seconds, McNabb misfired on a pass before throwing his second interception of the fourth quarter — this one into the hands of Harrison.

Nine seconds remained on the clock. Belichick and Romeo Crennel had come up with a defensive plan that intercepted McNabb three times, sacked him four times, and, of greater consequence, left him with zero rushing yards. Belichick could live with McNabb's 357 yards passing and three touchdowns — he wanted the Eagles' quarterback to try to beat New England with his arm — but was terrified of McNabb's mobility. "We wanted our fastest people out there to chase him down," Belichick said.

The chase was now over. Brady had his third ring, Branch (11 catches, 133 yards) had his MVP award, and Belichick had his place above the iconic Lombardi, with a 10-1 postseason record. Before Brady took a knee after the final snap, Belichick wrapped his arms around his two coordinators, Crennel and Charlie Weis, and pulled them in tight. Weis had accepted a six-year, $12 million deal to coach Notre Dame, and Crennel had accepted a five-year, $11 million deal to try to do what his boss couldn't with the Cleveland Browns.

Crennel was a dignified loyalist who Belichick thought outcoached people with fundamentals and basics rather than by trying "to outscheme everybody." Belichick credited him for taking control of the defense in 2001, after Dick Rehbein's death forced Belichick and Weis to handle Brady and Drew Bledsoe, and for developing rising young assistants the likes of Brian Daboll and Josh McDaniels. Weis, a card-carrying Jersey Guy, had spent much of Super Bowl week telling anyone who would listen how he was about to outscheme and out-recruit the competition at Notre Dame. One lineman perfectly summed up Weis this way: There were some days you wanted to hug him and other days you wanted to strangle him.

"They are two of the best coaches I've ever been around," Belichick said of Weis and Crennel. "It's been an honor to work with them."

Belichick and his coordinators locked themselves into this tight sideline circle, heads down, arms draped over shoulders, as they thanked one another for the memories and spoke of a secured lifetime bond. Before they broke up, Belichick placed his palms on top of the coordinators' heads. "And the New England Patriots will be the first dynasty of the 21st century," Buck said on Fox. The Patriots' coach then found his father, Steve, wearing a blue-and-white team cap and jacket, and wrapped his left arm around him. Tedy Bruschi ran up behind father and son holding a Gatorade bucket full of ice water above his head, and dumped it on the unsuspecting Belichicks.

Red, white, and blue confetti started falling from the Alltel Stadium sky. "If you knew Bill Belichick when he was coaching with the Cleveland Browns," Collinsworth said on the broadcast, "they had one winning season there. And to now say that his record in the playoffs would be better than the great Vince Lombardi, I don't know if there's a person in Cleveland that's not scratching their head a little bit and saying, 'Are you believing what we're seeing?'"

The Patriots had won three championships by a total of nine points, and Belichick had become the fourth coach to win three Super Bowls — and the first to do so within only four years. On the field, with fireworks exploding above, Fauria grabbed the coach and lifted him off the ground while shouting, "We did it." A seven-year veteran in Seattle, with a long history of significant injuries, Fauria had been beyond apprehensive about signing with the Patriots in 2002. "I heard so many bad stories about Bill," he said, "and how tough his camp was." Belichick had promised the tight end in advance that he'd give him the desperately needed time off from practice, and the coach honored that pledge. With a few exceptions, the new and improved Belichick had built tremendous two-way trust with his athletes and established a collegial work environment that was the envy of the league. "I was always searching for that college atmosphere," Fauria said, "where everyone is really connected and united and knows their roles . . . That was as close to a college brotherhood as I've ever seen."

Belichick worked his way from one delirious hug to another before telling reporters that he'd leave to them the comparisons to the all-time greats.

Soon enough he'd receive an email from the man who'd hired him in Cleveland, Ernie Accorsi, who told him: "I don't say these things cheaply. If you ask me for one idol in this business, I'd say Vince Lombardi. I named my third child after him. And I now have you in the same breath." Belichick emailed back. "I'm not in his class yet," Accorsi recalled him writing.

It had been a remarkable week for Belichick in Jacksonville, with testimonials to his genius coming from players and coaches alike. But there was one moment and scene from this night that would stay with him for the rest of his coaching life, a moment and scene that would make him emotional at a Super Bowl to be played ten years down the road.

That dousing by Bruschi. Belichick hadn't gotten to experience it after his first two Super Bowl victories, because they were decided by Adam Vinatieri field goals in the final seconds. Belichick said he hadn't felt water dumped on him in a long time, and that it felt good. On contact, he threw his head back, his mouth agape, and reached for his soaked hair with both hands. As Belichick staggered away, Bruschi grabbed the back of his hoodie and yanked him in for a hug. After he broke free, Belichick stopped and stared at his half-soaked father, who was trying to gather himself while being bumped by a photographer. Bill looked at Steve for only a second or two before turning toward the field to watch Brady take the snap and a knee.

But in that second or two, what did Bill see? Did he see an 86-year-old father in thick glasses stumbling about as he tried to shake his jacket sleeves dry? Or did he see an overwhelmingly decent man who had taught him to love the game of football, and who had lived long enough to watch his own flesh and blood become the Lombardi of his time?

On the night of November 19, 2005, Stephen Nickolas Belichick was watching the No. 1 college team in America, USC, play a Fresno State team coached by one of his son's former assistants, Pat Hill, when his heart suddenly stopped beating. The elder Belichick had attended Navy's victory over Temple that day and had enjoyed the company of some of his former academy players. He ate dinner, talked to Bill by phone, and then settled in for his usual round of Saturday night college football on TV. He died the way he had lived.

"So I'm sure that's the way he would have wanted it to end," his only child said the next day.

Steve Belichick was a Paul Brown disciple who thought his son might've fit in better back in Brown's day. "You didn't have to be a personality in the old days," Steve said. "[Television] changed the whole picture. Now you have to be a storyteller or have a TV presence in order to get hired." As great as Brown was, Steve said, "I don't think he ever walked into a room and took it over." He knew the same could be said of his boy, Bill, whom he'd never heard tell a joke.

The colorless Belichick had spent his career wiping out sideline personalities big and small, and it was a blessing that Steve was there to witness it. Bill didn't tell his players about his dad's death before they went out and defeated the New Orleans Saints in Gillette Stadium the next day. He didn't want to burden or distract them. He informed the team afterward in the locker room, where Robert Kraft awarded him the game ball before Belichick left his emotional players to address the news media.

"I coached this game with a heavy heart," he said. "My dad passed away. I found out about it in the middle of the night. Obviously, he had a tremendous influence on my life personally, and particularly in the football aspect. It was great to be able to share the tremendous memories with him and some of our recent successes, as I did when I was a kid when he was successful as a coach of the Naval Academy and that program." Through a thin smile, Belichick said of his gruff old man, "He went peacefully, which is unusual for him."

The wake was held that Tuesday afternoon and evening at the John Taylor Funeral Home, in Annapolis, and the funeral service was held the following morning at the Naval Academy Chapel. The program distributed at the service featured a cover photo of a younger Steve in a Navy cap, and described him as a devoted husband to his Jeannette for 55 years, as a campus institution for half a century, and as a golfer, squash player, and fisherman who also "loved to garden, paint, and care for his birds." Rick Forzano, the former Navy and Detroit Lions coach, spoke during the service of Steve's enduring loyalty to the academy. Tom Lynch, the retired rear admiral and former teammate of Roger Staubach's, relayed how the Heisman-winning quarterback described Steve as "the integrity of the team."

Bill Belichick delivered a moving eulogy to an audience of some 200 mourners that included Kraft and rows of familiar football figures. He said that even as a successful squash player at Wesleyan, he couldn't beat his old man, whose winning streak inspired Bill to smash his racquet. Belichick also spoke of his father's no-frills approach to running his football camp. "It was meet, practice, film, meal, then do it again," he said. "And when he said, 'Lights out,' he meant it." Sprints and push-ups on the lawn — even if the sprinklers were on — were the penalties for broken curfews.

"I know my dad felt, as important as football was, he fully understood what a midshipman's role was when he came here to serve, defend, and, if he has to, die for his country," Bill said. "He trained players to play football, to win, to beat Army, and to train to fight for their country."

At one point during his eulogy, Bill turned to his mother, Jeannette, and said, "You were the real strength behind two coaches in this family, and I love you." In his final address to his father, who rested in a casket covered by an American flag, Bill said, "Dad, may you rest in peace."

A Navy coach for 33 years, Steve Belichick, self-made son of the Depression, was buried in the academy cemetery. The first men who showed Bill how to coach football were all gone now. Al Laramore, Annapolis High, died of a heart attack in 1989, at age 53, while moving firewood with his son; he never got to see Bill as an NFL head coach. Steve Sorota, Phillips Academy, died in his Carrollton, Texas, home in April 2001, at age 87; he never got to see Bill as a Super Bowl–winning head coach.

Steve Belichick saw it all. He was right there, on the sideline, when the boy he taught how to scout and break down film conquered professional football. The head coach of the New England Patriots was already an all-time great in his early fifties, and there appeared to be only one grail left to claim.

Perfection. Bill Belichick would chase it, and some of his imperfections would surface along the way.

14

SPYGATE

In January 2007, a year after he suffered his first postseason loss as Patriots coach — to Denver — following 10 straight victories, Belichick lost the AFC Championship Game to the rival Indianapolis Colts, who had finally beaten New England in their previous two regular-season matchups. The Patriots held a 21–3 second-quarter lead inside the RCA Dome and appeared ready to harden the Colts' standing as big-game busts before Indianapolis staged an improbable comeback.

"We've got them right where we want them," Colts coach Dungy told his bewildered players at halftime. *Right where we want them?* "What the fuck is he talking about?" said one of those players, Dan Klecko. "We're down 21–6 to Tom Brady. That's not where I want to be."

Dungy had no choice but to play mind games with a locker room full of men who had no experience beating the Patriots when it mattered most. "You have to play them and not their mystique," Dungy said, "but that's hard to do, because all you hear about is their mystique and see their rings and know how good they are." Two Colts who would help Dungy send the Patriots home at last were players Belichick had sent on their way: Klecko and Adam Vinatieri.

Klecko never wanted to leave Foxborough, but his bosses thought he didn't quite fit. Belichick and Scott Pioli had so much respect for his work ethic and his father's New York Jets legacy that they sat with him for 45 minutes that September 2006 day he was cut to reminisce about their championship runs. Dungy and Colts GM Bill Polian picked up Klecko and turned some of Belichick's own coaching against him by using the 5′11″, 275-pound lineman's versatility at a most opportune time. With Indianapolis on the New England one-yard line late in the third quarter, Klecko was stationed at fullback when Peyton Manning backed away from center and shouted "Apple, apple" at the line of scrimmage, signaling a play the Colts had put in that morning, a play that sent Klecko into the right flat as a receiver.

"I'm thinking, *Oh, shit, there's no way he's throwing to me*," the lineman said. Sure enough, Manning threw it to him, and Klecko caught it and celebrated his touchdown with a hard spike. His love for the Patriots had been temporarily replaced by hate. "*Fuck it, you guys,*" Klecko thought to himself in that moment. "*I still wanted to be there, but this is what you get.*" In his gray hoodie with the sleeves hacked off below his elbows — a concession to his short arms, he said — Belichick paced the sideline with his hands on his hips before Manning completed a two-point conversion pass to tie the game.

Vinatieri was even more emotional than Klecko. He'd won two Super Bowls with field goals in the final seconds and he'd scored the winning fourth-quarter points in New England's third Super Bowl victory in four years, in the process becoming the NFL's Mariano Rivera — the best closer in the game. And yet, after the 2005 season, Belichick wouldn't give him the contract he thought he'd earned. "I felt like *You've rented me enough,*" said Vinatieri, who had shared an agent with Belichick, Neil Cornrich, before hiring a new representative and closing out the five-year, $12 million deal to sign with Indy.

Down 15 points at halftime of the AFC Championship Game matchup with his former team, Vinatieri did something he almost never did: He started shouting angrily in the locker room. He wanted this one badly. He wanted to beat Belichick to a fourth title, and he ended up 3 for 3 in field goal attempts, including a 36-yarder with 5:31 to play to make it a 31–31 game. "I think everybody in this town needed it for their own reasons," Vinatieri would say of the victory. "My reasons may be different than their reasons, but we all had to beat New England."

Nobody needed it more than the haunted Manning, who found himself on the wrong end of football's burgeoning Russell-vs.-Chamberlain rivalry. Peyton had already produced seven seasons of passing for more than 4,000 yards, yet he was 5-6 in the postseason and 0-2 against Brady, who was 12-1 in the postseason. Manning's father maintained that his son always felt he was competing against Belichick, not Brady, and Archie Manning knew how formidable the New England coach was as an opponent. In his first two years with the New Orleans Saints, in the early 1970s, Manning's offensive coordinator was Ken Shipp, who would later teach a young Belichick plenty about the more aesthetically pleasing side of the ball when they were together in Detroit in 1976. As the Patriots were winning big in the early 2000s, Shipp often spoke with Archie about young Bill's relentless quest for knowledge and about his extreme pride in Belichick's accomplishments.

Only this time, Belichick didn't come up with a defensive plan to stop Manning from throwing for 349 yards and driving the Colts 80 yards for the winning touchdown. Manning prayed on the sideline while the Patriots frantically tried to score in the final seconds, but this time it was Brady, for a change, who made the game-ending mistake on a pass intercepted by Marlin Jackson.

As it turned out, Belichick's biggest mistake wasn't letting go of the popular Vinatieri, whose departure was mourned by Patriots fans. It was trading holdout Deion Branch to Seattle for a first-round pick and leaving Brady with a first option like Reche Caldwell, whose drops against Indianapolis proved fatal. When this AFC title game was over and the Colts were on their way to a Super Bowl meeting with the Chicago Bears that they'd win, Belichick brushed past Manning in the postgame scrum, earning criticism from some media observers for showing a lack of sportsmanship. But Belichick did find Klecko and Vinatieri. "Go get a ring," the coach told Klecko. "If it's not us, I'm glad it's you guys," Belichick told Vinatieri. "Go win this thing."

The Manning snub came one week after San Diego Chargers star LaDainian Tomlinson suggested that Belichick was to blame for New England's postgame dancing at San Diego's expense, which the league MVP said showed "absolutely no class," and two weeks after Belichick shoved a photographer's camera into the man's face as the coach approached his former assistant, the New York Jets' Eric Mangini, for a surprising postgame hug. Belichick had been furious at Mangini for taking the head coaching job with the Jets, a franchise he hated, and he'd turned this postgame encounter into a big news event by offering his former defensive coordinator an overwhelmingly limp and lifeless handshake after their regular-season meetings, and by refusing to even speak Mangini's name before the Jets' stunning victory at Gillette Stadium. The New England coach did have to work his way through a swarm of cameramen to get to Mangini after the playoff victory, and he did call *Globe* photographer Jim Davis afterward to apologize for his own version of a postseason push. But the scene did nothing to soften the edges of a public image formed in his daily press conferences, where Belichick was only slightly more accommodating and human than he had been in his darkest Cleveland days.

Belichick knew how to play the media game; he proved that as an assistant with the Giants and the Jets. As the Browns' head coach, he chose not to play that game, or to not play it often enough. In Foxborough, the coach and his consigliere, Berj Najarian, would at times feed stories or confirmations of news items — not for attribution, of course — to writers they deemed fair or franchise-friendly. "The misnomer with him is that he doesn't care about the media or work the media. That's blatantly false," said one Patriots writer who got his share of stories from Belichick and Najarian. "He has his guys talk off the record . . . People say he doesn't care what people say or write, but he does care what they say or write. Every morning,

Berj would have a clip file, and on the treadmill Bill would read the newspapers. He keeps track, or Berj does, of what's being written and said and who's on whose side. I think there are times . . . before [Belichick] walks out to a press conference room and goes to the podium, he looks into the crowd and takes mental note of who's there."

Naturally, media members who were deemed enemies of the state weren't afforded the same off-the-record courtesies or background help that went to the franchise friendlies. Belichick wasn't unique in this context; just about every NFL head coach operated the same way.

As the Patriots prepared for a second straight off-season of deciphering why they hadn't reached the Super Bowl, Belichick needed all of his media savvy to deal with a couple of potentially damaging stories. One involved his relationship with a former New York Giants receptionist, Sharon Shenocca, whose divorce case put Belichick in headlines that had nothing to do with his winning percentage. BILL STOLE MY WIFE, read the screaming front page of the *Boston Herald* in the summer of 2006, when news first broke that Shenocca's husband had charged that she'd received "large sums of money and expensive gifts from Mr. Belichick, which she has used to purchase expensive clothing, pocketbooks, watches, a treadmill and maid service, most of which she initially hid from [her husband]."

Vincent Shenocca claimed that Belichick had limousines pick up his wife at her house and that he'd paid to send her to Houston for the Patriots' Super Bowl XXXVIII victory over Carolina, and he was seeking custody of their two children; Sharon Shenocca was seeking the same. The story resurfaced in February 2007 under the *New York Post* headline "Sugar Daddy Belichick," which cited court papers stating that the Patriots' coach had purchased for Shenocca a secret $2.2 million Brooklyn townhouse, had paid for her rental at the Jersey Shore, and had been wiring her cash payments for the previous 18 months. Sharon Shenocca claimed that her friendship with Belichick was platonic, but Vincent Shenocca alleged that his wife and the coach had engaged in "an adulterous relationship." His lawyer, Ed O'Donnell, planned to depose the coach as part of the custody fight.

The case was a great embarrassment to Belichick, who had separated from his wife, Debby, in 2005 — "quietly and amicably," wrote David Halberstam — though Vincent Shenocca said his wife, Sharon, had been in a relationship with the coach for years. Bill lived in Hingham, and Debby in Weston, and they divorced in 2006. Belichick was an intensely private man and a father of three who now had the most intimate details of his personal life splashed across the big-city tabloids. And at the office, his character was being assailed on an entirely different front. Ted Johnson, retired linebacker, had alleged in interviews with the *Globe* and the *New York Times*, published just before the Super Bowl, that Belichick had him engage in full-contact drills in practice in 2002 — against the trainer's advice — while still suffering from the effects of a concussion, which Johnson said resulted in another concussion.

This 2007 story was a nightmare for Belichick, who denied knowing that his linebacker wasn't prepared to hit in the 2002 practice session. Johnson had avoided selection in the Houston Texans' expansion draft but had to take a pay cut he didn't want to take to ensure his place on New England's roster. The contract turbulence set an uneasy training-camp tone between employer and employee even before Johnson suffered a concussion in a preseason collision with New York Giants running back Sean Bennett. "Bill's the one who actually pulled me off," the linebacker said, "when he saw me loopy."

Four days later, when the Patriots were scheduled to practice in full pads, Johnson assumed he'd find a red jersey in his locker — players in blue jerseys were cleared for full contact, players in red jerseys were not. He was stunned when he saw a blue jersey, and he approached the new head trainer, Jim Whalen, who agreed that the linebacker should be wearing red. But during the practice, an assistant trainer suddenly walked up to Johnson and handed him a blue jersey. "And I said, 'Who the fuck gave you that?'" Johnson recalled years later. "And he points three fields over, and there's Jim talking to Belichick." Fearing he might be cut if he didn't agree to engage, Johnson put on the blue and jumped into a nine-on-seven drill that required him to take on a blocking back, and the two met helmet to helmet. "And it was a warm sensation," Johnson said. "Everything slows down. Everybody's moving slow, my vision is blurred, and I'm going, *This is not good.*"

Johnson avoided contact the rest of the practice, and afterward he confronted Whalen. "What the fuck are you doing, man?" he asked him. "I got concussed on the first play I was out there." Johnson said he could see the blood drain from Whalen's face before the trainer sent him to an independent neurologist at Massachusetts General, where he was diagnosed with a second concussion and told to stay clear of contact for two weeks. Upon his return, Johnson was rendered inactive for the season opener against Pittsburgh. He was so angry he cleaned out his locker, then walked past Eric Mangini, who asked, "What are you doing? Are you moving out?"

"Yeah, I am, actually," Johnson responded. He walked out of camp for a few days, ignoring pleas from teammates to return to the facility, before he did return under the threat of a forfeited salary. Johnson said he told Belichick in a meeting, "I'm a team player. I've always been a team player. You can demote me, you can trade me, you can cut out my reps. But you can't play God with my health like that, Bill. You crossed the line. And you really fucked up."

According to Johnson, Belichick responded, "Well, I had to see if you could play." The linebacker shot back, "See if I can play? I've been a seven-year starter . . . Just trade me. You don't want me here. Just get rid of me."

Johnson recalled that his head coach finally relented and said, "All right, you know what, Ted? I did fuck up. I apologize." The linebacker likened Belichick's admission to Jack Nicholson's "You're goddamn right I did" courtroom admission in *A Few Good Men*. Belichick told the *Globe*'s Jackie MacMullan in 2007, "It was a watershed meeting for us. We had a long conversation and we both tried to see the other's position. I'm sure in part of that conversation I apologized for things I said or did, as he did for his actions and his emotions following his decision to leave the team. If I made a mistake or hurt Ted in any way, I don't feel good about that. I felt as though we left that meeting saying, 'We've both made mistakes. Let's move forward and get on a higher level.' And that's what we did."

That Belichick had put his veteran linebacker in harm's way was surprising to those who had seen him dramatically improve his player relations skills from his Cleveland days, and to anyone who knew how one of his old Wesleyan coaches had done virtually the same thing to a young Belichick — subjecting him to a dangerous practice technique that left him with a serious leg injury and a sense of disillusionment with the sport. Johnson made uncharacteristic assignment mistakes in the coming games that he attributed to his head trauma, but he lived up to a promise he'd made Belichick, that he'd be a low-maintenance Patriot for the rest of his playing days. Johnson was named a captain in 2003 and regained his starting job in 2004, and though he suffered additional concussions in those two championship seasons, he was a significant contributor to both titles.

"So we went from I wanted out of there, I hated that man, I resented him, I was angry, hurt, disgusted, to being a captain the next year," Johnson would say. "And honestly, we put it behind us."

Before the start of the 2005 training camp, Johnson visited Robert Kraft at the owner's house, and the two kicked their shoes off, put up their feet, and drank beers until midnight. The next morning, Johnson told Belichick he was retiring. The coach and the owner said kind things about Johnson (Belichick called him a "class act"), and, in a statement posted on the team's website, the linebacker referred to how the Kraft family had "believed in me from the beginning" and had "gone above and beyond in making me feel a part of their Patriots family." Johnson said he was proud to be associated with the Kraft legacy. He made no mention of Belichick.

He did mention that he could "no longer ignore the severe short- and long-term complications of the concussive head injuries I have sustained over the years." In additional remarks to reporters that day, Johnson said that he often couldn't get his bearings to call a play, and that doctors had told him his memory loss and sleep difficulties were the result of head trauma. By the time Johnson detailed his living hell to the *Globe*'s Mac-Mullan and the *Times*'s Alan Schwarz before the Colts–Bears Super Bowl, his neurologist was telling Schwarz that the retired 34-year-old Patriot was already exhibiting signs characteristic of early Alzheimer's disease. Johnson was speaking publicly two and a half months after former Philadelphia Eagles safety Andre Waters had committed suicide. Waters was later found to have been suffering from chronic traumatic encephalopathy (CTE), as a result, it was believed, of football-related concussions.

Johnson said that he suffered from depression and that he'd become addicted to Adderall after he started taking it in 2004 to improve his on-field focus. Johnson said his addiction was at least partly responsible for the demise of his marriage. He'd been arrested in July 2006 on domestic assault charges after the police responded to a dispute at his home; his wife, Jackie, recanted her claims before the two divorced.

Football had altered this 6′4″, 253-pound man. Johnson had savored the NFL life in his early days playing for Bill Parcells, who would sometimes hitch a ride with his linebacker on the drive back to the facility from the old practice fields. They talked about life on those short drives, about the player's father and family. Johnson loved being a Parcells guy, and though he was never a Belichick guy, he did come to appreciate the coach's incredible talent for putting his team in a position to win.

"Saturday meetings were my favorite with Belichick," he said, "because of what he does with a game plan. He narrows it down and makes it very simple so that we all understand what the main takeaways are for the team we're about to play . . . So he's got his pointer up there and he's like 'Look, Wayne Chrebet: We are going to hit this fucker on third down. Wayne Chrebet is not getting the ball on third down, OK?' Or 'Tony Gonzalez: When we get in the red zone, we're double-teaming his ass.' He'll say to the defense, 'You do these three things, we'll win the game.' Then he says to the offense, 'You do these three things, we'll win the game.' And sure as shit, we started winning the games."

But the games ended up leaving Johnson a broken man who came to believe that he'd suffered dozens of concussions that left him, he said, "in the darkest place for the longest time." Johnson's case helped force league elders, most notably commissioner Roger Goodell, to take the mushrooming concussion crisis more seriously than they had. The ex-linebacker took pride in that, too — the fact that he had the courage to tell his story. He could've been a made man in Boston for life, a TV personality, maybe a candidate for the team's Hall of Fame. "I knew when I told my story, I'd never get behind the velvet rope again," Johnson said. "But I felt I could really make a difference."

Belichick had been staggered enough by the onslaught of negative publicity that he agreed to sit down for a rare two-hour interview with a *Globe* features writer, not a sportswriter. Bella English opened her piece by citing Belichick's request that it be stated that he had not asked for this story to be written, and that he merely agreed to an interview request, because he wouldn't want readers to think "this is some type of a campaign trail." Nevertheless, his cooperation had Najarian written all over it; Berj knew that his boss desperately needed to open a small window on his softer side. So Belichick spoke in the interview of looking forward to spending more time with his three children, and more time reading, golfing, and fishing on Nantucket, where he owned three properties. Belichick's charitable causes were detailed, including his support of homeless shelters, Jim Brown's Amer-I-Can program for at-risk youth, an athletic and fitness program for the disabled, and his own foundation, which awarded college scholarships to graduates of his high school (Annapolis) and his father's (Struthers, in Ohio).

The *Globe* piece reported that the coach's friends "invariably say Belichick is a great father" to 22-year-old Amanda, a senior at Wesleyan; 19-year-old Stephen, a prep student at Northfield Mount Hermon; and 15-year-old Brian, a student at the Rivers School, in Weston. A Wesleyan classmate and good friend of Bill Belichick's, Rob Ingraham, told the story of how Belichick had "brought the house down" by singing "Love Potion No. 9" at his 50th birthday party on Nantucket. The sports marketing executive also said Belichick had given the executive's children a puppy and had treated his young son Tucker to a ride on the team plane to the Super Bowl and to regular email correspondence.

This profile helped stop the bleeding, at least for a while. But a quote in the story attributed to a law clerk for the judge in the Shenocca divorce case didn't help Belichick's longtime friend Sharon Shenocca. The law clerk for New Jersey Superior Court Judge Thomas Manahan told the *Globe* of the case, "The whole Bill Belichick issue is not really relevant. It's just about trying to destroy a reputation. What it's really doing is wasting money." Vincent Shenocca's attorney, Ed O'Donnell, said he asked for Manahan's recusal based on that quote, and that the request was granted.

O'Donnell had agreed to wait until after the 2006 season to depose Belichick, but the coach's attorneys kept maintaining that he wasn't available, due to team and league commitments. "This is when he had the wrong playbook, I guess," O'Donnell said years later. Sharon Shenocca wanted to move her children into the Brooklyn townhouse that "a friend" she didn't name (Belichick) had purchased for Shenocca and her sister, a singer named Terry Radigan, but she couldn't produce her friend, Belichick, as a supporting witness. The judge who replaced Manahan, Stephan Hansbury, wrote in his June 29, 2007, judgment that Sharon Shenocca, the defendant, "is relying completely on the whim of the friend to provide her and the children with shelter when he is not so obligated. Defendant also never produced this friend to testify at trial nor did she offer any reason or explanation why she should be the recipient of this financial bounty."

Hansbury continued, "Plaintiff contends only the friend could explain Defendant's entitlement to reside in the home. Plaintiff contends Defendant's friend could have provided knowledge as to his intentions, if any, to support Defendant and her children. Simply stated, Defendant has not met her burden of proof that there is a dependable home awaiting her and the children in Brooklyn."

The judge ruled that Vincent Shenocca was "correct in that the Court may draw an adverse inference" against Sharon Shenocca for failing to produce Belichick, who she said had given her about $150,000 since the complaint was filed, and that she could not move her eight-year-old son and six-year-old daughter from Morris Township, New Jersey, to Park Slope on what Hansbury called "a whimsical dream."

Had Belichick said under oath that he wanted Shenocca in the townhouse and would continue fully supporting her, and had he opened himself up to potentially embarrassing testimony that would be made public, Sharon might've had a chance to prevail in the case. But her husband, a contractor making a $55,000 salary, was awarded residential custody of the children. Sharon Shenocca was granted visitation rights every other weekend and for an occasional midweek dinner. She was ordered to pay Vincent $121 a week in support and $67,500 in legal fees.

O'Donnell said that he never saw direct evidence of a romantic relationship between Belichick and Shenocca. "But at the end of the day, if you want to see how good of a friend he was to her," the attorney said, "he did what was best for him." By sidestepping the deposition, Belichick basically protected Belichick.

He was only a few weeks away from the opening of training camp—his sanctuary, his place to hide from annoyances outside the boundaries of the NFL life he loved. His Patriots were loaded after some high-powered off-season additions, including an absurdly talented and troubled superstar named Randy Moss. Only the receiver wouldn't be the cause of the trouble that was just around the bend. The kind of trouble that made the Sharon Shenocca and Ted Johnson stories seem manageable.

The kind of trouble that only Bill Belichick could answer for.

Richard Seymour was sidelined after knee surgery, and Rodney Harrison had been suspended for using performance-enhancing drugs, and yet the 2007 Patriots entered their season opener against the New York Jets as slam-dunk favorites to reach the Super Bowl after a two-year absence. They had acquired Baltimore's Pro Bowl linebacker Adalius Thomas a year after pulling all-time great Junior Seau out of a brief retirement, and they'd decided to give Tom Brady some skill people worthy of sharing his huddle.

Belichick sent second- and seventh-round draft picks to Miami for Wes Welker, a rising receiver and valued return man, and a fourth-round pick to Oakland for Moss, who arrived as the most physically gifted talent Belichick had coached since Lawrence Taylor. Moss was 30 years old, and, because of injuries and a diminished focus while playing for losing Raiders teams, he hadn't been the same receiver he was as a five-time Pro Bowler in Minnesota. Moss had a long history of troublesome behavior dating back to his youth, which was why 20 NFL teams passed on drafting a receiver who had 174 receptions and 54 touchdown catches in two record-setting seasons at Marshall. As a pro, Moss confirmed some pre-draft fears by bumping a traffic cop with his car, squirting an official with a water bottle, verbally abusing a corporate sponsor, pretending to moon a Green Bay crowd, and leaving the field before the end of a game.

But Belichick figured that Moss was worth the same gamble he'd taken, successfully, on Corey Dillon. He thought the organizational culture was strong enough to absorb anyone and everyone and lead them on a path toward compliance. So he called Moss on the other side of midnight, while the receiver was out at a club, and when Moss heard the caller identify himself as Bill Belichick, he assumed it was a prank. "So I'm cussing him out," Moss recalled years later. "I'm like 'Man, get the hell out of here. Who the hell is this now?' So it went on until he kept saying, 'This is Bill Belichick.' And I'm like 'You're shitting me, man. I don't want to hear that, man. Now, who is this really?' And he said, 'No, Randy, this is Bill Belichick.' So I had to apologize, man, because I was basically taking it as a joke and the conversation went on from there."

Moss had accounted for 110 regular-season and postseason touchdowns, and yet New England had acquired him for a middle-round pick. "A lot of people are crediting Bill Belichick," Moss said, "and I think a lot of people really need to understand that if it wasn't for Myra Kraft, I would've never become a Patriot." Myra Kraft, the wife of the owner and a woman who firmly believed the Patriots should be a team of high-character men.

"She had a lot of influence on bringing me to New England," Moss said. "She's the female face of the franchise, and I think there was a lot of negative attention that I was receiving, and a lot of it was very false. And I think that Mrs. Myra Kraft really had to get to know me personally to really understand that a lot of the stuff that was said, the majority of it was lies. She told me she took a chance. It was just a gut feeling for her, and Mr. Kraft told me that he called her 'Mama.' And he said, 'Mama wanted you to come here.'"

Moss couldn't believe his good fortune. Tom Brady restructured his contract to allow New England to take on one of the game's signature receivers, and Moss agreed to downgrade the two years and $21 million left on his Oakland deal into a one-year deal for $3 million plus incentives. "I'm still in awe that I'm a part of this organization," Moss said after agreeing to the massive pay cut for a chance to win a ring. He had suddenly landed with the most successful coach and quarterback in the sport, and, after missing most of the preseason with a hamstring injury, he was ready to go on September 9, 2007, when the Patriots opened in the building where Belichick had first made a name for himself as an exceptional football coach: Giants Stadium.

As it turned out, Moss and the Patriots were hotter than the game-time temperature of 84 degrees. They ran the Jets off the field in a 38–14 rout highlighted by Moss's 51-yard touchdown against triple coverage and 183 receiving yards on nine catches. "He was born to play football," Brady said of his newest and most lethal weapon. The quarterback had it all now. He was getting serious with his relatively new girlfriend, Brazilian supermodel Gisele Bündchen (his ex-girlfriend, actress Bridget Moynahan, had just given birth to their son, Jack), and now he was being paired on the field with a perfect partner of a different kind. Brady wasn't seeing the Oakland Randy Moss. He was seeing the Minnesota Moss, the vintage Moss, the 6′4″ receiver who ran past defenders and jumped over them with ease. Brady had all day to throw to Moss and Welker, who caught the first of the quarterback's three touchdown passes. He wasn't sacked while posting a quarterback rating of 146.6, his best in nearly five years.

Man, this was a great day for the winning coach all around. On the other sideline, Eric Mangini had made a big mistake by sticking with his quarterback, Chad Pennington, a former teammate of Moss's at Marshall, when the outcome was no longer in doubt, subjecting his starter to some unnecessary hits as he played on an injured ankle. Pennington was annoyed enough to pull *himself* from the game with 6:51 left and New England leading by 17. "That was the first time I've ever done that," Pennington said.

Mangini played the fool on this Sunday, and Belichick surely got the biggest kick out of that. But the losing coach actually won a game within the game in the first half that the overwhelming majority of people inside Giants Stadium knew absolutely nothing about. It had started in the days before this opener, when Mangini informed his former boss that the Jets would not tolerate in their own stadium an illegal yet common Patriots practice: the videotaping of opposing coaches' signals from the sideline. The message to Belichick was simple: *Don't do it in our house.*

It was something of an open secret that New England had been illegally taping opposing coaches during games for some time, and yet the first public mention of improper spying involving Belichick's Patriots actually assigned them the collective role of victim. Following a 21–0 Miami victory in December 2006, a couple of Dolphins told the *Palm Beach Post* that the team had "bought" past game tapes that included audio of Brady making calls at the line, and that the information taken from those tapes had helped them shut out Brady and sack him four times. "I've never seen him so flustered," said Miami linebacker Zach Thomas.

Brady called the notion that he'd been duped "a big crock." Belichick's former Cleveland assistant, Nick Saban, in his second season coaching the Dolphins after leaving LSU, scoffed at the suggestion that he'd done anything improper and said his team had merely used TV tape of Brady and other quarterbacks to try to decipher their cadences. In fact, the Miami coach later revealed that he believed Belichick had figured out his defensive signals in a 2005 loss to the Patriots. "This is the most ridiculous thing I've ever seen in my life," Saban said. "Every guy on our team that I talked to about it says, 'Yeah, we've been doing this for ten years.' We did it in Cleveland [with Belichick] — watched TV copy of the game trying to get the cadence. I mean, now they've got us stealing stuff, buying stuff. I mean, like we're in the Mafia or something."

The story created an interesting debate around the league. Some coaches and players said that studying TV audio for play-calling clues was commonplace, others said it was not. Of the Dolphins' defensive adjustments in that 2006 game, one New England player said, "Every shift we made, they were calling out the plays at the line. It was like 'Wait a minute, how are you doing this?' . . . They knew exactly what we were doing offensively. If you watch them on film, you'll see it."

An NFL spokesman, Steve Alic, disclosed that the league had no interest in investigating the Dolphins. Alic told the *Palm Beach Post,* "The reaction around the NFL offices was 'That's football.'" Some invested observers referred to the case as "Audiogate," while others went with "Videogate." Either way, Zach Thomas maintained, the Dolphins beat the Patriots fair and square. "Everybody's thinking the only way we can beat the New England Patriots is if we steal their signals. There was no stealing signals. You watch tape."

Years later, this appeared as a remarkable, almost comical starting point in a case that would forever change the way much of America viewed Bill Belichick's football program. The New England Patriots were actually the aggrieved party, and their AFC East rivals were defending themselves against suspicions that they had benefited from an unfair competitive advantage. This was the subject of discussion on CBS when analyst Charley Casserly, former general manager of the Houston Texans and Washington Redskins and former member of the league's competition committee, became the first person with a major media outlet to report on a case that would come to be known as Spygate.

"The Patriots got caught doing something early in the year they weren't supposed to be doing," Casserly said. "They had a man on their sideline dressed in coaching attire, with a video camera, who was presumably videotaping the other team's signals. You can't do that. They were warned. If it happens again, they're going to be disciplined."

Of course, Belichick was asked about this in his Monday press conference. And of course, he was unhappy that the topic had been raised. "I haven't heard anything from the league," Belichick said. That wasn't a denial of illegal taping, nor was it a statement that the league hadn't contacted someone else in the organization. "Why don't you go talk to Charley Casserly," Belichick sniped. "He's the guy that has all the answers on everything." Two days later, Belichick took another unsolicited shot at Casserly as the so-called answer man. The back-and-forth was picked up in some markets here and there, but nationally, the story died on the vine. It was as if the Watergate burglars had been briefly detained by cops on the scene and then sent on their way.

But even if he didn't realize it, Mangini had turned himself into a one-man Woodward and Bernstein. His relationship with his former mentor had turned about as toxic as Belichick's was with Bill Parcells immediately following their Jets divorce, though Little Bill and Big Bill had recently met for a peace summit at Scott Pioli's home on Nantucket and had golfed together at the exclusive Nantucket Golf Club, before going out for dinner. (Belichick and Parcells also spoke warmly during a function at a Manhattan steakhouse for Harry Carson's induction into the Hall of Fame.) Belichick had raised Mangini in the NFL, promoted him in Cleveland from ball boy and public relations intern to offensive assistant, and then hired him with the Jets and the Patriots. Belichick had named him defensive coordinator — at age 34 — after Romeo Crennel left to become head coach of the

Browns, and after he'd spent only one year in that position, another former Belichick hire in Cleveland, Jets GM Mike Tannenbaum, hired him away from Foxborough.

Belichick had so much contempt for the Jets, he thought Mangini's eagerness to take that divisional job was an act of betrayal. Worse yet, Belichick believed that Mangini was quietly recruiting staffers to make the southbound journey with him to New Jersey, a claim the defensive coordinator denied. "Eric wasn't smart about it; he went behind Bill's back," said one Patriots official. "He didn't stick to the code. It's like *The Godfather*: He antagonized Bill, and it got messy."

When Mangini tried to clean out his office, he found that his boss had already put his key card for entry on the inactive list. Crennel and Weis had left Foxborough without this kind of hostility, but they'd been in place as coordinators for years and had helped Belichick win three titles. Besides, they'd started out as Parcells guys. Mangini was the ultimate Belichick guy, a Wesleyan noseguard, and he was leaving after one season as a coordinator — a 10-6 season followed by a divisional playoff loss to Denver — to join another Belichick guy (Tannenbaum) who worked for a franchise Belichick hated so much that, more than a decade later, when rattling off his shared résumé with Crennel, he'd call the Jets "another team" rather than actually speak their name.

Belichick did all he could to avoid speaking Mangini's name to the press after he took over the Jets. The border war that Parcells had declared over after the Jets agreed to trade Belichick to the Patriots in 2000 was suddenly back on. Shots were fired when New England filed tampering charges against the Jets in September 2006, after Belichick and Pioli had given training-camp holdout Deion Branch permission to talk contract terms (but not potential trade terms) with other teams. The Jets, who had offered a second-round pick, were cleared of the charges more than four months after Branch was dealt to Seattle. In a statement, after declaring that they were pleased that the commissioner had found New England's allegations to be "completely unfounded," the Jets said they'd remain competitive with the Patriots on the field "and partners off the field, working together to advance the interests of the league and its fans."

The Jets had a much better chance of winning four of the next five Super Bowls than they did of remaining cooperative business partners with the Patriots. Over the course of a 2006 season that saw the teams meet three times, Belichick set the juvenile tone for the Mangini handshake follies. To put more pressure on Mangini, he intentionally exaggerated the Jets' talent level and reminded everyone that their previous coach, Herm Edwards, had the 2004 team a field goal away from the AFC Championship Game.

In 2006, the Jets shut down a New England staffer who was trying to film from an unauthorized Giants Stadium position, but they didn't report the apparent infraction to the league. In Foxborough, Patriots security confronted and removed a Jets videographer who was shooting from the mezzanine level of Gillette Stadium — a place the home team said he wasn't allowed to be. The Jets countered that they did have New England's permission to film from the location in question — "For a double end-zone shot," a team official said — and that they regularly allowed opponents to film from two end-zone positions in Giants Stadium if they so desired. "It was bullshit," the official said of the Patriots' allegation.

Mangini decided the following season that he needed to warn Belichick of potential consequences for illegal videotaping, and he assumed that was that. The league had sent all 32 teams a letter the previous September that read, in part, "Videotaping of any type, including but not limited to taping of an opponent's offensive or defensive signals, is prohibited on the sidelines." The NFL had warned teams again before the start of the 2007 season, though it was believed that the second memo was specifically aimed at New England.

The NFL's game operations manual specifically stated that video-recording devices couldn't be used in the coaches' booth, on the field, or in the locker room during a game. In 2006, the Patriots had been caught trying to illegally film not just the Jets, but the Green Bay Packers, the Detroit Lions, and at least one other team. At Lambeau Field, Packers security confronted and removed a Patriots staffer who was filming without proper credentials. "From what I can remember," Packers president Bob Harlan told ESPN .com, "he had quite a fit when we took him out. We had gotten word before the game that they did this sort of thing, so we were looking for it."

Mangini was looking for it because he had lived it in Foxborough. His good friend Tannenbaum had hired him in part because he thought Mangini could relate well to people from different backgrounds. (The GM based this belief on the fact that Mangini had attended a Hartford, Connecticut, high school, Bulkeley, that was only 10 percent white.) The Jets were also buying a piece of the Patriots' puzzle, a piece of Belichick, the coach who had walked out on them and erected a dynasty. Mangini acted like Belichick in his press conferences, where he dodged everything, and in the locker room, where he implored his players to follow his robotic, say-nothing lead. He hammered home the notion that no detail was too small in preparing for a game. He was so much like his old boss that his quarterback, Pennington, was moved to say, "I thought his name was Eric Belichick sometimes, not Eric Mangini. That was what Eric saw succeed. He believed in establishing that culture with us."

What else did he learn from Belichick? Mangini had brought in a couple of recently released Patriots right before playing New England in 2007, including Reche Caldwell, just to discover a bit more about Belichick's latest adjustments. Meanwhile, Belichick brought in former Jets receiver Tim Dwight to conduct his own little reconnaissance of how Mangini was running his program in New Jersey. Former mentor and former protégé were still one and the same.

Special teams coach Mike Westhoff, who'd joined the Jets in 2001, had applied for the head coaching job that went to Mangini, and he stayed on as an assistant who one day was moved to explain his scouting methods to the new boss. "And I said, 'This is how I do things,'" Westhoff recalled. "I explained it to him, and I was telling him about my scouting report. And I thought it was as good as I've ever seen. I really liked it. I'd seen others, and I thought there was none better than mine . . . And Eric said, 'Yeah, I know, I've seen it before.' I said, 'What did you say?' He said, 'I've seen it.' Now, this was when he was first there . . . I didn't ask him exactly how it happened, but I was so mad. Did that mean someone had shipped it up to him before a game? I don't know. I never accused anyone, and he never told me. All I know is that was his exact quote. He looked me right in the face and said, 'I know, Mike. It is good. I've seen it before.' . . . It didn't come across to me as being innocent."

Early in New England's blowout of the Jets in the 2007 opener at Giants Stadium, this much was clear: Nothing looked innocent. Steve Yarnell, the Jets' vice president and director of security and a former FBI special agent, spotted a 26-year-old Patriots video assistant, wearing a photographer's vest, illegally filming the home team's coaches from the sideline. Square-jawed and built like an icebox, Yarnell, who played football for West Point during Bill Parcells's days as an Army assistant, notified NFL security and then moved in on Matt Estrella, a New Bedford, Massachusetts, native and Fitchburg State graduate with a degree in communications and media and a concentration in video production. Estrella was the same staffer who had been caught by Packers security shooting from an unauthorized field location the year before at Lambeau. He had started with the Patriots as an intern in June 2004 before being upgraded to full-time in July 2005, and he was about to get the scare of his young football life.

Yarnell confiscated Estrella's camera and tape, and soon enough he joined Jets senior vice president Bob Parente and Patriots security chief Mark Briggs in the Giants Stadium office of Pat Aramini, a longtime state trooper and an official with the New Jersey Sports and Exposition Authority who lorded over Meadowlands security. They were joined by FBI agent Bob Bukowski, who'd started working Meadowlands football and basketball games and horse races after the 9/11 attacks; Jim Crann, also a long-time state trooper and now a unit supervisor for the sports complex; and Rodney Davis, a former FBI special agent who'd become the NFL's security rep for Jets games. For about a half hour, these men talked, argued, debated, and fought for control of the camera and tape that were sitting on a credenza behind Aramini, who sat at his desk and played lead referee in a game with much higher stakes than the one being played on the field.

Briggs had one job in that meeting, and that was to persuade the men in the room to return to him Estrella's camera and tape. As a decorated British Army veteran who had been stationed in Northern Ireland and the Falklands and had run security at Wembley Stadium and at the 2000 Summer Games in Sydney, Australia, Briggs was a formidable spokesman for his cause. He had an engaging British accent, and Meadowlands security officials were comfortable with him. On game day, the NFL holds what's known as the 100-minute meeting, which takes place 100 minutes before kickoff and involves the referee and league, club, and stadium security and safety officials going over procedures in the event of an emergency or a stadium-ordered evacuation. Briggs participated in these meetings when the Patriots were in town, and Aramini, Crann, and Bukowski found him to be cooperative and reasonable.

Only Briggs was an infantryman for a reason: He had a certain bald-guy toughness about him, a hawkish look in his eye, that Aramini and others recognized as a force to be dealt with. As New England's head of stadium security since the spring of 2001, Briggs had pissed off more than a few people around the league. He could be ultra-aggressive with photographers and camera operators in clearing a path for Belichick on the way to a post-game handshake on the field — not that the coach needed the help.

As the meeting began, Aramini recalled, "Briggs was trying to say that it was theft, that we were keeping the Patriots' property. I said, 'No, if it's filmed at an NFL game, it's NFL property, and I'm keeping it.'" Aramini had never had any problems with the Patriots in all his years at Giants Stadium, and he considered Robert Kraft "a class act." But at one point in the meeting, according to Aramini, Briggs suggested that perhaps Aramini should be arrested. "He never asked for an arrest to be made," Crann countered. "He made suggestions there were criminal activities going on prior to us taking the camera. We didn't take the camera. We secured the camera so it couldn't be tampered with while the discussion was going on."

Meanwhile, the Jets' reps in the room — Yarnell and Parente — were furious that a Patriots official, of all people, could be claiming that his franchise was being wronged. "There were cross allegations being made," Crann said. "Steve was obviously aware that something was being done [by New England] that was inappropriate. Steve was mentioning things along the lines of corporate espionage, and I'm standing there going, *Hold on a second. Corporate espionage?* We called the NFL rep [Davis] in as well, because from where I was sitting . . . this was an NFL issue, not a criminal issue. We didn't want to make it a criminal issue regardless of what was being said by opposing sides."

Bukowski recalled that the neutral parties in the room were trying to determine whether the confiscated camera had been transmitting a signal to another location. "I think everything was being put out there to see if we'd get involved, and what was going to be done, and there were a lot of accusations going back and forth," Bukowski said. "[The Patriots] knew what was on it, and they wanted it back. They were trying any reason, but there was no way."

People in the room said that Davis, the NFL rep, allowed the discussion to unfold without taking a hard stand on the league's behalf. None of the parties had dealt with a case quite like this. Giants Stadium security officials were used to dealing with drunkenness, disorderly fans who needed to be ejected, and, in the wake of 9/11, the occasional threat on the building and the occasional plane from Newark or Teterboro Airport that flew a little too close to the packed house for comfort.

"We needed to get back to the business of handling 78,000 people," said Crann, who thought at the time that the fight for control of the camera and tape was "a Mickey Mouse thing" and "small potatoes."

As the only man in the room protecting New England's interests, Briggs seemed to know otherwise. He kept pressing for the return of Estrella's equipment, and if he was trying to intimidate the mediators, Aramini said, "he had the wrong three guys in the room."

Crann was a no-nonsense Irishman raised on a no-nonsense side of Newark, a trooper who did bomb squad and underwater recovery work and who was part of the Ground Zero rescue operations after the Twin Towers fell. Bukowski had been an FBI agent in Florida, New York, and New Jersey who had investigated the 9/11 terrorists and two Paterson, New Jersey, men with alleged ties to the hijackers. And the 56-year-old Aramini, raised poor in the projects of Frank Sinatra's hometown, Hoboken, was a walking Hollywood script.

Aramini's old man worked three jobs to support a wife and six kids before he saved up enough pennies to buy a shot-and-a-beer place called the Seven Seas. Before he spent his entire adult life around cops and killers, Aramini spent years around the longshoremen and railroad workers who drank at his father's bar on Hudson and Third, where more than a few of the regulars would've eaten Mark Briggs for lunch. As a state trooper,

Aramini worked undercover to infiltrate the Genovese crime family and to bring dirty cops to justice. He wore a wire for more than 300 hours, and he was in countless situations where armed wiseguys and corrupt police officers could've shot him dead on the spot. He feared for his life 24/7, and never more so than the night the recording device attached to his leg ran out of tape after three hours and began making a noise that somehow wasn't detected by the mobsters in his midst.

So Briggs, New England's security man, was up against a tough crowd. "I'm a street kid," Aramini thought to himself at the time. "You're not getting over on me." So Briggs didn't get over on him, or any of the other law enforcement men in Aramini's civilian security office, near the state police office on the east side of the building. The Jets insisted that Aramini keep the camera and tape, and Aramini reminded Briggs that possession is nine-tenths of the law. If Briggs wanted New England's property, he was going to have to run an all-out blitz to retrieve it. "He'd have to tackle me across the desk to get it from me," Aramini said, "and that wasn't happening."

Briggs wouldn't relent. "He continued to say, 'You're stealing the camera that's being taken from me,'" Crann said, "and it's like 'No, no, that's not what's being done here.'" Crann advised Briggs that it was time to secure the device and hand it over to the NFL.

Bukowski placed the camera in a box and sealed it up. "We signed it across the tape and said, 'We're going to treat this just like evidence,'" the FBI man said. "And then we handed it right to the NFL." The half-hour meeting was over, and Davis drove the sealed box to the league's Park Avenue headquarters that night, according to the mediators.

Despite being warned by Mangini and the league memo both, Belichick appeared to have done the unthinkable and ordered Estrella to proceed with his standard game-day operations. Dan Leberfeld, of Scout.com, was the first to report on New England's alleged wrongdoing, and on his weekly Monday radio appearance with Boston's WEEI, Belichick said he'd been informed at the game about the incident and refused to comment on the particulars. "It's a league thing," he said. "Whatever the deal is, which I don't really know the details of it, a lot of it, we'll comply."

Greg Aiello, NFL spokesman, released a statement confirming a league investigation into the Patriots and informing readers and fans that all teams "have been specifically reminded in the past that the videotaping of an opponent's offensive or defensive signals on the sideline is prohibited." Players and coaches around the league started weighing in. Kerry Rhodes, Jets safety, offered that Tom Brady "seemed like he knew what we were doing." In San Diego, LaDainian Tomlinson said he thought the Patriots "actually live by the saying 'If you're not cheating, you're not trying.'"

Was Belichick really arrogant enough to think he could get away with illegal spying on the Jets, even though they were on to him and prepared to act? Roger Goodell would answer that question in short order. Meanwhile, many longtime NFL people were left shaking their heads or laughing, or doing a little bit of both. They knew that pro football had a long history of gamesmanship and outright cheating, and that Bill Belichick was guilty of his fair share of both.

Steve Belichick and Ted Marchibroda, football mentors to Bill Belichick, were fine gentlemen greatly influenced by Hall of Famers Paul Brown (Steve Belichick) and George Allen (Marchibroda). The sport's most accomplished innovator, Brown was forever seeking an edge as he introduced playbooks, written aptitude tests, film grading, and taxi squads to the game. In 1956, he made his Cleveland Browns quarterback, George Ratterman, the first NFL player to wear a radio device in his helmet, and he later warned the New York Giants that they'd be fined by the Federal Communications Commission if they jammed the signal. (The Giants had earlier intercepted the Browns' signal by using a high-powered receiver on their sideline.) After fielding complaints from teams that thought the gadget gave Cleveland an unfair advantage, the league outlawed coach-to-quarterback radio communication.

In his years with the Los Angeles Rams and the Washington Redskins, Allen built a reputation as a coaching rogue without peer. He was once rebuked by the league for trading the same draft picks to different franchises in different deals, an outrageous form of double-dipping that Allen said had merely been the result of an oversight in his hectic workday. Allen was famous for planting a spying scout in a hotel room overlooking the Dallas Cowboys' practice field, and for obsessing over the possibility that enemy operatives were bugging his locker room or sitting in nearby trees and spying on Redskins workouts.

George "Papa Bear" Halas, patriarch and coach of the Chicago Bears, was said to have had itching powder applied to the opponents' soap bars and to have had a trained dog at the ready to run onto the field in the event that the Bears needed an extra timeout. Halas worried about Allen's spying, and Brown was concerned enough about Halas potentially taping his conversations in the visitors' locker room in Chicago that he talked to his quarterback in the showers. (Brown also checked the windows at his practice facility to make certain nobody was shooting unauthorized film.) Vince Lombardi of the Green Bay Packers fretted over the possibility that Halas spied on his practices; Lombardi had his players switch jerseys in an attempt to deceive the deceivers. In 1934, Halas's 13-0 Bears lost the NFL championship and an 18-game winning streak because the New York Giants put on sneakers at halftime—courtesy of the Manhattan College basketball team—to give themselves a huge advantage over a visiting team that might as well have been wearing skates on the frozen Polo Grounds field.

Oakland Raiders overlord Al Davis forfeited a couple of draft picks in the early 1980s for illegally stashing players and ignoring the roster limit, and in the 1960s he masqueraded as a reporter when probing an opposing player for valuable information. If the Raiders had a fast team visiting, Davis made sure his grounds crew either watered the grass or let it grow high to slow down the track. The coach of the San Diego Chargers, Harland Svare, once was so certain the Raiders had bugged his locker room inside the Oakland Coliseum that he looked up at a ceiling light fixture and shouted, "Damn you, Al Davis. Damn you, I know you're up there." (Davis later said, through a smile, "The thing wasn't in the light fixture, I'll tell you that.")

Davis was well known for filming opponents and for signing players released by division rivals to pump them for information. He was also known for offering $500 for a copy of an opponent's playbook, according to a rival scout. One of Oakland's linebackers, Matt Millen, said Davis had a sign, "The Raider Rules," posted above the locker room door. "Raider Rule No. 1: Cheating is encouraged," Miller said of the sign. "Raider Rule No. 2: See Rule No. 1."

In January 1983, the most prolific NFL winner of all time, Don Shula, won the AFC Championship Game over the fleet New York Jets on an Orange Bowl field turned into a mud pit by torrential rain and the decision to leave the field uncovered. Shula correctly argued that the choice to use or not use a tarp wasn't his to make, as the Orange Bowl was run by the City of Miami. But Shula was one of the most revered figures in Miami and the entire sport. It's hard to believe that one phone call from him wouldn't have ensured that the field was covered.

In the mid-1980s, during the Giants' two playoff victories over the San Francisco 49ers, Bill Parcells thought Bill Walsh broke the rules in a vain attempt to secure an early edge. Walsh used to script his first 15 plays, and Parcells said that in both playoff games, San Francisco's headphones suspiciously stopped working, which forced the other team to discontinue using its phones. "Now, let me get this straight," Parcells said. "You've got your script rehearsed, you know what you're going to do, the defense doesn't know what's coming, but they have to take their phones off?"

Bill Belichick, an admirer of Al Davis, was merely a creature of this culture. Spying was all the rage around the NFL, and so was the filming of opposing coaches. Some league executives, scouts, and coaches weren't even sure what was allowed and what wasn't when it came to Sunday surveillance, and some football lifers almost yearned for the day when pushing the envelope was considered a virtue, not a vice. They found a certain romance in the old-school tricks of the trade.

"Remember the prison guy who snow-plowed the field in New England for that field goal?" said John Teerlinck, maybe the NFL's all-time best defensive line coach, recalling the 1982 Patriots' victory over Miami. "That's how the game used to be played. Parcells in Giants Stadium opening the tunnel for the wind . . . People have been cheating or bending the rules or trying to get an edge from day one."

A former defensive end with the San Diego Chargers, Teerlinck was part of Bud Carson's staff in Cleveland before Belichick arrived. He said that in a 1989 game against Cincinnati, Browns defensive tackle Michael Dean Perry wore a wireless microphone in his pads for what was supposed to be a TV piece on the sounds of pro football. "And they said it would only last a quarter," Teerlinck recalled. "It will get hit and knocked loose and the wires will come off. It was bargain-basement stuff that was jerry-rigged. At the time, Cincinnati was having that no-huddle with Sam Wyche and Boomer Esiason calling everything at the line. We played them, and guess what? After listening to the tape, we could match up and we knew every goddamn call they were making at the line of scrimmage. Every play, every audible, every snap count."

Teerlinck admitted that he was not above taking liberties with league regulations. He was once summoned to Commissioner Paul Tagliabue's office to answer for all the quarterbacks his 1996 Detroit Lions were injuring — especially on shots to their legs.

"We knocked five quarterbacks out in six weeks," he recalled, "and they couldn't believe the stuff we were doing. We had our jerseys tailored, our pads cut down. I took the numbers off the jerseys and made them silk-screen so the offensive linemen couldn't hold them. There are so many games within the game, people have no idea . . . The media and the league office are so goddamn naive; they're afraid in the league office to know how the sausage is made. If they knew, they'd shit."

Floyd Reese, longtime NFL coach and executive, was coaching in Houston when a stranger from another team approached him in an elevator, introduced himself, and revealed that he'd been trying to steal his signals for three years. Kevin Gilbride was a Houston Oilers assistant in 1989 when one of Houston's video guys approached him with a strange question. "How would it feel to be a movie star?" the staffer asked. Gilbride didn't know what the man was talking about until he explained that the Oilers' upcoming opponent, the Browns, would have a camera trained on Houston coaches as they sent in signals from the sideline. "They'll be filming you so the next time they play you they'll have our signals," the staffer told Gilbride, who was in his first year in the NFL after coaching 15 seasons in the college game and in the Canadian Football League.

It was apparent that plenty of NFL coaches were playing loose with the rules. Belichick's friend Jimmy Johnson said he'd been told by a Kansas City scout years earlier that the Chiefs were filming opponents. "I did it with video," Johnson would say, "and so did a lot of other teams in the league . . . A lot of coaches did it. This was commonplace." Johnson also said that some NFL coaches "have selective amnesia, because I know for a fact there were various teams doing this."

Veteran scout and personnel man Dom Anile, first hired by Browns coach Sam Rutigliano in the early 1980s and later promoted by Belichick, was considered one of the better spies in the business. "I guess everybody cheats to some degree," he said. "You cheat and push the envelope until it's almost over the edge, and you hope to stay within the rules."

Hope. Anile studied tapes of an upcoming opponent to identify its signal caller, and then he'd attend that team's game on the Sunday before it faced the Browns. Anile didn't want to scout from the press box, the place everyone went to spy, so he'd enter the stadium and try to find a seat in the stands facing that signal caller. If it was a full house on a particular day, Anile had to get creative. One day at a packed Giants Stadium, desperate to find a seat that would give him a clear look at the coach in question, Anile approached a man with a young son at a hot dog stand, told the man he was a *Sports Illustrated* writer doing a story on NFL spying, and offered him $100 if he'd be willing to put his son on his lap and give Anile the boy's seat. Anile told the father he'd have his notebook and tape recorder out all game, so he needed to be left alone in exchange for that $100. The man took the deal, and the spy went to work.

Anile was working for the Browns' coach, Marty Schottenheimer, with offensive line coach Howard Mudd acting as the buffer. "Marty knows I'm doing this and likes the idea I'm doing it, but wants nothing to do with it," Anile recalled. "He turns it over to Howard. I would go back to Howard and sit down and go over the game with him . . . I would make stick figures for Howard to describe what I was seeing. I'd describe down, distance, the ball is here, and a coach would make like a Pac-Man move, clasping his hands together. And Howard would take all that information I gave him and go look at the tape of the game I saw and see that down and distance and the time I gave him. He may not have seen the guy on the film, but he knew what was a Pac-Man-designation play.

"What we looked for," Anile continued, "was a home-run ball, center field being vacated at the snap of the ball for whatever reason when they were going to blitz. Some guys around the league were doing this with cameras. I was working my tail off with a tape recorder doing this. Howard Mudd came to me on days the Browns were not playing, and we'd sit somewhere in the stands during a Cincinnati Bengals game . . . Howard was on the sideline on game day watching that guy across the way, and when he saw the Pac-Man figure, he knew there would be a vacant center field . . . The center would let [Bernie] Kosar know, and he would check off to any play we had to a center field pass. We would hit home runs all the time."

Anile described the signal caller's every motion on his tape recorder, and on Mondays he turned his information over to the coach assigned to make sense of it all. The coach matched up the opponent's Pac-Man signal with an empty middle of the secondary and presented it to Schottenheimer. During the game, the Browns' center looked to his sideline for the signal for zero coverage, and when he received it, he passed it on to Kosar through a sign or a word. The quarterback then alerted his wide receiver the same way. "And all of a sudden," Anile said, "six on the board. Boom, just like that."

Other scouts were known to pay scalpers for seats in the stands so they wouldn't be seen in the press box by fellow scouts and spies, and their intel was invaluable to a capable quarterback. Ernie Accorsi was working with the Baltimore Colts in 1977 when they used an administrative assistant to read lips to help them win the AFC East title. Bob Colbert was the former head coach at Gallaudet, a university serving the deaf and the hearing-impaired, and he had lip reading down to an art and a science. The Colts were playing the New England Patriots in the final regular-season game, and they needed a victory to finish 10-4 and win the divisional tiebreaker.

Down 24–10 in the third quarter, Baltimore faced a third-and-18 from its own 22-yard line when Colbert used binoculars to read the lips of Patriots assistant Hank Bullough from the press box. "Delayed double-safety blitz. Delayed double-safety blitz," Colbert saw Bullough call out to the New England defense. The lip reader relayed that call down to a coach, who relayed it to Colts quarterback Bert Jones, who then found Raymond Chester for a 78-yard touchdown. The Colts won the game, 30–24.

"From the films," Jones fibbed afterward, "I knew that Chester should be open down the middle if I could get the ball away. That was all there was to it."

Jones's former Baltimore colleague Bill Belichick was an active participant in the rampant rule-bending and rule-breaking going on in the NFL while he was coaching the Browns. One of his defensive starters said that a Cleveland staffer filmed signals and had an assistant coach on the side-line who "would put a certain hand up, and he had three or four wristbands on. That would mean we got the play and they'd send it in." This defensive starter said the signal was relayed to the Mike (or middle) linebacker, who then checked the defense into a proper alignment. Sometimes the Cleveland coaches were right, and sometimes they were dead wrong. On one play his coaches mistakenly thought they'd decoded against the Steelers, the Browns' starter said, a Pittsburgh offensive lineman blasted him into next week.

"He almost took my life on one play," the player said. "We thought we had their call on film, and they did something totally different . . . Belichick was filming in Cleveland, and without a doubt other teams were doing it, too. Everybody was doing it. I can tell you right now, in 1993 and '94, we were trying to pick up stuff. It was done through a VHS camera in the stands. I don't know who did it, but I know we got some signals . . . I would be at places and see guys filming, and they had the nerve to have an Oakland Raiders shirt on, looking at us and our coach from the stands. And I'd be like *These guys don't look like fans. They're putting a camera on us. Fans just tape. Fans don't shoot a play, put the camera down, and write down notes.* You could tell espionage from a mile away if you had half a brain."

Belichick asked one of his Browns scouts to attend a preseason game between the Giants and the Jets, and to keep working after the game was over, according to a Cleveland staffer with knowledge of the assignment. Belichick told the scout to wait for the Giants and Jets coaches to vacate their booths and then to enter them and "see if you can find anything in the garbage can." This was in line with a 1992 Marla Ridenour story in the *Columbus Dispatch* in which a Giants scout explained how Belichick had attended a playoff game with him and personally picked through garbage cans in the winners' and losers' booths for leftover material after the coaches had left. "We went home with two garbage bags," the scout said.

Belichick always believed that the espionage game was played on a two-way street. In 1991, with his 4-4 Browns preparing to play the 0-8 Bengals, Belichick announced that he was closing practice to the media and suggested that Cincinnati had gotten its hands on some classified Cleveland information. The Browns had beaten the Bengals 14–13 on a late Matt Stover field goal in September. "I just can't explain some of the things that happened in that game," Belichick said.

But his own dirty tricks inspired the league to summon a Cleveland executive to New York to answer for various suspected infractions, according to a Browns official, including stashing allegedly healthy players on injured reserve and preventing league checkers from having full and immediate access to his team. One Cleveland official questioned Belichick about his roster size in camp after realizing that, by his own count, the Browns were two or three players over the limit. Belichick told the official that it wasn't true and that he shouldn't worry about it. "I learned not to ask him about it anymore," the official said.

One prominent Browns player said that Belichick was "the master of stashing guys" who were healthy on injured reserve as a means of keeping them away from other teams. This was a fairly common practice around the league among coaches who saw potential in certain players but didn't have room for them on their rosters. One Browns source said that Belichick also had a way of outfoxing league checkers sent to camps to make sure teams were complying with roster limits and were not using players on IR in practice. The source said there was a time when Belichick decided practice jerseys should be just brown and white, with no assigned numbers to identify the players. At first the source thought this was a way of keeping information from the news media.

"But I figured out that when the league sends checkers to make sure injured reserve guys aren't practicing—and we had extra players at the time than you're allowed—that's why he did it," the source said. "So the league checker would go out to the field and he'd have a roster with numbers, and the deal in the NFL is you can't hesitate when a checker comes. He IDs himself, gives a badge, and goes right to the practice field. He gets a roster, and there are no numbers on our jerseys. He's trying to count. Seven guys go into the training room, five guys come out. Eight guys go into the training room, four guys come out. Pretty soon we quickly had numbers on our jerseys."

The league still embraced a Wild West mentality when it came to honor and sportsmanship, or lack thereof, through the 1990s, and Belichick wasn't about to be outgunned. "If the possibility of an advantage is greater than zero, we're going to do it," one of Belichick's players said. "The extent of how great the advantage is meaningless . . . The way he views the rules, in my opinion, is how you view the tax laws. You're going to interpret them as much in your favor as you can. And if the IRS comes knocking, you might be wrong, but you tried your best."

"I don't think Bill Belichick believes in cheating," one of his scouts said. "I got to know his dad a bit. That's not how he was raised in the game. But he was raised to know how to use rules to his advantage, and he does that better than anyone in the league."

On arrival in New England in 2000, Belichick had a staffer videotape the coaches' signals from the enemy sideline, and he had his personal mad scientist, Ernie Adams, study the filmed signals and match them up with the opponent's plays that had been dissected by Patriots scouts. From the press box, Adams had a direct line to Belichick down on the field. Though coaches on the sideline could communicate to quarterbacks via their helmet radio devices — introduced in 1994 — up until 15 seconds remained on the play clock, reducing the need for hand signals and the dummy cards with strange drawings and sayings prevalent in the college game, no defensive players were allowed to use such audio equipment. (New England was among the teams to vote against a proposal to allow one defensive player on each team the same radio device used by quarterbacks.) So if Adams recognized an opponent's defensive signal from a past game and relayed that information to the sideline in time for an adjustment, the Patriots could carry a significant competitive advantage into that play.

Over time, teams became aware of the Patriots' practice of taping their coaches, including the division rival Buffalo Bills, who defeated New England 31–0 in the 2003 season opener before losing the season finale at Gillette Stadium by the same score. New England had used a no-huddle offense in that second game, forcing Buffalo's defensive coaches to signal in their calls quickly and, at least theoretically, giving Tom Brady time to wait for his coaches to intercept those calls based on their surreptitious film work and then relay them to him before the snap. Brady had no touchdowns and four interceptions in the loss to Buffalo, and he had four touchdowns and no interceptions in the victory over Buffalo. Bledsoe was an abysmal 12 for 29 passing, for 83 yards, in the second game, and he was sacked three times and intercepted once before being replaced. As Bills offensive coordinator Kevin Gilbride was walking off the field that December day the season ended in a heap, he heard Bledsoe tell a New England player, "Man, you guys were great. It was like you knew just what we were doing." According to Gilbride, the New England player responded, "We did. We had you on film."

Two teams that had employed Belichick, the Giants and the Jets, were also aware of New England's taping, and of the ever-spreading rumors that scouting reports and play sheets were suddenly disappearing from the visitors' locker room in Foxborough or were being pulled out of conference room trash cans in the visitors' hotels. (Jimmy Johnson, a Belichick friend, admitted to instructing an intern to search trash cans when he coached.) NFL teams had come to see the Patriots' stadium the way NBA teams — especially the Los Angeles Lakers — used to see the old Boston Garden, where Red Auerbach was often accused of conducting some interesting plumbing and heating experiments in the enemy locker room. If nothing else, the Auerbachian effect on NFL teams worrying about Cold War tactics in Foxborough — real or imagined — likely showed up on the field. Any time spent chasing ghosts was time not spent preparing for Brady and the New England defense.

Herm Edwards, who coached the Jets from 2001 through 2005, was told by team officials that the Patriots were certainly filming him during games. "When you go to New England, I'm always on the 50-yard line, right?" Edwards said. "And I was like 'OK, if you think they're doing that, guys, we'll shuttle players in and out. That's easy.'" Before a game with the Patriots started, Edwards waved at a would-be Patriots camera across the field after the playing of the national anthem. "I don't know if they were filming me or not," he said. "But OK, I'd wave. And if you got me, OK, wave. But some coaches were paranoid about that. I wasn't.

"I knew this: You never left anything anywhere," Edwards continued. "Any building in the league, not just theirs. I always told the players, 'Make sure before you go out on the field, don't leave anything in this locker room that has anything to do with the game plan.' But you hear all this stuff with the Patriots. I never got involved in all that stuff. I just coached. Just coach your frickin' team.

"It was no different than when you went to go play the Raiders. If you had a walk-through on a Saturday at their place, shit, let me tell you something. You had guys up on the hills. It was 'Hey, man, you make sure . . . that there wasn't someone in the building filming you.' This was the Raiders, so that's what you thought. For me, it was laughable . . . But I think [Belichick's] been good in the sense of you have to be buttoned up. You've got to know 'Hey, man, there's something coming that you'd better be ready for, and when it comes, you'd better be able to adjust.'"

Westhoff, the Jets' special teams coach, said New York had issues with headphones malfunctioning in Foxborough at inopportune times during games — a common Gillette Stadium complaint made by visiting teams. Like Edwards, Westhoff was forever reminding the Jets under his watch to tuck away all notes and game plans before taking the field for warm-ups. The special teams coach delivered that reminder in every NFL stadium. "But always in New England," he said. "You'd better not leave it anywhere, but you really don't ever leave it there . . . All that miscellaneous bullshit, to me it's exactly that. They were a good, well-prepared football team . . . I respected everything they did. But they are doing this crap, what the hell for? To give Ernie Adams something to do? It's ridiculous. If they were doing that, Spygate, that's a bigger advantage than anybody knows. If they're filming and dissecting what the coordinator is doing, a signal, wow, that's a big advantage. A gigantic one."

Before Spygate broke, the Giants had played New England in six preseason games and one regular-season game since their former assistant,

Belichick, took over the Patriots, and the organizations had a certain respect and fondness for each other. Plenty of good football people had spent time working for both franchises, and deep down, in a place he couldn't reveal for public consumption, Belichick still thought of himself as a Giant. He admired the owning Mara family, adored nearly everything about Giants Stadium, and respected the franchise's historical standing in the league.

But the Giants also knew that Belichick wouldn't be filming their coaches for the sentimental value of a this-is-your-life video. Ernie Accorsi was about to start his final season as Giants GM in the late summer of 2006 when he was told that a New England video staffer had likely filmed Giants coaches in their final preseason game. "I was impressed they thought we were good enough to do that to," Accorsi said. "I was told he was doing it because he suspected we might be playing them [in the Super Bowl]. Somebody said something to Ray Anderson, who was in that VP-of-football-ops job, and he had said something to me. So I don't know if they were looking into it that night, but I'd heard it."

Six days later, Ray Anderson wrote the league letter to all teams reminding them that videotaping an opponent's signals on the sidelines is not permitted. "I didn't realize taping a coach's signals was illegal," Accorsi said. He wasn't the only member of the Giants' front office unaware of that rule; in fact, there were plenty of NFL executives, coaches, scouts, and players who weren't sure what was and wasn't allowed when it came to the century-old sporting tradition of stealing signs. And that's where Belichick and Adams seized opportunities, in the gray areas separating perception and reality.

The Giants had direct intel on the Patriots' videotaping operation, according to one team official who didn't think the illegal filming amounted to a big deal. The same official was more concerned about the possibility of a Patriots operative swiping something out of the Giants' locker room in Foxborough. "We were very conscious of that," the official said. "So we absolutely don't leave any practice scripts or game plans around the locker room. A lot of times you go there and the headset on the sideline goes out during the game, and we can't even communicate with people in the press box. We were getting air traffic control. We were hearing everything except what we were supposed to hear, and we weren't the only ones."

In January 2006, Jacksonville head coach Jack Del Rio said his team's coach-to-quarterback communication system had "mysteriously malfunctioned the entire first half" of a 28–3 playoff loss in Foxborough that saw Jaguars quarterback Byron Leftwich hit with two delay-of-game penalties in that first half. One longtime official from another team that faced New England in the postseason said that walking into Gillette Stadium felt very much like walking into a trap. "I can't remember the last time you ever went into a room up there and felt it was a secure area," the official said. "When you walk into the building, you assume not everything is aboveboard. I can't remember when I didn't feel that way about that place. You just know when dealing with that outfit, and I'm not even calling it cheating. You know if there's a way to push the envelope to the absolute edge, that's what they're going to do.

"You also know the coach is an extremely intelligent, innovative guy in terms of his football sense," this official continued. "You never underestimate that opponent. You're talking about a smart guy willing to do anything to achieve the ultimate objective: to win. He'll push the envelope and ask questions later. He's not going to ask questions up front. He'll rely on his own instincts and intelligence and then later say, 'This is the rule. This is how I interpreted it.'. . . Your antennae go up more in certain places, and they don't go up any more than they do in New England. They just don't . . . You make sure you don't leave anything behind there, that's for sure."

Peyton Manning was so fearful that Patriots operatives might've bugged the Indianapolis Colts' locker room in Foxborough that he moved all conversations about strategy into the hallway — a seemingly extreme precaution that his coach, Tony Dungy, said was at least partly shaped by his quarterback's conversations with former Patriots players. An executive with another AFC team said he didn't believe New England ever planted a listening device in enemy territory at Gillette Stadium, but that his team was forever on guard when it played the Patriots in their building. "We take precautions," the executive said. "We do it at a lot of away games. We try to bring as many of our own people as possible. You hear a lot of stories over the years [with the Patriots]. If your team is out for pregame, people could look through playbooks and play sheets for the first 20 plays of games . . . Yes, our antenna is up more in Foxborough than anywhere else." The executive said that the rumor that concerned him most involved a Patriots staffer entering the visitors' locker room and using the nearest copy machine to "copy the opposing team's first 20 plays on offense. And then in the game, Belichick, he's calling out what you do. 'Here comes a reverse. Here's a screen.' How he gets the plays, I don't know."

For all the fears, rumors, stories, and concerns, no Patriots employee was ever publicly identified by the league as having been caught entering another team's locker room to steal or copy game-related information, an act that would likely require the cooperation of stadium security personnel stationed at the doors. (The league didn't respond to a request for confirmation that no Patriots employee had ever been privately disciplined or reprimanded for stealing or copying information from an opponent.) New England was caught illegally videotaping opposing coaches in 2006, ignored the written warnings from the league and the verbal warnings from Mangini's Jets, and in September 2007 finally drew the wrath of the NFL and Commissioner Roger Goodell, who had succeeded Paul Tagliabue a year earlier. Goodell had already established himself as a law-and-order sheriff with a new personal conduct policy designed to come down hard on players who ran afoul of the law and embarrassed the league, including Atlanta Falcons superstar Michael Vick, who was suspended for his role in a dogfighting ring.

Spygate wasn't the same kind of case. No felonies were committed, and no prison time was imposed. This was about the integrity of the competition, and whether the Patriots had cheated on their way to becoming the sport's most successful franchise. Mangini had told people in the Jets' organization that the Spygate operation was conducted by "a closely held circle of people," that the Patriots were "really careful with their signal callers," and that low-level staffers reported straight to Adams when they were done filming. Mangini knew enough about the videotaping, and he'd just hired as his quarterbacks coach Brian Daboll, a Belichick aide since 2000 who was upset after being bypassed by fellow wonderboy Josh McDaniels, New England's offensive coordinator, whom Daboll had helped bring into the organization. Mangini also had on staff Steve Scarnecchia, son of Patriots assistant Dante Scarnecchia and a New England video staffer from 2001 to 2004, and Jay Mandolesi, who had been a New England video intern.

So, yes, the Jets were ready for the Patriots to cheat on that fateful day. "We were definitely looking for them to do it," one team official said. Mangini used multiple signal callers, including coaches sending out dummy calls, and got blown out anyway. But when Matt Estrella was caught filming from the sideline, Belichick immediately became the day's biggest loser. League officials essentially told the home team to stay out of it, that this wasn't just another Jets–Patriots dustup, and to let them handle the investigation. Surprised that Belichick had exposed his program against such ominous risk/reward odds, Mangini and the Jets said next to nothing about that investigation and moved on to their next opponent, the Baltimore Ravens.

Three days after the game, Belichick released a statement that said, "Although it remains a league matter, I want to apologize to everyone who has been affected, most of all ownership, staff, and players. Following the league's decision, I will have further comment." He then appeared at his usual Wednesday news conference and, after being blitzed by Spygate questions, pleaded for the gathered reporters to ask about his upcoming game with San Diego. He answered questions on the Chargers for ten or 15 minutes and batted away another Spygate query before the session ended.

The following day, after only four days of deliberations, Goodell announced that he was fining Belichick $500,000 (the maximum under the league's constitution, and a considerable chunk out of his reported $4.2 million salary), fining the team an additional $250,000, and taking away the Patriots' 2008 first-round draft choice if they made the playoffs, or their second- and third-round picks if they did not. Belichick's fine was the largest for a coach in NFL history, and the decision marked the first time a team had been sanctioned for videotaping signals and the first time a team's top draft pick was seized as part of a penalty.

"I specifically considered whether to impose a suspension on Coach Belichick," Goodell wrote in his letter to the Patriots. "I have determined not to do so, largely because I believe that the discipline I am imposing of a maximum fine and forfeiture of a first-round draft choice, or multiple draft choices, is in fact more significant and long-lasting, and therefore more effective, than a suspension."

Goodell concluded that Robert Kraft had no knowledge of the systematic cheating, and that the illegal taping had been stopped sufficiently early in the Jets game that it had no impact on the result. "This episode," the commissioner wrote, "represents a calculated and deliberate attempt to avoid longstanding rules designed to encourage fair play and promote honest competition on the playing field."

In response, Belichick released a statement saying he accepted "full responsibility for the actions" that led to the ruling and apologizing to the Kraft family, the fans, and everyone associated with the Patriots "for the embarrassment, distraction and penalty my mistake caused." Belichick reminded everyone in his statement that Goodell had acknowledged in his ruling that New England's sideline filming "had no impact on the outcome of last week's game. We have never used sideline video to obtain a competitive advantage while the game was in progress.

"Part of my job as head coach is to ensure that our football operations are conducted in compliance of the league rules and all accepted interpretations of them. My interpretation of a rule in the constitution and bylaws was incorrect."

Belichick said he would not offer additional comment on the ruling, and that was OK. Players and coaches who had been vanquished by the Patriots were speaking for him. Goodell didn't penalize New England for cheating in previous seasons, nor did he say he had evidence implicating the Patriots in past transgressions. But there wasn't anyone outside Massachusetts, New Hampshire, Maine, Vermont, Rhode Island, and Connecticut who believed this was a one-time offense. "They cheated; there should be an asterisk," said Steelers linebacker Joey Porter. Reno Mahe, a running back and special teamer on the Philadelphia team that lost a Super Bowl to New England after the 2004 season, said, "I think they should forfeit, man. We won the Super Bowl." Though Eagles safety Brian Dawkins, six-time Pro Bowler, didn't go quite that far, he did wonder aloud if his team had been duped out of a ring. "It's troublesome," Dawkins said. "There are obviously going to be questions about what happened. Yeah, it would bother me. The things they were able to do against us in that second half . . . I was giving them a whole bunch of credit for making halftime adjustments."

Philadelphia's defensive coordinator, Jim Johnson, among the best in the business, had attacked the Patriots with a series of blitzes, and the Patriots handled those blitzes with the greatest of ease. With the Eagles holding a 7–0 lead in the second quarter and with New England backed up to its own 13, Johnson ordered up back-to-back blitzes that were answered by Brady screen passes to Corey Dillon. The first screen was good for 13 yards and a first down, and the second was good for 16 yards, a first down, and a Joe Buck description on Fox as "a perfect call." People on the Philadelphia sideline grew suspicious as New England kept answering blitzes with screens. "There's no question they had our defensive signals," said one Eagles official, who didn't know if the signals were deciphered legally or otherwise. Steve Spagnuolo, linebackers coach, later said that Johnson firmly believed New England had decoded his team's signals and that two signal callers instead of one was a necessity when facing the Patriots.

Just about every former and current NFL coach copped to stealing signals, and to inspiring their counterparts across the field to cover their mouths with their play charts when giving a directive. Years later, Hall of Fame cornerback Deion Sanders would accuse Tony Dungy, a statesman of the game, of serial sign stealing, and Dungy didn't deny it. He said sign stealing had been going on in baseball since as far back as the 1800s, and that it was an accepted and natural part of sports. Sideline videotaping for the purpose of swiping signs? That was the illegal part, and, though many believed that other NFL teams participated in unlawful filming into the 2000s, it was widely thought that New England was the only franchise to continue the practice after the NFL's two written warnings.

So Dungy, no fan of Belichick's, likened the Patriots to record-breaking slugger Barry Bonds, who was hounded by steroid suspicions. The Steelers, who had lost two AFC title games at home to New England, were about as angry over the revelations as any NFL team. Receiver Hines Ward said he was certain the Patriots had cheated in their AFC Championship Game victory in Pittsburgh following the 2001 season. "They were calling our stuff out," Ward said.

In the first quarter of Pittsburgh's second AFC title-game loss to New England at Heinz Field, the Steelers went for it on a fourth-and-one at the

Patriots' 39. Jerome "the Bus" Bettis, Pittsburgh's 252-pound back, took the handoff and ran smack into the brick wall that was the New England defense, fumbling as he fell short of a first down. At least one Patriot defender on the field thought Belichick must've had advance intel on the Steelers' play, as the coach had a message relayed to his noseguard that he wanted him to shoot the gap left, to the center's right — precisely where Bettis was heading, behind the Steelers' guard who had pulled from the left. "How did he fucking know?" the Patriot said. "He called the perfect thing." On the very next snap, Brady hit Deion Branch for a 60-yard touchdown.

Everyone who had ever lost a big game to Belichick's Patriots was asking serious questions. Jacksonville defensive end Paul Spicer, a postseason loser to New England after the 2005 season, suggested that the NFL treat the Patriots the way the NCAA treats rule-breaking schools and put them on probation "and kick them out of the playoffs." The Rams (who lost to the Patriots in Super Bowl XXXVI) and the Panthers (Super Bowl XXXVIII) were upset and wondering if they'd been had. Ricky Proehl played for both teams and scored the tying fourth-quarter touchdowns in both Super Bowls. The St. Louis loss was more devastating than the Carolina loss, because the Rams were heavily favored and would've gone down as one of the great teams in league history. Proehl wasn't sure if he was cheated out of that distinction, but the Patriots did have staffers witness (but not videotape) the Rams' Saturday walk-through and did play a near-flawless game. "Definitely there were times we were like 'God, they really are in our huddle,'" Proehl said. "They had the perfect defense for where they needed to be. Where we would throw it, they were there."

Jets quarterback Chad Pennington, who had great respect for the Belichick-Brady Patriots, stopped short of saying the videotaping had provided them a significant advantage. "I think the right phrase is, it creates a more consistent advantage," Pennington said. "You still have to execute, but in our league the talent is so close, and for teams like New England who have been fantastic at playing with average NFL talent and getting great NFL results, that can become a great advantage. So even though you still have to have that execution, those small things can really separate teams in the NFL, because . . . these games come down to minuscule mistakes. It's different from a college or high school game, because the talent and preparation level is so high. So it's certainly an advantage. It's not the only reason a team wins, but it doesn't hurt."

If Belichick deserved the benefit of the doubt before Spygate, he'd surrendered it forevermore. Many prominent NFL figures and voices thought Belichick should've been suspended and didn't buy Goodell's rationale for not putting the coach on the bench. The prevailing thought in competing front offices? The commissioner had cut a break to Robert Kraft, an influential supporter who had endorsed his candidacy to replace Tagliabue. Many were also outraged that Belichick never answered material questions about his Spygate methods, and about the number of games and teams he improperly videotaped over the years. As it turned out, the commissioner was among the outraged. Years later, he'd tell *Sports Illustrated*'s Peter King that Belichick had assured him he'd apologize and hold himself more accountable than he did in his prepared statement, which focused too much on his alleged misinterpretation of a rule and the notion that the alleged misinterpretation hadn't helped him beat the Jets.

"I was given assurances that he would tell his side of the story," Goodell said. "He went out and stonewalled the press. I feel like I was deceived."

When the Patriots played San Diego the Sunday night after the penalties were announced, Belichick was treated to a standing ovation from the Gillette Stadium crowd. A franchise that was once barely an afterthought in the market had won enough to challenge the Red Sox for Boston-area supremacy and to develop a fan base with the passion and blind loyalty of those in the biggest college towns in America, and Belichick, who had just received a contract extension through 2013, was the people's choice. The Patriots won one for the skipper, prevailing by a 38–14 count for the second straight week, and in the locker room afterward the players came together in a huddle. "Bruschi would lead the postgame cheer," said Chad Brown, a linebacker in his 15th season, "and it was always 'How do we feel about blah-blah?' and the whole team would say, 'Aww, yeahhhh.' That Sunday, Bruschi said, 'How do we feel about kicking butt and having the greatest coach in the league?' And he got one of the loudest 'Aww, yeahhhhs' all year from us."

Brown had played for Pittsburgh and Seattle before first arriving in Foxborough in 2005, and Super Bowl champions Bill Cowher and Mike Holmgren were among his coaches. "I played in the NFL 12 years before I became a Patriot," he said, "and I think I learned more about football in year 13 than in the previous 12 years combined." Besides, the longtime linebacker said, he had firsthand knowledge of some of pro football's most prominent figures bending or breaking the rules. "I know very few athletes and coaches who have not pushed things to the line repeatedly," Brown said. "I know Hall of Famers who put silicone on their jerseys. Jerry Rice, I played with in Seattle. Maybe the greatest football player of all time. He used stickum."

After beating the Chargers in the first game of the rest of his coaching life, Belichick called the crowd's response to him "awesome." This was a good night across the board. Tom Brady had thrown two more touchdowns to Moss, suggesting that they were about to terrorize the league, before giving the beleaguered Belichick a pat on the ass. "After everything that went on this week," Brady said, "we wanted to do our best for him."

Bruschi was most vocal in how the Patriots felt about their coach, and this moment. The linebacker had suffered a stroke a few days after playing in the 2005 Pro Bowl, and he shocked many in the medical and football communities by returning to play a little more than eight months later. Bruschi was another Parcells guy turned Belichick guy. Belichick came to think of him as an exceptional player, not in terms of size and speed and physical talent but in terms of grit and reliability and intelligence — the things that separated the Patriots from the NFL pack. And Bruschi described this Week 2 victory as no less meaningful than the franchise's biggest postseason victories, because everything New England had accomplished was under siege.

But storm clouds were still gathering around the best coach in football. Fox's Jay Glazer had obtained a copy of the Matt Estrella tape and played it on the air; the video showed the Patriots' staffer shooting the hand signals of Jets coaches and then capturing the down and distance on the scoreboard. Glazer's colleague Terry Bradshaw, a four-time Super Bowl champion with the Steelers, called Belichick a "cheater" who had hurt his team and his fans "all because of your arrogance." Goodell was demanding that the Patriots turn over all tapes and notes relevant to any illegal filming of signals that took place before the 2007 opener, and warning that he could increase the team's penalties if the league discovered that the Patriots hadn't been entirely truthful and transparent during the investigation. Asked if he'd turn over all additional materials, Belichick said, "Of course."

Reports surfaced suggesting that the Patriots might've been miking defensive linemen to steal quarterback audibles (other teams had been accused of the same), that they might've been using an alternate radio frequency in the coach-to-quarterback communication system to override the 15-second cutoff on the play clock (a league official was responsible for that cutoff), and that they might've contributed to the communication system breakdowns that were hindering visiting teams at Gillette Stadium. It seemed the sturdy walls of the Patriot program were closing in on its founding father.

The broadcasting of the Estrella tape inflamed the crisis, and Goodell sent three league representatives to Foxborough to determine once and for all the full scope of New England's videotaping operation. Two days later, on September 20, NFL spokesman Greg Aiello released this statement: "The Patriots have fully cooperated and complied with the requirements of the commissioner's decision. All tapes, documents and other records relating to this matter were turned over to the league office and destroyed, and the Patriots have certified in writing that no copies or other records exist. League policies on in-game videotaping and audio communication will continue to be closely monitored and strictly enforced with all 32 teams."

The commissioner found no evidence that New England had committed audio or communication system infractions. But the questions that owners, executives, coaches, and players leaguewide were asking were ones that Goodell didn't have satisfactory answers for. Why in the world did he destroy New England's tapes and notes? Shouldn't the teams that were victimized by the cheating have a chance to see them? Didn't NFL fans have a right to know exactly what the Patriots were doing to alter what was supposed to be a fair-and-square competition? How many games and seasons were affected? Were New England's three Super Bowl titles, won by a combined nine points, the product of brilliant coaching and playing or the result of fraud?

"Let everyone know what was on the tapes," said the Steelers' Porter. "Why would you destroy them so fast?"

Indianapolis Colts president and GM Bill Polian said the question of why the Spygate tapes and notes had been destroyed was ultimately raised at a competition committee meeting. "They said they felt it was best to do so, and everyone shrugged their shoulders and said, 'OK,'" Polian said. "In retrospect, almost immediately in retrospect, that probably was not the wisest course of action. I think those [teams] that were taped deserved to know what was done to them."

Like the vast majority of his peers, Polian rejected Belichick's assertion that he'd merely misinterpreted a rule, since the league had twice emphasized it within the 12 months preceding Spygate. "And the idea that boys will be boys and everybody does it was refuted as only Marv Levy could refute it, by saying, 'No, everybody doesn't do it.' I think that's the appropriate statement . . . We had every reason to believe we were one of the teams taped, and as a result we felt we had the right to know what had been done to us, the scope and nature of it . . . You could point to any number of games, but without knowledge of the tape, how and when it was done, there's no way exactly to know how much it affected us.

"It's a great advantage," Polian continued. "The irony is that the people who did it legally, and we were one of them; we were great at stealing signals, and it had a significant advantage. No doubt about it. We had our advance scout watch the signal caller — that was one of his duties — and if you do it manually . . . you record on a tape recorder what signal is given and then you watch to match it on tape, it's laborious work. It takes a lot of time and effort, and many times you're wrong . . . Nobody cared that they were trying to get other people's signals. Shame on us if we don't take precautions to cover them up. But the fact it was done in a way that was patently illegal is the issue. We don't even know if it was used in the same game. That remains unanswered, though they contend it wasn't."

Goodell said he destroyed the tapes and notes to ensure that New England could never again use them, and to ensure that no other tapes could end up in the hands of a network partner looking to air them. If another video surfaced, Goodell reasoned, he'd know that the Patriots hadn't fully complied with his instructions. The commissioner minimized the advantage a filming team had over its opponent and maintained that the tapes and notes recovered were consistent with what New England claimed was in its possession — another reason, he said, that they were destroyed.

It was hard to find many people who were buying Goodell's explanation. The commissioner clearly wanted to stuff this scandal inside a box, tape it up, and store it in the deepest, darkest corner of the league's attic so it was never again seen or heard from. It would be eight years before a pair of investigative reporters uncovered exactly what had happened when those three league representatives descended on Foxborough — what they found and how they disposed of it — as Goodell saw no reason to offer any more specifics than he had to. He liked the idea of being the NFL's answer to Clint Eastwood, and he could deal with Michael Vick's dogfighting and Pacman Jones' run-ins with the law. But he couldn't deal with the notion that his three-time championship team amounted to counterfeit goods. He couldn't deal with New York Giants pass rusher Michael Strahan comparing Spygate to the NBA gambling scandal involving referee Tim Donaghy.

Goodell had to make it go away. But very few people outside of New England wanted that to happen. Spygate raged on as a tsunami of a sports story, and the man who started it all, Eric Mangini, came to regret the toll it took on his former boss's standing in the game. The day he was hired by the Jets, Mangini said of Belichick, "He was my mentor, my teacher, and I consider him a close friend that I will have for the rest of my life." This was the same Belichick who had locked Mangini out of his own office as payback for taking a job offer he told his assistant he should decline. Their families had been close, and Belichick had given a reading at Mangini's wedding. Mangini gave his son Luke the middle name William in honor of Belichick. He didn't want to firebomb the most important relationship in his football life, but that was what he did — for keeps — the day he turned in the Patriots over a system of cheating that he had profited from.

"If Eric had turned them in against Team X — Dallas or the Miami Dolphins or someone else — that violates the line of loyalty and family secrets," said one Jets official. "However, the thing that people miss a bit, Eric was employed by the New York Jets, and he had a loyalty and responsibility to the team he was employed by. To do it in our stadium against us — Eric would not have been doing his job for us if he didn't alert us. It's that fundamental."

Belichick didn't speak another word to Mangini. He had more important relationships to rebuild anyway, like the one with the man who hired him. Robert Kraft sat his coach down and asked him how much the illegal taping had helped the Patriots on a scale of 1 to 100. "One," Belichick said.

"Then you're a real schmuck," Kraft responded.

Opponents were calling Belichick far worse names than that. Yet he had something at his disposal that none of his antagonists had. He had Brady and Moss and an offense ready to do to the league what the Chicago Bears' defense had done to it in 1985. More than anything, Belichick had a locker room's worth of players planning to clear his name by delivering the greatest season the NFL had ever seen.

15

IMPERFECTION

The night before his Patriots played their first post-Spygate game, against San Diego, Bill Belichick figured he needed to lighten the team's load. He liked to show his team epic boxing matches, among other great sports events from the past, but this time he wanted to try something different. He thought a Boston-area comedian named Lenny Clarke could loosen up his players after an extremely tense week, and Clarke was a hit.

"It was just exactly what the team needed at that moment," Chad Brown said. "He was very funny. He poked fun at Bill and Tom. No one was unscathed by this guy's jokes." Belichick had come a long way since his less mature days in Cleveland, where two exotic dancers were once brought in to entertain the team.

The coach had so much equity built up with his players, largely due to his relentless work ethic. Brown said he had played for coaches who were out the door and heading home by 6 p.m. Belichick? Brown had spent parts of three seasons with the Patriots, arriving early and staying late. He had a key card to the facility and was there at all hours trying to extend his distinguished career. He would be released and re-signed three different times in 2007, his final season, and through all his comings and goings, there was one figure he couldn't escape. "Only one time in all the times I went to the facility was Bill Belichick's car not there," Brown said. "And by the time I left, it was there."

The hours devoted to his craft, to finding that elusive edge, were why Belichick was coming up with things other NFL coaches weren't. For one, he deployed an interesting, commonsense approach to critical short-yardage situations when the Patriots were on defense. "Bill would say, 'Let's go for a Kodak moment here,'" Brown said.

"We're going to let the other team break the huddle, start their cadence, go in motion, and right before they snap the ball we're going to call a time-out. Fourth and one, third and one — there are only like three or four plays on the offensive coach's play sheet, and that situation is only going to come up a few times in the game. So chances are he called his best play for that situation. By taking this Kodak moment, we've now seen the personnel, the formation motion. We got all that information. We've taken away their best play ... We practiced that. 'Chad, you're calling signals in this part of practice. OK, Chad, we're going to have a Kodak moment here. Practice it. Call time out right before they snap the ball.'"

Belichick had different, behind-the-scenes ways to reach and inspire his players. Gemara Williams, undrafted free agent out of the University of Buffalo, said there was a reason why players who were troubled elsewhere (Randy Moss, Corey Dillon) immediately conformed to the culture in New England. Inside Belichick's office, Williams said, lived a man the media and the fans almost never saw at a podium. "You go into his office and he's one of the coolest guys ever," Williams said. "He's not afraid to be a person. He's not afraid to connect with his players outside of football. He'll joke with you and laugh with you and tell you stories about his personal life that relate to something you're going through. He shows you that human side of him."

Brown said the coach allowed linebackers with at least ten years of experience to have rocking chairs in the meeting room. When Belichick showed his players films of his great Giants defenses, he allowed them to respond with firm, good-natured jabs. "We always pushed back," Brown said. "We were like 'Come on, Bill, that guard is 265 pounds, and Harry Carson is 250. The guard I'm playing this week is 335. I know the structure and A-gap and B-gap, but I can't do what Harry Carson did there. My guy is 80 pounds heavier.'"

In the team facility's auditorium, before he worked the room with his ample supply of sarcasm and dry humor, Belichick often opened his meetings with New England's most recent transactions. One player explained, "He would say, 'We cut so-and-so this morning,' or 'We signed so-and-so and he's in the room now.' He would do it in such a business-attitude way. It doesn't matter who it was or how surprising the move was. And oftentimes, after transactions, he would have news clippings."

Sometimes these news clippings inspired a humorous anecdote or a rebuke at some poor Patriot's expense. One day during the 2007 preseason, Belichick jumped all over cornerback Brandon Meriweather, his No. 1 draft pick, for committing the first-degree felony of praising Wes Welker in print. Belichick started reading the quote from a printout before looking up at Meriweather and saying, "What the fuck do you know? You're a fucking rookie. Have you ever gone against Wes Welker? What do you know about Wes Welker?" The entire room erupted in laughter.

One player said that the coach warned the team to stay clear of the "trifecta." The player quoted Belichick as saying, "Drugs, pussy, and alcohol. Don't get caught up in the trifecta." One morning, Belichick opened a meeting with a little story about potential, and how it related to his stacked 2007 team, that one player paraphrased this way: "There's a dad speaking to his son, and he says, 'Hey, son, I want you to go in the other room and ask your mother if she would have sex with anyone in the world for a million bucks.' The kid says, 'Dad, are you sure?' And the father says, 'Yeah, go ask her.' So the kid goes in and says, 'Hey, Mom, Dad wants to know if you'd have sex with anyone in the world for a million bucks.' And she says, 'Hell, yeah, I would.' The son runs back and the father says, 'Go in the other room and ask your sister the same question.' So he goes in and asks his sister, and she says, 'Heck, yeah.' The kid goes back to his father and says, 'Dad, she said yes, too.' And the father says, 'Well, son, here's the difference between potential and reality. Potentially, we're sitting on two million bucks. But the reality is we're living with two whores." The room fell apart again.

The Patriots came to understand that Belichick's favorite three words were "What the fuck?" Those three words were often heard during the showing of lowlights on Monday mornings, when the coach trained his red laser on the filmed images of players who screwed up this or that. One such lowlight featured fullbacks Heath Evans and Kyle Eckel, who had blown blocking assignments on a punt and nearly allowed the kick to be blocked. Belichick stopped the film, put the red laser on Evans and Eckel, and summoned the name of his fellow Andover football nerd, Ernie Adams. "Here's Heath and Eckel," Belichick said. "Put me and Ernie in here for Heath and Eckel. Let me tell you right now: It might not be any better, but it couldn't be any fucking worse."

The players loved these biting reviews, at least when they were aimed at Patriots other than themselves. During one full-contact scrimmage, Gemara Williams ran back a kickoff 100 yards for a touchdown. When the Patriots watched the return in a pitch-dark film room, Moss made everyone crack up by shouting, "That motherfucker is fast." But Belichick wasn't laughing over the next scene — that of an exhausted Williams catching the next kickoff in the end zone and taking a knee.

"Belichick stops the tape," Williams recalled, "and he goes, 'What the fuck? If a guy wants to find a way to go home, this is how you do it.' He cut into me for a good five minutes straight. He was ripping me, but he was being funny, and everybody was laughing. Afterward some coaches told me, 'Hey, don't take it hard. It's just Bill being Bill.' I'll always remember that moment."

Belichick wasn't an unforgiving overlord looking for reasons to terminate people. One day during the regular season, Eckel, an undrafted free agent, woke up to a *Boston Globe* article that detailed allegations of alcohol-fueled misconduct at his alma mater, the Naval Academy, where Belichick had grown up. Eckel showed up to work that day certain he was going to be fired. He wanted to keep a low profile and to avoid his coach as much as possible, but sure enough, he ran into Belichick in a hallway. "He pulled me over and says, 'Don't worry about it. I've had much worse written about me,'" Eckel said. "He cracked a small smile. It felt like a thousand pounds were lifted off my shoulders . . . I was a special teams guy who came in at the end of games when we were up 40 so nobody else had to get hit. I can't imagine what those interactions with Coach Belichick do for guys who play every down and make big plays in big games."

The player-coach relationship in New England was as healthy as any in the sport. Belichick felt that one of his primary jobs was to protect his players from external forces, from distractions that could undermine the mission statement. One sign on the top of a team facility door read WHEN YOU LEAVE HERE, then listed four instructions next to small Patriot logos: DON'T BELIEVE OR FUEL THE HYPE . . . MANAGE EXPECTATIONS . . . IGNORE THE NOISE . . . SPEAK FOR YOURSELF.

On Spygate, Belichick needed the Patriots to ignore the noise like never before. He told his players that the case had nothing to do with them and that they should focus on their jobs and let him deal with it. "We come in after destroying the Jets," said Evans, "and Bill's like 'Hey, guys, this was my doing. You guys knew nothing about it. I take full responsibility for it, and we're moving on. I'm sorry for my part in this.' And then, boom, it was never mentioned again."

Donté Stallworth, another talented receiver brought in with Moss and Welker, heard it this way from Belichick: "He pretty much told us . . . that we didn't break any rules, that everything that happened was legal but it's under question from the league's point of view. From a legality standpoint, I think he wanted us to know that everything that happened up to that point was not illegal; it was more frowned upon . . . The way I understood it, there were no broken rules; maybe bent rules. He told us, 'Listen, this is what happened and I'm taking responsibility for it. This is all on me.'"

The Patriots went on their own revenge tour anyway. Chad Brown lived near Bruschi, and the two would carpool together and talk about the damage done to New England's reputation. Bruschi had come back from a stroke and surgery to repair a hole in his heart, and now he had to listen to people challenge the legitimacy of a program that he embodied. "It wasn't just Bill Belichick being slammed," Brown said. "Everything those guys had worked for and built up was being questioned."

The Patriots answered the doubts on the scoreboard. They put up 38 points for a third consecutive week, shredding Buffalo in the process. They were 5-0 before they scored 48 against Dallas, and then 49 against Miami, and then 52 against Washington in a ruthless 45-point victory that left some critics assailing Belichick for running up the score on his old NFC East rival Joe Gibbs. While holding a 38–0 lead and still instructing Brady to throw in the fourth quarter, Belichick went for it on fourth-and-one at the Redskins' seven. "What did you want us to do?" he asked. "Kick a field goal?"

Gibbs didn't complain about the margin of victory; the Redskins did say their headsets malfunctioned inside Gillette Stadium, the apparent home office for malfunctioning headsets. The Patriots didn't lose any sleep over it. They were 8-0 and averaging more than 40 points a game. They had outscored their opponents by 204 points, and Brady had thrown 30 touchdown passes (he'd never thrown more than 28 in a season) against two interceptions. These were no longer your big brother's Patriots, the franchise that won with great team defense, a great kicking game, and a clutch quarterback who elevated workmanlike receivers. Suddenly New England was a fast-breaking NBA team with scoring options all over the floor. The Patriots were the Golden State Warriors a decade before their time, and Brady was the kind of stat machine Peyton Manning had always been.

One New England newcomer, Kyle Brady, was in awe of what he was watching. The tight end had played 13 years with the Jets and Jacksonville and was ready to retire his beaten-down body before Belichick persuaded him to take one last shot at winning a ring. Before the 1995 draft, Brady had run through some agility and catching drills for a Cleveland contingent that included Belichick and Ozzie Newsome, and he called it the most thorough and vigorous workout he'd ever endured. Belichick would deny a report that he threw a phone against a wall in disgust after the Jets took Brady with the ninth pick, one spot ahead of the Browns.

Either way, coach and tight end had worked together with the Jets and now were working together again with the Patriots, who had loaded up for another strong Super Bowl run. This was exactly what Kyle Brady was looking for to close out his career. "It was certainly the most unique year of NFL football that I experienced," he said. "It was such an amazing team, such a dynamic offense. You almost felt like you were in college again, and at times we felt we were playing teams that couldn't even offer us a challenge, especially in the first half. Every college team plays the first few games against Division I teams that don't have the same level of talent or depth, and it's usually a runaway and you've got backups in by the second or third quarter and you're drinking Gatorade on the bench, having a good time. That's how it felt [in New England]. It was as if we were at a completely different level than other professional teams."

Of course, it all started with the other Brady. The quarterback had never played with anyone whose skills approximated those of Randy Moss. One of Moss's first moves as a Patriot was to ask for the locker right next to the quarterback. "I wanted to know when he's studying, what he's studying, what he's thinking," Moss said, "so on Sunday we kind of made it look easier. So during the week, we would come in 5:30, 5:45 in the morning, get our workouts in, and then I might have a few questions about the game plan. Or I might have a few questions about practice the day before. And it was just more of *We do not want to let one another down.* And he's had his accomplishments, his notoriety . . . and I had mine. So I didn't want to let him down, knowing he's Tom Brady."

Moss regularly destroyed defensive secondaries with his size, speed, and athleticism. He ran effortlessly, his long strides eating up so much ground. His ability to track a ball and catch it at the highest possible point was unlike any other receiver's on the planet. Watching him compete against smaller and less skilled corners, Kyle Brady said, "was literally like watching a dad playing against his sons."

And yet Tom Brady wasn't forcing it to his otherworldly receiver. In an earlier season, after watching the quarterback hit Deion Branch 50 times in 51 training-camp attempts against the New England defense, Belichick ordered him to avoid throwing the ball to Branch for the rest of the week and to start spreading it around to his other receivers. Brady had other talented options beyond Moss in Welker and Stallworth — especially Welker, all 5′9″ and 190 pounds of him. Moss was going long and Welker was going short, running option routes and dusting the linebackers and nickel backs assigned to cover him.

The Patriots weren't filming anyone from the sidelines, and every post-Spygate team on the schedule had to have changed its signals as a precaution anyway. And yet Belichick was embarrassing the league with what was effectively a college spread offense. He was putting Brady in the shotgun for about half of his snaps, more than any other quarterback in the league, and he was using one-back formations and turning the slot receiver position into a weapon that would change the way offense was played in pro football. With the help of Josh McDaniels, Belichick, a defensive coach, had actually developed into an offensive mastermind. He was using a no-huddle attack with at least three wideouts to stretch defenses and force favorable matchups that Brady could exploit.

Meanwhile, Eric Mangini's Jets were a pathetic 1-7. Belichick was settling all old scores. Though the Patriots were slowed down by the defending champion Colts in Indianapolis, Brady threw two touchdown passes to overcome a ten-point fourth-quarter deficit and allow his coach to give Dungy, a Spygate critic, a drive-by handshake that made Belichick's postgame meetings with Mangini look warm and cuddly by comparison. The

Patriots reportedly complained that the Colts might've pumped artificial noise into the RCA Dome (no evidence was found to support this), and Belichick said the team's coach-to-quarterback communication system didn't work for much of the game — if only to show that when it came to suggestions of dirty tricks, two could play that game.

New England came back from its bye week to rout Buffalo, 56–10, in a Sunday night game to move to 10-0 and drive the conversation about a perfect season into high gear. Don Shula's 1972 Miami Dolphins were the only undefeated Super Bowl winners, but NFL teams were playing 14-game regular seasons back then. New England had a shot to become the league's first 16-0 regular-season team and its first 19-0 champ. That meant New England had a shot to become the greatest NFL team of all time.

Of course, Belichick would never let his team publicly talk about a game, possession, or snap that wasn't right in front of it. But the Patriots were human. And human nature dictated that they were thinking about 16-0 and 19-0, especially if it came at the expense of a coach, Shula, who said their achievements were "tainted." Belichick knew that. So when Pittsburgh safety Anthony Smith handed him a short-term distraction from the long-term goal, Belichick jumped on it. Smith channeled Joe Namath and guaranteed that the 9-3 Steelers would beat the 12-0 Patriots, and New England did a slow burn over that. Belichick read the safety's words to his team, and the Patriots responded as the Patriots often did. "Well done is always better than well said — that's been the motto of this team," Brady said.

Enraged by Smith's arrogance, Brady threw for 399 yards and four touchdowns, including two on deep balls over the top of the safety. During the game, the quarterback screamed profanities right into Smith's face. Gillette Stadium fans responded to a shot of Smith on the video board with a chant of "Gua-ran-tee . . . Gua-ran-tee." After the Patriots won, 34–13, Belichick said, "We've played against a lot better safeties than him, I'll tell you that." Smith had reawakened the tiring Patriots, who had played three consecutive night games and were starting to wobble under the weight of their pursuit.

New England had needed a late interception to barely beat Eagles backup quarterback A. J. Feeley, and then a streak-preserving mistake by Baltimore defensive coordinator Rex Ryan, who called a pre-snap timeout and negated a defensive stuff of Brady on a late fourth-and-one stop that would've secured the upset. Anthony Smith's foolish guarantee helped carry New England deep into the season and into another triumph over the Jets, this one in the rain and snow and wind of Foxborough, where Belichick broke into a sideline smile before meeting with his excommunicated protégé. "Great game," he told Mangini. "Awesome." At 14-0, Belichick had bigger concerns than the 3-11 Jets. His team would beat Miami the following Sunday to set Belichick up for the ultimate regular-season game against the ultimate team in the ultimate building.

He was going for 16-0 against the Giants in Giants Stadium. Belichick grew emotional every time he set foot in that place. He admitted that walking down the ramp and into the tunnel of this ballpark was a lot different "than it is for any other stadium in the league for me." His heart wanted him to turn left, toward the home locker room, when he entered, though his brain forced him to turn right. As a Giants assistant, he'd weathered Bill Parcells, the players' disrespect in the early years, and the disapproval of George Young, the general manager who never thought he'd become a successful head coach. And now Belichick had returned a three-time champ, with a chance to do something no NFL head coach had ever done.

He showed how much a perfect season meant to him by playing Brady, Moss, and his starters despite the fact that he'd long ago clinched the No. 1 seed and home-field advantage in the playoffs. The Patriots felt a bit liberated during the week to talk about 16-0, simply because the Giants represented their 16th opponent. They felt liberated to talk about Belichick's body of work, too. Bruschi, a Patriot since 1996, called 2007 "probably the best year I have seen him have as a coach." The linebacker reasoned that Belichick had more distractions to manage than ever before, "and with every distraction that he has had, he's come through it stronger."

For his trouble, Belichick had made the cover of *Sports Illustrated* for its Year in Sports holiday issue; the magazine's creative design people put the coach — or the coach's frowning face — in a Santa Claus costume over the headline "Perfect Season's Greetings." It wasn't perfect yet. Belichick warned his players that the Giants would be as physical as any team they had faced, and that proved true at the end of the game's first possession, when 6'4", 256-pound running back Brandon Jacobs took a short pass from Eli Manning and ran over Bruschi on his way into the end zone. The 10-5 Giants had nothing of postseason consequence to play for, either — they'd already locked down the NFC's fifth seed — and yet their coach, Tom Coughlin, a former colleague of Belichick's on Bill Parcells's staff, decided to play the banged-up Jacobs and the banged-up receiver Plaxico Burress, along with everyone else, in an attempt to derail New England's historic bid.

It turned out to be a wild game before a charged Saturday night crowd and a TV audience treated to a three-way national simulcast. Beyond the team milestone, Brady needed two touchdown passes to break Peyton Manning's record of 49 in a single season, and Moss needed two touchdown receptions to break Jerry Rice's record of 22 in a single season — though Rice had set his mark in 12 games in a strike-shortened 1987. The Giants held a 28–16 lead in the third quarter before the Patriots took control.

Down five points early in the fourth, Brady threw up a second-down heave down the right sideline to a wide-open Moss, who had to come back to the ball before dropping it. On the next play, Brady threw up the same kind of heave down the same sideline to the same wide-open Moss, who caught the ball in stride for a 65-yard score that gave New England the lead for good. Brady had his record, Moss had his record, and, after adding another touchdown, the Patriots had set the record for points in a season, with 589, and for points differential: 315. Thirteen months after making an in-season change at Gillette Stadium from grass to a synthetic surface, and six years after upsetting the offensive juggernaut that was the St. Louis Rams, Bill Belichick's New England Patriots had become the Greatest Show on Turf.

The Giants followed a late touchdown with an onside kick that was recovered by a fitting Patriot, Mike Vrabel. The perfect Belichick player had preserved the perfect Belichick season. Wearing his gray hoodie and a look of relief and contentment, Belichick hugged players and assistants as the clock bled to zero. Before the game, Peyton Manning had told his kid brother, Eli, that the Patriots were beatable, and Eli damn near beat them. John Madden was so moved by the effort that he left a voicemail for Coughlin the next morning telling him the decision to go all in was "one of the best things to happen in the NFL in the last ten years." The Giants played the game angry, too, according to center Shaun O'Hara, who accused the Patriots' trash-talking safety, Rodney Harrison, of "cheap-shotting everyone." One thing O'Hara took from the game, he said, was the fact that "every single guy in our huddle couldn't wait to play them again. Because we couldn't wait to kick Rodney Harrison's ass."

In the wake of this regular-season classic, both teams showed immense respect for each other; the Patriots–Giants relationship was the opposite of the Patriots–Jets relationship. Mike Pope, the Giants' tight ends coach and a former colleague, hugged Belichick on the field and told him, "I'll tell you what, that's an incredible thing. Nobody does that. Nobody does that." Belichick passed Giants owner John Mara in the stadium corridor and told him they were certain to meet again in the Super Bowl. Mara thought Belichick was just assuming the role of gracious winner.

Kevin Gilbride, the Giants' offensive coordinator, was waiting in the tunnel to congratulate New England linebackers coach Matt Patricia, who was a friend and former Syracuse colleague of his son's, when Roger Goodell grabbed his hand and told him what a great game it had been for the league.

"He was the happiest guy in America," Gilbride said. After the commissioner walked off, Tom Brady approached Gilbride to express his respect for the Giants. "He has his entourage of bodyguards protecting him," the offensive coordinator recalled, "and he says, 'Coach, what a great game. And what about some of those things you did in the red zone?' I said, 'Tom, you think I'm going to tell you this stuff?' I didn't know him at all. He just came over. So I was thrilled he came over, but I wasn't going to discuss that. He just said, 'Tell Eli I said he had a great game,' and that was it."

If Brady was attempting to do some early reconnaissance in the event of a possible rematch in the Super Bowl, Belichick would have been proud. The Giants walked off the field that night believing they had outhit the Patriots and that they could beat them if given a second chance. New England seemed to be aware of that.

One of the casualties of Coughlin's decision to play the Patriots for real, O'Hara was standing in the Giants Stadium tunnel after the game with New England guard Dan Koppen, with whom he shared an agent. Koppen asked O'Hara about his injured knee before saying, "You guys are the best team we played all year."

"I hope we get another shot at you guys," O'Hara said.

"I hope not," Koppen responded.

Bill Belichick's work with the 2007 Patriots was staggering. In his previous three NFL seasons, Wes Welker had a total of 98 receptions and one touchdown; he had 112 receptions and eight touchdowns in his first year in New England. Tom Brady threw for 22 more touchdowns than his previous career high. And Randy Moss, who arrived as a neon advertisement for trouble, accepted every tenet of the Patriots' culture and gave Belichick more receiving yardage (1,493) than he'd given any other coach.

"I think why I have so much love for him, admiration and appreciation for him," Moss said, "is because he brought me back down to the reality of: Everything that I've accomplished up to that point means nothing. And it was kind of like I had to refocus myself. He helped me refocus, the team helped me refocus, and then magical things happened. So I think it was just more of he knows how to get more out of his players no matter what type of level — Pro Bowl, All-Pro, free agent, whatever. He knows how to get the best out of any guy."

Belichick hit Moss with so many questions in team meetings about the defenses he was about to face, the receiver said, "it was like you couldn't study enough . . . When he starts talking, 80 to 90 percent of the team has a pen in their hands, ready to write." Truth was, Belichick grabbed Moss's attention in New England's very first team meeting of 2007. The Patriots were sitting by position, with the offense on one side of the room and the defense on the other, leaving Stallworth and Moss next to each other. Belichick started in by saying that nobody in his audience was a winner, because nobody in his audience was a member of the 2006 Indianapolis Colts, the defending champs.

Belichick would show the Patriots plays from their AFC Championship Game loss to the Colts, who had rallied from a 21–6 halftime deficit. He'd also prove to them that franchise players weren't entitled to any free lunches. Belichick played film of Brady passes that hadn't exactly hit their targets. "Very simple passes that a high schooler could make," Stallworth said. "Horrible throws. Bill looked back at us, played the film, looked back at us, and said, 'What the fuck is this? I could get Johnny Foxborough from down the street to make a better fucking throw than this, Brady.'"

Brady didn't flinch because, well, Brady never flinched when blitzed — by opposing pass rushers or his own coach. "But Moss and I looked at each other and said, 'Oh, shit,'" Stallworth said. "We sat up in our seats. We were like 'Holy shit.' Like a movie. We looked at each other at the same time. If Tom Brady gets this, everyone can. It set the tone for the season, and guys on that team were used to that . . . Nobody was safe from being coached up by Bill Belichick."

Including grinders the likes of Heath Evans, a 6′0″, 245-pound fullback from Auburn who had been picked by Seattle in the third round of the 2001 draft. Evans was barely used in his four seasons under Seahawks coach Mike Holmgren, and then in 2005 he was discarded by the Dolphins' Nick Saban after six games and a grand total of one rushing attempt for no yardage. When Belichick picked him up, Evans was, in his words, "a beaten-down dog." Holmgren and Saban always wanted to use him as a big-bodied fullback, a banger and nothing more. Belichick saw an athlete, not just a battering ram. "He knew my strengths more than I knew," Evans said, "and he knew my weaknesses more than I knew, from almost the jump."

Three weeks after Miami cut him, Evans suited up for the Patriots against the Dolphins. If only to stick it to Saban, Belichick made Evans the featured part of his offense, and the ex-Dolphin responded with 84 rushing yards on 17 carries plus 18 yards on three catches in a New England victory. The son of a Marine, Evans felt whole again as a football player. "I saw what a championship mentality is," he said. "I saw how to study film. I saw what real leadership was from players. I saw what real football discipline was. I also saw the pressure from day one to be overly prepared because of what Bill puts you through every day."

Evans recalled Junior Seau's first team meeting in New England in 2006. The legend was sitting in the back of the room, and Evans figured he hadn't been corrected or yelled at by a coach since junior high. And yet on this day, Belichick jumped him good, compelling Seau to get out of his chair and say, "Buddy?" in an incredulous voice. (Seau called just about everyone "Buddy" because he had a hard time recalling names.) "Junior didn't even know how to respond to Bill coaching him the way he was being coached, and being held to a different standard," Evans said. "He was a first-ballot Hall of Famer, and Bill was coaching him like he'd coach anybody." On the practice field, Seau sometimes aggressively approached the A-gap, bounced around, and then jumped offsides. Belichick didn't tolerate undisciplined mistakes, even from the sport's signature stars. "We don't guess here," he told Seau. In another practice, when Seau jumped offsides again, Belichick "ripped Junior apart in front of the whole team," one Patriot said.

It was a humbling experience for Seau, who nonetheless had the résumé to counterpunch in a team meeting before a bye-week break. Belichick asked him a question, and the linebacker responded, "Buddy, I have no idea." When Belichick followed up by pressing Seau on why he couldn't handle the question, the player said, "Seat 2A."

"What's Seat 2A?" Belichick asked.

"That's the first-class seat I have on a flight out of here," Seau responded. "I'll have the answer when I get back."

Belichick never stopped challenging his most accomplished stars. Forever sitting in the front row in meetings with his notebook open, Brady was under constant pressure from his coach, who sometimes made him prove his worth relative to his backup. "I saw Bill pit Matt Cassel against Tom Brady in a Q and A one time in front of the team," Evans said, "where Matt would answer a question and Bill would be like 'Brady, what do you think?' And he's like 'I don't agree.' And then Brady would have to give the right answer."

Every day, every classroom session, was an education in how to succeed in the NFL. Evans said that when he first got to Foxborough, he had no clue how to look at defenses, and how to value every precious inch of space separating a player from his adversary. Belichick taught Evans to ask himself, "What's the shade of the outside linebacker? What's the positioning of the 3-technique? What's the alignment of the safeties? How wide are they? Where are Randy Moss and Wes lined up, and according to Randy and Wes what's their coverage?" Evans would line up in the backfield with Kevin Faulk, and the two of them would talk about everything they were seeing. In five to ten seconds, they could diagnose everything coming their way. Belichick had given them the answers to every test by teaching them how to study.

And the lessons didn't stop at the classroom door. "Bill flat out asked you walking down the hallway, 'Hey, Heath, on first and ten in the tight red zone, what's Baltimore's favorite blitz?'" Evans said. "And you'd better know. Hallway, team meeting, at practice, wherever. And then he'd be like 'All right, smart-ass, what's their second-favorite blitz?' So it wasn't having one answer for him. It was having stockpiles of answers for him."

Belichick lit into players only if they committed unforced mental errors. He never asked players to do things they were physically unable to do, something Evans greatly appreciated after his miserable experiences in Seattle and Miami. Holmgren had won a Super Bowl in Green Bay, and Saban would later become arguably the greatest college football coach of all time. But after he was done with those coaches, Evans had no confidence. It took Belichick, he said, "to literally build a new version of me." That building of a new human being was done with a human touch.

"From what I knew of Nick . . . Bill is much more of a people person," Evans said. "People see the media persona, but Bill has an ability to coach in different ways. Mike Holmgren would just yell and scream at me and never really give me any way to get better, and it freakin' killed me on the inside, because I'm a pleaser. If you ask Bill, he'd know that I wanted to do well for the people I care about. I wanted to do well for my family. I wanted to do well for my coaches, and the people that took a chance on me or invested in me. Bill knew how to get to me and coach me so I could please him and make him happy. I couldn't make Mike happy for four years. And Bill is one of the funniest guys I ever met in my life. Everyone knows how smart he is, but he's also quick-witted."

In 2007, as he spread out defenses and emphasized the slot position, Belichick de-emphasized the fullback position. He told Evans that New England wouldn't be using two-back sets, told him he was needed on all special teams, and asked him to lose a little weight. But Evans did score touchdowns in the back-to-back games against Philadelphia and Baltimore that the Patriots nearly lost, and he did prove to be the kind of reliable role player Belichick cherishes. When Evans first showed up in Foxborough in 2005, he was fed up enough with Saban and the circumstances of his departure that he handed Belichick his Dolphins playbook as a form of payback. In return, Belichick developed him into a viable NFL player and offered up another small reason why he was going places no football coach had ever been.

By the time they made it to Super Bowl XLII, in Glendale, Arizona, for a rematch with the Giants, the 18-0 Patriots resembled a golfer who had squandered six shots of his seven-shot Masters lead as he trudged to the 72nd tee just hoping for a two-putt par. New England hadn't been the same unstoppable freight train across the final six regular-season games, nearly losing three of them. The Patriots were tied with Jacksonville at halftime of their divisional playoff game before winning by 11 on Brady's remarkable accuracy (26 of 28 passing for 262 yards and three touchdowns). They were leading San Diego by only two points entering the fourth quarter of the AFC Championship Game before winning by nine, having leaned on Laurence Maroney's second straight 122-yard rushing game to overcome Brady's three interceptions. Moss had only one catch in each playoff victory, and suddenly he was facing an allegation of domestic battery made by a woman who had obtained a temporary restraining order against him. (Moss vehemently denied the allegation.)

The Patriots expended a great deal of energy in the drive for a perfect season as opponents hoping to break up the streak attacked them with playoff intensity. "I think in the long run, that wore our team down," Kyle Brady said.

As much as seemingly everyone had rooted for the Patriots six years earlier, everyone was rooting against them now. Even Jon Bon Jovi was struggling to pull for his buddy Belichick over the Giants, his hometown team. "Everybody pulls for David, nobody roots for Goliath," Wilt Chamberlain once lamented. The Patriots had become Goliath, and Spygate made them less likable.

"When I went up there, that team had almost a persecution complex and used that to their advantage," Kyle Brady said. "Already before the controversy, you had a feeling that everyone outside New England and Patriots Nation hates them. So many people were so tired of their success and hearing about Brady and Belichick, and the haters gravitated toward an additional reason to hate them. It gave that team an energy and created a greater sense of resolve and determination to prove none of that stuff was necessary to win. 'This is the Patriot Way. We outwork you. We're better prepared, tougher, more disciplined.' They took pride in that."

As the Patriots closed in on the 1972 Miami Dolphins, reporters turned to some of those old Dolphins for comment. Mercury Morris, running back and return man, was known to throw a little party every time a previously unbeaten team lost late in the season. One day, Morris was on the TV in the New England locker room, essentially rooting for the Patriots to lose, and Kyle Brady recalled one player saying, "Man, let's shut this dude up. Let's go ahead and do this. This dude is too much. Everyone is tired of hearing him."

The more the Patriots pressed forward, the more resistance they met. Realizing that Tom Brady was having a season for the ages, teams had started blitzing him more to speed him up. New England was feeling the pressure between the lines, and also in the court of public opinion, where Arlen Specter, a Pennsylvania senator and the top Republican on the Senate Judiciary Committee, was demanding to know why Roger Goodell had ordered the destruction of the Patriots' tapes and notes relevant to their illegal videotaping operation. A devoted fan of the Philadelphia Eagles, the team that had lost Super Bowl XXXIX to New England, Specter told the *New York Times* that Goodell would be called before the committee, that the public had a right to know if the integrity of the game had been compromised and a right to know what was on those tapes. Later that morning, in his annual state-of-the-league news conference held on the Friday before the Super Bowl, Goodell fielded half a dozen questions on Spygate and maintained that he didn't believe New England's filming had had a significant impact on the outcome of any game. Of course, with Specter grousing about the NFL's antitrust exemption, it was in the commissioner's interests to downplay the entire episode.

Goodell said six tapes from 2006 and 2007 had been recovered from the Patriots, and that destroying them had been "the appropriate thing to do and I think it sent a message." Only very few people accepted the commissioner's explanation. A former Patriots video assistant named Matt Walsh suggested in an interview with ESPN.com that he was in possession of relevant and undisclosed Spygate information, and then the very next day, on the eve of the Super Bowl, the *Boston Herald* dropped a bombshell in the middle of Belichick's locker room. John Tomase of the *Herald* reported that the Patriots had taped the St. Louis Rams' final walk-through before New England's indelible upset in Super Bowl XXXVI, six years earlier. Though the team and the league denied having any knowledge of this, Tomase reported that after filming the Patriots' walk-through in the Superdome, a staffer remained behind and filmed the Rams. That staffer was later identified as Walsh, who acknowledged being present at the St. Louis session (he told Brian Daboll, then a coaching assistant, that Marshall Faulk was lining up as a kick returner) but denied videotaping it.

The *Herald* story only hardened the notion that nobody outside of New England wanted Belichick's team to win its fourth ring. As much as America had wanted the underdog Patriots to take down St. Louis in New Orleans, America wanted to see them fall to the underdog Giants in the Arizona desert. Belichick could tell his players every hour, on the hour, that they shouldn't worry about public perception and that Spygate was his personal burden to bear, but they were only human. And it was only human for athletes to feel stressed when their authenticity was being questioned.

As it was, the Patriots were buckling under the pressure to finish 19-0 even before those news stories broke near the end of the week. Troy Brown, a decorated Patriot and pro's pro who had been reduced to a practice squad player in his final season, would tell his biographer, Mike Reiss, that in his 15 years of professional football he "had never been part of a team that practiced as poorly as the Patriots did leading up to the most important game of their careers, which led them to being kicked off the field by Bill Belichick." Brown said that New England's first two practices after arriving in Arizona were "as bad as he's been a part of at any level" and that by week's end "things had picked up slightly but it was still an uneasy feeling."

Kyle Brady recalled a midweek practice at Arizona State's Sun Devil Stadium that went awry. "We went out and laid an egg," he said. "Balls were dropped. Guys were missing blocks. Balls were on the ground. That had not happened all season long. Bill brought us up at the end of practice and he said, 'Guys, let me tell you something. [The Giants] got ahead of you today.' He wasn't saying it to scare us. He really believed it."

Belichick didn't betray that truth in his mandatory sessions with the news media. He was actually cordial, semi-pleasant, and humorous enough for *Globe* columnist Dan Shaughnessy to label him "Belichuckle." It helped that the Spygate questions had been in short supply during the week, and when he was asked in a news conference about the latest developments, he did his usual deflecting, saying, "That's a league matter. I don't know anything about it."

Truth was, Belichick was in the habit of bringing his media A game to Super Bowl week. It was as if he knew he had to rise to the occasion and play along on the national stage. Catching Belichick's act during Super Bowl week was like catching Belichick's act on Fridays in Foxborough, when much of his preparation for the upcoming game was complete and the TV people and out-of-towners had already parachuted in and out. The coach knew his Friday audience consisted of the beat's day-to-day grinders, and for them he was often thoughtful and expansive — especially when the questions were about NFL history or the evolution of the tight end position or the ball flight for left-footed punters or the grit of old Giants warriors like Harry Carson, Carl Banks, and Lawrence Taylor.

Belichick was often Friday Bill times five at the Super Bowl, where he scoffed at the idea that he disdained his meetings with the press. "I think you have a job to do," he told reporters, "and you are our connection between our football team, our fans, and the people who have an interest in the game. I respect the job that you do and hope that you respect the job I do. I understand that sometimes I can't give you everything that you are looking for, but I do know that this is the conduit of information from the team to the fans, and the fans are what drive the game."

New England's players regularly saw the Super Bowl Belichick that he rarely trotted out for reporters and fans to see. But at the end of an emotionally and physically draining season, that side of Belichick wasn't motivating the Patriots during their most important practices of the year. Meanwhile, the Giants were looking and sounding like a refreshed and confident team with nothing to lose. Plaxico Burress didn't let his injured ankle stop him from predicting a 23–17 victory in the *New York Post,* and Giants co-owner Steve Tisch told a New Jersey columnist that he was also predicting an upset over the Patriots. "We'll have more points than they do," said Tisch, who believed the Giants were getting stronger by the week. "This is not a team that peaked at midseason," the owner said, in what seemed like a shot at New England.

In the AFC Championship Game, San Diego had held Brady to 209 yards passing while intercepting him three times. (Brady injured his right ankle in the victory.) The Chargers' defensive coordinator, Ted Cottrell, said that his players "were holding our looks right until the end and didn't show our hand." The Giants called Cottrell for advice before the Super Bowl. "I didn't give them all my secrets," he said. Cottrell did tell the Giants about certain tendencies Kevin Faulk showed when he entered the game. He'd also been a member of the Vikings' staff when Moss was in Minnesota, and couldn't believe the things he saw the receiver do in practice and games. Cottrell told the Giants that they needed to get their hands on Moss as much as possible and to prevent him from getting up in the air.

The Giants arrived at the Super Bowl site dressed in black for New England's supposed funeral. They had gone 0-3 against Dallas and Green Bay during the regular season, and yet, after opening the postseason with a road victory over Tampa Bay, the Giants beat the top-seeded Cowboys in their building before surviving Ice Bowl–ish conditions at Lambeau Field and outlasting Brett Favre and the Packers in overtime. The Giants had a good week of work in Arizona, outside of the fact that a backup receiver and special teams star, David Tyree, dropped everything thrown his way in the team's final full practice. "Balls were ricocheting off his helmet," Tom Coughlin said, "and Eli had to pat David on the butt and remind him he was a clutch player who could come through for us in the game."

Off their regular-season showing against New England, and off their charmed postseason run, the Giants were true believers in their ability to win this game. "We knew that if we played them again that we'd beat them," one Giants official said. "Physically, we beat the shit out of them in that regular-season game . . . They weren't looking forward to going through that again. Psychologically, even though it was a loss, that last regular-season game worked to the positive to an unbelievable degree, and also worked to the negative for them to an unbelievable degree. Literally walking off the field that night, our guys were saying to themselves and each other, 'If we play those fuckers again, we're going to beat the shit out of them, and they know it and we know it.'"

Though New England never would've agreed with that assessment, Kyle Brady did reveal that "a lot of guys on that team, if they were quite honest, would say they'd prefer to play the Packers, because we knew we matched up very well against them." Every NFL team knew that the only way to compete with the Patriots was to bring pressure — especially interior pressure — and move Brady off his preferred spot. The Giants of Michael Strahan, Justin Tuck, and Osi Umenyiora were more capable than anyone of executing that strategy, especially with Brady limited by the bum ankle that bothered him more than he let on.

At the same time, the Giants knew who and what they were up against. John Mara, team president and co-owner, had once been in the George Young camp when it came to Bill Belichick, Giants assistant. Mara didn't think Belichick had the personality to be a successful NFL head coach, and yet the Patriots' coach now stood next to Vince Lombardi and Tom Landry as former assistants the Giants never should've allowed to leave the franchise.

"George Young had spent his life in the National Football League," Mara said, "and he used to say to me all the time, 'I've been evaluating personnel all my life. That's what I do.' And he was wrong about Bill. I was wrong. A lot of us were wrong. Shame on us."

The Cleveland experience had made it appear that they were right, that Belichick didn't have the charisma and the commanding presence to lead. "That's exactly what I was thinking," Mara said. Belichick turned to Tom Brady in 2001, and everything changed. He had a chance now, in his eighth season in Foxborough, to join Pittsburgh's Chuck Noll as the only men to win four Super Bowls.

A Giants franchise that hadn't won it all since the 1990 season, or since Belichick left for Cleveland, was all that stood between the Patriots and an unimagined place. Yes, the Giants were riding a wave of momentum and, yes, they were talking a good game after that 38–35 shootout in the Meadowlands. But deep down, they knew they had lost six more games than New England. Six. They knew what they were facing at the quarterback and receiver positions. Of greater significance, they knew what they were facing at the position of head coach.

"So how are we going to do this?" Mara asked himself. "How are we going to beat him? He's got two weeks to prepare for us, so how can we possibly beat him?"

• • •

Eli Manning's ball was floating directly toward Asante Samuel, near the Giants' sideline inside University of Phoenix Stadium, which meant the Patriots were actually going to do this. They were going to win their fourth Super Bowl title. They were going to finish with the NFL's first-ever 19-0 record. They were going to finish as the greatest team of all time.

New England was leading 14–10, and there were only 80 seconds left, when Manning felt pressured by a blitzing Rodney Harrison and threw up a pass in the vicinity of David Tyree, who had scored the Giants' only touchdown. The receiver broke off the route earlier than Eli had anticipated, leaving Samuel all alone with the ball. And this is why the game was over: Samuel had 19 interceptions over the 2006 and 2007 seasons, playoffs included, the most in the league by far. He had picked off passes in five of his previous seven postseason games and returned three of them for touchdowns, including one against Peyton Manning in the previous year's AFC Championship Game.

"It would be great if I could pick off Eli one time," Samuel had said before the Super Bowl. "That would be real nice. Then maybe I could ask both guys for their jerseys so I could hang them in my trophy case."

He had every right to be confident, even cocky. Harrison called Samuel "the best corner in the league, hands down," and he was about to make a killing in free agency. A fourth-round pick out of Central Florida in 2003, Samuel had modest measurables among corners at the pre-draft combine, posting a 4.52 40-yard-dash time and a 35.5-inch vertical leap. But Belichick thought he had very good instincts and ball skills. "So when he gets his hands on the ball," the coach would say, "he intercepted most of them."

Belichick said he expected a good game out of Samuel, who expected the same from himself. "Big-time players step up in big-time games," he'd said, "and I consider myself a big-time player." He was right, too. Samuel would retire in six years with 58 regular-season and postseason interceptions, ten of them returned for touchdowns. "Hopefully Eli will play a bad game," he said that week in Arizona. "Hopefully I can be the reason."

The ball was right there. Eli was about to finish a bad game, and Samuel was about to be the reason. The 5'10" corner rose to make the catch, and the ball made contact with his ultra-reliable hands with 78 seconds to go. Somehow those ultra-reliable hands didn't hold on. Somehow the Giants had new life. With the team's season and legacy on the line, Samuel was the one Patriot not named Moss or Welker whom Belichick would've wanted in position to make a catch. And he didn't make it.

It wasn't an easy play. If Samuel were 5'11" instead of 5'10", he would've made the pick. If Samuel's vertical leap were 36.5 instead of 35.5, he would've made the pick. After the ball bounced off his hands and went flying into the Giants' sideline, Samuel leaned his head backwards, grabbed his helmet with both hands, and looked skyward, his mouth agape. "I don't know if Eli was trying to throw it away or something," he said later. "But it was a bad play on my part. I could have ended the game."

Instead, on the next play, Manning lined up in shotgun formation on third-and-five from the New York 44, with referee Mike Carey stationed 12 yards behind him and to his right. Manning took the snap and almost immediately found himself under duress. New England's furious four-man rush obliterated the Giants' front line, all but leaving the athletically challenged Eli to fend for himself. He stepped up in the pocket to avoid Adalius Thomas, swooping in from his left side, and stepped right into the vortex created by the stunt, or twist, that was run by New England's Jarvis Green and Richard Seymour, who steamrolled past Rich Seubert and Shaun O'Hara. Defending a stunt in football is like defending a pick-and-roll in basketball, and Seubert and O'Hara later blamed each other for not making a clean switch.

Green grabbed Manning's jersey with his left hand and then came over the top and grabbed it with his right while Seymour and O'Hara were locked in a Greco-Roman wrestling match inches away. The Giants' center said he saw Manning curl into his typical standing fetal position and thought to himself, *OK, we're probably going to lose this game.* Manning was so desperate to stay alive in the mayhem, he briefly considered throwing the ball to his best offensive lineman, Chris Snee, who wasn't blocking anyone. Somehow Eli spun out of Green's grasp, which left him open for Seymour to take down. Feeling he had nothing to lose other than the game, O'Hara planted his right hand around Seymour's throat.

"I said, 'Screw it,'" the center said. "I was squeezing his trachea as hard as I could and not letting go." The illegal chokehold disabled Seymour for a brief moment and likely allowed Manning to escape. The Patriots had been caught cheating at the start of their season, and a Giants lineman had just gone undetected cheating them at the end of their season.

As a manic Manning retreated to his 33-yard line, Carey ran up next to him, and then retreated himself when he realized the quarterback was alive and well and about to attempt a pass. The referee later admitted that he likely would have blown the whistle and ruled the play dead — with Manning in the Patriots' clutches — had he remained in his spot or taken a different path to the action. But Eli was free to make a play, and he had been making more than his share since his demonstrative Pro Bowl tight end, Jeremy Shockey, went down in December with a fractured leg. Shockey was a rare talent, but he was also a high-maintenance act who demanded the ball and wasn't afraid to show up Manning when he didn't get it. "I don't have a problem saying Jeremy Shockey was a pain in the ass," said Giants kicker Lawrence Tynes. "Eli was technically a young player, and the guy was constantly yelling at him when he'd come off the field. That's not conducive to a productive work environment. I could sense that Eli was a different player from that point on."

Manning sent up a prayer down the middle of the field, where the 6'0" Tyree and the 6'1" Harrison waited at the New England 24 to see who could jump higher. Tyree won the contest, made the initial catch as the safety swung his right arm at the ball, and then somehow secured it while being dragged to the ground by pinning it, with his right hand, against the top of his helmet. The same helmet that balls had been ricocheting off during the Giants' final practice. Before Coughlin could scramble onto the field for a second time on the drive, motioning frantically for a timeout, it was clear to all witnesses this was the most amazing Super Bowl catch they'd ever seen.

Some players on the field didn't realize just how absurd this sequence had been. Donté Stallworth was waiting for his luggage at the Fort Lauderdale airport the next day when he finally watched the play on his computer. "What the fuck?" he screamed out, and everyone at baggage claim immediately turned his way. Stallworth couldn't believe his eyes. "One of the best safeties in the league, not to be able to jar that ball loose from Tyree?" Stallworth said. "That probably happens maybe five out of 100 times."

This was one of the five. The singular Patriot the Giants wanted to defeat more than any other, Harrison, had been defeated. "We had hatred for Rodney Harrison going in," O'Hara said. "Not just him, but vengeance was on our mind." Every man, woman, and child inside the building had a feeling after the Tyree catch that this game had been decided right then and there. The Giants still had to cover 24 yards in 59 seconds to get into the end zone, but what team ever makes a play like that in the final minutes and then loses the game?

The Patriots had taken their 14–10 lead with 2:45 left, when Brady finished a workmanlike 80-yard drive with a short scoring pass to Moss, who was lined up on the right side against Corey Webster, man to man, before embarrassing him with his money move and making him fall down. On the New England sideline, Bruschi, a three-time champ, wrapped his arms around Seau, a legend without a ring. The Patriots needed just one stop.

They had so many chances on New York's final, fateful drive, and couldn't convert any of them. For the Patriots, it was a drive of nearlys. They nearly stopped Brandon Jacobs on a fourth-and-one. They nearly forced and recovered a Manning fumble. On the next play, they nearly intercepted Eli on the pass that headed right for Samuel. On the play after that, they nearly sacked Eli, and then nearly broke up his Hail Mary to Tyree. "Some unusual things happened that made you scratch your head and say, *What's going on here?*" Kyle Brady said. "We usually caught those breaks."

New England's Adalius Thomas actually ran down and sacked Manning on the snap following the Tyree catch, leaving an entire region of tormented fans to ask, *Where was that on the last play?* Coughlin had to burn his final timeout with 51 seconds left. Three plays and 12 seconds later, on third-and-11, Manning completed a 12-yard sideline pass to Steve Smith to give the Giants a first down at the New England 13. Burress was split wide to the left on the next play, and it was a small act of God that he was even on the field.

Burress had injured a knee ligament five days earlier by slipping in the shower, and the team didn't inform anyone about it. The receiver was sitting at his locker before the game, head down, praying that the painkillers he took would allow him to play with a bad knee and a bad ankle. Most of his teammates didn't think he'd be able to suit up, and the Giants had only minutes to play with before submitting their inactives. "Right up until the deadline," Coughlin said, "I didn't know if Plaxico would even dress. It was real." The Giants' coach was preparing to make Sinorice Moss active when he got word from trainer Ronnie Barnes that Burress was a go. Coughlin didn't need to be told twice; he handed his list of inactives to the team's PR man, Pat Hanlon, who brushed past Belichick on his way to making those names official.

The Giants were merely hoping the hobbled Burress could make a couple of big plays, and after managing only one 14-yard catch on eight targets, Burress finally gave them one. Matched up with Ellis Hobbs, who had already intercepted Manning, Burress faked a slant and froze Hobbs as he turned up the field, flawlessly executing what's called a sluggo route. Eli had a wide-open receiver to hit in the end zone, and hit him Eli did, with 35 seconds to go. His big brother Peyton, the previous year's Super Bowl MVP, started pumping his fists and clapping like mad in his upstairs suite.

As exhilarated wives and family members of the Giants started making their way downstairs for the on-field celebration, the stricken wives and family members of the Patriots passed them on their way back upstairs. (They had headed down after New England took the lead.) Tom Petty and the Heartbreakers had played at halftime; Tom Coughlin and the Heartbreakers were playing now. Coughlin and Belichick had engaged in some epic practice-field battles as Parcells assistants in the late 1980s, when Major Tom was coaching the Giants receivers and Captain Sominex, the Giants' defensive coordinator, was lording over the defensive backs. Parcells recalled his two assistants being locked in mortal combat as their units went after each other in red-zone drills. "That's where Tom and Bill got to know each other," Parcells said.

All these years later, Coughlin appeared to have won a far more significant battle. The Patriots seemed frozen in disbelief on their sideline. Bad omens were everywhere. New England's Laurence Maroney took the opening kickoff, and he was shut down at his own 26 by the Giants' Zak DeOssie, the former training-camp ball boy for Belichick and the son of one of Belichick's old Giants linebackers, Steve DeOssie. The Patriots' coach was gracious enough to greet his fellow Andover alum with a hug near midfield before the game, something Giants teammates razzed DeOssie about. During the game, veteran Patriots who remembered him as a camp kid, the Bruschis and Vrabels and Larry Izzos, were yelling at DeOssie as he prepared to perform his duty on punts. "Ball boy," they shouted, "you're going to get us a Gatorade after you mess this snap up."

Twenty-nine seconds remained when Brady took the field. Once a draft-day afterthought, Brady had grown into the NFL's most reliable player. It seemed the quarterback never did or said anything that hurt his team. Yet during the week, he'd stepped out of character by mocking Burress's prediction of a low-scoring Giants victory. "We're only going to score 17 points?" Brady asked incredulously. "OK. Is Plax playing defense? I wish he had said, like, 45–42, something like that. I wish he'd give us a little more credit for scoring a few points."

Brady had violated his own "Well done is always better than well said" code, and now he had a lousy 14 points on the board and a desperate need for three more just to buy himself overtime. The most prominent newcomer also deviated from the old New England playbook. "We'll see who has black on after the game," Moss had said in reference to the funereal attire worn by the Giants when they touched down in the desert.

The Patriots weren't ever supposed to get caught up in silly public banter, but they were on a seek-and-destroy mission all year, and their emotions had ultimately fractured their focus. Sloppy practices led to an uneven Super Bowl performance and an inability to finish huge defensive plays on the Giants' final drive. Wearing two sweatshirts with sleeves cut off near the elbows, including a blood-red Patriots hoodie on top, Belichick wasn't at the peak of his game, either. Rather than attempt a 49-yard field goal in the third quarter with his second-year kicker, Stephen Gostkowski, who had a career long of 52 yards and had made a 50-yarder in the playoffs the season before, Belichick chose to go with a Brady pass on fourth and 13, a pass that sailed out of the end zone. "I don't know why you don't kick that ball," said the Giants' Tynes, whose overtime 47-yarder in the NFC Championship Game had just become the longest postseason kick in Lambeau Field history. "That was a head-scratcher to me."

Belichick's decision also baffled some Patriots, including Bruschi, who, years later, as an ESPN analyst, cited the decision as a strike against Belichick in an on-air discussion about who should be considered the greatest NFL coach of all time. With the game being played indoors, Gostkowski would've had perfect conditions to work with.

Belichick had also abandoned the running game that was effective in New England's two playoff victories. The Patriots ran the ball only 16 times for 45 yards, almost all of it the work of Maroney, who'd rushed for a combined 244 yards on 47 carries against Jacksonville and San Diego. Belichick decided to put the Super Bowl on the right shoulder of Brady, who threw 48 times against those 16 handoffs. New England's lack of balance allowed the Giants' pass rushers to tee off and sack Brady five times, after they'd taken him down only once in December.

As the crowd buzzed with the anticipation of an indelible upset, the Patriots were left to confront the dire circumstances of a last-gasp possession. On first down, a rushed Brady threw waywardly downfield. Twenty-five seconds to go. On second down, Giants rookie Jay Alford beat right guard Russ Hochstein to his left and plowed into Brady's midsection for the sack. Nineteen seconds to go. On third-and-20, Brady and Moss flashed their historic greatness for the last time that season. The quarterback took the snap, rolled right to buy himself some time, stepped up, and launched the ball with everything he had toward the receiver streaking down the left side of the field. Moss had a step on cornerback Corey Webster, who'd helped win the NFC Championship Game by intercepting Brett Favre in overtime, and safety Gibril Wilson. If Brady had heaved it 69 yards in the air instead of 68, Moss might've caught it and either scored or put New England in position to tie or win on the next play. But Webster got his left hand on the ball, barely, deflecting it away. Ten seconds to go.

The camera found Belichick with his hands on his hips, licking his lips. He looked right and then swiveled his head quickly left, and his expression reflected the grim reality of the moment. It was fourth and 20, and Brady called time out. The Patriots had to try the obvious, again, a deep shot to Moss, and hope for a defensive pass interference call or a miracle catch. Brady lined up in shotgun formation as Belichick conferred with his offensive coordinator, McDaniels, and then lifted his right leg and planted his foot to signal for his last snap. He caught that snap and launched another pass down the left side of the field, but this time Moss didn't come as close to hauling it in as he encountered the same two defenders and went crashing out of bounds. One second to go. The Giants started to celebrate what John Mara would call the greatest victory in franchise history.

Madison Hedgecock, a Giants fullback, dumped a Gatorade bucket of ice water on Coughlin as Brady walked off the field, helmet in hand. Suddenly Belichick decided to jog across the field toward Coughlin while a credentialed functionary carrying a red flag chased him from behind, followed by New England's security chief, Mark Briggs. Carey, the referee, tried to intercept Belichick before he got to Coughlin, as the Giants had to take one more snap to make the game complete. The losing coach pushed past the ref and gave the winning coach a hug, then Belichick started walking off the field and toward the exits while surrounded by security and cops. "The official word from the NFL is a play has to be run," Joe Buck said on the Fox broadcast. "But it appears it will be run with Bill Belichick up the tunnel."

Eli Manning took a knee, and Coughlin pumped his fist in triumph. Much had been made of the head coach's transformation — under threat of termination — from an unforgiving tyrant to a more humane leader, and he, too, had spent the week in a stunningly jovial state. His young grandchildren had stormed his hotel room at 7 a.m. on Super Bowl Sunday to draw animals and other figures on his game plan, and he adored every second of it.

His Giants played loose and hungry, moving Moss to say that "their intensity from the beginning snap to the end of the game was really higher than ours." Moss also said the winners "just had a better game plan," and neither comment reflected well on his coach. The Giants had set up this result by burning nine minutes and 59 seconds of clock time on the opening 16-play drive. They would beat up the favored Patriots like the 2001 Patriots had beaten up the favored Rams, and, after winning three different Super Bowls by three points, New England finally lost one by the same margin. A Giants fan held up a sign afterward that said 18-1, and amid the delirium O'Hara surveyed the sheer devastation on the Patriots' faces. "Junior Seau was laying on his stomach, face flat on the ground," O'Hara said. "He couldn't believe he was that close. My heart went out to him."

So many poignant postgame scenes outside the stadium separated the winners from the losers. Giants linebacker Antonio Pierce boarded the bus back to the champions' hotel wearing most of his uniform — he simply didn't want to take it off. Kyle Brady ran into Coughlin, his former coach in Jacksonville, in the parking lot and congratulated him on the upset. "Brady," the winning coach responded, "we should've done this together." Patriots linebacker Rosevelt Colvin, out with a broken foot, was blaming himself for not being available as he took his endless trudge to the bus in a walking boot. Patriots guard Logan Mankins — who hadn't shaved during the winning streak — pulled some clippers out of his bag and started cutting his mountain-man beard right there on his team bus. His teammate Stallworth, feeling completely gutted in the back of that bus, wore headphones for the ride back to the hotel, which felt like it lasted days.

Before the Patriots pulled away from University of Phoenix Stadium, Belichick was sitting in the first row of bus No. 5642, staring at the final stats for the night. The matriarch of the Giants' ownership family, Ann Mara, saw the former Giants assistant and left her bus to board his and offer some words of comfort. "I didn't know if I should do it," she later told her son John, "but I saw him sitting there looking so unhappy. So I just wanted to go down and tell him what a great coach he was and what a great season they had."

The New England locker room had been a scene of unspeakable pain. This was the kind of misery that visited the St. Louis Rams when they lost to the Patriots six years earlier, and the Baltimore Colts when they lost to Joe Namath and the Jets decades before that. The 2007 Patriots had made 18 consecutive trips into postgame locker rooms laughing and joking and reveling in their own glory, and suddenly they were walking into a mausoleum. Their own.

Stephen Neal, the lineman who injured his knee in the defeat, recalled the looks on the faces of Seau, Moss, and Welker — the relatively new Patriots who had yet to win a ring — and the emptiness he felt for failing to win them one. Mostly the players in that godforsaken room remembered the deafening silence, occasionally pierced by the sounds of men weeping.

"I've never been in a locker room so quiet," Stallworth said. "They say you could hear a pin drop on the floor, but if that locker room floor was carpeted you could still hear a pin drop. Guys were crying. It was horrible. The atmosphere and feeling inside was . . . I can't explain it. Shock. Disbelief. Sadness. I hate to compare it to a funeral or say it was worse than that, but it was horrible."

Almost to a man, the Patriots were slumped at their lockers and silently blaming themselves. Even after a soul-crushing defeat, these players were wired to look in their own mirrors when assigning culpability. It was all part of the ethos of what would widely become known as the Patriot Way. Third-string quarterback Matt Gutierrez, an undrafted free agent who appeared in five games that year, was in the room wondering what he could've or should've done differently in practice to make Tom Brady better, or to make the first-team defense better. He didn't play a single down in the Super Bowl, yet he felt as responsible for this program-wide breakdown as Brady did. Ditto for Bam Childress, a practice squad receiver, who was asking himself if he could've done something else during the week to help Moss.

Into this dark abyss stepped the head coach of the New England Patriots. *What is he going to say?* players thought to themselves. *What can any coach possibly say in this moment?* Belichick stood among these shattered men and started to speak. "It's more emotional than I've ever seen Bill," said Heath Evans.

"I saw a defeated look on his face," said Stallworth, "and I'd never seen anything like it . . . I had never seen a coach that way before. He was just — he was not tearing up, but he was extremely upset. He didn't say much. Maybe he spoke for less than a minute."

Maybe he spoke for 45 seconds or 55 seconds, or 15 to 30 seconds longer than Stallworth recalled. The length didn't matter; the message did. And in that locker room, Belichick realized he had to coach his greatest team through one more possession. He had to ease his players' pain, and so he did what New England Patriots do. Belichick blamed himself.

"Other than my father," Evans said, "I've never had more respect for a man at any moment in my life as that man in that moment."

As low as he'd ever been, Belichick rose to his chief responsibility. "He said, 'We didn't prepare you guys well enough. The coaches didn't do a good enough job, and that falls on me. I didn't prepare you guys well enough, and I'm really sorry for that,'" Stallworth recounted. "He didn't blame the coaches. He blamed himself for everything and he apologized for that. He could've easily said, 'It sucks, but we didn't make enough plays.' He didn't mention the players at all . . . To me, that shows a lot about who he is as a person."

Evans said Belichick took specific responsibility for the offensive failures in the game. "He owned the situation, and it wasn't verbiage," the fullback said. "He was broken over the fact he had cost not himself, but his team, his coaching staff, and maybe most importantly his owner an opportunity to go down in history. He felt he mismanaged game-time scenarios and adjustments, and the truth is we had plenty of opportunities to win the game and the players didn't get it done.

"I've seen many coaches try to pull it off, and didn't pull it off, when trying to BS a bunch of grown men," Evans said. "I loved, respected, and honored Bill before that moment, and this magnified it after. With his powerful position, with everything he'd accomplished, he could've had a hard time saying he was sorry. Most prideful, arrogant people want to blame others, and that was never the case with him . . . The message was loud and clear, and especially guys on the offensive side of the ball fully understood what he meant and the ownership he took. I'd say, in my words, he took full ownership over the loose coaching decisions he made."

Belichick had started the season with his worst hour as a football coach, the Spygate scandal, and he had just finished it with his finest. He gave his heart to his men when he had nothing left to give them, and then it was time to leave. Stallworth made this one last observation about the undisputed leader of the best 18-1 team the NFL had ever seen:

"It was almost like he just faded to black when he walked away."

16

HERNANDEZ

On April Fools' Day 2008, Bill Belichick and Robert Kraft apologized to their NFL peers for New England's illegal videotaping practices. Roger Goodell had gathered owners and head coaches at the league meetings at the Breakers in Palm Beach, and no, they did not have the same reaction to Belichick that they had to Kraft.

"Robert was a lot more convincing than Bill," one owner said, "let's put it that way."

Kraft was a well-liked and respected steward of the game, someone who appeared genuine in his concern for the greater good of the league. He did not strike his audience inside the hotel's Ponce de Leon Ballroom as someone who was merely sorry his team had been caught cheating. He sounded like someone who was sorry that people in his franchise, on his watch, had embarrassed the NFL and called into question the integrity of the competition.

Kraft said that nothing outside of his family mattered more to him than the league, and that the Patriots would never again bring dishonor to the game. The room applauded him when he was done. Indianapolis Colts coach Tony Dungy was among the listeners who approached Kraft afterward to express how much they appreciated his contrition. Dungy called Kraft's speech "very sincere and heartfelt."

When Belichick rose to speak in the closed-door session, there was a different vibe in the room. Kraft wasn't the one responsible for Spygate, after all, nor did he have any knowledge of it before Matt Estrella's camera was confiscated in September. Belichick had orchestrated the entire thing, with Ernie Adams acting as co-conspirator, and he was facing a crowd of vanquished competitors who largely disagreed with Goodell's decision to destroy the Patriots' tapes and notes used in carrying out the operation. A league official who had heard Belichick address opposing coaches and executives in other settings described the typical reaction to him this way: "When he gets up, you can feel the loathing in the room." Part of that loathing was inspired by Belichick's perceived arrogance. And part was inspired by Belichick's winning percentage against those men in the room.

One owner in the audience said that loathing and skepticism hung in the air as Belichick claimed, again, that he had misinterpreted the rules and thought sideline videotaping of coaches' signals was legal as long as those tapes weren't used for a real-time advantage in the same game. "It's accurate to say there wasn't a single person in the room who believed what Bill said, that he misinterpreted the rule," the owner said. "That's one person in the league who doesn't misinterpret anything."

That morning, dressed in a Hawaiian shirt and sandals, Belichick met with reporters at the annual AFC coaches breakfast and actually broke news. He disclosed that he'd spoken with as many as five NFL representatives after the Super Bowl about the illegal filming of signals; neither the Patriots nor the league had previously disclosed that fact or the fact that other team officials were also interviewed.

The Patriots understood that this was serious business. In fact, when they hired former Panthers and Texans head coach Dom Capers in February as a special assistant/secondary coach, some figured they'd just purchased an insurance policy. Capers had finished the runner-up to Belichick in Foxborough in 2000, and if Belichick ended up getting suspended, Capers could have been an experienced hand to summon from the bullpen. Not that New England's head coach had any plans for getting suspended.

"I've addressed so many questions so many times from so many people," Belichick said, "I don't know what else the league could ask." He blamed himself for not getting a clarification on the videotaping rule from Ray Anderson in the league office. "That was my mistake," Belichick said. He also claimed that he "barely knew" former video staffer Matt Walsh, who was making noise about having new and important Spygate information in his possession, and remained adamant that New England had not taped the Rams' walk-through before Super Bowl XXXVI, contrary to the *Boston Herald* report.

"I've never seen a tape of another team's practice. Ever," Belichick said. The coach assured reporters that his program had become "more efficient, more streamlined" in the wake of Spygate — though he'd never use that word, "Spygate," to describe the case — to ensure that the episode wouldn't repeat itself. On a related matter, the league voted in a rule that allowed one defensive player to wear a communication device in his helmet, like the quarterback does on offense, to receive calls from the sideline. That device would dramatically reduce the need for hand signals and thus reduce the opportunity for spies to steal them.

Belichick voted for the proposal after voting against it in the pre-Spygate days. "It didn't pass last year and it did pass this year," Dungy said. "So you can draw your own conclusions."

This story wasn't about to go poof in the night. Goodell had met with Arlen Specter and told him that Belichick had been taping signals since 2000 (the commissioner had earlier suggested that the taping started in 2006) and that the Steelers had been illegally filmed in four games. The *Herald* report was still out there, and Matt Walsh was still out there, too. A low-level Patriots staffer from 1997 to 2003, Walsh had reinvented himself as a golf pro in Hawaii. He said he was willing to tell Goodell everything he knew about Spygate, but first he wanted protection. The commissioner had little choice but to give it to him. Had Goodell declined a meeting with someone who claimed to have fresh information about Spygate, his destruction of the Patriots' tapes and notes would become even harder to defend.

So Goodell reached an agreement that provided Walsh with indemnification against potential lawsuits and covered his legal fees and expenses as long as he turned over all tapes and other items relevant to the case. Walsh sent the league eight tapes of filmed signals from six games between 2000 and 2002, then met with Goodell for about three and a half hours on May 13. Walsh told the commissioner that he realized he was likely breaking NFL rules by videotaping signals and that after games he delivered the tapes directly to Ernie Adams. Walsh said that New England did not tape the St. Louis walk-through in February 2002 but that he witnessed it and did give coaching assistant Brian Daboll information on the Rams' use of tight ends, and did tell Daboll that Marshall Faulk was lining up as a kick returner. Daboll told league investigators he couldn't recall that conversation.

Walsh then met with Specter, who wanted the NFL to run the kind of independent investigation that Major League Baseball had asked George Mitchell, former senator from Maine, to oversee on the use of performance-enhancing drugs in the game. Goodell would do everything in his power to make sure that didn't happen. Walsh had given him no information that New England had bugged locker rooms or interfered with opponents' communication systems. (He did claim that the Patriots used a player on injured reserve in practice in 2001, their first championship season.) The commissioner said that, after conducting dozens of interviews, he didn't know where else to take the case. He even played Walsh's tapes for reporters, who seemed underwhelmed by the filmed images of coaches giving signals that were visible to any fan with good seats or a pair of binoculars. Some clips, not shot by Walsh, showed up-close views of San Diego Chargers cheerleaders performing during a game.

The next day, Belichick nailed down his biggest victory since the AFC Championship Game when the *Herald* ran front-page and back-page apologies to the Patriots in admitting that its story on the Super Bowl walk-through was false. SORRY, PATS, read the headline on the front page. OUR MISTAKE, read the one on the back. The triumphant feeling was short-lived. Walsh gave several interviews and described how he'd been instructed by superiors, including video director Jimmy Dee, on what to wear and what cover story to offer if questioned about his filming in another team's stadium. New England videographers were told to wear generic clothing, to cloak team logos, and to explain to security that they were shooting footage for the owner's media company, Kraft Productions. Walsh told HBO that the Patriots "went to great lengths to keep from being caught." He told the *New York Times* that his first illegal taping assignment occurred in 2000, in a preseason game against Tampa Bay, and that one of the New England quarterbacks observed that "probably 75 percent of the time, Tampa Bay ran the defense we thought they were going to run. If not more."

Belichick had to respond to those claims. For the first time, someone involved in the filming scheme had gone on the record to say what much of the NFL already believed—that Belichick lied when he said he was unaware that he was doing anything against the rules. Belichick agreed to a TV interview with a CBS reporter he respected, Armen Keteyian, who asked tough questions without losing the coach's trust. In the sit-down, Keteyian pressed the coach on the plausibility of his misinterpretation defense after the league had clearly spelled out the videotaping rule in writing.

Belichick countered that Walsh had never been instructed to wear what amounted to a disguise. "We weren't trying to be discreet about it," he said. Belichick claimed that he didn't think he could recognize Walsh, that the former staffer was "embellishing" his account of what had happened, and that Walsh had been fired for poor job performance and for secretly audiotaping a conversation with his boss, Scott Pioli. (Walsh's lawyer told the *Globe* that claim was a "complete fabrication.") Belichick reminded viewers that the signals were available to be seen by anyone who wanted to see them, and that the tapes were merely part of a "mosaic" of countless things Adams reviewed and considered in preparing for a game.

In the end, Goodell eagerly shut down the possibility of further investigation and additional sanctions. Even Specter lost his stomach for the fight, revealing in June that he was done trying to kick-start a congressional investigation into Spygate. Belichick and the Patriots had to pay their fines and surrender their first-round draft choice, No. 31 overall, but the coach would be eligible to do his job on opening day. He had won something by avoiding a suspension, and yet he had lost so much in the court of public opinion. In 44 states, Belichick was now branded a cheater, and in many precincts he was considered a liar for swearing he was guilty of an unintentional error, nothing more.

Football is a game of inches, not yards, and some suspected that Spygate advantages had allowed the Patriots to win three rings by a combined nine points. Yes, they did dominate in 2007, after the operation was shut down. No, they didn't win the whole thing. New England didn't have illegal film on the Giants from their regular-season game, and the Giants won the Super Bowl rematch by inches, not yards. Was cheating the difference between second place and first? Would the Patriots have won ring No. 4 if they'd stolen a few signs in Giants Stadium, in December, by way of a sideline camera?

The Patriots knew that the only way to silence those questions was to actually win ring No. 4. And as Bill Belichick rebounded from a near-lethal strike on his reputation, he didn't realize how forbidding a task that would prove to be.

Bill Belichick always met with his quarterbacks twice a week. And for nearly seven full years and four Super Bowl runs, his lead quarterback in the meeting room was Tom Brady, who had made 127 consecutive regular-season and postseason starts. That streak died at 128, in the first quarter of the 2008 opener against Kansas City, when Chiefs safety Bernard Pollard came in low and hit the quarterback's left leg, blowing out the ACL and MCL in his knee.

That Belichick went 11-5 that year with Matt Cassel at quarterback, only to become the first 11-win coach to miss the playoffs since the 1990 expansion to a 12-team postseason, amounted to a cruel injustice. But if nothing else, Brady's absence allowed Belichick room to reaffirm his greatness in a different way. His 11-5 record with Cassel (though Brady, the starter, was credited with the Kansas City victory) represented a necessary counterargument to those who pointed to his 5-13 record with Drew Bledsoe and his 36-44 record in Cleveland with Bernie Kosar, Vinny Testaverde, and friends as proof that Brady had made the coach, not the other way around. It also verified Belichick's system of finding and developing talent on the field, on the coaching staff, and in the front office.

His primary executive charged with identifying that talent, Pioli, left after the 2008 season to become general manager of the Chiefs. Out of loyalty to the man who raised him in the business, Pioli had rejected lucrative offers over the years from franchises that would have no Belichick for him to answer to. Like Josh McDaniels, the offensive coordinator who left to become head coach of the Denver Broncos, Pioli thought it was time to go out on his own. The system remained in place in Foxborough, with its founding father, just as it had when Thomas Dimitroff left his position as director of college scouting a year earlier to become the GM in Atlanta.

Belichick had moved people around his organization, most notably Nick Caserio, a coach and scout who was elevated to director of pro personnel and then director of player personnel. Caserio was typical of the young men Belichick often hired and groomed. He played small-college football at John Carroll, in Ohio, as did McDaniels, turning the Jesuit school into what would become a Triple-A farm team for New England coaches and staffers. McDaniels was the loser of a quarterback competition with Caserio, who was eventually hired as a personnel assistant by the Patriots, on McDaniels's recommendation. A Division III backup at Wesleyan, Belichick seemed to be looking for future Belichicks in the same kinds of places.

Eric Mangini had played at Wesleyan, Pioli had played Division II ball at Central Connecticut, and Dimitroff had played college ball in Canada, at the University of Guelph. Brian Daboll had played Division III football at the University of Rochester, and Matt Patricia did the same at Rensselaer Polytechnic Institute, in upstate New York. Josh Boyer, a defensive assistant elevated to defensive backs coach in 2009, had played his Division III football at Ohio's Muskingum University, and Monti Ossenfort, a rising scout in the organization, had been a Division III quarterback at the University of Minnesota–Morris.

Those who play small-college football normally do so because they adore the game. They are often hardworking, resourceful athletes forever finding ways to overcome their physical shortcomings, and they are often hungry to prove something and willing to work overtime to do it. The profile jibes perfectly with the Belichick ethos.

By hiring young applicants, and by generally avoiding retreads, Belichick didn't have to worry about deprogramming staffers who had been developed in less successful systems. He could teach the Patriot Way to a twentysomething assistant, teach him how to evaluate talent and identify players who could thrive in New England — even if they weren't likely to thrive for other teams. Belichick cared only about what a prospect could do, or couldn't do, in his program. He wasn't in the business of collecting talent, but of picking players who could form a highly functioning team. He despised groupthink, and he knew that lazy-minded, insecure scouts often shared opinions and information with peers in competing organizations in order to validate their evaluations and cover their asses.

Pioli's departure after the 2008 season left a significant front-office void and forced Belichick to rearrange his cabinet, installing Caserio as the franchise's lead personnel voice. Belichick promoted Jon Robinson from assistant director of college scouting to the director's chair and hired an old friend and colleague from his 1970s days in Detroit, Floyd Reese, who had built a Super Bowl team as GM of the 1999 Tennessee Titans, to help out with contracts as a senior football adviser. Belichick also rehired Jason Licht, who had left New England for Philadelphia after the 2002 season and later moved over to Arizona. Licht was proof that Belichick was willing to bring back into the organization people who had left him for other opportunities — he'd also rehire Daboll and McDaniels years later — as long as those people weren't named Eric Mangini.

In his nine years in New England, Pioli had been the most valuable Patriot outside of Belichick in shaping a championship roster, in acquiring players with strong character, and in allowing the head coach to do more delegating and big-picture, off-the-field managing of issues than he'd done in Cleveland. Pioli's eye for talent — or, more specifically, talent that would work in Foxborough — was unquestioned. But as a leader, he was more like his father-in-law, Bill Parcells, than Belichick. Some of his subordinates found him too demanding, too Parcellsian in his approach and tone. Many Patriots scouts and junior personnel types thought that Pioli had a big heart, a genuine concern for their family issues, and an engaging personality away from the office, but that his second-floor work environment was a full-pads experience. No matter how his management style was viewed, it was clear that his expertise would be sorely missed.

As he transitioned to the more even-tempered Caserio, Belichick was still surrounded by staffers who had made significant behind-the-scenes contributions to the culture that had landed New England in the Super Bowl four times in seven years. Belichick had always guarded his organization as if it were the Kremlin (some competing coaches actually referred to him as the Kremlin), and Spygate hadn't exactly inspired a new era of glasnost. So these front-office and support people remained more faceless than a Belichick long snapper. NFL sources with direct knowledge of the key people in those roles offered up the following composite scouting reports:

Nick Caserio, director of player personnel: "He's a great example of being born and bred in the Belichick system. Bill meets someone and he tries to identify the intangibles, your character and work ethic, and Nick epitomizes the Patriot Way . . . If you slice Nick's wrist, I don't think blood would come out. You'd see wires . . . Nick is a machine. His work ethic is off the charts. He's there at the crack of dawn, and he's not leaving until maybe an hour before the crack of dawn . . . When people see how dialed in he is, they don't see the human side. But when he gets you one-on-one, you see a good-hearted person."

Jason Licht, director of pro personnel: "Jason is the guy who says, 'Hey, let's get a beer after work.' In New England, if you have time for a beer after work, you have time to really watch more tape. Jason's a guy, in my opinion, that fights to find balance, because he's seen too many guys crash and burn. They put all their eggs in that basket and the family takes a back seat, and once that job is gone, they have nothing . . . Jason Licht, you can drop him in a cave in Afghanistan and he's going to talk to somebody. Jason has a lot more personality than Nick, who is very black-and-white. I'll say this delicately, but Nick is like a lot of those lifers with Bill, where they almost become institutionalized, where, when they leave, they can't operate in the wild."

Berj Najarian, director of football/head coach administration: "You know, that's Bill's right-hand man times a million. He's got personality, Berj, but you always wonder what he's thinking. I remember [Drew Bledsoe] on Secretaries Day sent Berj flowers and he was all pissed off. It was a joke . . . But you know his hands are in everything. He works a lot closer with coaches than the scouts. That's a guy people try to keep at arm's distance, because you get the sense that whatever we're talking about is being brought back and analyzed. So because of that, you're going to weigh every word. Guys are not really themselves around Berj . . . Berj worked his butt off to soften Bill's edges. He did a lot of sit-downs, a lot of people stuff that Bill would never do before, to help Bill. Berj is one of the unknowns, but he's done an incredible job of helping Bill with the media."

Jon Robinson, director of college scouting: "Bright. That man has earned it every step of the way. Treats people right . . . He had a rule for scouts, that they weren't allowed to be on the road any more than 12 days if you had a family, and if you had kids, you had to be home for their birthdays and for Halloween. And that was nonnegotiable. There are guys you work for because it's the job, and other guys you *want* to work for. He's one of those guys you want to work for."

Monti Ossenfort, national scout: "He's very similar to Jon Robinson. He has personality, and he's a guy people are loyal to. Monti was in New England, went to Houston, and then came back, so he's another guy Bill was willing to bring back to the organization . . . He's the next star coming. He's going to be a GM . . . He's a scout's scout . . . Great credibility."

Bob Quinn, assistant director of pro personnel: "Has a plan. A philosophical conviction on how to build a team. Smart, and has an air of confidence about him that doesn't manifest itself as arrogance . . . The one knock on him is you had to watch what you said around him. He's the guy who's going to run and tell the teacher."

Floyd Reese, senior football adviser: "Floyd's the best storyteller . . . A lot of young scouts think the more intricacies they can give in a report, and the more buzzwords and polish, made them come across as more intelligent and diligent. And Floyd is like 'Can he catch the ball or not? Can he run or not? Can he tackle or not?' . . . He was as old school and simplistic as you can imagine, but he had a tremendous way to take a whole lot of information, put it through a filter, and come up with one or two words and solve it."

Nancy Meier, director of scouting administration since 1975: "Love her. She's been through it all. What she means to that personnel department, you can't put a monetary value on it. She's the one common denominator in that department . . . She handles expenses, takes care of flights. 'I'm stuck in Omaha and I've got to get to San Francisco.' Boom, there it is. She minimizes stress for scouts."

Frantzy Jourdain, area scout: "Never a guy to go out there tooting his own horn . . . Frantzy was another one a lot like Floyd Reese. He's not going to come across great in his reports, but if you sit down and talk with him, you know he knows what he's talking about . . . Exceptional at getting background information about these guys in the SEC. Who's getting money from this one, who had this problem, who smoked weed and got pinched for it three times — he's that guy."

Brian Smith, assistant director of college scouting: "He's another guy who has a work ethic you can't even put on the chart . . . A consummate foot soldier. He's been institutionalized. He's a guy who will make sure he's the last one leaving the office, for fear of reprisal . . . He's as good a person as you'll ever be around. He's seen it all. He was an operations assistant before he got into scouting. He'd run around and make sure the food was right, and he talked about having to take Bill's car to get an oil change and you'd get in his car, open it up, and all kinds of wrappers and cups and water bottles came flying out."

Ivan Fears, running backs coach since 2003, receivers coach for Belichick's first two years: "Whatever running backs Bill brought in, he got up to speed . . . He doesn't have the same fire as others, but that's his personality . . . People wonder how much longer he can go, but he's there for a reason."

Kevin Anderson, football operations staffer since 2006: "Don't want to say he was a lackey. Consummate gofer."

Pepper Johnson, defensive assistant since 2000: "He's more the yeller and motherfucker and motivator than a technician. Bill never had anyone outside of Bill O'Brien [hired in 2007] who was that fiery . . . Pepper was like 'I'm going to motherfuck you to do it right,' rather than 'I want your feet here or your hands here.' Bill never had a high-level player like Pepper on his staff."

Johnson had started working with Belichick in 1986, his rookie year with the Giants. But the Patriots' head coach went back much further with another member of his staff, the former Andover classmate with the intentionally vague title of football research director. Of all the men and women under Belichick's employ, the most fascinating was Ernie Adams, a polarizing figure of sorts. Some coaches were clearly envious of the influence Ernie had on Belichick. In the early dynasty days, offensive coordinator Charlie Weis had very little use for Adams and believed that, when it came to deciphering signals and predicting plays, he was wrong as often as he was right.

"People in the building, mostly coaches," said one Patriots official, "got frustrated with some of Ernie's information . . . When Ernie was right, internally he got a lot of credit. When he was wrong, it never came up." The official said Mangini was another coach who grew frustrated with Adams's batting average.

Other staff members were put off by the fact that, in an organization shaped by accountability, Adams would fall asleep in meetings, without repercussions. One staffer recalled seeing Ernie out cold for the first time in a draft meeting, with his mouth wide open "like a Pez dispenser," and everybody else going about their business as if it were a common occurrence. "Sometimes Ernie would wake up and be right in the conversation," said a Patriots executive. One New England official said that coaches and personnel executives generally respected Adams's intellect and his knowledge of football strategy and history. Post-Spygate, information on opponents' signals — sans the illegal tapes — was still going straight to him.

"But he's not one of the guys embraced by the true meat-and-potatoes people," the official said. "He's got the late-seventies mustache, he still wears corduroys, he's got the brown bag lunch, and because of the packaging some guys can't look past that . . . He's definitely a guy whose value is greatest in the shadows."

In the team facility at Gillette Stadium, the shadows didn't provide much cover. Belichick knew what every staffer was doing, thinking, and saying, or at least it seemed that way. "Bill's got sleeper cells all over the place," one team official said. "You never know who you're talking to, and how the hell Bill ends up knowing what was said." His Big Brother presence aside, Belichick did not rule as an iron-fisted autocrat who spoke condescendingly to subordinates when discussing and debating personnel. Belichick's advisers and evaluators, from Adams and Caserio on down to the lowest-level scouts, were forever encouraged to think independently and to challenge a consensus opinion in the room about a player if they had done the homework to support their position. Listening was among Belichick's greatest strengths, and he allowed his scouts to talk him into, or out of, loving a prospect.

Belichick did have a defined philosophy on what the Patriots were looking for when hunting for talent. In meetings called to discuss players, Belichick said he asks himself and his cabinet members, "'What do we want them to do? What role do we envision them in? What spot do we see on the team that that player could perform?' and then try and find players that fit that criteria that can do the things that we want them to do. I think that gives them a lot better chance to succeed, as opposed to going out there and getting somebody and then saying, 'OK, now what are we going to do with them? Can he do this, can he do that?' We try to find somebody that can specifically fill a spot or do a job in our system that is pretty well defined. Whether that be a third receiver, a fourth corner, a swing tackle, sixth linebacker, fifth running back, whatever it happens to be. We try to define those spots on our team and then find players that will fit the criteria both physically and mentally and from an experience standpoint and so forth that we identify for that."

The Patriots identify the holes in their roster and then use their system of grading prospects to fill them. After Belichick was hired in New England, Pioli and Adams performed a makeover on the Patriots' scouting manual, which dated back to the franchise's Bucko Kilroy days. The system had some Kilroy in it, a little Gil Brandt from Dallas, a little Dom Anile from Cleveland. The uppercase letter that preceded the numerical grade represented a player's "type," and the lowercase letter that followed the numerical grade represented an "alert."

Among the uppercase letters assessing a prospect's type, an A signified greatness, a B signified that a player didn't have the desired bulk, and an S signified that a player didn't have the desired speed. Scouts used a Q for a player who didn't have the desired height, and a P for a player who would likely change positions in the NFL.

Patriots scouts grouped prospects into categories, such as a first-year or day-one starter, a "make it" player (one who's good enough to make a roster), and a reject. "A 7.0 is a first-year starter, a high-end guy," said one veteran Patriots scout. "An 8.0 is the Tom Bradys of the world, an elite player in the league. Once you get into the 6's, these are starters. A 6.8 or 6.9 would be a first-year starter. A three-down back would be a 6.9. A 6.2 for us would be like a center with guard flex . . . The upper 5's are backups, and the lower 5's are practice squad guys. Once you get to 5.4 and below, they're good for camp, but that's all they're going to be. And then you have your rejects."

The Belichick-Pioli standard for rejects was higher than most.

"When you put a grade on a player, it's always what he'll be in year two," said one scout. "The reason is that year one is a learning curve for everybody, but your grade is based on your specific role. He's a starter. He's a third guard. He's a third tackle. He's a center who has guard flexibility. He's a wide receiver who can only play in the slot. He's strictly a box safety. So Bill will be like 'Listen, we need a designated pass rusher. We need a slot corner only, so who are our slot corners?' Other places give these global instructions, and it's like 'How the hell do you know who's a second-round player?' Bill's thing is *role*. Everything is role-based. Bill also wants you, as a scout, to describe a player's body type to someone on the current or past Patriots roster. But the character part — that's where the heavy lifting is for us."

That's where the lowercase letters — after a player's numerical grade — come into play. These "alerts" can mean the difference between drafting a prospect and passing on him, so draft-eligible collegians wanted to have as few of these as possible printed after their numerical grades. A lowercase *c* identified a prospect as having a character issue, such as a history of marijuana use or a DUI arrest.

"And when there's a double *c*, that kid is a real shitbag," a Patriots scout said. "An *m* is there for mental issues, and if there's an injury history, you put down an *x*, like for a torn ACL as a sophomore. You put down double *x*'s with two major surgeries . . . But it's the guy with a double *c* that you stay away from."

In the 2010 NFL draft, the Patriots considered a player who certainly qualified for a double *c* designation. Aaron Hernandez, tight end at the University of Florida, was among the most talented and troubled college athletes in America.

"There was so much dirt on Aaron Hernandez," said one scout who had worked for Belichick, "it seemed you could dig up as much as you wanted. You could dig up enough to take him off your draft board, or you could stop at a certain point because you wanted to keep him alive on your draft board."

The Patriots had reasons to keep him alive on their board. They had just completed a near-disastrous 2009 (by their standards) that was highlighted by Brady's return to health, a record-setting 45–0 halftime lead over Tennessee in Week 6, and not much else. Belichick had traded away two of his longtime defensive leaders, Richard Seymour and Mike Vrabel, and watched two others, Rodney Harrison and Tedy Bruschi, retire before the start of what would be a 10-6 season defined by the coach's running conflict with Adalius Thomas and a blown 17-point fourth-quarter lead in Indianapolis, where Belichick gambled late and lost on fourth-and-2 at his own 28 with a six-point lead.

Seymour's departure was particularly painful, and yet, like Ty Law's (off to the Jets in 2005) and Willie McGinest's (off to Cleveland in 2006), it stood as another example of Belichick moving on from significant contributors if he believes they are about to become too expensive or too old. Brady was nothing like his monstrous 2007 self, after a year spent recovering from his knee injury, but he still managed to play at a Pro Bowl level while throwing to Randy Moss and Wes Welker, who combined for more than 2,600 receiving yards. (Welker wrecked his knee in the final regular-season game.)

Moss finished with 13 touchdowns, but he was held to five catches and 48 yards in New England's humiliating home playoff loss to the Baltimore Ravens, who intercepted Brady three times, strip-sacked him once, and took a 24–0 lead in the first quarter on the way to a 33–14 victory. Ravens running back Ray Rice took the first play from scrimmage 83 yards for a touchdown, and New England ended up with its first home playoff loss in nine games under Belichick. The fans were booing midway through the first quarter, and afterward Brady and others were being asked if this shocking blowout at home signaled the end of an era.

In the *Herald,* columnist Gerry Callahan shredded Belichick for dealing away Seymour for Oakland's No. 1 pick in 2011 and wasting a year of Brady's prime. In the locker room, nose tackle Vince Wilfork compared New England unfavorably to a high school junior varsity team. The Patriots' leadership void was obvious even outside the defensive unit; Belichick admitted that some of his younger assistants weren't as comfortable challenging him as his former coordinators Romeo Crennel and Charlie Weis had been. A few days later, Dean Pees, defensive coordinator, said he was leaving to pursue other opportunities, and Belichick declared that he'd keep the official job title open and assume a bigger role with the defense. (Bill O'Brien, quarterbacks coach, would continue to act as the unofficial offensive coordinator.)

Something else needed to give. Moss had caught 47 touchdown passes in 48 regular-season games with the Patriots, and yet he had only one touchdown catch and 142 receiving yards in four postseason games. As the Patriots were about winning championships, not division titles and playoff berths, they needed to try a different approach. They needed to start playing offense from the inside out rather than from the outside in.

Belichick decided to return to his early NFL roots, to a seminal moment in his career with the 1976 Detroit Lions, whom the young aide persuaded to use a two-tight-end set against a good New England team in what would be a stunning 30–10 victory for the sad-sack Lions. More than three decades later, Belichick was in the market for more than one tight end. And the best at that position in college football, Aaron Hernandez, happened to be coached by Urban Meyer, one of Belichick's close friends. Meyer was known for winning big and for seemingly having more of his players get in trouble with the law than any major-college coach around.

Hernandez was a habitual marijuana user who had reportedly failed multiple drug tests at Florida and yet had been suspended for only one game. Meyer hadn't suspended him for punching a Gainesville bar employee and rupturing the man's eardrum, despite teammate Tim Tebow's attempts to stop the assault. (The police recommended charging Hernandez with a felony before the case was somehow settled out of court.) The Florida coach apparently hadn't taken any action against Hernandez — a freshman still only 17 years old — for refusing to cooperate with police investigating a shooting that had left two men in a car wounded and one shot in the back of the head; an unharmed passenger initially told police that the shooter was a Hawaiian or Hispanic male who stood about 6'3" or 6'4" and had a muscular build and a lot of tattoos.

Meyer did lead Hernandez through Bible sessions and invite him into his family home, and he assigned Tebow as his de facto guardian. But he did not take away the thing Hernandez cherished most: football.

The record-setting high school star from the rough side of Bristol, Connecticut, caught 68 passes for five touchdowns his junior season at Florida and won the John Mackey Award as the nation's top tight end before declaring for the NFL draft. Hernandez's supporters painted him as the product of a devastating event in his life — the sudden death of his 49-year-old father, Dennis, a legendary high school athlete, when Aaron was 16 — and a dysfunctional home life that steered him into friendships with local criminals and drug pushers. Hernandez ran with a bad crowd, they said, neglecting this cold, hard truth: Hernandez *was* the bad crowd.

Originally intending to play at UConn with his older brother, D.J., widely viewed as the rare positive influence in his life, Hernandez was seen in Gainesville and on return trips from Connecticut hanging with Bristol friends who were not interested in Meyer's Bible study. Hernandez was already a wreck before his 20th birthday, which he celebrated a few months before taking a pre-draft psychological test administered by Human Resource Tactics, a scouting service that provided a number of NFL teams with assessments of a prospect's maturity, coachability, and dedication, and that advertised its tests as "proven predictors of subsequent performance in the league and delinquency off the field."

The Wall Street Journal reported that on a scale of 1 to 10, Hernandez scored the lowest possible number, 1, in the category of "social maturity," and that his responses suggested that he "enjoys living on the edge of acceptable behavior and that he may be prone to partying too much and doing questionable things that could be seen as a problem for him and his team." Hernandez actually received high marks for focus and mental quickness (a perfect 10 in both), self-efficacy, and receptivity to coaching. The report stated that the tight end saw himself "as a football player above all else" and predicted that he would "place a high priority on football and what it takes to be successful."

The Patriots wanted to bank on the possibility that Hernandez's desire to excel at football would overcome his self-destructive instincts. They had a private workout with the tight end and Tebow, attended by Belichick, Patriots linebackers coach Matt Patricia, and director of pro personnel Jason Licht. At 6′2″ and a chiseled 250, Hernandez showed off the dynamic athleticism that made him a first-round talent and a potential matchup nightmare for defensive coordinators in the NFL. "Bill thought he was the player missing on our team," said someone with knowledge of the workout.

A Drew Bledsoe fan growing up in Connecticut, Hernandez also showed what one Patriots source described as "great football intelligence" when Belichick quizzed him on situations in a classroom setting. Meyer did warn Belichick about Hernandez's behavior problems, though the depth of that warning was unclear. The Florida coach would say years later that he told his friend, "You just need to keep an eye on him." Only that was not what Meyer told some other NFL teams that inquired about his tight end.

One official with another team who asked about Hernandez said that Meyer told him, "Look, this guy's a hell of a football player, but he fucking lies to beat the system and teaches all our other guys to beat the system. With the marijuana stuff, we've never caught this guy, but we know he's doing it . . . Don't fucking touch that guy."

This team official was taken aback when Belichick, Meyer's friend, ended up drafting Hernandez in the fourth round with the 113th overall pick. "I never understood that," the official said. A number of NFL teams had taken Hernandez off their draft boards. They recognized that his skills made him a difference maker, but they just couldn't invest in a personality so volatile. The Patriots, meanwhile, practiced and played their games two hours from Bristol, where Hernandez could find trouble on every other block. Bringing him home magnified the risk.

"It seemed to us that [Hernandez] loved football," said one Patriots source. "Bill's had a lot of success with guys who have had problems elsewhere, so we thought Aaron could be successful with us. Usually if a guy has problems and he loves football, you can still work with him, because he doesn't want football to be taken away from him and be left with nothing."

A couple of weeks before the April draft, Hernandez sent out a letter to New England — through his agent, David Dunn, of Athletes First — in an attempt to allay the team's fears about selecting him. His letter was addressed to Nick Caserio, and in it Hernandez offered to take biweekly drug tests throughout his rookie season and to return some of his guaranteed salary to the team if he failed any of them. In the event that the collective bargaining agreement disallowed such a contractual agreement — which it would — Hernandez offered to donate some of his wages to the charities of New England's choosing.

"My coaches have told you that nobody on our Florida team worked harder than me in terms of workouts, practices or games," Hernandez wrote. "You have your own evaluation as to the type of impact I can have on your offense . . . In closing, I ask you to trust me when I say you have absolutely nothing to worry about when it comes to me and the use of recreational drugs. I have set very high goals for myself in the NFL, and am focused 100% on achieving those goals."

Belichick used his second-round pick in the draft on University of Arizona tight end Rob Gronkowski, who had missed his junior season in 2009 because of back surgery. Though Gronkowski was 6'6" and ran like a much smaller man, his back injury made him a gamble. Just not the kind of gamble that Hernandez was two rounds later. Despite the Florida star's considerable issues, the Patriots didn't think he'd still be on the board in the fourth round.

"I'm glad he was," Belichick said.

Meyer had delivered his friend perhaps his biggest draft bust in New England, Florida wide receiver Chad Jackson, the 36th overall pick in 2006, who caught only 13 passes as a rookie before a serious knee injury suffered in the AFC Championship Game derailed his career. And yet Meyer all but handpicked New England's 2010 draft, as Belichick selected Florida linebackers Jermaine Cunningham and Brandon Spikes in the second round (with Gronkowski), providing a measure of familiarity for Hernandez.

Floyd Reese was working contracts for Belichick, and he included some conduct clauses in Hernandez's deal that protected the team. Reese said that the Patriots were well aware of all of Hernandez's problems in Gainesville and that they had constructed a rookie deal in a way that would "make him understand he was going to get every cent that he was due at the draft slot . . . but that he was going to have to earn it. It was not going to come all at once just because you were picked in the fourth round . . . He had to stay on the straight and narrow. In the contract, he was going to be penalized for issues with drugs or being late or any of the things you look for."

Hernandez suited up as the youngest player in the NFL. In his first minicamp as a New England Patriot, winded after some reps, Hernandez jogged over to the sideline and approached the team's head trainer, Jim Whalen, with his mouth open. "I want water," the tight end said. Whalen grabbed the water bottle, threw it at Hernandez, and said, "This isn't fucking Florida. Do it yourself." Hernandez picked up the bottle, drank from it, then laughed as he threw it back down and walked away. The Patriot Way was about to be tested to the max.

If Bill Belichick was a talent evaluator without peer, he still had a couple of holes in his game. He had a hard time drafting the right defensive backs and wide receivers. Belichick also made underwhelming first-round choices at tight end in Daniel Graham (2002) and Benjamin Watson (2004), though he did prove himself at that position in the selections of Rob Gronkowski and Aaron Hernandez.

Off the alarming 10-6, one-and-done season in 2009, Belichick transformed his offense by shipping out the most lethal skill-position player he'd coached, Randy Moss, four games into the 2010 season. The receiver had reverted back to pre-Foxborough form by campaigning for a new contract and saying he felt unwanted. He also refused to engage fans in the team's annual charity Kickoff Gala, an event close to Robert Kraft's heart. Moss reportedly had a halftime confrontation with Bill O'Brien in the middle of a game at Miami and reportedly had a locker room argument with Brady over, of all things, the receiver's beard and the quarterback's long hair. The *Herald* said Moss had asked for a trade.

Belichick might have tried to work things out with a 27-year-old Moss, but not with a 33-year-old Moss, and especially not with a 33-year-old Moss who had put up marginal numbers in the postseason. Belichick dealt him back to his original team, Minnesota, and then went to work on reacquiring Deion Branch from Seattle to give Brady a fighting chance. But the coach's vision for this team clearly revolved around his explosive playmakers at tight end, Gronkowski and Hernandez, who returned the Patriots to legitimate championship contention.

Over the 2010 and 2011 regular seasons, Gronkowski and Hernandez combined for 256 receptions and 40 touchdown catches (27 by Gronkowski) as New England went 27-5. The Patriots suffered a crushing home playoff loss to Rex Ryan's Jets in between; the Jets sacked Brady five times and intercepted him once. Yet, according to a Patriots source, Belichick thought that over time the use of a "12 personnel" offense, or a two-tight-end set, would compromise some of the Ryan pressure packages that were giving New England problems.

"The transition from three wide receivers to a double tight end . . . came in response to Rex's overload pressure on one side," the source said. "With two tight ends, it makes it very difficult to do that. Or you could play 21 personnel and put Hernandez in the backfield; that versatility would get the Jets trapped in their base defense, and some of their exotic packages were then minimized to some degree. If you put 12 personnel on the field, you're leaving your base defense on . . . It's not like Bill sat down and said, 'We've got to get back at the Jets,' but he realized the Jets had schematic things that gave us problems, and that other people were going to duplicate it. Until we got hold of it, it wasn't going away. Once we got to more of a 12 personnel team with Gronk and Hernandez, those issues with the Jets went away."

The Jets had split with the Patriots in 2008 and 2009 and had taken two of three in 2010, including the divisional-round victory over the top seeds at Gillette Stadium that left Belichick and Brady feeling almost as gutted as they were after the Super Bowl loss to the Giants. But New England swept the Jets in 2011, outscoring them 67–37 in the process, and then swept them again the following year. It appeared that Belichick's roll of the dice with Hernandez had paid off. The combined numbers of Hernandez and Gronkowski in the 2011 season (169 catches, 2,237 yards) obliterated the previous NFL highs for a tight-end tandem. A personnel man who had worked with Belichick in a different organization said that Hernandez had "revolutionized" the Patriots' offense. "They had the no-huddle concept that destroyed everybody," he said. "You could never line up in the right defense."

With tattoos snaking up and down his exposed arms, Hernandez was quite a sight as he zigged and zagged across the field. One AFC general manager who had removed the Florida tight end from his draft board over character concerns was suddenly kicking himself for not picking him. "We were like 'Wow, I guess we blew that one,'" the GM said. "All those concerns were for naught." Hernandez scored a touchdown and gained 61 rushing yards, including a 43-yard run that set up the opening touchdown, in a 45–10 playoff rout of Denver, then had seven catches in the 23–20 AFC Championship Game victory over Baltimore.

"Every time we had him do something," Reese recalled of Hernandez, "it was shocking how well he did it. Near the end of his career, we were playing him as a running back, and we would turn around and give him the ball and it was shocking how well he ran it. He could do anything you wanted him to do."

Without Moss's length and acrobatics at his disposal, Belichick had found a different way to torment opposing defensive coordinators. The Patriots gained 6,848 yards in 2011, second most in the league, and they scored 513 points, third most in the league. They were returning to the Super Bowl for the first time in four years with a remodeled offense, and Belichick was ready to deploy it against the one football coach on the planet who seemed to have his number.

Tom Coughlin was never intimidated by Bill Belichick, and that was half the battle. The aura of Belichick and the power of his hundred-yard stare seemed to compel stressed-out opponents to do things they didn't ordinarily do. Coughlin knew better. He had known Belichick as an equal when the two went head to head in Giants practices under Bill Parcells's watch.

Side by side, they watched as Belichick's defensive backs tried to cover Coughlin's receivers. Belichick would ask his staffmate what he thought was the most challenging part of the secondary's coverage, and in turn Coughlin would ask his staffmate what he thought was the hardest part of defending the wideouts. Belichick said he worked more with Coughlin than he did with any other offensive assistant. They were forever trying to make each other better for the good of the team, and they were forever succeeding in that pursuit.

Belichick called Coughlin a good friend and a disciplined, hard-nosed coach whose teams reflected his approach. "I would say that, as an assistant coach," Belichick said, "it was the best relationship that I have ever had with another counterpart in that way." Coughlin returned the compliment in public settings when the two were about to face off. "I've got nothing but respect for Bill Belichick as a coach," he said. Coughlin added that he liked working with Belichick "because he was always about football, what he could do to make his players better," and spoke highly of Belichick's emphasis on toughness and preparation.

"We became good friends," Coughlin said. "We shared a lot of thoughts together."

So as these two fiercely determined men prepared to meet in Super Bowl XLVI, in Indianapolis, four years after their epic confrontation in Arizona, the storyline was set. Belichick and Coughlin, good friends and colleagues dating back to their Parcells days, were ready to compete for another championship before returning to their respective corners inside their mutual admiration society. Except that multiple people who had worked every day with Coughlin for years made some behind-the-scenes edits to that script. They maintained that, as much as Coughlin respected Belichick's football IQ and work ethic and had enjoyed matching wits with him in bygone Giants practices, he didn't have much use for Belichick the person. Tom didn't hate Bill; that was too strong a word. He just didn't particularly like him.

Coughlin had beaten Belichick in four of their five meetings as head coaches, including two when Tom was in Jacksonville and Bill was in Cleveland. In their most recent meeting, in November, Coughlin's Giants had ended Belichick's 20-game home winning streak and Brady's league-record 31-game home winning streak on Eli Manning's one-yard scoring pass to Jake Ballard with 15 seconds to go. Coughlin was hoisted in the air by Brandon Jacobs in the jubilant visitors' locker room. After surviving a four-game losing streak and more calls for his head, the Giants' coach had gotten hot at the right time. He'd turned a 7-7 record into a Super Bowl rematch with Belichick by beating the 15-1 defending-champion Packers in Green Bay and the 13-3 49ers in overtime in San Francisco. The Patriots had won ten consecutive games after their regular-season loss to the Giants, and they were about as tired of losing to this franchise as the old-guard Pats were of Belichick talking up Harry Carson, Carl Banks, and LT.

Even though Rob Gronkowski was severely limited by a high ankle sprain suffered in the AFC title game, Belichick had appeared relaxed during the week, advancing his trend of trotting out a kinder, gentler version of himself for the Super Bowl. He joked that he'd received a warm welcome from Indianapolis residents who appreciated his fourth-and-two gamble gone wrong against the Colts in the 2009 regular season, and was loose enough around the players that Wes Welker wondered if the change had been brought on by "a lady in his life." In fact, for about five years, Belichick had been dating the stunning Linda Holliday, a correspondent for the *StyleBoston* TV show and a thrice-divorced mother of twin girls. Holliday seemed to be doing a fairly good job on the human relations front. "Linda's fantastic for him," said Boston Celtics coach Doc Rivers, a Belichick friend who had spent some time in the couple's company. "Just a good person and fiery and funny and light, and I love watching games with her."

Rivers and Belichick had addressed each other's teams on occasion, and Rivers was impressed when he found Brady sitting in the front row with a notebook, as if he were a fifth grader eager to please the substitute teacher. Known as one of the more user-friendly coaches in professional sports, Rivers told anyone who would listen that Belichick was at heart a fun and agreeable personality. "I think Bill has that with the people he wants to have it with," Rivers said. "I think Bill's as engaging as anybody I know. I tell people all the time that he has a great personality and he's extremely funny. But Bill knows he's comfortable using it with people he trusts, his friends. The Bill Belichick you see in front of the media is the Bill Belichick doing his job. The Bill you see in other places is the Bill being a loving guy with friends and family."

The media tested Belichick at least once in Indianapolis. He fielded a Spygate question at the Super Bowl for the first time in a while, and it was a perfectly legitimate one. The Patriots hadn't won it all since they were caught breaking the rules, and that was becoming a thing. "We moved on from everything in the past," Belichick said in batting away the question. "We are focused on this game. That's it."

Coughlin was also busy validating the notion that he was no longer the oppressive ruler from the bad old days of 2004–2006, before he established a leadership council of veterans to connect with the locker room and before he actually interviewed local football writers on how he could improve his own tense relationship with the press. Given his head-to-head record against Belichick, and his team's belief that it could always find a way to beat New England, Coughlin had reason to feel good.

"I just think Tom and our coaching staff had their staff's number," said Giants kicker Lawrence Tynes, who had won the NFC Championship Game (against San Francisco) on an overtime field goal for the second time. "I think, as a player, and I'm not an X-and-O guy, but I think those guys believed because Tom had beaten Belichick and had a proven track record. So when Tom was presenting his plan for the Patriots, you've got 53 guys believing, and now it's going to be hard to beat them."

Then again, Bill Belichick had two weeks to prepare for the Giants. He was the best coach in football, and people up and down the Giants organization still couldn't believe what he had pulled off in 2007, going 18-0 with an offensive line they thought was mediocre at best. That line couldn't protect Brady against Coughlin's pass rush in Super Bowl XLII, inspiring one Giants executive to say, "It's the only time I've ever seen Brady get rattled. This fucking guy is fearless; he never flinches. That was the first time I've ever seen him imagine pressure that wasn't there."

Four years later, the Giants thought they had made Brady flinch again in their Week 9 victory at Gillette Stadium. "He was reacting to pressure that didn't exist," said second-year pass rusher Jason Pierre-Paul, who had 16.5 sacks in 2011, "and he was just throwing the ball places that there wasn't a receiver there. So imagine us just getting there even faster and we're actually doing our jobs and getting there and getting hits on him."

The Patriots' challenge was clear. They had to solve a defense that knew how to rattle the quarterback, and a leader, Coughlin, who had no love for, or fear of, the highly decorated coach on the other side of the field.

• • •

Tom Brady had the lead, the ball, and an open Wes Welker in Giants territory with a little more than four minutes to play and the trailing team in possession of only one timeout. Brady let go of a pass down the left side of the field, and suddenly New England's fourth title seemed as certain as it had when that Eli Manning pass was heading Asante Samuel's way in Super Bowl XLII.

Welker had even better hands than Samuel, and, while Belichick had staged his two-tight-end clinic all year, the receiver reminded everyone that his coach had revolutionized the slot position, too. Fully recovered from the knee injury he'd suffered two years earlier, Welker had career highs of 1,569 yards (on 122 catches) and nine touchdowns during the regular season. He'd also caught all seven passes Brady threw his way inside Lucas Oil Stadium and had run the ball twice for 21 yards. Welker was positioned near the Giants' 22 as the lofted pass came in for a landing with about 111 million Americans watching.

The Patriots were going to win No. 4 with Gronkowski making two catches on one leg, and with unwanted players all over the field. Welker was undrafted. New England's two featured running backs, BenJarvus Green-Ellis and Danny Woodhead, were undrafted, and the all-time great quarterback sharing their backfield was picked 199th. The starting center, Dan Connolly, was undrafted. On the starting defensive line, Kyle Love was undrafted, and Brandon Deaderick was a seventh-round pick. Among the starting linebacker group, Tracy White was undrafted and Rob Ninkovich was a fifth-round pick who had been cut by two other teams. In the starting secondary, Kyle Arrington was undrafted out of Hofstra and cut by two other teams, and James Ihedigbo was undrafted out of UMass and let go by the Jets.

Belichick always believed that his players determined the depth chart, not the coaches or the scouts. "One thing we tell all of the players at the beginning of the year . . . is if you look at our track record and history, it's true that I tell the team that I don't care how you got here," he said. "It's what you do when you get here. It doesn't matter if you were drafted in the second round, the fifth round, or not drafted at all. Ten years in the league, one year in the league, we are going to play the best players. Whoever that is is decided by you."

Mangini, Crennel, McDaniels, and Weis had all left New England for head coaching jobs in the NFL and major-college ranks (Weis), and they'd all failed. Some of them might've tried to act like Belichick, but in the end, they weren't Belichick. They couldn't bring Tom Brady with them, and they couldn't replicate the Patriots' equal-opportunity system.

That system was a split second away from being rewarded on the biggest stage one more time. But something very unfunny happened on the way to the championship ceremony stage. Brady had actually put his pass a little behind the 5′9″ Welker, and a tad high, and when the receiver rotated his body and extended his arms, his expert hand-eye coordination suddenly failed him. The ball bounced off his fingers as he started to fall down. Welker ended up on his knees at the 19-yard line, his helmet planted in the turf and both gloved hands planted on his helmet, with four minutes left on the clock.

On New England's bench, the defensive linemen reacted like fans, grabbing their own heads in disbelief. The referee, John Parry, told one of his fellow officials, "Well, that was the game." One incomplete pass later, the Patriots were punting the ball to the quarterback who had broken their 18-0 hearts in Arizona.

Eli Manning was not as good as his big brother Peyton; not even close. But in these situations he was the more dangerous player. Belichick had told his defensive players on the bench that the Giants' two best receivers, Hakeem Nicks and Victor Cruz, needed to be contained, and that the key to winning was forcing Manning to throw to his less appealing targets. "Make 'em go to [Mario] Manningham," he implored them. "Make 'em go to [Bear] Pascoe."

On the first snap of his final drive, pinned at his own 12 with 3:46 left and the Patriots holding a 17–15 lead, Manning followed Belichick's preferred plan and put a ball down the New England sideline for Manningham, who was covered by Sterling Moore and Patrick Chung. Somehow, someway, Manningham made a full-extension, over-the-shoulder catch while tapping down his right foot and then his left directly in front of Belichick before Chung knocked him out of bounds. The Patriots' coach challenged the call, if only because he had no choice. The review confirmed that the 38-yard catch was good, leaving New England with that sickening feeling of déjà vu all over again. Dressed in a checkered gray suit, David Tyree, the retired master of the helmet catch, was looking on from the Giants' sideline.

Manning picked away at the New England secondary, and the Giants advanced the ball to the New England 6 before Belichick took his second timeout with 64 seconds to play. He knew that Tynes would make the chip-shot field goal, and he needed to give Brady enough time to answer whatever points were scored. Belichick had only one call to make on second down, and it hurt him to the core to have to make it. Knowing he was violating every tenet of the Patriot Way, he told his defense to allow the Giants to score a touchdown on the next snap. The players had to repeat the order to themselves in the huddle just to make sure that they heard it right, and perhaps to give a teammate or two time to make an executive decision that overruled Belichick's.

"Gotta let them score. Gotta let them score," linebacker Jerod Mayo said.

"Gotta let them score," Vince Wilfork repeated.

Manning handed the ball to Ahmad Bradshaw, watched the New England defense swing open like a pair of ballroom doors, and started shouting at his running back, "Don't score. Don't score." Bradshaw tried to hit the brakes at the one-yard line. He lowered himself into a sitting position, but his momentum got the better of him as he turned toward his quarterback and fell gently into the end zone.

Belichick still had 57 seconds and one timeout to play with after the ensuing touchback, but now he needed a touchdown to win. Brady's first two passes were dropped by the reliable Branch (off a deflection) and Hernandez, adding to New England's long list of costly errors. On his very first snap of the game, Brady had been flagged for intentional grounding in the end zone, resulting in a safety. A Brandon Spikes recovery of a Victor Cruz fumble in the first quarter had been wiped out by a 12-men-on-the-field penalty two plays before a Cruz touchdown. The Patriots failed to recover two other Giants fumbles, and the hobbled Gronkowski failed to break up a jump ball in the fourth quarter that was intercepted by linebacker Chase Blackburn, who was giving away three inches in height. Welker later delivered the fatal drop.

The Patriots were always forcing other teams into mistakes and missed opportunities; the Giants were the one opponent who did the same to them. On third down, Brady was sacked by Justin Tuck and burned New England's last timeout with 36 seconds to go. Tuck had driven the quarterback's already injured left shoulder into the turf in the middle of the third quarter, and Brady — who had a run of 16 straight completions before the sack — wasn't the same player after that. But on fourth and 16, the quarterback summoned his greatness one last time. He escaped from pressure and fired a strike to Branch for a 19-yard gain and a temporary reprieve. Brady found Hernandez for another first down before spiking the ball with 19 seconds left. Back-to-back incompletions left the quarterback with five seconds left in the season, the ball on the New England 49, and one play to separate the winners from the losers, who would be quickly shepherded off the field by functionaries trying to set up the on-field coronation.

Fittingly, Brady's final two instructions were directed at his tight ends. "Run to the goalpost," he told Gronkowski before Gronk lined up in the slot to the right. "Run to the goalpost and catch it," he told Hernandez before the former Florida star split wide to the right. Brady took the snap and started dancing with light feet, as if he were Aaron Rodgers, just to buy his receivers enough time to get to the end zone. On the sideline, Belichick watched as his season came down to this desperation Hail Mary. Brady darted back, then forward, then back again, then forward again as Pierre-Paul finally broke free from New England's right tackle, Sebastian Vollmer, and closed in on him.

From his own 41, Brady launched the ball high just before contact, and it was a perfectly placed 65-yard pass — of course it was. Hernandez had beaten Gronkowski to the end zone, and as the ball descended toward the cursive Patriots logo, Hernandez gathered himself on the *r* and jumped with the small army of Giants defenders around him as his fellow tight end waited nearby. Coaches at all levels of the game practice what is called the "tip drill," sharpening a player's reaction to a tipped or deflected ball. Hernandez couldn't catch Brady's pass with the crowd around him in midair, but he did his job by contributing to the tip and keeping the ball alive.

A tremendous athlete for his size, Gronkowski might've been quick enough on two healthy feet to respond to the deflection and make a diving catch that would be remembered and celebrated forever. But his high ankle sprain and the heavy tape wrapped around it made him a step slow in this high-stakes tip drill, and his dive for the ball was fruitless. The season ended with Gronkowski and Hernandez on their backs in a Lucas Oil Stadium end zone, with Welker next to them on his hands and knees, his helmet buried again in the turf.

Criticized for his premature exit in Super Bowl XLII, Belichick headed straight for Coughlin and all but lunged into his arms, wrapping the winning coach in a meaningful hug. Ernie Accorsi, the Giants' GM emeritus and the executive who had hired Belichick in Cleveland, would later tell another Giants official, "Maybe this will keep me out of heaven, but I feel awfully good that we made a couple of choices years ago [in Coughlin and Manning] that gave him two defeats that I know bother him. And you don't overcome those. You don't forget them."

This one wasn't as crushing to New England as the first Super Bowl defeat, but it still hurt. A lot. "We just came up a couple plays short," Belichick said afterward.

New England had dedicated its season to the memory of Robert Kraft's wife, Myra, who died of cancer in July. To a man, the Patriots adored her. They wore a patch with her initials, MHK, on their jerseys, and after his touchdown pass to Hernandez, Brady tapped his patch and pointed skyward. Some players thought they'd let down their owner, but Kraft would hear none of that. He was proud of his team and gracious enough in defeat, for a second time, to wait with his son Jonathan for the Giants' owners to step down from the champions' stage so he could congratulate them.

John Mara was moved by the gesture after both Super Bowls, because he remembered not wanting to see or talk to anyone after the 2000 Giants were beaten by Baltimore for the Vince Lombardi Trophy. "There's nothing worse than losing that game," Mara said.

As part of his recovery, Belichick decided to get away from football and play in the AT&T Pebble Beach National Pro-Am, where he was teamed with tour pro Ricky Barnes, whose father, Bruce, punted for the Patriots in the 1970s. Barnes was impressed by how quickly the coach processed information on yardage and wind, picked a club, and fired away, and by how much he improved every day. "When he shows up, he's a 20 handicap," the pro said. "And when he leaves on Sunday or Monday, he's like a 12."

Belichick hadn't picked up a club since July, and yet he helped his two-man team finish in third place at 33 under, only two strokes behind the winners. Barnes kept the football questions to a minimum, and during the event, most players and fans knew enough not to ask Belichick about his second Super Bowl loss in five seasons. But Tiger Woods's caddie, Joe LaCava, a rabid Giants fan from Connecticut, couldn't resist getting in a shot on the driving range. LaCava spotted Belichick hitting balls next to Phil Mickelson and saw his opening. He walked up to Mickelson's caddie, Jim "Bones" Mackay, with a devilish grin on his face.

"How about my G-Men kicking the Patriots' asses again in the Super Bowl?" LaCava said out loud. "How great was that?" Mackay said that LaCava definitely saw Belichick and definitely wanted the coach to hear it.

Belichick's reaction? He had none. Tired of being a runner-up, the coach just kept his head down and kept pounding balls into the sky. Belichick knew what Ben Hogan knew: The secret was in the dirt.

On August 23, 2012, a prominent agent was sitting in a resort restaurant in the Tampa area with a starting member of the New England Patriots when he noticed a man covered in tattoos on the other side of the window.

"Who the fuck is that psychopath?" the agent asked the New England starter. He pointed toward the tatted-up man, who was reading a Patriots playbook in a hot tub on an extremely hot and humid day. "He looks like he's in a steam room," the agent continued. "He's drenched from head to toe in sweat."

"Oh, that's Aaron Hernandez," the starter answered.

"What?" the agent said. "Could I steal him?"

"He's OK," the starter said. "He's just weird."

"What do you mean, 'weird'?"

"That's the most different guy I've ever been around. One day he's super-cool and normal, and the next day he's acting like a thug, a gangster. He's got headphones on, and he doesn't talk to anybody, and he wants to sit at his locker and ignore the world."

Believing marijuana was the tight end's biggest problem at Florida, the agent had always thought the Patriots were geniuses for drafting Hernandez in the fourth round. He had a lot of clients who had told him that weed got them through the brutal demands of an NFL season. As long as Hernandez avoided suspension and kept using his multidimensional talents to New England's advantage, who cared if he liked weed as much as he liked football?

In the hot tub, on the surface, Hernandez didn't seem to have a care in the world. He was a few days away from wrapping up a contract extension worth a potential $40 million over five years, including $16 million in guaranteed money and a $12.5 million signing bonus, which was $4.5 million more than the bonus Rob Gronkowski had received in his six-year, $54 million extension, completed in June. The Patriots were no longer hedging their bets with Hernandez. Belichick thought so much of the young tight end that he decided to pay him instead of Wes Welker. The Patriots were convinced that their gamble had paid off even before Hernandez used the occasion of the team's annual Kickoff Gala to reveal that he was donating $50,000 to the Myra Kraft Giving Back Fund.

Robert Kraft called Hernandez "a first-class guy" and a super player. "Basically [he's] saying he wants me around here for the next seven years, he wants me to be a part of the family," Hernandez said of the owner. "So I'm a part of the Patriots family, and he wanted me to be set up for life. He didn't have to give me the amount he gave me. But he felt I deserved that and he trusts me to make the right decisions . . . All I can do is play my hardest for them and make the right decisions. And live like a Patriot."

Hernandez even maintained that the experience of playing in the Belichick culture had changed him as a human being. "You can't come here and act reckless and do your own stuff," he said. "I was one of the persons that I came here, I might have acted the way I wanted to act. But you get changed by Bill Belichick's way. You get changed by the Patriots Way."

Across his first two seasons, Hernandez had impressed some of his teammates and coaches with his passion for the game. Donté Stallworth, a ten-year veteran, was a teammate of Hernandez's for portions of the 2012 season. "To me," the receiver said, "he was on his way to being in the Hall of Fame. I've never seen someone so enthusiastic about practice and training. Who's enthusiastic about training? Nobody — but he was. He was one of the first to show up and the last to leave."

One Patriots scout said Hernandez was like a hyper little kid at practice who couldn't wait to get the running, catching, and hitting started. Chris

Simms, son of the former Giants quarterback Phil Simms and a Patriots coaching assistant in 2012, said Hernandez had earned widespread respect by logging Belichick and Brady hours at the office. "Aaron was one of the most loved guys in that organization," Simms said. "He was definitely one of my favorite guys on that team, too, and I know it sounds weird saying it. He was a real football player, this kid. He was into being great. He worked in the off-season when nobody was there. When nobody was looking, he was still going to get his work in. We lose the AFC Championship Game and three days later Aaron is in there watching film and working out.

"The coaches loved Aaron Hernandez," Simms continued. "That's not to say anything bad about the coaches; Aaron was very charismatic. You could cut up with him in the locker room, and he could talk crap to you, and you'd both laugh. He was extremely talented, he was 245 pounds, and he was quicker than [Julian] Edelman and [Wes] Welker. He could have been an all-time great."

But Hernandez did show signs of immaturity — and even a bit of misplaced hostility — at the team facility. The *Globe*'s Shalise Manza Young reported that within days of being drafted, Hernandez had told Welker, "I'll fuck you up" after the slot receiver refused to help the rookie figure out the equipment in the film room. Hernandez once called over *Herald* beat writer Ian Rapoport and said, "Hey, I just want you to know, you're my guy. If you need anything, let me know; I will help you out if I can. But I just want you to know, if you fuck me over, I'll kill you." Rapoport laughed it off.

Reporters laughed when Hernandez jokingly answered questions while chewing on a mouthful of food, and team officials weren't overly offended when the tight end neglected to show up for a couple of community service events he'd signed up for. Some in the organization noticed that Hernandez didn't seem to have many friends on the team and often left the building alone, but they thought he was a goofy, moody kid who needed time to grow up. Others started to realize that beneath his desire to become a great football player, Hernandez was driven by some darker force.

One Patriots staffer who had regular contact with the tight end thought he might've been suffering from bipolar disorder. "He had a charismatic smile ear to ear for seven days," the staffer said, "and on the eighth day he'd come in and, damn, he won't even look you in the eye. He's got a mean face on his head. It looks like, for lack of a better phrase, that he wants to kill someone."

Hernandez was back into the drug scene with his Bristol crew, and one Patriots source said that over time it became clear to people throughout the organization. "That element of his life kept creeping back in," the source said. "Everyone was aware of it. It was definitely a concern in the building."

Belichick did talk to his Patriots about avoiding off-field trouble, something he'd been doing for years. John Hufnagel, his quarterbacks coach in 2003, recalled being impressed at how often his boss preached to his players the need to represent their team and community in a positive way. "Bill coached them on how to be football players, but also how to be good citizens," Hufnagel said. "He made them aware of the potholes out there. When someone screwed up in the press, he'd bring it to their attention and say, 'Hey, is this how we want to be portrayed?' He made sure you fully understood where you were at and that you're a public person, and never forget that."

Only Aaron Hernandez was not going to be moved by any such lectures on civic responsibility. The new contract just gave him more money to spend on marijuana, angel dust, and whatever gun he thought he needed to protect himself while running with his circle of small-time criminals. Slowly, surely, Hernandez's life away from the team facility was unraveling. Police showed up more than once at a California apartment he shared with his fiancée, Shayanna Jenkins, in response to domestic disturbances that did not lead to an arrest.

In July 2012, Hernandez was involved in a dustup in a Boston nightclub with one of two Cape Verdean immigrants who were then gunned down outside the club. On May 18, 2013, Hernandez was reportedly involved in a confrontation with a taunting New York Jets fan outside a Providence club where, at around the same time, police saw an unidentified man placing a gun under a car. On June 13, 2013, a drug dealer and Hernandez friend named Alexander Bradley filed a lawsuit against the New England tight end, accusing him of shooting him in the face and costing him his right eye in February while the two were traveling in a car after an argument at a strip joint in Miami Gardens, Florida.

Were the Patriots and Belichick aware of the full extent of this behavior? They were clearly aware of some of it. Feeling that he was in danger, Hernandez had flown to the draft combine in Indianapolis ten days after he allegedly shot Bradley in the face, for the purpose of meeting with Belichick and requesting a trade. Belichick was not about to honor that request. A Patriots staffer named Kevin Anderson did later help Hernandez get a place in Franklin, Massachusetts, about ten miles from Gillette Stadium and eleven miles from his North Attleborough mansion; people close to the team saw it as a place for the tight end to lay low. Hernandez had a friend from Bristol, Ernest Wallace, move into the apartment.

Before Hernandez left Indianapolis, he again flashed the explosive side of his personality in the company of *Globe* beat writer Greg Bedard, who had been chatting with the Patriot in a bar before he looked outside and saw the tight end urinating on a running taxi, to the dismay of its driver. Bedard approached Hernandez and advised him to use the bar's restroom, and Hernandez didn't respond. The writer gently touched the player's elbow and said, "Aaron, come on, this is stupid," prompting Hernandez to wheel on him, jump in his face, curse him out, and shout, "I'm not a child. You're not my dad." Bedard told him he was acting like a child and returned to his friends. Hernandez walked back into the bar in short order and, assuming the role of Good Aaron again, reengaged Bedard and others in easy conversation.

Every NFL team employs security officials to identify potential problems with players and to head them off before trouble with the law and embarrassing news media coverage damage the brand. These security officials are charged with maintaining strong relationships with local and state law enforcement and nightclub owners for access to reliable information on players who might be behaving recklessly. Mark Briggs, the Brit who was head of Patriots security, had been in place for years. He would've been a complete incompetent if he didn't have some information suggesting Hernandez was careening down a path of self-destruction. So maybe the Patriots were merely hoping against hope that they wouldn't get the phone call they got on June 17, informing them that a man named Odin Lloyd had been executed in an industrial park about half a mile from Hernandez's mansion and that the cops thought the tight end might have been involved.

Lloyd was a semipro football player who had been dating the sister of Hernandez's fiancée, and two nights earlier Hernandez had gotten into a dispute with him over people Lloyd had been talking to inside a Boston club. Hernandez and two associates, including Wallace, had picked up Lloyd in the early-morning hours of the 17th, and in his final four texts to his sister, between 3:07 and 3:23 a.m., the victim wrote, "U saw who I'm with?" . . . "hello" . . . "Nfl" . . . "just so you know." At 3:25 a.m., Lloyd was executed by a cold-blooded killer who pumped six .45-caliber bullets into his body. The victim had keys in his pocket that belonged to a car rented by Hernandez.

Kraft and Belichick decided that if Hernandez were arrested for any charge in the murder case, even for obstruction of justice, he would have to be cut. Soon enough, the evidence started piling up against the tight end, and Gillette Stadium became the scene of a news media stakeout. On June 19, with reporters in the parking lot and news helicopters circling above, Kraft entered the facility and headed to the weight room to meet with Hernandez. Belichick was out of the country, so the owner had to take the lead on a situation that was spiraling out of control. Kraft took Hernandez into the office of assistant strength-and-conditioning coach Moses Cabrera and asked the man who had donated $50,000 to his wife's memory to look him in the eye and tell him if he had anything to do with Lloyd's murder.

"He said he was not involved, that he was innocent," Kraft would later testify in court, "and that he hoped that the time of the murder incident came out because I believe he said he was in a club." That revelation was not going to help Hernandez: How would he know the time of the murder unless he had been present when it was committed?

Owner and player spoke for five or ten minutes before Hernandez hugged and kissed Kraft and thanked him for his concern. The tight end had always hugged and kissed Kraft when they crossed paths. He didn't hug and kiss Briggs, the security chief, who also met with Hernandez and told him he'd tried to reach him three or four times on his cell phone before receiving a message that the player's voicemail box was full. Hernandez responded that the police had confiscated his phone and repeated that he had nothing to do with Lloyd's death. "He swore on his baby's life that he was telling the truth," Briggs said.

Hernandez told the security official that Lloyd was "like family." The player spoke to Briggs for five minutes, and Hernandez ultimately left the building and waited as his mother, Terri, drove over from Bristol to give him a ride home. Three years after Aaron's father, Dennis, had suddenly died from complications following what was supposed to be routine hernia surgery, Terri had married an ex-con named Jeffrey Cummings, who had been married to Dennis's niece. Cummings would later assault and slash Terri with a large kitchen knife and return to prison, and Terri divorced him.

The next day, June 20, Aaron Hernandez returned to Gillette Stadium and had another five-minute conversation with Briggs that wasn't as cordial as the first one. Briggs told the tight end that his presence was "bad for business" and asked him to leave the building. Hernandez finished up a phone call, shook Briggs's hand, and then left the stadium for the last time. On June 26, police showed up at Hernandez's North Attleborough home and found him wearing a white T-shirt and red gym shorts. They handcuffed him behind his back and walked him to a waiting car as his empty sleeves dangled in the breeze. Some 90 minutes later, the Patriots fired him. Two days after that, the team announced that any fan with Hernandez's No. 81 jersey could exchange it for a different New England jersey.

Meanwhile, investigators were working to connect Hernandez to the double murder in South Boston the previous July, and they were looking to revisit the circumstances of the 2007 shooting of two men in Gainesville, Florida. The Patriots thought they had drafted an uncommon talent, and it appeared they had drafted a common killer instead.

Years earlier, after the Patriots acquired Randy Moss, Kraft had promised that a player's character would remain an important factor in how the roster was assembled. But New England had taken on more and more character risks in recent seasons, on the assumption that the Belichick culture would have the conforming effect it had on Corey Dillon and, for the most part, on Moss. Not that the culture had changed them all. In 2006, the Patriots took a chance by drafting Baylor's Willie Andrews, who had once pleaded guilty to a misdemeanor gun charge. Two years into his employment, following an arrest on marijuana possession, Andrews was arrested again after allegedly pointing a gun at his girlfriend's head. He was cut the following day.

The Patriots seemed to take more risks as the non-championship seasons started to pile up. The team signed defensive tackle Albert Haynesworth, a two-time Pro Bowler who had been indicted on a misdemeanor sex abuse charge and had been suspended by Washington coach Mike Shanahan for insubordination, on the same day in July 2011 that it traded for high-maintenance receiver Chad Ochocinco, who would catch a grand total of 15 passes as a Patriot. New England released Haynesworth in November after he had a sideline confrontation with assistant coach Pepper Johnson. The following year, the Patriots acquired Aqib Talib, who had multiple run-ins with the law and had been indicted on a charge of firing a gun at his sister's boyfriend. (The charges were later dropped.) In 2012, New England reacquired Donté Stallworth, who had been suspended by the league for the entire 2009 season after going to jail for DUI manslaughter. In the 2012 draft, New England used its seventh-round pick on Nebraska's Alfonzo Dennard, who had been arrested for felony assault of a police officer and would later be convicted. Dennard also violated his probation when he was arrested for suspicion of DUI in the summer of 2013.

None of those cases could compare to the profound tragedy that was unfolding around the star tight end. Chris Simms, coaching assistant, had received a text message from Hernandez just before his arrest, asking for help contacting a trainer and muscle specialist. Simms couldn't believe it when he heard there was a warrant out for Hernandez. "I was like 'Man, I know he didn't pull the trigger' . . . I kept trying to tell myself all these things."

One high-ranking Patriots official thought that, in retrospect, Hernandez was the last prospect in America who should've been drafted by his hometown team. "When you think back on it," he said, "part of the reason he went to Florida was to kinda get away. Him going to Foxborough was maybe not an ideal location for him . . . He would've been better off in Seattle."

Chances are he would've found trouble in Seattle, too. An executive with another NFL team who had been warned by Urban Meyer to stay clear of his player in the draft said he wasn't at all surprised by the Hernandez crash and burn. "When I saw some of the shit he was able to get away with [at Florida]," the executive said, "we weren't taking him. He actually thought he was going to get away with murder. He always thought he could beat the system, and when he got arrested I thought, *Well, the system finally caught up with him.*"

On July 8, a dozen days after Hernandez was hauled out of his home, New England's owner finally made himself available to answer some hard, necessary questions about the alleged murderer he'd employed. Kraft had been vacationing in Europe and Israel, and instead of subjecting himself to a televised interrogation in a news conference, he invited some Boston writers into his Gillette Stadium office.

"If this stuff is true," Kraft said, "then I've been duped and our whole organization has been duped." The owner claimed that Hernandez was always polite and respectful at the facility, that he wanted to be a role model for the Hispanic community, and that the Patriots hadn't known what was going on in his life after he climbed into his car and left for the night. "We don't put private eyes on people," said Kraft, who conceded that Hernandez was immature. The owner said that the team would now have to reevaluate how it vetted players. Privately, Kraft told associates he didn't believe his head coach had given him a full accounting of Hernandez's behavior in college.

Sixteen days after the owner fielded questions, and five weeks after Odin Lloyd was shot dead, Belichick at last conducted a press conference, held before the start of training camp. He walked to a podium wearing a blue Patriots pullover. He had his omnipresent pencil tucked behind his right ear and was carrying the sheets of paper that contained the thoughts he planned to convey. He adjusted his microphone and said, "OK, going to address the situation involving Aaron Hernandez today. I felt that it was important enough to do that prior to the start of camp. It's a sad day. It's really a sad day on so many levels. Our thoughts and prayers are with the family of the victim, and I extend my sympathy really to everyone who's been impacted. A young man lost his life, and his family's suffered a tragic loss, and there's no way to understate that."

Belichick said he had been out of the country when he learned about the murder investigation. He referred to his notes as he somberly delivered an opening statement that lasted seven minutes and five seconds. On this day, he knew he couldn't assume the role of the news conference character he'd created at the media's expense. He knew he had to be human for this one. He took questions after completing his statement, though he warned reporters that he wouldn't be able to discuss specifics about the case or the player involved in it. The first time Belichick said the name Aaron Hernandez, in his opening remarks, was also the last time he said it.

The coach maintained that the team had "acted swiftly and decisively" in cutting Hernandez and took seriously the goal of making the Patriots "a pillar in the community." Belichick said that for 14 years in New England, he'd emphasized the need for his players to conduct themselves appropriately on and off the field. He said that he would examine the way the Patriots picked players but that he didn't expect substantive changes to the process. "Nobody knows better than you guys that all sources are not equal," Belichick told reporters. "You guys know that better than I do. So when you get information, you take information and you evaluate it and you do the best you can with it."

Belichick said he was "proud of the hundreds of players that have come through this program," though he acknowledged that he was personally hurt by the Hernandez arrest. He admitted that he'd made "plenty" of personnel mistakes over the years and promised that the Patriots would "learn from this terrible experience." Belichick answered a final question about his relationship with Kraft by saying that it had always been strong and was getting stronger by the year.

With that, he grabbed his papers and exited stage right to prepare for another camp and another season. The Hernandez case would haunt New England for a while, but once it became about football again, Belichick was back in control. He still had his system, and, more than anything, he still had his quarterback. Nobody had a winner at the game's most critical position like Belichick had. It seemed Tom Brady was the most reliable and authentic superstar in sports.

Until people started seeing evidence that he wasn't.

17

DEFLATION AND ELATION

Tom Brady was already worried about his job before he took the field in Kansas City for a *Monday Night Football* game in Week 4 of the 2014 season. He was telling confidants he felt that if he did not improve his play, Bill Belichick would not wait long before turning to the quarterback he had just drafted in the spring, a prospect from Eastern Illinois named Jimmy Garoppolo.

Maybe this was just Brady being Brady — still worrying unnecessarily that Drew Henson could walk through the door any day in Foxborough. Or maybe this was Brady expressing legitimate concern that Belichick was looking for an opportunity to do to him what he had done to decorated Patriots the likes of Lawyer Milloy, Ty Law, Adam Vinatieri, Willie McGinest, Deion Branch, Richard Seymour, Wes Welker, and, most recently, six-time Pro Bowl guard Logan Mankins: let them go while they were still productive and before they either declined or made too much money against the salary cap, or both.

Either way, Brady had been uneasy about his place in the Patriots' universe since Belichick used the 62nd overall pick to select Garoppolo. Jimmy's coach at Eastern Illinois, Dino Babers, raved about his accuracy and thought his prospect had the second-fastest release he'd ever seen, just a tick slower than Dan Marino's. When Belichick drafted Garoppolo, he announced that New England needed to address the quarterback situation for the future and that he wanted to be "early rather than late at that position." The Patriots had other holes on the roster to fill, but with his franchise quarterback turning 37 before the season started, the coach figured Brady would be creating the most conspicuous hole sooner rather than later.

"We know what Tom's age and contract situation is," Belichick said, a somewhat shocking remark from a man who almost never revealed anything of substance for public consumption.

Most great quarterbacks were battered shells of their former selves by their late thirties, though there had been exceptions like Brett Favre and Warren Moon. Brady wasn't shy about stating his desire to play into his forties, but his numbers had plunged in 2013, alarming those who wondered how long his Methuselah act could really last. Brady had thrown 25 touchdown passes, his lowest total in a full season since 2006, and had averaged 6.9 yards gained per attempt, also his lowest number since 2006. Brady had been sacked 40 times for the first time since he was dropped 41 times in 2001, and his passer rating (87.3) was his worst since 2003. If it wasn't yet time for Belichick to apply his year-too-early-rather-than-a-year-too-late dogma to the player who won him three Super Bowls, Brady's slippage surely put that thought in the back of the coach's mind.

Prior to 2014, Belichick had drafted half a dozen quarterbacks in the Brady era, none considered serious challengers to the throne. Garoppolo represented a radically different approach. He wasn't brought in to support Brady. He was brought in to someday replace him.

Was that someday suddenly closing on Brady like a freight train?

For a few years, Patriots coaches had noticed a dropoff in Brady's arm strength and velocity. In 2012, he averaged a full yard less per attempt (7.6) than in 2011, and his completion percentage, touchdown totals, and passer rating started to dip. In December of that year, Brady completed only 58.5 percent of his passes and averaged only seven yards per pass before following a strong playoff performance against Houston with a disastrous one against Baltimore in the AFC Championship Game, where he completed 53.7 percent of his passes, threw two interceptions, and averaged 5.9 yards per attempt in a 28–13 defeat.

The following season, when his numbers took a serious plunge, Brady averaged 1.7 fewer yards per attempt than he had in 2011. Sometimes in practice, frustrated coaches would shake their heads when Brady ignored open receivers downfield and threw short instead. "We all talked about that," one assistant said. "It was 'How can we get Tom to throw the go route?' He wasn't confident he could complete it . . . He was getting a little insecure about that. Bill would say, 'Hey, Tom, keep throwing deep. Keep working on it.'"

The assistant thought that after Aaron Hernandez's arrest, Belichick kept focusing on short- and mid-range options — Rob Gronkowski and Welker's replacement in the slot, Julian Edelman — in part because he didn't think Brady would or could consistently throw to an outside burner going deep. As a rule, New England coaches had tremendous respect for the quarterback's work ethic, consistency, and willingness to leave millions at the negotiating table in accepting team-friendly deals that made him the most underpaid franchise player in sports. And yet they were more willing than the general public might've suspected to break down Brady's game in critical ways behind closed doors.

Fairly or unfairly, a number of coaches thought Belichick's system elevated Brady, not the other way around. The general feeling among staff members, said one assistant, wasn't that the Patriot Way would make Super Bowl quarterbacks out of all 32 starters. "But if you gave us any of the top 15, we could do it," he said. "I don't think the coaches view Tom as special as everyone else in football does. Mr. Kraft thinks Tom is the greatest gift ever, but the coaches don't."

The assistant said that Belichick viewed Ben Roethlisberger and Joe Flacco as quarterbacks who could've had Brady's level of success in his system, and that he had a special place in his heart for Peyton Manning and Aaron Rodgers. "He's in awe of what they can do," the assistant said.

One Patriots staffer said that coaches scoffed when a personnel man who ranked the NFL starters from 1 to 32 slotted Brady at No. 1. "Tom's awesome, and I think he has better physical ability than he's given credit for," the staffer said. "In his prime, he had a special arm, even without the athleticism . . . But Aaron Rodgers may be the most physically gifted quarterback in the history of football. It's drop back for him, dance around, make seven guys miss me because my receivers and linemen suck, and then throw a 40-yard missile. Brady sees the first guy open and throws it right away."

Some coaches brought up Brady's upscale endorsement deals in recent years and whined that he'd "gone corporate" after fronting for Dunkin' Donuts in simpler, more modest times. Belichick had a different complaint of sorts. In sports-bar debates over the all-time greatest coaches, he knew there were still doubters and haters who liked to bring up his sub.-500 record without Brady under center, even after he finished 11-5 with Matt Cassel in 2008. As much as he appreciated everything Brady had done for him, Belichick was already telling people he looked forward to the day he could try to win a Super Bowl without him.

In that regard, Brady wasn't going to make it easy on his coach. He had teamed up with a controversial fitness guru and self-styled life coach, Alex Guerrero, as he pursued his goal of playing into his forties. In 2013, five years after Guerrero helped Brady recover from his knee surgery, the two opened the TB12 Sports Therapy Center at Patriot Place, an open-air mall adjacent to Gillette Stadium that featured shops, restaurants, bars, and the team's Hall of Fame. Brady had described Guerrero as one of his best friends, and he'd recommended him to other Patriots and to Pittsburgh Penguins superstar Sidney Crosby, who was battling neck and head injuries.

Brady had made an interesting choice for a business associate. Guerrero had studied traditional Chinese medicine at a California college that had since closed down. The magazine *Boston* reported that he had been sanctioned by the Federal Trade Commission for passing himself off as a doctor and for marketing a product that he falsely claimed could prevent or even cure cancer and other diseases. Brady had endorsed a Guerrero sports drink, NeuroSafe, which claimed to contain properties that expedited the brain's healing process after it was concussed, before FTC pressure compelled Guerrero to stop marketing the drink.

With the goal of reducing inflammation in the quarterback's aging body, Guerrero had Brady on a fun-free, plant-based diet that would've made a wild boar puke. Brady also performed workouts designed to make his muscles more pliable and less susceptible to injury, and the truth was, he hadn't missed a single start since blowing out his knee in 2008. For this he credited a man who admitted that conventional practitioners of medicine saw him as "a kook and a charlatan."

Brady had put his money on this wildly imperfect horse, and he was going to ride it into what he hoped was a distant sunset. Toward that end, the quarterback was staring down a difficult proposition. Dante Scarnecchia, the great offensive line coach, had retired, and the Mankins trade with Tampa Bay had left the line looking awfully young and thin. New England had brought in the star cornerback Darrelle Revis, formerly of the Jets and the Bucs, but didn't acquire any explosive playmakers on offense to give the old man a little extra help.

So Brady looked a little creaky in his first three games, winning two but failing to crack 250 passing yards in any. He wasn't happy with his performance, or with that of the offensive line under coach Dave DeGuglielmo, formerly of the Jets, Dolphins, and Giants. Before he played that Monday night game in Kansas City, Brady told people he was beginning to worry about his standing with Belichick. He went to work behind a line that included rookies Bryan Stork and Cameron Fleming, and he again looked dreadful. Brady was picked off twice and strip-sacked, setting up a Chiefs touchdown. He completed only one of seven throws of more than ten yards, leaving his completion rate on such throws (32 percent) as the worst in the NFL.

Belichick had seen enough after Brady threw a pick-six that gave Kansas City a 41–7 lead early in the fourth quarter. He benched the starter for Garoppolo, who had gotten off to a slow training-camp start before showing encouraging progress during preseason games. And, sure enough, Garoppolo immediately led the Patriots on a scoring drive, hitting Brandon LaFell for 37 yards before finding Gronkowski on a 13-yard scoring pass. As he returned to the sideline, Garoppolo received congratulations and high fives from teammates relieved that something positive had come out of this miserable night. Brady didn't appear to be among those giving him a hearty attaboy. In fact, Brady gave high fives to a number of offensive teammates, just not the one who had performed Brady's job better than he had.

It was garbage time in K.C., but still: Garoppolo completed six of his seven attempts on the night for 70 yards. The next morning, *Boston Globe* columnist Ben Volin published a piece under the headline "End Game Becomes Apparent" that declared it was time "to start wondering if the clock is running out on Brady's Patriots tenure a lot more quickly than we thought." Brady was statistically one of the worst quarterbacks in the league and the worst in the dreary AFC East. That was why Belichick was asked if the quarterback position would be evaluated during the week; he shot the reporter a look before dismissing the question with a snorting half laugh and a slight shake of the head.

Brady spent his benched portion of Monday night's game brooding and looking like the loneliest man on the planet. He was working on yet another contract that was well below market value, and he had to be incensed that this was how he was being thanked by Belichick—with a shaky offensive line, limited outside receivers who couldn't stretch the field, and a talented heir apparent replacing him in a national TV game. If Brady remained on the roster throughout the 2014 season, he would be guaranteed salaries of $7 million, $8 million, and $9 million over the following three seasons, at a time when Rodgers was making $22 million a pop. Brady, a three-time Super Bowl champ, ranked 16th among quarterbacks in average salary ($14.1 million) and made less than Alex Smith ($17 million average) and Andy Dalton ($16 million), who had combined to win one postseason game. (Brady had won 18.)

Suddenly the week leading into Sunday night's home game against the Bengals had become a referendum on whether Brady's days were numbered in New England. To complicate matters, Garoppolo was represented by Brady's agent, Don Yee. It wasn't common to see an agent juggle the best interests of a franchise player and those of the hotshot hired to take his job.

In a Wednesday press conference, Belichick was peppered with questions about Brady's age and the quality of the talent the coach had placed around him. Belichick created a stir by repeatedly answering, "We're on to Cincinnati," before elaborating with the much more expansive "We're getting ready for Cincinnati." Few NFL coaches could get away with Belichick's act in pressers, but the New England coach had done enough winning to operate by his own public relations playbook.

Belichick was a master of keeping his team focused on what was important, namely this game against the Bengals, and when kickoff arrived, Brady and the Patriots were ready to defy their obituary writers. The fans chanted the quarterback's name, and Brady responded with a vintage performance — a season-high 292 passing yards and two touchdowns in a 43–17 victory that felt just as profound as New England's 41–14 defeat in Kansas City. Brady had become the sixth NFL quarterback to pass for at least 50,000 yards. He acknowledged afterward that it had been a long week; ESPN's Chris Mortensen had reported that enough tension existed between the quarterback and the coaching staff over his diminished role in game planning to potentially send him to another franchise for the final seasons of his career. Brady denied the report and claimed that he had strong working relationships throughout the team facility. He did concede that he was aware of what people were saying and writing about his looming endgame in Foxborough.

"Well, it's hard to be oblivious to things," he said. "We all have TVs or the Internet or the questions I get and the emails that I get from people who are concerned. I'm always emailing them back like 'Nobody died. It's just a loss.'"

After the blowout of the Bengals, Belichick was surrounded by half-dressed Patriots as he stood in the middle of the locker room with a game ball in his hands. "We're certainly not big on individual stats around here," he said, "but 50,000 yards, Tom . . ." The players started applauding as Brady walked toward Belichick, who handed him the ball and then started to offer his right hand for a handshake. That wasn't going to be good enough this time. Brady had entered the locker room to a hug and a kiss on the cheek from Robert Kraft, whom he regarded as a second father; Kraft, in turn, regarded the player as his fifth son. Brady had a transformational relationship with the owner, and the quarterback was known to be a warm person who sometimes knocked his male friends off-balance by telling them he loved them.

But his relationship with Belichick was purely transactional; the two had never gone to dinner in all their years together. "They have a strictly professional relationship, 100 percent," said Brady's father, Tom Sr. "Bill's got many friends, and Tommy has many friends, and what Tommy needs from Bill is direction and coaching, and what Bill needs from Tommy is performance. They don't need to have a dinner."

An occasional victory hug wasn't asking for too much. So after taking the game ball from Belichick, Brady leaned toward him, wrapped his arms around him, and patted him on the back five times. The Patriots had started what would be a seven-game winning streak that would propel them to their 12th AFC East title in 13 seasons with a healthy Brady under center and silence all concerns that the quarterback was washed up. (Brady threw 22 touchdown passes and four interceptions in that winning streak.) Before they left the locker room on that seminal Sunday night against Cincinnati, Brady shouted, "Bring it down" as he lifted his right hand in the air and locked fingers with Belichick's. The players closed in on the coach and the quarterback, put their hands in the air, too, and shouted the desired response after Brady barked, "Team on three: One . . . two . . . three."

As the players dispersed, Brady and Belichick lingered for a second and exchanged a few words before going their separate ways. They had enjoyed one of the most successful business partnerships in NFL history. Before the 2014 season concluded, that partnership would be fractured by a controversy unlike any pro football had seen.

In the second quarter of the AFC Championship Game at Gillette Stadium, Tom Brady dropped back and underthrew a pass to Rob Gronkowski that was intercepted by the Indianapolis Colts' D'Qwell Jackson, who had picked off only one pass in his previous 48 games. Jackson wanted the ball as a souvenir, so he handed it off to the Colts' director of player engagement, who immediately handed it to an assistant equipment manager. New England already held a 14–0 lead, and unless the Colts established some momentum after the pick, it appeared they would lose a playoff game to their tormentors for the second consecutive year. Meanwhile, the equipment staffer noticed that the ball Jackson had intercepted seemed underinflated.

Ryan Grigson, the team's general manager, was notified of the ball's condition. The GM wasn't surprised: He'd been tipped off by his equipment manager, Sean Sullivan, that the Patriots were allegedly in the habit of manipulating game balls. The day before the game, Grigson had sent an email to Mike Kensil and Dave Gardi, senior members of the league's football operations department, that included an attachment from Sullivan that read, in part, "As far as the gameballs are concerned it is well known around the league that after the Patriots gameballs are checked by the officials and brought out for game usage the ball boys for the patriots will let out some air with a ball needle because their quarterback likes a smaller ball so he can grip it better, it would be great if someone would be able to check the air in the game balls as the game goes on that they don't get an illegal advantage."

Gardi responded that Kensil would take up the matter with the game officials at Gillette Stadium, and the Grigson email and Sullivan attachment were forwarded to game operations personnel and to senior members of the league's officiating department. The Colts had been suspicious of ball tampering since New England's 42–20 victory over them in November, when Mike Adams intercepted two Brady passes and brought the balls to the bench area, where equipment staffers found them to be soft and spongy and coated in what they described as a tacky substance. So, seven years after Spygate, the Colts and the NFL were ready for the Patriots in the event they cheated again. And when Indy's equipment staffers used their own hands and a digital pressure gauge to determine that the ball from the Jackson interception in the AFC Championship Game was similar to the balls from the Adams interceptions in Week 11, the mother of all NFL circuses was born.

Various officials were informed of the Colts' concern, and soon enough Grigson and Kensil had made their way down to the field from the press box and control booth. Kensil and Troy Vincent, a former star cornerback and the league's executive VP of football ops, decided that the footballs for both teams should be weighed. Alberto Riveron, from the officiating department, made the final call to collect the balls and test them at halftime to ensure that they complied with NFL regulations calling for game balls to be inflated to a pressure level between 12.5 and 13.5 pounds per square inch.

On the September day the Spygate case broke in Giants Stadium in 2007, New Jersey state troopers, FBI men, and security officials for the Patriots and the Jets engaged in a hidden high-stakes game for control of the confiscated camera while the teams battled on the field. On this night in Foxborough, seven years later, league and game officials conducted a hidden test that would shape the way much of America outside of New England looked at the Patriots' machine. In the dressing area of the officials' locker room, the balls were weighed with referee Walt Anderson's two pressure gauges.

New England's balls were tested first, and 11 of them came in below the 12.5 minimum PSI requirement on both gauges. The ball D'Qwell Jackson intercepted was measured three separate times — at 11.45, 11.35, and 11.75 PSI. With the start of the second half bearing down on them, the officials had time to measure only four of the Colts' balls. Those four were all at or above 12.5 on one gauge, while three of the four came in below 12.5 on the second gauge. The Patriots' balls were inflated to meet NFL standards, but no air was added to the Colts' balls because they were in compliance on at least one of the gauges. The balls were returned to the field for the second half, and Kensil, a former Jets executive, approached New England equipment manager Dave Schoenfeld on the sideline and reportedly told him, "We weighed the balls. You are in big fucking trouble." The Patriots then proved they knew how to play with properly inflated footballs, too. They outscored the Colts 28–0 in the second half and celebrated their sixth trip to the Super Bowl under Belichick before everyone went home happy.

Everyone except Grigson and other Indianapolis officials who felt they'd been had. In notifying the league the day before the game about the Patriots' alleged ball tampering, Grigson had said, "All the Indianapolis Colts want is a completely level playing field. Thank you for being vigilant stewards of that not only for us but for the shield and overall integrity of our game." Grigson wanted the NFL to act before the game started, not after. How in the world could the game officials allow New England's balls out of their sight after they were given advance warning that the Patriots might tamper with those balls?

These questions wouldn't be asked immediately, in a public forum, unless the story of what had gone down got out right away. Up in the Gillette Stadium press box, past midnight, wrapping up his column after finishing a postgame show for WTHR in Indianapolis, Bob Kravitz saw a text on his phone from a source telling him to call about something really important. Kravitz tried the source two or three times before finally reaching him and hearing that the NFL was investigating whether the Patriots had improperly deflated footballs that night. Kravitz thought the whole thing sounded outlandish, but he made some calls and got the story confirmed. He tweeted out the bombshell after he'd returned to his hotel, then finished writing and enjoyed a beer at the lobby bar. When he finally checked to see how his exclusive was doing on Twitter, he couldn't believe his eyes. "It was like, my God, we've broken the Internet," Kravitz said.

The columnist couldn't sleep that night; he was too busy staring at his ceiling and wondering what the hell he had gotten himself into. Kravitz arrived at the airport for his early-morning flight just hoping, praying, that someone would confirm his exclusive. He knew he'd gotten it right, but every journalist who has broken a major news story knows that feeling of dread when confronting the 2 percent chance that the reported story was false as a result of some misunderstanding.

And then Bob Glauber, of *Newsday*, printed confirmation from the league that an investigation was indeed underway, and Kravitz was in the clear. The Patriots, on the other hand, were not. Belichick said he didn't find out about the allegation and investigation until Monday morning — a claim that was extremely difficult to believe — and pledged to "cooperate fully with whatever the league wants us to do." As information started to trickle in, Belichick was trying to figure out who might've told the Colts that New England was allegedly taking air out of the footballs. The Baltimore Ravens were a pretty good place to start. The Patriots had just defeated the Ravens in Foxborough in a controversial divisional playoff game that saw the home team rally from two 14-point deficits to advance.

Baltimore's coach, John Harbaugh, had become the AFC's answer to Tom Coughlin as a Belichick stopper, which was a bit ironic, given that Belichick had recommended him for the Ravens job. Harbaugh said he was "incredibly awed" by the fact that Belichick called Ravens owner Steve Bisciotti on his behalf, and he honored that recommendation by beating the Patriots' coach in two road playoff games (by a combined 34 points) and by almost beating him a third time at Gillette Stadium in the AFC Championship Game following the 2011 season. Belichick knew he had to create opportunities to beat the Ravens in their latest postseason clash, and that was precisely what he did. He ran three third-quarter plays in their divisional playoff comeback with four offensive linemen and skill-position players reporting as ineligible receivers, and the Ravens had no idea how to react or whom to cover. Referee Bill Vinovich announced the ineligible Patriot on the play known as "Baltimore," running back Shane Vereen, who was on the line of scrimmage as a de facto extra lineman but split wide right and standing as if he were about to run a pass route. (Stretched wider on that side was the actual split end, Julian Edelman.)

Rookie linebacker C. J. Mosley came scrambling over to help on Vereen's side as Brady snapped the ball and found Michael Hoomanawanui — an eligible tight end lined up in the left tackle's spot — in the vacated space for 14 yards to the Baltimore 10. Harbaugh was so incensed that the officials, in his mind, weren't giving his defense enough time to adjust before the Patriots snapped the ball, he took his argument onto the field and drew an unsportsmanlike-conduct penalty. The Patriots scored, and then scored again on their next possession when Brady threw a pass behind the line to the former Kent State quarterback, Edelman, who fired a perfect strike to a wide-open Danny Amendola for a 51-yard touchdown.

Harbaugh had a hard time digesting this 35–31 defeat. "It's not something that anybody has ever done before," he said of the bizarre (but legal) formations. He criticized the officials for not giving the Ravens more time to identify the eligible and ineligible Patriots, and later said he felt that Belichick's status and reputation had overwhelmed the officiating crew. "And I absolutely respect that," Harbaugh said. "I have no beef with the Patriots or Coach Belichick." The Ravens' coach did have a beef with Brady for saying after the game, "Maybe those guys gotta study the rule book and figure it out."

When Harbaugh and Belichick communicated in the days to come, Belichick apologized for what Brady had said, according to a Patriots source, and Harbaugh assured the New England coach that the Ravens hadn't mentioned anything to the Colts about underinflated footballs. The Ravens would later say that their only communication with the Colts before the AFC title game had been a call between assistant coach Jerry Rosburg and head coach Chuck Pagano about another New England trick play (sending out its field goal unit and punting instead) and a text from kicking consultant Randy Brown to Pagano advising him that the Ravens weren't given the proper kicking balls during the divisional game.

This case was never about Baltimore. It wasn't about Indianapolis, either, even if the Colts would face some ridicule for lodging a fair-play complaint in a game they lost by 38 points. It was about the integrity of the most dominant franchise in the sport, same as Spygate, and it was propelled into a different orbit by a tweet from ESPN's Chris Mortensen reporting that the league had found 11 New England balls to be underinflated by 2 PSI. Belichick had a prior on his record; if it was found that he'd violated the rules again, he would be suspended by Roger Goodell and his reputation would be in tatters.

This was some way to begin preparations for a Super Bowl matchup with the defending champs, the Seattle Seahawks, and their top-ranked defense. On his weekly Monday appearance on WEEI's *Dennis and Callahan* show, Brady had called the early reports of underinflated footballs "ridiculous" and laughed when asked about the case that would come to be known worldwide as Deflategate. "I think I've heard it all at this point," Brady said. "That's the last of my worries. I don't even respond to stuff like this."

Only Brady would have no choice but to respond that Thursday, in his first press conference since the story broke. That same day, Belichick offered his first expansive remarks on Deflategate, opening with a long statement about how shocked he was Monday morning when details started coming in. He said he knew nothing of the process that delivered game balls from the officials' locker room to the field. He said he often used wet, sticky, cold, and slippery footballs in practice to make ball security more challenging than it would be in games, and to ensure that no Patriot ever used the condition of a ball as an excuse for not making a play. He said that in his entire coaching career he'd never once discussed a football's air pressure with any player or staffer.

But the most consequential words Belichick spoke that Thursday were these: "I think we all know that quarterbacks, kickers, specialists have certain preferences on footballs. They know a lot more about it than I do. They're a lot more sensitive to it than I am. I hear them comment on it from time to time, but I can tell you, and they will tell you, that there is never any sympathy whatsoever from me on that subject. Zero. Tom's personal preferences on his footballs are something he can talk about in much better detail and information than I could possibly provide."

Yes, Bill Belichick had just thrown Tom Brady under a double-decker bus.

Brady's friends and family members were not at all happy with this sudden turn of events. "I thought Bill handled it terribly, especially when it involved a guy who'd done everything to help your career as a coach, and you hung him out to dry," said one close Brady friend. "You weren't supportive of him, you didn't have his back, and you basically said, 'I don't know, ask Tom, I had nothing to do with it.' And you pushed it on him. When you think about it, that's not how [Belichick] ever wants players to act when they're asked questions in the media. It's the exact opposite of that. Bill tells them, 'Don't talk about in-house stuff, and don't talk about something that involves one of your teammates. Don't answer those questions.' And yet that's exactly what Bill did."

Belichick was angry at Brady, according to people in the Patriots' organization. He was angry at Brady because he had serious doubts about the quarterback's denial and because this crisis was the last thing the coach needed. Belichick had taken the full hit on Spygate, even though Brady and others benefited from the information gained through the illegal videotaping. The coach knew his legacy couldn't weather another damaging 'gate. If Spygate belonged to Belichick, Deflategate was going to belong to Brady.

The coach had come off as credible in his presser when he said he'd never had a single conversation about PSI in 40 years of coaching; it seemed that even rivals around the league were inclined to believe that Belichick had nothing to do with Deflategate. "There's no question they did it," one head coach said of the alleged ball deflation. "Tom was clearly lying, but I don't think Bill knew anything about it. Bill did his press conference and he was being honest, and I think he was really pissed about it."

Given the facts of the Spygate case and the leaguewide suspicions of continued black-ops tactics, it was odd that some inside the Patriots community viewed Belichick as a stickler for the rules. Chris Simms, the former NFL quarterback and a Patriots coaching assistant in 2012, called Belichick "the greatest rules follower I've ever been around in my career. Bill knows the rule book back to front. If we had a five-dollar pool on who's going to win the Masters and Bill got word of it going on, he put the kibosh to it. He sends an email, 'Hey, there's no gambling on the premises of any NFL facility.' He nixed our NCAA Tournament pool as well . . . I believe Tom did it, and I believe Tom did it by himself and with the ball boys. Of course he did it. We all know he did it. And I don't think Bill Belichick had anything to do with it."

Not every former NFL quarterback was so certain of that. Chad Pennington was the only starter not named Tom Brady to win the AFC East since Brady took over early in the 2001 season. (He won the division for the Jets in 2002 and for Miami in 2008, the year Brady missed.) In a 2008 meeting in Foxborough, the Dolphins scored four touchdowns on six snaps out of the Wildcat formation, which calls for a direct snap to a skill-position player other than the quarterback. New England wasn't prepared for that alignment and had no earthly idea how to defend it. Pennington maintained that in all his years of competing against Belichick's Patriots, that day represented the only time he saw a look of doubt on the faces of their defensive players. "I was almost in shock myself," he said. "They're always prepared for everything."

Pennington said that when he first met Eric Mangini, after the former Belichick coordinator took over the Jets, Mangini pulled out the Patriots' book on how to defend Pennington. The quarterback couldn't believe the detail. He also couldn't believe that a detail freak like Belichick wouldn't know his team was using underinflated footballs. "The only reason I can speak on that is because Mangini was my coach for almost three years," Pennington said, "and I know the level of preparation and detail the organization goes through. I have seen it with my own two eyes within the Jets organization when Eric was the coach. And, to be honest, I learned so much from Eric and the New England Way, and it made me a better player. And so it's just hard for me to fathom that they were unaware, or the coach was unaware. I can't fathom that, knowing I've never seen a stone unturned when it comes to the Patriot Way. To say you were unaware was an indictment of the Patriot Way, because the Patriot Way is to say, 'We're not unaware of anything. We know everything, from what we're eating in the cafeteria to who's serving food to who's coming to the complex to the amount of air in the football, to everything.'"

In that context, Brady also had an awful lot of explaining to do when he showed up in the team's interview room for his own Thursday press conference. His business manager, Will McDonough, had already emailed him an analysis of the Deflategate comments made by himself and Belichick. The Boston-based company Business Intelligence Advisors had concluded that the coach and the quarterback had "raised all sorts of behavioral flags" and had likely engaged in "an effort to withhold information" in their initial responses. "You should read this prior to any interviews you do about this," McDonough wrote Brady. "Belichick has really dropped this in your lap just now. Don't take this lightly."

The quarterback arrived at his presser wearing a white undershirt, a gray sweatshirt that hung unevenly around his neck, and a red-white-and-blue Patriots ski cap topped by a pom-pom. Given the circumstances and the stakes, Brady looked ridiculous. He faced a bank of cameras aimed his way and a packed room of reporters, not all of them familiar faces. And then Brady took the snap, took a five-step drop, and started dancing and dodging in the pocket.

He said that he'd much rather be talking about the Seahawks but that he wanted to face the news media's questions and to "provide the answers that I have, if any." Brady had answers. They just weren't very convincing ones.

He stood there for a half hour and looked uncharacteristically nervous, uncertain, afraid even. One Hall of Fame quarterback who was watching on TV, Fran Tarkenton, would say that Brady "looked like a deer in head-lights." At times the Patriots' franchise player had a slight tremble in his voice as he told a story that wasn't being warmly received across most of the country. "I didn't alter the ball in any way," Brady said in response to the opening question. He went on to explain the pregame process of picking out footballs he likes before the equipment staffers break them in. He said that the game balls are in ideal condition before kickoff and that he doesn't want anyone touching them before they're put in play.

Fair enough. But the second question was the one that started to move Brady off his spot. "This has raised a lot of uncomfortable conversations for people around this country who view you, a three-time Super Bowl champion, a two-time MVP, as their idol," the reporter said dramatically. "The question they're asking themselves is 'What's up with our hero?' So can you answer right now: Is Tom Brady a cheater?"

Brady laughed, then pursed his lips as he weighed the question. He ex-haled and said, "I don't believe so," before continuing a response that in-cluded six "um's" or "uh's" and two "you know's." "I feel like I've always played within the rules," he said. "I would never do anything to break the rules. I believe in fair play and I respect the league and everything that they're doing to try to create a very competitive playing field for all the NFL teams. It's a very competitive league. Every team is trying to do the best they can to win every week. I believe in fair play and I'll always believe in that for as long as I'm playing."

Not since Roger Mudd, of CBS, asked Ted Kennedy in 1979 why he wanted to be president had an answer done less to help a fair-haired son of Massachusetts. Brady had other tough moments in the presser, at one point saying, "This isn't ISIS. No one's dying." He also struggled to explain how a quarterback who is so particular in preparing a football to his liking had no idea that New England's balls were underinflated in the first half of the AFC Championship Game.

Before Brady had stepped into this inquisition, the team's lead PR man, Stacey James, had wanted to prep him. Brady told James he'd be fine on his own. And now that he was scuffling in the presser, Brady was ignoring James's repeated attempts to end it by calling for a final question. The quar-terback knew he had created a problem, and he wanted to stay out there to fix it. On the 61st question he fielded, Brady decided he'd had enough. "I think Stace said 'That's it' about ten minutes ago," he said. "So thank you, guys."

The reaction was swift and decisive. On ESPN's *NFL Live* show, former NFL players Mark Brunell, Jerome "the Bus" Bettis, and Brian Dawkins took turns criticizing Brady for telling a tale that wasn't believable. "Those who feared Belichick was throwing Brady under the bus by pointing the media to Brady," wrote *Hartford Courant* columnist Jeff Jacobs, "had to be relieved that The Bus didn't believe Brady either." Some commentators started lumping the quarterback in with noted sports liars and cheaters such as Lance Armstrong and Ryan Braun. ESPN's Damien Woody, a two-time champion with the Patriots, said he thought Brady was involved; the former lineman was called a turncoat and far worse by Patriots fans who demanded blind loyalty to Brady and the team. ESPN's Mike Wilbon, a widely respected national voice, had already called on the NFL to remove the Patriots from the Super Bowl if they were found to have tampered with the balls.

Hall of Fame quarterback Troy Aikman said the league needed to punish the repeat-offending Patriots more severely than it had punished the New Orleans Saints for the bonuses, or "bounties," paid to players for knocking out opponents in Bountygate. Sean Payton, the head coach, was suspended for a year in that case.

"It's obvious that Tom Brady had something to do with this," said Aikman. "Now the question becomes: Did Bill Belichick know about it?"

One NFL head coach said he thought Belichick would end up being cleared of any wrongdoing, "because I think he knows the rules so well and he's pissed that Tom and those equipment guys went behind his back, and because I think he wants to know everything. And he didn't know it." On the Brady side of the divide, one friend and former teammate was apoplectic that the quarterback had effectively been left to fend for himself.

"I think Belichick screwed him, totally left him out to dry," this friend said. "I don't think Kraft or Belichick handled it well. Who the NFL was really going after at the start of it was debatable. Were they really going after the golden child of the NFL, or was it Belichick and the Patriots? Ultimately it comes down to Tom being the fall guy. Belichick couldn't have screwed him more, if you ask my opinion."

Brady knew he'd just had a really bad day at the office. More than a few Patriots staffers and officials believed that he had been involved in the deflation scheme, and friends from different parts of Brady's life found it hard to believe the story he told—given the way he told it. The quarterback knew that he had to control the damage, and when pressed about the news conference — particularly about his weak, hesitant response to the "Is Tom Brady a cheater?" question — Brady had his answers ready.

He was adamant with co-workers, friends, and family members that he had no knowledge of any ball tampering. As to why he hadn't responded more forcefully to the cheating question, Brady told friends he was not thinking about Deflategate as he answered, but about the Spygate case and his own belief that at least some of the leaguewide suspicions about the Patriots — such as claims that staffers had pulled the opposition's stray or discarded scouting and game-plan material from vacated rooms — were likely true. If Brady was betrayed by a guilty conscience, said people close to him, it wasn't a feeling inspired by deflated footballs.

"Tom was terrible in that press conference," said one friend, "but his feeling was he didn't do anything with Deflategate. He wasn't involved. They asked him, 'Have you cheated?' and he knows the Patriots have not always done everything by the book, to say the least. To me, just come out and say that. Just say, 'No, I didn't instruct the equipment guys to do anything with the balls as part of any scheme.' Just don't say the second part about knowing the Patriots have done things in the past against the rules. But that's why he answered it the way he did."

The Patriots railed against the idea that they had lifted enemy material out of empty hotel or stadium rooms, but one accomplished longtime NFL veteran said that this was a regular source of conversation among his teammates. "Every team I was on, when we played the Patriots, they'd specifically say 'Don't leave anything out,'" the player said. "It was 'Be careful, don't leave it out somewhere in your hotel. Don't leave it in the locker room in Foxborough when you go out for warm-ups.' I think Bill Belichick would do everything he could to get an advantage. I think he feels if you're dumb enough to leave it out in your hotel or locker room, that's your problem."

Only now it was Brady's problem. And it would remain his problem for another 48 hours, until Belichick returned to the team facility's interview room for what seemed like a *Saturday Night Live* skit on Saturday afternoon.

Belichick's interactions with the media over 15 years in New England were far better than they were over his five years in Cleveland, hard as that was for fans observing this televised press conference to believe. His chief of staff, Berj Najarian, had a lot to do with that, though Najarian could also assume the role of hired muscle — forever lurking nearby — if he felt reporters looking for one-on-one time with the coach were pressing their cases a little too assertively. Over the years, Belichick had shown game films to writers and sent some of them Christmas cards. He joined some TV and print reporters out for dinner during Super Bowl week. He offered background information and off-the-record confirmations to media members he trusted and even occasionally let a columnist know that he'd read his or her most recent piece. Dan Shaughnessy of the *Globe*, the market's signature columnist, once wrote about all the old tension existing between Belichick and Bill Parcells, and after his subsequent daily presser, Belichick tapped Shaughnessy on the knee, acknowledged the surprised columnist by name, and said, "That was a great one today."

Belichick had softened a tad with age, with assists from his extroverted love interest, Linda Holliday, and the former chaplain turned Patriots character coach, Jack Easterby. He could still be brutally robotic, or robotically brutal, in his pressers, unless the questions involved special teams minutiae or the history of the single wing. Belichick created this character, and every time he stepped to the podium, he was an actor stepping onstage in his costume. Belichick as Quasimodo, his hunchback cloaked by a hoodie. This is why people were sometimes surprised when they encountered Belichick off campus and found the normal, somewhat engaging human being his friends knew. It would've been like stumbling into Carroll O'Connor back in the day and being surprised he didn't act like the bigoted Archie Bunker from one of Belichick's favorite shows, *All in the Family*. Belichick would shed that costume and that character for a special occasion here and there. But on this particular Saturday, he let down his hair, his guard, his everything, with the Super Bowl still eight days away and most of America still believing that the Patriots were guilty of producing, directing, and starring in a newfangled sequel to Spygate. Word had gotten around to reporters that something newsworthy and interesting would be forthcoming, and that it would be a good idea to stick around the facility for a while. And Belichick delivered. He entered a packed interview room and adjusted both microphones at the podium downward. He was wearing a nautical-blue team jacket over a striped, collared shirt. He looked up and actually smiled, asked reporters how they were doing, and when a couple of them asked him the same question, he said, "Good. Good. Good." This was going to be a hell of a good day for Bill Belichick.

He said that he wanted to share some information, that he'd spent the week educating himself about air pressure in footballs. Though he loved books on military strategy, and though he'd hung a sign on his locker room wall quoting ancient Chinese general Sun Tzu's *Art of War* — EVERY BATTLE IS WON BEFORE IT IS FOUGHT — Belichick wanted his audience to know that his team hadn't tried to win any simulated battle through pregame deflation. "I feel like this is important," Belichick said, "because there have been questions raised, and I believe now 100 percent that I have personally—and we as an organization—have absolutely followed every rule to the letter." He was just getting started on a filibuster that would last 16 and a half minutes and turn out to be as memorable as the rambling wreck of a presser he conducted when he bolted the New York Jets.

Belichick said the team had conducted its own tests, which found that the pregame rubbing of footballs (to break them in) had contributed to an artificially high PSI setting. That PSI number dropped when the balls reached their equilibrium and were exposed to the same cold weather conditions that decreased pressure in the tires of cars parked outside. In these tests, the coach said, his quarterbacks couldn't identify footballs with a difference of 1 PSI, and even struggled to identify footballs with a difference of 2 PSI.

In the end, Belichick said, New England's success was the by-product of hard work and physical and mental fortitude. He said the Patriots were the best team in the AFC in the regular season and had proved their conference superiority again by winning two postseason games.

"I'm embarrassed to talk about the amount of time that I put into this relative to the other important challenge in front of us," Belichick said. "I'm not a scientist. I'm not an expert in footballs; I'm not an expert in football measurements. I'm just telling you what I know. I would not say that I'm Mona Lisa Vito of the football world, as she was in the car expertise area, all right?"

The beat writers who already knew that Belichick loved watching Discovery Channel and the History Channel now knew he also loved Marisa Tomei's character in *My Cousin Vinny*. This was Belichick unplugged, and he wasn't finished.

"At no time was there any intent whatsoever," he continued, "to try to compromise the integrity of the game or to gain an advantage. Quite the opposite: We feel like we followed the rules of the game to the letter in our preparations, in our procedures, all right, and in the way that we handled every game that we competitively played in as it relates to this matter. We try to do everything right. We err on the side of caution. It's been that way now for many years. Anything that's close, we stay as far away from the line as we can."

These remarks didn't seem aimed just at Roger Goodell and NFL investigators, but at everyone who had quietly taken a complaint about the Patriots' alleged covert tactics to reporters or the competition committee. Belichick said he welcomed the league to investigate further and pronounced himself eager to move on from the subject so he could prepare for the Super Bowl.

He took 18 questions. The one that inspired the most meaningful response involved his statement that his organization always erred on the side of caution. A reporter wanted to know how that claim jibed with Spygate.

"I mean, look, that's a whole other discussion," Belichick said. "The guy's giving signals out in front of 80,000 people, OK? So we filmed him taking signals out in front of 80,000 people, like there were a lot of other teams doing at that time, too. OK? But forget about that. If we were wrong then, we've been disciplined for that."

Though the reporter didn't specifically challenge Belichick's assertion that there were "a lot of other teams" illegally videotaping in 2007, he did attempt to follow up by pointing out that Spygate had proved he was willing to cross the line. Belichick cut him short.

"The guy's in front of 80,000 people," he said. "Eighty thousand people saw it. Everybody saw it. Everybody sees our guy in front of 80,000 people. I mean, there he is. So, it was wrong, we were disciplined for it. That's it; we never did it again. We're never going to do it again, and anything else that's close, we're not going to do, either."

The reporter asked if this approach represented a shift in philosophy, a commitment to staying on the right side of the line. "We always do. We always have," Belichick said. "I mean, anything that's even remotely close, we're on the side of caution."

Belichick was asked if he'd consulted with any science experts in conducting his tests and arriving at his conclusions, and he said only that New England "talked to a lot of people." He took another handful of questions, then headed off to prepare for the Seahawks. The Patriots had quickly surrendered on Spygate, and Belichick had just served notice that his program would do no such thing on Deflategate. As for his serious reservations about Brady's denial, Belichick could set those aside. They had just become irrelevant. He could wrap his arms around science and hold on for dear life. He could get Brady ready for that angry Seattle defense and let the league try to make its case on its own.

Belichick couldn't waste any more time. He hadn't won the big one in ten years, and he was about to engage in a standoff with the man he'd replaced in Foxborough, Pete Carroll, that no witness would ever forget.

Belichick, call a fucking timeout!

Rick Young, a 46-year-old Patriots superfan from Fitchburg, Massachusetts, was among the many New Englanders screaming obscenities at their head coach from the University of Phoenix Stadium stands as precious time bled off the Super Bowl XLIX clock. Seattle Seahawks running back Marshawn Lynch had just powered the ball down to the Patriots' one-yard line and was poised to give his team the lead on the next play. All Seattle coach Pete Carroll had to do was give him the ball. And all Belichick had to do was call one of his two remaining timeouts, to give Tom Brady a fighting chance to drive for a field goal that would send the game into overtime.

But instead of taking that timeout with a minute left, Belichick just stood and stared across the field at Carroll, who was chomping away at his gum with his typical type A gusto and waiting for his opponent to stop the clock. Belichick sensed a little confusion on the Seattle sideline and didn't want to bail out the indecisive Carroll. So he let the clock run down to 50 seconds, 45, 40, 35, 30, while the fans cursed him and wondered if he'd lost his mind.

Young was sitting in the building's third level, around the 25-yard line on the Patriots' side of the field. "Everybody was going crazy on Belichick," Young said. "We were all screaming, 'We've got Brady. Just call a timeout and give us a chance. What the fuck is he doing?'"

In shotgun formation, the Seahawks snapped the ball with 26 seconds to play. The Super Bowl was about to deliver a bizarre ending to what had been a bizarre week.

It had started with Robert Kraft's bold and unannounced trip to the microphone after the Patriots had arrived in the desert the previous Monday, when he professed his belief that his coach and quarterback had done no wrong and that the outside investigator hired by the NFL to separate fact from fiction, Ted Wells, was destined to come up empty. Kraft said that if no wrongdoing was found, he would "expect and hope that the league would apologize to our entire team, and in particular Coach Belichick and Tom Brady for what they've had to endure this past week."

Fox Sports had just reported that the league had a low-level Patriots staffer on video carrying AFC Championship Game footballs from the officials' locker room into a Gillette Stadium bathroom, and *GQ* had just published a piece about the cozy relationship between Commissioner Roger Goodell and Kraft, whom one NFL executive called "the assistant commissioner." Kraft had been Goodell's most loyal advocate, helping him earn tens of millions in yearly wages and escorting him through the public relations disaster that was the initial two-game suspension of Baltimore Ravens running back Ray Rice, who had knocked out his future wife with a punch to the face in an Atlantic City elevator; Rice was later cut by Baltimore and suspended indefinitely by the league when TMZ aired a video showing that punch.

Seattle's star cornerback Richard Sherman had assailed Kraft's relationship with Goodell, and the cornerback and the owner exchanged verbal jabs at Tuesday's annual Super Bowl Media Day. Kraft also took the opportunity to announce that his players thought Deflategate was "a bunch of hogwash," a position that put Kraft at odds with his buddy Goodell. If nothing else, Kraft succeeded in making enough noise himself to take the pressure off his quarterback and his coach.

Yet on Super Bowl Sunday, his approach looked like it would be a losing one when Seattle carried a 24–14 lead into the fourth quarter. The Seahawks had seized control of the game when Chris Matthews, an undrafted 6'5" receiver who had no NFL receptions to his name, suddenly started making like Randy Moss. Matthews had spent time in the Arena Football League and the Canadian Football League and had worked as a security guard (before applying for a job at Foot Locker) when Seattle called, put him on the practice squad, and eventually made him a special teamer who recovered an onside kick in a stirring NFC Championship Game comeback victory over Green Bay.

Matthews had earned his team's trust, and Russell Wilson decided to throw him the ball in the last, and biggest, game of the year. Matthews's first NFL catch was an athletic, twisting 44-yarder over Kyle Arrington down the right sideline that led to a Lynch touchdown. On Seattle's next possession, Wilson found Matthews for an 11-yard score over Logan Ryan with two seconds left in the half. Matthews had two more catches in the third quarter, including a 45-yarder, leaving him with 109 yards before the 6'4" Brandon Browner, New England's tallest defensive back, finally shut him down. Belichick had benched the struggling Arrington in favor of his own answer to Chris Matthews, Malcolm Butler, the undrafted rookie from Division II West Alabama and a fifth corner who had made all of one start and who nonetheless made a significant difference in coverage.

Belichick's adjustments slowed Seattle's offense, allowing New England an opportunity for an even more improbable comeback than it had staged against Baltimore in the divisional round. Brady found Danny Amendola for a four-yard touchdown, and after a Seattle three-and-out, the quarterback drove the Patriots down the field one more time, completing eight consecutive passes to put the ball on the Seahawks' five-yard line. After a short carry by LeGarrette Blount, Brady faced a second-and-goal with a little more than two minutes to go and Seattle up 24–21.

The quarterback was finally in his element after the toughest two weeks of his career. He'd conducted an interview with NBC's Bob Costas that was no more convincing about his role or non-role in Deflategate than his presser in Foxborough had been, prompting Costas's colleague Cris Collinsworth to ask Brady to look him in the eye and tell him he'd never said something to a staffer about bleeding air out of a game ball. (Brady issued a firm denial, the announcer said.) The national debate over Deflategate had no place on the Super Bowl field. That was Brady's sanctuary, his office, his forum to do what made him rich and famous in the first place.

Edelman split out wide to the left. He'd absorbed a vicious head shot from Seattle's Kam Chancellor on a huge third-and-14, 21-yard gain on the previous scoring drive, and the Associated Press would report that the receiver was tested for a concussion and cleared to play on. The Seahawks had lost defensive end Cliff Avril to a concussion in the third quarter and had lost cornerback Jeremy Lane to a gruesome arm injury after he intercepted Brady at the goal line in the first quarter. The fact that Edelman remained in the game was a critical development in New England's favor. He was about to remind everyone that Belichick, the most brilliant of defensive minds, had used the slot position to showcase his ever-expanding creativity on offense; Welker to Edelman to Amendola (with Troy Brown as a founding father) had become his own Tinker to Evers to Chance.

On second-and-goal, the Patriots decided to run a play they'd put in the night before in a hotel ballroom walk-through. Edelman would sell a slant hard, stop on a dime, and then turn back toward the pylon after putting the covering corner on roller skates. Brady had missed his receiver earlier on the same play, but both knew it was available to them when needed. Now it was needed. Edelman sized up Lane's replacement, Tharold Simon, who had already surrendered a touchdown to Brandon LaFell. It was a mismatch, and as soon as Brady took the snap with 126 seconds to go, he exploited it. Edelman darted inside, used his left arm to push off on his plant and turn, and broke free for the easy three-yard score and his 26th reception in three postseason games.

The Patriots had their chance to win it all for the first time in ten years, and to do it in the building where they'd suffered their most haunting defeat, the Super Bowl XLII loss to the Giants. Only the Seahawks were defending champs for a reason; they'd shredded Peyton Manning's record-setting offense in Eli Manning's stadium in New Jersey the previous February. With a 36-12 record in the regular season and a 6-1 record in the postseason, Wilson had firmly established himself as an elite quarterback. He did nothing to harm his reputation on the first play of Seattle's final drive, when he hit Lynch for a 31-yard gain.

Wilson threw deep on the next play for Jermaine Kearse, who was successfully defended by Butler, before an expiring play clock forced the quarterback to burn the first of his three timeouts with 1:50 to go. On third-and-10, after Wilson missed Matthews for a long touchdown (Browner knocked the pass away), the Seattle quarterback found Ricardo Lockette for 11 yards and a first down at New England's 38. Wilson then hurried his teammates to the line, motioned to his receivers, and took the next snap with 74 seconds left. He quickly put the ball down the right sideline for Kearse, who went up with Butler at the New England 11.

The tipped ball fell into the inside of Kearse's left knee as he crashed to his back, then bounced from his knee toward his right hand. The receiver batted the ball as he tried to gain control of his body on the ground, then hit it again before grabbing it with both hands as he started to sit up. Patriots safety Duron Harmon hurdled Kearse as he was completing this amazing juggling act. Kearse, in disbelief himself, rose to his feet and turned toward the end zone before Butler pushed him out of bounds at the five-yard line.

A national TV audience was waiting for NBC's Al Michaels to deliver that signature line from the United States' upset of the Soviet Union's Big Red hockey machine at the 1980 Olympics: "Do you believe in miracles? Yes!" Instead Michaels described the play as a broken-up pass before saying, "And, is it, but somehow — what, did he wind up with the football?"

He wound up with the football.

Belichick had to check upstairs to confirm it was a catch. An ashen-faced Brady — his hair soaked with sweat, his eye black a bit smudged, his white jersey stained by grass — looked at the replay on the video board above and shook his head. The Patriots were all struck by the same ghastly thought: *How could this be happening to us again?*

Up in the stands, superfan Rick Young and his fellow New Englanders buckled under this devastating moment. "We were all trying to recover from another Tyree catch," he said. That would be David Tyree, the Giants receiver who had helped win Super Bowl XLII by pinning an Eli Manning heave against his helmet. "We were all thinking about the Manningham catch," Young said. That would be Mario Manningham, the Giants receiver who'd helped win Super Bowl XLVI with an improbable sideline catch in front of Belichick.

"All of those thoughts were in our head," Young said. "Including Billy Buckner, Aaron Boone. It all came back. *Here we go again.* That's all we were thinking."

The Patriots had won three Super Bowls and appeared in six since 2001, and the Red Sox had won three World Series titles since Boone hit his walk-off Game 7 homer for the Yankees in 2003, and yet fatalistic New Englanders were still confronting a legion of exorcised ghosts. This was their Kearse of the Bambino. Meanwhile, amid the chaos of the Kearse catch, another expiring play clock forced Seattle to take its second timeout with 66 seconds left. During the timeout, NBC aired a replay of the Tyree catch and showed Seahawks owner Paul Allen, seemingly ready to faint. "But they're not in yet," Collinsworth said on the air.

When play resumed, Wilson handed the ball to Lynch, who rumbled over left tackle before getting tackled at the one-yard line. It was a huge four-yard gain, and yet the Patriot Way was in full force on the stop. Patrick Chung, safety, aggressively filled the hole and sacrificed his body while getting pancaked by 272-pound fullback Will Tukuafu. Dont'a Hightower, a linebacker playing with a torn right labrum in his right shoulder, did a remarkable job by shedding 307-pound tackle Russell Okung and diving his injured body into Lynch's legs. Akeem Ayers, linebacker, got rid of his blocker (Luke Wilson) in just enough time to finish the tackle on Lynch with a minute to go.

Dressed in his PATRIOTS ESTABLISHED IN 1960 hoodie, Belichick stood there and thought about taking a timeout. Carroll, still looking as youthful as ever despite his snow-white hair, froze in anticipation of his opponent's next move. It was a Wild West showdown between supposed good and supposed evil. Belichick was cast in the role of diabolical overlord of a secretive empire that operated outside league rules, while Carroll was everyone's friendly next-door neighbor. Never mind that Carroll had left USC's storied football program to confront severe NCAA sanctions, or that his Seahawks were twice punished by the NFL for practice violations, in 2012 and 2014. Pete was fun and bouncy and goofy, and it pained Kraft to have to fire him after the 1999 season.

But fire him Kraft did, in favor of the coach who was letting the clock run and run and run with Seattle 36 inches from another Super Bowl title. Belichick studied Carroll's body language, studied the indecision of Seattle's players and assistants. "I don't know," he said, "something just didn't look right. They started on, and they started off, and now however many seconds had gone by, and I'm thinking, *All right, I'm not going to take them off the hook here by taking a timeout. If they want to use it, let them use it.*"

Meanwhile, Belichick's defensive coordinator, Matt Patricia, asked his boss more than once if he wanted to take a timeout, and the head coach didn't even look at him or answer him. "Yeah, I got it," Belichick finally said into his headset. He was effectively applying a full-court press to Carroll, and he decided to win or lose with his goal-line defense.

On New England's sideline, Matthew Slater, four-time special teams Pro Bowler, represented the conflicted mood of the players as Belichick let the clock run. "Tense. Tense," Slater said. "I may have been voicing my protest. I didn't know what was going on. I was just hoping we would do what we could to try to preserve time."

A couple of Patriots coaches lifted their arms, put their clenched fists near their ears, and flexed their biceps before putting three fingers in the air to signal a heavy goal-line package with three cornerbacks, or Goal Line

3 — the first time all year New England was using this personnel group. Butler had to get out there in Arrington's place, and the Patriots' safeties coach, Brian Flores, shouted, "Malcolm, go." Butler had been distraught over Kearse's acrobatic catch at his expense, and now he had a chance to do something about it.

During New England's final practice, Butler had struggled with the pass play Seattle was expected to run. Armed with blue and red team binders at his desk, buried behind his hayfield of a mustache and his Coke-bottle glasses, Ernie Adams had worked on the play in an office with handwritten memos and yellow Post-it notes to himself thumbtacked to a nearby bulletin board. After considerable study of the Seahawks, Adams labeled his diagram "14 Raffle Utah" and decided that New England might have to defend it in a big situation. Seattle would stack two receivers to a side of the field — one on the line, to essentially set a pick on his defender, the other off the line and outside the up-front receiver's shoulder and preparing to run a hard slant off the pick. Butler was having a rough time in practice covering the receiver running the slant, as the corner was chasing around the pick and compromising his ability to break up the pass.

The Patriots wanted Butler to jump the route and beat his man to the spot, in case Seattle lined up in that formation. And, sure enough, a rushed Carroll and offensive coordinator Darrell Bevell had Kearse and Lockette stacked on the right side, with Kearse on the line and Lockette off his right shoulder. Browner planted himself directly opposite Kearse, up close and personal, while Butler stood in the end zone, about a yard in front of the K in SEAHAWKS. Out of the shotgun, after receiver Doug Baldwin went in motion toward the left side, Wilson called for the snap with 26 seconds left. That meant Belichick had killed 34 seconds that could've been used by Brady on the following series.

That meant Belichick was going to get shredded by talk-show hosts and columnists if Seattle took a three-point lead and left too little time for New England to work its way into field-goal position. That meant Belichick was going to walk into his locker room inside University of Phoenix Stadium and blame himself as he had seven years earlier.

Carroll had been boxed in a bit by the wasted timeouts. Had two time-outs been available to him instead of one, he could have run Lynch twice, stopped the clock in the event both attempts failed, and then figured out whether to run or pass on fourth down. But even with one timeout, Carroll should have made the commonsense call. Football coaches can try to explain away almost anything with logic they think escapes the average fan or sportswriter, and, as it happened, Belichick would defend his opponent's decision to throw the ball on second down. Coaches tend to rush to each other's aid when under intense fire.

Lynch had made four consecutive Pro Bowl teams and had accounted for 1,306 rushing yards and 13 touchdowns in the regular season and for a combined 259 rushing yards and two touchdowns in the NFC Championship Game and the Super Bowl struggle he was one carry away from likely winning. Ricardo Lockette, the intended receiver on the play Carroll did choose? He'd managed 25 catches in his four-year career, postseason included.

Carroll called his number anyway. Across the field, with noise shaking the stadium at its core, Belichick was so calm and composed, it appeared he was gazing at a springtime sunset from his yard in Nantucket.

On the snap, Browner won the battle with Kearse by jamming him hard and rendering his pick useless. Lockette cut behind his teammate but didn't exactly move with the urgency of a man about to be involved in Super Bowl history. On cue, Butler charged from the rear as Wilson took his quick drop, swung open his shoulders to the right, locked in on Lockette, and fired a pass designed to lead the receiver into the end zone. Butler exploded toward the ball, blew up Lockette on contact just before the goal line, and made a remarkable catch before falling forward to the two-yard line. An undrafted Division II player who had worked the window at a Popeyes after being kicked off his junior college team had just won the Super Bowl.

The Patriots broke into a dizzying celebration. Belichick raised his right hand to the sky in triumph. Near his bench, a helmetless Brady did a 360 as he hopped up and down and squealed like a teenager at a boy-band concert. Across the field, Richard Sherman looked as if he'd just seen a family friend run over by a car. Wilson lowered his head, clapped his hands as he walked toward the sideline, and asked his head coach what had just happened. "They undercut the route," Carroll said. The Patriots had just undercut their former coach's shot at a two-Pete.

Before the final 20 seconds expired, fists and flags were thrown, Seattle's Michael Bennett jumped offside, and teammate Bruce Irvin was ejected. Collinsworth couldn't stop ripping Carroll for his incomprehensible call. Finally, Brady took the knee that ended the madness. Belichick had already embraced his coordinators and absorbed two Gatorade baths by the time he found his quarterback for a hug.

Belichick had feelings of empathy for the gutted Carroll, who he thought did a terrific job getting his teams to play hard for a full 60 minutes. Bill had been where Pete was at this very moment, in this very building. He knew it was a dark and lonely place.

Yet this was a moment of extreme relief for the winning coach. Belichick's championship drought had felt biblical to him, and now it was over. He'd seized his fourth Super Bowl championship, joining Pittsburgh's Chuck Noll as the only men to do it. He'd won without the sport's best offensive line coach, Dante Scarnecchia, who had retired a year earlier, and for the first time he'd won with his older son, Stephen, a 27-year-old defensive assistant, as part of his staff.

One of Belichick's childhood heroes, Joe Bellino, Navy's Heisman-winning halfback in 1960, was touched by the scene of Bill with his son Stephen as he watched from his Massachusetts home; it reminded Bellino of little Bill and his father, Steve, side by side at Navy practices back in the day. The Patriots' coach was thinking about his old man, too, and his 93-year-old mother, Jeannette, who was residing in an assisted living facility in Annapolis. Belichick's previous Super Bowl victory had come nine months before Steve died, and as Bill started to address the media in his postgame news conference, he was wondering what his father thought of him now.

"I guess the last thing I'll say before I open it up is, the last time I won and I got Gatoraded, my dad was here," Belichick said as his voice cracked with emotion. "I was certainly thinking about him tonight, and I'm sure he was watching. I hope my mom is watching, too, so — Hi, Mom."

On this memorable night in the Arizona desert, the head coach of the New England Patriots wasn't identifying himself as a four-time Super Bowl champ. He was, above all else, the proud son of Steve and Jeannette Belichick, and that was plenty good enough.

18

THE COMEBACK

The unbearable Deflategate saga lasted 544 days before Tom Brady announced on Facebook that he would not appeal his four-game suspension to the Supreme Court of the United States. Brady surrendered to the NFL on July 15, 2016, a Friday, the best day of the week for powerful corporations and rich and famous people to deliver bad news.

Only no summer getaway day could reduce the magnitude of this story. The most accomplished player in the league had just accepted Roger Goodell's penalty for being "at least generally aware" that low-level Patriots staffers John Jastremski and Jim McNally deflated footballs used in the AFC Championship Game victory over the Colts, according to the findings of attorney and lead investigator Ted Wells.

The Wells Report was released on May 6, 2015, and was followed five days later by the NFL's announcement that the Patriots would be fined $1 million, docked a first-round pick in 2016 and a fourth-rounder in 2017, and forced to play someone other than Tom Brady at quarterback for four games because the franchise player had engaged in "conduct detrimental to the integrity of, and public confidence in, the game of professional football." The battle that followed, in and out of courtrooms, left no winners on either side and did significant harm to long-standing relationships throughout the league.

Brady originally had his suspension overturned in New York by U.S. District Court Judge Richard Berman, who rebuked Goodell for enforcing "his own brand of industrial justice" and won himself a lifetime offer of free coffee from a Dunkin' Donuts in Maine in the process. After playing out the 2015 season, Brady saw his suspension reinstated by the United States Court of Appeals for the Second Circuit, in New York, which reinforced Goodell's broad disciplinary authority under the collective bargaining agreement. Brady's appeal of that ruling was denied before the quarterback decided against dragging his four-ring circus into the Supreme Court.

In the end, the people who believed Brady was involved in Deflategate seized upon the circumstantial evidence in the case. McNally, the officials' locker room attendant, popular among the refs for bringing them clam chowder (according to the league's former VP of officiating, Mike Pereira), had identified himself as "the deflator" in a text to Jastremski, an equipment assistant, before the Patriots countered with an absurd explanation for that nickname. (The team said McNally was referring to his own attempt to lose weight.) McNally had said in another text to Jastremski that he was "not going to espn . . . yet." He had taken the AFC Championship Game balls out of the officials' locker room (without permission) and into a Gillette Stadium bathroom for 100 seconds before carrying them to the field. Brady, who had said in a 2011 radio interview that he preferred deflated footballs, disposed of a cell phone that was used during a period Wells deemed relevant to his investigation.

The people who believed Brady was innocent of any wrongdoing in Deflategate seized upon the scientific evidence in the case — namely, that experiments using the applied principles of the Ideal Gas Law proved that Mother Nature, not the Patriot Way, represented the force responsible for New England's low PSI numbers. Those people also seized upon the Wells Report finding that the Patriots' footballs had not been as underinflated as first reported by ESPN's Chris Mortensen. Long regarded as one of sportswriting's most reliable news breakers, Mortensen had spent more of his time focused on the number of balls cited by his league source (the correct number, 11) before tweeting the news, rather than on the level of inflation. (The source's information of 2 PSI per ball was incorrect, though all 11 balls were under the minimum 12.5 PSI when measured on both of the referee's pressure gauges.) And yet the erroneous part of that report — left uncorrected by the league — shaped a narrative that the Patriots were as guilty as they were in Spygate.

New England assailed the NFL's claim that it had run an independent investigation, given that Jeff Pash, the league's executive vice president, played a significant role in Wells's inquiry and report. Robert Kraft was as angry at Pash as he was at anyone, and it seemed his days as "the assistant commissioner" and chief benefactor to Goodell were over. But eight days after the Deflategate penalties were disclosed, in May 2015, Kraft announced that he was reluctantly accepting the team's sanctions, for the best interests of the league. It was a painful concession for the owner to make, as he loved to be loved and he knew this move would be a most unpopular one with the fans.

The Patriots cared deeply about their feelings; network partners would hear more complaints from Patriots officials that included the words "our fans are not happy about this" than they'd hear from any other franchise. New Englanders are protective of their own, and Tom Brady, son of San Mateo, California, had very much become one of their own. So the fans were not happy with Kraft when he seemingly abandoned Brady and his planned appeal, and the quarterback's family and friends weren't happy with the owner, either.

One person close to Brady said the entire family was "miffed" at Bill Belichick for dumping Deflategate on the quarterback's shoulder pads three days after the story broke. "And we were very miffed with Kraft [in May]," the person said. "He hung Tom out there by saying he wasn't going to fight it with the league. And then later he realized that was a mistake. It was about money, and he's a billionaire. But over time we forgave him for that."

Some NFL owners weren't so quick to forgive Kraft for eventually pivoting away from his concession and resuming the fight, to the locals' delight. The owners' anger intensified over time as Kraft ignored the counsel of some associates to stand down for the good of the league and to remember that many believed that Goodell had gone easy on the Patriots in Spygate.

Kraft blistered Goodell's decision, in July 2015, to keep Brady's ban at four games — the owner had counted on a reduction after playing nice in May — and said that he was "wrong to put my faith in the league." Kraft directly apologized to the team's fans and declared that it was "completely incomprehensible to me that the league continues to take steps to disparage one of its all-time great players and a man for whom I have the utmost respect." The New England owner ripped the NFL again — after Brady called off the legal fight — when he said his quarterback had been denied a fair and impartial process.

"I was really unhappy with Robert's statement after the Deflategate case was settled," said one high-ranking executive with a rival team. "He went too far questioning the integrity of people in the league office . . . Of course they deflated the footballs. They're drinking the Kool-Aid [in New England], but there's nobody outside of New England who believes they didn't do it. I think some people have been sent to the electric chair on less circumstantial evidence than there was in this case. You're telling me that two equipment guys did this to the balls, with a Super Bowl trip on the line, without one of the greatest quarterbacks of all time being aware of it? . . . People say Roger wanted to go after the Patriots after Spygate. Do you really believe he wanted to do this? Why in the world would he want this?"

A September 2015 story by ESPN's Don Van Natta Jr. and Seth Wickersham answered that question definitively, citing sources saying that Goodell's relentless pursuit of Brady and the Patriots in Deflategate was effectively a "makeup call" for going soft on Kraft's franchise in Spygate. The investigative piece included the shocking and comical scene of three league officials, including Pash, literally stomping to pieces New England's Spygate videotapes in a stadium conference room and feeding Ernie Adams's

Spygate notes into a shredder. This was done under the watchful eye of the team's counsel, Robyn Glaser, who picked shards of the smashed tapes off the floor and threw them in the trash. Van Natta and Wickersham also reported that Goodell had asked former St. Louis Rams coach Mike Martz, loser of the epic Super Bowl encounter with Belichick after the 2001 season, to state publicly that he'd accepted the league's handling of Spygate in order to quiet Senator Arlen Specter's calls for a reopened case. Martz said he'd always believed "something happened" in his career-altering loss to the Patriots. Years later, when shown a copy of his statement suggesting that nothing untoward happened, Martz said he was certain someone had taken it and "embellished quite a bit."

Sources and documents in the ESPN story indicated that at least 40 games were illegally videotaped by the Patriots, dating back to 2000 — making the operation far more extensive than Goodell had admitted — and that the seized Spygate notes included detailed diagrams of the Pittsburgh Steelers' defensive signals from the January 2002 AFC Championship Game. It appeared Goodell had covered for his most successful franchise and one of his most ardent backers, Kraft, and other NFL owners let the commissioner know he had no choice but to even the score.

"People weren't happy with what Roger said about destroying the tapes and notes," one owner said. "His reasoning for doing it didn't make any sense. Of course the other franchises had a right to know the full extent of the cheating, and what was taken from them. But Roger knew that would be a great embarrassment to the league and the most successful team in it, and he wanted to minimize the damage. That was his priority, and I don't know if any owner or executive in the league was happy about it."

The Patriots responded to the ESPN story with a direct hit on the sports and entertainment giant, reminding fans and readers that the network had needed to apologize to the team for twice crediting the old *Boston Herald* report that falsely claimed the Patriots had taped the Rams' Super Bowl walk-through. "This type of reporting over the past seven years has led to additional unfounded, unwarranted, and quite frankly, unbelievable allegations by former players, coaches and executives," read the Patriots' statement. "None of which have ever been substantiated, but many of which continue to be propagated. The New England Patriots are led by an owner whose well-documented efforts on league wide initiatives — from TV contracts to preventing a work stoppage — have earned him the reputation as one of the best in the NFL. For the past 16 years, the Patriots have been led by one of the league's all-time greatest coaches and one of its all-time greatest quarterbacks. It is disappointing that some choose to believe in myths, conjecture and rumors rather than giving credit for the team's successes to

Coach Belichick, his staff and the players for their hard work, attention to detail, methodical weekly preparation, diligence and overall performance."

The Deflategate victim total kept piling up, and yet, almost miraculously, the one significant figure in the case who escaped relatively unscathed was none other than Bill Belichick. As much as Spygate didn't stick to Brady, Deflategate wasn't sticking to the head coach. The Wells Report might as well have been called the Brady Report. Belichick was cleared of any wrongdoing (as was Kraft), and many of the same people who thought the coach was lying when he swore he had merely misinterpreted a rule in Spygate found him to be believable this time around.

And as it turned out, there was one side benefit to Belichick that tempered the pain of losing a first-round pick: He would get to coach the first four games of the 2016 season without Brady under center. Belichick had long told associates he wanted a shot at winning a Super Bowl with another quarterback, and he was falling hard for the one he'd drafted in 2014, Jimmy Garoppolo, a good kid and a great-looking young player. One Patriots staffer said that people in the building believed in recent years that Belichick was asking himself, *Is Brady really going to have to be my quarterback until I retire?* Though he understood Brady's greatness better than anyone, Belichick yearned for a fresh challenge. The Deflategate suspension gave him a small window of opportunity to flex his coaching muscle in an entirely different way.

But before he got his opportunity with Garoppolo to start the 2016 season, Belichick opened the 2015 season with Brady on a distressing note. After New England's 28–21 home victory over Pittsburgh in the rain-soaked season opener (during which fans mocked the absent Goodell with chants of "Where is Roger?"), Steelers coach Mike Tomlin revealed that his team's headsets had been malfunctioning during the game. "That's always the case," Tomlin said of games he'd coached at Gillette Stadium. "We were listening to the Patriots' radio broadcast for the majority of the first half. On our headsets." Tomlin was listening to color man and former Patriots backup quarterback Scott Zolak, and he said the Steelers couldn't communicate coach to coach. Told he was indicating something very serious — that the Patriots were cheating again — Tomlin said, "I'm not indicating nothing. I'm telling you what happened."

Tomlin and his team were doing a better job than any journalist of advancing the ESPN story from two days earlier. The Steelers posted an article on their website accusing the Patriots of defying league protocol regarding malfunctioning headsets.

"This is the kind of stuff that happens to the visiting team in Gillette Stadium all the time," read the Steelers.com story. "From the start of the game through the opening 14 minutes of the first quarter, the Steelers coaches' headsets were receiving the Patriots Radio Network broadcast of the game. The broadcast was so loud that the Steelers coaches were unable to communicate, and the NFL rule is that if one team's headsets are not working the other team is supposed to be forced to take their headsets off. It's what the NFL calls the Equity Rule. Strangely enough, whenever an NFL representative proceeded to the New England sideline to shut down their headsets, the Steelers' headsets cleared. Then as the representative walked away from the New England sideline, the Steelers' headsets again started to receive the Patriots game broadcast."

Belichick had hit his breaking point. He'd had enough of the spoken and written claims of deflated footballs, jammed headset frequencies, pilfered play sheets, you name it. Hall of Famer Don Shula, the Miami Dolphins' legend, had taken to calling him "Beli-cheat," a shot clearly below the belt. *Sports Illustrated* had published a report of its own detailing the extreme methods teams used to protect their practices and locker rooms from real or imagined Patriot spies, including clearing out trash cans that might otherwise be searched for discarded intel and transporting their own sports drinks to Gillette Stadium so their hosts couldn't ensure the drinks were warm and/or late in arriving. On top of it all, Tomlin's sour grapes left a bitter taste in the winning coach's mouth. In a conference call with reporters the next morning, Belichick spoke of the common communication problems New England confronted in its stadium before firing off shots at Tomlin and other vanquished foes who had complained about alleged improprieties. He was clearly waiting for an opportunity to vent.

"I just think overall it's kind of sad, really, to see some stories written that obviously have an agenda to them with misinformation and anonymous-type comments and writing about warm drinks and trash cans and stuff like that," Belichick said. "I think it's just sad commentary and it's gone to a pretty low level. It's sunk pretty deep.

"First of all, let's say that I think our program here is built on competition and trying to improve every day and trying to work hard, and it's not built on excuses. We just try to go to work and improve and find a way to get better. This organization has won a lot of games, but particularly in reference to the great teams from '01, '03, '04, and back in there, all the great players that played on those teams . . . To take away from what those guys accomplished, what those teams accomplished, how good they were, how many great players we had, how well they played in big games, how they consistently showed up and made big plays and game-winning plays — it's just not right."

Belichick had punched back by accusing Tomlin of being an excuse maker and sent a message to the rest of the league that future accusations would be met with forceful reminders of New England's long-running dominance. The NFL actually came to Belichick's aid by announcing that the problems in the Pittsburgh game had resulted from a "stadium power infrastructure issue, which was exacerbated by the inclement weather." League spokesman Michael Signora said that the coaches' headsets were provided by the NFL as part of standard operating procedure, and that once the stadium power issue was addressed, the Steelers (and Patriots) had no additional problems with their communication equipment.

On the subject of rule-bending and rule-breaking in pro football, everything seemed to circle back to Foxborough. It seemed the Patriots were involved even when they weren't involved. An example: Following a 2010 game against Miami, a New York Jets strength coach, Sal Alosi, was suspended and fined for tripping a Dolphins gunner on punt coverage as part of a human wall of Jets that Alosi had set up close to the sideline. The Patriots weren't even playing in this AFC East game, and yet they were dragged into the controversy when Mike Westhoff, the Jets' special teams coach, told ESPN 1000, in Chicago, that New England had been guilty of similar tactics — remarks that contributed to the NFL's decision to fine the Jets $100,000.

Westhoff swore that he had no knowledge of what Alosi was doing on the sideline, but he maintained that he'd watched tape of New England that showed Patriots players lining up on the sideline when they were returning punts. "New England had it organized — look at any film," Westhoff said. "It was like the [Texas] A&M marching band, and we had four idiots in sweatpants doing it."

Westhoff shared his concerns with NFL officials during the Alosi investigation, and the next time he saw Scott O'Brien, New England's highly regarded special teams coach, O'Brien let Westhoff know he was upset about it. "Scott said, 'I've been coaching more than 20 years and I never once did this, and I got my ass reamed by my owner,'" Westhoff recalled. "I said, 'I apologize to you, Scott, but it's still the New England Patriots who did this. So fuck you guys.' They did it for years."

Truth was, many other NFL franchises had been punished for breaking league rules involving illegal practices, tampering, injury-report violations, salary-cap violations, and creating artificial stadium noise when the visiting team had the ball. So some veteran players, coaches, and executives did not necessarily see the Patriots as rogue outliers. Michael Huyghue, an agent who had been an executive with the Detroit Lions and Jacksonville Jaguars, was among those who believed that Brady knew that staffers were deflating footballs for his benefit, but he compared the misdemeanor to someone stealing a cherry while shopping in the fruits section of a super-market.

"Technically you're not supposed to do that, but who cares?" Huyghue said. "I don't think Bill Belichick knew about it. Could Brady have gone to the equipment guys and done this on his own? Yeah. It's the kind of thing Belichick could've known about, but didn't know about. If you have a 15-year-old son and you go through his drawers, you might find something you don't want to find, so you tell him what the right thing to do is, but you're not going through his stuff.

"The nature of this game," Huyghue continued, "is to get every advantage you can . . . Bill's nature is to turn over every rock, and that's led him sometimes to turn over some rocks he shouldn't have turned over. He's just a machine that gobbles information. He's drawn to figuring out your weaknesses. I don't believe he's a guy who sets out and says, 'Let's cheat. Let's go and see if we can get a copy of your playbook.' He wants to say he can beat you and let you know he beat you, but he doesn't want to gimmick-beat you. He wants to outprepare you and beat you. It's the same way guys use bankruptcy laws to save you financially, and use loopholes in the tax code to maximize income. That's what Bill does."

Huyghue pointed out that NFL teams are forever signing players off upcoming opponents' practice squads for the express purpose of learning those opponents' calls and audibles. A senior vice president of the Jaguars' football operations from 1994 through 2001, Huyghue also estimated that during that period, five to seven NFL teams were illegally videotaping opponents before games on any given Sunday. "Back in the day," Huyghue said, "when teams came in on Friday or Saturday and did a walk-through in the stadium, the home teams were required to leave the venue. But teams would routinely stand up in the back of sky boxes and watch or film the walk-throughs. It's prohibited, and they did it."

To many, the perpetual hunt for an edge was an ingrained part of NFL culture hardly confined to New England. Tim Green, a former first-round draft pick and an eight-year linebacker and defensive end in Atlanta, called rules-bending "inherent" in the game. "It almost feels like law school to me," said Green, a lawyer, author, and broadcaster, "where you start going down that rabbit hole. When is it bending the rules and when is it breaking the rules? Who makes that judgment call? Even Deflategate: Was that breaking the rules or bending the rules? People who get on their soapbox and thump their Bibles on that, I think it's hypocritical.

"I played against offensive linemen that put silicone on their jerseys and didn't get caught, and linemen who held me intentionally and didn't get caught. Before they had a flinch rule on the goal line, I would flinch when the crowd noise was crazy to try to draw that offensive lineman offsides . . . Was I cheating or taking advantage of the situation? I bet you Bill Belichick would say 'Hey, that's smart. You're using your surroundings. You're like the American military fighting the British. You're using your environment and getting any edge you can have.'"

As a Fox analyst, Green had only limited access to Belichick; he worked a couple of Patriots games and sat in the usual briefings Belichick and other NFL head coaches had with network announcing crews. But Green came away from those briefings with the strong impression that Belichick's Naval Academy upbringing had shaped his approach to competition. "I wouldn't be surprised, if you could get him to go under hypnosis, that he sees himself as a general," Green said, "and that football is merely a variation of a campaign of war . . . Unquestioned obedience is imperative. Hierarchy is imperative, and by outworking, outplanning, and outthinking your opponents, you can win. And I really don't mean this in a disparaging way, but I believe that espionage is also a part of that. It's all theoretical speculation, but my read of him was that to take someone's plays, to take their signals, and to spy on them — I would think on a psychological level, for him, that's not only all right, but it's appropriate and the right way to do things."

In the end, New England's alleged actions in Deflategate represented a high football crime to some, and another day at the office to others. The first NFL quarterback Belichick worked with, Baltimore's Bert Jones, said he always manipulated game balls by asking the officials to rub them down with hot, wet towels to remove the balls' sheen and to create higher, more defined seams. Decades later, Arizona's Jeff Blake claimed that every NFL team used pins to bleed air out of footballs before kickoff. Blake said he couldn't understand why Deflategate had become such a big deal. "It's not something that's not been done for 20 years," he said.

The Patriots couldn't believe that this had become a major national story, and their quarterback couldn't believe that his good name had been soiled. Did Brady do it? Did he conspire with the two staffers, Jastremski and McNally, to create a small ball that would be easier to grip and rip? Or did a league office full of suits who were eager to hammer the Patriots and who hadn't given the Ideal Gas Law a second thought since junior high lose sight of a reasonable explanation for deflated balls on a cool New England night?

Exponent, the scientific consulting firm hired by the NFL, conducted tests that in its view demonstrated that the Ideal Gas Law couldn't fully account for the drop in PSI in New England's footballs. The Patriots countered with a parade of experts who poked a million holes in Exponent's findings. One search for the truth led to Timothy Gay, a professor of physics and astronomy at the University of Nebraska. Gay had authored a book,

The Physics of Football, and it happened to include a foreword from his Andover schoolmate Bill Belichick. The book was published a decade before Deflategate, but it included a breakdown of how the Ideal Gas Law relates to football.

Gay had been the football team manager at Andover when Belichick and Ernie Adams played on the offensive line. When his book came out, he wrote them an email about it, and one of the two responded by saying that both were too busy to read it. "I said, 'If you read this book, you'll get an extra three points every six years,'" Gay recalled, "and they said, 'Yes, we'd want to read that.'"

As a physicist and football junkie with a distant connection to the Patriots' coaching staff, Gay followed Deflategate very closely. He initially told reporters that he believed the Ideal Gas Law could explain the drop in the footballs' air pressure. But his opinion was later altered by the timeline described in the Wells Report. Gay focused on the estimate by Wells's firm (Paul, Weiss) that the testing of New England's footballs at halftime of the AFC Championship Game had started after the balls began to warm up and therefore should've produced higher PSI numbers than were reported that night. The report states that testing began "no sooner than 2 minutes after the balls were brought into the locker room and was estimated to have taken approximately 4 to 5 minutes (leading to an ending time of between 6 and 7 minutes, and thus, an average measurement time of between 4 and 4.5 minutes, assuming a start time of 2 minutes) . . . Given the likely timing of the testing, one would expect the average halftime pressure measured for the Patriots footballs on Game Day to be higher than what was actually recorded."

The way Gay saw it, if the reported timeline was correct, the Ideal Gas Law couldn't explain the inflation levels of New England's footballs. "Because the balls had time to warm up and reinflate," he said. "That's the best evidence I've seen that something fishy happened and someone cheated, and the circumstantial evidence points to two guys in the equipment room, two flunkies."

Gay had watched his old schoolmate's *My Cousin Vinny* press conference, and he reviewed all the data from experiments that concluded the Patriots were blameless in the whole mess. But the physicist kept coming back to the timeline. "I don't think Bill or Tom cheated," Gay said. "The ball boys took it on themselves.

"Bill has done me a huge professional favor [by writing the book foreword], and I'm very grateful to him. But I'm going to tell the physics like it is. And when you factor in the timeline, the best evidence is that somebody cheated."

• • •

The 2015 season started heading south in an overtime loss to the hated New York Jets at MetLife Stadium two days after Christmas, and six weeks after a giddy victory over the New York Giants in the same building, on Stephen Gostkowski's 54-yard field goal with one second left. Belichick had made a bizarre decision to give the Jets the ball after winning the overtime coin toss, and the home team needed only five plays to score and, ultimately, cost New England home-field advantage in an AFC Championship Game it would lose to Peyton Manning and the Broncos.

On the verge of retirement, Manning hugged Belichick on the field afterward and told him, "Hey, listen, this might be my last rodeo, so it sure has been a pleasure." Belichick responded by pulling Manning close and telling him, "You're a great competitor. You're a hell of a player." Denver would beat the Carolina Panthers in the Super Bowl, and Manning would finish his career with two championship rings, a record five MVP awards, and three consecutive conference-title-game victories over Brady, who was 11-6 overall in the head-to-head.

Belichick called the loss in Denver a "crash landing" after Brady absorbed 20 hits (the most on any NFL quarterback all year) and four sacks, and after Gostkowski missed his first extra-point kick in nine years and 524 attempts. The Patriots were manhandled, and yet, in a testament to their resourcefulness, they somehow had a chance to tie Denver in the final seconds on a two-point conversion pass that failed. Belichick responded by firing his offensive line coach, Dave DeGuglielmo, just as he'd fired his punt returner, Chris Harper, after his November fumble in Denver prevented New England from improving its record to 11-0.

Failure was not an option in Foxborough. Belichick cleaned up another problem in March when he traded Pro Bowl defensive end Chandler Jones, a 2012 first-round pick, to Arizona for guard Jonathan Cooper and a second-round pick in the 2016 draft. Jones had effectively traded himself in the middle of the playoffs when he stumbled into the Foxborough police station's parking lot, shirtless and disoriented, after suffering from an adverse reaction to synthetic marijuana; he dropped to his knees and put his hands behind his head, though not on police orders. Jones was hospitalized, released, and back at work the next morning, but he was shipped out as soon as his coach could get some value for him.

Belichick sent that second-round pick to New Orleans for third- and fourth-rounders used to take two potential starters in guard Joe Thuney and receiver Malcolm Mitchell, adding to his long history of trading down in the draft. He'd done a fair amount of trading up, too, and, like every other strong evaluator, he had his share of draft-day misses. But Belichick didn't just repeat the cliché that the draft is a crapshoot; he devised a strategy around that truth. Trading down allowed Belichick to add picks, and the more picks a team had, the better its chances of finding a productive player in that class. And the later a rookie was selected in the draft, the less the Patriots had to pay that rookie at the expense of veterans who had earned their keep.

As he entered the 2016 season, his 17th in New England, the 64-year-old Belichick had everything about his program completely under control. He regularly took scrap-heap players from other franchises and made them significant contributors to the league's best team. Belichick was proficient at acquiring bargain contracts, at working the restricted free-agent market, and at identifying moderately talented players whose intelligence made them more valuable than their more skilled contemporaries.

Patriots who wanted to stick around needed to subjugate their egos; Belichick was not about to suffer any fools. "At this point in my career," he would later tell his old friend Urban Meyer at Ohio State, "I want to coach guys I like. I want to coach guys I want to be around, and that's it, and I'm not going to coach anybody else."

He'd earned the right. It said so on the side of his Nantucket fishing boat, which once carried the name *V Rings* (counting the two he won as a Giants coordinator) before the Super Bowl victory over Seattle mandated a fresh paint job and a new name: *VI Rings*. Belichick was living large in his Nantucket and Hingham, Massachusetts, homes, and in his Foxborough fiefdom. He often showed up for work in jeans and wrinkled sweatshirts, and he did it his way. Over the years, if he felt like calling up a friendly AFC coach one day and telling him to cut his kicker for missing a crucial field goal attempt, he called him. If he felt like ripping the Eagles one day for firing Chip Kelly after three seasons, he ripped away. If he felt like cutting Tim Tebow one day, shortly after asking him to decline a $1 million endorsement gig that required 24 hours of work (for the sake of fitting into the team, of course), he sure as hell cut Tebow.

Belichick had established his authority the hard way. His assistants couldn't complain on Thursday night that they hadn't seen their wives and kids for more than 20 minutes since the previous Sunday night, because he was working more hours than all of them. Sometimes when Belichick headed home a tad early, one staffer said, he would "bring a backpack so big you could fit six bowling balls in it, and it was stacked with offensive and defensive playbooks."

He never stopped, even after winning a Super Bowl in heart-stopping fashion. In the weeks after beating the Seahawks on Malcolm Butler's goal-line interception, Belichick visited Indiana University basketball coach

Tom Crean before the draft combine to exchange ideas and watch some Indiana football film with his Patriots coaching assistant and former Cleveland personnel director, Mike Lombardi. Belichick told Crean's basketball players that the Butler play had initially been installed in a May minicamp, and that January and February games are sometimes won the previous spring. As if to prove his point, Belichick broke out his cell phone and started taking photos of the motivational signs and pictures Crean had on his facility walls — in case one or two would work in Foxborough. He'd just won his fourth Super Bowl title, and he was trying to get 1 or 2 percent better in a college basketball gym.

That was classic Belichick. So were his conversations with fellow Wesleyan alum Thomas Kail, the Broadway director of *Hamilton,* about the similarities between teamwork on the stage and on the field. Friends and enemies alike were blown away by Belichick's willingness to learn and improve despite his absurd success rate. One of his old full-time rivals and part-time critics, Bill Polian, came to fully appreciate Belichick's greatness after leaving the Indianapolis Colts and joining ESPN as an analyst. He had never had a true conversation with Belichick ("The rivalry dies hard," Polian said), and past controversies had done nothing to soften the edges of Patriots–Colts ("Spygate put a lot of gasoline on the fire," Polian said), but the former executive was amazed by what Belichick had willed into existence.

"The way he put it all together, managed the game, created a game plan, and the way they adjust and tie all facets together — they're in a league of their own in that regard," Polian said. "And that's all him. The coaching staff does exactly what he wants, and it works so well in terms of both strategy and tactics that it's really amazing. I hate the term 'cutting edge,' because it isn't; it's really sound football and taking it to an organizational and strategic and tactical level that we haven't seen in the NFL.

"What's interesting about it," Polian went on, "is he's adapted to the rules and the players. Bill Parcells, for whom I have great respect, is a power football guy. And Bill Belichick and the Patriots are anything but that, and that's because of a combination of the rules and the ability to have Brady and all these other players around him . . . If I had a Hall of Fame vote — and I don't, and Spygate is a part of his history you can't write without it, but it wouldn't change my vote one iota — I think Bill Belichick is a first-ballot Hall of Famer, and that's how I would vote. I think his record speaks for itself."

Belichick started running things on his own terms and on his own time after winning his first title. In those early years, he had a job candidate in to interview for a position on staff. The man sat outside the coach's office and waited and waited and waited, and Berj Najarian popped in on occasion to apologize for the delay and to explain that Belichick had gotten tied up with work. The candidate went to visit another employee he knew in the building, and on the way he passed Belichick, working out on an exercise machine. Finally the coach saw his guest at around 3:30 p.m., some seven hours after the scheduled interview time. The candidate realized he'd been tested by a potential employer who wanted to see just how badly he wanted the job. He left the team facility thinking he'd had a good two-hour showing; Belichick thanked him and assured him he'd be brought back in for a second interview. The candidate never heard another word from the Patriots. It wasn't the last time someone booked for an appointment with the head coach was put through that kind of experience.

Belichick was successful enough and powerful enough to treat people as he saw fit. At the league meetings in the spring of 2016, Jeff Howe of the *Herald* tweeted out the scene of Roger Goodell giving a speech to owners and head coaches in a banquet room while Belichick was walking down the hallway in the opposite direction. The Patriots' coach had no use for league executives, league functions, league logos, league anything, after the Spygate and Deflategate cases. Belichick was the only head coach whose name and likeness didn't appear on EA Sports' *Madden NFL* video game — according to Yahoo!'s Dan Wetzel, he'd declined to join the NFL Coaches Association, thereby declining to cash in on its deal with *Madden*. Belichick had also mocked the league's policy on injury updates by listing Brady as "probable" for years, for a shoulder injury that didn't actually exist.

Mike Pereira, the Fox analyst and former game official who had become the NFL's vice president of officiating, used to have semi-regular and always professional phone conversations with Belichick about rules, until the coach stopped calling after Spygate. The confiscated tapes were played on Pereira's machine at league headquarters, but he had no meaningful role in the case. His apparent offense, in Belichick's eyes, was that he worked for the NFL.

The news media could feel the deep freeze, too. Belichick did have his charming moments in pressers, and he did show respect to most network announcers in pregame production meetings (though he often rolled his eyes over the heavily detailed questions asked by one particular network reporter). One radio reporter and columnist who covered Belichick in his Cleveland days, and again in New England, Mike Petraglia, said the coach was more helpful and showed much more personality in media settings with the Patriots than he had in those settings with the Browns.

"But if you said A and you did B," said another reporter who knew Belichick, "you were excommunicated from the church of Bill Belichick."

Those production sessions with network partners in New England could be tense, as nobody knew which Belichick was coming through the door on a weekly basis.

"There's a sense of trepidation as you're waiting for him to walk in," said one veteran of these meetings. "You don't know what kind of mood he's in. Dick Vermeil might give you a bottle of wine, Jim Fassel will bullshit with you, and Mike Shanahan was great in those meetings, but Bill was different. It was like trying to pick a lock. You're not quite sure what the combination is. If you ask the wrong thing, you could get that sideways look from Bill that said, 'What the fuck was that question?'"

In every way, Belichick had won the media war that many coaches fight and lose badly. His star tight end, Rob Gronkowski, was injured in a joint August practice with the Chicago Bears, and Belichick's next media availability was the following morning. In that press conference, not one question was asked about the injury or the status of an irreplaceable player who could end up in the Hall of Fame. Reporters knew the coach would give them nothing on it, so they didn't bother. Nor would there be much point in asking Gronkowski's teammates for an update, as Belichick was forever schooling his players on the messages he wanted them to deliver — or, more important, not deliver — to the news media.

On the practice field, while twirling his whistle, Belichick had the same hold over his players. One Patriots veteran who had played for an NFC North team on which his teammates openly laughed at a head coach trying to assume a tough-guy stance shuddered when imagining what would happen to players who laughed at New England's head coach.

"There's not many more intimidating figures in sports than Coach Belichick," Gostkowski said. The kicker had done a hell of a job for his boss, replacing perhaps the greatest kicker of all time, Adam Vinatieri. And yet Gostkowski had long felt every ounce of the pressure Belichick puts on his players in the leadup to Sundays. In his first couple of days on the team as a rookie, in 2006, Belichick set the tone for Vinatieri's successor by pointing to a picture of a Patriots player on the wall and asking him to identify the man. Gostkowski had no idea who it was, and Belichick lit into him and told him the player's name was Don Davis, and that he might want to get to know Davis, since he'd be covering his kickoffs.

"Personally," Gostkowski said, "I get more nervous kicking in front of Coach Belichick in practice than I do in front of fans in the game."

As intimidating as his glare and presence can be, Belichick never believed in governing with volume. "He's going to make it tough," said safety Devin McCourty, "but he's not going to degrade you. He's not going to disrespect you." The players appreciate that approach as much as they appreciate Belichick's consistency. He's virtually the same person every practice, whether it's an August training-camp session or a late January day in preparation for the AFC title game. That the Patriots know what they're going to get from him, McCourty said, "helps players know exactly how they need to perform."

Belichick would keep it fairly simple when breaking down opponents, giving his players a few things they needed to do to win and a few they needed to avoid so they wouldn't lose. Even though players sometimes arrived at the team facility on Wednesday morning—after an off day on Tuesday—to find a game plan that didn't resemble anything in their playbooks, Belichick didn't believe in overwhelming his team with information. He normally quizzed his players on Wednesdays on the upcoming opponents' tendencies and strengths and backstories, and followed the full-team meeting with unit and positional meetings before running an afternoon practice that focused on first- and second-down plays. (Third down is generally handled on Thursdays.) Players watched tape of practice afterward, and Belichick started dialing back his demands on Friday. But he never stopped coaching situational football, which the Patriots practice, preach, and master unlike any other team.

Through 2008, Belichick kept an aging three-time Pro Bowler, Larry Izzo, productive on kick returns by allowing him to chip-block early in coverage to hide his diminishing speed. In 2010, Belichick explained to the rookie McCourty how the Gillette Stadium wind dragged a fade-pattern pass back to the inside on a certain corner of the field. Sure enough, in New England's next home game, McCourty found himself defending that very pattern Belichick had talked about. "I had an interception where the ball was sailing that way and it just kind of stopped," McCourty said. Just as his head coach had predicted.

As much as he insisted that pro football was a players' game, Belichick had established himself as the NFL's MVP—most valuable person. On a certain level, it was funny that Belichick had ascended to such heights in a game dominated by big, powerful, and remarkably swift men. He had been a mediocre high school football player and a lousy Division III college player. In the words of one longtime NFL evaluator who had watched Belichick work out prospects, he was "maybe the worst fucking athlete I've ever seen. The players used to laugh at him . . . He would move along and show the players drills, shuffling laterally, and he was just a terrible athlete. I remember one big offensive lineman saying, 'Did this guy play anywhere?'"

Belichick could joke about his own lack of athleticism, in part because his historic career amounted to such a decisive victory of brains over brawn. He wasn't going to have Tom Brady for the first four games of 2016, which was the kind of development that would ruin most teams' seasons, and yet Belichick was so confident in his program and in his ability to coach up the young second-stringer, Jimmy Garoppolo, that he spent the morning of the September 11 season opener, in Phoenix, talking baseball with his friend Tony La Russa, the former Cardinals, Athletics, and White Sox manager and current Arizona Diamondbacks executive who had just been inducted into the Hall of Fame.

La Russa didn't want to bother Belichick on the day of his big Sunday night opener in the desert. "But he said, 'Get your ass down here,'" La Russa recalled. "So I walked in, the Patriots are about to play the Cardinals to open the season without Brady, and we had this talk and Bill was more concerned about our disappointing season and how to fix it and what's ahead. I was in there for an hour and a half, and for an hour and 15 minutes of that, he was checking on me. Geez, what a friend."

What a coach. That night at University of Phoenix Stadium, where he had won his most recent Super Bowl title, Belichick walked in as a 9.5-point underdog, the biggest spread against his team since it had upset the Rams 15 years earlier. He walked out as the proud owner of an apparently worthy successor to Tom Brady.

Garoppolo, 24, completed 24 of 33 passes for 264 yards and a touchdown in the 23–21 victory, showing mobility, touch, and toughness in finding a way to win without the injured Gronkowski. (By comparison, a 24-year-old Brady had been 13 for 23 for 168 yards and no touchdowns in his NFL debut as a starter.) Garoppolo took smelling salts before the game — just to get himself going, he said — and then did nothing to disabuse anyone of the notion that he was a star in the making.

"Good" was Belichick's underwhelming assessment of his quarterback. Asked for a little bit more than that, Belichick said, "It's been good. He made some plays. It's not perfect, but he made a lot of good plays." The Patriots' coach wasn't going to get carried away, because the Patriots' coach never got carried away. He'd already guaranteed that Brady would take over as the starter when his suspension was complete, removing any possibility that Garoppolo could effectively unseat the incumbent the way Brady had unseated the injured Drew Bledsoe in 2001. As it turned out, Garoppolo couldn't make it through two full games without getting injured; he threw three touchdown passes against Miami before exiting with a 2-0 record and handing the job to the third-stringer. Jacoby Brissett, a Bill Parcells favorite, beat Houston before getting shut out by the Buffalo Bills. Brady returned in Week 5 to pick apart the hapless Cleveland Browns, throwing for 406 yards and three touchdowns after former Browns tight end Aaron Shea, Brady's friend and former Michigan teammate, said that a pissed-off Tommy was bad news for the rest of the NFL and that "Deflategate hurt Tommy a lot more than he'll let anyone know."

Even without the first-round draft pick they forfeited in Deflategate, the Patriots were whole again. Brady was back. Dante Scarnecchia, their invaluable offensive line coach, was back from a brief retirement. Their defense would lead the league in points allowed (250) for the first time since 2003, and the 39-year-old quarterback would throw 28 touchdown passes against two interceptions while winning 11 of 12 starts. Garoppolo threw only four passes in those 12 games, but he'd already served notice that a confrontation with Brady was coming, and sooner rather than later.

Belichick didn't have to worry about that for now. He didn't have to worry about much over the course of a 14-2 regular season other than trading another talented defender, Jamie Collins, whose expiring contract and reported desire to be paid like an All-Pro were shipped to Cleveland for a draft pick. In fact, Belichick's biggest concern in 2016 had nothing to do with football and everything to do with a political football.

Donald Trump had scored a much bigger upset than the Patriots did in Super Bowl XXXVI, and by beating Hillary Clinton and winning the presidency, he'd put his longtime friends and the holy trinity of pro football's most impressive dynasty—Belichick, Brady, and Kraft—in a most uncomfortable position. Trump was only the most polarizing and divisive force in the modern history of American politics. He had led the birtherism movement in a failed attempt to prove that the nation's first black president, Barack Obama, was not born in the United States. He had called for a ban on Muslim immigration and had made a series of offensive comments about African Americans and Mexicans.

Belichick, Brady, and Kraft found out it was much easier being Donald Trump's friend when he was building skyscrapers, running beauty pageants, and hosting The Celebrity Apprentice. Brady had judged the Miss USA pageant for Trump in 2002, played many rounds of golf with him over the years, and, in September 2015, had effectively endorsed him by keeping a red MAKE AMERICA GREAT AGAIN cap in his locker. Kraft had long spoken of how kind Trump was to him in the wake of his wife's death, in 2011, constantly checking on the Patriots' owner, and though he'd been a lifelong Democrat, he would donate $1 million to Trump's inauguration celebration.

But the president-elect turned a hotter spotlight on Belichick than anyone else in Foxborough. He was the leader of the best team in a sport that's roughly 70 percent black, and there he was in Instagram photos posted by his girlfriend, Linda Holliday, posing with her and Trump after a March dinner at Trump's Palm Beach resort, Mar-a-Lago, where the coach was reportedly a member. Within days of the photos' appearance, the *Globe* published two letters from outraged readers, under the headlines "How Can Owner, Coach and Star Pose with Him?" and "Happily Aligning with Hate." One published letter, from a Tessa Yesselman of Cambridge, criticized the coach for his association with Trump. "Belichick has made millions of dollars largely off the labor of black athletes on the Patriots," it read. "Public figures are entitled to their opinions and private lives, but when you stand happily next to a man who makes weak and insincere denouncements of the Ku Klux Klan, and consent to pictures with that man on social media, you align yourself with the vitriol and hate he embodies."

Yesselman, who worked for a New York agency that investigated police misconduct, was a passionate Patriots fan who had admired what she called the "grumpy genius" of the team's head coach. "But after the election letter," Yesselman said, "I was done with him."

The election letter. At a New Hampshire rally the night before the voters went to the polls, Trump said he had been handed a letter from Belichick a couple of hours earlier on his plane. The Republican candidate had someone call the coach for permission to read the letter at the rally, and Belichick asked if he could send a revised version for that purpose. Trump told his supporters that he assumed the coach would tone down his praise in the second letter, "like most gutless people do. Gutless. But he's the opposite. He's a champ. So he sent me the new letter, and it was much better. It was stronger."

Trump shared Belichick's second version with the crowd:

> Congratulations on a tremendous campaign, he read. You have dealt with an unbelievable slanted and negative media and have come out beautifully, beautifully. You've proved to be the ultimate competitor and fighter. Your leadership is amazing. I have always had tremendous respect for you, but the toughness and perseverance you have displayed over the past year is remarkable. Hopefully tomorrow's election results will give [you] the opportunity to make America great again. Best wishes for great results tomorrow, Bill Belichick.

The crowd cheered. Trump barely lost New Hampshire, but he shocked the world by winning the election. The following day, Belichick stepped to his news conference podium in a striped, collared shirt with the top two buttons left unfastened. He opened by talking about how much respect he had for that week's opponent, Seattle, and after two minutes on the Seahawks he pivoted on his own to Trump. Belichick said that the president-elect had been a friend for many years, but that he himself was not a political person who makes politically motivated comments.

"I have a friendship and loyalty to Donald," Belichick said. "A couple of weeks ago, we had Secretary of State [John] Kerry in our locker room. He's another friend of mine. I can't imagine two people with more different political views than those two, but to me friendship and loyalty is just about that. It's not about political or religious views. I write hundreds of letters and notes every month. It doesn't mean I agree with every single thing that every person thinks about politics, religion, or other subjects. But I have multiple friendships that are important to me and that's what that was about."

With that, Belichick said he wanted to focus on New England's big game with Seattle. Asked immediately if he felt happy or annoyed that Trump had read the letter at the rally, Belichick responded, "Seattle." As another reporter tried to ask if he'd talked to his players about Trump and if he was concerned about "locker room rancor" resulting from his stated support, Belichick said the word "Seattle" four times before requesting the next question.

As it turned out, Belichick didn't vote for Trump or Clinton or anyone else. Brady refused to say whether he had voted for Trump; he said only that his supermodel wife had ordered him to stop talking about politics. (Gisele did post a flat "NO!" in response to an Instagram question about whether the couple had supported Trump.) One of New England's two African American captains, Devin McCourty, didn't say anything in his Wednesday media availability that suggested Belichick would have trouble reconciling his loyalty to Trump with his responsibility to inspire the black players on his team.

"I think the one thing that's certain is everybody has their own opinions in our locker room," McCourty said, "but politics aren't going to divide our locker room. We're here to do a job, but I think everyone is entitled to their own opinion and who you support."

Martellus Bennett, the tight end acquired in an off-season trade with Chicago, wrote an emotional Instagram letter to his young daughter that he opened with these words: "Daddy how will this effect [sic] my future? Jett, I'm not totally sure my love." Back in September, on opening night in Arizona, Bennett and McCourty had raised their fists high during the playing of the national anthem, in support of San Francisco 49ers quarterback Colin Kaepernick, who since the preseason had been taking a stand by taking a seat, and then a knee, during the anthem to protest police brutality, the deaths of unarmed African Americans at the hands of cops, and systemic oppression of people of color. These were two New England Patriots — two of Bill Belichick's players — who were joining a growing protest on the 15th anniversary of the 9/11 attacks, and it was a powerful visual.

It caused no apparent discord inside the Patriots' facility. Despite his friendship with Trump, Belichick seemed well equipped to relate to the experience and burdens of the African American athlete. He was the son of the only white man on Okinawa during World War II who initially accepted and befriended Samuel E. Barnes, one of the first black officers in the U.S. Navy and a hero who called Steve Belichick "one of the most unprejudiced persons I'd ever met." Bill Belichick had also lived through the turbulent desegregation of Annapolis high schools, and he reveled in the fact that his unified football team — under an inclusive coach, Al Laramore — had represented the best of what black and white could accomplish when working together.

Race was never an issue with the head coach of the New England Patriots. Players, agents, and sportswriters did sometimes talk about the makeup of Belichick rosters and how he seemed to have more white players at the offensive skill positions long dominated by black athletes — particularly wide receiver — than any coach in the NFL. But that truth was likely the result of Belichick exploiting yet another market inefficiency, and a culture of coaching, from the youth leagues through the pros, that had undervalued good white athletes at positions they were no longer supposed to be qualified to play. (Just as vile racial stereotypes once compelled ignorant coaches to steer black athletes away from the quarterback position.) If fellow AFC East teams didn't know what they had in Wes Welker (Miami) and Chris Hogan (Miami and Buffalo), and if other franchises couldn't see that the small and undrafted Danny Amendola and the small seventh-round quarterback, Julian Edelman, could be dynamic postseason receivers, Belichick would be more than happy to educate them.

He would get that chance to educate them again in his 14th postseason appearance in New England. Belichick would need Hogan, Amendola, and Edelman to again crash through their projected NFL ceilings if he was going to do something on Super Bowl Sunday that no coach had ever done.

Julio Jones made the lunging, full-extension catch near the right sideline and somehow tapped down both feet as he fell out of bounds with 4:38 left in Super Bowl LI. Suddenly the Patriots were confronted with that familiar haunting feeling. David Tyree. Mario Manningham. Jermaine Kearse. Now it was Jones, the 6′4″ receiver for the Atlanta Falcons who looks and plays like a superhero, making a you've-gotta-be-kidding-me catch inside NRG Stadium, in Houston. Leading 28–20, ball at the New England 22, the Falcons were in easy field-goal range for Pro Bowl kicker Matt Bryant, who had made 37 of 40 attempts during the regular season and postseason and 31 of 32 from distances shorter than 50 yards. If Atlanta made it a two-score game on this series, the Patriots would almost certainly lose.

Jones was the most likely Falcon to make a decisive play against New England, and perhaps the most fitting Falcon, too. Before the 2011 draft, Atlanta general manager Thomas Dimitroff, the Patriots' former director of college scouting, asked for Belichick's opinion on whether he should trade up from No. 27 to No. 6 to take the Alabama star. Dimitroff was preparing to send Cleveland the 27th pick, his second- and fourth-rounders in the same draft, and his first- and fourth-rounders in 2012. Belichick told his former employee that he shouldn't do it, that it was the kind of deal destined to stay with him forever. Dimitroff listened, then decided that he knew his organization better than Belichick or any outside voice did. He thought his franchise quarterback, Matt Ryan, needed an explosive and athletic target, and so Dimitroff did the deal.

Jones had made his GM look smart in ignoring Belichick's advice; he'd accounted for 323 receptions, 4,873 yards, and 20 touchdowns over the past three regular seasons. And now he'd just made the biggest play of his career and was threatening to send the Patriots home to something other than a parade.

This was what Dimitroff had called his "dream game" ever since he arrived in Atlanta, in 2008: a chance to face Belichick in the Super Bowl. He was his own man, with his own personality as a snowboarder, mountain biker, and all-around fitness freak, but Dimitroff had mixed a little Foxborough into his own Deep South system. He had as his director of pro personnel Joel Collier, the son of Joe Collier, the former Denver defensive coordinator who taught Belichick everything he knew about the 3-4 defense. Belichick had hired Collier's son as a Patriots secondary coach in 2005 and let him go after the 2007 season, much to the chagrin of Joel's old man.

Dimitroff had also brought in, as an assistant to head coach Dan Quinn, Dante Scarnecchia's son, Steve, who'd worked in New England's video department in the early Spygate years. As a staffer for Josh McDaniels in Denver, amazingly enough, Steve had been caught illegally filming a San Francisco walk-through before a game in London. Dimitroff had decided to give him a last NFL chance.

He also decided to revive the career of Scott Pioli, who had been Belichick's chief personnel man before he left to run the Kansas City Chiefs in 2009. Pioli was fired after four mostly stormy seasons, and a month after witnessing the suicide of linebacker Jovan Belcher, who had murdered his girlfriend before he arrived at the Chiefs' facility, thanked Pioli for giving him a chance, and then shot himself in the head.

Dimitroff hired Pioli a year later, and together they built a program that was on the verge of beating their former boss for the heavyweight championship of their sport. All the Falcons had to do was run the ball three times, force the Patriots to exhaust their timeouts, and then kick the field goal to effectively end New England's shot at completing the greatest comeback in Super Bowl history.

The Falcons had held a 28–3 lead late in the third quarter, showing why their offense had outscored Belichick's by nearly 100 points during the season. Brady had helped Atlanta's cause by throwing a ghastly pick-six before halftime to give the underdogs a 21–0 lead. His parents, Tom Sr. and Galynn, were in the stands watching, and it was Galynn's first appearance of the year. She wore a bandanna around her head and a No. 12 shirt that read BRADY'S LADIES on the back, and she was praying like hell for her quarterback to turn it around. Galynn had been in a grueling fight with breast cancer, and before the game her only son told Robert Kraft, "Let's win one for her." As the game started to fall apart for Brady, Kraft thought of Galynn and wondered what must've been running through her Tommy's mind.

But the Patriots never betray a sense of panic. When the Falcons took their 25-point lead, Belichick looked as if he were observing a disappointing performance in a non-contact training-camp drill. His even sideline temperament had always been among his more obvious strengths, and it helped keep his team calm and focused when confronting overwhelming odds. Brady, meanwhile, exhorted his teammates to play harder and tougher, to give more. Soon enough he was hitting Amendola for 17 yards on fourth-and-3, and then lumbering for a first down on third-and-8 before finding James White for New England's first touchdown, nearly 43 minutes into the game.

Gostkowski missed the extra point but kicked a field goal with 9:44 left in the fourth, before the Patriots made the play that reminded the world why they're the Patriots and everyone else is not. On third-and-1 in the middle of the fourth quarter, still holding a 16-point lead, Quinn and offensive coordinator Kyle Shanahan elected to pass, despite the fact that their running backs would finish the game averaging 5.78 yards per carry. Linebacker Dont'a Hightower rushed in from the Falcons' right, running back Devonta Freeman whiffed on the pickup, and Hightower pancaked Matt Ryan and sent the ball into the arms of New England tackle Alan Branch. Five plays later, Brady hit Amendola for a touchdown. White took a direct snap on the two-point-conversion attempt — he made a terrific catch above his right shoulder that would be overlooked amid the dizzying events to come — and carried the ball across the goal line to make it a one-possession game.

Atlanta appeared to rediscover its legs on its first snap when Ryan found Freeman for a 39-yard gain. The running 27-yard throw to Jones two plays later had the feel of a dagger, just as the Kearse catch had in the Super Bowl two years earlier. Only coaches often do the strangest things when standing across the field from Bill Belichick in a big game. With his fanatical devotion to minutiae, Belichick makes competing coaches work and think for 3,600 game-clock seconds. The Super Bowl is a draining experience to begin with, complete with an endless intermission to account for the megawatt halftime act (in this case Lady Gaga's). Belichick's ominous presence in this setting can leave his counterparts feeling in the fourth quarter like suspects willing to say anything after a ten-hour interrogation.

Just as Pete Carroll had made the indefensible choice to throw the ball on second-and-goal from the 1, two plays after the Kearse catch — an offense that some team members never forgave him for — Quinn and Shanahan decided to throw two plays after the Jones catch. Of course Ryan was sacked by Trey Flowers for a loss of 12 yards, turning the potential clinching kick into a 53-yarder, and of course the Falcons were flagged for holding on the next pass (a nine-yarder to Mohamed Sanu to compensate for the previous mistake), to set up a third-and-33 and the eventual punt.

Brady had to start at his own 9 with 3:30 left, but every witness knew this drive would be exactly what it turned out to be — a monument to the Patriot Way and Belichick's ability to identify talent that would work in his system better than it would anywhere else. Seven Patriots would touch the ball on this 10-play, 91-yard possession, and none was among the top 100 players taken in his draft class. Center David Andrews, Amendola, and Hogan had gone undrafted. Brady was famously picked 199th in 2000. Edelman, the Kent State quarterback, went 232nd in 2009. White was taken 130th out of Wisconsin in 2013. Malcolm Mitchell, part of the eventual yield of the Chandler Jones trade, went 112th out of Georgia in 2016.

A lacrosse player at Penn State who played a year of football at Monmouth, Hogan had been let go by four NFL clubs, including two AFC East teams and the only franchise (the Giants) to beat Belichick's Patriots in a Super Bowl. Hogan had helped send New England back to Houston, where it had won it all a dozen years earlier, by shredding the Pittsburgh zone for 180 yards and two touchdowns in the AFC title-game blowout, and he helped kick start this drive against Atlanta with a 16-yard catch on third-and-10.

Mitchell followed with an 11-yard catch on second-and-10 before Brady fired his next pass over the middle into what Belichick would ordinarily call a "fucking team meeting" while reviewing his Monday morning lowlights. The throw was intended for Edelman and was batted in the air by Robert

Alford, leaving the Patriots' receiver and three Atlanta defenders, including Alford, to go for the rebound at the Falcons' 41. In an unwieldy tangle of 16 arms and legs, with the pass hitting Alford's right leg and left foot, a diving Edelman somehow gathered the ball before it hit the ground. It was a catch that made Tyree's look like a five-yard square-out. Quinn had almost no choice but to challenge, and, in losing the review, he burned his final time-out with 2:03 left.

At that moment, the Falcons surely knew they were going to lose. On the next three plays, Brady hit Amendola for 20 yards, White for 13, and White again for 7. On his way to a 20-point game, a Super Bowl record (he also set a record with 14 receptions), White scored on a one-yard carry on the next play. New England still needed the two-point conversion to tie, and converting two such attempts on back-to-back possessions would usually be a long shot. But Atlanta was a broken team, and Belichick and offensive coordinator Josh McDaniels had worked on two-point plays all week.

"I don't know," Belichick said, "just Josh and I had a sense that we may need a couple of them." Lined up on the left side, Amendola went in motion, caught a bullet from Brady, and got the ball across the goal line before two defenders could stop him. The same Amendola who had taken a $4.4 million pay cut in May to remain a Patriot and to have a chance to do what he had just done.

The Falcons had at least a 99 percent chance to win at 20 different points in the game, according to ESPN Stats and Information, and they couldn't finish off Belichick and Brady. The Patriots won the overtime coin toss when Matthew Slater called heads, and it was all Amendola, Hogan, Edelman, and White again, all the way down to the Atlanta 2, as New Englanders in the crowd flipped NRG Stadium on its ear. On second-and-goal, Brady took his 99th snap and pitched the ball deep to White, who headed for the right corner, cut back at the 5, and plowed his way through two tackles and into the end zone to give the quarterback and Belichick their record fifth Super Bowl title.

Matt Patricia bear-hugged Belichick and lifted him off the ground. Brady and running back LeGarrette Blount were on their knees, surrounded by photographers and camera operators, when Belichick found them amid the confetti on the field. He leaned down to hug them both, and they rose together as one. Soon enough Brady fell into the arms of his mother, who had motivated him on this night far more than Roger Goodell's Deflategate suspension ever could. The only imperfect part of Brady's perfect night would unfold in the locker room, where a credentialed Mexican journalist would swipe his game jersey from his bag.

On the stage for the trophy presentation, Terry Bradshaw told Belichick,

"Well, there's so much debate about who's the greatest coach in the history of the NFL. Tonight that got solved, and that would be you, my young man. Congratulations." Wearing a blue jacket minus the standard "Flying Elvis" team logo missing from his upper left chest — likely a hard jab at a league office demanding conformity on its biggest night — Belichick thanked Bradshaw. "But look," he said, "it's all about these players. We've got great players. They're tough and they compete. We thought they competed for 60 minutes, but it took more tonight."

It had taken everything Belichick had inside him to turn a 28–3 deficit into a 34–28 victory. It had taken a little of Steve Belichick's attention to detail, Al Laramore's focus on fundamentals, and Steve Sorota's ability to adapt to overcome the challenges he faced in this game. Belichick also needed to elevate his players the way his first NFL boss, Ted Marchibroda, had during Baltimore's comeback season in 1975. Marchibroda had died, at 84, some 13 months before Super Bowl LI, and he would've been awfully proud of Billy on this night.

Belichick was booked for another parade in Boston, for a rally that would feature him leading the crowd in a chant of "No days off" as he held the Lombardi Trophy in his left hand. But before he left Houston, before he could savor his place as the only coach to have won a Super Bowl ring for every finger on his left hand, Belichick had the number five in his mind for a different reason.

"As of today," he said the morning after his breathless comeback, "and as great as today feels, as great as today is, in all honesty we're five weeks behind in the 2017 season to most teams in the league."

Belichick was already prepared to play catch-up, prepared to start grinding for next year. But next year was going to be different, radically different. Much to everyone's surprise, the 2018 season was going to be turbulent enough to challenge every last virtue and value of the Patriot Way.

19

HUMAN BILL

Is Belichick really as big a prick as he seems?

Most national football writers have likely fielded that question a few times at family barbecues and weddings, at least those family barbecues and weddings held outside of New England. Bill Belichick might be the most disagreeable figure in sports, and his real and/or manufactured contempt for the news media makes his press conferences must-see TV for executives, coaches, and fans everywhere.

If Belichick cared about how he came across to much of the country, he had a funny way of showing it. Though in recent years he had replaced the trademark hoodie with relatively stylish outfits at pressers (undoubtedly at Linda Holliday's urging), Belichick had long abandoned any meaningful attempt to burnish his public image. He could have made millions upon millions as a product endorser for companies that found creative ways to monetize his dark genius, and yet he didn't bother to profit off the character he created when the cameras were on. The modern entertainment-industrial complex had rewarded Kardashian-esque figures who were famous for being famous, people who had built empires on almost no discernible accomplishments. Belichick stood on the other end of that spectrum. He had won five Super Bowls. He had so much to capitalize on.

And there was a period in the spring of 2007 when he considered doing just that. He started Bill Belichick Inc. as a for-profit company that would specialize in "consulting, entertaining and endorsing," and he appeared ready to build his brand and act as a paid corporate spokesman and guest speaker. Around the same time, Belichick met in a Boston restaurant with two New Jersey executives from 16W Marketing, Frank Vuono and Steve Rosner, who had counted Lawrence Taylor and Phil Simms among their clients. Belichick wanted to discuss a possible representation agreement. Vuono said that he found Belichick less interested in the extra cash than in the potential impact on his image and legacy, and that he had heard the coach do a strong impersonation of Bill Parcells at the Pro Bowl and found him witty enough to be an effective pitchman.

"It would be easy for him to poke fun at himself if he did go into endorsements," Vuono said. "He'd be the perfect Oscar in *The Odd Couple*." Rosner told Belichick that assuming a tongue-in-cheek role in a commercial would be a good way of showing people a different side of him. "When I said that," Rosner recalled, "a smile came across his face."

The marketing execs knew that a hard sell would not work with Belichick, so they kept it light for a couple of hours, headed home, and waited for a signal. A couple of weeks later, the coach called to say thanks but no thanks. Time commitment might've been a concern for someone who all but lived at the office, and perception could've been an issue, too. Even if it meant limiting his net worth to $35 million (by *Forbes*'s estimate) down the road, did Belichick really want any Patriots fan thinking that success had made him a bit soft, even a little distracted?

In the end, the bad-guy routine was really working for him. Bobby Valentine, who was all but eaten alive by the Boston media during his disastrous one-and-done season managing the 2012 Red Sox, had been among those who watched in awe as Belichick played that media role to the hilt. "I don't really get it," Valentine said. "I don't know how it's allowed. It's more envy than anything else. I tip my hat to him for his complete dominance of the situation. I don't get how he's been able to do it, but it's been spectacular to watch. It's well rehearsed, it's well disciplined, and he stays within his boundaries better than anybody I've ever seen."

Robert Thompson, a trustee professor of television and popular culture at Syracuse University, likened Belichick to Simon Cowell in the early days of *American Idol*. Cowell would say cruel things about auditioning performers and seemed to find pleasure in doing so. "Yet there was a sense, when anybody got a yes vote from him," Thompson said, "that was the thing they always talked about: that Simon said yes. It's like a really dysfunctional family, when your mean dad finally says something good about you and it means more to you than all the people who were helpful to you. I'm not saying Bill Belichick is Simon Cowell or a dysfunctional father, but there are all kinds of ways to treat people that get them to be motivated to do their best.

"My guess," Thompson continued, "is if we're going to wait for people to say what a great guy Bill Belichick is, what a warm human being he is, we might have to wait for people to write his eulogy. Those stories are probably out there, but in many ways we don't want those stories. He's played a certain role in this grand drama. It would be like if J. R. Ewing in *Dallas* suddenly started becoming a philanthropist, or if Walter White in *Breaking Bad* gave money to a detox center."

People who were interested in humanizing Belichick found that he had no apparent interest in being humanized. One reporter's request to Berj Najarian and the coach's agent, Neil Cornrich, for details on acts of kindness and generosity that might have gone unrecognized — ordinarily a dream request for someone representing a public figure — was met with stone-cold silence. Even Patriots officials hoping to soften his image over the years ran into a wall of stern resistance.

Before the 2017 season started, those officials were likely stunned when a cleaned-up Belichick posed with Holliday ("the rose next to the thorn," the coach called her) for a photo shoot for *Nantucket Magazine,* which published an accompanying cover story on his love for his girlfriend and his eastern-end 'Sconset compound under the cover line "Belichick & Holliday: America's Winningest Team." Nantucket was the seaside retreat where, for decades, Belichick had gone for his boating, fishing, biking, golfing (at Sankaty Head), and unwinding between seasons, and the *Globe* reported that the coach's growing collection of cedar-shingled homes was assessed at more than $10 million; he'd transferred two homes to his ex-wife, Debby, as part of their divorce settlement.

Belichick valued his privacy along the towering bluffs of 'Sconset, and the locals respected his space. Occasionally a story or two would leak out from the island, like the one told by Vito Capizzo, a former teammate of Joe Namath's at Bear Bryant's Alabama who became a legendary coach at Nantucket High School. After Belichick won his first Super Bowl title, Capizzo asked him if he would speak to the school's athletes and cheerleaders as part of a fund-raiser for Nantucket's library. Capizzo had owned a Thrifty Rental Car place on the island and had seen Belichick here and there, and he always thought the Patriots' coach was more down-to-earth than the distant Bryant. Belichick immediately agreed to speak to the students at the fund-raiser, which raised $5,000 for the library. "I had a check for him for $1,000," Capizzo said, "and he wouldn't take it. He said, 'It's for the kids.' He was still married, and we went over and had a drink. We talked about football and he told me, 'I wish I had your record.'"

As much as Belichick preferred to keep stories of his common decency buried, they were there to be unearthed, from the early stages of his coaching career through the championship years in New England. In August 1980, before Belichick's second season with the New York Giants, backup quarterback Randy Dean was traded to Green Bay. Dean had made all of three starts in three seasons, and after the Packers cut him, his NFL career was over. On his way out, his former racquetball partner, Belichick, sent him a video of his highlights with the Giants. Dean was a marginal football player, perhaps easily forgotten, and he joked that the highlight tape was fairly short. "But Bill's the only coach who ever did that for me," Dean said. "My kids enjoyed it. It meant a lot to me."

While with the Giants, Belichick visited the Sing Sing Correctional Facility, in Ossining, New York, and spent a couple of hours talking football with dozens of inmates. In order to better understand the urban environments that produced many of his players, Belichick also rode along with Drug Enforcement Administration agents in impoverished pockets of New Jersey. In Cleveland, Bill and Debby funded a financially strapped homeless shelter for women and children, and the coach lent his time to Jim Brown, whose Amer-I-Can Program provided life skills to at-risk youths. Belichick had visited prison inmates with Brown and met with reformed gang members in Brown's homes and in hotel rooms.

The coach was beyond generous with his assistants, too, giving them his TV and radio money and greeting low-level staffers with hundred-dollar handshakes. "There were always two sides to Bill Belichick," said one of his Cleveland scouts. "He was an emperor who can be incredibly aloof, condescending, and arrogant, which was always in there. But fundamentally, deep down inside, there's a good guy who was raised by good parents."

That person was alive and well in Foxborough, but living in the shadows by choice. Belichick's support of a young staffer, Mark Jackson, after Jackson's father died on Christmas Day of 2000 was something that the future athletic director at Villanova would never forget. In March 2002, after Williams College coach and future College Football Hall of Famer Dick Farley dropped him a congratulatory note on beating the Rams in the Super Bowl, Belichick replied with a handwritten letter that read, in part, "Dick — my goal in coaching is to have your record! Congratulations on your continued success." A couple of years later, after cutting Farley's son, Scott, Belichick offered to write Scott a letter of recommendation if he wanted to pursue a job in the industry.

In July 2002, Belichick invited the media to a two-hour film session in the new stadium's auditorium, treating reporters like players and showing them, among other things, how the Patriots had defended Atlanta's mobile quarterback (Michael Vick) and its relatively immobile quarterback (Chris Chandler) in a game the previous season. In 2003, Anthony Pleasant, 35-year-old defensive end and a pro's pro in his final NFL season, believed he had been kept on the Patriots' roster by Belichick solely as a show of appreciation for his efforts in Cleveland and Foxborough.

In the summer of 2004, the year the New York Jets would retire Joe Klecko's number, Belichick spoke to the Patriots about Klecko's greatness as a defensive lineman while he locked eyes with Dan Klecko, Joe's son and a

New England nose tackle, and gave the kid goose bumps he could still feel a dozen years later. Klecko reported that Belichick gave punter Josh Miller a book of children's poetry, *Where the Sidewalk Ends,* as a gift after Miller and his wife had a baby.

Before his Super Bowl XXXIX victory over Philadelphia in Jacksonville, in February 2005, Belichick received a note from his lacrosse coach at Wesleyan, Terry Jackson, whose wife was undergoing chemotherapy for ovarian cancer. Karen Jackson used to cook meals for Belichick and the other Wesleyan players, and, in turn, Bill and his friend and teammate Mark Fredland would babysit for her. Jackson wrote that his wife's bucket list included trips to the Kentucky Derby and the Super Bowl, and that he was wondering if Belichick could scratch one of those items off the list.

"The tickets have already been purchased," the coach wrote back. "We'll see you after the game." Jackson and Karen cherished their time at the Super Bowl; she died months later. Over the years, Jackson deeply appreciated the many notes Belichick kept sending him from Foxborough, thanking his Wesleyan mentor for his kindness and for teaching him the meaning of teamwork. "I know I wouldn't be in this position without your help and the great example you set for me and all the other players you coached," Belichick wrote him years later. "Thanks for providing such a great role model for all of us when we needed it most."

In 2005, Belichick helped turn a reunion for his Andover football team into what teammate Dana Seero called a show of support for the former star quarterback at Phillips and Harvard, Milt Holt, who'd gone on to become a state senator in Hawaii before serving prison time on federal mail fraud charges involving campaign funds, and for failing a drug test while awaiting trial. Belichick gave Holt a tour of New England's Gillette Stadium facility as part of the reunion weekend. Months later, Belichick got word that the wife of his former Wesleyan football teammate Jeff Gray had been hospitalized for nearly a year, after suffering burns over 60 percent of her body when a spark from their woodstove set her robe on fire. Belichick immediately contacted Gray, apologized for not knowing about his wife sooner, and hosted him and his two sons at practice on the same night he hosted Terry Jackson and his family.

That October, two days before a game against Buffalo, Belichick left his team to attend the funeral of Giants owner Wellington Mara, a gesture that left a lasting impression on Mara's son John. When Belichick signed Junior Seau in 2006, he made a mark on the star he'd just released, Willie McGinest, by calling him and asking if it would be OK for Seau to wear his number, 55. (McGinest gave his permission—he'd initially worn that number at USC because it was Seau's.) At an August 2008 preseason game with the

Giants, just months after that team handed him his most devastating defeat as a head coach, Belichick approached Giants offensive lineman Chris Snee, tapped him on his shoulder pads, and told him he'd played a hell of a game in Super Bowl XLII. "Those words stayed with me," Snee said. That same year, a theater executive named Josiah Spaulding Jr. was attending a function for the Marquis Jet company at the Four Seasons in Boston when a man approached and told him that the guest speaker, Bill Belichick, would like him to sit at his table.

Spaulding was a member of a prominent Boston family, but he was flabbergasted that the legendary coach of his favorite team wanted to be seated with him. As he approached Belichick, the coach rose from his seat and said, "Joe, it is so great to see you again." Spaulding was a bit starstruck and completely confused. "Have we met before?" he asked.

"Yeah, you punched me and knocked me down and scored the winning goal against us," Belichick responded. Suddenly, 34 years later, the memory hit Spaulding between the eyes. Wesleyan. The defender who had cheap-shotted him with his stick, an unprovoked whack across his left leg, before the hulking and bearded Bowdoin star decked him and then scored. Spaulding never knew the defender's name. "You were that asshole?" Spaulding asked Belichick. "Because I still cannot feel anything on the left side of my leg from my knee to my ankle." They laughed a lot that night and exchanged cell numbers, remaining in touch afterward.

In 2009, Frank Edgerly, a first-year Patriots scout whose previous job was as head coach at New Jersey's Red Bank Catholic High School, found himself dealing with a profound family crisis: His 45-year-old sister, Debbie, had been diagnosed with breast cancer four years earlier, and she was fighting for her life in a hospital in Des Moines, Iowa. Even though Belichick never made him feel like a high school coach who needed to stay in his lane, Edgerly was only months into the job and was still, in his words, "walking on eggshells" around the facility while learning the NFL trade. He didn't tell his superiors about his sister's crisis, not in the middle of the season. But word got to Belichick anyway and, through Nick Caserio, the Patriots arranged for plane tickets, a hotel, and a rental car for Edgerly and his wife to spend time with Debbie. It was the last time the scout saw his sister alive. "It makes you wonder sometimes if Bill really wants to be the villain," Edgerly said.

Belichick called his former fullback Heath Evans to offer comforting words after he blew out his knee while playing for New Orleans in 2009, a call that meant everything to Evans and his family. Around the same time, Belichick was campaigning for the Wesleyan teammate who beat him out as the starting center, Bob Heller, to get inducted into the school's hall of fame. A Seattle attorney who was a two-time All-American, Heller said Belichick had been a consistent and supportive presence from afar as he endured treatments for multiple myeloma. Heller was inducted into the Wesleyan Hall of Fame in 2010. "Bill is loyal to a fault," Heller said. "If you're his friend, he's got your back."

Doc Rivers became a friend of Belichick's when he was coaching the Celtics, and the Patriots' coach agreed to address his team during a playoff series. (Belichick kept it short and bittersweet after one victory, telling the Celtics to kick ass in every upcoming game and drawing a rousing locker room response.) Rivers also asked Belichick to take part in a video to inspire his team as it started one postseason run. "It was a cool video about toughness and being a warrior, and this guy was reading it with a hood on," Rivers said. "The players couldn't see who it was, and at the very end the hood was taken off and it was Bill, and the guys went nuts. That was a big ask for him to do that, and he did it. That was the coolest thing he ever did for us." Belichick commiserated with Rivers over big losses, he skated with Bruins coach Claude Julien in advance of the NHL Winter Classic at Gillette Stadium, and, though Valentine's stay at Fenway Park was turbulent and brief, he remained forever willing to contribute Patriots items to fundraisers for Sacred Heart University (where Valentine became athletic director) and to host friends of Valentine's and the school's at games.

Belichick does have a heart; he just prefers to keep that fact classified. In May 2011, he signed autographs and visited kids at the Franciscan Children's Hospital, in Brighton, but declined to discuss his appearance with reporters. That same year, after cutting tight end Garrett Mills — a 2006 fourth-round pick who never played in a regular-season game for the Patriots — Belichick wrote letters of recommendation for him for the graduate programs at Northwestern and Stanford; Mills earned his M.B.A. at Northwestern. In 2013, Belichick started a foundation that focused on football and lacrosse programs and provided coaching, mentorship, and, according to its website, more than half a million dollars to organizations in need. A foundation grant made possible the building of Bill Belichick Field and the creation of a lacrosse program for children in Uganda.

Contrary to popular perception, many Patriots players and coaches had a certain fondness for Belichick that transcended his unmatched ability to put them in position to succeed on the field. Before New England's Super Bowl victory over Atlanta, an ESPN.com reporter approached numerous Patriots assistants and asked them this question: "What is the nicest thing Bill Belichick has ever done for you?" Running backs coach Ivan Fears, who had worked under Belichick for his entire term, said there was a Media Bill and a Genuine Bill. "The guy you guys are seeing isn't Bill," he told the reporter. "That's the guy up there to do the press conferences. No, you've got to know Bill. No, no, no, you've got to know Bill. If you know Bill, you understand why the players love him and you understand why we love working for him. Bill is a hell of a dude, I'm telling you . . . Get away from the media thing and know Bill."

Patriots assistants often measure every syllable when talking about Belichick, knowing that he has little use for the humanizing process. Brian Flores, linebackers coach, did say Belichick told him at halftime of a hotly contested divisional playoff game against Houston that he could leave the building after his pregnant wife's water broke while she sat in the stands. (Jennifer Flores called from the ambulance to say that she wasn't having contractions and that Brian could stay for the second half.) Brendan Daly, defensive line coach, said that Belichick had arranged for a car to race him to the airport after a game in Denver so he could meet his wife and kids for his father-in-law's funeral services the next day, and that the coach told him to take as much time as he needed away from the team. Brian Daboll, tight ends coach, recalled the time Belichick lent him a car for his first six months on the job, in 2000. Chad O'Shea, receivers coach, said his head coach showed genuine concern for his assistants' families. "I think he's outstanding that way," O'Shea said, "and it's far from probably what people think of him. He's very good with our children. He's very generous on holidays in terms of gifts. It's not uncommon for him to get football cards for the coaches who have sons. There's not a day I go in there that I don't genuinely enjoy and want to work for Bill Belichick. I feel strongly about that, because he cares about you both as a coach and as a person."

In May 2017, Belichick attended services for Kathy Berman, wife of his friend Chris Berman, of ESPN, after she died in a two-car accident in Woodbury, Connecticut. A few months earlier, after his historic comeback at the Falcons' expense, Belichick made his way to ESPN's on-field set, put on a headset, and gave long, insightful answers to questions from Berman, Randy Moss, and Steve Young. As the interview wrapped up, Berman said, "Listen, just another night at the office, right, Bill?" Belichick laughed. "It was an amazing night, Chris, unforgettable night," he responded as he gave him a hearty handshake and explained how winning a title with his sons Stephen (safeties coach) and Brian (scouting assistant) on staff made it more special.

Then Belichick wrapped his left arm around Berman's shoulders, stepped into him, and said, "And this is, you know, on your farewell tour. I'm glad I can make a stop on that, too." Berman had accepted a reduced role at ESPN after 38 years of building the company into a global juggernaut, and Belichick figured he wasn't terribly thrilled about it. "And you gave me overtime," the broadcaster said. "You didn't want to let me go." The winning coach laughed again. That Belichick, in his most glorious moment, took the time to acknowledge a likely wounded industry giant with millions watching was a pretty damn nice thing to do.

Belichick was human after all, not a joyless automaton. But as he pursued a sixth ring as head coach of the Patriots in 2017, his job became more joyless than it had been in a long, long time. He had a problem, a big one, and it was being caused by the two most unlikely opponents he'd ever faced.

Tom Brady and Robert Kraft.

At 3:03 a.m. on April 19, 2017, five days after he was acquitted of murdering Cape Verdean immigrants Safiro Furtado and Daniel de Abreu, Aaron Hernandez was found naked and hanging by a bedsheet tied to his cell window inside the Souza-Baranowski Correctional Center's general housing unit, in Shirley, Massachusetts. Serving a life sentence for the shooting death of Odin Lloyd, Hernandez, 27, had used cardboard to jam the tracks of his cell door to prevent guards from thwarting his suicide attempt.

The onetime Patriots star was found with a fresh cut on his right middle finger and with blood on adjacent fingers and in large circular marks on his feet. He had JOHN 3:16 written in ink on his forehead and in blood on the wall. (The Bible verse reads: "For God so loved the world, that he gave his only begotten Son, that whosoever believeth in him should not perish, but have everlasting life.") Hernandez had also made drawings on the wall in blood and had placed under them a Bible opened to John 3, with the 16th verse marked in blood. Three handwritten notes were found next to the Bible, and their messages were redacted from the police report on the inmate's death. Hernandez had placed a large amount of shampoo on the floor to ensure that the area beneath his dangling feet inside cell No. 57 was as slippery as possible.

Hours later, the New England Patriots visited the White House and presented President Trump with a No. 45 jersey and, eventually, a commemorative championship ring. Neither Trump nor his favorite football team said a word about the Good Friday death of Aaron Hernandez, whose attorney, Jose Baez, had spoken hopefully about getting the Lloyd conviction overturned on appeal. Hernandez's brain would later be studied by researchers at Boston University, and it presented the most severe case of chronic traumatic encephalopathy ever found in a person his age. It was yet another alarming headline for the NFL, already weighed down by the CTE and concussion crisis and the fear that the football-caused brain damage cited in the premature deaths and suicides of some prominent players would encourage more and more parents to steer their young sons toward safer sports.

For the Patriots, Hernandez was a haunting thought they tried to delete from memory. Bill Belichick was asked about Hernandez during a CNBC interview conducted before the player's gruesome death. When the interviewer, Suzy Welch, mentioned Hernandez as part of a word-association game, Belichick said, "Tragedy." When Welch responded by saying, "Heartbreaking," Belichick countered with "Yes, that would be another word."

Sheriff Thomas Hodgson, of the Bristol County House of Correction, where Hernandez was jailed after his 2013 arrest, said that the former tight end was "a master manipulator, probably the best I've ever seen." Hodgson said he told Robert Kraft that the owner shouldn't blame himself for believing in Hernandez and giving him a big contract, that Hernandez had a diabolical gift for deceiving people. "When you talk to him, you think everything is coming from the heart," Hodgson said. "Sociopathic people can do that and do it very well."

Even if the sheriff's words offered the owner a small measure of reassurance, Kraft wasn't the one who had brought Hernandez into the organization. That was Belichick. He decided Hernandez and his behavior issues were worth the fourth-round gamble in 2010, and it turned out to be the worst personnel decision of his life.

The Hernandez disaster did not temper Kraft's faith in Belichick as an evaluator, however. In fact, ever since he allowed his coach to start Tom Brady over his $100 million favorite, Drew Bledsoe, in 2001, Kraft had never regretted giving Belichick full personnel control. He had stripped away some of Bill Parcells's authority before Parcells's stormy departure, but he would never do the same to Belichick. Kraft had imposed his will on his coach only once since New England starting winning championships, and the player involved was Troy Brown.

Once an eighth-round pick in the 1993 draft, Brown was a lifer Patriot, admired and respected by all. But with the receiver turning 36 before the start of the 2007 season, Belichick wanted to cut him loose. Kraft insisted that Brown be made an exception to the coach's practice of getting rid of players too early rather than too late, and Belichick relented. But just because he agreed to keep Brown a Patriot didn't mean he agreed to play him. New England had just acquired receivers Randy Moss, Wes Welker, and Donté Stallworth. Of the 19 regular-season and postseason games the Patriots played that season, Brown failed to see action in 18 of them.

Kraft suspected this might've been Belichick's way of paying him back for interfering, but a source close to the coach contended that there was no payback involved, that Belichick watched a descending punt bounce off Brown's facemask and decided his return man was washed up. The thing was, that punt didn't bounce off Brown's facemask until the 15th game of the season, a road victory over the Dolphins. The 15-year veteran also recovered from that embarrassment to return the next punt 28 yards; it was the last time he touched a football in an NFL game.

Kraft and Belichick had no meaningful personnel clashes after that one. The owner was heavily involved in Brady's new four-year, $60 million contract completed in March 2016, and Kraft and the quarterback had developed a relationship that each described in father-son terms. Then again, Bledsoe was also close enough to Kraft to be called the owner's fifth son. Belichick ran him off to Buffalo and then did the same to Lawyer Milloy, starting a pattern that extended all the way through Vince Wilfork in 2015 and Chandler Jones and Jamie Collins the following year. Belichick was either keeping or shipping out players with one thought in mind: what he thought was best for the New England Patriots. That included the quarterback position and a franchise player like none other, Brady.

For his part, Brady had long said he knew he could be traded just like his childhood idol, Joe Montana, had been dealt from San Francisco to Kansas City to clear the way for Steve Young. "Yeah, absolutely," he said. "You can't be around this long and not realize that the world will keep spinning and the sun will come up tomorrow without you . . . It could happen to anybody. You just have to show up for work, do the best you can do every day, and let your performance just speak for yourself."

Brady's family always believed that Belichick would trade Tommy in the twilight of his career, and that it was just a matter of where and when. In the winter of 2013, after Brady took a three-year, $27 million deal that was $30 million below market value, he was furious that his salary-cap discount didn't compel Belichick to keep Welker from signing with Denver and teaming up with Peyton Manning, who had been cut by Indianapolis after undergoing a series of neck surgeries. Brady's sister, Nancy, told people then that her brother felt that "Belichick will definitely do to him someday what the Colts did to Peyton."

Tom Brady Sr. had the same feeling. Asked if he thought his only son would have a happy ending in Foxborough, Tom Sr. said, "I don't think so. I would hope he would have a happy ending, but very few people really go out the way they want to go out. In Tommy's particular case, I think he wants to play another four to five years. I think it's up to Bill to determine whether Tommy is the horse he wants to bet on. Everybody seems to believe that 40 years old is a cliff that, once you reach it, you fall off it. I don't think Bill's ever had an athlete as dedicated to being a complete football player as he has had with Tommy, because of Tommy's wholesale commitment, 365 days a year, to nutrition, to conditioning, to actively becoming a better performer. As such, I don't think that they're necessarily prepared for what Tommy is going to be capable of at age 43, 44, or 45."

Or were they? On October 30, 2017, after off-season reports suggested that New England could land a first-round pick for Jimmy Garoppolo, if not two, Belichick shocked the football world by trading Brady's backup to the 49ers for a second-rounder in the 2018 draft. A second-rounder for a quarterback projected to be a surefire star. Garoppolo was in the final season of his four-year deal, leaving the Patriots in a jam as they approached the trade deadline and as the backup approached his 26th birthday. Brady was set to make $14 million in 2018, with a salary-cap hit of $22 million. If the Patriots chose to use the franchise tag on Garoppolo, they would've been investing $45 million in the quarterback position for that one season, or ultimately trying to trade a high-priced Jimmy G. to teams that might leverage the Patriots' desperation against them.

Belichick had hedged his bets when he didn't deal Garoppolo before the draft, holding on to him in case Brady did show signs of decline after turning 40, on August 3. (Quarterbacks generally don't respond well to their 40th birthdays — if they're good enough to play that long — and Belichick wasn't certain Brady's superhuman devotion to fitness and healthy eating and sleep habits would make him an exception to the rule.) But at the time Belichick had to make his decision, Brady had a 6-2 record, the league lead in passing yardage, and 16 touchdown passes against two interceptions, as well as 51 touchdowns against seven interceptions over the 23 regular-season and postseason games he'd played since his suspension ended.

As it turned out, Belichick should have done a few things he didn't do. He should have gambled that Brady — a freak of nature who had stated his desire to play until at least age 45 — would play at a high level into his forties and traded Garoppolo in the off-season for at least one first-rounder. He should have kept his promising third-stringer, Jacoby Brissett, whom he traded to Indianapolis in September for receiver Phillip Dorsett. Hindsight being 20/20, he also should have selected Garoppolo in the first round in 2014 (instead of draft bust Dominique Easley), which would have given New England the right to pick up a fifth-year team option on Garoppolo's contract and to buy another year of monitoring Brady's battle with the aging process.

It was too late for any of that in the middle of the 2017 season. The ultimate salary-cap manager, Belichick wasn't about to commit $45 million to one position, even the most important position, in the event that he couldn't find a trade partner for Garoppolo that didn't lowball him because of Jimmy G.'s upgraded wage. Belichick had met with Robert Kraft, Jonathan Kraft, and Nick Caserio in the early summer to discuss the quarterback situation, and the men left their meeting committed to an attempt to sign Garoppolo to a manageable new contract. Between that meeting and late October, Robert Kraft told associates that he'd occasionally ask Caserio if there was any update on Garoppolo and that the longtime director of player personnel would tell him there was no progress to report.

Garoppolo's agent, Don Yee, needed to keep his signature client Brady happy, which meant keeping him in Foxborough, and he needed to grant Garoppolo his ultimate wish, a starting job in the NFL, which meant moving him to another franchise. Yee was never going to do a long-term deal with the Patriots that kept Garoppolo on the bench, no matter what Belichick offered, and that was why negotiations didn't get serious.

So Belichick did what he had to do, much as he didn't want to do it. He moved Garoppolo out of the AFC to ensure that the quarterback couldn't cancel any future Patriots trips to the Super Bowl, though he didn't hold an NFC-only auction and wait for the highest bidder. Belichick handed him to a coach (Kyle Shanahan) and executive (John Lynch) he respected. He also did right by Yee, who had signed off on a series of deals with Belichick that paid Brady tens of millions less than what other elite quarterbacks were making in order to provide the team with cap flexibility. (Brady could offer these discounts in part because his wife had been the world's highest-paid supermodel every year since 2002.) Belichick wouldn't exactly have thanked Yee for his help and understanding had he sent his client to Cleveland.

In explaining the Garoppolo trade to the news media, and by extension to a surprised and confused fan base, Belichick said the quarterback situation was "just not sustainable given the way that things are set up. It's definitely not something that we wanted to walk away from and I felt like we rode it out as long as we could. We, over a period of time, explored every option possible to try to sustain it, but just at this point felt like we had to make a decision. It's a very complex situation on multiple levels, and this is really the last window that we had, and we did what we felt was best for the team."

Belichick made it clear that he had strong feelings for Garoppolo. "The 49ers are getting a good player, and they're getting a good person," the coach said, "and they're getting a great teammate and they're getting a good quarterback . . . He's a talented individual, was a great person to coach. I met with him weekly and, again, have a tremendous amount of respect for him." Somewhere Brady must've been asking himself, *Would it have killed the guy to have said these things about me every now and then?*

Not that it mattered anymore. Forget the record five Super Bowl rings; Brady had accomplished the unthinkable. He'd become the first Patriot to defeat the same Belichick machine that had ultimately traded, released, or forced into retirement every star player before him. The machine had identified Garoppolo as his future replacement in the spring of 2014, and Brady defied it by winning two more championships in three years and forcing the kid to go take his ball somewhere else.

It pained Belichick to deal Garoppolo. This was his Steve Young, after all. This was the quarterback who would forever silence the discussion about Belichick needing Brady as much as Parcells needed Belichick. This was the quarterback who would end the debate over which titan was more important to the dynasty, Belichick or Brady.

And now he was 2,700 miles away. Belichick was left with an ageless and freshly empowered Brady, and with a nonthreatening, Tommy-deferring journeyman, Brian Hoyer, as a backup. He was also left with the task of finding another Garoppolo to develop (good luck with that) and with the burden of confronting a procession of published stories that detailed the escalating tension among Belichick, Brady, and Kraft and the internal power struggle that was won by the quarterback.

It started with a bulletin from a Golf Channel host, of all people, though Ryan Burr had spent seven years at ESPN. "Brady camp 3 days ago felt privately TB could be traded by Bill after 17," he wrote on Twitter after the Garoppolo trade. "This was a Kraft decision to make it clear Brady finishes as a Pat." Burr then tweeted, "Told TB relationship with BB not great and all his loyalty is too [sic] Mr. Kraft." These tweets were largely dismissed as long-distance spitballs from an outsider. They shouldn't have been.

In December, Bob Hohler of the *Globe* wrote that Belichick weeks earlier had stripped Brady's body-and-life coach, Alex Guerrero, of the privilege of flying on the team charter, standing on the sideline during games, and treating players not named Tom Brady in the Gillette Stadium office the coach allowed him to have. Over time, Guerrero had added many of New England's players to his roster of clients — one Patriots source said that nearly two-thirds of the roster was "going up the hill" from the stadium to see Guerrero at the nearby facility he opened with Brady in 2013, the TB12 Sports Therapy Center.

"Say what you want about Alex Guerrero," said one team source, "but he knows how to manipulate the body."

One invaluable TB12 convert, Rob Gronkowski, believed he'd been able to make a big catch on a painfully low Brady throw against Pittsburgh, in a December game that would decide home-field advantage in the playoffs, that he wouldn't have made without embracing Guerrero's emphasis on flexibility over the team's emphasis on strength. Gronk's fellow tight end Aaron Hernandez had been among the earliest high-profile Patriots who had decided Guerrero did a better job of getting him ready to play than the team's training staff did.

It was no secret that Guerrero traded in unorthodox methods of injury prevention and treatment and that his advice to players often conflicted with advice they were getting from New England's medical staff. Belichick came to believe he had made a mistake in granting extensive access to Guerrero, and he had become uncomfortable with the depth of his influence. So he kneecapped him. In the process, of course, he kneecapped Brady, too.

There was a time when Belichick would approve of anything Brady wanted when it came to preparing for a game. Years earlier, when Belichick visited the New York Yankees in spring training, he'd had a conversation with Yankees officials in their weight room. GM Brian Cashman recalled that they discussed equipment and what worked and did not work when training athletes. "Belichick told a story that Tom Brady wanted specific equipment, and their strength coach didn't want it," Cashman said. "Belichick said, 'If Tom Brady wants it, Tom Brady gets it.' If you get a player at that level, you get him what he needs, even if the strength coach says otherwise."

In this case, Belichick was tired of other Patriots choosing Brady's guy over the team's staff. The quarterback was wounded by Guerrero's demotion. They had just collaborated on a book, *The TB12 Method,* and Brady continued to hold up Guerrero as the primary reason he hadn't missed a game because of injury since the 2008 season. The self-styled fitness guru, who had a dubious past littered with financial disputes, lawsuit settlements, and bankruptcy filings, was godfather to Brady's son Ben and could be seen sitting at the quarterback's locker after a game, waiting for him to shower and dress. As business partners with a grand vision of millions around the globe frequenting TB12 facilities and living on TB12 diets, it seemed Guerrero needed Brady a whole lot more than Brady needed him.

Only the quarterback didn't treat his partner as if that were the case. So when Belichick demoted Guerrero, that development, Hohler wrote, "created some friction in Foxborough." In the wake of the *Globe* report, Greg Bedard, of *Boston Sports Journal,* wrote that the Guerrero situation "has absolutely become a source of friction between Brady and Belichick" and that an attempt to arrange a peace summit involving the quarterback, the coach, and Kraft — before the December 11 loss at Miami — failed, at least for the time being. The following week, under the headline "Patriots Run Feels Like It's Winding Down," NBC Sports Boston's Tom E. Curran observed that the 2017 season had felt like the end of a party. "Like people are gathering up their coats and saying their goodbyes," he wrote.

The coordinators, Josh McDaniels and Matt Patricia, were expected to leave for head coaching jobs, and the special teams coach, Joe Judge, was among the aides expected to depart for promotions elsewhere. But Belichick's likely staff reconstruction was hardly the only reason that the late stages of 2017 felt like goodbye; whispers that Belichick and/or Brady might walk away were growing a bit louder. And that possibility was taken to Defcon 1 by a story published by ESPN's Seth Wickersham on January 5, 2018, headlined, "For Kraft, Brady and Belichick, Is This the Beginning of the End?" An artful writer and dogged reporter, Wickersham surveyed the trees already planted and explained why they represented a forest.

Wickersham added detail and context to the Belichick/Brady-Guerrero divide and wrote of how some Patriots felt that the decision to see or not see Guerrero for treatment was really a choice between aligning with the league's most powerful quarterback or the league's most powerful coach. The ESPN story stated that Brady had several October meetings with Kraft to reaffirm his desire to play into his forties, that a separate meeting between the quarterback and Belichick ended with a "little blowup," and that during Brady's Deflategate suspension, an injured Garoppolo arrived at a scheduled TB12 appointment to find the doors locked and his phone calls going unanswered. (The quarterback denied freezing out his heir apparent and reminded associates that Garoppolo had made dozens of trips to TB12 and that Brady had invited him along on his most recent trip to the Kentucky Derby.) Of greater consequence, Wickersham wrote that Kraft and Belichick had a meeting two weeks before the trade deadline that ran a half day long, and that "a furious and demoralized" Belichick left with a "clear mandate" to trade Jimmy G. and anoint none other than Tommy B. as the 40-year-old quarterback of the future.

The piece caught fire on the Internet, and the Patriots responded with what had to be an NFL first: a joint statement from an owner (Kraft), a coach (Belichick), and a quarterback (Brady):

> For the past 18 years, the three of us have enjoyed a very good and productive working relationship. In recent days, there have been multiple media reports that have speculated theories that are unsubstantiated, highly exaggerated or flat out inaccurate. The three of us share a common goal. We look forward to the enormous challenge of competing in the postseason and the opportunity to work together in the future, just as we have for the past 18 years. It is unfortunate that there is even a need for us to respond to these fallacies. As our actions have shown, we stand united.

Kraft would deny much of the ESPN story to Peter King of *The MMQB* and call the reported claim that he'd met for half a day with Belichick and ordered the code red on Garoppolo "a total fabrication and fiction." Kraft said that his first conversation with Belichick about Garoppolo's status since their early-summer meeting had unfolded the day the deal was made with San Francisco. The owner said he was initially taken aback by the coach's news that he had a trade in place with the 49ers and that he consulted with his son, team president Jonathan Kraft, before giving Belichick his blessing to proceed.

Did Kraft really direct Belichick to move Garoppolo and interfere with a personnel decision for the first time since 2007, when he insisted that an aging Troy Brown remain on the roster? This was the central question that lingered as New England prepared to transition from a 13-3 regular season and its ninth consecutive AFC East title to another postseason run at the Lombardi Trophy. No credible source was doubting that Guerrero had created a chasm in the organization or that Brady was a bit paranoid about his gifted backup. When asked by an ESPN.com reporter the previous spring if he was annoyed by Garoppolo's presence on the roster the way Joe Montana was once annoyed by Steve Young's presence, Brady answered, "That's a great question," before delivering a lengthy response that didn't include the word *no*. Sources said Brady did tell Kraft that he was concerned Belichick might trade him after 2017 and that he felt he deserved a secure place on the 2018 roster after all the winning he had done on bargain-basement deals.

But competing narratives emerged about whether Kraft had protected Brady and, by pushing out Garoppolo, prevented Belichick from using a potential postseason loss and even the smallest sign of decline to trade Brady before the 2018 season. It was clear that the owner respected Belichick's control of the roster. When someone asked Kraft if he thought a second-round pick was really enough of a return for Garoppolo, the owner responded, "Don't you think Bill's earned the right?"

Belichick had certainly earned the right to make these calls. He'd proven to be the best of the best in the fields of talent evaluation, acquisition, and development, and if he thought the deal with San Francisco was a good one — even if many saw it as better for Garoppolo than for New England — he likely had sound reasons. Kraft understood that.

But Brady was the one exception to all Patriot Way ordinances. He wasn't Lawyer Milloy or Richard Seymour or Wes Welker or Logan Mankins. Brady was the greatest football player ever, still performing at an MVP level. He also had a relationship with Kraft that was warm and transformational; his relationship with Belichick was always cold and transactional.

Brady had been turning to Kraft for help and guidance for a long time. In the early years, if he was concerned about the presence of some people in the locker room he thought didn't belong there, he asked Kraft to step in. The owner visited Brady at his locker right before every game, every season, for a little heart-to-heart. They spoke and texted often, exchanged birthday gifts, and even lived in neighboring mansions near Pine Manor College, in Chestnut Hill. Sometimes Kraft signed messages to his biggest star with the valediction "Much love."

Kraft desperately wanted Brady to retire a Patriot. When someone mentioned that the quarterback had left open the possibility of playing even beyond age 45, Kraft said, "Then he'll be a Patriot beyond age 45." Belichick knew how his employer felt. He didn't have to ask Kraft about Brady and the possibility of replacing him. Sources said that Kraft never specifically ordered Belichick to trade Garoppolo. But if the coach had asked the owner if he could trade Brady and go with the kid, sources said Kraft would have rejected the request.

Those who argued over whether there was an actual "mandate" were playing a game of semantics. Belichick watched from afar as Garoppolo turned the 1-10 49ers into the 6-10 49ers, winning all five of his starts with impressive command while devaluing New England's acquired second-rounder. A popular working theory in the Patriots' building was that Garoppolo's play was making the trade look more confounding by the week, moving Belichick to defend it more vigorously to confidants and to assign more and more blame to Kraft's man crush on Brady. Voilà: A mandate was born.

The Kraft-Belichick relationship was no less interesting to examine than the Brady-Belichick relationship. It had gotten off to a good start in the early years — Steve Belichick, military man, liked his son's boss because he always kept his shoes shined. On the other hand, sometimes Steve Belichick's only child would pass Kraft in the hallway and not say a single word to him. Over the years, many players and aides experienced the same silent drive-by, and most came to realize that the coach didn't care to waste three seconds on a useless greeting that could otherwise be devoted to a thought about Sunday's game. Only Kraft wasn't a player or an aide. After all these seasons together, he was a billionaire paying Belichick more than $10 million a year.

Sometimes in meetings, Belichick would treat Kraft like a reporter when he asked for an injury update. Though the owner wished his coach showed him and his son Jonathan more respect at times, Kraft had long ago come to terms with Belichick's flaws. He'd been roughed up by Parcells, who taught him that the NFL isn't for the sensitive and weak. (Stacey James, Kraft's PR man, told associates that he'd gone 16 years without being yelled at by Belichick, and that he hadn't gone 16 days without being yelled at by Parcells.) One owner who wasn't a fan of Belichick's once asked Kraft, "When are you going to fire that asshole?" Kraft responded, "When he goes 8-8."

Belichick ripped off 17 consecutive winning years, averaging 12.3 regular-season victories along the way. Kraft had learned to wall off Belichick's weaknesses and focus on his immense strengths. He'd been angry at his coach here and there — over Spygate, over unnecessary confrontations, over his high-profile role in the Shenocca divorce case — but he understood that managing geniuses in sports, the arts, business, politics, whatever, meant putting up with their maddening idiosyncrasies. One league source said Roger Goodell told Kraft that he was the only owner who could have successfully dealt with Belichick for as long as he had.

Their partnership was without peer in the NFL, and Brady's durability had allowed it to flourish for as long as it had. Tommy might've nudged his preferred targets — Rob Gronkowski, Julian Edelman, Danny Amendola — Guerrero's way (or else). Tommy might've gone corporate, as some coaches had complained, and he might've worn people out with his pliability-over-density lectures and his increasing interest in growing his personal brand in the United States, China, Japan — everywhere. Tommy might've become the NFL's answer to Tom Cruise and entered the jumping-into-Scientology-and-onto-Oprah's-couch phase of his career with his devotion to Guerrero and the doctrine of TB12.

But Brady was still the chief reason why Belichick and Kraft were the best at what they did. As long as Brady was upright and productive, it would've been crazy to let Jimmy G. or Alex G. break up the band. The Chicago Bulls of Michael Jordan, Scottie Pippen, and Phil Jackson broke up prematurely after winning their sixth NBA title, in 1998, when they all had more basketball to play and coach, and that is a regret they will carry to their graves. Belichick, Brady, and Kraft needed to reboot and realize how remarkable it was that they had gone 17 years before they got a little sick and tired of one another and had a season that amounted to a slow week for George Steinbrenner's Yankees in the middle of their last dynasty.

The Patriots had run out of external opponents to conquer, so, out of boredom, they took the fight within. Brady beat Belichick, or the Belichick machine, and maybe the coach evened the score by marginalizing Brady's go-to guy. Either way, the Patriots said they stood united in the face of these public disclosures. And yet their unity could manifest itself only in the one mandate that truly mattered in New England: winning the whole thing.

On another AFC Championship Game Sunday in Foxborough, as Patriots fans walked by a few hours before kickoff, a man with a thick Boston accent hawked clothing products outside the nearby TB12 Sports Therapy Center, wedged between a Pure Barre workout studio and a Green Tangerine Spa & Salon at Patriot Place. The sun was out, the sky was blue, and the temperature was a surprisingly comfortable 48 degrees. The man stood near an oversize picture of a screaming Tom Brady, below the words WELCOME TO TB12. WE GOT THIS. He sounded like a beer vendor at Fenway Park when he barked, "Get your TB12 gear heeee-ah. Hats, Shirts, Scaaaaahves."

The stadium experience had come a long way since the early stages of Robert Kraft's ownership, though the drive in on Route 1 — home to small industrial shops and motor inns — was still as gray and grim as ever. The owner's company, the Kraft Group, opened Patriot Place in 2007, and Bass Pro Shops, Five Guys, Bar Louie, and a Showcase Cinema de Lux were among the establishments competing for consumers' disposable income. But the most reliable product on the grounds was Patriots football. And the lead spokesman for that brand, doubling as the face of TB12, was about to play the Jacksonville Jaguars, after suffering a bloody injury to his throwing hand only four days earlier.

Brady had attempted a handoff to Rex Burkhead in practice, and somehow came away from the exchange screaming as he surveyed a money hand that looked like a zombie's half-eaten lunch. For a while the franchise player wasn't sure he'd be there for the franchise on Sunday. The gash near his right thumb required a dozen stitches and compelled Brady to wear red gloves to his Friday press conference to prevent photographers from getting a shot of the cut.

"I'm not talking about it," the quarterback said when asked about his hand. He would do his talking on the field against a Jacksonville team coached by Doug Marrone and managed by Tom Coughlin, the head of football operations who had denied Brady and Belichick two additional rings as coach of the Giants. Though a three-touchdown blowout of the Tennessee Titans in the divisional round had quieted talk of the dynasty's impending doom, the Patriots couldn't get to kickoff against the Jaguars without a reminder of the tension within. Kraft did a pregame interview with the NFL Network, and he was asked by Willie McGinest, the first Patriot to seek treatment from a young Alex Guerrero years earlier, how important it was to keep Belichick and Brady together for another three, four, or five years.

"Life is difficult," the owner said, "especially if you're doing things at a high level. Having continuity, keeping things going, you know, the fact that Tommy and Bill Belichick and my family have been together for 18 years . . . There's a lot of strong-minded people, but when you have something good going, everyone's got to get their egos checked in and try to hold it together."

A friend of Belichick's said the coach was unhappy with Kraft's "egos" comment and felt it was directed at him. Belichick and his employer were going to meet in the off-season to hash out their issues. Meanwhile, this AFC Championship Game represented what appeared to be the final time Belichick's staff would be together at Gillette Stadium. Josh McDaniels, offensive coordinator, was expected to take over the Colts, and Matt Patricia, defensive coordinator, was expected to take over the Lions. The last time Belichick had faced an exodus this significant, he beat the Eagles in Super Bowl XXXIX and bade farewell to defensive coordinator Romeo Crennel (Cleveland Browns) and offensive coordinator Charlie Weis (Notre Dame) with an emotional group hug. At the time, Brady told a friend, "Bill does everything. He's in control of everything. He runs everything. Don't worry — as long as Bill's here, we're not going to miss a beat."

Thirteen years later, Brady's sentiment on that front wasn't quite as strong. McDaniels had been a miserable failure as a too-young, too-soon head coach in Denver, where he alienated co-workers throughout the organization with immature and imperious behavior. Like Eric Mangini before him, he tried to act like Belichick without producing Belichick results. McDaniels got himself fired 12 games deep into his second season. On the rebound in Foxborough, he had reestablished the bond he had with Brady before leaving in 2009. They were some 16 months apart in age, and they spoke of their brotherly love before and after their sideline confrontation in Buffalo in December, when McDaniels rebuked Brady for throwing behind Brandin Cooks and the quarterback responded by profanely screaming at him. McDaniels understood what it meant to be a quarterback in a high-pressure environment; he'd played for his father, Thom, an Ohio coaching legend, at Canton McKinley. George Whitfield Jr., a quarterbacks coach who once played on the opposite side of the famous McKinley–Massillon rivalry, recalled McDaniels as a miniature version of Brady — resourceful, über-competitive, and in complete command of his system as he barked out orders and audibles at the line of scrimmage. Brady was going to miss him.

Patricia had been an aeronautical engineering student at Rensselaer Polytechnic Institute, where he played on the offensive line, before picking coaching over a job working on nuclear submarines for Westinghouse. He was a grad assistant at Syracuse when Belichick interviewed him for a coaching assistant's position with the Patriots. Belichick interrogated Patricia the way he'd interrogated Kirk Ferentz on technique and philosophy while coaching the Cleveland Browns — the way he'd interrogated scores of job candidates in between — and Patricia held his own. McDaniels and Brian Daboll were running point on the hire, and McDaniels asked George DeLeone, Syracuse's associate head coach, for a recommendation DeLeone was happy to give.

Known for his thoroughness in vetting potential hires, Belichick apparently missed a serious incident that had unfolded during Patricia's time as a student at RPI: He had been indicted by a Texas grand jury on a 1996 charge of aggravated sexual assault after a 21-year-old woman accused Patricia and his friend and teammate Greg Dietrich of forcing her to engage in sex while on spring break on South Padre Island, a story broken by the *Detroit News* years later. The charge was dismissed reportedly at the alleged victim's request, and after the case came to light Patricia vehemently maintained his innocence. Belichick said the Patriots were never aware of the incident.

They recruited him in 2004 as if they had no concerns about his character. One friend of Patricia's said that soon after the Syracuse assistant returned from the Belichick interview, the Patriots called him to offer the job, for a salary of $20,000. Patricia was thrilled, but he said he just needed to run the offer by his wife. "And they said, 'Don't bother — you don't have the job anymore,'" Patricia's friend recalled. "The fact that he had to talk to his wife, they took the job away. Matt called me and I said, 'Don't ever tell anyone that again. Take the job and then go talk to your wife.'"

DeLeone confirmed that friend's account. "Yeah, that happened," he said. "I called Josh back, or he called me . . . and the next thing I know, Matt comes in and he's really nervous and says, 'Coach, Coach, they took the job away. I thought I had a little time to make a decision.' I told him, 'Matt, no, that's not the way it works. You don't get on the phone with those freakin' people unless you've already made your decision.'" DeLeone was among the Syracuse coaches and Patricia friends who called Foxborough to lobby for the reinstatement of the offer, and their efforts were successful.

Patricia moved from assistant offensive line coach to linebackers coach in 2006, following the preferred Belichick path of learning both sides of the ball, and after a couple of years calling the plays, he earned the official title of defensive coordinator in 2012. In his red jacket and red cap, he looked like a mall Santa on the sideline — only with a darker beard. Patricia had very little to work with in 2017, and his defense was an embarrassment over the first quarter of the season. It wasn't rocket science, but it took a former rocket scientist to figure it out. Even though his unit suffered from the Chandler Jones–Jamie Collins talent drain and from Rob Ninkovich's retirement and from Dont'a Hightower's season-ending injury in October, Patricia pieced together a prototypical bend-but-don't-break defense that finished 29th in yards allowed (5,856) but fifth in points allowed (296).

And now Belichick was about to lose his most valuable defensive asset. He did have good young coaches on staff, as always. Brian Flores, a linebackers coach and a product of the housing projects in Mike Tyson's Brooklyn neighborhood, Brownsville, was widely respected as a developing leader, motivator, and tactician and appeared in line to assume Patricia's defensive play-calling duties. On the offensive side, receivers coach Chad O'Shea and assistant quarterbacks coach Jerry Schuplinski, from the John Carroll pipeline, were the clubhouse leaders to take over McDaniels's responsibilities. Belichick's older son, Stephen, was drawing strong reviews from the safeties he coached and the colleagues he worked with, and his younger son, Brian, had just made the switch from scouting assistant to coaching assistant. Time would tell if they were destined to become head coaches like their father and their highly regarded sister, Amanda, who was running the women's lacrosse program at Holy Cross, or if they would find their callings as vital career assistants, like their grandfather Steve.

Even if McDaniels and Patricia departed, Bill Belichick would have three of his most important aides in place, in Ernie Adams, Berj Najarian, and Nick Caserio, who does more coaching during practice and on game days than any director of player personnel in the sport. Adams and Najarian were still occupying their unique roles of football research director and director of football/head coach administration, and Najarian had enough clout with his boss to inspire Belichick to wear an Armenian flag pin on his lapel in a 2015 trip to the White House, where Najarian confronted President Obama on his failure to publicly call the Ottoman government's mass murder of 1.5 million Armenians in the early 20th century what it was: a genocide.

Belichick would also keep on his staff Jack Easterby, a relentlessly upbeat chaplain hired in the wake of the Aaron Hernandez arrest who was still managing players' emotions and personal issues as the league's only character coach. Sean Harrington, a former Tufts University football player and computer whiz, would still be in place as the league's only senior software engineer in personnel. Belichick had the NFL's most eclectic and unique coaching and scouting staff, and assuming that Caserio didn't follow McDaniels and Patricia out the door, it seemed strong enough to weather a transition year and keep the Patriots in contention in 2018.

One high-ranking NFL executive suggested that Mangini would be an ideal fit as a returning defensive coordinator, giving Flores more time to develop. That was a nonstarter for Belichick. Mangini was dead to him, and the former assistant's public pleas for a repaired relationship only served to seal his fate. When Belichick's friend Chip Kelly took over the 49ers in 2016, he inherited Mangini as defensive coordinator. Belichick pushed for Mike Vrabel to take Mangini's job, and even after Vrabel chose to remain with Houston Texans coach Bill O'Brien, Kelly fired Mangini.

Belichick's reach extended far beyond Foxborough. He had friends, protégés, grown-up staffers, executives, people who owed him favors all over the league. He became the most powerful coach in American sports by winning more than anyone else and by game-planning exclusively to his players' strengths and coaching them to do things their pre-Patriots résumés suggested they weren't capable of doing.

"They know he's always telling the truth," said Ivan Fears, the lifer assistant. "He's not in there to blow smoke up their rear end. He tells it like it is. Most of the times he's an asshole when he's doing it, because he's really frank. But it works."

On a Sunday when Tom Brady played with black kinesiology tape wrapped around his right hand, when Rob Gronkowski was concussed in the first half by a fierce Jacksonville defense, it worked again for the Patriots. They were down ten points in the fourth quarter when Brady completed a third-and-18 pass to Danny Amendola for 21 yards, a play that altered the vibe of a game the Jaguars had physically controlled. Brady hit Amendola for a nine-yard touchdown four plays later, and after three punts — two from Jacksonville — Brady found Amendola again for a four-yard score; the receiver had played a brilliant all-around game. Up in the press box, sitting among many writers who had covered his epic victories over New England, Coughlin could only mutter to himself, complain like a fan, and forcefully write down notes about everything that was going wrong. With 55 seconds left in the first half and Jacksonville in possession of two timeouts and the ball at its own 25, Marrone had decided that his quarterback, Blake Bortles, should kneel out the clock and take a 14–10 lead into halftime. It was a dreadful mistake. No opponent can give away possessions against the Patriots in January, in their building. The Jaguars were playing not to lose long before they lost.

New England made the expected defensive stop in the end, Dion Lewis ran for the clinching first down, and then Belichick slid down his headset, clapped his hands enthusiastically, and pumped his right fist toward the sky while shouting, "*Whooooo.*" Belichick wrapped his arms around the departing Patricia, and the two awkwardly and passionately squeezed each other as if they weren't ever letting go. The Patriots were going to have an opportunity to win three championships in four seasons, 13 years after they did it the first time around. On the field after surviving the Jaguars, Belichick and Brady shared a warm embrace that belied the stress in their relationship.

It was a fleeting moment. In his postgame press conference, when asked about Brady's ability to perform despite the hand injury, Belichick said, "Tom did a great job, and he's a tough guy. We all know that, all right? But we're not talking about open-heart surgery here."

Belichick had just sent his quarterback to their eighth Super Bowl together with a swift kick in the ass. Tom Brady, former seventh-stringer at Michigan, had grown accustomed to the feeling.

Bill Belichick stepped off the team plane in Minnesota wearing his father's fedora. The last time Belichick had faced the Philadelphia Eagles in a Super Bowl was also the last time Steve Belichick attended the big game. Father and son were doused by Gatorade after that victory in Jacksonville, and then nine months later Steve was gone.

This game could have been billed as an overwhelming coaching mismatch, as Belichick was facing a second-year head coach in Doug Pederson, a former journeyman quarterback who, as offensive coordinator of the Chiefs, had directed their baffling slow-down offense while trailing the Patriots by two scores in their divisional playoff game following the 2015 season.

Pederson had been a head coach for 34 games, or four fewer games than Belichick had coached in the postseason alone. Yet with his work in 2017, Pederson strongly suggested he'd be a worthy adversary. Somehow he had led the Eagles to their first Super Bowl appearance in 13 years despite losing to injury all-world quarterback Carson Wentz and a nine-time Pro Bowler at left tackle, Jason Peters, among other significant Eagles. Pederson had kept his team loose, aggressive, and confident enough to block out the critics expecting the top seed to be toppled on the NFC side of the draw. He also had quickly molded backup quarterback Nick Foles into a reasonable facsimile of Wentz; Foles shredded the Vikings for 352 yards and three touchdowns in the NFC Championship Game rout in Philly, preventing the visitors from becoming the first team to play a Super Bowl in their home building.

It appeared to be an intriguing matchup, and one that could produce the classic game the NFL sorely needed. The league had been under siege all year. African American players were protesting systemic injustices in society by kneeling or raising fists during the national anthem, and President Trump had tossed gallons of gasoline onto the fire at a September rally by advising NFL owners to handle your average protester this way: "Get that son of a bitch off the field right now. Out. He's fired. He's fired!"

The league couldn't defend the indefensible position of keeping Colin Kaepernick unemployed while lesser quarterbacks were signed, and couldn't adequately explain why their television ratings were tanking, or how much the decline was related to the protests. Malcolm Jenkins of the Eagles had been among the more prominent and thoughtful voices of dissent, leading a coalition of players to hash out issues with the owners and meeting with community, police, and congressional leaders in pursuit of reform. His white teammate Chris Long, a former Patriot, had created one of the year's more unifying snapshots when he wrapped his arm around Jenkins during the anthem. On the New England side, things were a bit more complicated. Trump's good friend Kraft said he was "deeply disappointed by the tone" of the president's remarks about the players. Two days after those remarks, while some Patriots players (including Brady) linked arms in solidarity during the playing of the anthem before a game against Houston, 16 black Patriots took a knee while many in the Gillette Stadium crowd booed.

Belichick waited until the following morning to release a statement on the controversy. "I have coached football for over four decades," it read, "and one of the greatest things about being in this environment is the diversity of people, backgrounds, viewpoints and relationships we are fortunate to experience. As with any large group of people, there is a variety of perspectives and opinions on many topics." Belichick said he'd keep private his conversations with players about any issues involving the team. One Patriots source said that some African American players had expressed concerns privately about the Kraft-Belichick-Brady friendship with Trump. "There was a little bit of 'Are they with us or are they with him?'" the source said. But that feeling didn't fester, the source added, as the protesting players felt that all three had earned the benefit of the doubt.

Winning is a great unifier, and Belichick's methods had won with all colors and creeds, over and over again. He was coaching in his 11th Super Bowl, and his most interesting response to a question in the leadup to the game might've come when he was asked about possibly breaking his tie with Vince Lombardi and joining George Halas and Curly Lambeau as the only men to win six NFL titles. How did it feel to be linked with the sport's enduring icons?

"It's hard for me to really picture that," Belichick said. "They're such great, legendary coaches. I don't really see myself . . . I don't think of it that way. I just think of how great they were, what they meant to the game, what they accomplished, and how much respect I have for them.

"I'd certainly put Paul Brown in there," Belichick continued, "for all that he has done for this game. When you're talking about all the great coaches, I don't see how you can leave him out of it." Belichick once wore a fedora in Brown's honor, too — on the 2010 day he tied the former Browns and Bengals coach on the all-time victories list with No. 170.

Done with his press conferences, Belichick was the Thursday night co-star of an ESPN *30 for 30* documentary titled "The Two Bills," produced by NFL Films' Ken Rodgers, who'd persuaded Belichick and Parcells to sit together in the New York Giants' locker room in June to tape their first joint on-camera interview since 1991. Their relationship had evolved from the time when one of Belichick's teammates at Wesleyan, Art Conklin, said he'd attended a birthday party for Belichick where there were charts on the walls showing "all statistics of Parcells's record with Belichick, and Parcells's record without Belichick, and how much Belichick did alone." (Conklin said Parcells was not present at the party.) Big Bill and Little Bill had patched up things enough to live peacefully for part of the year in the same Jupiter, Florida, building. They could even laugh about the time a leak from Belichick's unit ran into Parcells's and caused some damage. "Not just my apartment," Parcells would say in a 2016 interview, "but everybody down below me, too. Happened about five years ago. I knocked on his door to let him know. I think it came from his fridge. Part of my ceiling came down, but it wasn't just me."

Parcells, a Hall of Famer, had come to terms with the fact that his former assistant had surpassed him on the list of all-time greats. In the ten Super Bowls he'd coached in, seven of them victories, Belichick had done some unconventional things that helped his team win. He planned for Buffalo's Thurman Thomas to gain more than 100 rushing yards, and his Giants defenders thought he'd lost his mind. He refused to call a timeout with Seattle on the goal line in the final seconds, and Patriots assistants, players, and fans thought he was positively mad.

So it was no surprise that Belichick planned to throw a curveball at the Eagles. The only surprise was that Doug Pederson was ready to hit it out of the park.

His head bowed on the sideline, Malcolm Butler was weeping during Leslie Odom Jr.'s moving rendition of "America the Beautiful." He was rubbing his crying eyes with his gloved left hand while safety Jordan Richards rested a hand on his shoulder pads. The hero of Super Bowl XLIX had just been told he wasn't in the game plan for Super Bowl LII.

Belichick had decided to start Eric Rowe, a third-year cornerback from Utah, instead of Butler, who had played 97.8 percent of New England's defensive snaps in the regular season and all 141 defensive snaps in the playoff victories over Tennessee and Jacksonville. Butler's benching promoted Rowe, who'd been in the rotation against the Titans and the Jaguars, and moved up Richards and cornerback Johnson Bademosi. Richards had played only six defensive snaps in the AFC title game. Bademosi was a healthy scratch against Tennessee and didn't play any defensive snaps against Jacksonville.

Butler had been sick enough to miss New England's team flight to Minnesota on Monday, but he arrived the following day and joined his team at practice. By all accounts, he was ready to play. As the first half of the Super Bowl unfolded and it became clear that Butler wasn't in Belichick's game plan, people assumed the star corner must've violated a team rule to force the coach's hand. Did he break curfew? Did he do something worse? If he'd ever exhibited a poor attitude after New England gave Buffalo's free-agent cornerback Stephon Gilmore a big contract in the off-season (five years, $65 million), it hadn't compelled Belichick to bench him.

So why sit him on the biggest Sunday of the year? On a certain level, Butler was the reason Belichick and Brady were considered the greatest ever at what they did. If he hadn't intercepted Russell Wilson's pass at the goal line three years earlier, Belichick would've been crucified for failing to call a timeout. The Patriots would've suffered their third consecutive Super Bowl defeat, and their championship drought would've covered ten full seasons and counting. Brady gave Butler the Chevy truck he won as the game's MVP for a reason. He knew how much better a 4-2 record in the big game looked on his résumé than 3-3.

But the way Belichick saw it, whatever Butler did against Seattle then wasn't going to help him beat Philadelphia now. He would say this move was based on football reasons only. Belichick thought Rowe and the other defensive backs gave him the best chance to win, so those were the men he put on the U.S. Bank Stadium field.

And on the game's first series, Rowe was in coverage on the Eagles' first two third-down conversions, though he recovered to break up a potential third-down touchdown pass from Foles to Alshon Jeffery and hold Philly to a field goal. On the Eagles' next series, after New England kicked a field goal of its own, Rowe wasn't so fortunate. Foles threw a perfect pass toward the back of the end zone, and Jeffery rose high to beat Rowe's otherwise tight coverage and gather in a 34-yard touchdown pass.

Early in the second quarter, New England's chances were further compromised when Brandin Cooks made a 23-yard catch and then zigzagged his way into a brutal helmet-to-helmet shot from Malcolm Jenkins, which sidelined the receiver for the balance of the game. Belichick had acquired Cooks from New Orleans for his 2017 first-round pick; the deal marked the first time the Patriots had dealt their first-round pick for an established NFL asset since Kraft made the deal with the New York Jets for Belichick himself. Now Brady would have to beat the Eagles without Cooks or Julian Edelman, who'd been lost for the year in August, just as he beat the Falcons a year earlier without Gronkowski.

Brady had taken a helmet shot to the midsection on the Cooks play that left him doubled over in apparent pain, and yet two snaps later, on third-

and-5 at the Philly 35, he was asked to sneak out of the backfield and run a pass route so Danny Amendola could throw him the ball. Brady was wide open near the right sideline, and Amendola threw a near-perfect pass, but the ball bounced off the quarterback's fingers and fell to the turf. Brady couldn't blame the drop on the injury to his right hand; he wasn't wearing the tape he had worn against Jacksonville. Belichick decided to go for it on fourth down, and a rushed Brady lobbed up a wobbly ball to Gronkowski that never stood a chance.

The Eagles would face their own fourth-down decision at New England's one-yard line with 38 seconds left in the half. Pederson immediately decided to answer Belichick's gamble with one of his own, dismissing three easy points for a chance at the kind of dagger Jacksonville had been afraid to fire. The coach called time out, and Foles asked him, "You want Philly Philly?" Pederson looked down at his oversize play chart, hesitated for a second, and said, "Yeah, let's do it, let's do it."

Foles returned to his huddle and said, "Philly Special, Philly Special, ready . . ." The Eagles clapped and broke the huddle. Foles lined up in shotgun formation, and running back Corey Clement shifted to a position next to him. Foles faked as if he was calling for the snap, moved up behind right tackle Lane Johnson, and stood tall and relaxed his body for a second — as if he were out of the play — when Clement took the direct snap. As the running back ran left, Foles suddenly reengaged and sprinted toward the right side of the end zone. Clement flipped the ball to tight end Trey Burton, a former high school and college quarterback, and Burton made the easy throw to a wide-open Foles for six points.

Foles caught the ball that Brady had dropped. Pederson won the fourth-down gamble that Belichick had lost. Philly took a 22–12 lead into halftime, and NBC's camera focused on the trailing coach trotting off the field. Belichick was wearing a hoodless Patriots sweatshirt with sleeves cut off below his shoulders, over a shirt with sleeves cut off at mid-forearm; he looked like a weekend warrior in a flag football league. "Belichick back to the locker room," play-by-play man Al Michaels said, "beginning to make his adjustments, which he makes all game long." Color man Cris Collinsworth responded, "And he's pretty good at halftime, too." Michaels: "I'll say." Collinsworth: "Twenty-eight to three last time around, they came back and won. Ten-point deficit, nothing."

Belichick's revamped secondary had been picked apart by Foles, who passed for 215 yards in the first half. If Belichick had planned to force Foles to beat him through the air, it seemed that Foles was prepared to do just that. Belichick sat the 5'11", 190-pound Butler in favor of a corner (Rowe) who was two inches taller and 15 pounds heavier, and in favor of a three-safety nickel package that included Richards (20 pounds heavier). Safety Patrick Chung was also ten pounds heavier than Rowe, whom he replaced in the slot. If the idea was to persuade the Eagles to keep the ball in Foles's hands rather than in the hands of punishing running backs LeGarrette Blount and Jay Ajayi, who weighed in at a combined 473 pounds, the strategy wasn't working.

With Justin Timberlake's halftime show providing all the time he needed to review his options, Belichick decided his three-cornerback sets in the second half should include Bademosi instead of the shorter and lighter Butler, who also happened to be the better football player. Asked later why he made the call to go with Bademosi in that role, Belichick would say, "He practiced it the most."

Rowe actually played fairly well; in addition to breaking up a touchdown pass, he also broke up a two-point conversion attempt. But on the Eagles' first possession of the second half, Belichick's decision to go with Bademosi, a six-year veteran out of Stanford, hurt his team. On a night when the Eagles would badly damage the Patriots on third down (10 out of 16 successful conversions) and fourth down (2 of 2), Foles threw short of the first-down marker to Nelson Agholor on a third-and-6, and Bademosi whiffed on a Pop Warner tackle that absolutely had to be made. Philly scored on that drive to take a 29–19 lead, compelling Brady to try to win his sixth ring on his own.

Brady found Chris Hogan for a 26-yard touchdown on his second third-quarter series, after hitting Gronkowski for a five-yard score on his first, and the league's two teams tumbled into the fourth quarter and toward an indelible finish. Win or lose, this couldn't be Brady's farewell to pro football. Though he'd recently told a friend that "winning three out of four a second time would be a great way to go out," Brady couldn't possibly leave the Patriots after Belichick traded Garoppolo and Brissett, could he?

Why would he leave, anyway, when he'd just been named league MVP for the third time, and when the Eagles were having a harder time defending him than the Patriots were defending Foles? Brady remained on fire by punctuating his third consecutive possession with a touchdown pass, this one his second to Gronkowski, before Stephen Gostkowski gave New England its first lead, at 33–32 with 9:22 to go.

So many times over the years, it seemed the Patriots had been outplayed and/or outhit by their opponents, only to hang in there and steal a victory with fourth-quarter execution, conditioning, and poise. They never, ever panicked, a direct reflection of their ever-stoic coach.

Only these Eagles were on the kind of magical ride the Patriots had been on 16 seasons earlier. Foles led a 14-play, slow-death drive that included a conversion on fourth-and-1 and a touchdown pass to Zach Ertz, who beat Devin McCourty and then survived the ground and an official replay review after losing control of the ball upon landing. The Eagles failed on the two-point try, and Brady got the ball back with 2:21 to play, down five points, with fans on both sides of U.S. Bank Stadium expecting anything but precisely what happened next.

On second down, as Brady was about to make his throw, a fellow Michigan man named Brandon Graham rushed in, reached up with his left hand, and knocked the ball loose and into the arms of teammate Derek Barnett with 2:09 left. Brady sat on the field in a state of disbelief, knowing the Tuck Rule couldn't bail him out of this one. The Eagles ran Blount three times, kicked the field goal, and dared New England to score eight points against a defense built by coordinator Jim Schwartz, who had been given his first NFL job in Cleveland, by the Patriots' head coach.

Belichick tried his second trick play of the night, a kickoff-return reverse run by Dion Lewis and Rex Burkhead, and it didn't exactly mirror Pederson's Philly Special near the end of the first half. Burkhead was tackled at the New England nine-yard line, leaving Brady 58 seconds to cover 91 yards with no timeouts. The best the quarterback could do was move the Patriots to their own 49 with nine seconds left, giving them one crack at a Hail Mary. Brady took the shotgun snap, spun out of Graham's attempted sack, and let the ball fly before absorbing one last shot to the rib cage from Fletcher Cox. In the front of the end zone, Gronkowski and half the city of Philadelphia fought for the ball and batted it about before it dropped harmlessly to the turf as time expired. At last, the Eagles had their first Super Bowl title and their first NFL championship since 1960.

Belichick winced as the final play met its demise, tossed his headset to the ground, and bent over to pick up his papers before weaving his way through a manic maze of photographers and congratulating a Gatorade-soaked Pederson through a warm embrace. Brady had thrown for a Super Bowl–record 505 yards, and it wasn't enough to compensate for the 538 yards surrendered by the defense, the most ever allowed by a Patriots team coached by Belichick.

The losing coach left the field with Philly's green and white confetti falling around him. In his postgame press conference, Belichick said he was proud of how his players and coaches had competed. "We weren't able to perform at our best," he said. "Obviously didn't do a good enough job coaching. Missed a lot of opportunities offensively in the first half, didn't play good enough defensively, didn't play good enough in the kicking game . . . Tough way to end a lot of really good things that happened this season, but that's what this game's about."

Belichick maintained that Malcolm Butler's benching hadn't been disciplinary in nature and that the cornerback had been healthy enough to go. "We put the players out there and the game plan out there that we thought would be the best tonight," he said. "Like we always do."

When he was done answering questions, Belichick stepped off his podium and walked down the hallway behind a wall of dark curtains. Before he reached his locker room, he stopped at his team's postgame food spread, grabbed something small off one of the tables, and spoke for a few minutes with Robert Kraft.

In 48 hours, Belichick and Kraft would dine together at a Patriots Place restaurant, Davio's, in an attempt to reach a détente on their most pressing issues. Social media photos of this summit at an open table invited speculation that they wanted to be seen peacefully breaking bread; the truth of it was, the private room they'd requested for the meal wasn't available. Between their chat on the losing side of U.S. Bank Stadium and their Tuesday night dinner, so much had gone down. Belichick and Kraft had persuaded Josh McDaniels to rescind his verbal agreement to coach the Colts and remain as offensive coordinator. Belichick was criticized and questioned over his Butler decision not just by commentators and columnists but by former Patriots (Ty Law, Rob Ninkovich, and Brandon Browner). Butler released a statement denying that he'd missed curfew or committed any team violation during Super Bowl week, and he apologized for the language he'd used in the only interview he gave after the game.

"They gave up on me," Butler had told ESPN's Mike Reiss. "Fuck. It is what it is."

Butler said he didn't know why Belichick sat him, and that he felt he "could've changed that game." In the days before Super Bowl LII, one of Belichick's old favorites, Rodney Harrison, had complimented his 65-year-old coach for changing his style over the years to better relate to millennials. "Oh, he's different," Harrison said. "And you have to be different, because the mentality is different. These kids nowadays, they're different. They're not hard-nosed kids like we were back when we were winning Super Bowls, so he had to change his coaching style, become a little softer, have more personality, because these younger players can now relate to him. I think he's done a great job relating to the players."

Only now Belichick's players were angered and confused by the move he'd made. Browner, the former Patriots cornerback, ripped the coach over the Butler decision and called the locker room "divided" in an Instagram post that was liked by Patriots linebacker Dont'a Hightower. Butler's own statement on Instagram was liked by a number of current and former New England teammates, including Brady, who added this comment to the post:

"Love you Malcolm. You are an incredible player and teammate and friend. Always!!!!!!"

Brady's support put pressure on Belichick to give the fans something more than his boilerplate response that he plays the people he thinks give his team its best chance to win. Benching Butler was likely his most puzzling Super Bowl decision since trying a fourth-and-13 pass against the Giants ten years earlier rather than asking Gostkowski to attempt a 49-yard field goal, and Patriots fans deserved an explanation.

But they weren't getting one anytime soon. If Belichick had out-Belichicked himself this time, the fans would have to live with it. His coaching quirks had worked out for them far more often than not.

Not that Belichick wasn't hurting this time around. Upon leaving his locker room on Sunday night, dressed in a dark gray suit with a purple shirt and tie, Belichick was feeling what Marv Levy and Mike Martz and Pete Carroll had felt on the wrong side of some of his more memorable NFL moments. He was eating a slice of pizza he'd pulled from the team spread as he walked with Linda Holliday, who was wearing a shirt with her boyfriend's surname embroidered in silver sequins on the back. Holliday still had a strand of Eagles confetti in her hair when a team staffer pointed the couple toward the team bus.

Bill Belichick had no parade to plan for, so he did the only thing a losing Super Bowl coach could do. He loaded his sorry, second-place ass on that bus on this bitterly cold Minneapolis night and started the drive toward the combine, free agency, the draft — the endless, all-consuming search for players who could ensure that this would never again happen to his team. Truth was, even if the rest of the league didn't know it, Belichick seemed to have his opponents right where he wanted them.

The greatest football coach of all time was only five weeks behind.

EPILOGUE

Tom Brady felt trapped. He still wanted to play football, but he was not sure he wanted to play anymore for Bill Belichick. If Belichick wanted a chance to win it all with another quarterback, well, maybe Brady wanted a chance to win it all with another coach.

Two could play that game.

"If you're married 18 years to a grouchy person who gets under your skin and never compliments you, after a while you want to divorce him," said a source with knowledge of the Brady-Belichick relationship. "Tom knows Bill is the best coach in the league, but he's had enough of him. If Tom could, I think he would divorce him."

Brady was no less interested in playing for Josh McDaniels than Belichick was in keeping and playing Jimmy Garoppolo, said one team source. So it was no surprise that Brady threw some passive-aggressive social media jabs at Belichick in the weeks after their crushing Super Bowl defeat. To his comments on Malcolm Butler's Instagram post he added a telling remark to Rob Gronkowski's advice for Danny Amendola, who decided against taking another hometown discount and signed with Miami. In describing the honor of playing with someone so tough, Gronk advised Amendola to "Be FREE, Be HAPPY" in a 60-word Instagram post that included 58 lowercase words. "Well said gronk!!!!" was Brady's response, punctuated by handclap emojis.

The quarterback also starred in a Gotham Chopra documentary called *Tom vs. Time*, on Facebook Watch, which opened with Brady referring to his coach in the first episode as "Belichick" and then closed without his ever referring to him again. Belichick is barely seen over six episodes; he's almost treated as a bit player in the drama, a midlevel staffer. Until the final scenes.

"These last two years have been very challenging for him in so many ways," Brady's wife, Gisele, said of her husband as she drove her car. "And I think he tells me, 'I love it so much and I just want to go to work and feel appreciated and have fun.'"

Tom Brady just wants to go to work and feel appreciated and have fun.

"It's a big commitment," he said in the next scene, "sitting here, laying here, three days after the year getting my Achilles worked on and my thumb. And you go, 'What are we doing this for?' You know, 'What are we doing this for? Who are we doing this for? Why are we doing this?' You got to have answers to those questions, and they have to be with a lot of conviction. When you lose your conviction, then you probably should be doing something else."

Brady had been badly wounded by Belichick's decision to shut down his fitness guru and life coach, Alex Guerrero, whom he credited with his longevity. "Tom felt it was just a mean thing to do," said someone close to him. Brady was wounded enough to consider retiring rather than playing another season for Belichick. A source close to the quarterback said in late March, with the draft rapidly approaching, that Brady still wasn't sure if he was going to return.

But in the end, even if he wanted to, Brady could not walk away from the game, and he could not ask for a trade. The moment Belichick moved Garoppolo to San Francisco, and banked on Brady's oft-stated desire to play at least into his mid-forties, was the moment Brady was virtually locked into suiting up next season and beyond. Had he retired or requested a trade, he would have risked turning an adoring New England public into an angry mob. Brady was not about to take that risk. He was not about to leave the fans and Robert Kraft with a hole the size of Boston Common at quarterback.

That didn't mean Brady had to like the circumstances of his return. Beyond his anger over Belichick's marginalization of Guerrero, he was sick and tired of the unforgiving way he was being coached. In the middle of *Tom vs. Time,* Brady said of his teammates, "My connection with them is through joy and love. It's not through fear. It's not through insults. That's not how I lead." One Brady confidant said those comments were made with Belichick in mind.

At the end of April, after the Patriots declined to use either of their two first-round picks to select Louisville's Lamar Jackson or another available quarterback to fill the Garoppolo void (they drafted LSU quarterback Danny Etling in the seventh round), Brady sat down with broadcaster and friend Jim Gray at the Milken Institute Global Conference, in California, and stated publicly for the first time that he would play in 2018 and beyond. But when Gray asked Brady if he felt appreciated by Belichick and Robert Kraft, and if he felt they had the "appropriate gratitude" for what he had achieved, the quarterback said, "I plead the Fifth!" A smiling Brady paused and then said, "Man, that is a tough question."

Gray did not need to add Kraft to the conversation, as the owner and quarterback were still enjoying as warm an employer-employee relationship as there was in the NFL. Brady's issue was with Belichick, and only Belichick.

"I think everybody in general wants to be appreciated more in their professional life," the quarterback said, "but there's a lot of people that appreciate me way more than I ever thought was possible as part of my life . . . I think what I'm learning, as you get older, it comes from within — the joy, the happiness, those things come from inside. To seek that from others, to seek that from outside influences, people you work with . . . I feel like it comes from within for me. So I'm trying to build up what's within me, so that I can be the best for me, so that I can be the best for other people. That's part of growing. I'm learning these things, too."

Brady did call Belichick the best coach in league history and "an incredible mentor to me," and he did say he could not have built his legendary career without him. "We've had a great relationship," Brady said, "a very respectful relationship for a long time." And that relationship was tested as never before.

"He has a management style [with] players," Brady said of Belichick, "and he would say, 'Look, I'm not the easiest coach to play for.' I would agree. He's not the easiest coach to play for."

Especially when the Patriots weren't winning the whole thing. Brady's most dangerous target, Gronkowski, had clearly reached his own limit with Belichick, fueling reports that he was weighing a jump to Hollywood and/or the world of professional wrestling. Boston insiders Tom E. Curran and Mike Giardi reported on Gronk's extreme frustration with Belichick and his insistence that the team's strength coaches and trainers offered his beaten-up body the best path to a productive and relatively healthy season. The *Herald*'s Karen Guregian wrote that Belichick had "chastised Gronk in front of the players for being a TB12 client" early in the 2017 season.

Gronk was miserable. Brady was miserable. Some fans and current and former Patriots were still miserable over Belichick's decision to sit Malcolm Butler in the Super Bowl. Asked about social media in his 2017 CNBC interview, Belichick had said he did "all I can to fight it" and that his goal — as it related to his players — was to "try to stamp it out." But he was losing that social media war, and his intentional bungling of popular forum names (referring to Snapchat as "Snapface") was not helping his cause. Belichick's two best players, Brady and Gronkowski, had used the Internet as a weapon against him, and in his Twitter goodbye to the Patriots, Amendola mentioned "Mr. Kraft, teammates, staff and all of Pats nation." He did not mention his head coach.

Amendola was a lot less subtle about his feelings for Belichick in an April interview with ESPN's Mike Reiss. Asked about the Butler benching, Miami's newest receiver said, "I have my thoughts about it, because I was out there putting my blood, sweat, and tears out on the field that night, and one of our best players wasn't on the field. To tell you the truth, I don't know why. I did ask, but I didn't get any answers. I can't make decisions like that, so I don't necessarily worry about it, but I know Malcolm is a great player and he could have helped us win."

Amendola also said he sensed that Belichick's decision to sit Butler hurt his teammates. "Nobody really got an explanation for it," he said. "He's a brother of ours . . . And I hate to see a guy who worked so hard throughout the season not get a chance to play in the biggest game of the year and really get no explanation for it."

Three years earlier, Seattle coach Pete Carroll made a baffling Super Bowl decision that helped the Patriots to their fourth title and effectively ended the Seahawks' chances of establishing their own dynasty. Seattle never recovered from that goal-line call. In some ways, Carroll never recovered from that goal-line call.

Is it possible that the Butler benching signaled the beginning of New England's end by magnifying every hidden and unhidden conflict inside Belichick's program? Is it possible that the head coach who forever gave his players the credit for victories and blamed himself for defeats had lost his compass and allowed his ego to run amok with all the talk of greatest this and greatest that?

Amendola told Reiss that Belichick is "an asshole sometimes." His assessment echoed the words left tackle Nate Solder wrote for the Players' Tribune website after he left for a big free-agent deal with the Giants. Though Solder praised Belichick and McDaniels for freeing him to miss practices and meetings if he needed to tend to his cancer-stricken son, the tackle described the Patriots' work environment as a "cold" place where everything is "predicated on performance." That culture was sustained, and tolerated, because the players knew that, more than any other NFL coach, Belichick gave his team its best chance to win.

But with the Butler call, he failed to give the Patriots their best shot against the Philadelphia Eagles. Mr. Do Your Job didn't do his, and Brady, Gronkowski, and other winning Patriots who had long overlooked whatever problems they might've had with Belichick started acting out. Suddenly the coach of the Patriots was starting to resemble Humphrey Bogart's Philip Francis Queeg in *The Caine Mutiny*. Brady and Gronkowski didn't show up for voluntary offseason workouts, another sign that Belichick's approach was under siege. Citing a need to spend more time with his family — though he did his fair share of corporate jet-setting in places such as Monaco while teammates were toiling in Foxborough — Brady didn't even show for organized team activities in late May; he was the NFL's only starting quarterback who didn't attend OTAs, voluntary practices that Brady had called vital in the past for building chemistry with his receivers. Like Gronkowski, he finally appeared for mandatory mini-camp in June, when he cited "personal reasons" for his absence and claimed that his relationship with Belichick was "great" and that he'd "loved" playing for him in 2017.

Sources disputed that characterization and maintained Belichick had lost his firm hold on the team. "Bill has worn thin on everybody," said one team source who added that Belichick was "very lucky to have Bob Kraft and Tom Brady in his life, because they're the only owner and quarterback who could've put up with him for this long."

Kraft told reporters in March that he had met with his coach and Brady, as planned, and he tried to downplay the significance of the sit-down by saying they "have meetings all the time." Only this meeting was different — far different. By any objective measure, the unity the Patriots swore they had in January was going, going, gone.

Suddenly Belichick was staring down one of the most daunting challenges of his career. He had lost championship veterans in Butler, Amendola, Solder, and Dion Lewis in free agency, but Belichick always knew how to replace talent. That wasn't going to be a problem too burdensome to overcome. The much bigger off-season issue was whether Belichick had lost his locker room and his team . . . perhaps for good.

He was 66 years old, and people were wondering if Belichick's days as the league's most imposing force were over. It was a stunning fact, really, as Belichick had just appeared in his record eighth Super Bowl as a head coach, and his 11th overall, and he had nearly won three titles in four years for the second time. In some ways it was the ultimate compliment — Belichick's Patriots had established such an absurdly high standard that a season ended by a one-possession defeat in a Super Bowl that saw Brady throw for more than 500 yards could be characterized as a disaster.

In the lead-up to his 19th season in Foxborough, Belichick faced the toughest questions he had faced since taking over the Patriots, in 2000, and answering for the specter of failure — as a head coach — that had followed him from Cleveland. Could he win back his players after the Butler benching as he'd won them back after the Lawyer Milloy trade in 2003? Could he recover from a devastating defeat and a relatively dysfunctional season to break his tie with Vince Lombardi and win championship No. 6?

On one level, the reaction to Belichick's coaching in the Super Bowl was unfair — he knew his team best, after all, and his postseason records suggested that he was the most qualified person on the planet to determine whether Butler would help or hurt the cause. On another level, Belichick had never cut anyone around him a break. Why should he get a pass now?

It was going to take time for the fractures in Foxborough to heal. But if nothing else, Belichick had earned that time. He had earned everyone's benefit of the doubt. He had earned the right to fix his relationship with Brady, Gronk, and the fan base. More than anything, he had earned the faith of all New Englanders that he could lead the Patriots to another Super Bowl, where the next critical choice he made would notarize his greatness one more time.

In a stormy early spring that promised to make for a fascinating 2018 season, the coach of the Patriots still seemed more likely than not to win that sixth title before he was done. And as for any old Lombardi fans who bet against Bill Belichick in 2000, at least one — an older, wiser columnist from St. Cecilia High — wouldn't be making that same mistake again.

AFTERWORD

I ran into Jon Bon Jovi near the delirious New England locker room after the Patriots' 13–3 victory over the Los Angeles Rams in Super Bowl LIII, and as I introduced myself — Jersey Guy to Jersey Guy — he did a double take. Bon Jovi had just read this book in hardcover form. He had a few thoughts on my project, and a few more on what he had just witnessed. His longtime friend Bill Belichick had just won his sixth championship as a head coach after spending much of the season running a team that looked entirely capable of flaming out in the playoffs.

First, the championship. The 56-year-old rocker and former owner of the Arena Football League team in Philadelphia had been around success long enough to know that chemistry, for a rock band or a football team, matters almost as much as talent. Bon Jovi had known Belichick for 30 years, back to his days with Bill Parcells's Giants. He had become a confidant and a regular guest at Belichick's practices over the decades, and he saw what he saw and he knew what he knew when it came to comparing New England's improbable Super Bowl champs of 2018 to its most immediate and dysfunctional predecessor, which lost to Philadelphia in the big game.

Bill Belichick, Tom Brady, and Robert Kraft were again the picture of relative harmony.

"The organization is just running well these days," Bon Jovi said as the Patriots danced to "Mo Bamba" in their packed locker room inside Atlanta's Mercedes-Benz Stadium. "Tommy is getting along with Bill, [Bill's] getting along with Kraft, and Kraft's being nice to him. It seems like they're peacing it out. Winning will do that to you."

It took a Rock and Roll Hall of Famer to become the first Belichick friend, or Patriots associate, to confirm publicly what was nowhere to be found in the team's published unity statement 13 months earlier: that there were real fractures, if only temporary fractures, in the relationships among the best coach, quarterback, and owner in football. Certainly time helped heal those wounds, as did a couple of tweaks in Belichick's approach. He eased up on Alex Guerrero, for one, after he tired of the long line of Patriots heading to see Brady's fitness guru and business partner inside Gillette Stadium, and then removed him from team flights and the game-day sideline. Belichick restored some of the stripped access, and Guerrero was seen during the season eating with the team's training staff, and then, of course, on road trips and again on the Super Bowl field, hugging Brady as the postgame confetti fell from the stadium rafters.

Belichick also eased up on Brady, whose offseason message to the coach had been heard. The quarterback was thrilled when Belichick and Kraft talked Josh McDaniels into rejecting the Indianapolis head coaching job he'd already agreed to take, but Brady needed more than the return of an offensive coordinator who almost always had his back. He needed more from the only NFL head coach he'd ever known.

Toward that end, nearly everyone in and around the team facility noticed that Belichick seemed to be going out of his way to praise his quarterback — or at least to praise him more than he normally had (a low bar, indeed). "If you used a scale of 1 to 10," said someone inside the building who noticed, "it went from a 1 to a 2 or a 2.5." But that small gain was a big difference maker with Brady. One source with direct knowledge of the Belichick/Brady relationship said "things were much better between them" during the 2018 season than they had been in 2017, and that the coach's decision to — as ESPN's Jeff Darlington put it — "treat Tom more like a 41-year-old man" helped keep alive a season that often appeared to be teetering on the edge of a cliff.

The Patriots were 1-2 following an embarrassing Sunday night loss to Matt Patricia's Detroit Lions (Julian Edelman was serving a four-game suspension for PED use) before they pieced together a six-game winning streak, including home victories over Patrick Mahomes and Aaron Rodgers. New England was 9-3 when it traveled to South Florida to face the Dolphins, an opponent that forever gives Belichick and Brady fits at home, and sure enough, Miami's final offensive play sent the Patriots reeling. Taking the snap from his own 31 with seven seconds left, Miami quarterback Ryan Tannehill threw a pass over the middle to Kenny Stills, who lateraled to DeVante Parker, who lateraled to Kenyan Drake, who zigged and zagged and blew past a defender Belichick should have never put on the field, a stumbling, bumbling Rob Gronkowski, and raced into the end zone for the walk-off touchdown.

A tough loss the following week to Pittsburgh, a team the Patriots owned as much as the Rooney family owned them, inspired some to conclude that the dynasty was likely over for real this time. New England scored a grand total of 10 points in that game and committed 14 penalties and allowed a rookie fifth-round draft pick, Jaylen Samuels, to run for 142 yards on 19 carries. The Patriots were 3-5 on the road. Brady didn't look the same. Gronk didn't look the same. To make matters worse, the troubled Josh Gordon, who had been acquired in a September trade with Cleveland (an act of desperation by the playmaker-starved Patriots), would be suspended yet again by the league for violating its substance-abuse policy.

But even though they were suddenly 9-5, the Patriots couldn't be dismissed as a serious contender as long as Belichick and Brady were upright. Under an ESPN.com headline that read, "Don't Bury the Patriots Yet: Why Their Playoff Path Isn't Daunting," I wrote after the Pittsburgh defeat that they would surely beat the Bills and the Jets at home to finish 11-5 (they did), that the Texans could still lose one of their last two games to hand back New England the two-seed and much-needed first-round bye (they did), and that the Patriots could still end up in Kansas City for their eighth straight appearance in the AFC Championship Game (they did).

"Any other franchise would be dead and buried," I wrote. "But these are the New England Patriots. They still have the greatest coach and quarterback of all time and a reasonable enough postseason path to somehow make this thing work."

The resting Patriots caught a break in the wild-card playoff round when the Los Angeles Chargers beat the Baltimore Ravens, who knew how to play postseason football in Foxborough better than any other AFC franchise. The Chargers were never going to beat New England after making back-to-back trips across the country to play 1 p.m. Eastern playoff games. The Chiefs? The Patriots had defeated them in a regular-season shootout, 43–40, and Belichick held a 6-2 career advantage over Chiefs coach Andy Reid in head-to-head meetings, including a 2-0 record in the postseason and 1-0 in Super Bowls. On the other hand, the Patriots' last trip to Arrowhead Stadium ended in a 2014 Chiefs rout that inspired Brady (and many others) to believe he might get replaced by rookie Jimmy Garoppolo sooner rather than later (Brady recovered that season to win his fourth Super Bowl title).

Though the AFC title game in January 2019 was no rout, the Chiefs appeared to have beaten Belichick and Brady at home one more time. I'll never forget folding shut my laptop and starting to pack up my things in the Arrowhead press box after Brady's final-minute pass bounced off Gronk's hands and into the arms of Kansas City's Charvarius Ward, apparently sealing the Chiefs' first trip to the Super Bowl in nearly half a century. And then I saw the flag. And then I heard the referee announce that the Chiefs' Dee Ford had lined up in the neutral zone. And then I knew the Patriots were going to win this game (Rex Burkhead, a prototypical Belichick player, would barrel into the end zone in overtime) and reach the Super Bowl for the fourth time in five seasons and for the ninth time in the Belichick/Brady years.

Brilliant as 33-year-old Sean McVay was, it was hard to imagine him beating a legendary coach twice his age in Belichick, who was an old acquaintance of McVay's grandfather John. It was just as hard to imagine Jared Goff, a third-year pro, beating Brady, especially with the Rams' otherworldly running back Todd Gurley limited with a bum knee. Then again, Philly's Doug Pederson and Nick Foles weren't supposed to beat Belichick and Brady either.

Even though the Patriots had embraced a nobody-believes-in-us, everyone-says-we're-too-old-and-too-slow mentality, they were favored to defeat the Rams. The game turned out to be as ugly as most of Goff's passes. Brady was hardly on fire himself, but with the score 3–3 midway through the fourth quarter he made the one throw he had to make — a 29-yarder to the rejuvenated Gronkowski down to the Los Angeles 2. (It was fitting that Gronk, widely ridiculed after his role in the Miami miracle, was the man who put the Patriots in position to win.) Sony Michel carried the ball into the end zone on the next play, and Goff responded on the following drive by cracking under blitz pressure and throwing a dreadful pass toward the end zone that was picked off by Stephon Gilmore.

Belichick's de facto defensive coordinator, Brian Flores, the Dolphins' head-coach-in-waiting, had come up with a masterful plan and a pass rush that had been nonexistent for much of the season to keep the high-flying Rams from scoring a touchdown. A year after benching Malcolm Butler in the Super Bowl loss to Philadelphia, Belichick did not make any bizarro moves against Los Angeles; in fact, he was so locked in, at one point NFL Films caught him stalking the sideline and looking across the field, urgently talking through his headset to McDaniels. "Josh," Belichick said, "where's McVay? I can't find him." Belichick found him, and the whiz kid all but melted under his death stare.

When Brady took a knee on the last play to make the 13–3 score a final, Belichick threw up his arms in touchdown form before shouting, "We're champions." He worked his way down the sideline shouting "Ha-ha" and "We're champs, man, we're champs" as he hugged coaches, players, and Berj Najarian. Belichick was doused with blue Gatorade before hugging his daughter Amanda on the field, and soon enough he would embrace Brady and the game's MVP, Edelman, and assure them, "We'll be back too." Of course, Belichick could not leave the field without holding his granddaughter Blakely in his arms, sharing an unprecedented level of winning with yet another generation.

On the other side, McVay was gracious enough to state the obvious for the record. "I'm pretty numb right now," he said in his postgame news conference, "but definitely I got outcoached."

In the winners' locker room, the Patriots seemed to be having a whole lot of fun — the kind the Eagles' Lane Johnson said they never had in Belichick's "fear-based organization" in an appearance a year earlier on *Barstool's Pardon My Take* podcast. One team source said Belichick made this championship possible by taking a kinder, gentler approach not just with Brady, but with the entire team — choosing to boost its confidence in delicate and vulnerable times, rather than slashing and gashing players after a bad week like he did in the old days.

Honestly, I was glad this team made good on the final words I wrote about Belichick in the epilogue and went on to win its sixth title.

No, I wasn't naive enough to think that this forecast made up for my 2000 Belichick forecast gone terribly awry — and countless Patriots fans on social media made sure to remind me of that. But for any fan of greatness, it was good to see the Patriots neutralize the damage they inflicted on themselves a year earlier. Super Bowl LII would not have been a worthy epilogue for the most remarkable football story ever told.

Almost immediately after Super Bowl LIII washed away that stain, Jon Bon Jovi told me he was a fan of this book. "I thought 80 percent of it was a love letter to Belichick," he said, "and you were very fair to him." Bon Jovi contested my characterization of his rooting interests in Super Bowl XLII in Arizona, where his beloved Giants denied his beloved friend Belichick a 19-0 season, but he said that was his only quibble. We laughed a bit about it and shook hands, and then the rocker headed off into the night as I made my way to the press box to write that the Patriots had secured their standing as the greatest dynasty in the history of American sports, college or pro.

I never heard directly from Belichick about the book; I asked him a handful of questions about his team in press conferences, and he answered them without incident. Before I covered my first Patriots game after the book's publication — the marquee Sunday night game against Green Bay and Aaron Rodgers — I contacted their PR chief, Stacey James, and offered to drive up a couple of days early and make myself available to Belichick, Kraft, Brady, or anyone else in the organization who might have an issue with me or the contents of the book. If anyone cared to dispute something, I wanted that person to have a face-to-face opportunity before I covered another game in Gillette Stadium. James got back to me later and said nobody in the organization had given him reason to believe such a meeting was necessary. As I wrote ESPN columns and features about the Patriots over the balance of the season, I was treated professionally by the members of the organization I came in contact with, just as I had been before I wrote the book.

New England's offseason should have been one long and blissful parade in celebration of a sixth title in 18 years, even though Gronkowski retired, as expected, before leaving open the possibility he could turn that retirement into a vacation that ended late in the 2019 regular season. But instead the offseason devolved into something of an unholy mess. Greg Schiano, a longtime Belichick friend, suddenly resigned as Flores's expected replacement about a month after he accepted the job, citing a need to "spend more time on my faith and family."

This chaotic turn of staffing events was nothing compared to the Defcon 1 nightmare five weeks earlier that was the arrest of the 77-year-old Kraft in Jupiter, Florida, on charges of soliciting sex at a massage parlor. The police said that Kraft had made two trips to the parlor, including one on the day of the AFC Championship Game, and that the team owner paid for sexual acts that were videotaped as part of an undercover investigation. Kraft denied that he engaged in any illegal activity, and put up a fierce legal fight in the hope of getting the charges dropped.

The owner rejected the prosecution's offer of expunged charges in exchange for an admission that he would've been found guilty in court of soliciting prostitution. Kraft's fight seemed to do him more harm than good, as it kept alive the story and the possibility that the videotape would be released publicly. Once again, the Patriots were leading the league in on-field conquests and off-field crises.

Meanwhile, Kraft's 67-year-old head coach went about his business like he always had — as if nothing in his world was out of order. Belichick was preparing for yet another NFL draft in April, and yet another opportunity to start defending his Super Bowl title in training camp.

In between the draft and camp would surely be some downtime in the sun and sand of Nantucket. And maybe a few hours for Bill Belichick, pro football's most decorated grandfather, to finally figure out how much longer he can keep outworking and outcoaching men half his age.

ACKNOWLEDGMENTS

A number of books served as helpful roadmaps to understanding Bill Belichick and the New England Patriots' system, and none were more valuable than the late, great David Halberstam's *The Education of a Coach* and Michael Holley's *Patriot Reign* and *War Room.* NFL Films documentaries and highlights were terrific resources, as were newspapers including, but not limited to, the *Boston Globe,* the *Boston Herald,* the *Providence Journal,* and the *Hartford Courant* in New England, and the Cleveland *Plain Dealer,* the *Akron Beacon Journal,* and the *Columbus Dispatch* in Ohio.

I learned so much about Belichick's Patriots by reading and watching the dedicated men and women who have covered them over the years. Their ranks include, but are not limited to, Greg Bedard, Ron Borges, Albert Breer, Bill Burt, Nick Cafardo, Tom E. Curran, Mark Daniels, Kevin Duffy, Michael Felger, Chris Gasper, Mike Giardi, Karen Guregian, Ryan Hannable, Bob Hohler, Jeff Howe, Doug Kyed, Kevin Mannix, Shalise Manza Young, Tony Massarotti, Jim McBride, Phil Perry, Mike Petraglia, Christopher Price, Ian Rapoport, Mike Reiss, Michael Smith, Ben Volin, and Michael Whitmer.

Heavyweight columnists Dan Shaughnessy and Jackie MacMullan were always among my most reliable role models. Steve Buckley taught me a ton about professionalism when I was a kid reporter at the *National Sports Daily,* and Gerry Callahan was one of the best columnists anywhere before he left newspapers for radio. In Cleveland, the great Mary Kay Cabot was a tremendous resource, and Tony Grossi, Bud Shaw, and Peter John-Baptiste were most kind with their time. In New York and New Jersey, old colleagues Mark Cannizzaro, Rich Cimini, Brian Costello, Vinny DiTrani, Mike Eisen, Bart Hubbuch, Gary Myers, Tara Sullivan, and David Waldstein were a major help. Nationally, Jarrett Bell, Greg Bishop, Kevin Clark, Peter King, Tim Layden, Chris Mortensen, Bill Simmons, Jenny Vrentas, and Dan Wetzel were among the industry titans whose significant works informed me.

At ESPN, rising star Steve Ceruti was always there when needed. My über-talented teammates Seth Wickersham and Kevin Van Valkenburg did far more than pitch in, and the accomplished author and TV reporter Gene Wojciechowski was a valued sounding board. Bill Hofheimer, Allie Stoneberg, and the distinguished storyteller Greg Garber helped when they didn't have to. Of course, I will always remain indebted to Rob King and Leon Carter for bringing me aboard.

Murray Bauer, Joe Favorito, Jay Flannelly, Geoff Hobson, Andrew Howard, Steve Kennelly, Jim Kleinpeter, Andrew Korba, Joe Posnanski, Dick Quinn, Peter Reilly, Avis Roper, Jim Saccomano, Paul Santangelo, Don Sperling, and Matt Turk all made notable contributions. Thanks to the Joe Andruzzi Foundation, which does God's work for cancer patients. And a special thanks to those who put their trust in me and anonymously aided my pursuit of the truth — you know who you are.

My literary agent, David Black, is the best in the business by a country mile, in addition to being a tough and brave man. At Houghton Mifflin Harcourt, Megan Wilson was a fierce advocate of my work, again, and Will Palmer was everything you could ask for in a copy editor and more. Jenny Xu made the entire process much smoother than it could have been, and the outstanding Susan Canavan, editor for three of my four books, was a smart and reassuring voice even as she was instructing me to cut 30,000 words from my original document.

Finally, my wife, Tracey, and son, Kyle, deserve some sort of commendation for putting up with my disengagement for the past three years. They are the best friends I've ever had, and I could not have carried this project into the end zone without their unconditional love and support.

A NOTE ON THE AUTHOR'S INTERVIEWS AND SOURCES

Bill Belichick did not agree to be interviewed for this project. His quotations throughout are primarily from the thousands of news conferences and mass media availabilities he has participated in during his NFL coaching career and from the print and broadcast outlets cited in these pages. The author interviewed more than 350 people exclusively for this book, and those interviews served as the foundation of the narrative. The following is a chapter-by-chapter summary of additional sources that made important contributions.

1. The Teacher

Paul Stillwell, *The Golden Thirteen: Recollections of the First Black Naval Officers* (Annapolis, MD: Naval Institute Press, 1993).

David Halberstam, *The Education of a Coach* (New York: Hyperion, 2005).

"John J. Bell," *Progress-Index* (Petersburg, VA), December 3, 2006.

Anthony G. De Lorenzo, "Steve Belichick Pressed into Service After Lloyd Cardwell, Hard-Running Regular, Is Hurt in Game with Cleveland," United Press, November 15, 1941.

Dan Daly, "Bill Belichick's Old Man Was Pretty Amazing, Too," *Washington Times,* August 29, 2002.

Vardy Buckalew, "Belichick Joined Carolina Staff with Top Pass Defense Record," *Daily Tar Heel* (Chapel Hill, NC), November 6, 1953.

Bob Hohler, "Belichick Family Tree Filled with Surprises," *Boston Globe,* July 18, 2017.

"Belichick to Take Over Commodore Backfield," *Nashville Tennessean,* August 21, 1949.

"Belichick-Munn," *Palm Beach Post* (FL), August 24, 1950.

Ken Rodgers, dir., *A Football Life: Bill Belichick* (Mount Laurel, NJ: NFL Films, 2011).

Rich Cimini, "It's Belichick to Patriots' Defense: Has Been Scheming for This Day Since Age 6," *Daily News* (New York), February 3, 2002.

Bill Belichick, interview by Armen Keteyian, *NFL Today,* CBS Sports, October 3, 2005.

Ian O'Connor, "Invincibility of Belichick Enhanced by His Invisibility," *USA Today,* January 20, 2004.

Steve Belichick, *Football Scouting Methods* (New York: Ronald Press Co., 1962).

2. Big Al

Robert Fachet, "With the Belichicks, the Apple Hasn't Fallen Far from the Tree," *Washington Post,* February 7, 1991.

Ron Borges, "What Makes Bill Belichick Tick?" *Boston Globe Magazine,* September 10, 2000.

Ken Rodgers, dir., *A Football Life: Bill Belichick* (Mount Laurel, NJ: NFL Films, 2011).

Rick Maese, "Full Speed Ahead for Belichick, Just a Chip off the Navy Block," *Washington Post,* January 21, 2007.

"Annapolis Invades Severna Park Tomorrow: Panthers Assured of Title," *Evening Capital* (Annapolis, MD), November 27, 1968.

3. Andover

Bill Burt, "'I Owe This School a Lot'; Belichick Holds 1 Year at Phillips in High Regard," *Andover Townsman* (MA), February 2, 2015.

Ron Borges, "What Makes Bill Belichick Tick?" *Boston Globe Magazine,* September 10, 2000.

Bill Burt, "Phillips Andover Honors Belichick," *Eagle-Tribune* (North Andover, MA), June 12, 2011.

David Halberstam, *The Education of a Coach* (New York: Hyperion, 2005).

"PA Football Sets Back Tufts Freshmen, 26–12; Blue Passing Attack Accounts for 219 Yards," *Phillipian,* October 7, 1970.

Buzzy Bissinger, "Andover Football Trips Lawrenceville," *Phillipian,* October 21, 1970.

Buzzy Bissinger, "Unbeaten PA Football Trounces Exeter, 34–8; Takes First Home Win Over PEA Since 1958," *Phillipian,* November 18, 1970.

Bill Belichick, "Coach Bill Belichick Day" speech to Phillips Academy student body, Andover, MA, February 27, 2002.

Michael Kranish, "Jeb Bush Shaped by Troubled Phillips Academy Years," *Boston Globe,* February 1, 2015.

Jeb Bush, interview by Clay Travis, *Fox Sports Live: Countdown to Kickoff,* FS1, October 10, 2015.

Terry Pluto, "The Man Behind the Mask," *Akron Beacon Journal,* December 18, 1994.

4. Wesleyan

David Halberstam, *The Education of a Coach* (New York: Hyperion, 2005).

Bill Newell, "Trinity Holds Cards, 21–15," *Hartford Courant,* November 17, 1974.

Rich Cimini, "Belichick, Bon Jovi in Perfect Harmony," *Daily News* (New York), January 25, 2004.

Al Hopkins, "4 on the Path of Prominence," *Capital* (Annapolis, MD), June 6, 1975.

5. Billy Ball

Bill Belichick, interview by Armen Keteyian, *NFL Today,* CBS Sports, October 3, 2005.

Seth Wickersham, "Shipp Shaped Belichick's Thinking," ESPN.com, September 4, 2009.

Bill Belichick, interview by Suzy Welch, *Power Lunch,* CNBC, April 13, 2017.

Ron Jaworski with Greg Cosell and David Plaut, *The Games That Changed the Game: The Evolution of the NFL in Seven Sundays* (New York: ESPN Books, 2010).

Woody Paige, "Belichick's Roots in Denver," *Denver Post,* January 29, 2008.

6. Little Bill

Barrie Dawson, "Giants Turn Dramatic Victory into Defeat," *Journal News* (White Plains, NY), November 16, 1981.

Michael Eisen, "Exploring the Legacy of Bill Parcells," Giants.com, August 3, 2013.

Ken Rodgers, dir., "The Two Bills," ESPN *30 for 30,* NFL Films, February 1, 2018.

Bob Papa, "Bill Parcells," *Giants Chronicles* video, July 16, 2014.

Bob Papa, "Bill Belichick," *Giants Chronicles* video, March 21, 2012.

Lawrence Taylor with William Wyatt, *My Giant Life* (Chicago: Triumph Books, 2016).

Lawrence Taylor with Steve Serby, *LT: Over the Edge* (New York: HarperCollins, 2003).

Ian O'Connor, "Patriots' Coach Establishing His Legacy As Best of a Generation," *Journal News* (White Plains, NY), February 6, 2005.

Bernie Miklasz, "Friendly Rivals: Belichick Got Start Under Marchibroda," *St. Louis Post-Dispatch,* January 26, 1991.

Greg Garber, "Being Driven Takes Them Far: Giants' Belichick, Bills' Marchibroda: Roads Meet Again," *Hartford Courant,* January 24, 1991.

Ian O'Connor, "Belichick Battle Plan a Key to Victory," *Asbury Park Press* (NJ), January 17, 1999.

"Bills' Offensive Coordinator Is Hoping Belichick Gets Opportunity with Browns," *Buffalo News,* January 28, 1991.

7. Cleveland

Steve Love, "Ten-Hut! Mr. Belichick! New Leader for Gen. Modell's Squad," *Akron Beacon Journal,* February 6, 1991.

Bill Belichick introductory press conference, WEWS-TV News 5, Cleveland, February 5, 1991.

Ed Meyer, "Coach Grasps the Details: 38-Year-Old Takes 'Hard Way' to Browns," *Akron Beacon Journal,* February 6, 1991.

Associated Press, "Saban Named to Browns' Staff," *Lancaster Eagle-Gazette* (OH), February 14, 1991.

Tony Grossi, "Belichick Insightful When Paid to Talk," *Plain Dealer* (Cleveland), August 29, 1991.

Joe Schad, "Friends Draw Line in Sand," *Palm Beach Post* (FL), January 9, 2005.

Dan Shaughnessy, "Saban's Disguises Look Very Familiar," *Boston Globe,* December 11, 2006.

Jeffrey Brodeur, "Michael Dean Perry Ends Holdout," Associated Press, August 27, 1991.

Dan Shaughnessy, "The New Bill Belichick Is Wise Enough to Know He's Not Changing," *ESPN the Magazine,* September 2000.

Ed Meyer, "Victory at Any Cost: Belichick Has Powers of Persuasion," *Akron Beacon Journal,* September 4, 1992.

Tony Grossi, "Langhorne: Worst Year of My Life," *Plain Dealer* (Cleveland), March 31, 1992.

Associated Press, "Browns Defensive Lineman Perry Angered by Belichick's Comments," *Lancaster Eagle-Gazette* (OH), July 24, 1992.

8. Mistakes by the Lake

Mary Kay Cabot, "Modell: Success or I'll Leave," *Plain Dealer* (Cleveland), December 31, 1992.

Marla Ridenour, "Belichick: Browns Need Tuneup, Not Overhaul: Coach Admits Making His Share of Mistakes," *Columbus Dispatch,* December 30, 1992.

Terry Pluto, "The Man Behind the Mask," *Akron Beacon Journal,* December 18, 1994.

Marla Ridenour, "Belichick: Testaverde Earned Shot," *Columbus Dispatch,* October 12, 1993.

Mary Kay Cabot, "Belichick Deal Extended to '97," *Plain Dealer* (Cleveland), October 22, 1993.

Ed Meyer, "Bernie Gets Sacked: Browns Waive Kosar, Citing Diminished Skills. Belichick Takes the Heat," *Akron Beacon Journal,* November 9, 1993.

Mary Kay Cabot, "Mrs. Coach: Debby Belichick Is No Bench Warmer for the Cleveland Browns," *Plain Dealer* (Cleveland), May 14, 1995.

John McClain, "Browns' Belichick Unpopular with Everyone," *Houston Chronicle,* November 19, 1993.

Chuck Heaton, "Modell Says Byner Trade Was 'Lousy,'" *Plain Dealer* (Cleveland), October 9, 1991.

Bill Belichick, interview by Mike Veneman, "Sports Mock Live," *Browns Insider,* 1994.

John Curran, "For Boardwalk Popcorn Store, a Brisk Mail-Order Biz," Associated Press, December 13, 2003.

Jon Saraceno, "Browns Fans Still Blue: Belichick Tunes Out Dawg Pound," *USA Today,* December 2, 1994.

Michael Holley, "Not the People's Choice; All the Success in the World Can't Turn the Fans On to Coach Belichick," *Boston Globe,* December 30, 1994.

David Ginsburg, "Art Modell Moves Browns to Baltimore," Associated Press, November 6, 1995.

Tony Grossi, *Tales from the Cleveland Browns Sideline* (New York: Sports Publishing, 2004).

Greg Frith, "Cleveland '95: A Football Life," NFL Films, October 3, 2012.

Brad Parks, "That's All, Folks," *Star-Ledger* (Newark, NJ), January 4, 2000.

9. Border War

Will McDonough, "Parcells to Leave; His Poor Relationship with Kraft Cited — Contract Controversy Looms," *Boston Globe,* January 20, 1997.

"Patriots Owner Scolds Parcells," *New York Times,* August 28, 1996.

Michael Holley, *Patriot Reign: Bill Belichick, the Coaches, and the Players Who Built a Champion* (New York: William Morrow, 2004).

Michael Felger, *Tales from the Patriots Sideline* (Champaign, IL: Sports Publishing, 2004).

Rich Cimini, "As Head Guy, Beli Checks Out," *Daily News* (New York), February 12, 1997.

Rich Cimini, "Tuna Take on Time Sounds a Bit Fishy," *Daily News* (New York), September 2, 2000.

David Halberstam, *The Education of a Coach* (New York: Hyperion, 2005).

Bill Parcells with Nunyo Demasio, *Parcells: A Football Life* (New York: Crown Archetype, 2014).

Wayne Parry, "Sacked Again: Judge Denies Belichick Request to Negotiate with Pats," Associated Press, January 25, 2000.

Peter King, "Robert Kraft Made a Mistake and Turned It into a Dynasty," *The MMQB,* SI.com, January 30, 2017.

Bill Parcells to Robert Kraft, January 27, 2000, posted on Twitter by Levan Reid (@LevanReid), WBZ-TV CBS, Boston, January 27, 2016.

10. Brady

"Not So Special Start," Patriots.com, July 17, 2000.

Michael Smith, "Patriots Make Brady No. 2 QB," *Boston Globe,* September 5, 2001.

Kevin Mannix, "Patriots QB Coach Dead; Heart Condition Claims Rehbein," *Boston Herald,* August 7, 2001.

Michael Felger, "For Pats, Life Looks Better — Positive Signs Everywhere," *Boston Herald,* July 29, 2001.

Pepper Johnson with Bill Gutman, *Won for All* (New York: McGraw-Hill, 2002).

Ian O'Connor, "Surpassing Michael Jordan As Ultimate GOAT Is Brady's Last Challenge," ESPN. com, May 15, 2017.

Ian O'Connor, "The Ravens Coach Who Pushed to Pick Tom Brady in 2000 Draft," ESPN.com, January 14, 2017.

George Kimball, "Debate Ends Quickly," *Boston Herald,* October 8, 2001.

Ken Powers, "Brady Leads N.E. to Win in Overtime Against San Diego," *Telegram & Gazette* (Worcester, MA), October 15, 2001.

Shalise Manza Young, "Belichick: Moss Traits Are Like 2 of the Greats," *Providence Journal,* November 7, 2009.

Steve Buckley, "The Metamorphosis of Bill Belichick," *Boston Herald,* December 9, 2001.

David Pevear, "Emotional Rescue at the Old Gray Stadium," *Sun* (Lowell, MA), December 22, 2001.

Mark Cannizzaro, "Patriots' Title Hopes Are Snowballing," *New York Post,* January 20, 2002.

11. Champion

Pepper Johnson with Bill Gutman, *Won for All* (New York: McGraw-Hill, 2002).

Tim Casey, "Fans in Foxboro Turn Out in Force," *Boston Globe,* January 28, 2002.

Nick Cafardo, *The Impossible Team: The Worst to First Patriots' Super Bowl Season* (Chicago: Triumph Books, 2002).

Steve Buckley, "The Metamorphosis of Bill Belichick," *Boston Herald,* December 9, 2001.

Michael Wilbon, "Belichick Is a Changed Man, and Change Is Good," *Washington Post,* February 3, 2005.

Gordon Edes, "Head Games: Patriots Coach Has Well-Earned Reputation for Stopping Whatever's Thrown His Way," *Boston Globe,* February 2, 2002.

Michael Felger, "Believe It: Pats Super; Vinatieri, Brady Deliver in Thrilling Championship Win," *Boston Herald,* February 4, 2002.

Charlie Weis and Vic Carucci, *No Excuses: One Man's Incredible Rise Through the NFL to Head Coach of Notre Dame* (New York: HarperEntertainment, 2006).

Pat Summerall and John Madden, Super Bowl XXXVI broadcast, Fox, February 3, 2002.

Greg Garber, "Brady-to-Brown Puts Pats in Position," ESPN.com, February 3, 2002.

Phil Sheridan, "Belichick Dared Pats to Take It to the Rams," *Philadelphia Inquirer*, February 5, 2002.

George Kimball, "Belichick Wins a New Image, Too," *Boston Herald*, February 4, 2002.

Michael Holley, *Patriot Reign: Bill Belichick, the Coaches, and the Players Who Built a Champion* (New York: William Morrow, 2004).

12. Bigger Bill

Jimmy Golen, "Patriots Cut Four-Time Pro Bowler Milloy," Associated Press, September 2, 2003.

George Kimball, "Lawyer Collects His Fee," *Boston Herald*, September 8, 2003.

Kevin Mannix, "Self-Paralysis; Belichick's Gamble on Milloy Could Cut Legs Out from Under Him, Pats," *Boston Herald*, September 7, 2003.

Jimmy Golen, "Patriots Say They Don't 'Hate' Belichick," Associated Press, September 15, 2003.

Bill Belichick, "O.K., Champ, Now Comes the Hard Part," *New York Times*, January 26, 2003.

Jackie MacMullan, "Pioli and Belichick a Nice Team," *Boston Globe*, January 26, 2004.

Karen Guregian, "Hate Is Strong Word," *Boston Herald*, September 15, 2003.

David Pevear, "Patriot Players Maintain They Remain Solidly Behind Belichick," *Sun* (Lowell, MA), September 15, 2003.

Michael Holley, *Patriot Reign: Bill Belichick, the Coaches, and the Players Who Built a Champion* (New York: William Morrow, 2004).

Dan Shaughnessy, "Efficient Win Engineered by Team of Experts," *Boston Globe*, November 17, 2003.

Mark Cannizzaro, "The Great Escape; Belichick Knew What He Was Doing When He Bolted Jets," *New York Post*, January 16, 2004.

Bryan Burwell, "Dungy Proves You Can Be Calm and Win in NFL," *St. Louis Post-Dispatch*, January 16, 2004.

Dave Goldberg, "Patriots 24, Colts 14," Associated Press, January 19, 2004.

Rich Cimini, "Belichick, Bon Jovi in Perfect Harmony," *Daily News* (New York), January 25, 2004.

Adam Schefter, "Fox, Belichick on Cutting Edge," *Denver Post*, January 29, 2004.

Steve Serby, "Fresh Despair for Delhomme," *New York Post*, January 29, 2016.

Bill Belichick, Super Bowl speeches, NFL Network *Sound FX*, NFL Films.

Greg Gumbel and Phil Simms, Super Bowl XXXVIII broadcast, CBS, February 1, 2004.

Bob McGinn, "Belichick Most Fascinating NFL Figure," *Milwaukee Journal Sentinel*, February 4, 2017.

13. Dynasty

Bill Belichick, speech at Sports Medicine and the NFL symposium, quoted in Mike Reiss, "Belichick's Keynote Address: Passion Plus," ESPN.com, May 10, 2013.

Michael Wilbon, "Belichick Is a Changed Man, and Change Is Good," *Washington Post*, February 3, 2005.

Jarrett Bell, "Piecing the Patriots Together," *USA Today*, April 22, 2005.

Todd Jones, "Belichick Has Come a Long Way in 10 Years," *Columbus Dispatch*, December 6, 2004.

Tim Warren, "Mystery Man," *Northwestern*, Winter 2008.

Les Carpenter, "'Football Researcher' Ernie Adams Is Biggest Mystery Behind Bill Belichick's Secretive Patriots," Yahoo! Sports, February 2, 2012.

"Sports People; Syzmanski Quits Colts," *New York Times*, May 8, 1982.

Pete Thamel, "Low-Key Adams Makes High Impact on Patriots," *New York Times*, January 16, 2004.

Bob Hohler, "Adams's Role? It's Top Secret," *Boston Globe*, February 3, 2008.

Kevin Lynch, "Belichick Fits the Bill, in More Ways Than One," *San Francisco Chronicle*, January 2, 2005.

Bill Belichick, Super Bowl speeches, NFL Network *Sound FX*, NFL Films.

Michael Currie Schaffer, "In Case of a Win, a Major . . . Event; Just Don't Call It a Parade," *Philadelphia Inquirer*, February 3, 2005.

Jeff McLane, "10 Years Later, Recalling Eagles' Last Super Bowl Appearance," *Philadelphia Inquirer,* January 31, 2015.

Ian O'Connor, "Patriots' Coach Establishing His Legacy As Best of a Generation," *Journal News* (White Plains, NY), February 6, 2005.

Stephen N. Belichick, funeral order of service, Annapolis, MD, November 23, 2005.

Dan Shaughnessy, "Given Proper Naval Sendoff," *Boston Globe,* November 24, 2005.

Bill Ordine, "A Final Navy Salute; Annapolis Coaching Legend Remembered As Tough, Compassionate," *Baltimore Sun,* November 24, 2005.

14. Spygate

Ian O'Connor, "Adam Vinatieri's Journey to Becoming the NFL's Old GOAT," ESPN.com, December 16, 2016.

Jackie MacMullan, "'I Don't Want Anyone to End Up Like Me,'" *Boston Globe,* February 2, 2007.

Alan Schwarz, "Dark Days Follow Hard-Hitting Career in N.F.L.," *New York Times,* February 2, 2007.

Bella English, "After a Bruising Year, Belichick Opens Up; Patriots' Head Coach Admits He Made Some Mistakes," *Boston Globe,* March 4, 2007.

Vincent J. Shenocca v. Sharon M. Shenocca, Dual Final Judgment of Divorce, No. FM-14-1181-05 (Superior Court of New Jersey Chancery Division, Morris County, NJ, June 29, 2007).

Greg A. Bedard, "Dolphins: Eavesdropping Not Unusual," *Palm Beach Post* (FL), December 13, 2006.

Chris Mortensen, "Sources: Camera Confiscated After Claims of Pats Spying on Jets," ESPN.com, September 11, 2007.

John Stark, *Troopers Behind the Badge* (Bellmawr, NJ: New Jersey State Police Memorial Association, 1993).

Christine Brennan, "City, Names May Change for Raiders, But the Image Remains the Same," *Washington Post,* September 26, 1984.

Matt Millen, NFL Films interview excerpted in "The Raider Rules," YouTube video, uploaded by jen1454, August 15, 2011.

Michael David Smith, "Bill Parcells Still Thinks Bill Walsh Cheated During 1980s Playoffs," *ProFootballTalk,* NBCSports.com, September 25, 2011.

Jimmy Johnson, *Fox NFL Sunday,* Fox, September 16, 2007.

Marla Ridenour, "Browns Have What Giants Fans Want: Coach Belichick," *Columbus Dispatch,* August 17, 1992.

Jarrett Bell, "'Spygate' Lingers Even with Closure; Goodell's Briefing Satisfies Committee," *USA Today,* February 22, 2008.

Tony Dungy, interview by Dan Patrick, *The Dan Patrick Show,* NBC Sports, August 20, 2015.

Steve Spagnuolo, interview by Anthony Gargano and Bob Cooney, *The Morning Show,* 97.5 the Fanatic, Philadelphia, January 29, 2018.

John Nalbone, "'Spygate' and the Super Bowl; Dawkins: Pats' Tactics 'Troublesome,'" *Times of Trenton* (NJ), September 14, 2007.

Dave Goldberg, "New England Acknowledges 'Spygate' Helped," Associated Press, November 11, 2007.

Joey Porter, interview by Trey Wingo, *NFL Live,* ESPN, May 23, 2008.

Gary Myers, *Coaching Confidential: Inside the Fraternity of NFL Coaches* (New York: Crown Archetype, 2012).

15. Imperfection

Michael Holley, *War Room: The Legacy of Bill Belichick and the Art of Building the Perfect Team* (New York: It Books/HarperCollins, 2011).

Bob Hohler, "Troubled Waters," *Boston Globe,* November 18, 2007.

Dan Salomone, "2007: Coughlin Receives Voicemail from John Madden," Giants.com, September 10, 2013.

Ken Rodgers, dir., "The Two Bills," ESPN *30 for 30,* NFL Films, February 1, 2018.

Dave Hyde, "Let the Game Begin! Pats, Dolphins Scrap on Waiver Wire," *Sun-Sentinel* (Broward County, FL), September 4, 2014.

Greg Bishop and Pete Thamel, "Senator Wants N.F.L. Spying Case Explained," *New York Times*, February 1, 2008.

Troy Brown with Mike Reiss, *Patriot Pride: My Life in the New England Dynasty* (Chicago: Triumph Books, 2015).

Kevin Paul Dupont, "Belichick; Patriots-Giants Super Bowl XLII," *Boston Globe*, February 3, 2008.

Paul Schwartz, "Com-Plax Numbers — Bold Burress Calls For 23-17 Giant Win," *New York Post*, January 29, 2008.

Ian O'Connor, "Beware of Underdog; Confident Tisch Predicts a Big Blue Win," *Record* (Bergen County, NJ), January 26, 2008.

Ian O'Connor, "Coughlin's Super Bowl Sunday for the Ages," *Record* (Bergen County, NJ), February 6, 2010.

Rich Cimini, "Pats' Samuel Ready to Pick His Next Spot," *Daily News* (New York), February 1, 2008.

Ian O'Connor, "How Tom Coughlin Solved the Bill Belichick Riddle," ESPN.com, November 12, 2015.

Joe Buck and Troy Aikman, Super Bowl XLII broadcast, Fox, February 3, 2008.

16. Hernandez

Judy Battista, "Patriots Were Questioned on Videotaping Claims," *New York Times*, April 2, 2008.

Jamison Hensley, "Reed Likely to Wear Radio Helmet for 'D'," *Baltimore Sun*, April 2, 2008.

Greg Bishop, "Videotaper's Inside View of the Patriots' Spying," *New York Times*, May 16, 2008.

Bill Belichick, interview by Armen Keteyian, *CBS Evening News*, May 16, 2008.

Michael Holley, *Patriot Reign: Bill Belichick, the Coaches, and the Players Who Built a Champion* (New York: William Morrow, 2004).

Gerry Callahan, "No Defense for Belichick; Trust Starts to Rust After Bad '09," *Boston Herald*, January 12, 2010.

Albert R. Breer, "Hernandez Has History of Drug Use," *Boston Globe*, April 27, 2010.

Jonathan Clegg, "Aaron Hernandez: An Early Warning in 2010 NFL Draft Profile," *Wall Street Journal*, July 3, 2013.

Mike Reiss, "Sources: Moss, Coach in Exchange," ESPNBoston.com, October 7, 2010.

Ian O'Connor, "The Trial of Aaron Hernandez Might Just Be Getting Started," ESPN.com, April 18, 2017.

"Super Bowl XLVI Mic'd Up: Manning's Game-Winning Drive & Giants D Holds Off Brady," NFL Network *Sound FX*, NFL Films, NFL.com, 2012.

Greg A. Bedard, "Aaron Hernandez, an Enigma on Trial," SI.com, March 25, 2015.

Mark Briggs court testimony, "Aaron Hernandez Murder Trial pt. 380 Mark Briggs," YouTube video, uploaded by TheCount.com, March 31, 2015.

Robert Kraft court testimony, "Raw Video: Robert Kraft Testifies at Hernandez Trial," YouTube video, uploaded by CBS Boston, March 31, 2015.

17. Deflation and Elation

Chris Sweeney, "Tom Brady's Personal Guru Is a Glorified Snake-Oil Salesman," *Boston*, October 9, 2015.

Mark Leibovich, "Tom Brady Cannot Stop," *New York Times Magazine*, January 26, 2015.

"Postgame Locker Room Speech and More," video, Patriots.com, October 6, 2014.

NFL Players Association, on behalf of *Tom Brady v. National Football League*, No. 0:15-cv-03168-RHK-HB (U.S. District Court for the District of Minnesota, 2015).

Ted Wells, *Investigative Report Concerning Footballs Used During the AFC Championship Game on January 18, 2015*, May 6, 2015.

Greg A. Bedard, "Pats Sources: Strong Statements by NFL Officials Left Out of Wells Report," SI.com, May 11, 2015.

Brent Schrotenboer and Jim Corbett, "Are Legacies Tarnished?; Greats Weigh In on How History Will Judge Pats' Belichick, Brady," *USA Today,* January 29, 2015.

Jeff Jacobs, "Who Let the Air Out?; Brady, Belichick Know Nothing," *Hartford Courant,* January 23, 2015.

Troy Aikman, interview, KTCK the Ticket SportsRadio 1310 podcast, Dallas, January 22, 2015.

Al Michaels and Cris Collinsworth, Super Bowl XLIX broadcast, NBC, February 1, 2015.

"2014 New England Patriots, Super Bowl XLIX," NFL Films, 2015.

Bill Belichick, quoted in "Do Your Job: Bill Belichick & the 2014 Patriots," NFL Films, 2015.

18. The Comeback

Ted Wells, *Investigative Report Concerning Footballs Used During the AFC Championship Game on January 18, 2015,* May 6, 2015.

Don Van Natta Jr. and Seth Wickersham, "Spygate to Deflategate: Inside What Split the NFL and Patriots Apart," ESPN.com, September 8, 2015.

Bob Labriola, "Steelers Come Up Short vs. Pats, 28–21," Steelers.com, September 10, 2015.

Greg Bishop, Michael Rosenberg, and Thayer Evans, "Suspicions of Bill Belichick's Patriots Regime Persist Among Opponents," SI.com, September 8, 2015.

Jeff Blake, interview, WGFX 104.5 the Zone, Nashville, January 28, 2015.

Patriots–Broncos AFC Championship Game, NFL Films, January 24, 2016.

Ben Axelrod, "Ohio State Football Coach Urban Meyer Learned New Recruiting Philosophy from New England Patriots' Bill Belichick," Landof10.com, April 13, 2017.

Dan Wetzel, "Bill Belichick's Stiff-Arm of Camouflage Campaign an Unlikely Coincidence," Yahoo! Sports, November 18, 2015.

Ian O'Connor, "'Now You've Pissed Off the GOAT': An 'Angry' Tom Brady Returns," ESPN.com, October 7, 2016.

Nicholas Confessore, Maggie Haberman, and Eric Lipton, "Trump's 'Winter White House': A Peek at the Exclusive Members' List at Mar-a-Lago," *New York Times,* February 18, 2017.

Tessa Yesselman, "Happily Aligning with Hate," letter to the editor, *Boston Globe,* March 10, 2016.

Joe Buck and Troy Aikman, Super Bowl LI broadcast, Fox, February 5, 2017.

19. Human Bill

"Belichick Playbook: Incorporation," *Boston Business Journal,* March 5, 2007.

Robert Cocuzzo and Bruce A. Percelay, "Winning Combination," *Nantucket Magazine,* July 2017.

Bob Hohler, "For Coach, Nantucket's the Place to Unwind," *Boston Globe,* February 1, 2018.

Michael Holley, "It's Just Another Sideline," *Boston Globe,* April 28, 2000.

"Financial Assistance," Bill Belichick Foundation, BillBelichickFoundation.org.

Ian O'Connor, "Uncovering the Humanity Behind the Belichick Machine," ESPN.com, February 5, 2017.

Massachusetts State Police, "Death Investigation of Aaron Hernandez," police report, May 4, 2017.

Bill Belichick, interview by Suzy Welch, *Power Lunch,* CNBC, April 13, 2017.

Bob Hohler, "Belichick Pushing Back on Brady's Guru," *Boston Globe,* December 20, 2017.

Greg A. Bedard, "How Much of a Concern Is This Alex Guerrero/Bill Belichick Rift for the Patriots?" *Boston Sports Journal,* December 20, 2017.

Tom E. Curran, "Patriots Run Feels Like It's Winding Down," NBC Sports Boston, December 29, 2017.

Seth Wickersham, "For Kraft, Brady and Belichick, Is This the Beginning of the End?" ESPN.com, January 5, 2018.

Peter King, "Robert Kraft Responds: Patriots' Owner Denies Report of Extended Meeting About QBs with Bill Belichick," *The MMQB,* SI.com, January 6, 2018.

Robert Snell, "Lions' Patricia Indicted, Not Tried in '96 Sex Assault," *Detroit News,* May 9, 2018.

Stephen Kurkjian, "Belichick's Armenian Flag Pin at Obama Meeting Takes Center Stage at St. James Men's Club Talk," *Armenian Mirror-Spectator* (Watertown, MA), June 4, 2015.

Kevin Duffy, "Patriots Won't Say What Sean Harrington Does; Meet 'Genius' Who Rejected Google for New England's Scouting Department," MassLive.com, January 8, 2018.

Al Michaels and Cris Collinsworth, Super Bowl LII broadcast, NBC, February 4, 2018.

Super Bowl LII, NFL Network *Sound FX,* NFL Films, 2018.

Mike Reiss, "Malcolm Butler on Super Bowl Loss: I Could Have Changed That Game," ESPN.com, February 5, 2018.

Epilogue

Gotham Chopra, *Tom vs. Time,* Facebook Watch, January–March, 2018.

Tom E. Curran, *Boston Sports Tonight,* NBC Sports Boston, February 26, 2018.

Mike Giardi, "Source Says Patriots Players Are Miserable," NBCSportsBoston, March 15, 2018.

Karen Guregian, "Rob Gronkowski Debate Wearing Thin," *Boston Herald,* April 8, 2018.

Mike Reiss, "Now a Dolphin, Danny Amendola Says Patriots' Contract Offer Fell Significantly Short," April 14, 2018.

Nate Solder, "Thank You, New England," Players' Tribune, April 12, 2018, https://www.theplayerstribune.com/en-us/articles/nate-solder-patriots-giants-thank-you.

BIBLIOGRAPHY

Books

Belichick, Steve. *Football Scouting Methods.* Mansfield Centre, CT: Martino, 2011.

Brown, Troy, with Mike Reiss. *Patriot Pride: My Life in the New England Dynasty.* Chicago: Triumph Books, 2015.

Burke, Monte. *Saban: The Making of a Coach.* New York: Simon & Schuster, 2013.

Cafardo, Nick. *The Impossible Team: The Worst to First Patriots' Super Bowl Season.* Chicago: Triumph Books, 2002.

Felger, Michael. *Tales from the New England Patriots Sideline.* Champaign, IL: Sports Publishing, 2004.

Grossi, Tony. *Tales from the Cleveland Browns Sideline.* New York: Sports Publishing, 2004.

Halberstam, David. *The Education of a Coach.* New York: Hyperion, 2005.

Holley, Michael. *Patriot Reign: Bill Belichick, the Coaches, and the Players Who Built a Champion.* New York: William Morrow, 2004.

———. *War Room: The Legacy of Bill Belichick and the Art of Building the Perfect Team.* New York: HarperCollins, 2011.

Jaworski, Ron, with Greg Cosell and David Plaut. *The Games That Changed the Game: The Evolution of the NFL in Seven Sundays.* New York: ESPN Books, 2010.

Johnson, Pepper, with Bill Gutman. *Won for All: The Inside Story of the New England Patriots' Improbable Run to the Super Bowl.* New York: McGraw-Hill, 2002.

Myers, Gary. *Coaching Confidential: Inside the Fraternity of NFL Coaches.* New York: Crown Archetype, 2012.

Parcells, Bill, with Nunyo Demasio. *Parcells: A Football Life.* New York: Crown Archetype, 2014.

Pierce, Charles P. *Moving the Chains: Tom Brady and the Pursuit of Everything.* New York: Farrar, Straus and Giroux, 2006.

Price, Christopher. *The Blueprint: How the New England Patriots Beat the System to Create the Last Great NFL Superpower.* New York: St. Martin's Press, 2008.

Stark, John. *Troopers Behind the Badge.* Bellmawr, NJ: New Jersey State Police Memorial Association, 1993.

Stillwell, Paul. *The Golden Thirteen: Recollections of the First Black Naval Officers.* Annapolis, MD: Naval Institute Press, 1993.

Taylor, Lawrence, with William Wyatt. *My Giant Life.* Chicago: Triumph Books, 2016.

Taylor, Lawrence, with Steve Serby. *LT: Over The Edge: Tackling Quarterbacks, Drugs, and a World Beyond Football.* New York: HarperCollins, 2003.

Weis, Charlie, with Vic Carucci. *No Excuses: One Man's Incredible Rise Through the NFL to Head Coach of Notre Dame.* New York: HarperCollins, 2006.

Magazines

Boston Globe Magazine
Boston magazine
ESPN the Magazine
Nantucket Magazine

New York Times Magazine
Northwestern magazine
Sports Illustrated

Newspapers and Wire Services

Akron Beacon Journal
Andover Townsman
Armenian Mirror-Spectator (Watertown, MA)
Asbury Park Press (NJ)
Associated Press
Baltimore Sun
Boston Business Journal
Boston Globe
Boston Herald
Buffalo News
Capital (Annapolis, MD)
Daily News (New York)
Daily Tar Heel (Chapel Hill, NC)
Denver Post
Eagle-Tribune (North Andover, MA)
Hartford Courant
Houston Chronicle
Journal News (White Plains, NY)
Lancaster Eagle-Gazette (OH)
Milwaukee Journal Sentinel
Nashville Tennessean
Newsday

New York Post
New York Times
Palm Beach Post (FL)
Philadelphia Inquirer
Phillipian
Plain Dealer (Cleveland)
Progress-Index (Petersburg, VA)
Providence Journal
Record (Bergen County, NJ)
San Francisco Chronicle
Star-Ledger (Newark, NJ)
St. Louis Post-Dispatch
Sun (Lowell, MA)
Sun-Sentinel (Broward County, FL)
Telegram & Gazette (Worcester, MA)
Times of Trenton (NJ)
United Press International
USA Today
Wall Street Journal
Washington Post
Washington Times
Wesleyan Argus

Websites

BillBelichickFoundation.org
BostonSportsJournal.com
ESPN.com
ESPNBoston.com
Giants.com
Landof10.com
MassLive.com
NBCSports.com/Boston
NewsLibrary.com

Newspapers.com
Nexis.com
NFL.com
Patriots.com
Pro-Football-Reference.com
SI.com
Steelers.com
The MMQB
WEEI.com

Videos and Broadcasts

CBS, FOX, NBC (Super Bowl broadcasts)
Giants Chronicles
NFL Films (Sound FX; A Football Life; game clips; Patriots features and documentaries)

Patriots.com (Patriots postgame locker room videos)
"The Two Bills," ESPN 30 for 30

INDEX